JOHN FOSTER

John Foster as Chancellor of the Irish Exchequer at Westminster, *c.* 1805, from
a contemporary engraving of unknown provenance

JOHN FOSTER

The Politics of the Anglo-Irish Ascendancy

A. P. W. MALCOMSON

'*No man can know Ireland by inspiration*'
Robert Ross to Lord Downshire, 9 July 1798
referring to the new Lord Lieutenant
Lord Cornwallis

Published for
THE INSTITUTE OF IRISH STUDIES
THE QUEEN'S UNIVERSITY OF BELFAST
by
OXFORD UNIVERSITY PRESS
1978

Oxford University Press, Walton Street, Oxford OX2 6DP

OXFORD LONDON GLASGOW
NEW YORK TORONTO MELBOURNE WELLINGTON
KUALA LUMPUR SINGAPORE JAKARTA HONG KONG TOKYO
DELHI BOMBAY CALCUTTA MADRAS KARACHI
IBADAN NAIROBI DAR ES SALAAM CAPE TOWN

© *A. P. W. Malcomson 1978*

British Library Cataloguing in Publication Data
Malcomson, A P W
　John Foster
　1. Foster, John, b. 1740　　2. Statesman – Ireland
　– Biography
　I. Queen's University of Belfast. Institute of Irish Studies
941.507'092'4　　　DA948.6.F/　　　77-30449
ISBN 0-19-920087-4

*Printed in Great Britain
at the University Press, Oxford
by Vivian Ridler
Printer to the University*

To my
Mother and Father

CONTENTS

ACKNOWLEDGEMENTS

THIS book is based principally on MS. material in the Public Record Office of Northern Ireland, above all on the Foster/Massereene MSS. there. To Viscount Massereene and Ferrard, the direct descendant of John Foster, I am especially indebted, not only for permission to quote from the letters of John Foster and other members of the family, but also for the interest he has taken in my work, for the hospitality he has shown me, and for the oral family traditions which he has imparted. I should like to thank Mr. Brian Trainor, Deputy Keeper of the Records, P.R.O.N.I., for permission to quote from the Foster/Massereene MSS., and to record a more personal debt, both to him and to his predecessor, Mr. Kenneth Darwin. I also owe much to all my colleagues on the staff of P.R.O.N.I., among whom it would be invidious to single out individuals, with the exceptions of Miss Gertrude Hamilton and Miss Geraldine Hume.

For permission to draw on other MS. material, I should like to thank the following owners and depositors of family collections, in P.R.O.N.I. and elsewhere: the Duke of Abercorn, the Marquess of Anglesey, Messrs. Babington & Croasdaile, Mr. R. B. Beaumont, the Trustees of the Bedford Estates, the Earl Belmore, the late Mr. J. G. C. Spencer Bernard, Lady C. Bonham-Carter, the Trustees of the Broadlands Estates, the Earl of Caledon, the Marquess Camden, Lord Congleton, the Earl of Courtown, the Marquess of Downshire, the Marquess of Dufferin and Ava, the Misses Emma and Sylvia Duffin, the Earl of Dunraven, Lord Egremont, the Earl Erne, Lord Farnham, Mr. Adrian FitzGerald, the late Mrs. O. J. Fortescue, Viscount Gage, Mr. F. E. Hart, the Marquess of Headfort, Mr. David Holland, Mr. B. Y. McPeake, Mrs. A. C. May, Capt. R. Neall, the Earl of Normanton, Miss Faith O'Grady, Mr. Dermot O'Hara, Mr. Arthur Pack-Beresford, Lord Redesdale, Mr. Noel Ross, Lord Rossmore, Lord Sackville, the Earl of Shannon, Mr. H. W. B. Stewart, the late Major-General Sir Eustace Tickell, and the late and present Duke of Wellington.

I should also like to acknowledge the permission and the assistance of the following institutions: the Armagh Diocesan Registry; the British Library Board; the Buckinghamshire County Record Office; the Genealogical Office, Dublin; the Gloucestershire County Record Office; the Hampshire County Record Office; the House of Lords Record Office; the Keele University Library; the Kent Archives Office; the National Library of Ireland; the National Library of Scotland; the Public Record Office, London, and the Comptroller, H.M. Stationery Office; the Public Record Office of Ireland; the Royal Irish Academy, Dublin; the State Paper Office, Dublin Castle; the Suffolk County Record Office; and the West and East Sussex Record Offices. On some of these institutions I made fairly unreasonable demands, and for help beyond the call of duty, I should like to thank: Sir John Ainsworth, Bt., Mr. Michael Hewson, and Mr. Donal O'Looney, of the National Library of Ireland; Mr. Hugh Hanley, Buckinghamshire County Archivist; Mr. Breandan McGiolla Chiolle, Keeper of the State Papers, Dublin Castle; Mr. Iain Maciver of the National Library of Scotland; Mr. E. K. Timings and Mr. J. A. Walford of the Public Record Office; and all the staff of the Queen's University Library with whom I have come in contact.

Where MS. material in another institution has been photocopied by P.R.O.N.I., I cite either originals or photocopies, depending on which gives the more precise reference. Where MS. material has been printed, in whole or in part, I cite the printed in preference to the MS. source. In quoting from MS. material, I have been faithful to the original, except that I have eliminated archaisms of purely antiquarian interest and have clarified confusing punctuation unless I was too confused myself to be able to do so with confidence. Unless otherwise stated, Acts of Parliament are Irish Acts, acres are Irish Plantation acres, and pounds are Irish pounds (even after the equalization of the British and Irish currencies in 1826).

Many friends and colleagues have contributed to this book, though in no way to its shortcomings. Where my debt can be related to a specific part of the text, I acknowledge it in a footnote. At this point, I should like to acknowledge only my more general debt to the following: Mr. P. F. Watkinson and Mr. D. H. Newsome, who first gave me the appetite to do a piece of research; Mr. A. B. Cooke, who provided much inspiration and provoked much thought; Dr. D. W. Hayton and Dr. P. J. Jupp, without whose generous advice the last chapter would be much worse; Professor E. M. Johnston, whose suggestions crucially influenced the structure of the book; and Professor J. C. Beckett, who supervised the Ph.D. thesis on which part of it is based, guided me through subsequent drafts and re-drafts, and generally helped in more ways than I can record or shall ever know. To Miss Esther Hewitt my special thanks are due for her help with the proofs and the index.

A. P. W. Malcomson

Public Record Office of
Northern Ireland, 1977

ABBREVIATIONS

B.L. Add. MSS.	British Library, Additional Manuscripts
C.L.A.J.	*County Louth Archaeological Journal*
D.N.B.	*Dictionary of National Biography*
E.H.R.	*English Historical Review*
F.P.	Foster/Massereene MSS.
H.M.C.	Historical Manuscripts Commission
H.O.	Home Office
I.H.S.	Irish Historical Studies
K.A.O.	Kent Archives Office
N.L.I.	National Library of Ireland, Dublin
N.L.S.	National Library of Scotland, Edinburgh
P.R.O.	Public Record Office, London
P.R.O.I.	Public Record Office of Ireland, Dublin
P.R.O.N.I.	Public Record Office of Northern Ireland, Belfast
Q.U.B.	The Queen's University, Belfast
R.I.A.	Royal Irish Academy, Dublin
R.O.	Record Office
S.P.O.	State Paper Office, Dublin
T.C.D.	Trinity College, Dublin
U.C.D.	University College, Dublin

INTRODUCTION

In Great Britain, and even in Ireland, John Foster's name is no longer a household word. A simple statement of the facts of his career is, therefore, by no means superfluous. Born in 1740, he died in his eighty-ninth year, in 1828, and was politically active almost to the end. He first entered the Irish Parliament in 1761, when not quite of age, as member for the family borough of Dunleer, co. Louth. In 1768, two years after his father's retirement from the House, he succeeded him as M.P. for co. Louth and represented the county uninterruptedly till his elevation to the peerage of the United Kingdom as Lord Oriel in 1821, by which time he was the Father of the House of Commons at Westminster[1] (Chapter Three). His career as a prominent figure in national politics, and more specifically his official career, was understandably not so long and not so uninterrupted; but it was still, by any reasonable standards, both (Chapter Two). He served first as Chairman of the Committee of Supply and Ways and Means, 1777–84, then as Chancellor of the Exchequer, 1784–5, then as Speaker of the House of Commons, 1785–1800, and finally, returning to a former office, as Chancellor of the Irish Exchequer at Westminster, 1804–6 and 1807–11. As will be apparent from these dates, the only long interruption in his official career came in the years immediately following the Union in 1800, after he had distinguished himself as the most influential opponent of that measure. With the exception of these years, and of the year 1806–7, it can fairly be said that between 1784 and 1811 he held the highest political offices (the Irish speakership being a political office) to which under normal circumstances an Irish politician could aspire.[2]

[1] List of Irish constituencies and their M.P.s, 1818, Peel MSS., B.L. Add. MS. 40298, fol. 30. Peel was not sure about this; but Mr. Roland Thorne of the History of Parliament Trust confirms that, if service in the Irish Parliament is reckoned along with service in the United Kingdom Parliament, Foster was the longest-serving member by 1818.

[2] During the years of Foster's official career, two equally high or higher offices were held by Irishmen: the lord chancellorship by John Fitzgibbon between 1789 and 1802, and the chief secretaryship by Lord Castlereagh between 1798 and 1801

It can also fairly be said that he lived through a period of exceptionally rapid and dramatic political change, especially in Ireland. When he entered the Irish Parliament, there was no compulsory limitation on its duration except the duration of the life of the sovereign, and it was roughly co-equal in legislative importance with the British and Irish Privy Councils; while he sat in the Irish Parliament, it was invigorated by statutory octennial dissolutions, and emancipated in theoretical though not practical terms by 'the Constitution of 1782'; when he died, the Irish Parliament, having come briefly into its own in the period 1782–1800, had been extinguished almost thirty years previously by the Union, which had transferred the representation of Ireland to Westminster. When he entered the Irish Parliament, it was so far from being reformed that its entire membership could have held places and pensions, had there been room for them all on the Irish establishment; when he died, an Irish Place and Pension Act had been in operation for thirty-five years, the Irish borough representation had been subjected to what was, in effect, a drastic measure of reform almost thirty years previously, and the Great Reform Act lay just round the corner. When he entered the Irish Parliament, the Irish Roman Catholics were not only debarred from any form of direct participation in political life, they were also debarred from acquiring property for any longer than a thirty-one year tenure, the exercise of their religion was proscribed by the letter of the law, and theoretically their hierarchy and even their priesthood should not have existed; when he died, the disabilities of the Catholics in matters of property and religion had been removed for nearly fifty years, the Catholics had enjoyed the parliamentary franchise for thirty-five years, and they were soon to be admitted to an almost equal participation in political life with the Protestants. (Foster did not quite live to see this last event, 'Catholic Emancipation', which took place in 1829; but he lived to recognize its inevitability.[1]) If these events do not qualify for

and (more debatably, since the Wellesleys were only debatably Irishmen) by the Wellesley brothers between 1807 and 1812. However, I do not regard these as 'normal' appointments, in that they departed from an old precedent and did not set a new one.

[1] F. T. Foster to Lord Oriel, 20 Feb. 1827, F.P. D.207/73/199.

the description of rapid and dramatic political change, it is hard to imagine what events would; and Foster lived and was politically active through almost all of them.

He was also opposed to almost all of them. He publicly, and perhaps privately, supported the Octennial Act of 1768. He publicly (though belatedly) supported the Constitution of 1782, and he later came to see and to exploit its potential; but at the time he was privately fearful of the consequences and very uneasy at the nature of the agitation which extorted the Constitution of 1782 from the British Government. He was either indifferent or hostile to the Place and Pension Acts of 1793. He led (as has been seen) the opposition to the Union in 1799–1800. And though he supported and contributed to the measures of 1778 and 1782 removing the disabilities of the Catholics in matters of property and religion, he made the most effective speech against their readmission to the parliamentary franchise in 1793, and thereafter he was the Anglo-Irish Ascendancy's most effective spokesman against Catholic Emancipation (notably in the first post-Union debate on the subject, in 1805), until succeeded in that role by his nephew and political heir, John Leslie Foster. To all these measures Foster applied the touchstone, would they undermine the Anglo-Irish Ascendancy, either indirectly by weakening the British connection, or directly by reforming the Irish representation or admitting Catholics to a participation in political power. For all his political importance, he was always on the defensive (except sometimes in his cherished sphere of economic affairs). His characteristic political posture was making the best of what he considered a bad job—even as bad a job as the Union—and his political career was in effect a series of rearguard actions fought on behalf of the Anglo-Irish Ascendancy (Chapter Eight).

The term Anglo-Irish Ascendancy requires definition. The Anglo-Irish were the descendants of people of English origin who had settled in Ireland during the fifteenth, sixteenth, seventeenth, and eighteenth centuries, usually after receiving grants of land for military or other services to the British Crown. In religion they were not only Protestant, but Anglican, in distinction to the Protestant Dissenting families of Scottish origins who were planted in Ulster in the early seventeenth century, or who planted themselves in the late seventeenth

century. The Anglo-Irish were a social élite rather than a strictly
ethnic group. Thus, the humbler English settlers in Ireland—
for example the other ranks in successive British armies sent
thither—belong ethnically but not socially to the Anglo-Irish,
or rather were Anglo-Irish but not part of the Anglo-Irish
Ascendancy—unless like Foster's family they rose to membership of it (Chapter One). By the same token, many families not
ethnically Anglo-Irish were part of the Anglo-Irish Ascendancy
by Foster's time: 'Old English' families like the Geraldines
(the dukes of Leinster, knights of Glin, Kerry, and so on) and
the earls of Clanricarde; Gaelic families like the Malones of
Baronston and the Quins of Adare; and Scottish families like
the Macartneys of Lissanoure and the Stewarts of Newtownards.
These families, whatever their ethnic background, had become
part of the Anglo-Irish Ascendancy by conforming to the
Anglican communion, just as several Old English and Anglo-
Irish families excluded themselves from it by adhering to the
Catholic faith—the various Catholic Plunket families of co.
Meath, and the Brownes of Kenmare, for example. For most
of the eighteenth century, the Anglo-Irish Ascendancy held
a virtual monopoly, legal or practical, of political power:
a legal monopoly in that Catholics were excluded by law from
Parliament, the parliamentary franchise, and the corporations,
and Protestant Dissenters from the corporations; a practical
monopoly in that Protestant Dissenters, though never excluded
by law from Parliament or the parliamentary franchise, numbered only a handful of members in any House of Commons.
(With regard to the corporations, the practical monopoly of
the Anglo-Irish Ascendancy remained almost intact until
municipal reform in 1839, although Protestant Dissenters were
legally admissible to corporations from 1780 and Catholics
from 1793). However, it must again be stressed that only the
higher echelons of the Anglo-Irish as an ethnic group really
belonged to the Anglo-Irish Ascendancy and really profited
from this virtual monopoly. A very few of the lower echelons
were members of corporations (always as the yes-men of who-
ever controlled the corporation politically), but the rest were
on the same political footing as the Protestant Dissenters, who
could vote in borough elections if they were freemen or in
county elections if they were 40/- freeholders.

The Anglo-Irish Ascendancy was therefore a narrow social and political élite, to be defined along social and political, rather than ethnic, lines. Indeed, but for the handful of Protestant Dissenting M.P.s, and but for a few Protestant Dissenting and Catholic landowners who had proprietary interests in county elections, the Anglo-Irish Ascendancy could be defined as comprising those who themselves sat in the Irish Parliament or who exercised significant influence over the return of the 300 members to the House of Commons. The Protestant Dissenters and Catholics in these categories are so few that the definition may perhaps be allowed to stand.[1]

In 1782, during the debates on the Catholic Relief Act (or rather Acts) of that year, Grattan described Ireland as 'a Protestant settlement' which these measures, if carried, would transform into 'an Irish nation'.[2] Ireland was not a Protestant settlement in 1782: it was still an Anglo-Irish Ascendancy. The act of 1780 readmitting Protestant Dissenters to corporations and all other offices of trust and profit under the Crown had nominally produced a situation of political equality among Protestants of all descriptions, but granted the narrowness of the franchise in the boroughs and the strength of the Ascendancy proprietary interests in the counties, the equality was only nominal. Foster, partial though he was to Protestant Dissent and particularly to the linen weavers of Ulster, wanted it to stay that way; a parliamentary reform, even on exclusively Protestant lines, was unacceptable to him. Likewise, when he supported the Catholic Relief Acts of 1782, the last thing he thought he was bringing into existence was 'an Irish nation': for him, as for Swift at an earlier period and Barrington at a later, the only Irish nation was the Anglo-Irish Ascendancy. In 1782 the limit of the concessions which the Ascendancy could safely make had, in Foster's view, been reached, and he was not prepared for meaningful political concessions to Protestant Dissenters (or even to the Anglo-Irish who lay outside the Ascendancy proper), or for any political concessions

[1] For the Anglo-Irish generally, see J. C. Beckett, *The Anglo-Irish Tradition* (London, 1976), *passim*.

[2] Quoted in Maureen Wall, 'The United Irish Movement', *Historical Studies*, v (London, 1965), 136. This is an extremely important article, which dispels much of the careless rapture which nineteenth-century nationalist historians infused into the movement.

to the Catholics (the first act of 1782 stipulated that Catholics could not own or hold freehold land in boroughs where the freeholders had the vote[1]).

Whether the Anglo-Irish Ascendancy of 1782 was a maintainable political institution is problematical. Foster thought that it was, because he thought that political discontent and indeed political awareness was confined to a number of middle-class agitators, who enjoyed no support among the masses of the people, particularly the Catholic masses. More constructively, he hoped to prevent the spread of political discontent by means of the material prosperity which, in the years between 1779 and the outbreak of war in 1793, he did more than anyone else to achieve (his political thinking is always to be considered in the light of the emphasis he placed on economic considerations). The worsening economic situation from 1793 onwards, caused mainly by the war and the disturbed state of the country, nullified the constructive element in his policy. However, he may have been justified in questioning the validity of the other constructive alternatives. Would a parliamentary reform of the sort that would have found favour with the Irish parliamentary Opposition (which was the utmost which could conceivably have been granted) really have prevented the United Irishmen from advancing on to revolutionary politics? Also, was the Catholic Relief Act of 1793 really necessary to prevent the leaders of the Catholic Committee from combining with the United Irishmen in a genuinely united United Irish movement? There was possibly more life in the Anglo-Irish Ascendancy of 1782 than nineteenth-century historians or, more important, the late eighteenth-century British government, allowed.

In terms of practical politics, it was on the attitude of the British government that the maintenance or otherwise of the Ascendancy depended. Foster was well aware of this. But he assumed that the dependence of the Ascendancy on the British government was reciprocal, in that the British government could not maintain control of the Irish Parliament and, ultimately, maintain the British connection, except by means of the Ascendancy. Logically, the validity of this assumption was strengthened by the Constitution of 1782, which made it

[1] 21 & 22 Geo. III, c. 24, s. 1. The second act was c. 62.

much more important that the British government should be
able to control the Irish Parliament, since it could no longer
browbeat it: psychologically—from the point of view of the
psychology of British governments—the validity of the assumption was weakened by the Constitution of 1782, which had been
extorted by a revolt of the Anglo-Irish Ascendancy, in alliance
with elements outside the Ascendancy, to whom it might be
profitable for the British government in the future to make
a direct appeal. Foster was probably right in assuming that the
British government could not have maintained control of an
Irish Parliament which had been rationally reformed, and the
British government never tried the experiment; but it did
break in on the Ascendancy to the extent of an irrational
reform—the readmission of 40/- Catholic freeholders to the
county franchise in 1793. The effects of this concession were
not felt until after the extinction of the Irish Parliament, and
had they been felt before then, could easily have been counteracted by the preponderating representation enjoyed by the
close boroughs—the strongholds of the Ascendancy. However,
before making the concession, the British Prime Minister, Pitt,
had made the calculation that, if by-passing the Ascendancy
proved an unsuccessful policy, the British government had
the additional safeguard that it could by-pass Ascendancy and
Irish Parliament alike by carrying a Union.[1] The Ascendancy,
or more specifically those Irish politicians who followed
Foster's line in upholding it, had no such room to manœuvre.
Since they would not cease to be an Ascendancy by widening
the basis of their power, they could have '. . . no other God
but English Government . . .' It was this unequal inter-
dependence of the Ascendancy and the British government
which characterized the Irish politics of Foster's day, and
committed Foster personally to a series of rearguard actions.

Moreover, even in former days of equal or more nearly
equal inter-dependence, it had proved impossible to translate
the community of interest between the Anglo-Irish Ascendancy
and the British government into community of sentiment.
The marriage had been loveless long before the Constitution
of 1782: a marriage of convenience dictated by the cold fact
that '. . . Ireland is too great to be unconnected with us, and

[1] Wall, *United Irish Movement*, p. 132.

too near us to be dependent on a foreign state, and too little
to be independent . . .'[1] British commercial selfishness had
produced the usual colonial response among the Ascendancy,
and in the political sphere the heavy-handedness of the British
government or its Irish representatives had twice produced
crises, in 1724–5 and 1753–6, in which an Anglo-Irish national-
ism had come near to the surface. In 1765, a time of comparative political calm, the appointment of a new lord lieutenant
was thus received by John Ponsonby, Speaker of the House of
Commons, scion of one of the most powerful Ascendancy
families, and the British government's chief parliamentary
manager among the Irish politicians:

. . . I have the satisfaction to find that the terms upon which I
proposed to serve Government have been approved: I mean that
nothing new or extraordinary was to be asked from the Country,
and that the pretensions of Gentlemen here should have more
attention paid to them than has of late been shown to Irish
recommendations. The public as well as private character of Lord
Hertford [the new Lord Lieutenant], together with the great property
which he has in Ireland, are the best securities which we can have
for his good behaviour. There could not have been found a person
to govern us who in all respects would be so likely to use us well,
and I for one shall do my best endeavours to support his Administration upon those terms which I have premised, and *upon none other.*
. . . If anything truly destructive to Ireland shall be attempted,
no man will be more ready to oppose than myself. But peevish
opposition is the most destructive thing that can be, as it must
make every Lord Lieutenant our bitter enemy, and consequently
we must be represented in England as a people whom it is impossible
to please. . . . I am now for looking forward. What matters it to us
who are Ministers in England? Let us stick to our own circle and
manage our own little game as well as we can.[2]

The uneasy arrogance, the suspicion of 'destructive' British
measures, and the claim to speak on behalf of 'the Country'—
these were typical 'Ascendancy' attitudes (though probably
expressed nowhere else with such cynical frankness). There
is an even more uneasy arrogance in Foster's description of
a subsequent Lord Lieutenant, the Emancipationist Lord
Fitzwilliam, as '. . . the weakest, [most] well-meaning, good

---

[1] C. T. Greville to Duke of Rutland, 3 Dec. 1784, *H.M.C. Rutland MSS.* iii. 155.
[2] Ponsonby to Foster's father, Anthony, 14 Aug. 1765, F.P. D.562/1757.

man I have met . . .'—a description penned in March 1795, *after*, and not before, the British Government had recalled Fitzwilliam; also in his description of Lord Cornwallis, the Lord Lieutenant who carried the Union, in September 1798 as 'a damned silly fellow'.[1] Foster had good reason for greater uneasiness. In Ponsonby's day the only issue was, by what agency should the alliance between the British government and the Ascendancy be maintained: in Foster's day, the British government had decided that it needed to look for allies outside the Ascendancy. The lovelessness of the marriage, which had always been there, became more apparent as its convenience unilaterally diminished.

This, then, is the context in which Foster's political career has to be set. The context is peculiarly, but not exclusively, Irish. The Irish administration had a peculiarly narrow sphere of legislative initiative and action, because it was not responsible to the Irish Parliament (after the Constitution of 1782, as before), and because matters of high policy were still decided in Great Britain; Foster and the Irish politicians of the 1790s, misleadingly known as 'the Irish Cabinet', were administrators rather than cabinet ministers (in even the contemporary British sense of that term), because they had no other God but an English government which was unsympathetic to their 'Ascendancy' views. Yet, in Great Britain, too, in the late eighteenth and early nineteenth century, the legislative sphere of government, though it was widening under the pressures of the war and the industrial revolution, was still very narrow by modern standards; in Great Britain, too, it was not unknown for cabinets to hold together only because they agreed to differ on certain major matters of policy and principle like parliamentary reform and, later, Catholic Emancipation. The really important distinction between the politics of the Anglo-Irish Ascendancy and contemporary British politics was the difference in the intensity of conviction which such major matters of policy and principle evoked. For Ascendancy politicians of Foster's stamp, parliamentary

[1] Foster to Lord Sheffield, 23 Mar. [1795], printed in A. P. W. Malcomson (ed.) *An Anglo-Irish Dialogue: a Calendar of the Correspondence between John Foster and Lord Sheffield, 1774–1821* (Belfast, 1975), p. 18; Marquess of Buckingham to Lord Grenville, 10 Sept. 1798, quoted in G. C. Bolton, *The Passing of the Irish Act of Union* (Oxford, 1966), p. 69.

reform for Ireland was no mere matter of internal regulation, but a threat to the British connection: parliamentary reform for Great Britain did not possess this dimension. Again, for Foster, as for his almost exact contemporary, George III, Catholic Emancipation was a question of conscience and a challenge to their whole concept of the constitution; but for Foster it was also another threat to the British connection and, in effect, a question of political life and death. Foster's career is of British significance because the intensity of his convictions, not actually on Catholic Emancipation, but on the Union, transformed him in 1798–9 from an extreme form of eighteenth-century administrator-politician, indeed 'man of business', into a leader of 'Party'. He himself denied the change, and after the Union reverted to type; also, the party was formed round the one issue, and narrowly fell short of 'General Opposition'. However, it was a very unusual and un-eighteenth-century opposition, for all that, and the wonder is that it was mounted by a man of Foster's political type and previous record. Intensity of conviction alone explains this, and explains also why contemporary or remotely contemporary British politics furnish no parallel.

In the local sphere, the politics of the Anglo-Irish Ascendancy—at least as practised by Foster in Louth and Drogheda (Chapters Three and Four)—are not so distinct from contemporary British politics under the unreformed electoral system. In this sphere, too, Foster's career is of British significance, because top-rank British politicians of his day usually did not represent popular constituencies; and although top-rank Irish politicians often did, few of them have left papers, or at any rate have left papers which have not been 'weeded' of local detail. In Foster's case papers about the chancellorship of the Irish exchequer jostle with papers about the Dundalk gaol and the Louth infirmary, in indiscriminate profusion. With the probable exception of Henry Dundas, Foster is the only top-rank politician of his day, in either Great Britain or Ireland, whose papers permit an equal coverage of the national and the local contexts, and a study of the interaction of the two and the contrasts between them.

The chief contrast is the virtual absence of political issues from the election politics of Louth, though not of Drogheda, in spite of Foster's prominence in national politics on the issues which threatened the Anglo-Irish Ascendancy. The issues were aired at Louth grand jury and county meetings or on other inter-election occasions, and Foster's conduct on them was of general importance to his 'interest' in the county; but by and large they did not feature in Louth elections until 1826. Since Foster foresaw at least as early as 1795 that the chief practical danger of the Catholic Relief Act of 1793 was that Protestant aspirants to represent counties would play to the Catholic vote, it is not surprising that he kept the Emancipation issue out of Louth elections for as long as in him lay. However, since his forecast came true in virtually every county with a largely Catholic electorate sooner than it came true in Louth, and since the revolt of the Catholic freeholders in Louth and else-where against their Protestant landlords was the proximate cause of the granting of Emancipation in 1829, his methods of keeping Louth politically apathetic and obedient up to 1826 are of much more than local significance. When every allowance has been made for the patronage and the number of freeholders at his command (Chapters Six and Seven), it is clear that the answer does not lie solely in 'real estate' factors of this kind. At least part of the answer lies in Foster's reputa-tion as 'the best grand juror, magistrate, improver and country gentleman in the Kingdom': in other words, in his personal popularity and successful paternalism.

This is an important conclusion, and if true of the Foster interest in Louth, has far-reaching implications; after all, Louth was the smallest county in Ireland, and the most likely to be reducible to a proprietary borough; Foster sat for it for longer than any other Irish county member in the days of the unreformed electoral system;[1] the Foster family enjoyed as long an uninterrupted run in its representation as any other Ascen-dancy family in any other county;[2] and it was almost certainly

---

[1] His nearest rivals were John Beresford, M.P. for co. Waterford, 1761–1805, Thomas Conolly, M.P. for co. Londonderry, 1761–1800, and James Stewart, M.P. for co. Tyrone, 1768–1812.

[2] The Beresford family represented co. Waterford without interruption from 1757 to 1826, and Lord George Beresford was elected again in 1830, after losing his seat in 1826. The Stewart family, father and son, represented co. Tyrone without interruption from 1748 to 1812. These are probably the nearest rivals to the Fosters, but the basis of comparison is rather phoney, since a family interest could return an M.P. who did not bear the family patronymic.

the only Irish county which was uncontested for so long a period
as fifty-eight years (1768–1826). Irish county elections in this
period are usually regarded as in some sense less popular than
English (though not Scottish) county elections, because of the
alleged absence of a substantial yeomanry in Ireland, the
presence on the great estates of armies of very dependent freeholders (particularly after 1793), and the consequent emphasis
on coercion rather than cajolery. The case of Louth does not
substantiate this view, although it may be that Louth was an
unusual and particularly English kind of constituency, because
it contained no really great estate (Foster's included) and
a numerous, resident gentry. However, it is unlikely that the
view will be substantiated by the study of any county which is
well documented in terms of family papers emanating from
electoral interests concerned in its politics. The view, in fact,
derives from too much concentration and reliance on central-
government sources: on the numerous and bewilderingly
interconnected 'lists' of the Irish House of Commons which stud
the period 1769–93 (and have no exact British counterparts),
and on the papers of British politicians serving in the Irish
administration in Dublin Castle. The central government
usually received a picture of county politics (and not county
politics only) which was either innocently over-simplified, for
purposes of ready reference, or else deliberately misrepresented,
for purposes which were decidedly less innocent. In general,
the picture which emerges from the central-government
sources is more static than it ought to be; the counties are more
'sewn-up' than they actually were; the strength and internal
cohesion of a few big interests is exaggerated; the strength and
importance of the unpredictable 'independent interest', based
on the minor gentry and the more substantial yeomanry, is
correspondingly played down; and insufficient account is
taken of the fact that a popular element in county politics was
always present to a greater or lesser extent, and made itself
felt with greater or lesser effect. The impression gained from
the Foster/Massereene MSS. is that Louth politics were not so
very different from English county politics, and that in general,
when allowance is made for differences in electoral law
(notably the unique Irish registration system, which had no
British counterpart until 1832), the local politics of the Anglo-

Irish Ascendancy were not so very remote from their English counterpart.

In the sphere of national politics, too, Foster's eminence cannot be accounted for on the basis of 'real estate' factors, of the sort which the twentieth century delights in predicating for the eighteenth. Chapter One discusses, among other things, the extent of his inherited advantages, and Chapter Five discusses in more detail the extent of one of them, his electoral influence (and the extent to which electoral influence helped a career politician to attain high office). There is, however, no reason to suppose that he attained high office on any basis other than merit. He was highly regarded by successive British governments and/or their Irish representatives for his experience and industry as a 'man of business', for his expertise in economic affairs, and for his effectiveness as a parliamentarian—assets particularly necessary after 1782, when the British government lost the power to amend Irish legislation, and assets which in its eyes outweighed the inconvenience of his 'Ascendancy' views. He was also highly regarded by the independent country gentlemen of the Irish House of Commons, including many people often to be found in opposition to the government, who recognized in him a kindred spirit (as indeed did many of the country gentlemen at Westminster, his brogue notwithstanding), and elected him their Speaker accordingly. Indeed, his country gentleman ethos was probably his leading political characteristic, in British as well as in Irish terms. It is a well-known truism that country gentlemen very seldom came to the fore in the parliaments which collectively they dominated. Indeed, Foster was arguably the first true country gentleman to attain top political eminence, in either Great Britain or Ireland, since Walpole. Other politicians of his day possessed country-gentleman characteristics: Addington was plain-spoken, but then his background was professional; Dundas was positively uncouth, but he was tainted by the orientalism of the Board of Control (to say nothing of the skulduggery of managing the Scottish electoral machine); and Castlereagh was at home among the Presbyterian farmers of co. Down, on whom his election depended, but was also at home among European crowned heads. Foster, alone, was separated from the class from which he came by nothing but ability; and it was the combination of first-rate ability, particularly in the sphere of economic affairs, with the style and manner of a country gentleman, which ensured him such success as he enjoyed.[1]

[1] Citation of authorities has been given at this stage only for quotations and points which do not occur in the body of the text. The quotation on the title-page is taken from the Downshire MSS., P.R.O.N.I. D.607/F/309.

CHAPTER ONE

A New Family among the Anglo-Irish

In the words of Professor Namier, '. . . English history, and especially English parliamentary history, is made up by families rather than by individuals; for a nation with a tradition of self-government must have thousands of dynasties, partaking of the peculiarites which in other countries belong to the royal family alone. . . .'[1] The same is of course applicable to Irish history and to the Foster family in particular. Although easily the most distinguished individual of his family, Foster was profoundly influenced by the type of family he came from: by its origins, traditions, sources of income, local influence, marriage connections, and so on; and the Foster family as a whole possessed distinctive, indeed unusual, characteristics, which were bound to leave a mark on any individual member of it, no matter how personally distinguished he might be.

The popular image of the Anglo-Irish Ascendancy family of the second half of the eighteenth century is not flattering; it is one of decadent descendants of some small-time *conquistador*, dissipating a property which had been easily come by; it is one of trafficking in parliamentary seats and scrambling for honours and places; above all, it is one of irresponsibility, improvidence, and absenteeism. The reality is far different in many cases, and particularly in that of the Fosters. They numbered no *conquistador* among their ancestors; they devoted much energy to the augmenting and improving of a property which they owed to their own industry alone; they controlled only one seat outright, which they never sold; the honours and places which they obtained were hardly commensurate with their deserts; and they were not irresponsible, not improvident, and not absentee. Indeed, it seems likely that John Foster's only

[1] L. B. Namier, *England in the Age of the American Revolution* (London, 1961), p. 19

improvidences were the scale on which he invested in agricultural improvement, and his choice of an active political career.
In the present-day process of glamourizing eighteenth-century
Anglo-Irish society, the Fosters receive no mention, and for
the good reason that they were middle class in their origins
and in their virtues. Foster, no doubt, predicated these virtues
for the Anglo-Irish Ascendancy as a whole, and in so doing
was misled into overstatement by the record and tradition of
his own particular family. Perhaps, without that record and
tradition, he would not have become the champion, or rather
the rearguard, of the Ascendancy. Certainly, his family
background is extremely important to an understanding of his
successful paternalism in the sphere of local politics; it was
successful because it was not lofty, and it was not lofty because
the Fosters were not themselves so far removed from the soil.
His family background is also important to an understanding
of his abiding Anglo-Irish patriotism and provincialism, even
after the Union, in the sphere of national politics.

The most important single fact about the Fosters is that they
were a new family. The newness of any Anglo-Irish family
must of course be viewed in the light of the wholesale displace-
ments and confiscations of the sixteenth and seventeenth
centuries. Yet even when viewed against this background, the
Fosters stand out as a new family. The tradition is that they
came over to Ireland in the 1660s as mowers of hay. When
they settled in co. Louth is not clear. The 1666 Hearth Money
return for Dunleer parish, where they lived from at least the
1680s to the 1740s, contains the[1] name Samuel Foster;[1] 'Samuel'
occurs once in the eighteenth century as a family Christian
name, so the likelihood is that this Samuel was John Foster's
great-great-grandfather. If so, he will have been the father of
Anthony Foster of Dunleer, who in 1683 was named by the
charter of Dunleer borough as one of the thirteen original or
'charter' burgesses.[2] This Anthony's date of birth is unknown,
but he must have been of age in 1683 and he died in 1722. He
is the earliest Foster mentioned in *Burke's Peerage*. In successive

---

[1] A. P. W. Malcomson, 'The Foster Family and the Parliamentary Borough of
Dunleer, 1683–1800', *C.L.A.J.* xvii. 156. All subsequent references to Dunleer
borough are taken from this source.

[2] Copy charter of Dunleer borough, 1683, F.P. D.207/19/2.

editions of that work he is hopefully styled 'Colonel' Anthony
Foster, but there is no other evidence besides *Burke* of his
military rank. Indeed, *Burke* is largely responsible for obscuring
the important fact of the Fosters' humble origins. In *Burke's
Peerage* they are always described as 'of the Cumberland family'
and in *Burke's Landed Gentry*, with equal, if inconsistent,
grandiloquence, as 'of the Berkshire family'.[1] When the Chinese
wished to honour a man, they used to ennoble his ancestors:
the British custom has been to ennoble the man himself, and
leave the ennobling of his ancestors to his own ingenuity.
Certain of our ruling families have been particularly active
in this direction—notably the Russells and the Foxes—and it
must be assumed that the Fosters, too, went in for a mild form
of self-ennoblement. If Anthony Foster was a colonel, his
services were very scantily rewarded. Up to 1698 he seems to
have held no land except a customary tenancy of a 270-acre
farm in Dunleer; in 1698 he was for the first time granted
a lease of his farm.[2] He may have been something more than
a mower of hay, but he must certainly have been something
less than an erstwhile colonel. The point is settled fairly
decisively by the fact that John Foster himself could trace his
family no further than one generation beyond 'Colonel'
Anthony Foster,[3] probably to the Samuel Foster of the Hearth
Money return.

The newness of the Foster family is of course a point which
can be overstated. There is not, for example, any reference to
it in all John Foster's voluminous correspondence, except for
one anonymous letter written in 1810 which, amid the common
form of threatening his life and sending him to the devil,
throws in a reminder of his 'low birth'.[4] No doubt this was
just a lucky hit. The correspondence of other people is equally
silent; it must have been widely known, but it seems not to
have been mentioned, or perhaps thought worthy of mention.
The only all-out attack on John Foster for his plebeian origins
appeared in an English newspaper in 1786 (and suggests that
the English press would have benefited from Foster's Irish

[1] *Burke's Peerage and Baronetage* (1933 edn.) p. 1633; *Burke's Landed Gentry* (1862 edn.), p. 503.
[2] Chancery bill filed by John Foster, [*c.* 1738], F.P. D.562/5108.
[3] Count De Salis to John Foster, 7 Sept. 1810, F.P. T.2519/4/1657.
[4] Anonymous letter to John Foster, Aug. 1810, F.P. D.562/11584.

Libel Act of 1784).[1] It recounts how John Foster's 'grand-father' (great-great-grandfather would be nearer the mark) 'followed the laborious profession of a *mower*' and made his fortune by winning a mowing match to which his employer had challenged some neighbouring landowner:

. . . In wagers of this nature, all advantages may be taken, and the advantage which Foster's opponent took was that of mixing a very strong purgative in his drink. This had the desired effect, and Foster was very soon seized with a complaint in his bowels that threatened the loss of his promised victory. But . . . he took off his drawers, tucked his shirt round his middle, and in this manner suffered the physic to work as he worked, and won the wager, to the great diversion of many hundred spectators. . . .

It is remarkable that, while a most abject servility marks the character, the features of a monkey seem to have been stamped on the visage, of this family; so that many people who know the mower's descendants better than myself, do not hesitate to declare that they are as servile as lawyers, and as mischievous, as the animal they so nearly resemble. . . .

It must be acknowledged that the only extant likeness of John Foster in which he is not disguised in speaker's wig and robes, bears out the comparison to a monkey (see the Frontispiece). This scurrilous newspaper attack would appear to be an exceptional case; certainly, John Foster never had to endure taunts about his mean extraction thrown out in the heat of parliamentary debate, as did the British politicians, Charles Jenkinson, President of the Board of Trade, and Lord Thurlow, Lord Chancellor of England.[2] The Jenkinson and Thurlow episodes were also exceptional, and their significance lies in the fact that in both cases the victim had very much the best of the encounter. It is needless here to dwell on the truism that the eighteenth century paid more than lip-service to the doctrine of social mobility. Among Foster's contemporaries and near-contemporaries there were many men of similar origins to himself, and this was particularly true of men who like himself

---

[1] Cutting from an unnamed English newspaper, [1786], Leinster MSS., P.R.O.N.I. D.3078/11. For Foster's Libel Act see pp. 49, 382, 407.
[2] Namier, *The Structure of Politics at the Accession of George III* (London, 1929), i. 15; Lord Campbell, *The Lives of the Lord Chancellors and Keepers of the Great Seal of England*, 3rd edn. (7 vols., London, 1849–50), v. 539.

came from professional families which had come to the fore through a combination of legal and parliamentary ability.

The list of such men includes many of the most distinguished figures in Irish political history in the second half of the eighteenth century. It includes Anthony Malone; Henry Flood; John Hely-Hutchinson; Henry Grattan; John Scott, 1st Earl of Clonmell; John Fitzgibbon, 1st Earl of Clare; John Philpot Curran; and Barry Yelverton, 1st Viscount Avonmore. Of these, Hely-Hutchinson, Scott, Curran, and Yelverton were virtually self-made men. Yelverton was apparently 'the quondam usher of a boarding-school'; Curran's father was the seneschal of the manor of Newmarket, co. Cork; Scott's brother, at the time Scott was Attorney-General, was agent for an estate belonging to a Mr. Butler; and it was said of Hely-Hutchinson in 1773 that '. . . he would prostitute his conscience to advance his relations, who are very poor, for he is of but mean rank and birth . . .'[1] The others on the list, including John Foster, were the sons of men who had made fortunes at the bar. Indeed, in the case of Fitzgibbon's father, the fortune was reckoned at the colossal figure of £100,000.[2] It would perhaps be unfair to call Malone, Flood, Grattan, Foster, and Fitzgibbon 'second generation' men. In particular, Malone and Fitzgibbon pose insuperable problems for the sociologist, because their fathers were converts from the Roman Catholic religion and their families had been prominent before the days of forfeiture and attainder.[3] What can fairly be said about the whole five is that their families had been put on the map through the exertions of their fathers. Along with the four virtually self-made men they show that undistinguished origins were not a disqualification for success in the Law and Parliament in the days of the Anglo-Irish Ascendancy. None of them at any stage shared the fate of C. M. Warburton,

---

[1] Dr. William Drennan to Dr. William Bruce, Dec. 1783, Drennan-Bruce MSS., P.R.O.N.I. D.553/17; W. O'Regan, *Memoirs of the Legal, Literary, and Political Life of . . . John Philpot Curran*, (London, 1817), p. 2; extract of a letter from Mr. Scott to [?], 1 Jan. 1779, Downshire MSS., P.R.O.N.I. D.607/B/46; M. Bodkin (ed.), 'Notes on the Irish Parliament in 1773', *Proc. R.I.A.*, vol. 48, Sec. C, No. 4 (1942–3), 183.

[2] E. Fitzgibbon, *The Earl of Clare: Mainspring of the Union* (London, 1960), p. 41.

[3] Ibid., pp. 39 f.; Edmund Burke to Richard Burke, 20 March 1792, printed in T. W. Copeland and others (ed.), *Correspondence of Edmund Burke* (9 vols., Chicago/Cambridge, 1958–70), vii. 101.

B

Dean of Ardagh, whose application for a bishopric in 1804, though countenanced by the Irish Government, was rejected by George III on the grounds that '. . . he was a Roman Catholic originally; his name Mongan, and his father an Irish harper. . .'[1]

Where the Fosters differed from the other families is that they were a borough-owning family. Of the others, only Flood followed the example of the Fosters by making a determined effort in the middle years of the century to capture control of a borough (Callan, co. Kilkenny), and after a round of duels, contests, and election petitions, failed. The Fosters' effort in this respect took place earlier in the century, in the period 1715–35. They were probably no more scrupulous in their methods than Flood, and that they were more successful was probably the result of good luck rather than anything else. As has been seen, Dunleer, where they lived and held land, was a parliamentary borough, and the first Anthony Foster among its original burgesses. The patrons of the borough, the Tenison family, were also the Fosters' landlords in Dunleer, but as the Fosters prospered they grew increasingly independent of landlord control. The Tenisons were negligent patrons, and eventually the Fosters took advantage of their negligence and gained control, by sharp practice if not by actual treachery, of the return for the two seats for the borough. In 1735 they voluntarily surrendered one seat to the Tenisons, and reached a written partition agreement with them which held good until Dunleer was disfranchised at the time of the Union. Possession of half a borough meant that the Fosters entered the category of 'inevitable' House of Commons men. John Foster's father, another Anthony, sat for Dunleer, 1737–60, John Foster himself, 1761–8, and other members or connections of the Foster family for the rest of the century. The importance of the Dunleer seat to the Foster family is a matter of conjecture. There was no parliamentary tradition in the family prior to 1737, and perhaps Anthony Foster would never have entered parliament or pointed his eldest son in the same direction, if he had not possessed a seat of his own. Thanks to Dunleer, John Foster

---

[1] List of Union engagements, 26 Sept. 1804, printed in M. MacDonagh (ed.), *The Viceroy's Post-Bag* (London, 1904), p. 43. Even Warburton, however, achieved his bishopric in 1806.

had the advantage of a very early parliamentary apprenticeship, of a long-stop (which he never needed) in case of defeat
in co. Louth, and of one additional vote in parliament besides
his own. Such advantages are hard to measure, but they must
have played a significant part in his career.

Borough-ownership was not a normal characteristic of new
families, because such families had *ipso facto* not been prominent
in the first three-quarters of the seventeenth century, when
boroughs were being incorporated for the benefit of prominent
individuals, and because in the second half of the eighteenth
century, when boroughs began to come on to the market with
some frequency, demand always exceeded supply. The Fosters
owed their borough-seat simply to the fortuitous situation of
their leasehold property and to the negligence of their landlords. In other respects, however, they were typical of the
successful, new, professional families. John Foster's father,
Anthony (1705–79), was the first member of his family to
possess—or at least to display—the required combination of
legal and parliamentary ability. His father, another John
Foster and the son of 'Colonel' Anthony Foster, had been
a country attorney, but not a barrister, nor had he been an
M.P. (although *Burke's Peerage*, needless to say, states that he
was). Anthony Foster was a barrister, and a barrister, moreover, whose surviving papers indicate an extensive practice and
an august clientele. He was, as has been seen, the first of the
Fosters to enter the House of Commons, and he was also the
first to represent co. Louth—from 1761 to 1766. In the latter
year he retired from the House on appointment as Lord Chief
Baron of the Court of Exchequer. Yet, although he retired
from the House, he did not retire from politics; nor perhaps
was it in the nature of high judicial office in Ireland at this
time for a judge to do so. In 1767, for example, the year after
Anthony Foster's appointment, the English Lord Chancellor,
Lord Camden, noted that '. . . the Chancellor, Chief Baron
and Chief Justice are called to the [Privy] Council in Ireland,
in the quality of statesmen, and . . . the Council in that country
is an assembly of equal importance with either branch of the
legislature. . . .'[1] Anthony Foster was the outstanding figure on

[1] Lord Camden to Duke of Grafton, [July?] 1767, quoted in E. M. Johnston,
Great Britain and Ireland, 1760–1800 (Edinburgh, 1963), p. 236.

the Irish bench of his day because of the range of his extra-professional activities, including politics. He was credited with influence over a number of members of the 1768 Parliament, and was a valuable intermediary between the Government and the numerically important 'squadron' which followed the uncertain leadership of his remote kinsman and political associate, the Duke of Leinster.[1] All the same, he was first and foremost a lawyer, and only secondarily a politician. Prior to his appointment to the bench he had aspired to the solicitorship-general, an office which if anything made greater demands on a man's parliamentary than on his professional ability.[2] The Government, however, seem to have considered him 'fitter' for his existing office, that of First Counsel to the Revenue Commissioners, which he had held since 1760, and whose duties were more exclusively professional.[3]

Anthony Foster was an able man whose misfortune it has been to be overshadowed by an even abler son. Yet, it is important to remember that, at the outset of his career in public life, it was John Foster who was very much in his father's shadow. In 1773, a Government-compiled list of the members of the Irish Parliament noted that there was '. . . no man of more worth [than Anthony Foster], and indeed the son takes entirely after the father: a sensible, prudent young man . . .'; and Anthony Foster's retirement in 1777 made possible the series of promotions which in turn made possible John Foster's elevation to his first office.[4] As his father's son, it was inevitable that John Foster should be groomed to shine in the allied spheres of the Law and Parliament. However, partly because of differences of temperament between the two men, and partly because of the difference which had taken place in the wealth and status of the Foster family since Anthony Foster's young days, the balance which John Foster struck between the Law and Parliament was different from

[1] F. Elrington Ball, *Judges in Ireland, 1221–1921* (London, 1926), ii. 150 ff.; William Hunt (ed.), *The Irish Parliament in 1775* (London, 1907), pp. 31, 36, 44; Walter Burgh to John Foster, 29 Apr. 1776, F.P. D.562/4568.

[2] John Beresford to Lord Auckland, 8 Apr. 1795, Westmorland MSS., S.P.O., fols. 113.

[3] Memo. by Lord Shannon of an interview with the Lord Lieutenant, [17–21 Apr. 1764], Shannon MSS., P.R.O.N.I. D.2707/A/1/12/7.

[4] Bodkin, *Notes*, p. 205.

the balance struck by his father. Anthony Foster had first entered Parliament long after he had been called to the bar, but John Foster entered it five years before he was called to the bar, and indeed before he was quite of age; where Anthony Foster was primarily a lawyer and only secondarily a politician, John Foster was the reverse. As early as 1766, relations between them were strained because of John Foster's alleged neglect of his profession; and although another list of the Irish Parliament, compiled in 1775, considered him to be a 'very rising young man in the Law and Parliament', the likelihood is that even at this early stage he regarded the law as '. . . but a nominal profession . . ., applied himself to other studies, and no doubt had higher game in view than the humble situation of a practising barrister or even the more dignified one of a puisne judge. . . .'[1] In 1779, the Lord Lieutenant included among John Foster's qualifications for office the fact that '. . . he has no professional avocations to take him from Parliamentary and Cabinet attendance. . . .'[2] All the same, just as Anthony Foster remained a politician even after his appointment as a judge, so John Foster remained a lawyer to the end of his political career. His most celebrated office, the speakership, almost indispensably required the talents and training of a lawyer; and when he was Chancellor of the Irish Exchequer at Westminster, it was a common ground of complaint against him that he was always ready to pit his own opinion in legal matters against that of the Law Officers of the Crown, and sometimes of the Irish Lord Chancellor as well.[3]

In the sphere of local as well as national politics, John Foster's career began in the shadow of his father's. This was literally true, in the sense that John Foster succeeded him as M.P. for Dunleer in 1761, and as M.P. for co. Louth in 1768 (after Anthony Foster's elderly brother-in-law had acted as a seat-warmer during the 1767–8 session). It was also true in the less obvious, but more important, sense that under Anthony Foster the Foster family interest in co. Louth already enjoyed

[1] Mrs. Foster to John Foster [her stepson], 27 Feb. 1766, F.P. D.562/3215; Hunt, *Irish Parliament*, p. 22; *Public Characters of 1798–9*, 3rd edn. (London, 1801), p. 375.

[2] Lord Buckinghamshire to Lord George Germain, 13 May 1779, Heron MSS., N.L.I. MS. 13037/12.

[3] See, for example, Lord Hardwicke to Lord Hawkesbury, 19 July 1805, Hardwicke MSS., B.L. Add. MS. 35710, fol. 124.

to some extent the prestige of high position in national politics, which it was later to enjoy to a very much greater extent under John Foster. Anthony Foster's political influence and command of patronage naturally grew as his political and official career progressed; but from the beginning he had had influential contacts in government circles. The first of these was Theophilus Bolton, Archbishop of Cashel, 1730–44, whose nephew and heir married Anthony Foster's sister in 1734. Too little is known about Archbishop Bolton. He was a protégé of King, Archbishop of Dublin, and therefore an object of suspicion to the Primate, Boulter—an Englishman—as a potential leader of 'the Irish interest'. He was a member of the linen board. His papers show, in addition, that he was the author of pamphlets on such topics as the wool trade, proposals for a recoinage, the utility of premiums, the causes of the increase in Ireland's national debt, and so on—which, if they were published at all, must have been published anonymously, since the only printed work with which he has been credited is a sermon on the wellworn theme of the Irish rebellion of 1641.[1] To some extent the link between Bolton and his nephew's brother-in-law, Anthony Foster, is conjectural. But the conjecture is based on the community of their interests, on the fact that Bolton made Foster the guardian of his great-nephew and eventual heir,[2] and on the additional fact that Foster thought highly enough of Bolton's writings on political and economic subjects to preserve Bolton's drafts among his own papers. There is no concrete evidence to show that Bolton assisted Foster's advancement in any respect: for example, Foster did not become a member of the linen board till 1750, six years after Bolton's death. But it may be significant that when he did join it his associates there were Lord Chief Justice Henry Singleton and Edward Synge, Bishop of Elphin, two men who had been close friends of the late Archbishop.[3] Singleton, who came from the Louth–

[1] W. A. Phillips, *A History of the Church of Ireland* (3 vols., Oxford, 1933), iii. 198, 206, 221; draft pamphlets in Archbishop Bolton's hand, [1730s], F.P. D.562/ 937–41, D.207/3/13–15; Henry Cotton, *Fasti Ecclesiae Hibernicae* (2 vols., Dublin, 1851), i. 18 f.

[2] Bolton to Foster, 8 Apr. 1741, F.P. D.562/1123.

[3] Bishop of Elphin to Lord Limerick, 7 June 1753 and 12 Feb. 1754, Roden MSS., P.R.O.N.I. Mic.147/9, vol. 17, pp. 97, 119; copy of Bolton's will, 29 Feb. 1744, showing that Synge was a witness and Singleton the sole trustee, F.P. D.562/ 1115.

Meath area, and had been M.P. for Drogheda, was also a close friend of the Foster family, as was another local man prominent in legal and political circles, Philip Tisdall, successively Solicitor- and Attorney-General. Through them, Foster entered the orbit of an even more influential *politique* than Bolton, George Stone, Archbishop of Armagh, 1747–64, and by at least the early 1750s was numbered among Stone's intimate followers.[1] With contacts at national level of the importance of Bolton, Synge, Singleton, Tisdall, and Stone, Foster must have been recognizable from an early date as an up-and-coming man and as a channel through whom the favours of the Castle were likely to flow. From 1750, as has been seen, he held a seat at the linen board, membership of which was notoriously an object of ambition among county families because of the patronage the board commanded; and as the draftsman, and to a considerable extent the architect, of its legislation, Foster's share of the patronage must have been commensurate with his share of the responsibilities.[2] From 1760 to 1766 he must have enjoyed in addition the share of the patronage of the revenue board which fell to the disposal of the First Counsel to the Commissioners, and from 1766 to 1777 the lion's share of the patronage of the court of exchequer, which fell to the disposal of the chief baron.[3] After 1777, when Anthony Foster's official career ended and John Foster's official career began, command of this species of departmental patronage became an even more prominent feature of the Foster interest in co. Louth; but it was not a new feature, and the difference after 1777 was one of degree rather than of kind.

If Anthony Foster was the member of the family who first introduced the prestige of high position in national politics into the Foster interest in co. Louth, the building up of the local, or territorial, element was the combined work of several generations, starting with the first Anthony, and still in progress—though with much diminished intensity—in the early nineteenth century. The Foster estate began in Dunleer, and extended ultimately to 1,200 or 1,500 acres in that vicinity,

[1] Foster to Lord Limerick, 9 May 1752, Roden MSS., P.R.O.N.I. Mic.147/9, vol. 17, 75–6.
[2] Bishop of Elphin to Limerick, 29 May and 15 Dec. 1753, ibid., pp. 90, 105.
[3] The most valuable offices in the court of the exchequer, for example the much-coveted clerkship of the pleas, were in the gift of the lord lieutenant.

all held on such favourable leasehold terms as to be virtually
fee simple.[1] Well before the Dunleer estate was complete,
however, the Fosters' centre of gravity had shifted westwards
and southwards, towards and over the Louth–Meath border.
It is not possible to trace, acre by acre, the process by which
this estate, consisting of a solid bloc in the south-west corner of
co. Louth and overspilling into Meath, was built up. But it
is clear that the vast majority of it came from one source, the
Moore family, who at the dissolution of the monasteries had
received an enormous grant of well over 50,000 acres in Louth
and Meath. The head of the Moore family was the Earl of
Drogheda, but it was with a cadet branch, the Moores of
Ardee, co. Louth, that the Fosters had their first dealings.
The Moores of Ardee possessed at the end of the seventeenth
century an estate worth about £5,000 a year, lying for the
most part in and around the town of Ardee. However, in the
first thirty years of the eighteenth century they ran the whole
gamut of the insolvent landowner, starting with mortgages
and foreclosures and ending with a private Act of Parliament
to allow them to break their family settlement and sell land
for debt. The first John Foster and his son, Anthony, figured
in this process of disintegration in the dual role of lawyers
acting on behalf of the Moores, and speculators in land. By
1746, they had acquired in fee simple virtually all the remaining
estate of the Moore family, after a series of extremely complicated transactions and at a total cost of at least £12,000.[2]
Sizeable though this sum was, it was nothing compared to the
sums which they are known to have laid out in buying land
from the head of the Moore family, Lord Drogheda. Their
first step in this direction took place in 1714, when John
Foster obtained a 59-year lease from Lord Drogheda of the
lands of Grangegeeth and Cadrath, co. Meath, totalling
1,862 acres. Two years previously, John Foster's brother-in-
law, Thomas Fortescue, had obtained a lease for the same
period from Lord Drogheda of the lands of Collonmore and
Collonbeg (usually abbreviated to Collon), co. Louth. In

---

[1] Malcomson, *The Fosters and Dunleer*, p. 160, n. 3.

[2] Philip Gayer to Anthony Foster, 29 Dec. 1746, F.P. D.562/969; statement of
title to the unsettled estate of Lord Ferrard, [1836], Kirk MSS., P.R.O.N.I.
D.2121/7/33. The rest of the information about the Moores of Ardee comes from
C.L.A.J. vii. 476 ff.

1729 Foster and Fortescue purchased jointly the fee simple of all these lands for £10,786, and in 1741 partitioned them so that Foster should have Collon and Fortescue the lands in Meath. Also in 1729, Foster acquired in fee simple the lands of Glasson and Ballysillagh (508 acres) for £1,290, and in 1734 the lands of Strinagh (708 acres) for £2,300. These lands were in co. Meath and had all formerly belonged to Lord Drogheda; like the Moores of Ardee, he was obliged to sell them with Collon, Grangegeeth, and Cadrath, in order to clear his debts. All told, it appears that the Fosters acquired something like 2,500 acres either directly or indirectly from Lord Drogheda.[1] No acreage figure can be put on the land acquired from the Moores of Ardee, but the likelihood is that well over half the Foster estate in Louth and Meath, which totalled 6,500 acres in 1778,[2] came from the Moore family as a whole.

By 1778 the estate was approaching its maximum extent. The gross rental, which in 1778 was £4,854, more than doubled between then and roughly 1820, to £10,120; but additions to the acreage accounted for only £1,223 of this increase.[3] Indeed, it could be said that the acreage already approached its maximum extent by about 1750, when it stood at roughly 6,000.[4] Since the Fosters were a new family, none of the estate had come to them by patent or by inheritance. It had all been pieced together painfully, by purchase, often in units smaller than a townland, and the process of purchasing had started

---

[1] The information on the Fosters' transactions with Lord Drogheda comes from the following sources:

a. *C.L.A.J.* viii. 197, 200, 203. The Collon estate leased to Fortescue in 1714 contained 2,236 acres, while the Fosters' Collon estate according to a 1778–82 rental (see 31*n*) contained only 1,952. This discrepancy is probably explained by the fact that the 1778–82 rental seems not to include the Collon demesne, so whenever this source is cited an addition of 284 acres is made to the figure it gives for Collon.

b. Foster family settlement, 19 Feb. 1736, F.P., Chilham deed room.

c. Deed of partition, 29 Apr. 1741, F.P. D.562/889.

d. Tripartite deed, 18 Feb. 1729, F.P., Chilham deed room.

e. Agreement between the Rt. Hon. William Graham and others and John Foster, 11 Dec. 1734, F.P., Chilham deed room.

[2] H. G. Tempest (ed.) 'Rental of the Foster Estate, 1779–81', *C.L.A.J.* x. 222 ff. The period covered by the rental seems actually to be 1778–82.

[3] Rough rental of the Foster estate, [*c.* 1820], F.P. D.562/14568.

[4] Statement of John Foster's title to lands in Co. Louth, 12 May 1808, F.P., D.207/8/6; statement of Lord Ferrard's title to his unsettled estates, [1836], Kirk MSS., P.R.O.N.I. D.2121/7/33.

only in the very late seventeenth or very early eighteenth century. This was a remarkable achievement—though not unique among the new professional families with whom the Fosters were earlier compared. The estate which Flood inherited from his father was reckoned at £5,000 a year in the 1760s, and the estate which Fitzgibbon inherited from his father at £6,000 in the 1780s; and in the same decade Scott could pride himself on being worth £15,000 a year which, though it must have included his official income, still left him much richer than the Fosters.[1] All the same, even if the Foster estate was unique neither in its size nor in the rapidity with which it had been assembled, in both respects it was an achievement which had severely stretched the Fosters' limited resources. It is significant that, by as early as 1740, the first John Foster was getting anxious about the extent of his indebtedness.[2] The lull in purchasing after roughly 1750 is not, however, to be attributed to anxiety on this score; for once the period of heavy purchasing was over, the period of heavy expenditure on improvements began. This was the work of Chief Baron Anthony Foster (although the process was continued by his successors), and earned him Arthur Young's celebrated epithet of 'great improver, a title more deserving estimation than that of a great general or a great Minister . . .' Young's account of Collon, the Fosters' seat and the nerve-centre of their estate, suggests that Anthony Foster poured his professional earnings (which can hardly have exceeded three thousand guineas a year)[3] into the improvement of the estate on an altogether staggering scale. From what Young says, and what he implies,

[1] J. A. Froude, *The English in Ireland in the Eighteenth Century* (3 vols., London, 1895), ii. 55; Fitzgibbon, *Earl of Clare*, p. 42; Ball, *Judges in Ireland*, ii. 175.

[2] John to Anthony Foster, 13 Nov. 1740, F.P., T.2519/4/2415.

[3] This is the figure put by Henry Grattan Junior on Anthony Malone's professional earnings—Henry Grattan Junior, *Memoirs of the Life and Times of the Rt. Hon. Henry Grattan* (5 vols., London, 1839–46), i. 61. Malone must surely have been in even bigger practice than Anthony Foster; against this, it must be noted that Grattan's figure relates to an early stage of Malone's career (though he does not suggest that his earnings rose later on), and may not be a reliable gauge of what Anthony Foster might have been earning in, say, the 1750s and early 1760s. Tisdall was earning £3,000 a year at the bar in 1760 (Duke of Bedford to Duke of Newcastle, 8 Jan. 1760, Bedford MSS., P.R.O.N.I. T.2915/9/2); this figure seems to refer to his private practice only, and it would presumably have been much higher if he had not had a great deal of (underpaid) work to do for the Crown as Solicitor-General.

the sums which Foster spent in this way must have been in the region of £50,000, spread over a period no longer than twenty or twenty-two years. No wonder Young declared that the improvements 'were of a magnitude I have never heard of before'.[1]

Young accepted Chief Baron Anthony Foster's testimony that they had been 'exceedingly profitable'. This would certainly have been the case if the £50,000 had been Anthony Foster's own; but the likelihood is that much of it had to be borrowed. This was the popular belief, recorded by the author of the scurrilous 1786 newspaper attack: '. . . The Chief Baron . . . purchased . . . a very considerable landed estate . . ., when land was at a low price, with money he contrived to borrow, the repayment of which he kept so secret that his enemies have suspected, and even declared, that it is not repaid at this hour. . . .' Moreover, Young must have been mistaken in saying that the Fosters' land was leased at only 3*s.* or 4*s.* an acre before the improvements, since this would have been an impossibly low return on the money they are known to have invested in purchasing their Louth (though not their Meath) estate; so it may be that he overestimated the financial advantages from the improvements because he underestimated the income which the Fosters were getting from their estate before the improvements began. Certainly, a rental of the estate for the years 1778–82[2] suggests (though it is a difficult document to interpret) a far from healthy financial situation. It suggests in particular that the Fosters were so burdened with debt that they were unable to live within their landed income over this four-year period. In 1789 the unkind couplet

> Foster in public expense stands alone,
> Blasts the national credit as well as his own

was penned; by 1799 John Foster's debts were popularly reckoned at £30,000—which was an understatement; and by 1810 they had reached the alarming figure of £72,000.[3] The cost of acquiring the estate in the first place, and the cost of the continuing process of improvement, probably accounted

---

[1] Arthur Young, *A Tour in Ireland* (2 vols., Dublin, 1780), i, pp. 146 ff.

[2] See p. 13, *n.* 2.

[3] Grattan, *Life*, iii. 417; Bolton, *Union*, p. 18, n. 3, brief for the plaintiff in the chancery case of Lord Massereene *v.* Lord Ferrard, 1838, F.P. D.1739/3/15.

for a high proportion of this sum. This certainly was the opinion of Foster's son and successor, Thomas 2nd Viscount Ferrard, who referred in 1838 to '. . . the heavy debts incurred by the late Lord Oriel [as John Foster became in 1821] in . . . improvements on the estates in Louth and Meath far exceeding all assets and unsettled property left to . . .' Lord Ferrard. Ferrard's cousin, Revd. W. H. Foster, concurred in this opinion, and attributed 'many, if not all' of John Foster's debts to his expenditure on the Louth estate.[1] The melancholy truth suggested by both these testimonies is that the financial advantages accruing from the Fosters' improvements were swallowed up in interest charges, and that this particular family tradition, which—like most of the other family traditions—John Foster followed, was not healthy.

One highly expensive aspect of improvement to which the family tradition, fortunately, did not run, was building. In an era of building mania, symbolized most spectacularly by the activities of the Fosters' connection by marriage, the Earl-Bishop of Derry, the Fosters were content to remain in the small and ungainly house which Anthony Foster had put up in the main street of Collon in the early 1740s and which still stands today, diagonally opposite another Foster-inspired building, the Protestant church.[2] About 1766, Anthony Foster, writing to his cousin, James Fortescue, to invite him to stay, warned him that he would have to share a room because of the limited accommodation in the house.[3] During the 1770s, John Foster had some discussion with James Wyatt about building,[4] but it seems that nothing came of this, unless indeed Wyatt had something to do with the Greek Doric temple which was built in 1780 or 1781 on the top of a hill in the middle of the Collon demesne. This temple was gradually extended to provide sleeping accommodation at least for the family; in 1786 John James Barralet did a pastel of the Fosters

---

[1] Brief in Lord Massereene *v*. Lord Ferrard, 1838, F.P. D.1739/3/15.

[2] Extract from Isaac Butler's journal, 1744, quoted in *C.L.A.J.* v. 97. I am indebted to Fr. Colmcille, O.C.S.M., of Mellifont Abbey (formerly Oriel Temple), Collon, for this reference and for much oral information about Collon. I am also indebted to Mr. Hal Sloan, the present (1977) owner of the house, for a fascinating conducted tour.

[3] Anthony Foster to James Fortescue, [1766?], F.P. D.562/1771.

[4] John Foster to John Baker Holroyd, 5 July 1776, *Anglo-Irish Dialogue*, p. 3.

posing with uncharacteristic languor on its steps; and in 1787–9
Beranger and De Grée worked on the decoration of its interior.[1]
When guests came to stay, they were entertained at Oriel
Temple (as it was called) during the day, and were then jogged
in an old coach down to the house in the main street, where
they slept. This arrangement, according to John Foster's
daughter, '. . . was so uncomfortable as soon to banish all
visitors, even of our own family. . . .'[2] Nevertheless, the arrangement was to be permanent, except that the temple was further
extended in 1811 to serve as an inexpensive residence for John
Foster's newly married son.[3] In 1790, with Mrs. Foster's
elevation to the peerage as Baroness Oriel, the Fosters sprouted
their first coronet, but this event was not commemorated in
masonry. Instead, the lords lieutenant and other dignitaries
who regularly stayed at Collon during the parliamentary
recess (because of its proximity to Dublin and John Foster's
high official position), were presumably subjected to the
rigours described by his daughter. Foster was very interested
in building, and indeed played a conspicuous part in the
introduction and encouragement of the Greek revival in Irish
architecture. In his public capacity, he took much more than
an *ex officio* interest in the successive re-vamps to the Irish Parliament House.[4] In his private capacity, however, he left no
monuments to his pioneering taste, apart from Oriel Temple
(which is possibly the earliest Greek Doric portico in Ireland),
and the nearby stables, which were built about 1812 by Edward
Parke, the architect whom he favoured most, both as Speaker
and in his other public capacities.[5] With these exceptions,
there was nothing of architectural distinction at Collon; and
the explanation must lie in Foster's parlous financial situation.
Collon was one place where it was never, even for a moment,

---

[1] Ann Crookshank and the Knight of Glin, *Irish Portraits, 1660–1860* (London,
1969), p. 59; notebook kept by Foster, 1787–91, F.P. D.2681/1/5.

[2] 'Recollections of a beloved mother', by Lady Dufferin, 1824, F.P. T.2519/4/
1818.

[3] Thomas to John Foster, 24 Mar. 1811 and 17 Mar. 1813, F.P. D.562/3392,
3395.

[4] A. P. W. Malcomson, 'John Foster and the Speakership of the Irish House of
Commons', *Proc. R.I.A.*, vol. 72, Sec. C, No. 11 (1972), p. 280.

[5] Parke to Foster, 13 Apr. 1812, F.P. T.2519/4/1289. I am indebted to Dr. E.
McParland for the information about Oriel Temple and Foster's part in the Greek
Revival in Ireland.

imagined that George IV would stay during his visit to Ireland in 1821, though he did of course stay very close at hand, at Slane Castle. On that occasion, Lords Londonderry (formerly Castlereagh) and Sidmouth, but not the King, came over to see the Oriel Temple nursery and plantation, which were probably the most celebrated privately owned institution of the kind in Ireland. On it, Foster must have spent large sums of money; but nothing in comparison to what he would have had to spend if he had indulged his enthusiasm for architecture.

The fact that Foster did not build himself a mansion in keeping with his official position and high rank is important in two respects. The first is the financial. Expenditure on the scale which would have been necessary would have bankrupted the Fosters and forced them to sell at least part of their estate. The example of the 1st Earl Belmore, for whom Wyatt built Castle Coole, near Enniskillen, in 1788–98 at a cost of £54,000, and who died £70,000 in debt, is well known.[1] However, the comparison with Lord Belmore is perhaps misleading, since Belmore had a much greater estate and landed income, and since even in his wildest dreams Foster would never have contemplated building on the scale of Castle Coole. A more modest mansion and more realistic example than Castle Coole is Rokeby Hall, co. Louth, which Francis Johnston built for Archbishop Robinson of Armagh in the 1790s for the huge sum of £30,000.[2] If Foster had built at all, he would surely have had to build on that scale? The first consequence of his abstention from building was, therefore, the negative one that it kept him solvent: the second was the positive one that it kept him, as far as outward appearance went, in the ranks of the modest Irish country gentleman. The lack of grandeur at Collon—indeed, the lack of common amenity—was of a piece with Foster's down-to-earth, approachable manner. The importance of his country-gentleman ethos has already been mentioned, and he would have lost it if he

---

[1] Constantia Maxwell, *Country and Town in Ireland under the Georges* (Dundalk, 1954), pp. 90 f.; an account in Belmore's papers records that £49,269 was spent between May 1788 and April 1795, and this seems to include everything, including the major item of freight—Belmore MSS., P.R.O.N.I. D.3007/D.2.

[2] Francis Johnston to J. N. Brewer, 29 Feb. 1820, Johnston of Kilmore MSS., P.R.O.N.I. D.1728/23/2.

had gone 'grand' (and if he had been raised to the peerage in 1811, when he wanted to be). The two architecturally distinguished houses in co. Louth, Beaulieu, built for the Tichborne family in the second half of the seventeenth century, and Townley Hall, rebuilt for the Balfour family in the late 1790s, were the seats of two of the Fosters' defeated county rivals.[1] It was characteristic of Foster that he should have been satisfied with the substance of having defeated them, without being tempted into emulating them in matters of outward show. Nor was Collon even third among the 'big houses' of co. Louth. Rokeby Hall must certainly have been more impressive; also Clermont Park, the main seat of the main branch of the Fortescue family; Ravensdale Park and Stephenstown, the seats of cadet branches of the Fortescues; Drumcar, the seat of the Fosters' kinsmen, the McClintocks; and no doubt the seats of other county families besides. The plain fact was that no one seeing Collon house (the temple was out of sight from the town) for the first time would ever have guessed that it was the seat of the first commoner of Ireland, whose wife was a viscountess. No doubt it was because the Fosters did not flaunt their newly acquired greatness that they were spared unkind contemporary comment on the newness of their family. Whether the decision not to flaunt their greatness in bricks and mortar was a conscious one, or whether it was simply an instinctive response to their financial difficulties, is a moot point. Probably a conscious desire to preserve their country-gentleman ethos had a good deal to do with it.

In fact, they were very slow to respond to their financial difficulties, in the practical sense of taking steps to ensure that things at least did not get worse. One reason for this was that they had grown accustomed to enjoying a sizeable income from extra-landed sources. In the days of the first John Foster, the country attorney, their dependence on extra-landed income was probably not very great. It then assumed major proportions during Anthony Foster's years at the bar and on the judicial bench. Under John Foster it again assumed major, and this time alarming, proportions. Professional earnings were neither stable nor dependable, but they were better in both respects than the earnings from political office. At least

[1] *C.L.A.J.* v. 303.

judges were certain of a pension: prominent politicians were
not (Foster's friend and protégé, Sir John Parnell, received no
pension in 1799 after fifteen years' service in Foster's former
office of Chancellor of the Exchequer).[1] The total income which
Anthony, John, and Thomas Foster drew from official—as
distinct from professional—sources over the period 1760–1816
can be estimated as being in the region of £213,000 (see
Appendix, Table Five). If this figure seems large, it can be put
in its British perspective by comparison with the £900,000
which the 1st Marquess of Buckingham and his two brothers
are alleged, on dubious authority, to have drawn from their
various offices over a period of half a century; or with the
£3,400 a year which another celebrated British pluralist,
Horace Walpole, was drawing in 1745, and the £6,000 in
1785, from sinecures which he held for life and had done
nothing to merit except be born the son of a prime minister.[2]
The Fosters' average income from office was lower than
Walpole's—something short of £4,000. To take the average
is, however, to miss the important points that it fluctuated
very considerably, that it was disproportionately concentrated
in the one period, 1798–1811, and that it petered out sharply
thereafter. These fluctuations made budgeting difficult, and
were particularly dangerous in the case of a family which had
a relatively small landed income to fall back on. With a gross
rental which rose from just under £5,000 in 1780 to over
£10,000 in 1820, the Fosters were inadequately cushioned
against the loss of an official income which at its peak touched
£10,000 a year. As Hely-Hutchinson's son, the 1st Earl of
Donoughmore, sneered to John Foster in 1804: '. . . I can
resign my place when I like, for I can live without it; which is
more than you can do. . . .'[3] The Fosters' problem was that
they were often threatened with loss of place, because the
offices they held were mostly high political ones which lay

[1] Henry Parnell to Hardwicke, 20 June 1804, S.P.O. 521/175/12. This was of
course caused by the circumstances of Parnell's departure from office; he was dismissed in 1799 for his opposition to the Union.

[2] Rachel Leighton (ed.), *Correspondence of Charlotte Grenville, Lady Williams Wynn*
(London, 1920), p. 8; R. W. Ketton-Cremer, *Horace Walpole* (London, 1964),
p. 98; W. S. Lewis, *Horace Walpole* (London, 1961), p. 20.

[3] Marsden to Hardwicke, 17 Nov. 1804, Hardwicke MSS., B.L. Add. MS.
35725, fol. 84.

in what John Foster's nephew aptly described as 'the hurricane sphere' in the event of a change of administration.[1] Incomes from such offices were, as Thomas Foster's prospective father-in-law put it in 1810, '. . . so uncertain that I think they must . . . be put out of consideration . . . '.[2]

Not only were they uncertain; they were also subject to heavy deductions for necessary official entertaining. Anthony Foster's predecessor as Lord Chief Baron, Edward Willes, an Englishman, noted and lamented the fashion in Ireland of keeping '. . . near double the number of servants for what gentlemen of the same rank and fortune keep in England. . . . '[3] The inadequacy of their salaries was the constant lament of high office-holders in Ireland in the late eighteenth and early nineteenth centuries; and this was especially true of the Englishmen among them, some of whom, notably Lord Chancellor Lifford in 1768 and Lord Lieutenant Camden in 1797, admitted that they had not realized in advance the extent of the profusion and display which would be expected of them in their official capacities.[4] The same profusion and display were expected of Foster, particularly while he was Speaker.[5] His other offices must have been less expensive, but it is significant that Sir John Newport, his successor as Chancellor of the Irish Exchequer in 1806, claimed in the following year to be '. . . quitting office a poorer man than I entered into it . . .', and a subsequent Chancellor, William Vesey FitzGerald, complained in 1816 of the 'tremendous expense' of the situation.[6] The Fosters themselves, though their testimony on such a point is of course suspect, were in no doubt that high office had damaged John Foster's private affairs.[7]

This was not true of all high office-holders. But those of them who made money did so, not out of the salaries ostensibly

[1] J. S. Rochfort to John Foster, 3 Feb. 1806, F.P. D.207/33/67.
[2] C. Skeffington to John Foster, 6 Nov. 1810, F.P., T.2519/4/1670.
[3] Quoted in B. Trainor and W. H. Crawford (ed.), *Aspects of Irish Social History, 1750–1800* (H.M.S.O., Belfast, 1969), No. 1.
[4] Lifford to Duke of Grafton, 31 Mar. 1761, Grafton MSS., W. Suffolk R.O. 423/308; Camden to Pitt, 10 Oct. 1797, Chatham MSS., P.R.O. 30/8/326, fol. 215.
[5] Malcomson, *Foster and the Speakership*, pp. 282 ff.
[6] Newport to William Elliot, 28 Mar. 1807, Newport MSS., Q.U.B. MS. 7, fols. 17–18; FitzGerald to Andrew Stacpoole, 4 Mar. 1816, Vesey FitzGerald MSS., N.L.I. MS. 7846, pp. 166–8.
[7] Thomas to John Foster, 18 Feb. 1811 F.P. D.562/3389.

annexed to their offices, but out of sinecures or other forms of provision for a life or lives which they held on the side. In 1779 John Beresford, Foster's colleague and rival for most of his official career, pointed out that the incomes from offices '... in the efficient departments are ... too small.... The most lucrative employments in the Kingdom . . . are sine-cures . . .'.[1] The Fosters, however, only once held a sinecure office—the customership of Dublin Port, which John Foster enjoyed from 1779 to 1784—and their only provisions for a life or lives were Anthony Foster's retirement pension as Lord Chief Baron and John Foster's pension in compensation for the abolition of the speakership. The first, Anthony Foster lived only two years to enjoy; and the second, though worth the large sum of £5,000 a year, came too late to retrieve John Foster's financial situation. It was conferred on him in 1800, and by 1806 he had been forced to sell it for a lump sum on what proved to be highly disadvantageous terms. The Fosters were in fact the victims of a system which gave a dispropor-tionate amount of political rewards to those who served the government with their votes rather than with their voices. For a man like John Foster who controlled a couple of seats in Parliament, it seems to have been more remunerative to be 'a strenuous supporter of His Majesty's Ministers . . . upon every occasion'[2] than to hold high political office. Cases in point are Foster's Louth neighbours, the Earls of Clermont, Clanbrassill, and Roden. None of them had any more parlia-mentary interest than he had. Yet because they put their interest to purely mercenary use and were prepared to do a deal with virtually every administration of whatever political complexion,'. . . no man in Ireland (hardly excepting Hely-Hutchinson) . . . had such favour from Crown and Castle . . .' as Lord Clermont; Lord Clanbrassill enjoyed for forty-two years a sinecure which over that period brought him in some-thing in the region of £125,000; and the Roden family held for four generations a semi-sinecure of only slightly lesser value, and numerous other offices besides.[3] Because the offices

---

[1] Beresford to Sir Richard Heron, 3 Oct. 1779, F.P. D.562/8611.

[2] P. J. Jupp, 'Irish M.P.s at Westminster in the Early Nineteenth Century', *Historical Studies*, vii (London, 1969), 77. The M.P. who made this his proud boast was William Handcock, later 1st Lord Castlemaine.

[3] Lord Buckingham to Pitt, 28 Sept. 1788, Chatham MSS., P.R.O. 30/8/325,

of these three peers were all non-political they had the advantage, firstly, of lying outside 'the hurricane sphere', and,
secondly, of requiring no expensive official entertaining: two
advantages which most of the Fosters' offices lacked.

On the whole, then, the Fosters—and particularly John
Foster—did badly out of office, and office certainly did not
provide the solution to their financial difficulties. The other
possible solution was advantageous marriage. Advantageous
marriage, however, was something which was less easy to
encompass than historians often assume. Both parties to any
marriage settlement were on the make, and one party seldom
gained significantly over the other unless some event subsequently took place which had not been anticipated at the
time the settlement was being drawn up. Settlements followed
a pre-ordained pattern. Their purpose was to provide in
advance portions for the younger children of the forthcoming
marriage, and a jointure (or widow's annuity) for the bride
if she outlived her husband. The portions and the jointure
were secured on the estate of the bridegroom's father (or of the
bridegroom himself, if he had already inherited). Usually they
bore a direct relationship to the marriage portion which the
bride brought with her, and this relationship usually was that
the bride's jointure represented ten per cent per annum of her
marriage portion, and that her marriage portion was expected
to cover the portions for all the younger children.[1] For any

fol. 168; A. P. W. Malcomson, 'The Struggle for Control of Dundalk Borough,
1782–92', *C.L.A.J.* xvii (1970), pp. 34 f.

[1] John Stewart to Abercorn, 7 Jan. 1816, Abercorn MSS., P.R.O.N.I. T.2541/
IB3/22/3; draft marriage settlement of William Foster and Patience Fowke, 1743,
F.P. D.562/5112; marriage settlement of Chichester Fortescue and Elizabeth
Wellesley, 1743, F.P. D.562/5115; draft mortgage from the Revd. Joseph Pratt to
John McClintock, 1773, F.P. D.562/5117; petition of Frederick Hamilton, 1772,
F.P. D.562/14614, p. 14. This relationship between portion and jointure was
always liable to be varied if there were special circumstances in the case. For
example, if a bride was an heiress presumptive, this fact might be reflected in her
jointure, but not in her portion (this was the case with Thomas Foster's wife—see
Appendix, Table Two). Also, if there was significant disparity of rank between the
bride and groom, and therefore 'condescension' on the part of one, the condescension might be paid for by the other in cash terms; when Viscount Crosbie, eldest
son of the Irish Earl of Glandore, married one of Lord George Germain's daughters,
Lord Crosbie felt that it was appropriate for his father to provide a jointure of
£2,000 in return for a portion of only £10,000—D. Large, 'The Wealth of the
Greater Irish Landowners, 1750–1815', *I.H.S.* xv (1967), 39 f. On the other
hand, in the same year plain Mr. Richard Quin of Adare, co. Limerick, secured

family on the look-out for an advantageous match, the only hope lay in the marriage of their eldest son. Daughters were always a financial drain, and younger sons little better. For, although the wives of younger sons brought portions with them, these almost invariably went towards purchasing an estate for the newly-weds; and if a younger son married a well-portioned girl, this only meant that his father had to increase his portion accordingly.[1] The eldest son, on the other hand, was due to inherit all his father's estate in any case; so if he married advantageously, the most his father could be expected to do was make a more generous provision for him during the father's own lifetime. In this event, the loss to the estate was temporary and the gain permanent.

The whole system of marriage settlements was weighted against a family like the Fosters (see Appendix, Table Two). They did not have sufficient rank to make their eldest son an attractive prospect for an heiress of similar descent to their own, and they were obviously beneath the notice of an heiress of superior descent. Partly because of this, and partly because of imprudent choice, Chief Baron Anthony Foster and his son John made bad matches. Anthony Foster's marriage in 1736 did not come up to the financial expectations of his father,[2] and John Foster's in 1764 can be called without exaggeration a financial disaster. A bad match made by the eldest son subjected the family estate to heavy settlement charges for the future; if the portion which his bride brought with her was insufficient to provide portions for their younger children, the estate of the husband had ultimately to pay the difference. In the case of the Fosters it was almost inevitable that there should be a difference to pay: not only were they a new family, they were also a rising family, and they were rising fairly rapidly in both wealth and status. This meant that a settlement which had been regarded as adequate at the time of the eldest son's marriage would be inadequate and obsolete by the time his children reached marriageable age twenty or

a daughter of the British Earl of Ilchester at the more usual tariff of a portion of £10,000 and a jointure of £1,000 (marriage settlement of Quin and Lady Frances Strangways, 9 June 1777, Dunraven MSS., Adare Manor, co. Limerick.

[1] John to Anthony Foster, 4 Dec. 1737, F.P. T.2519/4/2330.
[2] John to Anthony Foster, 20 May 1736, F.P. T.2519/4/2285.

thirty years later. Since for two generations the Fosters' eldest sons had made matches which even at the time had been deemed unremunerative, it is not hard to see how the weight of settlement charges fell with crushing effect upon the Foster estate.

The jointure provided for Mrs. John Foster well illustrates this point. The portion she brought with her at the time of her marriage would have entitled her to a jointure of only £200. In 1777, when the Fosters were re-settling their estate, it was decided to add to this £200 a further £600 from Foster sources. By 1810, however, even this was judged inadequate. In the intervening years Mrs. Foster had been created first a baroness and then a viscountess in consideration of her husband's political services, and it was assumed that she would require a jointure of £2,000 a year (the difference of £1,200 coming once again from Foster sources) to support her rank in the peerage with appropriate dignity during the years of her widowhood. Fortunately for the Foster estate, she did not in fact live to be a widow. Indeed, in this respect the Fosters were consistently fortunate, for the wife of the eldest son in each generation either pre-deceased him or else did not long survive him. The longest term for which the Foster estate had to pay a jointure was twelve years. If, however, John Foster's eldest son, who died in 1792, had lived to marry, the estate would have been saddled with a jointure of £1,000, or perhaps £2,000, for a period of possibly fifty years; which was more than it could have borne. On the other hand, the Fosters were unlucky in that their cadet branches in the male line were all prolific. Most families could expect that at least one estate settled on a younger son would some time or other revert to the main branch through failure of direct heirs.[1] The fact that this never happened in the Foster's case tended to cancel out the advantage they enjoyed of short-lived dowagers. On the whole, therefore, the Fosters, partly through imprudent choice and partly through difficulties inherent in their situation, were consistently the losers instead of the gainers by the system of marriage settlements.

They were however the gainers in terms of political connections. Indeed, it almost looks as if, realizing that they were

[1] For the estates settled on or acquired by the cadet branches, see p. 286 and Appendix, Table Two.

not in a strong position for capturing an heiress, they determined on marrying for connections rather than for money. The most important of these connections was with the Burgh family of Bert and Oldtown, co. Kildare (see Appendix, Table Three). The Burghs were a family of splendid lineage. They were descended from the old De Burgh earls of Ulster, and they also claimed descent, more questionably, from Charlemagne. But they were far from affluent. Heedless of this last disadvantage, the Fosters married into them on four separate occasions between 1738 and 1764. John (Speaker) Foster's mother was a Burgh; so were his step-mother and his aunt; and he himself married another, Margaretta Burgh of Bert, his first cousin.[1] Through the Burghs the Fosters were connected with the celebrated politician and orator, Walter Hussey Burgh (who, as well as being maternally a Burgh, was married to Mrs. John Foster's sister); more remotely they were also connected with the Burghs' kinsman and patron, the powerful Duke of Leinster; and with the Parnells of Queen's co., headed by Sir John. It was therefore in the sphere of national politics that the connection with the Burghs proved serviceable: the connection which was to be of most service in the local sphere was an earlier one, John Foster's marriage in 1704 to Mary Fortescue of Newragh, co. Louth (see Appendix, Table Four). The Fortescues were cadets of the well-known English family of that name.[2] From small beginnings they had made themselves important people in co. Louth—at least compared to the Fosters. From the Fosters' point of view, the marriage was financially unremunerative; but it later brought other, less tangible rewards. The Fortescues were their partners in the representation of co. Louth for the first forty-five years of the Foster ascendancy, from 1761 to 1806, and well before then the two families had entered into close political alliance. The marriage connection was not of itself sufficient to bring this alliance about, nor were the Fosters indebted to the Fortescues for the county seat they first won in 1761. But thereafter the connection between the two families served to

---

[1] Pedigree of the Burgh family, Genealogical Office, Dublin, MS. 176, pp. 467–79.

[2] Lord Clermont, *History of the Family of Fortescue in all its Branches* (London, 1869), pp. 131–6.

strengthen their political alliance and to smooth out potential jealousies.

The Fosters' marriage connections had the one limitation that they did not stretch across the Irish Sea, or provide the Fosters with an entrée into British politics. This was an important limitation. A high proportion of the information, or misinformation, which penetrated British political thinking, penetrated because it was conveyed through private channels. Some of the greatest Irish magnates or proprietors occupied a sufficiently prominent position in British politics to be channels of communication in themselves: the Prime Ministers, Rockingham and Shelburne, the 1st Marquess of Downshire, the 1st Marquess of Abercorn, and so on. Other lesser and more exclusively Irish families had no personal position in British politics, but were related to English families who had, and derived their channel of communication from such family relationships. Obvious examples of this are the relationships between the Duke of Leinster and Thomas Conolly of Castletown, co. Kildare, on the one hand, and the Duke of Richmond and Charles James Fox, on the other; the Stewarts of Newtownards and Lords Hertford and Camden; the Ponsonbys and the Duke of Devonshire and Lord Fitzwilliam; and so on. That the Fosters lacked such relationships was not entirely due to their newness as a family. The Conollys, for example, were no older, though they compensated for their newness by boasting a rentroll four or five times the size of the Fosters'. Even the Stewarts were not as old a family as they later made out (nor was Stewart their proper patronym), their immediate background was mercantile and they had not established themselves as an important landed family until the 1740s. Like the Conollys, however, the Stewarts were considerably richer than the Fosters, and in any case possessed an almost Hapsburg genius for matrimony, which they retained into the early nineteenth century.[1] The Fosters suffered from being at once a new family and a not particularly affluent one.

Lacking family connections in British political circles, John Foster was slow in establishing personal connections of his

---

[1] B. Fitzgerald, *Lady Louisa Conolly, 1743–1821: an Anglo-Irish Biography* (London, 1950), p. 72; H. Montgomery Hyde, *The Rise of Castlereagh* (London, 1933) pp. 9 ff.; oral information from Dr. Hyde.

own—or perhaps failed to recognize the importance of so
doing. The fact that his schooling took place locally, at Drogheda grammar school, did not help in this respect. His younger
rival, Sir John Newport, who came from an even newer
family than Foster, owed much of his future political success
to an education at Eton, where he was lucky enough to establish
a lasting friendship with W. W. Grenville, afterwards Lord
Grenville and Prime Minister.[1] After leaving Drogheda
grammar school, Foster proceeded to Trinity, and then to the
Middle Temple (in both respects following in his father's
footsteps). However, in this period study at a London Inn of
Court did not betoken English orientation, as it was obligatory
on anyone wishing to be called to the Irish bar; and Foster's
only contact derived from his Inn of Court days seems to have
been John Baker Holroyd, later 1st Earl of Sheffield, whose
family were already long-standing friends of the Fosters. There
was community of interest between the two men in everything
to do with agriculture and economics. Politically, they were at
one time in opposite camps, but in spite of this Sheffield
remained Foster's strongest family or private link with important British political circles (not that Sheffield's own footing in
that quarter was all that sure). Also, it so happened that two
of the chief secretaries of the 1790s were Sheffield's brothers-in-
law: Sylvester Douglas, Chief Secretary, 1793–4, and Thomas
Pelham, Chief Secretary, 1795–8. Foster's letters to Sheffield
are the most important single source of information about
Foster's broad political thinking, and some of them were
intended for more penetrating eyes than Sheffield's, particularly for Pitt's. If Foster unashamedly used his friendship with
Sheffield as a channel of communication with British Ministers,
Sheffield repaid him by being at best a half-hearted political
ally and at worst a treacherous friend. He was not himself
in a strong enough position to fight Foster's corner with effect,
and perhaps he did not have the inclination to do so. It is,
however, worth noting that, although he was a Unionist, in
January 1799 he spoke in the British House of Commons
against the timing of the measure, and to that extent was

---

[1] P. J. Jupp, 'Irish Parliamentary Representation, 1800–20', Reading Ph.D.
thesis, article on Newport; Newport to Buckingham (Grenville's brother), 3 Aug.
1788, Joly MSS., N.L.I. MS. 39/118.

perhaps representing views which Foster had expressed to him in November or December 1798.[1]

The advantages to an Irish politician of political or family connections in British politics are obvious. Lords lieutenant and chief secretaries were appointed from London, and much of the Irish administration's most valuable patronage could not be apportioned without prior consultation with the British government.[2] Moreover British governments of the last third of the eighteenth century generally speaking lasted longer than Irish viceroyalties (though the reverse was true of the last years of Foster's career in national politics, the period 1801–11). This meant that an Irish politician's best long-term prospects for promotion lay in having good connections in British ministerial, rather than in Irish viceregal, circles. It was no coincidence that the only men who in the period from 1768 to 1812 broke through the taboo against Irishmen filling the office of chief secretary were Irishmen with extremely good English connections—Sir George Macartney, Lord Castlereagh, and the Wellesley brothers. It would be wrong to suggest that Foster was unique in the poorness of his connections, although Parnell and he certainly were worse off in this respect than the other members of the Irish Cabinet. It would also be wrong to suggest that he never acquired connections in British ministerial circles. He did, particularly in the persons of the second-raters in British politics who were sent to govern Ireland in the years 1790–4 and 1795–8: the Lords Lieutenant, Lords Westmorland and Camden, and their Chief Secretaries, Robert Hobart and Pelham. These connections were important in his political come-back after the Union, and Camden acted as principal intermediary between Pitt and him in 1804. However, it is important to remember that they were connections derived from office, not family or private ones; that they were formed in Ireland, not Great Britain; and that they came late in his career.

Most men are influenced, for good or ill, by the kind of family they come from; and Foster was no exception. It was his

[1] For Foster's relations with Sheffield, see Malcomson, *Anglo-Irish Dialogue*, passim.

[2] For example, Lord North had to be consulted before the office of Customer of Dublin Port, worth roughly £1,000 a year, could be conferred on Foster—Heron to Buckinghamshire, 17 Apr. 1779, Heron MSS., N.L.I. MS. 13037/9.

peculiar family background which made him that very rare combination of the true country gentleman and the true career politician: a combination which virtually dictated his style of politics. He was, on the one hand, a country gentleman, endowed with personal ability far above the average for his class, and on the other a career politician without the faintest tinge of the adventurer. Had the Fosters been a family of longer lineage, broader acreage, and more extended constituency influence, Anthony Foster would probably have been raised to the peerage late in his life, or John Foster early in his, and John Foster's political career would never have taken place. As things were, John Foster, being the eldest son of a borough-owning but parvenu family, which needed an extra-landed source of income, almost inevitably entered the House of Commons; and because he was the even abler son of an able father, it was almost as inevitable that he should have chosen the precarious path of the career politician, in preference to the safe path of the silent supporter and sinecurist. His financial dependence on official income was a dangerous liability for a career politician, and lowered him in the estimation of contemporaries—certainly in the estimation of Lord Donoughmore. In reality, it probably had little influence on his political course, and none at the time of the Union. Other aspects of his family tradition influenced his political course, and style, more significantly. The family tradition of improving landlordism made him a paternalist in local politics, and in national politics the apostle of the paternalist role of the Anglo-Irish Ascendancy as a whole; it also made him the kind of chancellor of the exchequer who did not have to learn about agriculture and linen from the appendices of the *Commons' Journals*. His parvenu background probably contributed much to his assertiveness and intractability: qualities which took him to the top, but did not smooth his relations with his colleagues in high politics, particularly those of them who were English. Finally, his lack of English connections intensified his suspicions of British governments, and his aggressive Anglo-Irish patriotism and provincialism. Lacking in aristocratic finesse, he was never at home in the post-Union round of London political dinner parties; but by the same token, as the Irish country gentleman with an assured place in Irish landed society, he did not fall for the blandishments lavished on such occasions—as O'Connell was later wont to do. His self-appointed role in politics was that of a kind of permanent secretary for Ireland, ever at hand to correct the wildest English misreadings of the Irish situation.

CHAPTER TWO

The 'Ministerial Patriot': Foster's Official Career 1777–1811

THE soubriquet 'Ministerial Patriots' was coined by Attorney-General Scott in June 1780,[1] and was obviously intended primarily as a sneer at Foster. It is probable that Foster would have considered it apt. Its aptness, however, depends on careful definition. Foster was not a 'Patriot' in the special Irish sense of that term: a member of the 'Patriot' group in the Irish House of Commons, which emerged at the beginning of George III's first Irish Parliament under the leadership of Lord Charlemont and Flood, and which campaigned for a redress of Ireland's constitutional and political grievances. With the exceptions of Union and Emancipation, Foster was not roused to fervour by constitutional and political issues: his patriotism was apparent mainly in the economic sphere. Also, in the striking sense already mentioned,[2] he was less of an Irish patriot than even Pitt; he never contemplated Irish parliamentary reform or political concessions to the Irish Catholics, and his patriotism related, not to Ireland, but to the Anglo-Irish Ascendancy (though he himself would have drawn no distinction between the two). Again, he was not strictly speaking a Minister, except in the years 1784–5, 1804–6, and 1807–11; when Chairman of the Committee of Supply and Ways and Means, 1777–84, he specifically denied being a Minister, and when Speaker, 1785–1800, he repeated the denial,[3] and was theoretically supposed to be the servant of the House, not that of the Crown. Moreover, although he was a responsible Minister during his first tenure

[1] Scott to John Robinson, 4 June 1780, printed in William Beresford (ed.), *Correspondence of the Rt. Hon. John Beresford* (2 vols., London, 1854), i. 136.
[2] See pp. xvii ff.
[3] See pp. 41, 62.

of the chancellorship of the Irish exchequer, his responsibility was not to the Irish Parliament—a body to whom no Minister was responsible—but to the Irish Administration in Dublin Castle, and through it to the British Government in Whitehall. Quibbling apart, he was in effect a Minister, except during the period 1799–1804, but a Minister ever watchful and suspicious of his political masters in London.

Foster's career of 'Ministerial Patriotism' began in 1777 with his election to the chairmanship of the committee of supply and ways and means. Because of the paucity in Ireland of offices with parliamentary duties attached, the Irish chairmanship of committees was far more important than its contemporary British counterpart (though Foster wilfully exaggerated its importance when he claimed in 1782 that he had 'always considered [it] as a probable step towards the . . . [speakership]'.[1] The previous nominee was no less a figure than Attorney-General Tisdall (who had been preceded by Anthony Malone), and the other aspirant, besides Foster, was the extremely influential John Beresford, a Commissioner of the Revenue, and Chief Commissioner from 1780 to 1802. Beresford, an almost exact contemporary but a more experienced man than Foster, considered his election as good as certain,[2] and was disappointed only because circumstances and luck favoured Foster. At the end of 1776, the Earl of Buckinghamshire had been appointed Lord Lieutenant of Ireland. It so happened that Buckinghamshire was the brother-in-law of Thomas Conolly, and that Conolly, in turn, was the brother-in-law and close political confrère of the Duke of Leinster. Buckinghamshire was led (or as it turned out, misled) by these family connections to look for support beyond the normal confines of the Castle. The first circumstance which brought Foster to his notice was Foster's family and political connection with the Leinster 'squadron', particularly with Walter Hussey Burgh. The second was the family and political connection

---

[1] Foster to W. W. Grenville, 18 Nov. 1782, Additional Dropmore MSS. in the possession of the late Mrs. O. J. Fortescue, Ethy House, Lostwithiel, Cornwall. I am indebted to Dr. P. J. Jupp for drawing this source to my attention. For the Irish chairmanship of committees, see also Malcomson, *Isaac Corry, 1755–1813: 'An Adventurer in the Field of Politics'* (Belfast, 1974), pp. 10 f.

[2] Beresford to E. S. Pery, 26 Sept. 1777, Emly MSS., Huntington Library, California; photocopies in P.R.O.N.I. T.3087/2/16.

between Foster and Tisdall, who Buckinghamshire intended should conduct the parliamentary session due to start in the autumn of 1777; Tisdall described Foster as possessing '. . . the best abilities for business of any man in the House of Commons. . . .'[1] Finally, Foster's father, the Chief Baron, had reached retiring age, and Buckinghamshire wanted his office for the then Prime Serjeant, so that he might give the prime serjeantcy to Hussey Burgh. Conolly, Leinster, and Tisdall all recommended Foster for office, and the Chief Baron made office for his son a condition of his own retirement. The Chief Baron's 'complicated terms' were acceded to; accordingly, Hussey Burgh was appointed Prime Serjeant and Foster was promised that he 'would succeed upon a vacancy to an office of business'.[2] The office of business which seems to have been in mind was a seat at the revenue board,[3] but in fact the first appropriate office to fall vacant was the chairmanship of committees. (Tisdall not only recommended Foster for office, but himself provided the office by his unexpected death.) Foster was elected Chairman with the support of the Administration at the opening of the session, and in April 1779 he was also given the semi-sinecure of the customership of Dublin Port.[4] The Administration were careful, however, to keep tabs on him by granting him the office during pleasure rather than for life, as his predecessor had held it. They sweetened the pill later in the month by making him an Irish Privy Councillor.

He remained Chairman of Committees and Customer of Dublin Port until 1784 when at last an 'office of business' materialized in the form of the chancellorship of the Irish

---

[1] Edward Tighe to [William Eden?], 12 Aug. 1781, *H.M.C. Carlisle MSS.*, 515; Richard Heron to Robinson, 13 Oct. 1777, Heron MSS., N.L.I., MS. 13035/12. Tisdall's part in the official arrangements of the Buckinghamshire Administration has tended to be overlooked because of his death in September 1777, before the parliamentary session. Two months before Buckinghamshire's appointment, Tisdall had recommended that Hussey Burgh be brought into office, as Solicitor-General—Robinson to the King, 7 Oct. 1776, Robinson MSS., B.L. Add. MS. 37833, fols. 79–80. Thus, it does not seem that the decisive factor in Hussey Burgh's appointment to the prime serjeantcy was Buckinghamshire's family connection with Conolly and Leinster.

[2] Earl of Shannon to James Dennis, 21 Feb. 1777, Shannon MSS., P.R.O.N.I. D.2707/A/2/3/42; Buckinghamshire to Germain, 27 June 1777, Heron MSS. N.L.I. MS. 13035/7.

[3] Tighe to Heron, 11 Apr. 1779, ibid. MS. 13037/8.

[4] See p. 29, *n.* 2.

exchequer. Yet although the office he held remained the same from 1779 to 1784, his position in national politics varied considerably over the period. His influence was at its height in the last year of the Buckinghamshire Administration and at its nadir during the short-lived lord lieutenancy of the Duke of Portland in 1782.

In large measure he was indebted for the commanding position he had reached by the end of 1779 to the exceptional difficulties which beset the Buckinghamshire Administration, and to the Buckinghamshire Administration's exceptional unfitness to cope with them. The American war had drained Ireland of troops and crippled its revenue. It had also intensified the demand of the 'Patriots' that the commercial restraints by which Great Britain still shackled the Irish economy should be taken off. Inadequate concessions were made in 1778, but they fell far short of 'Free Trade'. Free Trade, though much clamoured for, was a term used by different people to mean different things until as late as November 1779; it then became defined as the right for Ireland to export its produce and manufactures direct to the British American and West Indian colonies, on the same terms as Great Britain itself, and to export wool, woollens, and glass to the European countries with which Great Britain was on trading terms. (At no stage had it anything to do with Free Trade in the nineteenth-century sense of the term.) In 1779, the demand for Free Trade assumed a much more threatening form, as it was now backed by the Volunteer movement and by widespread agreements not to accept British imported goods.[1] The Buckinghamshire Administration was incompetent to deal with the situation. The Chief Secretary, Sir Richard Heron, a man of no previous political experience, was the most inept holder of the office during the years of Foster's official career, and was popularly known as 'Sir Richard Wigblock'.[2] Tisdall's successor as

[1] For the general background see M. R. O'Connell, *Irish Politics and Social Conflict in the Age of the American Revolution* (Philadelphia, 1965), *passim*; J. A. G. Whitlaw, 'Anglo-Irish Commercial Relations, 1779–85, with Special Reference to the Negotiations of 1785', Q.U.B. M.A. thesis, 1958, *passim*.

[2] J. M. Mason to Robert FitzGerald, 2 Jan. [1781], FitzGerald MSS., in the possession of Mr. Adrian FitzGerald, 16 Clareville St., London S.W. 7, vol. 4/38. The reference number relates to P.R.O.N.I.'s calendar of this collection, which is to be published under the title, *The FitzGerald Papers: a Calendar of the Papers of Robert and Maurice FitzGerald, Knights of Kerry, 1750–1850.*

Attorney-General, John Scott, was not afraid to face the parliamentary music, but probably had an unrealistic faith in the power of parliamentary management. In any case Scott and Beresford (who shared this faith) were bitterly resentful of Buckinghamshire's policy of heaping honours and offices on former opponents of the government.[1] The Beresford–Scott group turned therefore into what Buckinghamshire foolishly dismissed as 'a paltry faction inimical to me', and used their by no means 'paltry' influence via their contacts in the British Government to discredit him in the eyes, not only of Lord North, but of the King. These contacts were below cabinet level, and with the men of business of the so-called 'Treasury group', particularly John Robinson, Joint Secretary to the British Treasury; however, in the confused last years of the North ministry contacts at this level were extremely effective, certainly as a means of bringing matters to the notice of the King.[2]

It was as a result of these exceptional economic and political difficulties, and of Buckinghamshire's problems in finding someone capable of conducting the forthcoming session on the Administration's behalf, that the comparatively inexperienced Foster came to the fore. Hussey Burgh, Buckinghamshire had good reason to fear, was not to be depended upon. Scott, the obvious choice by virtue of his office, was ready to play a supporting role in the House of Commons, but not to take the lead. John Hely-Hutchinson, as usual, was ready for anything, but Buckinghamshire shrank from him, rather as the King and Bute had shrunk from Henry Fox; besides, Hussey Burgh, Scott, and Foster all refused to co-operate with Hely-Hutchinson, as had Tisdall while he lived.[3] As long as Hussey Burgh and Foster remained united in the service of government, Foster was bound to be the junior partner of the two; where one was acclaimed for his 'glorious feelings', the

[1] See, for example, Beresford to Robinson, 14 Mar. 1780, *Beresford Correspondence*, i. 130 ff.

[2] Buckinghamshire to Lord Barrington, 13 Feb. 1780, Heron MSS., N.L.I. MS. 13039/3; the King to Robinson, 29 Nov. 1778 and 21 Nov. 1779, and Robinson to the King, 9 Oct. 1779, Robinson MSS., B.L. Add. MSS. 37834, fol. 40, 37835, fol. 30, and 37834, fol. 154. It is not clear whether Beresford and Scott knew that their letters to Robinson were being shown to the King.

[3] Buckinghamshire to Germain, 10 Oct. 1779, Heron MSS., N.L.I. MS. 13038/14.

other was merely commended for '. . . that strain of good sense, candour, and honesty that calls upon the thanks of every Member of Parliament, and the gratitude of his Country. . . .'[1] By April 1779, however, Buckinghamshire was anticipating Hussey Burgh's defection. He told Heron that it was his intention 'that Mr. Foster should stand forth, under you, the leading man in all matters of Finance', and Buckinghamshire was hopeful '. . . that if he [Foster] cannot steady the conduct of the Prime Serjeant, his own will not be shaken by that gentleman. . . .'[2] This optimism was justified as far as Foster was concerned. In July, Hussey Burgh and he reached the parting of their political ways: Hussey Burgh declared, at first privately and then publicly, that the connection between himself and the Castle was severed,[3] while Foster went ahead with preparations for the budget which it would be his job to 'open' when Parliament met in October.

Foster was convinced of the immediate political necessity that substantial commercial concessions should be granted to Ireland: because of the war and the other causes of Ireland's economic distress which commercial concessions would not remove, he probably doubted whether they were an economic necessity, except in the longer term. He knew that Buckinghamshire was well-disposed. He must also have known that already, in March, Buckinghamshire had urged concessions over the importation of West Indian sugar and the exportation of Irish woollens, upon the British Government, and been rebuffed.[4] Foster's draft for a 'Free Trade' address to the Lord Lieutenant at the opening of the session,[5] was rejected by Buckinghamshire as too sweeping. But the subject of Ireland's economic distress was wide open to enquiry (indeed, it was the Irish Administration's plan that Foster should move for and chair a committee of the whole House for this purpose); also, the

---

[1] Earl-Bishop of Derry to J. T. Foster, 17 Apr. 1782, J. L. Foster MSS., R.I.A. MS. 23 G. 39—photocopies in P.R.O.N.I. T.2519/7/2/10; reference to Foster in a speech of Grattan's, 16 Dec. 1777, reports attributed to Sir Henry Cavendish of debates in the Irish House of Commons, Library of Congress, Washington—photocopies in P.R.O.N.I. Mic.12, iv. 176.

[2] Buckinghamshire to Heron, 17 Apr. 1779, Heron MSS., N.L.I. MS. 13037/9.

[3] Buckinghamshire to Heron, 28 July 1779, ibid. MS. 13038/10.

[4] Buckinghamshire to Heron, 6 Mar. 1779, and Heron to Buckinghamshire, 9 Mar. 1779, Heron MSS., N.L.I. MS. 13037/2.

[5] Draft address by John Foster, [*c.* 1 Aug. 1779], F.P. D.562/8332A.

session opened without precise instructions having arrived
from London as to the extent of the concessions which
Buckinghamshire might make.[1] The circumstances of the
opening of the 1779 session were thus peculiarly propitious for
Foster's first essay in 'Ministerial Patriotism', and certainly he
was not the man to throw up a position of practical influence
in an administration, in furtherance of a yet unspecific opposition demand.

The course he pursued through the ensuing chaos, was
subtle. He never compromised in debate on the principle of
commercial concessions, and declared himself to be their
firm supporter.[2] But as a supporter of the Administration he
exerted himself to save them from being beaten on the two
most ignominious issues on which an administration could be
beaten, the address and the supplies. In neither instance was
he successful: in the first because of the unexpectedly violent
temper of the House, and in the second because of Heron's
stupidity.[3] Nevertheless, the political exigencies of the moment
required that Foster's tactic be at least tried. Since an adverse
vote of the Irish House of Commons could not bring down an
Irish administration, in the circumstances of the late autumn
and early winter of 1779 the Irish Administration was simply
being used as a whipping-boy for the British Government.
Foster knew that Buckinghamshire needed no further convincing of the necessity for Free Trade, and that the decision
lay, as it had always done, with the North Ministry in Great
Britain. The question now was, how long would the North
Ministry take to make up their minds, and would the Volunteers wait. While the North Ministry were making up their
minds Foster tried, without prejudice to the principle of Free
Trade, to prevent a deadlock between the Irish Administration
and the Irish House of Commons. Even if Heron had been
a more effective leader, this was the kind of lead which was
more effectively taken by a native politician. Nor were Foster's
motives in taking it necessarily time-serving. He believed that
the Irish economy was deriving much greater immediate

[1] O'Connell, *Irish Politics and Social Conflict*, pp. 158 ff.
[2] *Dublin Journal*, 12–14 Oct. 1779.
[3] Buckinghamshire to Lord Weymouth, 13 Oct. 1779, Grattan, *Life*, i. 391 ff.;
Beresford to Robinson, 13 Oct. 1779, *Beresford Correspondence*, i. 53 f.; Buckinghamshire to Weymouth, 25 Nov. 1779, Grattan, *Life*, ii. 8 f.

advantage from the non-importation associations, which though intended as blackmail were achieving the objects of protectionism, than it would from Free Trade. As he later wrote to the Under-Secretary at the Castle, Sackville Hamilton, after Free Trade had been conceded: '. . . I am thoroughly convinced that the non-import associations . . . have done us more service than the whole of the Free Trade will do these fifty years. They have opened to us the first and best market for every Nation, its own supply. A market certain, steady, and within our power at all times, but which like fools we had given away [to Britain], and looked only to the speculative gain of hunting beyond seas for uncertain precarious markets . . .'[1] Ironically, this view was later endorsed by Grattan.[2] It is interesting that Foster should have held it; after the winning of Free Trade, and especially after the winning of the Constitution of 1782, he was to be the firmest exponent in Ireland of prosperity by Act of Parliament:[3] so it might be expected that he would have accepted the obverse—that adverse Acts of Parliament had been the primary cause of Ireland's previous economic distress.

At the beginning of December the North Ministry at last made up their minds. Impelled more by considerations of British party politics than by parliamentary and extra-parliamentary pressures from Ireland, they conceded the principle of Free Trade. The most important consequential legislation was British. But Irish legislation was necessary to regulate the terms of the future trade between Ireland and the British colonies, Ireland and various European countries, and Ireland and Great Britain itself. Foster was responsible for piloting this legislation through the Irish House of Commons, as Heron, Hamilton, and (ominously for Foster) Beresford departed for London early in 1780 to hammer out the details with the British men of business. This meant that some of the whipping and lobbying duties of the Chief Secretary devolved on Foster, who was well-qualified for the task because of his contacts with the Leinster 'squadron' and other independent

[1] Foster to Hamilton, 29 March 1780, F.P. D.562/8371; Whitlaw, 'Anglo-Irish Commercial Relations', pp. 28 f.

[2] *Parliamentary Register* (Irish), i. 138.

[3] For Foster and 'prosperity by Act of Parliament', see pp. 361 ff.

and unpredictable elements in the House.[1] However, it also meant that Foster played only a postal part in the stage of the business to which his talents and cast of mind were peculiarly fitted.[2] The biggest single point of difficulty was the duty on British refined sugar imported into Ireland, and in April Foster actually spoke and voted against the Administration on this apparent side-issue, after Heron had failed to represent his views effectively, or at any rate successfully, in London. In reality it was not the side-issue it appeared. Future trade between Ireland and the British West Indian colonies depended on West Indian raw sugar for the only possible 'back freight' to Ireland; and due to the usual combination of British competition and native incompetence, the Irish sugar refining industry was in embryo and was likely to remain so unless protected against imports of refined sugar from England. The level of duty was raised dramatically by the Irish Parliament, and then reduced again—though not to the level originally intended by the British Government—when the bill came before the British Privy Council under the Poynings's Law procedure.[3] Another measure of Foster's which attracted the hostile attention of the British Privy Council, was a bill '. . . by which bounties are given to certain species of Irish linens exported to Africa, America, Spain, Portugal, Gibraltar, and Minorca, and also to Irish sailcloth exported to any place except Great Britain . . .' In effect, the bill, by establishing in Ireland the same bounties as were paid in Great Britain on the export of both British and Irish linen from there, tended to deprive Great Britain of its re-export trade in Irish linen and to raise the price of Irish linen in the British market. The British Privy Council considered these implications, but did not alter the bill, although Attorney-General Scott had written privately to Robinson remonstrating against it.[4] The

[1] Buckinghamshire to North, 14 Dec. 1779, Macartney MSS., P.R.O.N.I. D.572/7/36; Heron to Buckinghamshire, 18 Jan. 1780, Heron MSS., N.L.I. MS. 13039/1.   [2] See, for example, Hamilton to Foster, 7 Feb. 1780, F.P. D.562/8357.

[3] Heron to Robinson, 20 May 1780, Grattan, *Life*, ii. 429 f.; Whitlaw, 'Anglo-Irish Commercial Relations', pp. 60 ff.

[4] Copy report of the board of trade to the British Privy Council on the Linen Bill, 17 July 1780, Chatham MSS., P.R.O. 30/8/321, fols. 68–80; Scott to Robinson, 4 June 1780, *Beresford Correspondence*, i. 137. For Foster's views on the significance of this bill, see *Speech of the Rt. Hon. John Foster . . . on Thursday the 11th day of April 1799* (Dublin, 1799), pp. 84 f.

significance of these two episodes, the sugar duty and the Linen Act, is that they show that Foster's patriotism, apparently dormant while Free Trade was a vague abstraction, sprang to life when Free Trade became a matter of concrete detail.

Even before his hostile vote on the sugar duty, his conduct during the Free Trade crisis had not satisfied Lord North, who reminded Buckinghamshire that the only servant of the Crown in Ireland who had remained steady throughout was Scott.[1] Buckinghamshire, while paying due tribute to Scott's plucky support in the House of Commons,[2] was still filled with justifiable suspicion of the Beresford–Scott group. For once, Foster's lack of connections in British politics proved an advantage to him. Buckinghamshire felt that Foster would be his man, while Scott or Beresford would owe their primary allegiance to their contacts in the British Government. It was for this reason that he had turned to Foster in December 1779,[3] and from then on Foster was regarded by everyone as his 'Minister' in the House of Commons. Indeed, Buckinghamshire even insisted that the King should be clearly informed that Foster was 'the real efficient man of business'.[4] Foster denied all this. He lamented to Sackville Hamilton that '. . . from my situation in the Chair of Supply and Ways and Means people seem to look to me for proceedings on subjects conversant in money or trade; and as I am no Minister, and meddle as little as I can in other business or Administration, I wish to avoid the imputation of neglect where certainly none is due to me . . .'[5] This was disingenuous, but understandable. No one with an eye to his future career prospects would have wished to be too closely associated with the measures of the Buckinghamshire Administration. As Beresford scathingly remarked in March 1780:

. . . His Excellency may very truly say, so far as his experience goes, that Mr. Foster is the only man of business, for I am sure he has tried no other. Let the business which has been done answer for itself.

[1] North to Buckinghamshire, 18 Feb. 1780, Heron MSS., N.L.I. MS. 13039/1.
[2] Buckinghamshire to Germain, 29 Nov. 1779, *H.M.C. Stopford-Sackville MSS.*, i. 262.
[3] Heron to Buckinghamshire, 23 Jan. 1780, Heron MSS., N.L.I. MS. 13039/2.
[4] Lord Hillsborough to Buckinghamshire, 4 Mar. 1780, ibid. /4.
[5] Foster to Hamilton, 8 Feb. 1780, F.P. D.562/8356.

I am sure that I do not know any man who wanted a recommendation to English Government that would dispute for the honour of
having planned or executed the business of the present Administration in Ireland; for my own part, I claim no part of the credit. . . .[1]

Beresford, who had recently returned from London, must have
known that Lord North had recommended him to Buckinghamshire to succeed Heron as Chief Secretary. The idea of an
Irishman as Chief Secretary was not new. There had been the
recent instance of Sir George Macartney; more significantly,
there had been the earlier instance of Theophilus Jones,
a connection of the Beresford family, who had become Chief
Secretary in 1767, as part of an extremely shortlived, but
fascinating, experiment in Irish cabinet-making. Beresford,
with his very good English connections, would have conformed
to these precedents, but Buckinghamshire was emphatic that
'. . . upon such an arrangement, no informed person would any
longer consider me as Lord Lieutenant',[2] and refused to accept
North's recommendation. Whether he countered by recommending Foster, is not clear. It was rumoured in mid to late
March 1780 that he had done so;[3] and it is almost certain that
he would have done so in the previous December or January,
but for the fear that, if he subscribed to the principle of an
Irish chief secretary, this would only increase the pressure on
him to appoint Beresford. Perhaps hopes of the chief secretaryship influenced Foster's disclaimers of being a Minister, and
disappointment of the chief secretaryship, his conduct over
the sugar duty and the Linen Act. If so, he was being remarkably short-sighted for a clever man. The Buckinghamshire
Administration clearly did not have long to run; and in
November Buckinghamshire was recalled and replaced by
the Earl of Carlisle.

Foster's future was far from assured. He had come to the
fore under exceptional circumstances and under the auspices
of an Administration which by any standards had been a
conspicuous failure. Under any in-coming administration his

---

[1] Beresford to Robinson, 14 Mar. 1780, *Beresford Correspondence*, i. 130 ff.

[2] Instructions from Buckinghamshire to Heron, 5 Mar. 1780, Heron MSS.,
N.L.I. MS. 13039/4.

[3] Archbishop of Cashel to Lord Macartney, 26 Mar. 1780, Macartney MSS.,
P.R.O.N.I. D.572/7/53; Beresford to Robinson, 14 Mar. 1780, *Beresford Correspondence*, i. 130 ff.

influence was bound to be diminished because it had hitherto to some extent derived from the peculiar incapacity of Heron. Besides, the new Chief Secretary, William Eden, was friendly with Robinson, Beresford's principal English confidant, and could reasonably be expected to have imbibed some of Beresford's resentment against Foster. Yet in spite of these unfavourable auguries, Foster survived the transition, his influence reduced but not eclipsed. An anonymous character sketch of him which had been circulated in British ministerial circles in September 1780 shows the light in which he was regarded in that quarter. It reckoned him 'wanting in sagacity and political courage, and inadequate to the management of a party', but 'a great master of business, intimately connected with the Aristocracy, and affable'.[1] The section of the aristocracy with which he was most intimately connected was of course the Leinster 'squadron'; but as Lord Carlisle prided himself on the 'broad-bottom' of his Administration,[2] this was no disadvantage to Foster. He was no longer 'Minister'; but he held his own amid the bevy of talent which the Carlisle Administration attracted into its orbit (including independent and even opposition talent); and he continued to play the leading part, next to the Chief Secretary, in commercial and economic affairs, for example by co-operating closely with Eden on the preliminaries to the founding of the Bank of Ireland.[3] In October 1781, Eden was able to report to North that 'the Attorney-General and Mr. Beresford and Mr. Foster are all perfectly zealous and much attached to us'.[4]

The period between 1779 and 1783 witnessed the agitation of a series of popular questions which it is convenient to deal with *en bloc*. What were as significant as the measures themselves were the attempts of constituencies and other extra-parliamentary organs of opinion to influence the way M.P.s voted on them. Co. Louth had been active in November 1779, when it instructed its M.P.s to vote for a short money bill if Free Trade was not conceded,[5] and Foster's support of

---

[1] Hillsborough to Robinson, 19 Sept. 1780, *H.M.C. Abergavenny MSS.*, 37.
[2] Carlisle to Lord Gower, 23 Nov. 1781, *H.M.C. Carlisle MSS.*, 534.
[3] Foster to Eden, 26 Dec. 1782, Auckland MSS., B.L. Add. MS. 34419, fol. 80.
[4] Eden to North, 13 Oct. 1781, *Beresford Correspondence*, i. 176.
[5] Address of the Louth freeholders to their M.P.s, 8 Nov. 1779, FP. D.562/14657. For a discussion of this episode, see pp. 226 f.

Free Trade had not been sufficiently open or decided to satisfy
the Volunteer element among his constituents. His conduct
over the other popular questions of the period was even less
satisfactory. In January 1780, he made it clear that he had
no time for 'speculative abstract points of constitutional right',
and accordingly, as Lord Buckinghamshire's 'Minister',
opposed Yelverton's motion for the modification of Poynings's
Law at the end of April.[1] He favoured an Irish Mutiny Bill,
but only because of his conviction that magistrates could not
be prevailed on to act under the British one;[2] and the amendment to the Irish Mutiny Bill which he proposed and carried
at the end of May was designed to avoid an explicit admission
that Britain lacked the power to legislate for Ireland. When
the British Privy Council refused to accept his compromise
clause, he did not hesitate to support their perpetual Irish
Mutiny Bill, which became law in August;[3] and he resisted
Grattan's attempt to get it repealed in November of the
following year. The blunt home truths of his speech on that
occasion are characteristic, and memorable:

... Tonight we have frequently heard it repeated that the Hereditary
Revenue alone was sufficient to maintain such an army as might
destroy our liberties. How monstrously has this revenue increased
in a few days! Within this week it was asserted that all our revenues
in time of profound peace, were scarcely equal to our military
establishment. How then should it be sufficient in such a time of
commotion as we must suppose—and indeed the whole danger is
suppositious? In a time of civil war, will the revenue increase? ...
We have lived under the influence of the Mutiny Law for eighty-eight
years, without feeling any inconvenience from it, though during that
time it was the law of another country. But now that it is become our
own law, shall we suppose that consequently it is become injurious? ...[4]

Foster could, and did, claim that he had supported the Declaration of Rights in 1782 which led immediately to the modification of Poynings's Law, the repeal of 6 George I, and the
establishment of the Constitution of 1782. But his support came
too late to make him popular, or win him credit with the

[1] Foster to Hamilton, 16 Jan. 1780, F.P. D.562/8346; Buckinghamshire to
Hillsborough, 29 Apr. 1780, Grattan *Life*, ii. 79.
[2] Buckinghamshire to Hillsborough, 8 May 1780, ibid. ii. 87.
[3] Grattan, *Life*, ii. 98, 125.   [4] *Parl. Reg.* (Irish), i. 68.

Opposition. He had opposed similar declarations during the Carlisle Administration (whom he loyally extolled in his speech in April 1782), and the declaration of that month had already been reluctantly backed, as a government measure, by the newly arrived Administration of the Duke of Portland.[1] His support of the Act of Renunciation in 1783 was similarly lukewarm; privately he remarked (and again the remark was characteristic) that he thought the measure necessary, but not for the satisfaction of reasonable people.[2] All attempts at parliamentary reform, he steadfastly resisted, and was prominent among those M.P.s who denounced the proceedings of the Volunteer National Convention in November 1783.[3]

Portland's succession to Carlisle in the spring of 1782 marked a more significant change than Carlisle's succession to Buckinghamshire at the end of 1780. Buckinghamshire and Carlisle had both been appointed by the North Ministry, but Portland came over as a result of the fall of North and of a change of government in Great Britain. At this particular period, links between the Irish Opposition and the former British Opposition, of which Portland had been a leading light, were especially close, and in these circumstances it was inevitable that some supporters of previous Irish administrations should be dismissed, to make room for some of Portland's connections in the Irish Opposition. The two most prominent martyrs were Attorney-General Scott and Sackville Hamilton's junior colleague as Under-Secretary, John Lees. Foster was not martyred, but he was not among the 'private confidential men' of the Portland Administration.[4] Nevertheless Hussey Burgh was, which no doubt assured Foster of at least an indirect hearing. Portland himself distrusted and underrated him, and turned instead for advice on economic affairs to Portland's kinsman, George Ponsonby, second son of ex-Speaker Ponsonby and a member of that Ascendancy dynasty which

[1] Ibid. i. 67 f., 344, and v. 410.
[2] Foster to Eden, 26 Dec. 1782, Auckland MSS., B.L. Add. MS. 34419, fol. 80.
[3] Lord Northington to C. J. Fox, 30 Nov. 1783, Grattan, *Life*, iii. 157 f. *The Parliamentary Register* makes scant mention of Foster's speech, and attributes it to a 'William' Foster (ii. 241). This must be a mistake for 'John' since John Foster's cousin, John William Foster, M.P. for Dunleer, had been a member of the Convention.
[4] Foster to Buckinghamshire, 27 May 1782, *H.M.C. Lothian MSS.*, 415.

possessed all the advantages lacking to the Fosters of good connections in British politics.[1] In fact, there was little scope during the Portland Administration for Foster's particular talents; the continuing fermentation in popular opinion, and the unmanageability of Portland's Irish advisers, prevented him from following up the Constitution of 1782 with the commercial adjustment between Great Britain and Ireland which he had intended.[2] In any case, his stay in Ireland was short. In July 1782 the death of the Prime Minister, Lord Rockingham, led to a reorganization of the British Government and to many secessions from it, including that of Portland. The new Prime Minister was the Earl of Shelburne, and the new Lord Lieutenant, Earl Temple. The effect of the change was to strengthen Foster's position, although Temple to some extent echoed Portland's distrust of him; '. . . I find Foster very useful to me,' he wrote to his brother, 'but more in Finance than in politics, though he swears through thick and thin.'[3] Not long afterwards, in April 1783, the Shelburne Ministry was driven from office, and Portland assumed the figurehead premiership of the notorious Fox–North Coalition. After a delay which exasperated him, Temple was succeeded as Lord Lieutenant by the Earl of Northington. The change was of importance to Foster. Northington did not confine his confidence, to the same exclusive extent as Portland had done, to the Irish connections of the British Ministry, and he soon formed a much higher opinion of Foster's ability than either Portland or Temple. By October 1783 he was reporting to Portland that Foster's 'services are of great consequence, and absolutely necessary for Mr. Pelham [the Chief Secretary] to have'. Northington accordingly recommended that Foster be appointed to the office of chancellor of the Irish exchequer.[4]

The recommendation was not new. It had been made by both Lords Buckinghamshire and Carlisle while they were in

---

[1] Portland to Northington, 6 July 1783, Northington MSS., B.L. Add. MS. 38716, fol. 46; Jupp, 'Parliamentary Representation', article on G. Ponsonby. The Ponsonby family had also supported the Carlisle Administration. For a discussion of their political role, see pp. 202 f., 354 ff., 396, 401 ff.

[2] See pp. 394 f.

[3] Temple to W. W. Grenville, 15 Jan. 1783, *H.M.C. Dropmore MSS.*, i. 183.

[4] Northington to Portland, 21 Oct. 1783, Northington MSS., B.L. Add. MS. 38716, fol. 95.

office. Moreover, Foster had in practice been carrying out the duties of the office since 1777, with the possible exception of the short-lived Portland Administration in 1782. There were various reasons why this anomalous situation had been allowed to go on for so long. The office had been conferred in 1763 on a chief secretary, William Gerard Hamilton (best known as 'Single-Speech' Hamilton). Hitherto it had always been granted during pleasure, but to Hamilton it was granted for life. When approached by the successive Irish administrations who wanted to buy back the office, Hamilton proposed exorbitant terms. Though he was a minor British politician and Foster a major Irish one, British governments were more concerned about offending Hamilton than they were about obliging Foster.[1] The situation was complicated by the three changes of British government between February 1782 and April 1783, and the consequent changes of lord lieutenant; no lord lieutenant wanted to incur the odium of accepting Hamilton's terms unless he was going to be in Ireland for long enough to have the advantage of Foster's support. Indeed, shortly after Northington made his recommendation, the Fox–North Coalition fell from power; and once again it looked as if Foster was going to be baulked of the chancellorship of the exchequer.[2] But Northington, not without reluctance, persevered in the recommendation, and his Pittite successor implemented it. The sorry history of these negotiations illustrates well the kind of obstacles which were placed in the way of an efficient conduct of Irish affairs by the fact that the Irish administration depended on the votes of the British, not of the Irish, Parliament.

The chancellorship of the exchequer was only one of many offices which in the period between 1760 and 1800 was brought back to Ireland. The most important were the secretaryship of state, the mastership of the rolls, one of the vice-treasurerships and, above all, the lord chancellorship. However, the bringing of these other offices back to Ireland did not alter the nature of their duties, if they had any; it merely altered the nationality

---

[1] Portland to Northington, 27 Dec. 1783, Pelham MSS., B.L. Add. MS. 33100, fol. 501.
[2] Northington to Pelham, 27 Feb. 1784, Pelham MSS., B.L. Add. MS. 33100, fol. 60.

of the incumbent. In the case of the chancellorship of the exchequer the alteration was more profound. Hamilton had in fact been the first English absentee to hold it in recent years. But even when held by a resident Irish politician it had had no duties attached to it; Henry Boyle, for example, John Ponsonby's predecessor as Speaker, had held it along with the speakership in the 1730s and 1750s, and in his day it had been described as 'a place of honour and dignity, and very little to do'.[1] Since 1763 there had been several suggestions about conferring it on 'a leading member of the Irish House of Commons', in accordance with the principle 'that the patronage of Ireland should be confined as much as possible to Ireland'.[2] But nobody had said anything about the duties of the office which were, until 1777, performed by, of all people, the attorney-general,[3] and only devolved on Foster in 1777 because of Attorney-General Tisdall's death. The significance of the chancellorship of the exchequer as conferred on Foster in 1784 was that it was to be '. . . a responsible office, which, in conformity to the practice in England, may for the future be considered here as entrusted to a person speaking the sentiments of Government in the House of Commons on these two subjects [finance and commerce] . . .'; from the Irish point of view, and with Irish magniloquence, it was 'one badge of our imperial consequence'.[4] It was certainly an important constitutional and political development.

The Northington Administration was succeeded by that of the Duke of Rutland, a personal friend of Pitt's, who brought over as his Chief Secretary Thomas Orde. After an uncertain beginning,[5] Foster's relations with the new Administration soon became close and cordial. By June 1784 the well-informed private secretary to the Lord Lieutenant, Edward Cooke,

[1] E. and A. Porritt, *The Unreformed House of Commons* (2 vols., Cambridge, 1903), ii. 397; Dr. Marmaduke Coghill to Edward Southwell, 27 Sept. 1735, Southwell MSS., N.L.I. MS. 875

[2] Cabinet minute delivered by Lord North to Sir John Blaquiere, [c. 18 Aug. 1773], Blaquiere MSS., N.L.I. MS. 877, fol. 1; Heron to Buckinghamshire, 5 Apr. 1777, Heron MSS., N.L.I. MS. 13037/7.

[3] Beresford to Lord Westmorland, 8 Apr. 1794, Westmorland MSS., S.P.O. fol. 113.

[4] Northington to Lord Sydney, 20 Feb. 1784, Grattan, *Life*, iii. 186 f.; *Parl. Reg.* (Irish), iii. 31.

[5] Sydney to Rutland, 28 Apr. 1784, Sydney MSS., N.L.I. MS. 51/C/7.

noted that he was '. . . taking a lead everywhere and extending his influence on all sides. He has weathered the storm with great firmness. . . .'[1] The storm had blown up over the Dublin manufacturers' demand for protecting duties against British competition, which Foster had been foremost in resisting. He had thus been particularly marked for assassination by the Dublin mob and for abuse by the Dublin press. The first menace he narrowly escaped in November 1783; and the second he minimized by pushing through the House of Commons in April 1784 a controversial Libel Bill, declared by its opponents to be 'a bill of resentment, not of redress' and 'a most desperate and violent aim to effect the subversion of the Constitution'.[2] Foster's unpopularity in Dublin and the country was at its height in 1784 (ironically, the year of his celebrated Corn Law): a height it never again reached until his widely-execrated budget of 1810. The *Dublin Evening Post* declared in January 1784, 'honest Jack prefers his employment to the good opinion of his countrymen':[3] his part in the celebrated commercial propositions of 1785 was to lend currency to the largely unfounded charge.

The Irish starting-point for the commercial propositions was an opposition address at the close of the stormy 1784 session calling for 'a wise and well digested plan for a liberal arrangement of commercial intercourse between Great Britain and Ireland',[4] which Foster and Orde accepted with modifications. In September, Foster submitted to Orde two most able and lucid memoranda on the detailed form which he considered this arrangement should take: there should be a re-interpretation of the Navigation Act (to which Foster was already pledged in Parliament[5]) so that Ireland would be permitted to re-export British colonial goods to Great Britain itself; articles of home growth or manufacture should, generally speaking, pass between Great Britain and Ireland

---

[1] Cooke to Eden, 1 June 1784, Auckland MSS., B.L. Add. MS. 34419, fol. 396.
[2] Temple to Grenville, 23 Nov. 1783, *H.M.C. Dropmore MSS.*, i. 223; *Parl. Reg.* (Irish), iii. 157 f. After scrutinizing the bill, the British Attorney- and Solicitor-General remarked on its stern character, but did not feel justified in recommending that it be 'respited'. For the Libel Bill, see also pp. 382 f., 407.
[3] Quoted in *C.L.A.J.* vi. 121.   [4] *Parl. Reg.* (Irish), ii. 217.
[5] *Parl. Reg.* (Irish), ii. 274.

at the lower rate of duty currently chargeable, if there was
a difference in the rate (and usually there was, and it was to
Ireland's disadvantage); Irish linen should continue to be
imported into Great Britain duty-free (and Pitt reckoned that
the value of Irish linen imported into Great Britain was
roughly the same as the value of total British exports to Ireland);
and though bounties on exports from one kingdom to the
other were generally to be eliminated, the bounty system
which was the basis of Foster's Corn Law was not only to be
preserved, but was to be rounded off by 'a reciprocal preference
of taking corns, etc., from each other before either apply to
foreign states for a supply'.[1] Pitt, however, had for some time
been thinking in terms of an arrangement which, although
along the same commercial lines as Foster's, was not exclusively
commercial in scope. To Pitt, this was the moment, not only to
supply the commercial counterpart of the Constitution of
1782, but also to strengthen the constitutional connection
between Great Britain and Ireland by enacting that Ireland
should provide a defined, annual contribution towards imperial
charges—later narrowed to naval charges.[2] Foster was opposed
to the idea of a defined, annual contribution. He wrote to
Grattan: '. . . it were better for Britain to leave the affair to
the liberality and ability of the moment when our aid might
be necessary . . .'; and two years after the failure of the commercial propositions, when a scheme was afoot to revive them,
he put the point even more plainly in a letter to Beresford:
'. . . My opinion always was that it was the best policy to keep
the commercial subject by itself, and to leave the Imperial
concerns to the general unexplained but well-understood
situation in which they are. If Irish Government fails at any
day to carry them, it fails to be a Government—it cannot
carry Establishments, Taxes, Revenue, or any subject of
moment. . . .'[3] All 'the confidential friends of Government' in
Ireland shared Foster's reservations, as did Rutland himself,

[1] Foster to [Orde], 15 and 28 Sept. 1784, Melville MSS., N.L.S.; photocopies
in P.R.O.N.I. T.2627/1/1/6, 9; Pitt to Rutland, 6 Jan. 1785, printed in Duke of
Rutland (ed.), *Correspondence between the Rt. Hon. William Pitt and Charles, Duke of
Rutland, Lord Lieutenant of Ireland, 1781–1787* (London, 1890), p. 64.

[2] John Ehrman, *The Younger Pitt: the Years of Acclaim* (London, 1969), pp. 199 ff.

[3] Foster to Grattan, 20 Jan. 1785, Grattan, *Life*, iii. 236; Foster to Beresford,
5 Oct. 1787, *Beresford Correspondence*, i. 328.

who urged Pitt in November 1784 '. . . to abandon your idea of a compensation [i.e. contribution], which I protest to you I think will render all advantages which you expect to derive from your liberal compliances abortive . . .'[1] Thus, from the outset, there was an important divergence of private opinion between the Irish and British Administrations. Foster was no doubt unreasonable in expecting the British Government to rely for the security of the compact on the good disposition of the Irish Parliament, when the British Government had had so much recent experience of the contrary; but Pitt, too, was unreasonable in holding out for an elaborate legislative security, for the ensuing crisis revealed that, though he had little faith in the good disposition of the Irish Parliament, he had an unrealistic faith in its manageability.

In the late autumn of 1784, Foster and Beresford set off for London, where they hammered out with Pitt and others ten commercial propositions which Foster introduced into the Irish House of Commons in February 1785. In the face of opposition, notably from Grattan, the propositions were expanded to eleven, and two important modifications were made. First, the Irish Parliament was given a greater degree of control over the manner in which Ireland's contribution was to be applied to naval charges; and second, it was specified that in time of peace Ireland would not be called upon for any contribution unless its budget balanced. Foster did not inspire these amendments (indeed, he endeavoured unsuccessfully to persuade Grattan to drop them), but thereafter he was active behind the scenes, along with the other 'confidential friends of Government' in convincing Rutland and Orde that, without the amendments, it would be impossible to defend and carry the propositions 'in the face of the country'.[2] The eleven propositions, as amended, passed the Irish Parliament and were transmitted to Westminster, where no such conviction of that impossibility was felt by Pitt and his Cabinet. The Irish Parliament's largely nominal control over the application of the contribution was retained, but the clause providing for

---

[1] Rutland to Sydney, 23 Jan. 1785, and Rutland to Pitt, [Nov. 1784], *H.M.C. Rutland MSS.*, iii. 153, 165 f.

[2] V. T. Harlow, *The Founding of the Second British Empire, 1763–1793* (London, 1952), i. 579 ff.; Rutland to Sydney, 12 Feb. 1785, *H.M.C. Rutland MSS.*, iii. 179.

a balanced budget was struck out.[1] Other equally important changes were also made. The difference between the eleven Irish propositions and the twenty resolutions which emerged from the British Parliament was, in essence, that the former extended no further than the commercial relations between Great Britain and Ireland, whereas the latter extended to the commercial inter-relationship of the whole British Empire—an inter-relationship over which Great Britain, the constitutional sensitivities of the Irish parliament notwithstanding, had of necessity to be the superintending power.[2] It was this change in the scope and nature of the commercial propositions, rather than (as is commonly supposed) the unreasonable jealousy of British commercial and manufacturing interests, which gave rise to most of the amendments made by the British Parliament, most of the behind-the-scenes objections of Foster and the 'confidential friends of Government' in Ireland, and most of the opposition which the twenty British resolutions encountered in the Irish Parliament when they were introduced there in the form of an Irish bill in August 1785.

British commercial and manufacturing interests, particularly those of Lancashire and Clydeside, were extremely vociferous in their protests, which were articulated and to a considerable extent orchestrated by two members of the Northite section of the British Opposition—Eden, the former Chief Secretary, and Lord Sheffield.[3] The latter denounced 'my friend, Chancellor Foster's *wicked* attempt', which he summarized as 'Delightful work—Ireland to have every advantage of an Union without taking upon her any of the disadvantages'.[4] However, the Foxite section of the British Opposition tried, in addition, to play the scarcely consistent role of Irish 'Patriots', epitomized in Fox's celebrated piece of sophistry: '. . . I will not barter English commerce for Irish slavery; that is not the price I would pay, nor the thing I would purchase. . . .'[5] The cause of the British commercial and manufacturing interests

[1] The eleven Irish propositions and twenty British resolutions are printed, inaccurately, but except for the eleventh British resolution intelligibly, in Grattan, *Life*, iii. 489 ff., 495 ff.

[2] For the argument of Lord Thurlow, the English Lord Chancellor, on this head, see Daniel Pulteney to Rutland, 19 July [1785], *H.M.C. Rutland MSS.*, iii. 226 f.

[3] Ehrman, *Pitt*, pp. 207 ff.; Paul Kelly 'British and Irish Politics in 1785'. *E.H.R.* xc, No. 356 (July, 1975), pp. 536 ff.

[4] Quoted in *Anglo-Irish Dialogue*, xv.   [5] Quoted in Grattan, *Life*, iii. 257.

was thus not championed as effectively, or at any rate as singlemindedly, as it might have been; and these interests were on the whole more vociferous than influential. The principal concession to them was a provision, under the twelfth British resolution, to prevent Irish manufacturers from deriving an unfair advantage over them as a result of the generally lighter rates of taxation in Ireland. However, no concession was made to the argument—largely fallacious in the case of skilled labour—that Irish wage-rates were generally lower than British; and the stipulations of the British resolutions to prevent smuggling (which was notoriously prevalent in Ireland) and ensure that the re-export trade was genuinely carried on in British colonial goods, were not unreasonable.[1] It is not correct, though frequently asserted, that the ninth British resolution excluded Ireland from trade to 'countries beyond the Cape of Good Hope to the Straits of Magellan': Ireland was already excluded from direct trade with the British possessions in the East, which came within the East India Company's chartered monopoly; the ninth resolution prevented Ireland from trading with *foreign* colonies in the East, except on the same basis as Great Britain, and in return permitted the company to allow Ireland a share of its monopoly if it wished.[2]

The twenty British resolutions, in fact, retained all the commercial essentials of the eleven Irish propositions. To this the very petitions against the British resolutions from Irish commercial and manufacturing interests bear witness; all the petitions except one denounced them as destructive to the constitution as well as the trade of Ireland, and clearly were more concerned about the constitution than the trade. The one exception, a petition from the cotton, calico, and linen printers of Dublin, confined itself to the alteration in the duties on British and Irish manufactures passing between the two kingdoms, which was effected by the eleventh British resolution—an alteration which Beresford, for one, thought was either going to be harmless to Ireland, or 'highly disadvantageous to England', depending on how it was to be interpreted.[3] The effects of the

---

[1] Whitlaw, 'Anglo-Irish Commercial Relations', pp. 164 ff.

[2] Ibid. pp. 190 ff.; *Parl. Reg.* (Irish), v. 380.

[3] Whitlaw, 'Anglo-Irish Commercial Relations', 182; Beresford to Pitt, 9 July 1785, *Beresford Correspondence*, i. 285 ff.

British resolutions on the purely commercial provisions of the settlement, were very much as described by one of Rutland's members in the British House of Commons in May 1785:

... Another violent opposition was made against the Irish being allowed to grant, as is their present custom, a bounty on the sale of a manufacture without our being able to lay on a countervailing duty here to balance such bounty. But on this, as well as on every division in the Committee, we beat them. ... I can only say in one word that Pitt never suffered any sort of amendment or comment unfavourable to Ireland to be directly or indirectly introduced in the course of this affair, of which Your Grace may with confidence assure the Irish, except they should deem such the explanation relative to the E[ast] Indian trade, and our declaring their trade in general to be subject to any regulations we may make for the benefit of both. ...[1]

Pitt himself, later in the month, was able to give Orde a convincing account of the British Government's success in resisting amendments designed to remould the commercial provisions to Ireland's disadvantage.[2] In general, he took the line that the best way to counter the argument that Britain was conferring too many commercial benefits on Ireland, was by tightening the stipulations whereby Ireland was riveted into place in the imperial scheme of things.[3]

Foster did not disapprove of the place allocated to Ireland but, as in the case of the imperial contribution, he disapproved of the riveting. In his view, the fourth, fifth, and seventh British propositions—those relating to Ireland's trade with the Empire—required no further security than 'mutual good faith and understanding' between Great Britain and Ireland; in any case, he argued that, sentiment apart, Great Britain already possessed a better security for Ireland's good faith than Ireland did for Great Britain's, because under the Constitution of 1782 Ireland could not alter any part of the settlement 'without the assent of the Crown and the responsibility of the British Minister and the Keeper of the Great

---

[1] Daniel Pulteney to Rutland, 26 May [1785], *H.M.C. Rutland MSS.*, iii. 208 f. The particular example of the bounty on the sale of a manufacture did not in fact support Pulteney's argument, as this amendment was subsequently admitted, and became part of the fifteenth resolution.

[2] Pitt to Orde, 29 May 1785, *H.M.C. Rutland MSS.*, iii. 210 f.

[3] Pitt to Rutland, 21 May 1785, *Pitt–Rutland Correspondence*, pp. 103 ff.

Seal of England'. Foster particularly objected to the notorious fourth proposition, which bound the Irish Parliament to enact in the future such 'laws for regulating trade and navigation, . . . [and] imposing the same restraints and conferring the same benefits on the subjects of both Kingdoms', as were enacted by Great Britain. He foresaw the Irish Parliament's outraged reaction to this attempt to bind it, while at the same time he considered that the stringent wording in fact failed of its object:

> . . . Britain . . . does not ever propose to bind herself that Ireland shall enjoy every exclusive privilege, or not [to] make a law at any time which shall not confer equal benefits: we are to rest on her good faith for this, and it is the only solid ground to rest on. . . . The resolution providing no means of ascertaining whether they [the laws] do or not [confer equal benefits and equal restrictions], the whole treaty, notwithstanding the caution to the contrary, becomes dependent on . . . mutual good faith and understanding. . . . If the fourth resolutions [*sic*] . . . , after declaring the principle [of enacting the same laws for the future], adopted all the present British system of law, they would answer every purpose of permanency and would be such as no reasonable man could object to . . . Nay, if they were qualified with the condition that Ireland should cease to enjoy every benefit of colonial trade whenever she omitted to keep her laws similar, no constitutional objection could be made, and her legislature would be unaffected. . . .[1]

Foster, and the Attorney-General, Fitzgibbon, were to employ this last qualification in explanation of the fourth proposition during the subsequent debate on the Irish bill embodying the substance of the British resolutions.[2] But the qualification would have been more effective if written into the bill, than it was as a gloss upon it. On the whole, it is hard to see how Grattan and the Irish Opposition could have objected to Foster's form of words, or why Pitt and the British Government did object to it.

In the mood in which the Irish House of Commons was by 13 August, when Orde introduced the Irish bill, it is probable that Grattan and the Opposition would have found something

---

[1] Rough draft of a memo. by Foster, [June/July? 1785], F.P. D.562/8512.

[2] Foster's speeches are in *Parl. Reg.* (Irish), v. 408 ff., 473 ff.; Fitzgibbon's speech is at pp. 377 ff. The Irish bill is given in full in Whitlaw, 'Anglo-Irish Commercial Relations', pp. 214 ff.

else to object to, even if Foster had succeeded in drawing the sting of the fourth resolution. The Irish debate was unreal, in that the Opposition debated the twenty British resolutions, while what was in fact before the House was an Irish bill—the counterpart of a British bill which had just received its first reading at Westminster—both of which differed significantly from the twenty resolutions and ostensibly had no connection with them. This procedural device of the two bills was a compromise hammered out at the last moment between the British and Irish Administrations; the British had at first intended that the twenty resolutions themselves should be laid before the Irish Parliament, while the Irish had at first argued that nothing short of a British act would give satisfaction, since resolutions, or even a bill, would arouse the suspicion in Ireland that the British Administration had more amendments up its sleeve.[1] The changes in wording were even more eleventh-hour than the change in procedure: as late as 8 August, Pitt wrote to Orde reporting that the British bill had just been modified to meet some of the objections made (though he did not name him) by Foster:

... We have taken infinite pains to put everything, and particularly what relates to the Fourth Proposition, in the light most unexceptionable and most flattering to the feelings of Ireland. The principle of a necessary uniformity of Navigation Laws is admitted. The Bill, in order to obtain it, stipulates that all the laws to be made by Great Britain shall confer equal benefits, *etc.*, and that Ireland shall enact laws to do the same there. Our legislative rights are surely as much bound as yours, and Ireland, instead of having to *register* edicts, will have always as free a judgement as England whether the laws in fact are equal. . . .[2]

Moreover, Foster's copy of what is obviously a first draft of the Irish bill,[3] is covered with insertions in his handwriting specifying which clauses were 'fundamental and essential', and therefore not capable of unilateral alteration by Great Britain. These insertions are all present in the Irish bill introduced by Orde. Finally, the Irish bill differed from the resolutions, and

[1] Lord Ashbourne, *Pitt: Some Chapters of His Life and Times* (London, 1898), pp. 134 f.
[2] Pitt to Orde, 8 July 1785, Ashbourne, *Pitt*, pp. 136 f., 142.
[3] F.P. D.562/8502.

particularly from the twentieth resolution, in more than verbal respects. The twentieth resolution had contained a provision for making perpetual the regulations under which the Irish Hereditary Revenue was collected (the Hereditary Revenue was the fund on which the naval contribution was to be charged); these included penalties for contravention, some of them capital, and Foster, Beresford, and Rutland himself had at first anticipated that this part of the twentieth resolution would arouse greater opposition than the whole of the fourth.[1] The perpetuation clause was not present in the Irish bill. What was present in the Irish bill, and absent from the twentieth resolution, was a clause which went some of the way towards satisfying the requirement of the eleventh Irish proposition for a balancing of the Irish budget in peacetime. These hard-won concessions from the British Administration served no purpose. Grattan not only concentrated on the twenty resolutions, but showed little comprehension even of them. Among other things, he condemned the prohibition of the export of English wool to Ireland (which had been part of the eleven Irish propositions), denounced the perpetual revenue regulations 'under which you are no longer a Parliament' (and which were no longer part of the measure), and misstated the nature of the restrictions on Ireland's trade with the East.[2] In the debate on the commercial propositions, argument was overcome by rhetoric, and the men of business, eloquent though they were, by the mere orators.

Reporting on the debate, his sometime political ally, Conolly, made sneering reference to Foster's zeal to do the bidding of his 'employers'.[3] Yet, there is slender foundation for this charge of time-serving. Granted the breadth and complexity of the arrangement, and the number of concessions made to his and his associates' views in the final Irish bill, Foster had as much reason as any of the principal protagonists of the commercial propositions to feel substantial satisfaction at their content— certainly as much as Pitt. Long after the event, when there was no particular reason for him to do so, Foster continued to

---

[1] Ashbourne, *Pitt*, pp. 124 f. (at this stage, the future twentieth resolution was the eighteenth); Rutland to Pitt, [*post* 13 July 1785], *H.M.C. Rutland MSS.*, iii. 215 f. The date tentatively suggested for this letter by the editor of the volume, 12 June 1785, appears to be a mistake.

[2] See p. 53, *n.* 2.

[3] Conolly to Buckinghamshire, 29 Aug. 1785, Heron MSS., N.L.I. MS. 13050/3.

praise in public and in private the 'offers of solid and substantial benefit to trade' which the propositions had held
out, and which misrepresentation and 'objections . . . on the
score of the constitution', alone had frustrated.[1] The obvious
antidote to Conolly's sneer at Foster's ministerialism is Sheffield's
distaste for his patriotism; it was inevitable that a politician
occupying Foster's difficult middle ground should be mis-
construed, in opposite senses, on opposite sides of the Irish
Sea. Of the two misconstructions, Sheffield's—that Foster
sought all the advantages of a Union without any of the
disadvantages—was nearer the mark. At the time of the Union,
in 1799, Pitt was to argue that Foster had advocated the commercial propositions on grounds which made their failure an
argument in favour of Union: Foster, however, was able to
retort with effect that, since 1785, Ireland had obtained most of
the solid and substantial benefits to trade which the commercial
propositions had offered; as he would not have accepted Union
as the price of them all in 1785, there was all the less reason
for him to accept Union as the price of the remnant in 1799.[2]

The benefits to trade acquired by Ireland between 1785
and 1799 (actually, between 1786 and 1793), can most conveniently be summarized at this point, when the terms of the
commercial propositions are fresh in mind, and before economic
considerations are swamped by the political developments of
the 1790s: from Foster's point of view, the benefits to trade
were an important offset to these unwelcome political developments. The immediate sequel to the commercial propositions
was the British Navigation Act of 1786, which had in fact
been envisaged by the fourth British resolution. Under Lord
North's Act of 1778, Irish ships and seamen counted as British
for purposes of the British navigation system; but a new system,
and in particular tighter regulations for the registration of
shipping, was required as a result of the loss of the American
colonies;[3] the problem was to incorporate Ireland in it, without

---

[1] *Foster's Speech of 11 Apr. 1799*, pp. 44 f.; Foster to Sheffield, 1 Aug. 1793, *Anglo-Irish Dialogue*, p. 13; Bolton, *Union*, p. 90; Whitlaw, 'Anglo-Irish Commercial Relations', p. 199.

[2] *Speech of the Rt. Hon. William Pitt in the House of Commons, Thursday Jan. 31, 1799*, 4th edn. (London, 1799), pp. 20 ff.; *Foster's Speech of 11 Apr. 1799, passim*, especially pp. 45 ff.

[3] Whitlaw, 'Anglo-Irish Commercial Relations', p. 137; Ehrman, *Pitt*, pp. 339 ff.

once again offending the constitutional sensitivities of the Irish Parliament. This was solved by skilful drafting. The British Navigation Act avoided any pretension to bind Ireland and simply left it to the Irish Parliament to pass a Navigation Act if it thought fit; and the Irish Navigation Act (of 1787) repeated the provisions of the British, without purporting to do so, and without linking either the provisions or the duration of the Irish Act to future British legislation.[1] The lesson of the commercial propositions had been learned. Likewise, the Irish Parliament in 1786 and 1787 passed acts adjusting the terms of Irish trade with the United States and France respectively, in the light of the latest British developments in these sectors;[2] these two Irish Acts were annually renewed thereafter, in the same way that Irish Free Trade with the remaining British American and West Indian colonies was kept in line with the British navigation system by the Irish money bill of each session. As Foster had observed in 1784, if the Irish government failed to carry such things, as the need arose, it failed to be a government. It was symptomatic of Ireland's new role in the network of British trade and navigation that Portugal, which since the granting of Free Trade had refused to recognize Irish woollens as British under the Methuen Treaty,[3] in 1787 waived its objections. In 1793 a further British Navigation Act at last permitted the re-export of British colonial goods from Ireland to Great Britain; and in the same year, when the East India Company's monopoly was renewed, Ireland was admitted to a compulsory participation in its trade—Foster's 'hobby as to the East Indies'[4]—nothing very substantial, but more substantial than the permissive participation which had been embodied in the ninth British resolution of 1785. By 1793, therefore, Ireland was in enjoyment of most of the benefits which the commercial propositions had held out, except in relation to the trade in home produce and manufactures between Great Britain and Ireland. In this latter sphere, a start had been made in 1792, when the substance of

---

[1] 27 Geo. III, c. 19 (British); 27 Geo. III, c. 23. For a more detailed discussion of this navigation legislation, see pp. 367 f.

[2] 26 Geo. III, c. 16; 27 Geo. III, c. 9.

[3] Whitlaw, 'Anglo-Irish Commercial Relations', p. 57.

[4] Fitzgibbon to Beresford, 14 May 1793, *Beresford Correspondence*, ii. 13 f.; 33 Geo. III, c. 63 (British); 33 Geo. III, c. 31.

Foster's reciprocal preference in corn had been established, subject however to some stipulations which he deemed whims and absurdities.[1] An equalization of duties, though much mooted, was not in fact established till the Union; but things did not remain precisely as they had been in 1785. In 1793, the Irish Parliament placed heavy duties on imported cotton, including—exceptionally—imports from Great Britain;[2] which meant that in any future adjustment it could no longer be maintained that an equalization of duties would redound solely to Ireland's advantage. In 1793, too, the Hereditary Revenue was commuted to a Civil List granted for the King's life; which meant that in any future adjustment there would be no convenient means of clogging the commercial concerns with an imperial contribution.[3] Besides, the indications were that Pitt was no longer disposed so to do. In November 1794, he echoed Foster's language of 1785 to a group of Irish politicians which did not include Foster: if an equalization of duties was established, Great Britain would hope in return for additional military assistance from Ireland; '. . . but here Mr. Pitt disclaimed all ideas of condition or positive bargain, and thought it should rest on the more liberal ground of mutual regard and reciprocal good offices. . . .'[4]

These were the remote sequels to the commercial propositions, and they are crucial to an understanding of Foster's political thinking and political course:[5] the immediate sequel was his unanimous election to the speakership of the House of Commons, which took place on 5 September 1785.

He was the government candidate for the speakership.[6] To this extent, and because as far as is known the Irish Administration had no prior commitment to him, his part in the com-

[1] 32 Geo. III, c. 20; Foster to Sheffield, 4 Nov. 1795, *Anglo-Irish Dialogue*, p. 23.

[2] Whitlaw, 'Anglo-Irish Commercial Relations', p. 7. For a previous precedent for imposing additional duties on imports from Great Britain, see ibid. 87.

[3] Foster to Sheffield, 1 Aug. 1793, *Anglo-Irish Dialogue*, p. 13. For a discussion of the Civil List, see pp. 380, 396, 429.

[4] Memo. of a discussion between Pitt, on the one hand, and Lord Fitzwilliam, [the Ponsonbys?, and Parnell] on the other, mainly about the equalization of duties, 29 Nov. 1794, Pratt MSS., K.A.O. U.840/o.153.

[5] For a further discussion of them, see pp. 364 ff.

[6] The information on which this paragraph is based is taken from Malcomson, *Foster and the Speakership, passim*, but especially p. 303. For the circumstances behind the resignation of Foster's predecessor, see Malcomson, 'Speaker Pery and the Pery Papers', *North Munster Antiquarian Journal*, xvi (1973–4), 42 f.

mercial propositions contributed to his elevation. However, the Irish speakership, unlike its contemporary British counterpart, was attained only after a genuinely popular election, over which the government had limited influence. Foster was the government candidate, but in an important sense he was the popular candidate as well. His very widely acknowledged ability and his country-gentleman ethos, were important ingredients in his success, and won him the support of elements in the House not normally amenable to government influence, notably 'the independent country gentlemen' and even Grattan. The popular basis of elections to the Irish speakership, together with the prestige traditional to the office as the mouthpiece of the legislature in its dealings with the executive, meant that it enjoyed a remarkable degree of independence of the government, and placed its holder in an extremely strong constitutional and political position. It was a kind of *imperium in imperio*, which in Foster's day had gone only a short distance towards the non-partisan office of modern times—nor was it even clear that this was the direction in which it was heading. The contemporary British speakership had gone further, though not so far as was once imagined. The old idea of its evolution was that the modern British speakership was foreshadowed by Speaker Onslow in the mid-eighteenth century, but that because of the unworthiness of Onslow's successors, the position reached at the time of Onslow's retirement was not resumed until the 1820s or 1830s. More recent work, however, has shown that Onslow's concept of the speakership was far removed from the modern one, and that the unspoken principle of 'active impartiality' on which he acted, made the speaker at times arbiter of the fate of measures and ministries. Paradoxically, it was the unworthiness of his successors, in the sense of their comparative mediocrity, which prepared the ground for the emergence of the modern, non-partisan office; in a sense, the speakership could only become a non-partisan office when it ceased to be filled by a man of Onslow's great ability. In Ireland, by contrast, it continued to be held by men of great ability. Indeed, Foster and his immediate predecessor, Edmond Sexten Pery, were men of much greater ability than their mid-eighteenth century predecessors, Boyle and Ponsonby. Foster, though perhaps not Pery, was as active a political leader as Boyle and Ponsonby had been. His influence was more 'personal', theirs more 'real'; he was not formally connected with the executive, they were. Yet at times he wielded the influence he had, differently based though it was, with all their factious and unscrupulous zeal. To a modern way of thinking, independence of the executive is the hallmark of the non-partisan speakership. But the independence which the Irish, though not the British, speakership possessed in Foster's day, rested on its ability to embarrass the executive: in other words, to be partisan.

In immediate, practical terms, the Irish speakership opened up to Foster honours and offices which up to then had been beyond his reach. He was made a British Privy Councillor and, more important to Foster, became an *ex officio* member of the British board of trade.[1] He was also in line for the most dignified office which an Irishman could hold, the lord justice-ship. Up to 1768, when the lord lieutenant resided in Ireland only during the time that Parliament was sitting, the two or three lords justices appointed to act for him in his absence had possessed very considerable power; after 1768, when the lord lieutenant resided all the year round, lords justices were only needed for interregnums or temporary periods of absence. However, on the second occasion when Foster held the office, in 1789, he and his colleague, Fitzgibbon, the recently appointed Lord Chancellor, ruled the country during an interregnum of six months' duration, when Foster successfully exerted their joint authority to prevent an embargo on the export of Irish corn which the British Government was in favour of imposing.[2] In theory the speakership withdrew its possessor from 'the active scene of politics', with the possible exception of his short bursts of office as a lord justice. Foster claimed in August 1794 that he knew '. . . little of the present Ministerial system, and am almost as retired a country gentleman as if I never had been engaged in public measures. . . .'[3] In practice, however, he continued to exercise a good deal of influence over measures, particularly in his old sphere of economic affairs. His successor

    [1] Rutland to Pitt, 24 Aug. 1786, *H.M.C. Rutland MSS.*, iii. 339; Lord Liverpool to Foster, 3 Mar. 1801, F.P. D.207/28/111H.
    [2] Beresford to Hobart, 27 Nov. 1789, F.P. D.562/1413; Foster and Fitzgibbon to Lord Westmorland, 8 Dec. 1789, S.P.O. Private Official Correspondence books.
    [3] Foster to Sheffield, 11 Aug. 1794, *Anglo-Irish Dialogue*, p. 16.

as Chancellor of the Exchequer, Parnell, was his friend and
political protégé.[1] Where Foster was 'an enterprising, able,
busy man',[2] Parnell was notoriously indolent; and the upshot
was that Foster never completely gave up the duties of the
chancellorship of the exchequer. In August 1786 Rutland
handed over the Irish part of the negotiations for an Anglo-
French trade treaty to the trinity of Foster, Parnell and Beresford, 'the three fittest men in Ireland for the task'.[3] Foster
corresponded direct with Eden, now reconciled to Pitt, and
the British negotiator in Paris (and infuriated Eden by the
obstinacy with which he held out for concessions to the Irish
linen industry). A decade later Foster was still playing as
prominent a role as Parnell, and seems, for example, to have
been the moving spirit behind the Irish Administration's
appeal to Pitt in 1796-7 to negotiate for it a loan of £1,500,000
from the Bank of England.[4] Clearly, the speakership, while
opening to him new spheres of influence, never withdrew him
altogether from his old sphere. He remained a regular and
influential member of the lord lieutenant's informal 'cabinet'—
much more regular and influential than his predecessor, Pery,
had been.

Naturally, the extent of his influence continued to vary from
one administration to another. He does not, for example,
seem to have been fully confided in by Rutland's successor,
the Marquess of Buckingham, who as Lord Temple had been
Lord Lieutenant, 1782-3, and had had reservations about
Foster's political reliability. During the Regency crisis in
1789 Foster told Buckingham to regard him 'as owing all to
Mr. Pitt, as fearing all from Mr. Fox, and determined to fight
to the last drop if attacked'.[5] The threat of attack arose probably
from the Opposition's allegations that he had shown partiality
from the chair;[6] this threat, combined with the fact that one

---

[1] Scott to Robinson, 29 July 1780, *Beresford Correspondence*, i. 139; Buckingham
to Grenville, 18 Dec. 1788, *H.M.C. Dropmore MSS.*, i. 389.
   [2] Sheffield to Eden, 6 Sept. 1785, Auckland MSS., B.L. Add. MS. 34420, fol. 105.
   [3] Rutland to Pitt, 24 Aug. 1786, *H.M.C. Rutland MSS.*, iii. 338 f.
   [4] Foster to Pelham, 1797, F.P. D.562/9594; Foster to Pelham, 31 Dec. 1796,
S.P.O. 620/26/202; Lord Camden to Pelham, [*c.* 1 Feb. 1797], Pelham MSS.,
B.L. Add. MS. 33103, fol. 132; Pelham to Camden, 16 Feb. 1797, Pratt MSS.,
K.A.O. U.840/C.122/11.
   [5] Buckingham to Grenville, 18 Dec. 1788, *H.M.C. Dropmore MSS.*, i. 389.
   [6] Grattan, *Life*, iii. 513.

of the leading members of the Opposition, George Ponsonby's elder brother, William, was at this time canvassing for the next speakership election, no doubt stiffened Foster's resolve to stand by Buckingham. All the same, Buckingham—as before—did not altogether believe his vows. At the height of the crisis, Buckingham took the strong step of refusing to transmit the Irish Parliament's addresses to the Prince of Wales inviting him to assume an unrestricted Regency of Ireland. It may be that, as spokesman of the House of Commons, Foster was excluded, or excluded himself, on constitutional grounds from the discussion of this tactic.[1] However, it is probably a truer indication of his position that, for one brief moment just after this, his ally, Parnell, deserted Buckingham and voted with the Opposition.[2] In short, Foster's support during the Regency crisis was at worst uncertain, and at best by no means as decided as Fitzgibbon's.[3]

With Buckingham's successor, the Earl of Westmorland, who arrived in Ireland early in 1790, Foster's relations were soon much closer. Westmorland immediately saw in him 'a very able man and considerable connection', and gratified him by obtaining a peerage for Mrs. Foster.[4] He was again the government candidate for the speakership at the start of the 1790 Parliament, defeating William Ponsonby by a comfortable majority; and he was unfailingly included in the deliberations of the 'Irish Cabinet' which emerged during Westmorland's Administration, and which was composed of Fitzgibbon, Beresford, Parnell, Archbishop Agar of Cashel and, to a lesser extent, the Attorney- and Solicitor-General, Arthur Wolfe and John Toler. All lords lieutenant had had cabinets of some sort. But Westmorland's possessed a uniform composition and a continuity which were unusual, perhaps unprecedented.[5] He himself acted more as the Irish Cabinet's representative in Great Britain than as the British Government's representative

---

[1] Buckingham to Grenville, 25 Jan. 1789, and Scrope Bernard to Grenville, 21 Feb. 1789, *H.M.C. Dropmore MSS.*, i. 402, 416 f.

[2] Buckingham to Grenville, 21 Feb. 1789, ibid., i. 418.

[3] For Fitzgibbon and the Regency crisis, see p. 388.

[4] Westmorland to Grenville, 20 Mar. 1790, *H.M.C. Dropmore MSS.*, ii. 158.

[5] Lord Cornwallis to Maj.-Gen. Ross, 16 Aug. 1798, *Cornwallis Correspondence*, ii. 387; Henry Dundas to Westmorland, 16 Jan. 1792, Westmorland MSS., S.P.O. fol. 44.

in Ireland. The strength of the Irish Cabinet lay in the ability and experience of its members, especially when compared to the ineptitude and inexperience of Westmorland and, to a lesser extent, of his Chief Secretary, Robert Hobart: its weakness was that in the last resort it could not survive without the support of the lord lieutenant's power and patronage, which derived immediately from the power and patronage of the Crown. This weakness was exposed to the full by the most important measure of the Westmorland Administration— Catholic Relief—which was strongly pressed by the British Government and as strongly resisted by the Irish Cabinet. By the time the trial of strength was over, even Westmorland had come to see 'how little can be done here against the English Government': while the trial of strength was still on, he commented to Pitt, in a rare moment of intuition, that Fitzgibbon 'has no other God but English Government, and will not distress us.'[1]

The British Government's policy of Catholic Relief for Ireland was initially inspired by British legislation of 1791 in favour of non-Irish Catholics:[2] it very rapidly gathered momentum from the obvious imminence of war against Revolutionary France. On the idealogical level, the British Government viewed the Irish Catholics as a conservative force, predisposed towards monarchical institutions, who were natural allies against the anti-clerical Revolution and, within Ireland, against Presbyterian republicanism; on the practical level, the British Government wanted to take positive steps to make Ireland a fruitful field for British recruitment, and an uninviting arena for French invasion. They may be criticized for taking too European a view of a situation which, because of the nature of Irish Catholicism, was peculiarly Irish: Foster, on his side, may be criticized for taking too narrowly Irish a view of a situation involving much wider considerations of strategy and manpower. Foster had supported the Irish Catholic Relief Act of 1778, and though he had not spoken on it, had helped to draft Luke Gardiner's Relief Acts of 1782.[3]

---

[1] Westmorland to Pitt, 30 Mar. 1793 and 11 Jan. 1793, Lord Lieutenant's Union Correspondence, N.L.I. MS. 886, fols. 159, 109.
[2] See pp. 407 f.
[3] Luke Gardiner to Foster, [Nov.?] 1781, F.P. D.207/5/47.

In 1782 he reached his *ne plus ultra*; and thereafter the whole weight of his ability was exerted against further concessions to the Catholics, and especially against the concession of the elective franchise. '. . . He would', he said in a well-known passage, 'allow them property, with equal security [with the Protestants] for that property; civil liberty, with equal security for that civil liberty, and everything which could tend to their ease, their happiness, and personal welfare; but he would draw a line round the Constitution, within which he would not admit them while their principles were, he would not say hostile, but certainly not as friendly to the Constitution as those of Protestants. . . .'[1]

At the close of 1791 and the beginning of 1792, acrimonious correspondence passed between London and Dublin on the principle and extent of Catholic Relief. Pitt, and more particularly the Home Secretary, Henry Dundas, proposed the concession of some form of qualified franchise, but Westmorland, echoing the sentiments of the Irish Cabinet, warned them that it was a concession which 'every servant of the Crown and every man in Parliament (except an agitator or two) would revolt at'.[2] There was partiality, no doubt, but substantial accuracy, in his reading of the situation: in their prejudices and passions on the Catholic Question as in much else, the Irish Cabinet were fairly representative of the private sentiments of a large majority of the Irish House of Commons,[3] indeed of the Anglo-Irish Ascendancy. In 1792 the influence of the Irish Cabinet was strong enough to ensure that the Relief Act which passed did not extend to the Catholics either the franchise or, almost as contentious, the right to carry arms; also, that it was not sponsored directly as a government measure. The only important respect in which the views of the British Government prevailed, was that no resolution was passed barring the door to a future concession of the franchise.[4] After this success, the Irish Cabinet exerted themselves to demonstrate to the British Government the impossibility of pressing further concession in the present temper of both Parliament and the country. In this next phase of their campaign, Foster

[1] *Parl. Reg.* (Irish), xiii. 337.
[2] Westmorland to Pitt, 18 Jan. 1792, Westmorland MSS., S.P.O. fol. 45.
[3] For the change in these sentiments, see pp. 353 ff.
[4] Lecky, *History of Ireland*, iii. 38 ff.

played a prominent part. In April 1792, when it was his duty as Speaker to present the money bills of the session for the royal assent, he gave a strong 'Ascendancy' bias to a speech which ought to have been formal and non-controversial; in May he was accused by Edmund Burke's son, Richard, the agent to the Catholics of Ireland, of abruptly leaving the chair in order to forestall the presentation of a Catholic petition; and in September, the co. Louth grand jury, of which he was foreman, passed strongly worded anti-Catholic resolutions, which Burke Senior called 'Mr. Foster's declaration of war' and denounced as 'an infamous libel'.[1] In spite of these and similar manœuvres staged by the other members of the Irish Cabinet, the British Government, bent on rallying the Catholics behind the war effort and weaning them away from radical reform, decided in December 1792 to be no longer deflected from their resolve to push through the Irish Parliament the franchise and the right to carry arms. Accordingly, Hobart was instructed to introduce, as a government measure, a bill to that effect at the beginning of 1793. Having probably ascertained in advance that the Irish Administration had 'the good sense' not to resent his 'maintaining an opinion which he could not yield, upon one single point',[2] Foster openly opposed the bill in Parliament. In February he exercised what seems to have been an unspoken right of the speakership, and made at committee stage a second-reading speech, denouncing the whole principle and policy of the measure in what Hobart admiringly described as 'a chain of able statement and observation, which made a deep impression on the house.'[3] The impression it made, however, was not deep enough to defeat the bill. This, the Irish Cabinet could hardly have achieved if they had been united in opposition to it; as it was, they were not. Only Foster and Archbishop Agar spoke against it in Parliament; even Fitzgibbon back-handedly supported it at second reading, though he then ambushed it in committee with

---

[1] Grattan, *Life*, iv. 65 f.; Richard Burke to Dundas, May 1792, Melville MSS., P.R.O.N.I. T.2627/2/1/2; Edmund to Richard Burke, 1 Oct. 1792, *Burke Correspondence*, vi. 224. For the Louth grand jury resolutions, see also pp. 230 f.

[2] Foster to Sheffield, 20 Mar. 1799, *Anglo-Irish Dialogue*, p. 30.

[3] Hobart to Sir Evan Nepean, 28 Feb. 1793, S.P.O. 510/30/4; *Parl. Reg.* (Irish), xiii. 332 ff. For some discussion of the speaker's unspoken right to make a second-reading speech in committee, see Malcomson, *Foster and the Speakership*, p. 281.

a successful amendment raising the property qualification which entitled Catholics to carry arms. As a result, the bill had an unexpectedly (and, from Westmorland's and Hobart's point of view, embarrassingly) easy passage; its most contentious clause, the franchise, passed the House of Commons by the comfortable majority of 144:72.[1]

The significance of Foster's open opposition in Parliament is that it showed, not quite for the first time, that his 'Ministerial Patriotism' applied only within certain limits; also, that it anticipated his future opposition to the Union, though by no means the full extent of that opposition.[2] Foster had gone into open opposition once before, on the sugar duty in 1780. In 1793, as in 1780, he was nominally an officer of the House, not a Minister of the Crown, and so enjoyed considerable freedom of manœuvre—to say nothing of the great practical independence of the government which the speakership afforded him in 1793. Moreover, in 1793, for the first time in his career, the Government he served had sponsored a measure directly challenging the cardinal point of substance in his political thinking—the maintenance of the Anglo-Irish Ascendancy. The economic was the usual sphere for his 'Ministerial Patriotism'; even in that sphere his previous experience had taught him that tactical withdrawal was often productive of strategic advance, and his characteristic attitude was that 'all difficulties may be settled by negotiation much better than by debate'.[3] Since even in that sphere he had once before renounced the way of negotiation and gone into opposition, it was almost inevitable that he should have gone into opposition on a matter, to him, of conviction, where ground, once given, could never be regained. It is doubtful if he was capable of accommodating his convictions to considerations of prudence or policy. Even if he had been, there would have been no point in his doing so in 1793. The measures of that session which he valued, and which were under discussion behind the scenes while Catholic Relief was before the House, were the compulsory participation of Ireland in the East India Company's monopoly, and the

[1] Hobart to Nepean, 16 Mar. 1793, S.P.O. 510/30/4; Lecky, *History of Ireland*, iii. 141.

[2] See pp. 81 f., 418 ff.

[3] Foster to Pelham, 5 Apr. [1784]. Pelham MSS., B.L. Add. MS. 33101, fols. 75–6.

re-interpretation of the Navigation Act to permit the re-export of British colonial goods from Ireland to Great Britain. These, however (along with the, to Foster, unwelcome Place and Pension and Responsibility Bills), were under consideration because the British Government wished to conciliate, not the Irish Cabinet, but the Irish Opposition; and it was as sops to the Opposition that they were ultimately carried.[1] There was, therefore, no prudential reason for Foster, their real champion, to worry about the loss of his behind-the-scenes influence in their favour. He accordingly—and almost certainly he would have done it anyway—attacked the Catholic Relief Bill with inflexible vigour, and with pointed criticism of the British Government, whom he blamed, not only for the bill, but for the agitation in the country in its favour.[2] The bill, in his view, was so bad in principle that no amount of softening in matters of detail could make it acceptable. In particular, he rejected the suggestion that the time-honoured 40/- qualification for the county franchise should be changed to a uniform £10, and did not refer to the alternative, and more plausible, suggestion that a special £10 or £20 qualification should be created for Catholic voters alone.[3] In 1793, and again in 1799-1800, he failed to follow the line which was characteristic of him when his convictions were not involved: he failed to seize a possible opportunity of palliating what he deemed a bad measure.

The Catholic Relief Act of 1793 restored to the Catholics the right, which they had been deprived of since at least 1728,[4] of voting in parliamentary elections on equal terms with the Protestants. However, as Foster had warned (not altogether prudently), there were no grounds for saying that men who were fit to elect were unfit to be elected. Catholic agitation at once concentrated on the right to be elected, and with the recall of Westmorland and the appointment of Earl Fitzwilliam to succeed him at the end of 1794, it seemed near to fulfilling

---

[1] See pp. 378 ff. [2] See pp. 416, 431.

[3] His only contribution to the details of the measure was to support a suggestion for the form of oath to be taken by Catholics qualifying themselves under the Act (*Burke Correspondence*, vii. 364, *n*. 7).

[4] See J. G. Simms, 'Irish Catholics and the Parliamentary Franchise, 1692–1728', *I.H.S.* xii (1960–1), 28 ff. By an Act of 1704, Catholics could vote if they took an oath of abjuration which was debatably still compatible with the tenets of their religion.

its aim. This time, however, the Irish Cabinet were united among themselves, and were spurred into intense political activity by Fitzwilliam's precipitate dismissal of Beresford as Chief Commissioner of the Revenue and of Edward Cooke and Sackville Hamilton as Under-Secretaries at the Castle. Moreover, they had good enough contacts in British ministerial circles to know that Fitzwilliam had exceeded his instructions on Emancipation as well as in the matter of dismissals, and that there was a fair chance of his being disavowed and recalled. By January 1795, Fitzwilliam was arguing that the public mind was so agitated that it was no longer safe to delay Emancipation; yet it could also be argued that the state of agitation of the public mind was to a great extent of his own fomenting. This gave the Irish Cabinet their cue, and they exerted themselves to get up a combination against the Emancipation Bill, which Fitzwilliam's political allies, the Irish Whigs, had introduced into the House of Commons with his consent and approbation. Together, Foster and Fitzgibbon persuaded him to make it an 'open' question (in other words, one which office-holders could oppose without fear of dismissal), and then set about building up an opposition to it among the traditional supporters of the Castle. According to one source who was biased in their favour, they were so far successful in this that they had marshalled 120 votes against it (with 'a strong probability' of 20 more) by the time Fitzwilliam was recalled towards the end of February.[1] All prospects for the bill's success departed with him.

The Fitzwilliam episode shows up the strength and durability of Foster's position in national politics. Although he openly headed a coalition against a measure which the Lord Lieutenant thought necessary to avert rebellion, he was still not ostracized politically. Even in the midst of Fitzwilliam's rage and humiliation at being recalled, Foster was able to exercise some degree of influence over him: Foster and Fitzgibbon convinced him, where Fitzgibbon alone had failed, of the absolute necessity of adjourning Parliament before he appointed lords justices and made his departure from Ireland.[2] To a great extent the

---

[1] John Pollock to Westmorland, 15 Apr. 1795, Westmorland MSS., S.P.O. fol. 111. For the Fitzwilliam débâcle, see also pp. 376, 403 f., 424 ff.
[2] Fitzgibbon to Westmorland, 25 Mar. 1795, ibid. fol. 114.

durability of Foster's position was due to the independent status of the Irish speakership. Fitzwilliam could dismiss Beresford, Cooke, and Hamilton, he could arrange for the compulsory retirement of the Attorney- and Solicitor-General, he could even contemplate the removal of Fitzgibbon; but he could not get rid of Foster without a general election. This gave Foster a strong bargaining position. Informed rumour had it that Fitzwilliam offered him Beresford's office of Chief Commissioner of the Revenue along with the secretaryship-of-state, if he would agree to resign the speakership and so make way for William Ponsonby to succeed to it.[1] These were handsome terms to offer to a declared enemy. However, the independent status of the Irish speakership does not alone explain why they were offered to Foster: a contributory explanation is to be found in the importance attached to his services, even by Fitzwilliam. Both Foster and Parnell were no longer allowed to exercise their old influence; but Parnell was described as 'growing confidential', and Foster was reported to be 'extremely intimate' with Grattan who, next to the Ponsonbys, was the most prominent of Fitzwilliam's Irish supporters.[2]

Under Fitzwilliam's successor, Earl Camden, who was later described as 'not the most decided character in public or private matters',[3] the Irish Cabinet returned to the plenitude of power they had enjoyed in the period up to 1793. Yet, early on in the Camden Administration at any rate, Foster's relations with it were strained. The clash came over Foster's demand that his brother, by then Bishop of Kilmore, be translated to a better (and borough-owning) bishopric, that of Clogher, which was backed up by 'a threat of his declining to be any longer one of your [Camden's] Cabinet'.[4] To this Camden reluctantly consented in December 1795. In the same month the Chief Secretary, Thomas Pelham, who had previously held that office under Northington, cited Foster's blackmailing methods in the matter of patronage as a major factor in Pelham's disgust at Irish politics and disinclination to continue as Chief

---

[1] Marcus Beresford to Beresford, 6 Feb. 1795, *Beresford Correspondence*, ii. 67 f.

[2] Ibid.; Cooke to Westmorland, 18 Jan. 1795, Westmorland MSS., S.P.O. fol. 132; Cooke to Nepean, 27 Jan. 1795, Chatham MSS., P.R.O. 30/8/327, fol. 147.

[3] Lord Essex to Lord Lowther, 10 Mar. 1806, *H.M.C. Lonsdale MSS.*, 174.

[4] Pelham to Camden, 20 Dec. 1795, Pratt MSS., K.A.O. U.840/o.189/5; Camden to Pelham, 19 Dec. 1795, Pelham MSS., B.L. Add. MS. 33101, fol. 354.

Secretary.[1] The principal feature of the Camden Administration was a policy of special powers and counter-revolutionary draconianism, which has been blamed for driving innumerable otherwise well-disposed peasants into rebellion, and of which, more than any other member of the Irish Cabinet, Foster was the architect.[2] In particular, it was Foster who in February and March 1798 strongly urged the bold (and successful) policy of arresting the known United Irish leaders on suspicion. It was also Foster who in March and April won the Irish Cabinet's last, and as it proved Pyrrhic, victory, by heading the agitation against the Irish Commander-in-Chief, Sir Ralph Abercromby, who had issued an indiscreet, demoralising and, in one part, illegal, general order on 26 February, describing the army in Ireland as being in 'a state of licentiousness which must render it formidable to everyone but the enemy.'[3]

In the ensuing complex and fast-moving crisis, which ended up by discrediting the Irish Cabinet in the eyes of the British Government, there was little difference of policy between them. Condemnation of the general order was unanimous, and began with the British Government, the Irish Administration and Irish Cabinet having previously maintained a discreet silence on the subject, in the hope that it would attract no attention.[4] The policy of draconian measures was confirmed by Pitt, who urged Camden on no account to abate 'those exertions by which you have hitherto saved the country'.[5] There was some divergence of view as to who should implement these 'exertions': Abercromby believed that the regular army should not be dispersed and dissipated in local dragonnades, which were the job of the gentry and their yeomanry corps, and his general order had instructed the generals under him accordingly; Camden, Pelham, and some members of the British Government were sympathetic to this view; the Irish Cabinet opposed it,[6] and Pitt, too, doubted '... whether anything but the vigorous

---

[1] Pelham to Camden, 1 Dec. 1795, Pratt MSS., K.A.O. U.840/C.122/6.

[2] Thomas Pakenham, *The Year of Liberty: the Story of the Great Irish Rebellion of 1798* (London, 1969), pp. 42 ff., 53 ff.; Grattan, *Life*, iii. 401, and v. 271.

[3] Pakenham, *Year of Liberty*, pp. 43 ff., 51.   [4] Ibid., pp. 54 f.

[5] Pitt to Camden, 13 Mar. 1798, Chatham MSS., P.R.O. 30/8/325, fols. 5–6.

[6] The attitude of Fitzgibbon, now Lord Clare, is doubtful. He had long lamented the dispersal of the regular army, and had hoped that the establishment of an Irish yeomanry would obviate the necessity for it—Clare to Camden, 28 Aug. 1798,

exertion of military force, under military and not civil direction, can restore quiet to the country. . . .'[1] On the more immediate question of what to do about Abercromby, however, there was unanimity between the British Government, the Irish Administration, and the Irish Cabinet; the political embarrassment and military danger which would ensue if Abercromby were to resign, must if possible be averted; but Abercromby must subscribe to a compromise formula by which the damaging and illegal parts of his general order would be explained away.[2] Abercromby refused, and tendered his resignation, which Camden still hesitated to accept. At this point, and not before, the Irish Cabinet mustered their parliamentary forces with a view to making Camden implement the agreed consequence of the failure of negotiation; on 24 March Foster held a meeting in the Speaker's Chamber for this purpose, and turned a presenting speech into a reaffirmation of the policy Abercromby had undermined. Camden reported Foster's move to the British Government, adding that the move had had no bearing on Abercromby's decision to resign, which had been taken previously. In reply, the British Government did not animadvert on Foster's conduct, and instead gave Camden 'distinct and explicit' instructions to accept Abercromby's resignation, and negotiate with him no further.[3]

Then the focus shifted, as it so often suddenly did in dealings between Whitehall and Dublin Castle. The influence of Dundas, a favourer of more conciliatory methods for Ireland and a friend of Abercromby, began to make itself felt in the British Cabinet. By an illogical thought-process, Abercromby's

Pratt MSS., K.A.O. U.840/O.183. In 1801, in a debate at Westminster, he pointed to the dispersal of the regular army as one of the greatest initial difficulties which Lord Cornwallis had to cope with after the outbreak of the rebellion—*Parl. Reg.* xv. 542. The problem was that, although dispersal was bad for the discipline of the regulars, a stiffening of regulars was good, and perhaps necessary, for the discipline of the largely Orange yeomanry. Clare, certainly, recognized the problem long before Abercromby appeared on the Irish scene.

[1] See p. 72, *n.* 5.
[2] Camden to Portland, 15 Mar., and Portland to Camden, 19 Mar., 1798, Home Office MSS., P.R.O. H.O. 100/75, fols. 225–8, 253–6; Camden to Pitt, 17 Mar. 1798, Chatham MSS., P.R.O. 30/8/326, fol. 268.
[3] *Commons' Journals* (Ireland), xvii. 309; Camden to Portland, 26 Mar. 1798 (two letters, one official and one private, of the same date), and Portland to Camden, 31 Mar. 1798, H.O. MSS., P.R.O. H.O. 100/75, fols. 299–302, 319–22, 357–8; Pitt to Camden, 31 Mar. 1798, Pratt MSS., K.A.O. U.840/O.190A.

original sin came to some extent to be mitigated in the British Government's eyes by the subsequent, and by no means precipitate, campaign of the Irish Cabinet against him.[1] Abercromby himself, with a skill which casts doubt on his supposed, and boasted, political *naïveté*, was careful to extol Camden's 'virtuous character' and to lay all the blame for his resignation on the Irish Cabinet, without ever consenting to specify what action they had taken against him between 26 February and 24 March, and without ever admitting that it was not they, but he, who had rejected a compromise solution.[2] Myth soon superseded reality in the minds of the British Government —and of the King, who was hypersensitive to civilian interference in matters military. Camden was praised for his efforts to '. . . heal the mischief which has been industriously created on what he [the King] terms the ill-advised wording of Sir Ralph's orders . . .' (the mildest epithet so far applied to them); and Camden was also urged to persevere in what had been previously forbidden, his attempts to persuade Abercromby to withdraw his resignation.[3] However, the policy of draconian measures, carried out 'under military and not civil direction', was at the same time confirmed and persevered in:[4] only its Irish upholders, and particularly Foster, were discredited. Over a year later Lord Castlereagh, who had been Camden's private secretary at the time of the Abercromby crisis and shortly afterwards succeeded Pelham as his Chief Secretary, reminded Camden of the conduct of 'your own friends, but particularly the Speaker, in driving Sir R. Abercromby from the country'; in Castlereagh's view, Foster's '. . . open hostility was infinitely more compatible with the stability of Government than the interference and embarrassment which both you and Pelham experienced from the period of that meeting in his own

---

[1] Portland to Dundas, 29 Mar. 1798, Melville MSS., N.L.I. MS. 54A/129.

[2] Abercromby to Dundas, 1 Apr. 1798, ibid. /131; Abercromby to Camden, 24 Mar. 1798, H.O. MSS., P.R.O. H.O. 100/75, fol. 307.

[3] Portland to Camden, 10 Apr. 1798, ibid. fol. 58.

[4] Pitt's letter of 31 March (see p. 73, *n.* 3) urges Camden to 'a well-concerted effort for crushing the rebellion by the most vigorous military exertions in all the disturbed provinces', and recommends as Abercromby's successor General Lake, a greater 'hawk' than Foster, and a man who had been openly critical of Abercromby and laudatory of the Irish Cabinet. In this letter, however, Pitt also urges that the local gentlemen and their yeomanry corps should give more active assistance to the regular army.

Chamber, in which, from being a member of your Cabinet, he became a member of a faction to control it. . . .'[1]

The outbreak of the '98 Rebellion determined the British Government to do what Camden had been urging on them since the spring of 1797: combine the offices of lord lieutenant and commander-in-chief, and appoint to the combined office Great Britain's foremost soldier-statesman, the Marquess Cornwallis. Cornwallis's appointment betokened a change of system. He was '. . . not to preclude the hopes of clemency towards those who may submit, and must ultimately and as soon as possible have in view some permanent settlement which may provide for the internal peace of the country and secure its connection with Great Britain . . . by an Union.'[2] In other words, on the question of military and security measures, the British Government took the (probably sensible) view that draconianism was the best available means of dealing with a situation of smothered rebellion; but once rebellion had burst out, and had been defeated in the military sense, the best available means of extinguishing it was lenity. Cornwallis combined this view with a strong, preconceived prejudice against the Irish Cabinet—in part derived from the Abercromby crisis. He regarded them as men, insignificant in themselves, who had become significant only because of the improper use they had been allowed to make of the influence of the Crown. He thought, incorrectly, that their power was 'founded on the grossest corruption', and took pride in having 'totally set [them] aside'.[3] He was the more easily able to set them aside because they did not present a united front against him. As in 1793, Fitzgibbon (now Earl of Clare) deserted his colleagues and, after some hesitation, threw in his lot with the new Lord Lieutenant, especially on the controversial issue of the bargain Cornwallis made with the United Irish leaders arrested on suspicion, that their lives would be spared if they made a full confession of their treasonable connection with France.[4]

[1] Castlereagh to Camden, 24 July 1799, Pratt MSS., K.A.O. U.840/C.98/7.
[2] Pitt to Camden, 11 June 1798, ibid. /O.190A.
[3] Cornwallis to Ross, 23 Nov. and 16 Aug. 1798, *Cornwallis Correspondence*, ii. 445, 387.
[4] Clare to Auckland, 1 Aug. and 26 Nov. 1798, printed in Bishop of Bath and Wells (ed.) *The Journal and Correspondence of William Lord Auckland* (4 vols., London, 1861–2), iv. 39, 70.

As Foster's not-very-loyal friend, Lord Sheffield, declared—with much exaggeration—if Clare and '. . . the Speaker could have agreed, the consequences would have been worse than the existing rebellion. . . .'[1] Clare was by no means converted to Cornwallis's general policy of lenity. But on the particular issue of the United Irish leaders he took a broad view, and appreciated the value of a full confession which would discredit the claim of the British Opposition that the rebellion had been caused, not by an aspiration for an Ireland separated from Great Britain, but by the British Government's failure to concede Catholic Emancipation and Irish parliamentary reform. Foster, by contrast, characteristically took the narrowly Irish view that sparing the lives of the leaders would hearten the rebels and dismay the loyalists. Clare's attitude was also shaped by the all-important consideration that he strongly approved of the principle—though he disapproved of the timing[2]—of the projected Union.

Foster's stand against the Union is the most celebrated episode of his career. However, it is important to remember that his hostility to the Irish, though not yet the British, Government dated from a time when Union was nothing more to him than the vaguest rumour. From the day after his arrival in June 1798, Cornwallis ostracized Foster politically—something which, as has been seen, not even Fitzwilliam in 1795 had done to Foster, although in its precipitancy it resembled Fitzwilliam's treatment of Beresford; and Foster, on his side, roundly denounced in letters and conversation Cornwallis's 'speculative nonsense of conciliation'.[3] Foster would always, whatever the immediate circumstances, have opposed the Union in Parliament. It was a measure in which his deepest convictions were involved and by which they were knocked over like so many skittles. His grounds for opposing it, financial, economic, political, and constitutional, are set forth at great length and with great effect in his orations in the House of April 1799 and February 1800; and to them must be added the very important ground, which he deliberately

---

[1] Sheffield to Auckland, 12 Aug. 1798, Auckland MSS., B.L. Add. MS. 34454, fols. 431–2.

[2] For Clare and the Union, see p. 389.

[3] Foster to Sheffield, 7 and 23 July 1798, *Anglo-Irish Dialogue*, pp. 26 ff.

refrained from mentioning publicly (until the debate on the Catholic Petition of 1805), that the Union, by disfranchising most of the Ascendancy strongholds, the close boroughs, would ultimately lead the Irish Catholics to agitate for a separate Irish Parliament in which, this time, they would be dominant.[1] With grounds such as these, he would always have opposed the Union with the inflexibility which he had displayed over the Catholic Relief Bill of 1793. He himself saw, or affected to see, a strong similarity between the circumstances of 1793 and 1799–1800, and was pained that Cornwallis did not show the forbearance of Westmorland. However, the circumstances were widely different. The Irish Administration of 1793, though not the British, had much sympathy with Foster's 'Ascendancy' outlook, and no doubt privately welcomed his opposition as taking some of the absurdity out of their previous prognostications about the impossibility of carrying the franchise. Between Foster and Cornwallis, on the other hand, there was no kind of sympathy; and Foster abhorred Cornwallis, not just as the promoter of the Union, but as the man who he thought had mishandled the military side of the rebellion, and whose treatment of the defeated rebels had been nothing less than a betrayal of the loyal. Again, Foster's opposition in 1793 was a magnificent failure: in 1799 it was a success. After the event, as will be seen, Pitt claimed that he would not have resented Foster's opposing the Union in Parliament. But it is at least questionable whether he would have taken this attitude in the hour of defeat in 1799. The circumstances of 1799–1800 were such that Foster's inevitable opposition, and the Government's reaction to it, could not be temperate and free from rancour.

There were faults of personality on both sides. At the end of March 1798, when deciding *against* the appointment of Cornwallis, Pitt had expressed 'great doubts whether his

[1] Foster to Sheffield, 5 Feb. 1801, ibid. 36; *A Detailed Report of the Speeches on the Irish Roman Catholic Petition from the 25th of March 1805 ... to the 14th of May following* ... (London, 1805), p. 296. Earlier, however, Foster had expressed doubts about the effectiveness of the close boroughs of the Irish Parliament as strongholds of the Ascendancy, because of the likelihood that needy or unscrupulous Protestant proprietors would sell them, or at least their seats, to Catholics—draft resolutions in Foster's handwriting for a committee [which he hoped would be set up after the defeat of Emancipation in early May 1795], F.P. D.207/5/10.

temper of mind and prejudices on Irish subjects, make him qualified for the task'.[1] Foster, on his side, was notorious for his assertiveness and intractability. If these characteristics were resented by men like Camden and Pelham, who had some personal regard for him, how much more must they have been resented by Cornwallis—not that he acquired much first-hand experience of them. Informed contemporaries of such varied stamp as Lords Sheffield, Grenville, and Clare, Edward Cooke, and Euseby Cleaver, Bishop of Ferns, all concurred in blaming Cornwallis for wantonly antagonizing Foster.[2] Both Castlereagh, whom Cornwallis had continued as Chief Secretary, and Portland, now Home Secretary, a man who had never had much regard for Foster, showed a greater appreciation than Cornwallis of the importance of his attitude and a greater inclination to soothe his ruffled feelings by taking him into their confidence.[3] Pitt invited him in the middle of October 1798 to come over to London, and in the first week of November Foster, not without reluctance,[4] set out. Just before his departure Cornwallis at last sent for him, but appears to have been fairly non-committal on the subject of the Union. The outcome of this interview suggests that there was more of stupidity than antipathy in Cornwallis's behaviour towards him, since Cornwallis thought they had parted good friends 'after an amicable explanation', while Foster proclaimed himself much dissatisfied at the way he had been received.[5] It seems that the Irish Administration first got round to asking formally for Foster's views on the Union as late as 24 November, when he was already in London conferring with Pitt on the subject.[6] This was not the way to handle a man of Foster's

[1] Pitt to Camden, 31 Mar. 1798, Pratt MSS., K.A.O. U.840/O.190A.

[2] Sheffield to Auckland, 12 Aug. 1798, Auckland MSS., B.L. Add. MS. 34454, fols. 431–2; Grenville to Buckingham, 28 Jan. 1799, printed in Duke of Buckingham (ed.), *Memoirs of the Court and Cabinets of George III* (4 vols., London, 1853–5), ii. 429 f.; Clare to Auckland, 15 Nov. 1798, *Auckland Correspondence*, iv. 67; Cooke to Auckland, 2 Nov. 1798, Auckland MSS., B.L. Add. MS. 34455, fol. 26; Bishop of Ferns to Egremont, 19 June 1799, Petworth House MSS., P.H.A. 57/26.

[3] Castlereagh to Camden, 4 Oct. 1798, Pratt MSS., K.A.O. U.840/C.98/3; Portland to Pitt, 19 Oct. 1798, Lord Lieutenant's Union Correspondence, N.L.I. MS. 886, fol. 396.

[4] Foster to Pitt, 21 Oct. 1798, Chatham MSS., P.R.O. 30/8/328, fol. 47.

[5] Cornwallis to Ross, 8 Nov. 1798, *Cornwallis Correspondence*, ii. 431; Clare to Auckland, 15 Nov. 1798, *Auckland Correspondence*, iv. 67.

[6] Castlereagh to Foster, 24 Nov. 1798, *Castlereagh Correspondence*, ii. 17.

temper, especially a man whose influence Castlereagh, at any rate, recognized would be 'prodigious'.[1]

Foster's discussions with Pitt in London were also unfortunate in their consequences. At this early stage Pitt's guesses as to how Irish politicians were likely to react to the Union were far from inspired: he thought, for example, that Beresford was more likely to oppose it than Parnell,[2] though the reverse proved to be the case. Between Foster and Pitt there appears to have been a complete misunderstanding. Foster afterwards said that he had distinctly forewarned Pitt in December 1798 that he must publicly oppose the Union unless 'the real, uninfluenced sense of the country' should come out in favour of it; and had specified that by this he did not mean 'a small or influenced majority in the House'.[3] Perhaps he meant November rather than December, because in early to mid-November both Clare and Camden formed an impression of his attitude which agrees with this in substance.[4] Pitt, however, formed in mid-November a completely different impression. He thought that Foster was opposed to the principle of a Union, but that he saw no '. . . material difficulty or objection likely to arise in the detail . . . I think I may venture to say that he will not obstruct the measure; and I rather hope if it can be made palatable to him personally (which I believe it may) that he will give it fair support. . . .'[5] The discrepancy between the two versions is glaring. Foster in December 1799 attributed it simply to a misunderstanding.[6] But one of Pitt's political associates reported in April 1799 that 'Mr. Pitt thinks the Speaker deceived him'; and in 1801 another reported Pitt as saying that '. . . Foster had broken faith with him upon the Union: not by opposing it (for he had always professed his objections to it), but by taking a lead against it, which he had distinctly promised not to do. . . .'[7] The nub of the matter was probably

---

[1] Castlereagh to Wickham, 23 Nov. 1798, *Cornwallis Correspondence*, ii. 448.

[2] Pitt to Cornwallis, 17 Nov. 1798, ibid. pp. 441 f.

[3] Foster to Pelham, 8 Dec. 1799, Pelham MSS., B.L. Add. MS. 33106, fol. 322.

[4] Clare to Pitt, [c. 10 Nov. 1798], Lord Lieutenant's Union Correspondence, N.L.I. MS. 886, fol. 515; Camden to Castlereagh, 16 Nov. 1798, *Castlereagh Correspondence*, i. 449.

[5] Pitt to Cornwallis, 17 Nov. 1798, *Cornwallis Correspondence*, ii. 441 f.

[6] Foster to Pelham, 8 Dec. 1799, Pelham MSS., B.L. Add. MS. 33106, fol. 322.

[7] Lord Liverpool to Blaquiere, 19 Apr. 1799, Blaquiere MSS., N.L.I. MS. 877,

that Foster considered himself free to influence the sense of the country *against* the measure, while Pitt considered him bound to remain neutral until the sense of the country had declared itself. The misunderstanding (which, for convenience's sake, it may be called) had important consequences, because, as Foster afterwards admitted, nothing did so much to harden his attitude to the Union as the strong and personal terms in which Pitt alluded to him in the British House of Commons in February 1799, to which he replied with equal asperity in the Irish House in April.[1] Whatever passed between them in November and December 1798, Pitt was no doubt influenced in his assessment of Foster's probable conduct by the 'Ministerial Patriotism' of most of Foster's previous political course, and presumably did not realize that Foster was inflexible where his convictions were involved. Even Camden, who knew Foster well and had not misunderstood his sentiments on the Union, shared in mid-November 1798 Pitt's optimistic view, at least to the extent of thinking that Foster 'will not take an active part against it'.[2]

Foster returned to Ireland early in January 1799, and Castlereagh heard immediately that his language was very hostile.[3] Foster, on his side, complained that the Irish Administration '. . . withdrew their confidence from me before I ever expressed an opinion publicly, and they did it with many unpleasant circumstances from the very day I landed from England. . . .'[4] By 'publicly' he presumably meant, in Parliament; and it was scarcely reasonable in him to expect them to ignore his open opposition in all other quarters, and in particular to ignore the anti-Unionist petition sent up by co. Louth even before the parliamentary session opened, which the Administration regarded, with some exaggeration, as almost exclusively Foster's handiwork. They did in fact show restraint by not dismissing any of his dependants, particularly his son, Thomas Foster: a restraint they did not show in the case of Parnell and the anti-Unionist Prime Serjeant, James Fitz-

fol. 23; Lord Colchester (ed.), *Diary and Correspondence of Charles Abbot, Lord Colchester* (3 vols., London, 1861), i. 269.

[1] Foster to Camden, 3 Aug. 1799, Pratt MSS., K.A.O. U.840/O.81/4.
[2] Camden to Castlereagh, 16 Nov. 1798, *Castlereagh Correspondence*, i. 449.
[3] Castlereagh to Portland, 9 Jan. 1799, *Castlereagh Correspondence*, ii. 85.
[4] Foster to Camden, 3 Aug. 1799, Pratt MSS., K.A.O. U.840/O.81/4.

Gerald. Indeed, Foster's dependants were left unmolested until after the 1799 session was over. This did not mollify him; and Thomas Foster, when finally he received his dismissal in June, expressed surprise and indignation at the harshness of the measure. Foster took the same line, and persisted in regarding his opposition to the Union as of a piece with his opposition to the Catholic Relief Bill of 1793. To the last he claimed that he was in opposition, on conscientious grounds, to one single measure of government: all thought of 'General Opposition' he indignantly disclaimed.[1]

This was not strictly true. His efforts to turn a Bill for the Better Suppression of the Rebellion into a Union question,[2] and his attempt to knock the ground from under the Government by supporting a Regency Bill designed to render impossible a recurrence of the Regency crisis of 1789, were actions which bordered on, if they did not actually constitute, 'General Opposition'. Moreover, even if his opposition was not general, it was certainly factious and violent. There is a wide consensus of contemporary opinion that his partiality in the chair was 'gross and glaring',[3] and Pitt did not hesitate to accuse him of this in the strong personal attack he made on him in the British House of Commons in February 1799. Foster's alliance at the beginning of February with the Ponsonby party also smacked of factiousness. It bore that perceptible stigma which, in spite of the apologies of recent historians, has never been effaced from the Fox–North Coalition in Great Britain. In particular, it suggested, incorrectly, a trading-in of Foster's 'Ascendancy' principles, and gave rise to Grattan's unjust jibe that 'Foster will be delivered of his religion with as much facility as a lady lying-in, in a hot climate . . .'[4] The other

---

[1] Thomas Foster to Castlereagh, 10 June 1799, Castlereagh MSS., P.R.O.N.I. D.3030/820; John Foster to Camden, 3 Aug. 1799, Pratt MSS., K.A.O. U.840/O. 81/4; Foster to Sheffield, 20 Mar. and 19 Sept. 1799, *Anglo-Irish Dialogue*, pp. 30 f.

[2] Cornwallis to Portland, 28 Feb. 1799, *Cornwallis Correspondence*, iii. 69.

[3] William Crosbie to Lord Mornington, 31 Jan. 1799, Wellesley MSS., B.L. Add. MS. 37516, fol. 38; Clare to Auckland, 23 Jan. 1799, *Auckland Correspondence*, iv. 80; Camden to Castlereagh, [Jan. or Feb. 1799], *Castlereagh Correspondence*, ii. 138; Beresford to Auckland, 16 Feb. 1799, *Beresford Correspondence*, ii. 215; Cornwallis to Portland, 12 Feb., 14 Mar., and 7 June 1800, *Cornwallis Correspondence*, iii. 187, 212, 248 f. See Malcomson, *Foster and the Speakership*, pp. 298 f.

[4] 'J.W.' [Leonard McNally, an informer known as 'Lord Downshire's friend'] to Downshire, 23 Feb. 1799, Downshire MSS., P.R.O.N.I. D.607/G/83.

unfortunate feature of the alliance was that it was cemented by the raising of a subscription among the Ponsonby party and the Dublin bankers (or the passing round of a 'begging-box', as Cornwallis called it) for the payment of Foster's debts.[1] The subscription was in fact called off (though not before £16,000 had been collected); which meant that Foster suffered the odium of it, but derived from it no advantage.[2] Still greater odium attached to the tactics resorted to by the 'patriotic Speaker' when he visited Harrogate in the autumn of 1799, ostensibly because his wife was taking the waters, but in reality to see what he could do to play on the commercial jealousies of the Yorkshire woollen manufacturers. As has been seen, such jealousies—though not from Yorkshire—had played their part, at least psychologically, in wrecking the commercial propositions in 1785, and Foster now tried, with some success, to marshal them against the Union.[3]

Foster would have argued that the methods he resorted to were justified by the many unconstitutional practices employed by the Government in order to carry the Union. It may be doubted whether he was perfectly sincere in denouncing the compensation for disfranchised boroughs as a 'monstrous and unconstitutional offer', and certainly he was in no financial position to refuse the £7,500 for his half-share in Dunleer;[4] but his indignation at the use made of the Place Act—'such a question as a total change of our Constitution being so openly connected with the disposal of the emoluments of the Crown'— was probably sincere, and accords with the laudable vigilance he had always exercised as Speaker against attempts by the executive to tamper with the legislature.[5] What is more questionable about his conduct over the Union is his failure to make

[1] Cornwallis to Ross, 13 Feb. 1799, *Cornwallis Correspondence*, iii. 59 f.; Beresford to Auckland, 26 Jan. 1799, *Beresford Correspondence*, ii. 199 f.; Henry Alexander to Pelham, [c. 12 Feb. 1799], Pelham MSS., B.L. Add. MS. 33106, fol. 209.

[2] Buckingham to Dundas, 5 Apr. 1799, Melville MSS., N.L.I. MS. 55, fol. 166.

[3] Cornwallis to Ross, 5 Apr. 1800, *Cornwallis Correspondence*, iii. 225. For an account of reaction in the Midlands to Foster's speech on the Regency Bill, see Mrs. Edgeworth to Dr. Beaufort, 23 Apr. 1799, Beaufort MSS., N.L.I. MS. 13176. I am indebted for this reference to Mrs. Marilyn Butler.

[4] Malcomson, *Fosters and Dunleer*, p. 162.

[5] Foster to Sheffield, 12 Dec. 1799, *Anglo-Irish Dialogue*, p. 35; Malcomson, *Foster and the Speakership*, p. 293.

much, if any, constructive contribution to the detail of the measure, though it is clear that the Government would have welcomed his assistance in this respect, and possibly gone out of their way to meet some of his points, simply because they came from him.[1] However, like Catholic Relief in 1793, the Union was in Foster's eyes so wrong in principle that nothing would avail to soften or palliate its effects. The chief critic of the commercial clauses was Foster's nephew and political follower, John Maxwell Barry, and it is not improbable that in his behind-the-scenes discussions with the Government, he relayed his uncle's sentiments.[2] Even so, the sentiments would have come with greater effect from Foster direct. In any case, the most important result of these discussions, concessions to the Irish cotton industry, had been denounced in advance by Foster in the House as merely condemning the industry to a lingering death instead of the sudden one originally proposed. In his speech in February 1800 he dismissed every one of the financial and economic clauses, apart from the two by which Britain waived duties amounting to £26,000 a year on British goods going to Ireland, as either injurious or useless to Ireland.[3] Up to the last, his criticisms were couched in this sweepingly destructive vein.

Nevertheless, if he did not influence, or seek to influence, the content of the measure, the influence which he had on the size and strength of the opposition to it was, in Edward Cooke's view, 'amazing'.[4] Clare, too, expressed the opinion in March 1800 that the fierceness of the struggle arose 'principally, if not altogether, from the part taken by Foster'.[5] This being so, a concerted effort was made, in the summer and winter of 1799, to win him round at least to assisting with the economic and financial details of the Union. The effort was concerted, because there was no shortage of eager and busy intermediaries, notably Lords Camden and Sheffield and Thomas Pelham. The extent to which Pitt authorized these overtures has not

---

[1] Elliot to Castlereagh, 11 Sept. 1799, *Castlereagh Correspondence*, ii. 397 f.
[2] Bolton, *Union*, pp. 194 f.
[3] *Speech of the Rt. Hon. John Foster . . . Delivered in Committee on Monday the 17th Day of Feb. 1800* (Dublin, 1800), *passim*.
[4] Cooke to Camden, 7 May 1799, Pratt MSS., K.A.O. U.840/O.81/3.
[5] Clare to Lord Wellesley, 9 Mar. 1800, Wellesley MSS., B.L. Add. MS. 37308, fol. 283.

hitherto been established, particularly since Camden went out of his way to becloud the issue by stressing that he was writing to Foster without 'the previous knowledge of anyone' (as if Foster would have believed that a lightweight like Camden would have taken such an important step without the sanction of Pitt).[1] However, a letter from Pelham to an Irish crony and fellow-Unionist, establishes the point beyond doubt. Writing on 4 November 1799, Pelham reported (and the letter deserves extensive quotation):

... I must tell you in confidence that I have been trying to reconcile him [Foster] to Mr. Pitt, and as far as the latter is concerned, I have been successful. I have satisfied him that no one in the Irish House of Commons can cope with him in the details of commerce, and that it would be highly advantageous to secure his neutrality at least when the propositions are discussed in the Committee. Pitt's conversation and sentiments about Foster were liberal and manly. He acknowledged frankly his indignation at Foster's conduct upon his return to Ireland, and especially at his answers to the Louth and Dublin Addresses. At the same [time] he acknowledged with equal fairness his talents and merits, and disclaimed with equal warmth and liberality the idea which has been circulated here of Foster having proposed inadmissible terms of personal advantage.[2] All this will be reported to Foster, who seems by his letters to Lord Sheffield and others to wish to explain his conduct and soften Pitt's hostility to him, without however abandoning his opposition to the principle of Union. If he is sincere in his wishes to be well with Government and not to persist in opposing the Union in the details, if the principle is once adopted by the country, he has a fair opportunity of coming round, and I think that the Administration in Ireland will feel the advantage of having his neutrality at least. . . .[3]

This letter shows that, although a typically eighteenth-century misunderstanding (of the sort which produced the Fitzwilliam débâcle) contributed to Foster's opposition to the Union and to the bitterness and asperity of that opposition, the element of misunderstanding and 'personal animosity' had been removed,

---

[1] Camden to Foster, 25 July 1799, Pratt MSS., K.A.O. U.840/O.184/5.
[2] See, for example, Francis Plowden, *History of Ireland from the Union* (3 vols., Dublin, 1811), i. 145.
[3] Pelham to Sir George Shee, 4 Nov. 1799, Shee MSS., in the possession of Capt. Richard Neall, 57 Orchard Avenue, Chichester, Sussex, who kindly made them available to me via the N.R.A., where they were being sorted and listed in 1974.

at least on Pitt's side, before the session of 1800 began. Foster was given every opportunity to return to the government fold, and was not required to recant or to profess support for the principle of the Union. That he remained in unconstructive opposition, was his own decision entirely.

In view of the importance attached by contemporaries, and especially by Unionist contemporaries, to Foster's role on the Union issue, he was obviously a man whom the post-Union Government, in both London and Dublin, sought to cultivate and appease. Accordingly he was included in the amnesty which was granted to most of the anti-Unionists, even though he had sinned more irremissably than most. His compensation for the abolition of the speakership was fixed at the generous figure of £5,000 a year for life;[1] and Pitt was magnanimous in the line he proposed should be adopted towards him: Foster was to be made to understand that he was not to govern Ireland, '. . . but that his assistance in promoting its internal improvements and local interests should be cordially accepted . . .'[2] Just before the fall of Pitt's Ministry in February 1801, the Earl of Liverpool (formerly Charles Jenkinson), President of the Board of Trade, either forgetting or affecting to forget that Foster had been a member of the board only by virtue of the speakership, consulted him on the prospects for promoting the cultivation of hemp in Ireland.[3] In September 1801, Thomas Pelham, now Lord Pelham and Home Secretary, advised Cornwallis's successor, the Earl of Hardwicke, to ask Foster's opinion about the policy of restricting the Irish distilleries.[4] In December, Pelham himself wrote to Foster direct about the trade in corn between Great Britain and Ireland, and met with a not-very-encouraging response.[5] Finally, at the beginning of 1802, Hardwicke, acting on a suggestion of Pelham's, conferred with Foster about the Irish militia, in which Foster had always taken a keen interest since its establishment

---

[1] Malcomson, *Foster and the Speakership*, pp. 274 f.

[2] Abbot to Hardwicke, 29 June 1801, quoted in McDonagh, *Viceroy's Post-Bag*, p. 90.

[3] Liverpool to Foster, 29 Jan. and 3 Mar. 1801, and Foster to Liverpool, 8 Feb. 1801, F.P. D.207/28/111B, 111H, 111F.

[4] Pelham to Hardwicke, 24 Sept. 1801, Pelham MSS., B.L. Add. MS. 33108, fol. 48.

[5] Pelham to Foster, 4 Dec. 1801, and Foster to Pelham, 10 Dec. 1801, ibid. fols. 407, 435.

in 1793.[1] Shortly after this audience Foster crossed over to London to take his seat for the first time in the United Parliament, and in spite of the blandishments he had received from both the Irish and the British Administrations, had moved decisively into the camp of opposition by the spring of 1802.

In view of the height from which Foster had fallen and the impossibility of providing him with an 'office equal to the rank and situation he formerly held', it was perhaps inevitable that he should go into opposition, especially since the pressure of Union engagements made it difficult to find offices of suitable standing for any of his anti-Unionist dependants.[2] Besides, marked differences of principle and policy separated him from the Hardwicke Administration. Hardwicke inherited not only Cornwallis's system of lenity but also his antipathy to the old Irish Cabinet. The King himself had stressed to Addington, who succeeded Pitt as Prime Minister in March 1801, that it must be made clear to the Irish that the Union had closed 'the reign of Irish jobs'.[3] Hardwicke was therefore over-sensitive to the unreal danger that the Irish Cabinet or, worse still, the so-called Undertaker system of pre-1768 days, would revive under post-Union conditions; and his first Chief Secretary, Charles Abbot, launched into a reform programme which immediately brought him into collision with Lord Clare.[4] Clare died early in 1802 and was succeeded by an Englishman, the overbearing Lord Redesdale, who echoed Cornwallis's claim that he alone could speak for the Irish nation and liberate it from the bondage of Irish party: what worried Redesdale was that Great Britain might be ruined by the Union if the spirit of Irish jobbery got into British politics.[5] Abbot's successor as Chief Secretary, William Wickham, endorsed these sentiments: 'It is *necessary*', he wrote, 'to be without ceasing on our guard against everybody and everything that is Irish. . . .'[6] Foster alone was left to pick up the gauntlet thrown down by

[1] Hardwicke to Pelham, 28 Jan. 1802, ibid. Add. MS. 33114, fol. 101.

[2] Hardwicke to Pelham, 17 Dec. 1801, ibid. fols. 91–2.

[3] George III to Addington, 11 Feb. 1801, McDonagh, *Viceroy's Post-Bag*, p. 3.

[4] Hardwicke to Addington, 24 Oct. 1801, *Colchester Diary*, i. 324; Clare to Pelham, 5 Sept. 1801, Ashbourne, *Pitt*, pp. 271 f.

[5] Redesdale to Lord Eldon, 19 July 1802, printed in H. Twiss (ed.), *The Public and Private Life of Lord Chancellor Eldon* (3 vols., London, 1844), i. 432.

[6] Wickham to Addington, 18 Dec. 1802, Wickham MSS., Hampshire R.O.; photocopies in P.R.O.N.I. T.2627/5/D/33.

the Hardwicke Administration. Parnell had died in 1801, Clare in 1802; Beresford, typically, had made a graceful and remunerative exit into retirement; and Archbishop Agar had allowed himself to be muzzled by a combination of temporal and spiritual honours. Foster was thus the only actual or political survivor of the old Irish Cabinet.

Foster's parliamentary campaign of 1802 was not very successful, although it must be admitted that the evidence for its lack of success is almost entirely to be found in the correspondence of his enemies. He was torn between a strong personal animosity towards Isaac Corry, who had succeeded Parnell as Chancellor of the Irish Exchequer in 1799, and a desire to avoid saying anything disrespectful about Addington,[1] whom he respected for having saved the King from Pitt and the country from Emancipation. This cramped his tactics and his choice of issues in the early part of the year. On 7 May, he came out into the open by introducing the methods by which the Union had been carried as an additional topic for a retro-spective motion of censure on the Pitt Ministry.[2] But though roughly half the Irish members then sitting at Westminster had opposed the Union, Foster's amendment made a difference of only eight or ten votes to the division.[3] The Union as a politi-cal issue was clearly dead, and Corry was able to exult in the feeble effects of 'the explosion of the great anti-union battery'.[4] This failure was hardly compensated by Foster's success in June in rattling Chief Secretary Wickham on a militia question where the Irish Administration had been led astray by an erro-neous opinion of the Irish Law Officers.[5] Abbot, the ex-Chief Secretary, was of opinion at the close of the session that '. . . Foster has quarrelled with Ministers, made no Opposition friends, and by his uncandid manner has given a very un-favourable impression of his character to all the English country gentlemen, who thought much of him before they

---

[1] Abbot to Hardwicke, 17 Mar. 1802, Hardwicke MSS., B.L. Add. MS. 35712, fol. 115.

[2] *Parl. Reg.* xviii. 281.

[3] Jupp,'Parliamentary Representation', p. 142; Wickham to Hardwicke, 10 May 1802, Hardwicke MSS., B.L. Add. MS. 35713, fol. 92.

[4] Isaac Corry to Alexander Marsden, 30 Mar. 1802, S.P.O. 620/61/134.

[5] Wickham to Hardwicke, 1 June 1802, Caledon MSS., P.R.O.N.I. D.2433/D/5/68.

saw and heard him. . . . '[1] The problem from Foster's point of
view was that his political connections lay among the Irish
members, who since the Union had been cut adrift in a House
where nine-tenths of the subjects under discussion did not
directly concern them, and who consequently had a natural
tendency towards venality and subservience. Wickham put the
point well when he stated '. . . that the formation of a *Party* on
Irish politics only is a thing impracticable, . . . as long as Government has any favours to grant or any titles to bestow . . .';[2] and
the Marquess of Sligo came to the bitter conclusion that
'the worst enemies of this country [Ireland] in England are
the Irish'. Even Corry, with all the advantages of office, had no
following among the Irish members, and indeed seems to have
received from them nothing but abuse.[3] In these circumstances,
Foster could do no more than give the United Parliament some
impression of what he was capable of, if enlisted in a better
cause and fighting on firmer ground. He did not again appear
at Westminster until the beginning of 1804.

This, if it was intentional, was a prudent move. Left to his
own devices, Corry 'exposed his deficiency on every occasion',[4]
and no longer derived advantage from the 'uncandid manner'
in which Foster had in the previous session attacked him.
Corry's relations with the Irish Administration deteriorated;[5]
which naturally raised the question whether Foster, who would
make a better Chancellor of the Exchequer, could possibly
be a more troublesome colleague. In August 1803, Wickham,
on the advice of Addington, Hardwicke, and even Redesdale,
opened up negotiations with Foster.[6] Nothing came of this,
probably because Foster insisted on the proscription of Corry,
and in any case expressed the view that the chancellorship
of the Irish exchequer ought to be abolished.[7] Nevertheless
negotiations seem to have continued, on and off, until March

[1] Abbot to Marsden, 28 June 1802, S.P.O. 521/136/2.
[2] Wickham to Addington, 3 Sept. 1802, Wickham MSS., P.R.O.N.I. T.2627/5/
D/23.
[3] Sligo to Marsden, 11 June 1803, S.P.O. 620/18A/7.
[4] Theophilus Jones to Beresford, 29 Mar. 1804, *Beresford Correspondence*, ii. 283.
[5] Malcomson, *Isaac Corry*, pp. 26 ff.
[6] Wickham to Addington, 29 Aug. 1803, Wickham MSS., P.R.O.N.I. T.2627/5/
D/69.
[7] Wickham to Castlereagh, 29 Sept. 1803, ibid. T.2627/5/G/53; Marsden to
Hardwicke, [Jan. 1804?], Hardwicke MSS., B.L. Add. MS. 35723, fol. 186.

1804. Lord Sligo, a friend of Foster's and indeed of everybody, was acting as intermediary in February, and seems to have been instrumental in preventing him from supporting a motion of censure on Hardwicke's handling of Emmet's insurrection of 1803.[1] Between December 1803 and March 1804, Foster displayed restraint and a conciliatory spirit on another question on which he might have attacked the Irish Administration: the volume of paper currency in circulation in Ireland, and the consequent differential between the London and Dublin rates of exchange. Foster resisted the temptation, as others did not, to twit Corry for paying his own salary at par; he gave the Government every opportunity to set up its own committee to enquire into these monetary and exchange difficulties; and only as a last resort did he move for a committee himself, of which he was appointed chairman at the beginning of March. His initiative and moderation on this issue, and his efficiency and sweet reasonableness as chairman, raised his political stock considerably and earned him the respect even of certain Whigs.[2] Moreover, early in the year a new element had entered into the situation, when Foster met Pitt at a private dinner party in London. To everyone's surprise they got on well together. This was the more surprising in view of the fact that Foster had initially regarded the hostility of the Hardwicke Administration towards him as instigated by Pitt.[3] On 15 March, Foster and two of his cronies, Edward Hardman and Nathaniel Sneyd, voted in the minority on Pitt's motion for a naval enquiry, and Foster's influence 'materially led the La Touches to vote' in the same minority.[4] By 21 March, Lord Sligo was lamenting that the Hardwicke Administration had missed its chance of acquiring Foster, since he was now definitely ranged with the new, combined opposition to Addington.[5] Foster's exactly contemporary chairmanship of the Irish currency committee served to bring to the forefront his pretensions

[1] Sligo to Marsden, 16 and 19 Feb. 1804, S.P.O. 620/13/180/2, 3.

[2] F. W. Fetter, *The Irish Pound, 1797–1826* . . . (London, 1955), pp. 27 ff. But not the respect of Charles Abbot—Abbot to Redesdale, 19 Apr. 1804, Redesdale MSS., Gloucester R.O.; photocopies in P.R.O.N.I. T.3030/2/3.

[3] Wickham to Addington, 29 Aug. 1803, Wickham MSS., P.R.O.N.I. T.2627/5/D/69.

[4] *Parl. Debs.* i. 927; Jones to Beresford, 29 Mar. 1804, *Beresford Correspondence* ii. 283.

[5] Sligo to Marsden, 21 Mar. 1804, S.P.O. 620/13/180/7.

to office (though, once in office, he seems to have been slow to respond to the recommendations of his own committee[1]), and when Addington fell at the beginning of May, Pitt offered Foster the chancellorship of the Irish exchequer. Having formerly advocated its abolition, Foster now refused to accept it unless it was coupled with the first lordship of the Irish treasury. Pitt agreed to this, and Hardwicke was left shrugging his shoulders and reflecting that 'Mr. Addington might have had him on the same terms'.[2]

All the same, Hardwicke welcomed Foster's appointment. He assumed that the combination of the chancellorship of the exchequer and the first lordship of the treasury was largely a matter of prestige and emolument. It never occurred to him, though he was well aware of Foster's assertiveness and intractability, that Foster would construe his powers under the Irish Treasury Act of 1795 as he afterwards did. The Treasury, or Responsibility, Act had been passed as a popular measure designed to bring the issue and expenditure of public money under the control of a treasury board responsible to Parliament.[3] It had been founded on resolutions of the Irish House of Commons recommending that the Irish treasury should be modelled

[1] Fetter, *Irish Pound*, p. 50.

[2] Hardwicke to Charles Yorke, 13 June 1804, Hardwicke MSS., B.L. Add. MS. 35706, fol. 56.

[3] 35 Geo. III, c. 28, ss. 14–16, 20–3; T. J. Kiernan, *History of the Financial Administration of Ireland to 1817* (London, 1930), pp. 277 ff. The treasury board had been set up in December 1793 (becoming operational in March 1794) as a by-product of 33 Geo. III, c. 34, by which the King had surrendered the Hereditary Revenue for his lifetime in return for a fixed Civil List (see also pp. 380, 396). In 1793 a Responsibility Bill had been introduced, but it was decided that the matter was best dealt with by administrative means (the prerogative of the Crown to place the lord high treasurership of Ireland in commission), rather than by statute. For most of 1794, disputes raged over the extent of the treasury board's powers *vis-à-vis* the lord lieutenant. The Responsibility Act of 1795 which the Fitzwilliam Administration sponsored, was thus an act of explanation only (though it left much unexplained); there was no Responsibility Act of 1793, as is commonly stated. See John Hely-Hutchinson to Lord Loughborough, 18 Mar. 1793, *H.M.C. Donoughmore MSS.*, p. 327; Fitzgibbon to Hobart, 4 Apr. 1794, Chatham MSS., U.L. Cambridge Add. MS. 6958, fol. 1428; Sylvester Douglas to Pitt, 20 Aug., 16 and 27 Oct. 1794, Chatham MSS., P.R.O. 30/8/327, fols. 367–70, 249–51, 276–8. It is significant that Douglas, the then Chief Secretary, reported that Parnell was at the head of the party who wanted to put a wide interpretation on the powers of the treasury board—significant not only because Parnell was Chancellor of the Irish Exchequer, but because he got most of his ideas from Foster. At the time, however, Foster professed his innocence and ignorance of these disputes—Foster to Sheffield, 29 Mar. 1794, *Anglo-Irish Dialogue*, p. 14.

on the British, and that it should be given 'full powers of control and superintendence over all officers of receipt and expenditure', including revenue officers. The wording of the Act had fallen short of these recommendations. The 'superintendence' was there, but the 'control' was not, if by 'control' was meant the power to proceed against and punish offending officers; this power, in the absence of any specification to the contrary, remained with the lord lieutenant—even the immediate officers of the treasury and the exchequer were 'answerable' to the king, in other words to the lord lieutenant. Moreover, the accounting officers—clerk of the pells, accountant-general, and auditor-general—were required to furnish accounts, not just to the treasury board, but to the lord lieutenant as well. In practice, the workings of the treasury board had fallen still further short of the Commons' resolutions. A great borough proprietor, the 2nd Earl of Shannon, had been made First Lord of the Treasury in 1793, on the grounds that a prestigious office was required to cement his recent return to the government fold, and that he had hereditary claims to the lord high treasurership as a representative of the 'great' Earl of Cork.[1] Also, the responsibility established by the Treasury Act was in practice somewhat impaired by the invariable appointment of the chief secretary as one of the lords of the treasury. Thus, the first lordship of the treasury was largely an office of *otium cum dignitate* until Lord Shannon was bought out to make way for Foster; also, the 'control' and even 'superintendence' of the treasury board over the revenue officers was largely nominal, as it depended on the authority of the lord lieutenant, who generally exercised his authority in this sphere through the former channel of the chief secretary. There was presumably no practical obstacle to his by-passing the treasury board, since any returns which were not furnished to him, as lord lieutenant, under the Act, were furnished to the chief secretary as a lord of the treasury.

Under these circumstances, Foster could reasonably claim that the practice he inherited was a deviation from the Treasury

[1] The Lord High Treasurer in 1793, at the time the office was put in commission, was the 5th Duke of Devonshire, another representative of the Great Earl. In 1764, before Devonshire's appointment, Shannon's father had been hankering after the office—1st Earl of Shannon to 2nd Earl, then Lord Boyle, 20 Oct. 1764, Shannon MSS., P.R.O.N.I. D.2707/A/1/5/53.

Act; and in his cooler moments, he did not deny the overriding
authority of the lord lieutenant (in other words, the imperfect-
ness of the responsibility), and sought only to establish the
principle that all communication between the lord lieutenant
and the revenue boards should be via the treasury.[1] However,
in his wilder moments, he himself deviated far from the Treasury
Act, in the opposite direction to the practice he inherited.
He construed the board's 'control and superintendence' over
the revenue boards as empowering it to dismiss revenue
officers and remit fines imposed on members of the public,
without reference to the lord lieutenant.[2] Still less defensible
was his construction of the clause of the Treasury Act providing
that all warrants signed by the lord lieutenant for new salaries,
gratuities, and pensions in the revenue departments should be
'countersigned' by at least three commissioners of the treasury;
he construed it as empowering himself alone, as First Lord,
to approve or reject them, and at one point detained nineteen
such warrants signed by Hardwicke.[3] With substantial accuracy,
he was said to consider '. . . himself as holding a situation exactly
similar to that of the First Lord of the Treasury in England in
every respect but patronage . . .'[4] In fact, the two offices were dis-
similar in most respects but name. Alexander Marsden, the
Under-Secretary in the Civil Department of the Castle, put
his finger on the most important point of dissimilarity when
he stressed that 'the Minister is at the head of the Treasury
in England; and he is not so in Ireland. . . .'[5] In Ireland, the lord
lieutenant was the 'Minister', though, as Hardwicke rightly
saw, he would not long remain so unless a stop was put to

[1] Foster to Charles Long, 16 Oct. 1805, and Long to Foster, 17 Oct. 1805, H.O.
MSS., P.R.O. H.O. 100/131, fols. 237, 241.
[2] Case for the opinion of counsel in a dispute between the treasury and the board
of excise, 16 Dec. 1804, H.O. MSS., P.R.O. H.O. 100/123, fols. 257–68.
[3] Hardwicke to Hawkesbury, 19 July 1805, Hardwicke MSS., B.L. Add. MS.
35710, fol. 124; 35 Geo. III, c. 34, s. 21.
[4] Nicholas Vansittart to Hardwicke, 17 June 1805, Hardwicke MSS., B.L. Add.
MS. 35716, fol. 105.
[5] Marsden to Vansittart, 4 June 1805, Vansittart MSS., B.L. Add. MS. 31320,
fol. 124. In December 1804, Redesdale had written, with characteristic vigour and
venom, to Spencer Perceval, his brother-in-law: '. . . You have given us . . . the
most profligate, the most dishonest, the most lying, the most crafty, the most violent,
the most acute, and the most wild man of talent whom Ireland has produced, as
the Prime Minister of this country, the Viceroy over the King's Vicegerent. . . .'
Redesdale to Perceval, 17 Dec. 1804, Redesdale MSS., P.R.O.N.I. T.3030/7/30.

Foster's usurpations. Redesdale and the Law Officers confirmed Hardwicke's opinion that Foster's conduct was illegal. At the same time they saw no point in trying to set him right in his construction of the Treasury Act, since his misconstruction of it was in their opinion deliberate and was calculated 'to take into the hands of certain Irish leaders the power of Government in this country'.[1] In other words, it was the English versus the Irish interest.

In this struggle, the strength of Foster's position lay not so much in the wording of the Treasury Act as in the weakness of Pitt's second ministry. Pitt, as Hardwicke had frequent cause to complain, 'never thinks of Ireland except when he is pressed for votes in Parliament'; and because he was under constant pressure throughout his second ministry, he hesitated to drop a man like Foster, who was 'necessary in Parliament'.[2] Under-Secretary Marsden, who hated Foster, reckoned that he did not stand high among the Irish members; and in October 1805, the newly arrived Chief Secretary expressed the view that Foster was 'thought of much more importance in England than he is here [Dublin]'. But even Marsden admitted that Foster's 'manner' in debate had been successful in selling his ideas for Irish revenue reform to the English members; and Henry Grattan Junior commented favourably on Foster's mode of conducting the Irish business, especially as compared to Corry's.[3] Foster was certainly more than a match, both in the House of Commons and behind the scenes, for Nepean and Vansittart, the two men who were successively Chief Secretary during his first year of office, and upon whom Hardwicke, remote in Dublin Castle, had to depend to keep Foster in check during the parliamentary session. Both were found wanting in this respect:[4] had Wickham remained as Chief

[1] Hardwicke to Hawkesbury, 23 Dec. 1804, H.O. MSS., P.R.O. H.O. 100/123, fol. 244.
[2] Hardwicke to Yorke, 24 Aug. 1805, Hardwicke MSS., B.L. Add. MS. 35706, fol. 276; Marsden to Hardwicke, 25 Dec. 1804, ibid. 35725, fol. 122.
[3] Charles Long to Pitt, 29 Oct. 1805, Chatham MSS., P.R.O. 30/8/328, fol. 259; Marsden to Vansittart, 20 June 1805, Vansittart MSS., B.L. Add. MS. 31230, fol. 57; Grattan, *Life*, v. 106. For Foster and the Irish members, see pp. 445 ff.
[4] Redesdale to Hardwicke, 4 July 1804, Hardwicke MSS., B.L. Add. MS. 35718, fol. 14; Marsden to Vansittart, 17 June 1805, Vansittart MSS., B.L. Add. MS. 31330, fols. 49–51; Henry Alexander to Lord Caledon, postmarked 16 Oct. 1805, Caledon MSS., P.R.O.N.I. D.2433/C/6/3.

Secretary, Foster would probably not have been allowed to range so widely, just as he would probably have been stopped in his tracks if Pitt had succeeded in getting the able George Tierney to accept the chief secretaryship early in 1805.[1] Hardwicke was further handicapped by the fact that, although he had been retained in office by Pitt, he owed his original appointment to Addington:[2] Foster had been Pitt's own choice and Pitt could not repudiate him without loss of face. It became even less likely that Pitt would want to repudiate him after the Addingtonians seceded from the ministry in June 1805, leaving Hardwicke without an ally in the Cabinet. Foster, for his part, continued to have reasonably powerful and loyal allies there in the persons of Lords Westmorland, Hobart (now Buckinghamshire), and Camden—all viceregal contacts of the 1790s—and more surprisingly could also look to his former antagonist, Castlereagh, for some measure of support. Wickham had '. . . always considered the meddling of ex-Lord Lieutenants and ex-[Chief] Secretaries as very mischievous to the good government of Ireland . . .'[3] Westmorland, Buckinghamshire, Camden, and Castlereagh each had his own motives for meddling, but together they constituted what Lord Redesdale called 'a miserable Irish faction in England'.[4] They had all been Unionists. But once the Union was passed and had ceased to be a political issue, they made common cause with Foster and provided him with what he had lacked for his whole career in the Irish Parliament—a 'backgame' to play in Great Britain.[5] They, especially Camden, helped him back to office in 1804 and helped to keep him there.

Foster's term of office as Chancellor of the Irish Exchequer and First Lord of the Irish Treasury lasted from May 1804

[1] Frederick Robinson to Hardwicke, 14 Feb. 1805, Caledon MSS., P.R.O.N.I. D.2433/D/5/81.

[2] Pitt to Hardwicke, 15 May 1804, ibid. D/5/76; J. S. Rochfort to Foster, 5 Sept. 1805, F.P. D.207/33/49.

[3] Wickham to Redesdale, 5 Feb. 1806, Redesdale MSS., P.R.O.N.I. T.3030/4/9. Foster's other contact of this kind, Pelham, had been dropped by Pitt.

[4] Redesdale to Vansittart, 25 June 1805, Vansittart MSS., B.L. Add. MS. 31230, fol. 65.

[5] Cooke to Camden, 7 May 1799, Pratt MSS., K.A.O. U.840/O.81/3; Redesdale to Spencer Perceval, 4 Nov. 1804, Redesdale MSS., P.R.O.N.I. T.3030/7/26; Marsden to Hardwicke, 3 June 1804, Hardwicke MSS., B.L. Add. MS. 35724, fol. 144.

(though he was not officially appointed until July) to February 1806. On the whole it is a sorry episode. That he had constructive plans for administrative and financial reform, is undeniable; he was afterwards able to claim publicly that he had taken successful measures to eliminate speculation on the London–Dublin exchange, to reduce the volume of the Bank of Ireland's circulating paper, and to diminish the quantity of small notes in circulation by an issue of silver tokens, and that he had come near to effecting an equalization in the British and Irish currencies.[1] But most of his reforms were inseparable from his more dubious plans for increasing the powers of the treasury. In particular, his bill for dividing the board of customs from the board of excise was one of several which, after repeated remonstrances from Hardwicke, were stopped by Pitt at the end of June 1805 because of the extension they gave to the authority of the treasury.[2] The result was that the division of the revenue boards, which had been Foster's 'favourite measure' for 'many years past',[3] was postponed until the following year, when it was effected by his rival and successor, Newport. Foster's one solid achievement was the setting up of a commission of enquiry into the fees of the public offices in Ireland. But even this could be seen as another vehicle of his self-aggrandisement, and the head of the commission, his nephew, J. S. Rochfort, was probably too deeply dyed in his political colours to be capable of objective recommendations.[4] Most of Foster's measures during this period could be represented by his opponents as 'jobs for himself, with some public advantage and more public expense and influence . . .' (as Grattan said of the bills which were stopped by Pitt at the end of June 1805).[5]

In Foster's eyes, however, these particular bills were designed to establish 'nothing but the constitutional English practice',

[1] *Substance of the Speech of the Rt. Hon. John Foster in Committee on the Irish Budget on May 7 1806* (London, 1806), pp. 11 ff., 28; Foster to Pitt, 12 Nov. 1804, Chatham MSS., P.R.O. 30/8/328, fols. 55–6.

[2] Grattan, *Life*, v. 270; Hardwicke to Yorke, 1 June 1805, Hardwicke MSS., B.L. Add. MS. 35706, fol. 246.

[3] Henry Alexander to Caledon, 17 Oct. 1805, Caledon MSS., P.R.O.N.I. D.2433/C/6/5.

[4] Nepean to Pitt, 8 Dec. 1804, Lord Lieutenant's Union Correspondence, N.L.I. MS. 887, fol. 237; Rochfort to Foster, 10 July 1805, F.P. D.207/33/43.

[5] Grattan to McCan, 15 July 1805, Grattan, *Life*, v. 271.

and he resigned in protest at their being stopped.[1] There then followed a long interregnum during which Pitt tried to persuade him to remain upon terms, Hardwicke at the same time declaring that he would resign forthwith if a 'temporising compromise' were reached with Foster.[2] The deadlock lasted from the end of June till the end of October, and eventually it was decided that Hardwicke should go and Foster stay; that all communication between the lord lieutenant and the revenue boards should be made via the treasury; and that '. . . the Revenue Boards are to be divided, and the authority of the Treasury over all subordinate Boards admitted. . . .'[3] But Foster's victory was far from complete: as part of the conditions on which he remained in office, he had to concede that the treasury in turn operated under the authority of the lord lieutenant, and that the chief secretary should henceforth be one of the quorum of three required for the countersigning of warrants.[4] Equally significant, in terms of practical politics, the successor to the Addingtonian, Vansittart, as Chief Secretary, was Charles Long, a Pittite and one of Pitt's inner circle of acolytes. Long was a watchdog over Foster whose warnings would be heeded; and he soon came to the (unfair) conclusion that Foster's importance derived principally from the fact that 'few persons here [Ireland] have attended to financial matters at all . . .'

There was more behind the depressing wrangles of Foster's first term of office as Chancellor of the Irish Exchequer at Westminster, and in particular more behind his attempt to extend the powers of the Irish treasury, than Foster's aggressive Irishness and well-known defects of personality. The very bad personal relations between Foster and Hardwicke should not be allowed to conceal the important fact that, at bottom, theirs was an institutional, not a personal, clash: or, more precisely, a clash over finding the institutional means to attempt a solution of Ireland's central problem in the period

[1] Rochfort to Foster, 16 July 1805, F.P. D.207/33/45; Foster to Pitt, 29 June 1805, Chatham MSS., P.R.O. 30/8/328, fol. 65.

[2] Hardwicke to Hawkesbury, 9 Sept. 1805, Hardwicke MSS., B.L. Add. MS. 35710, fol. 144.

[3] Henry Alexander to Caledon, postmarked 31 Oct. 1805, Caledon MSS., P.R.O.N.I. D.2433/C/6/9.

[4] Long to Foster, 22 and 26 Oct. 1805, and Foster to Long, 27 Oct. 1805, H.O. MSS., P.R.O. H.O. 100/131, fols. 247, 251, 259; Long to Pitt, [1?] and 29 Oct. 1805, Chatham MSS., P.R.O. 30/8/328, fols. 261–3, 259.

1801-17. This was the problem of Ireland's failure to come anywhere near meeting the financial obligations which the Act of Union had imposed.

The financial provisions of the Act had been based on the premise that, in 1800, Ireland was in too weak an economic condition to bear taxation on equal terms with Great Britain.[1] It was accordingly enacted that the treasuries, revenues and debts of the two kingdoms should be kept separate until Ireland was in a condition to bear equal taxation and until the debts of the two kingdoms should be in the proportion of 1 on the part of Ireland to $7\frac{1}{2}$ on that of Great Britain. In the meantime, Ireland's contribution to imperial expenditure was tied to British expenditure in the same proportion, subject to a revision after twenty years if, within that time, financial amalgamation had not taken place. With greater prescience and accuracy than anyone else exhibited at the time of the Union, Foster had prophesied in 1800 that Ireland would be unable to meet its proportion of contribution; that the $1:7\frac{1}{2}$ proportion of debts would be reached by an increase in the Irish debt, not a decrease in the British; and that one of the conditions for financial amalgamation would thus be fulfilled at a time when the other could not, because Ireland would by then be much less capable of bearing equal taxation than it had been in 1800. Even Foster, however, had not foreseen the duration or the financial effects of the war; the event only deepened the gloom of his prophecy. Over the period 1801–17, Irish taxation roughly speaking doubled, but the Irish debt

[1] The information on which this paragraph is based, unless otherwise attributed, is taken from Earl of Dunraven, *The Finances of Ireland Before the Union and After* (London, 1912), pp. 39 ff., and Kiernan, *Financial Administration*, pp. 297 ff. These authorities disagree, in that Dr. Kiernan takes the view that the British Government deliberately fixed Ireland's Union contribution too high, with a view to running up the Irish national debt and so forcing Ireland prematurely into equal taxation with Great Britain. (In other words, Dr. Keirnan would award Foster no prizes for prophecy.) Lord Dunraven (pp. 56–9) takes account of one of Dr. Kiernan's authorities for this supposition—a speech of Castlereagh's in 1800—but while stressing the unfairness of the burden imposed on Ireland and criticizing subsequent British governments for making no reparation, he does not attribute to the British Government of 1800 the surely fantastic machiavellianism of which Dr. Kiernan believes it capable. Also, he points out, which Dr. Kiernan does not, that the practical effect of financial amalgamation, when it came in 1817, was to halve Ireland's Union contribution, and that equal taxation for the whole of the United Kingdom was not the immediate or even the ultimate result (pp. 78, 86–9).

nontheless quadrupled. The logical solution to this problem which hindsight would suggest, is that the proportion of Ireland's contribution should have been revised in Ireland's favour long before the twenty years specified by the Act of Union had elapsed. However, British parliamentary, to say nothing of public, opinion would never have tolerated such a step, while the war lasted, its outcome was uncertain and its effects on the British economy all too apparent. Even as things were, 'the English', according to J. S. Rochfort, 'think we are not half taxed'.[1] Moreover, in the very early nineteenth century it was 'considered a very great experiment to infringe upon so great a compact as the Union',[2] even in matters of no consequence when compared with the level of Ireland's contribution.

In these complicated political and financial circumstances, Foster was confronted with the wellnigh impossible task of raising as much as he could by taxation, while at the same time ensuring that taxation did not bear so heavily that, when financial amalgamation came, Ireland would be less able to bear equal taxation with Great Britain than it had been in 1800. He assumed—pessimistically, as things turned out— that when the debts had once reached the Union proportion, equal taxation, with the loss of the temporary protecting duties which Ireland enjoyed under the Act of Union would follow immediately. In consequence, he did not take the short-term view that his best course was to borrow as much as the British Government would allow him, in the confident expectation that Great Britain would ultimately have to shoulder the liability for this debt.[3] Instead, he appealed to the English members to recognize

[1] Rochfort to Foster, 4 Mar. [1809], F.P. D.207/34/65.

[2] Lord Glandore to Lord Radnor, 7 Apr. 1806, Talbot-Crosbie MSS., N.L.I. The matter of no consequence to which he referred was the post-Union status of the Irish peers.

[3] Henry Grattan Junior is not precise in his statement on this point, but this would appear to be the policy he attributes to Foster (Grattan, *Life*, v. 311). Newport complained in 1806, with considerable exaggeration: '. . . I have leaned very lightly on Ireland [in his budget], for which Mr. Rose and Mr. Foster have highly censured me, as not raising the supplies within the year—a course never pursued by Mr. F., though so warmly urged on me his successor. . . .' (Newport to William Elliot, 9 May 1806, Elliot of Wells MSS., N.L.S. E.W.30). In fact, Foster had only censured him for introducing no new tax or duty (*Foster's Speech on the 1806 Budget*, p. 3). The problem was the inelasticity of Irish taxation: the increased

. . . how deeply themselves and their constituents are interested in watching over the finances of Ireland, and forcing the Minister into such measures for that country as may ward off, not accelerate, so untimely an approach [to the 1 : 7½ proportion of debt]. They may rely upon it that, if the Irish debt accumulates in the manner it is going on, a joint debt will be an encumbrance to them, and equal taxes will not only not produce proportionate Revenue from Ireland, but will bring a poor and impoverished country, instead of a prosperous and rising nation, into joint stock and joint partnership. . . .'[1]

His own blueprint for measures to ward off the untimely approach of the debts, was a thorough reform of the Irish revenue laws and revenue boards. Whether he was right in theory in arguing that Irish taxation, if properly productive, need not be burdensome, is a matter for students of government finance and economic policy to determine. In practice, his policy was compromised by the fact that the authority to bring the revenue boards to book was split between the chancellor of the Irish exchequer on the one hand and the lord lieutenant and chief secretary on the other. It was presumably his perception of this difficulty which had led him to advocate in 1803–4 the abolition of the chancellorship. The alternative he had then proposed is not clear: it may have been a merger of the chancellorship with the chief secretaryship, which would have unified the authorities and was briefly tried after his final retirement from office in 1811; or it may have been a merger of the Irish and British treasuries and exchequers, which could have preceded financial amalgamation (and was in fact recommended by Foster's enquiry board in 1813), and which would have brought to bear on the Irish revenue boards the more effective authority of the British, as opposed to the Irish, treasury.[2] The formula of combining the chancellorship with the first lordship of the Irish treasury, must have been Foster's next proposal for creating an authority strong enough to grapple with the boards. Whether, at the time, Pitt grasped

rates of duty in Corry's budget of 1803 and Foster's of 1810 (the stiffest he had to introduce) in fact produced less than the previous rates (Dunraven, *Finances of Ireland*, p. 70). The excise revenue hardly increased between 1800 and 1810, although the rates of duty were considerably increased (Kiernan, *Financial Administration*, p. 322).

[1] *Foster's Speech on the 1806 Budget*, p. 8.
[2] Newspaper cutting attacking W. W. Pole, [Aug./Sept. 1812], F.P. D.562/9342; Kiernan, *Financial Administration*, pp. 219 f.

the implications for the lord lieutenant's position as 'Minister', is not known.[1] In stating his reasons for declining the chancellorship on its own, Foster must surely have made clear to him the role he had in mind for the chancellorship and the first lordship combined? This 'misunderstanding', like their misunderstanding over the Union, is redolent of the Fitzwilliam débâcle.

Foster's term of office, and Pitt's second ministry, came to an end with Pitt's death in January 1806. The 'Ministry of All the Talents' which succeeded, was in many respects antithetical to Foster, particularly on the Emancipation issue, and Fox, especially, was suspicious of anyone who had been connected with 'the old Castle'.[2] However, the new Ministry were conscious of the numerical importance of the Irish members and loath to alienate one of the very few who was personally distinguished. The Prime Minister, Lord Grenville, and even Fox, were reported to set some store by Foster's usefulness in economic affairs, and negotiations of some kind took place between the Talents and him, probably after Grattan had refused the chancellorship of the Irish exchequer and it was proving difficult to reach agreement on any other successor.[3] Nothing came of these negotiations, although Rochfort for one was of the blunt opinion that Foster 'could not be on more disagreeable terms with them [the Talents] than you were on with the last Government'.[4] Instead, Grenville's old friend, Newport, was eventually appointed to the office. The terms on which he was appointed, showed that the Talents had learned from the mistakes of their predecessors: Newport was to have a seat at the Irish treasury board, but like Parnell and Corry before him he was only to be Second Lord; Grenville, as Prime Minister, was to be First Lord of the Treasury in both Ireland

[1] For a discussion of the point, see pp. 440 ff.

[2] Fox to Duke of Bedford, 9 June [1806], transcript from the Holland MSS., B.L. Add. MS. 47569, fols. 293–6, made by the late Professor A. Aspinall, and placed at my disposal by Dr. P. J. Jupp.

[3] Grenville to Spencer, 8 Feb. 1806, Aspinall transcript from the Althorp MSS.; Rochfort to Foster, 10 Feb. 1806, F.P. D.207/33/70; J. L. Foster to Foster, 17 Feb. 1806, F.P. T.2519/4/314; Long to Marsden, 17 Feb. 1806, S.P.O. 531/225/3; Revd. H. B. Dudley to Foster, [pre 18? Feb. 1806], F.P. T.2519/4/313; Grenville to Foster, 18 Feb. 1806, F.P. D.207/67/21; Canning to his wife, 21 Feb. 1806, Aspinall transcript from the Canning MSS.; Lord Henry Petty to J. L. Foster, 25 Feb. 1806, J. L. Foster MSS., P.R.O.N.I. T.2519/7/3; Grattan, *Life*, v. 286, 297, 418.

[4] Rochfort to Foster, 1 Feb. 1806, F.P. D.207/33/66.

and Great Britain. This new arrangement was presumably designed to foreshadow financial amalgamation, and in the short term to prevent Newport from empire-building like Foster.

The arrangement was to be permanent, even though the Ministry of All the Talents was short-lived. When they fell from power in March 1807 and were succeeded by the 'no Popery' Ministry of the Duke of Portland, Foster, though he returned to office as Chancellor of the Irish Exchequer, was not allowed to hold it along with the first lordship of the Irish treasury. He was from the start at a disadvantage during the negotiations over the new Government's Irish arrangements. He had not attended Parliament since the summer of 1806, and consequently was caught napping in Ireland when the Talents fell.[1] Moreover, there were in 1807 other runners for the chancellorship of the Irish exchequer: Lord Clancarty, Sir Laurence Parsons, and Foster's own nephew, John Maxwell Barry.[2] In these circumstances, Foster's most influential ally, Camden, advised him to lower his terms;[3] and in the end he did so, although the terms he obtained were nominally more generous than Newport's. They were that, in addition to holding the chancellorship of the Irish exchequer and the second lordship of the Irish treasury, he was to be a supernumerary Lord of the British Treasury. The seat at the British board was hailed euphemistically by his brother-in-law, Thomas Burgh, as betokening 'a real blending of the money interest of these two countries'.[4] But it was at least a generous sop, made more generous in 1809 when Perceval, on succeeding Portland as First Lord, advanced Foster to the second lordship of the British treasury. It is probably an indication of Foster's preoccupation with Irish, to the exclusion of British, affairs that he never, apparently, attended the British treasury board.[5]

[1] John Maxwell Barry to Rochfort, 27 Mar. 1807, F.P. D.207/52/15.

[2] James Corry to Foster, 20 Apr. 1807, F.P. T.2519/4/341; Elliot to Under-Secretary James Traill, 11 and 17 Apr. 1807, Elliot of Wells MSS., N.L.S. E.W. 26.

[3] Camden to Foster, 18 Apr. 1807, F.P. T.2519/4/340.

[4] Burgh to Foster, 23 Apr. 1807, F.P. D.562/12101.

[5] Denis Gray, *Spencer Perceval: the Evangelical Prime Minister, 1762–1812* (Manchester, 1963), p. 319. After 27 January 1809, a record of attendances at treasury board meetings ceased to be kept (with several exceptions in 1811, when Foster was never present). Mr. Gray (p. 269) attributes the vacancy for Foster's supernumerary lordship in 1809 to his resignation from the board, instead of to his

Foster returned to office imbued with a determination to effect 'all the measures I have had in contemplation for the Revenue and for Ireland'.[1] Without the first lordship of the treasury, he had no longer any pretext for doing so except by the authority of the lord lieutenant. His dominance over the treasury board remained, however, though without formal recognition; as John Maxwell Barry observed of a later period: '. . . The Board of Treasury are inefficient; . . . in all Revenue superintendence the Chancellor of the Exchequer only acts. . . .'[2] This was because membership of the board was compatible with membership of Parliament; and as all its members were in fact M.P.s, it was consequently almost impossible to formalize the board's proceedings and obtain a reasonable attendance at Treasury Chambers, Dublin Castle, even during the recess; it was hard enough to assemble the three members necessary as a quorum to sign certain documents.[3] (The contemporary British treasury board was in much the same situation, in spite of the proximity of its chambers to the House of Commons.[4]) In these circumstances, the treasury board as a whole was in no position to assert its general right of 'control and superintendence' over the revenue boards, which were slightly less haphazard in their proceedings because their members were ineligible for Parliament.[5] The very impotence of the

promotion in it. The promotion was purely a matter of prestige, and meant no increase in influence or emolument. See the treasury board minutes, 1807–11, P.R.O. T.29/89–110.

[1] Foster to Rochfort, 22 Mar. 1809, F.P. D.207/34/76.

[2] James Crofton to Vesey FitzGerald, 4 Dec. 1813, Vesey FitzGerald MSS., N.L.I. MS. 7824, p. 146.

[3] Sir Charles Saxton to Robert Dundas, 15 May 1809, Melville MSS., N.L.I. MS. 55/251; Vesey FitzGerald to W. W. Pole, 17 Sept. 1810, Peel MSS., B.L. Add. MS. 40407, fols. 1–17. This eligibility to sit in Parliament derived from the old and by now threadbare principle of 'responsibility'.

[4] Gray, *Spencer Perceval*, pp. 318 f.

[5] All the same, the Irish revenue boards were not composed, like the English, 'of gentlemen who make their business their principal employment, and who have, as well by law as by inclination, no concern in politics . . .'—Sir Arthur Wellesley, the Chief Secretary, to Lord Hawkesbury, 13 Nov. 1807, printed in Duke of Wellington (ed.), *The Supplementary Despatches and Correspondence of the Duke of Wellington* (7 vols., London, 1860), v. 180 f.; Wellesley was speaking specifically of the excise board. Foster's view, expressed in 1809, was that 'the misfortune of both boards' was not a lack of zeal and efficiency, but 'their acting under their officers and venturing little in chief'—Foster to Rochfort, 20 Mar. 1809, F.P. D.207/34/74.

treasury board might have made it a convenient instrument for Foster's reforms and their concomitant, his self-aggrandizement. However, the Lord Lieutenant, the Duke of Richmond, and his successive Chief Secretaries (forgetting the short-lived Robert Dundas), Sir Arthur Wellesley and William Wellesley Pole, had no intention of allowing this to happen, and were swift to counteract what Wellesley called in June 1807 Foster's 'first effort to supersede the authority of the Lord Lieutenant by that of the Irish Treasury . . .'[1] Moreover, under the Portland and Perceval ministries there were not the same divided counsels as regards Irish policy as had existed during Pitt's second ministry; and the generally steady support which Richmond received from Whitehall, combined with the generally harmonious relations between his Chief Secretaries and himself, prevented a recurrence of the events of 1804 and 1805. Accordingly, the treasury did not again become the channel of communication between the Irish administration and the revenue boards, as Foster had previously tried to make it and still thought it ought to be.[2] Foster also did not renew his claim that the treasury was entitled to remit fines on its own authority (or possibly a compromise was reached over the level of fine it could remit without the authority of the lord lieutenant), and was entitled to dismiss (or restore) revenue officers.[3] As a result, the success of his revenue reforms depended almost entirely on the degree of support he received from the lord lieutenant and chief secretary and, more remotely, from Perceval.

Some limited reforms were effected, though possibly nothing which would not have been effected without Foster. In June 1808 an act was passed abolishing fees in the customs department, pursuant to a recommendation of his enquiry board. It was a source of much frustration to him that this bill was rejected on a technicality by the House of Lords in July 1807,

---

[1] Wellesley to Long, 6 June 1807, *Wellington Supplementary Despatches*, v. 73. Long had presumably been tutoring Wellesley on the basis of Long's own experience of Foster.

[2] Vesey FitzGerald to Pole, 17 Sept. 1810 (see p. 192, *n*. 3).

[3] Ibid.; James Crofton to Foster, 30 Aug. 1809, F.P. D.562/15238; Foster to J. Fairtlough, 26 Jan. 1810, F.P. T.2519/4/777. In fact, the treasury during Foster's second term of office failed to carry out its primary function of ensuring that all public money was paid punctually into the teller of the exchequer's account in the Bank of Ireland (Kiernan, *Financial Administration*, pp. 325 ff.).

and thus made ineligible for reintroduction during that session.[1]
Great benefits to the Revenue were claimed for this act, though
in the short term additional revenue had to be raised to
compensate customs officers appointed prior to the enquiry
board's recommendation of 1804.[2] A similar reform was carried
out by administrative means in the excise department, and in
both excise and customs some progress was made, not always
along the lines marked out by Foster, in increasing salaries,
reclassifying offices, rotating officers, and reorganizing the
system of promotion.[3] In 1809, Foster succeeded in giving
effect to a previous enactment of his, dating from 1804,
whereby the treasury board was charged with the duty of
submitting the public accounts to Parliament by a stipulated
date.[4] In other respects, however, the treasury seems to have
had the utmost difficulty in extracting accounts and returns
from both the excise and customs boards.[5] These bodies were
also prone to quarrel as violently with each other as each
from time to time did with the treasury: in 1808, for example,
Foster had to lament a farcical row between the excise and
customs boards over the erection of 'a staircase, whether the
landing shall be right or left'.[6] The business of the excise board
stopped altogether in the spring of 1810 when the Chairman,
Lord Annesley, who had hitherto given general support to
Foster's measures and general obedience to the treasury's orders,
had some kind of nervous breakdown which manifested itself in
persecution mania and necessitated his compulsory retirement.[7]

[1] Foster to Robert Bradshaw, 5 Aug. 1807, F.P. D.562/12414; Foster to John
Croker, 30 Nov. 1809, F.P. D.207/71/18.

[2] James Arbuckle to Foster, 1 Feb. 1809, F.P. D.562/11099; Wellesley to Saxton,
29 Jan. 1809, *Wellington Supplementary Despatches*, v. 548 f.; Foster to Bradshaw, *n* 1.

[3] Wellesley to Hawkesbury, 13 Nov. 1807, Wellesley to Foster, 1 Dec. 1807 and
5 Jan. 1808, and Wellesley to Saxton, 28 Jan. 1809, *Wellington Supplementary
Despatches*, v. 180 f., 211, 284, 546; Lord Annesley's minutes of and observations
on the excise board's proceedings, Jan.–Apr. 1810, Annesley MSS., P.R.O.N.I.
D.1854/4/18; Edward Hardman to Foster, 12 Oct. 1810, F.P. T.2519/4/741. In
1800 the cost of collecting the revenue was 8% or 9%, which had risen to 14½% by
1810 (Kiernan, *Financial Administration*, p. 322); presumably salary-increases and
short-term compensation accounted for the rise.

[4] Foster to Pole, 9 Aug. 1811, F.P. D.207/38/78.

[5] Foster to George Cavendish, 7 July 1808, F.P. D.562/10607; Foster to John
Croker, 30 Nov. 1809, F.P. D.207/71/18.

[6] Foster to Rochfort, 28 Aug. 1808, F.P. D.207/34/48.

[7] Foster to Rochfort, 20 Mar. 1809, F.P. D.207/34/74; Pole to Richmond,

His successor, Alexander Marsden, the former Under-Secretary, was an old personal enemy of Foster. However, in this instance Richmond and Pole took Foster's part, and stipulated that Marsden must act in harmony with the Chancellor of the Irish Exchequer, or go.[1] Marsden, in fact, supported Foster well, but by this time the customs board had gone into open revolt against the treasury.[2] Foster's last months in office were spent in combat with that board, and he resigned in 1811 still lamenting '. . . the inefficacy and impolicy of the present system in Ireland under which the Revenue stands, and its total inadequacy to a full collection or an economical or satisfactory management . . .'[3] This considered statement was made in a letter to Perceval in April 1811; earlier, in February, he had reported to Perceval, '. . . Revenues have fallen so as to have cleared into the Treasury in the last year not quite £3,850,000, and our quota of two-seventeenths for the last year was £6,614,000. . . .'[4]

In the matter of increasing the revenue by taxation, as in the matter of increasing its net yield by reform, Foster was not given a free hand. The most important, and recurrent, disagreement between the British Government and him was over distillation from grain in Ireland. Foster regarded distillation from grain as both a painless and a productive source of revenue, as well as an important encouragement to tillage.[5] In 1808, however, the British Government decided to prohibit it throughout the United Kingdom, fearing a scarcity in England and a famine in Ireland, and also to some extent yielding to parliamentary pressure from the West Indian sugar planters.[6] Foster resisted this 'desperate attempt . . . on our agriculture' in vain. He failed to induce the Irish distillers to come to

20 May 1810, Richmond MSS., N.L.I. MS. 73, fol. 1763. On 7 April, Annesley had announced to the Commissioners that 'I kept a journal [cited in p. 104, *n*. 3], not for occupation, but to justify myself . . .'

[1] Pole to Richmond, 3 May 1810, Richmond MSS., N.L.I. MS. 73, fol. 1683.

[2] Marsden to Foster, 4 Dec. 1810, F.P. T.2519/4/649; Edward Hardman to Foster, 4 Feb. 1811, F.P. D.562/11708; Foster to George Cavendish, 1 May 1811, F.P. D.562/10782.

[3] Foster to Perceval, 13 Apr. 1811, F.P. D.207/69/16.

[4] Foster to Perceval, 9 Feb. 1811, F.P. D.207/69/1.

[5] Foster to Rochfort, 14 Mar. 1808, F.P. D.207/34/32.

[6] Gray, *Spencer Perceval*, pp. 364 f.

London and put their case before a parliamentary committee on the subject ('. . . I always dreaded that the removal of our Parliament would deaden all true Public feelings, or at least put them to sleep . . .'), and he failed to convince Perceval of the impolicy of the prohibition. To his arguments, Perceval replied blandly: '. . . You perhaps have a better estimate of the Irish feeling, but it is by the English one that our conduct will be judged. . . .'[1] In the event, Foster spoke and voted against the Government of which he formed a part, in an acrimonious debate and a narrow division in May 1808.[2] (He did not on this occasion go to the extreme of taking his seat on the opposition benches, as he had in July 1805;[3] but these hostile demonstrations, together with his vote on the sugar duty in 1780, are reminders that even on measures which did not threaten the Ascendancy he was not necessarily a pliable ministerial tool.) The prohibition was, nonetheless, enacted, and Foster redoubled his efforts to get it lifted from Ireland. By February 1809, he had obtained authority from Perceval to introduce, as part of his Irish budget, a bill to that effect, but in March the bill was thrown out in a thin House and in circumstances which gave rise to the suspicion that Perceval had given him only 'a hollow and delusive support'.[4] In the same month, another component of his budget, a Malt Tax Bill, was also defeated, causing him to exclaim against the 'laxity' of the Government in leaving him '. . . unsupported as Chancellor of the Exchequer in those measures previously arranged between him [Perceval] and me . . .'[5] The practical consequence was that Foster was left with the unpleasant choice of either taxing things which he thought could less easily bear taxation, or of borrowing the expected yield of the distillery and malt taxes.[6] In 1810 the battle over the distilleries was re-joined, and this time Foster won (the prohibition was lifted from Ireland in 1810 and from Great Britain in 1811, but

---

[1] Foster to Rochfort, 2 Apr. 1808, F.P. D.207/34/37; Perceval to Foster, 9 Apr. 1808, F.P. D.562/2147.

[2] *Parl. Debs.* xi. 428 ff., especially p. 445.

[3] Grattan, *Life*, v. 270. This story may be apocryphal.

[4] *Parl. Debs.* xii. 1128 ff.; James Corry to Foster, 8 Mar. 1809, F.P. D.562/6441.

[5] Foster to Rochfort, 22 Mar. 1809, F.P. D.207/34/76.

[6] Rochfort to Foster, 29 Mar. [1809], F.P. D.207/34/77.

then reimposed over the whole of the United Kingdom in 1812[1]). However, he won only after a series of acrimonious wrangles with the Irish Law Officers and the excise board over the Distilleries Bill and associated legislation; also only after he had had to abandon his policy of fining townlands and whole parishes where illicit stills had been found but no offenders had been brought to book.[2] This last was not, to Foster, a point of detail but a point of principle; he had long contended that Great Britain and Ireland could not be subjected to a uniform taxation system, not only because of the inferior taxable capacity of Ireland, but because the laws to enforce the collection of the Revenue in Ireland had to be too draconian to be acceptable in Britain.[3] The townland and parish fines (which had first been introduced by Foster in 1785) were thus only one facet of a system of draconian revenue laws. It may be doubted whether they were workable, even in Ireland, except in counties as small and as well-peopled with resident gentlemen as Louth. Certainly, in obliging Foster to give them up, Perceval and Pole were acting on local information from parts of Ireland where draconianism had not worked, notably Inishowen, co. Donegal.[4]

Foster's second term of office as Chancellor of the Irish Exchequer at Westminster was thus a scene of largely frustrated endeavour. If it escaped the spectacular collisions of his first term of office, it was still characterized by a great deal of muffled acrimony, particularly at administrative level. Both Richmond and Pole privately thought that Foster was a man with whom it was impossible to get on harmoniously, and both disapproved of his 'finance principles' (though it is not clear what they were).[5] On one thing Richmond, Pole, and Foster were all agreed, and that was on the inexpediency and indeed

---

[1] Peel to Vesey FitzGerald, 4 and 5 Dec. 1812, Vesey FitzGerald MSS., N.L.I. MS. 7813, pp. 41, 240.

[2] Edward Hardman to Foster, 12 Mar. 1810, F.P. T.2519/4/683; copies of correspondence involving Foster, the Law Officers and the excise board, 7–14 May 1810, F.P. T.2519/4/709A, B; Pole to Richmond, 23 Feb. 1810, Richmond MSS., N.L.I. MS. 73, fol. 1716; Foster to Rochfort, 22 Mar. 1810, F.P. D.207/34/118.

[3] [Thomas Burgh] to Foster, 22 Mar. [1808], F.P. D.562/12258.

[4] Abercorn to Perceval, [16 Nov. 1810], and Sir John Stewart to Abercorn, 7 Apr. 1815, Abercorn MSS., P.R.O.N.I. T.2541/IK/19/80, /IB3/21/6.

[5] Pole to Richmond, 16 Mar. 1811, Richmond MSS., N.L.I. MS. 65, fol. 751; Richmond to Pole, 19 June 1811, Whitworth MSS., K.A.O. U.269/O.214/5.

impossibility 'of the Chancellorship of the Irish Exchequer continuing as it is'.[1] Foster at this stage probably favoured financial amalgamation and the abolition of the office: Pole was convinced, '. . . from the present state of our financial system, and from the jarring interests that have been created by Foster between the Treasury and the Castle, that there is no hope of doing any good or of restoring the authority of Government, but by having the Office of Chief Secretary and Chancellor of the Exchequer held by the same person. . . .'[2] The only disadvantage of Pole's scheme, from the point of view of an English lord lieutenant and chief secretary, was that it meant that the odium of necessarily stiff and unpopular budgets would no longer fall on a native Irish politician.[3] Whatever plans were in train for the chancellorship of the Irish exchequer were disrupted by the Regency crisis at the end of 1810 and beginning of 1811, and while the restricted Regency lasted, Perceval was unwilling to undertake a reorganization of the Irish administration. In the end it was Foster who took the initiative, in February 1811, by tendering his resignation— perhaps in the hope that he would be cajoled back into office on more advantageous terms.[4] His specific grievance was that a batch of revenue officers had been appointed over his head and without his knowledge. This was not a mere pretext, as the appointments ran counter to a new warehousing system for the excise, which he wanted to introduce and on which part of his 1811 budget depended.[5] In general, he felt himself to be 'no more than a mere clerk to propose taxes', and descanted on the '. . . £90,000,000 debt, 4½ million interest—a tremendous situation, with discordant Boards and a Chancellor of the Exchequer unsupported by the Irish Government. . . .'[6] Whatever his hopes may have been, his resignation was in fact accepted, with expressions of regret and the request that he

---

[1] Thomas Foster to Foster, 19 Feb. 1811, F.P. D.562/3390.

[2] Pole to Richmond, 15 June 1811, Richmond MSS., N.L.I. MS. 73, fol. 1730.

[3] Foster to J. L. Foster, 24 July 1810, F.P. D.562/2215; Foster to Perceval, 12 Aug. 1810, F.P. D.562/2101; Pole to Richmond, 2 Mar. 1811, Richmond MSS., N.L.I. MS. 65, fol. 744.

[4] George Tierney to Earl Grey, 5 Mar. 1811, Aspinall transcript from the Grey of Howick MSS., kindly placed at my disposal by Mr. Roland Thorne.

[5] Foster to Pole, 13 Feb. 1811, F.P. D.207/38/42.

[6] Ibid.; Foster to Frederick Geale, 11 Mar. 1811, F.P. D.562/11754.

would continue in office until the end of the session.[1] This he agreed to do—probably a serious mistake. By announcing his intention of resigning, he reduced his potential influence over the proceedings of the committee set up in that session to investigate Ireland's ability to fulfil its Union obligations, though he had been secretly assembling accounts for use on that committee since October 1810:[2] by staying in office *pro tem.*, instead of resigning at once on the issue of principle he had raised, he deprived himself of an opportunity to justify his measures as a finance Minister and to disassociate himself from 'the system and miserable course' which had led Ireland to national bankruptcy.[3] It would appear that the miserable course which he himself pursued over his resignation was influenced by the hope of a U.K. peerage and a provision for life.[4]

A full and uninhibited statement by Foster of his plans for post-Union Irish finance would have been a more flattering

[1] Pole to Foster, 19 Feb. 1811, F.P. D.207/38/44; Perceval to Foster, 26 June 1811, F.P. D.207/69/32.

[2] Foster to Marsden, 26 Oct. 1810, F.P. T.2519/4/619; Foster to Perceval, 9 Feb. 1811, F.P. D.207/69/1; Foster to John Barry, 16 Mar. 1811, F.P. D.207/52/37; Pole to Richmond, 20 Mar. 1811, Richmond MSS., N.L.I. MS. 65, fol. 74; Foster to Richard Nevill, 17 May 1811, F.P. D.562/11859; William Houghton to Foster, 2 July 1811, F.P. D.562/11922. It is clear that Foster had some plan up his sleeve, but not clear precisely what. By 1811, the British and Irish debts had reached the proportion envisaged by the Act of Union as a condition for financial amalgamation, although this was deferred until 1817. In 1816, John Leslie Foster, Foster's nephew, said in the debate on the subject, '. . . the necessity for the consolidation of the exchequers of both countries existed some years back, as it was impossible that Ireland could bear additional taxation . . .' (Kiernan, *Financial Administration*, p. 315). It is almost certain that John Foster favoured financial amalgamation in 1811, although he was extremely guarded in even his private correspondence on the subject (cited above). His successor (apart from the Pole interregnum), Vesey FitzGerald, who inherited many ideas from him, also favoured financial amalgamation, but had great difficulty in getting the Cabinet to come to a decision on the subject while the war and the peace negotiations lasted. In the end, Castlereagh's seems to have been the decisive voice in favour of the policy; which is ironical in view of the fact that Castlereagh more than anyone else had been the author of the $1:7\frac{1}{2}$ proportion. For Vesey FitzGerald's efforts to bring about financial amalgamation earlier than July 1816 (the date of the Act, which became effective in January 1817), see Vesey FitzGerald to Lord Liverpool and Vansittart, (both) 23 Feb. 1814, and to James Crofton, 14 Apr. 1814, Vesey FitzGerald MSS., N.L.I. MSS. 7828, pp. 49–55, and 7830, pp. 40–1. For the extent to which he was, in general, influenced by Foster's ideas, see Vesey FitzGerald to Foster, 1, 7, and 15 May 1813, Vesey FitzGerald MSS., N.L.I. MS. 7818, pp. 200–2, 247, 278.

[3] Thomas Foster to Foster, [?25] May 1811, F.P. D.2681/12.

[4] Thomas Foster to Foster, 22 Feb. 1811, F.P. D.2681/10; Pole to Richmond, 24 Feb. 1812, Richmond MSS., N.L.I. MS. 67, fol. 994.

epitaph than those which were penned—most of them by his political enemies. Newport, writing in early June 1811, was particularly scathing:

> . . . Foster and I have been on very bad terms, from my endeavours, used not unsuccessfully during the whole sessions in the House and the [Irish Finance] Committee, to detect and expose his jobbing, and destructive waste of the public revenues. . . . He has . . . now retired from office, and he asked me whether I would accept it. My answer, you may easily guess; it applied to the claim which the community had on the author of the conflagration, to extinguish it. . . .[1]

Grattan was kinder: '. . . Foster has closed his political career. It was a varied day, clouded not a little; brighter in his own country than in England; splendid at the time of the Union; obscure at the close. . . .'[2] This leaves out of the reckoning things which, while they were arguably not 'bright' in Grattan's eyes,[3] were much more darkly 'clouded' in Foster's: the re-admission of the Catholics to the franchise in 1793 and the disfranchisement of most of the Irish close boroughs in 1800—both of them staggering blows to the Ascendancy, and both of them blows which Foster tried in vain to deflect. Again, although Grattan, with his sense of the theatrical, was right in saying that Foster would have ridden off into retirement with much greater éclat[4] in 1800 than in 1811, there is a certain dignity in Foster's post-Union failure, since it was a failure to surmount difficulties which he had been almost alone in foreseeing. The contrast between 'his own country' and England, is also too facile. The consistent message of Foster's career is, how limited were the influence and the sphere of action of the merely Irish politician. These limitations operated in College Green almost as effectively as at Westminster, and operated even in the case of an Irish politician of Foster's intellectual calibre and adeptness at the art of 'Ministerial Patriotism'.

---

[1] Newport to Knight of Kerry, 4 June 1811, FitzGerald MSS., 10/63.
[2] Grattan to James Grattan, July 1811, Grattan, *Life*, v. 449.
[3] For Grattan's 'Ascendancy' outlook, see pp. 352 ff.
[4] To adapt a phrase of Thomas Foster's—Thomas Foster to Foster, 18 Feb. 1811, F.P. D.562/3389.

CHAPTER THREE

'Good Words and Kind Promises': Foster and Co. Louth 1768–1828

To extrapolate a consistent message from Foster's official career is not to deny that the Ireland of 1811, when it ended, was a very different place politically from the Ireland of 1777, when it began; his long political survival was only made possible by a series of painful adjustments to what he regarded as 'unaccountable alterations in our constitution'.[1] In the sphere of Louth politics, his career lasted longer—from 1768 to 1821 as M.P. for the county, and from 1821 to 1828 as the head of the family to which one of the county M.P.s belonged. In this sphere, dramatic political change did not occur till almost the end of his career; but significant and subtle change was under way all the time. The Fosters, along with the Beresfords, have been cited as the textbook example of an Ascendancy family in local politics, crushing their county under the dead weight of an unassailable proprietary interest which suddenly became assailable when their own freeholders revolted against them. But this is not the picture which emerges from a detailed study of co. Louth politics. The picture is one of paternalism rather than brute proprietary force. Moreover, it is not simply a picture of paternalist politics being overtaken by the politics of issues, in particular by the all-absorbing issue of Catholic Emancipation; for the Foster interest in Louth at various earlier stages in its existence had been either strengthened or weakened by local reaction to the Fosters' behaviour on the political issues of the day. Yet, even though the Foster interest in its early days and prime was far more popularly based than the circumstances of its overthrow would suggest, and even

[1] See p. 371, *n*. I.

though it was affected by eddies rather than by a consistent current of change, the overall impression remains that by 1828 Louth politics had undergone a transformation. To compare the Hogarthian affray which took place after John Foster's first election for Louth in 1768, with the mobbing and intimidation of his freeholders at the famous election of 1826, is to compare two different political worlds.[1]

In order to explain the circumstances of his election in 1768 and the origins of the county interest established by his father, Anthony, it is necessary to go back to the year 1745, when Anthony Foster's first cousin, William Henry Fortescue of Reynoldstown (afterwards Earl of Clermont), was returned unopposed at a by-election, and also to make a quick review of county politics earlier still in the century. Fortescue was the first member of his particular branch of the Fortescue family to represent Louth, but the Fortescues were a numerous and prolific local tribe, one branch of which, the Fortescues of Corderry, had preceded William Henry Fortescue in the representation of the county (see Appendix, Table Four). The other local families who had hitherto rung the changes in its representation were: the Tichbornes of Beaulieu, headed by Henry Tichborne, Lord Ferrard, the Governor of co. Louth; the Astons of Richardstown, the head of whom, William Aston, was Ferrard's son-in-law; the Moores, headed by Lord Drogheda, a dwindling influence because their estates, as has been seen, were dwindling under pressure of debt; the Tenisons of Thomastown, the Fosters' landlords in Dunleer and the victims of the Fosters' surprise attack on the political proprietorship of that borough; the Ludlows of Ardsallagh, co. Meath, whose principal territorial strength lay in that county, not in Louth; the Tisdalls of Bawn, the most famous of whom was Philip Tisdall, the future Solicitor- and Attorney-General; and the Bellinghams of Castle Bellingham. To this list should be added two other families, whose claims to represent the county were at least as good, but who never actually did so: the Townleys, afterwards Townley Balfours, of Townley Hall, and the Hamiltons of Dundalk, afterwards Earls of Clanbrassill. There is no obvious reason why the Townleys never sat for Louth; one of them was, briefly, a candidate for

[1] See pp. 125, 149.

the vacancy filled in 1745,[1] but those of the family who entered
Parliament did so as representatives for the local borough of
Carlingford. The Hamiltons did not sit for Louth, in spite of
being probably the biggest single political interest in the county
during this early period, because their head, James Hamilton,
1st Earl of Clanbrassill, opted for a career in British politics,
and did in fact distinguish himself as a leading light in the
opposition to Sir Robert Walpole.

It was once remarked, not of co. Louth, but of co. Kerry,
that '. . . when the honours of the County are a little varied, . . .
it prevents the County from being agitated, which otherwise
must be the case. . . .'[2] In co. Louth, where the honours of the
county were very much varied in the period up to 1745, this
remark seems to have been valid. There was a contest for one
of the two county seats at the general election of 1727, in which
the Tisdalls were defeated by the Tichbornes and the Astons,
after a petition to the House of Commons. Apart from this,
there is no mention of a contest in the period up to 1745.
However, this conclusion must be regarded as very tentative:
contests which went the length of an election petition—disputed
elections—are recorded in the *Commons' Journals*; contests
which did not go that length are to be traced only in the
manuscript sources, and there are virtually no manuscript
sources for Louth politics in this early period. From the
evidence of the *Commons' Journals*, it is possible to hazard
the guess that the four boroughs within co. Louth—Dundalk
(the county town), Ardee, Carlingford, and Dunleer—led a
more active political existence than the county itself. There
were disputed elections for Carlingford in 1705, Dundalk in
1707, Ardee in 1727, and Dunleer (not solely due to the Fosters)
in 1715 and 1727.[3] By at least the 1730s the era of contests
in the boroughs was, for the time being, over. Each of them had
fallen under the influence of one or more patrons, and this
influence held firm for the rest of the eighteenth century
(although in Ardee, Carlingford, and Dundalk it did not
go unchallenged). No county ever fell under the influence

---

[1] Paper headed, 'Answers to some paragraphs relative to Mrs. Walsh and her
conduct . . .', [*c.* 1760], Holloden MSS., Holloden, Bagenalstown, co. Carlow.

[2] Lord Ventry to Lord Glandore, 11 Nov. 1801, Talbot-Crosbie MSS., N.L.I.

[3] *Commons Journals* (Ireland), ii. 439, 511, and iii. 467, 473, 486, 586.

of a couple of family interests in the fairly decisive sense in which boroughs often did. But co. Louth was unusual in two respects in the period up to 1745: the number of family interests was large, and it was not clear whether one particular group of them would be politically dominant in the future, and if so, which group it would be.

One reason for this uncertainty was that the landownership of the county was in a very fluid state. The local land market was booming, and three families at least were brisk speculators in land, the Fortescues of Reynoldstown, the Fosters, and the Tisdalls (who do not seem to have held on to many of their purchases). The break-up of the estates of the Moore family—Lord Drogheda and his cadets—has been referred to, and Lord Ferrard's estate was going the same way. Ultimately three other estates—the then largest in the county—went this way too. These were the estates of three Catholic peers, Lords Bellew, Carlingford, and Louth, who had escaped the Williamite confiscation and still owned, the first two 6,000 acres each, and the last 4,000.[1] Because these families were Catholic they were themselves barred from Parliament, and they contributed to the instability of co. Louth politics by putting the votes of their Protestant freeholders to fairly mercenary use (between 1704 and 1728 it was at best uncertain whether Catholic freeholders could vote, and from 1728 onwards quite certain that they could not). This, the Bellews continued to do even after they conformed to the Church of Ireland in 1707: in 1734, for example, John Foster the Elder remarked sourly about some transaction with Lord Bellew, 'I should be much better pleased with the abatement of the rent than the compliment of the freeholders'.[2] This element in the instability of co. Louth politics was gone by the 1740s, by which time most of the estates of the three Catholic or ex-Catholic peers were also gone, due to a combination of financial difficulties and failure of direct heirs. The Fosters, and to an even greater extent their cousins, the Fortescues of Reynoldstown, benefited from this

---

[1] J. G. Simms, 'Co. Louth and the Jacobite War', *C.L.A.J.* xiv. 141 ff.; MS. opinion of Thomas Lefroy, written on the blank leaves of *A Statement of Title of Robert, Earl of Roden, to Lands in Co. Louth*, March 1838, Roden MSS., P.R.O.N.I. Mic.147, vol. 4; John to Anthony Foster, 26 Feb. 1735, F.P. T.2519/4/2240.

[2] John to Anthony Foster, 9 Feb. 1734, F.P. T.2519/4/2199.

process. Reynoldstown itself and the surrounding lands were purchased by the Fortescues from Lord Louth,[1] and the Fosters acquired small parcels of land from each of the three estates. Once the break-up of these and the Moore and Ferrard estates was complete, a political structure corresponding to the landed structure of the county could emerge.

In the political structure which did emerge, the Fortescues were the dominant family; which is why a Fortescue, not a Foster, was elected at the by-election of 1745. This the Fortescues owed to two things: their land and their connections. With something in excess of 11,000 acres (probably greatly in excess of it), they were in 1745 the largest landowners in the county. They also occupied a central position in county politics by virtue of their marriage connections: on one side they were cousins of the second-largest landowners in the county, the Fosters, and on the other of the third-largest, the Hamiltons of Dundalk. The Fortescue/Foster/Hamilton alliance was to dominate co. Louth politics from 1745 to 1755, and again from 1761 to 1809 (when the alliance temporarily split); but the more significant development during that period was the shift within the alliance which placed the Fosters in the position of the dominant partner. The elements which brought about this shift were present in 1745, but latent. At that stage the Fosters had only recently acquired outright possession of Collon, the biggest single unit in their estate and the part of it which was later most productive of freeholders (up to 1741 they had owned Collon jointly with the Fortescues).[2] Moreover, in 1745 and for a decade thereafter, the Fosters had not started on the process of improving which in the end they carried to such (possibly uneconomic) heights that their estate, though second to the Fortescues' by a long chalk in terms of acreage, was very far ahead of it in terms of the number of freeholders it could accommodate. The Fosters' subsequent improvements were vital, not just in terms of real political estate, but in

[1] For more information about the Fortescues and their purchases, and a discussion of the size, value, and descent of their estates, see A. P. W. Malcomson, 'The Earl of Clermont: a Forgotten Co. Monaghan Magnate of the Late Eighteenth Century', *Clogher Record*, xiii. 24 f., 46 f., 51. Clermont was a co. Monaghan magnate in right of his wife.

[2] Deed of partition between John Foster and Thomas Fortescue (among other parties), 29 Apr. 1741, F.P. D.562/14568.

terms also of the personal popularity which accrued to the family as a natural result of their unprecedented paternalism.

Between 1745 and 1755, the Fortescues and the Fosters, with the Fosters still very much the junior partners, carried Louth 'as they pleased', as a contemporary put it.[1] In 1755 another by-election became necessary, and unfortunately for them coincided with the aftermath of the celebrated Money Bill Dispute of 1753.[2] This was a political crisis of such importance that it dominated the local politics of most constituencies where elections took place during the years 1753–6, boroughs no less than counties, and in some boroughs affected the course even of municipal elections. The proximate cause of the crisis was the attempt by George Stone, Archbishop of Armagh, to oust Henry Boyle, the Speaker, as the principal manager of the House of Commons; the reason for its duration and intensity was that Boyle almost at once became a focal point for the quasi-nationalist aspirations of Anglo-Ireland. By the time of the Louth by-election of 1755, it was tolerably clear that the British Government, perhaps aware of the selfishness of Stone's motives, or perhaps—as was characteristic of British governments in their dealings with Ireland—wanting peace at any price, had decided to purchase peace by sacrificing Stone and buying off Boyle. Nevertheless, Stone and Boyle were as anxious as ever to demonstrate their strength at constituency level, and so increase their bargaining power; and in any case engagements had been entered into over the Louth by-election before there had been any clear prospect of a settlement. Stone's allies in the county were the coalition which had carried the last by-election; and three Louth men had been prominent at national level in the power-struggle against Boyle: Henry Singleton, Philip Tisdall and, to a lesser extent, Anthony Foster. However, the power-struggle, and the apparent likelihood of Stone's discomfiture in it, had encouraged 'the major part of the gentlemen of that county' to form 'themselves into an independent company to oppose the former interest'.[3]

[1] James Rooney to Sir Nicholas Bayly, 27 May 1755, Anglesey MSS., P.R.O.N.I. D.619/21B/129.
[2] For the Money Bill crisis see J. L. McCracken, 'The Struggle between the Irish Administration and Parliament, 1753–6', *I.H.S.* iii (1942–3), 159 ff.
[3] Rooney to Bayly, 27 May 1755 (cited in *n.* 1). The term 'independent' requires some comment. The 'independent interest', as it is always called in

Their candidate was Thomas Tipping, William Aston's son-in-law, who had purchased Beaulieu from Lord Ferrard's heirs, and was the representative of the old Tichborne/Aston interest. More important, he was also a client of Boyle's. The Stone party's candidate was probably William Foster, Anthony Foster's youngest brother. After a very sharp contest, Tipping won by the narrow majority of twenty-six. His victory was grandiloquently hailed by his supporters as 'the Revolution of Louth', and subscriptions were got up by 'the Louth Independent Club' to strike commemorative medals for distribution among the freeholders who had voted for him.[1] The Fosters and their allies contemplated a petition, but abandoned the idea. Tipping remained in possession of his hard-won seat until 1760, when Parliament was dissolved on the death of George II.

At the time of the general election of 1761, the sitting members were Tipping and William Henry Fortescue. Both Tipping and Fortescue declared themselves candidates, but so did Anthony Foster, who probably tried to enlist Fortescue in a full-scale offensive against Tipping. Fortescue, however, hesitated. He knew that, after the violence of the contest in 1755, the desire was widespread among the leading interests in Louth, notably Blayney Townley Balfour of Townley Hall, '. . . to avoid ill blood, to save the expense of a disputed election, to avoid perjury among the lower kind of voters, and that we should live in unity, harmony and good neighbourhood in our County . . .'[2] This widespread desire, and his own anxiety

contemporary election literature and correspondence, was composed of the smaller landlords in any county, who because of the smallness of their estates were obliged to band together in coalitions which were unworkably wide in their basis, in order to have any chance against the leading interests in the county. The independent interest is often synonymous with the 'popular interest'—this was the case in Louth —and espoused popular political causes. Yet the independents, as Dr. P. J. Jupp has emphasized, were not so popular in their politics as to allow their tenants any more freedom than that enjoyed by the tenants of the leading interests; 'independence' began and ended with the landlord or gentry class.

[1] Rooney to Bayly, 26 Nov. 1755 and 27 Jan. 1756, ibid./142, 150; *C.L.A.J.* i. 50, and v. 303; *Belfast News-Letter*, 13 Jan. 1756.

[2] Blayney Balfour to Anthony Foster, 5 Dec. 1760, F.P. D.562/916. This frequently expressed horror of perjury 'among the lower kind of voters', ought not to be treated with too much scepticism. After all, the Protestant Constitution in Church and State, which was the constant theme of the Ascendancy's encomia, was hedged about on all sides by oaths, ranging from the monarch's coronation oath of 1689 to the freeholder's oath, established in Ireland in 1715.

to stand well with all parties in Louth, seems to have led
Fortescue to enter into a compromise agreement with Tipping
—on a most bizarre basis, if the following vivid account is to
be believed:

> . . . There is a new practice here of selling Counties. The selling of
> boroughs has been long practised. Messrs. Fortescue, Foster, and
> Tipping were candidates for the County of Louth, and they came
> to an agreement to deposit £400 each, that Fortescue should be
> one Member, and that Foster and Tipping should toss up which of
> them should be the other, and the loser to get the £1,200 to enable
> him to purchase a seat for a borough, and this agreement was
> approved by the first man in this Kingdom. The toss has been made,
> and Foster won it. Perhaps you will think that £1,200 is a large
> sum for a seat in our Parliament. I assure you, it is not sufficient,
> for they sell from £1,600 to £2,000. . . . The gentlemen of the County
> of Louth are greatly dissatisfied at coughing up for the County . . .[1]

'The first man in this Kingdom' was none other than Primate
Stone, who had written an almost panic-stricken letter to
Foster, urging him to '. . . accede to the terms proposed.
Perhaps it may be a sufficient reason to such of your friends
who are disposed against your making a concession, that you
make it solely to oblige me. . . . I put my whole weight and
credit with you now upon your ready and cheerful compliance
with Fortescue upon the accommodation proposed. . . .'[2] It is
hard to believe that the accommodation provided for a literal
toss-up. More probably, recourse was had, as was usual on
such occasions, to the register of freeholders, to ascertain the
probable outcome of the poll, had a contest taken place.
Whatever was done, it incensed 'the independent gentlemen
of the County', who '. . . have had a meeting, and intend to
set up two gentlemen for that County in opposition to Fortescue
and Foster. William Brabazon is to be one. I do not know the
other. Several are named, but our friend [Balfour], they tell
me, has lost all interest, as the scheme of tossing up for the
County is laid to his charge.'[3] Nothing came of this, as Fortescue
and Foster were returned unopposed.[4] However, this was not

---

[1] Richard Wilson to his wife, 11 Dec. 1760, Holloden MSS.
[2] Primate Stone to Anthony Foster, 1 Dec. 1760, F.P. D.562/4631.
[3] Richard Wilson to his wife, 27 Jan. [1761], Holloden MSS.
[4] *Dublin Journal*, 9–12 May 1761.

the end of the matter, for they failed to keep their side of the bargain by contributing to buy a borough seat for Tipping— or perhaps the £1,200 proved inadequate, and they refused to contribute their share of the difference. This may or may not have been Foster's doing; but the likelihood is that he was half-hearted in implementing what he had been so reluctant to agree to in the first place. Balfour held Fortescue responsible, and threatened to challenge him to a duel if he did not compel his friends to honour Balfour's interpretation of the agreement.[1] Whether this duel was ever fought is not known, but the reference to it is a reminder of the 'gladiatorial' element in Irish political life (which Sir John Blaquiere was to note and experience on his appointment in 1772 as Chief Secretary).[2] Even without the duel, feelings in co. Louth ran high as a result of the violated agreement: so high, indeed, that for a couple of years after 1761 the county had to go 'without sheriffs or grand jurymen'.[3]

In these circumstances another election was to be dreaded.

---

[1] Balfour to Anthony Foster, 5 Dec. 1760, F.P. D.562/916. The Irish election duel is usually regarded as an instance of banditry and barbarism. However, it was the *ratio ultima* of the gentleman's code of honour, and the gentleman's code of honour, rather than the statute book, was what kept elections, even in Ireland, fairly pure. (The fact that Ireland had a more comprehensive and on the whole better code of election law than England up to the Union, is probably a proof of greater need in Ireland rather than of greater virtue.) Election duels were sometimes fought over trivial things, such as a candidate's canvassing tenants without their landlord's permission, but they were not shoot-outs between rival candidates; even Barrington, who generally presents a picture of the Anglo-Irish landed class which is at once sensationalized and degrading, expresses horror at the one election duel which gave the appearance of being such a shoot-out, the Wexford election duel of 1807. The important function of the gentleman's code of honour and, ultimately, of the election duel, was by and large to prevent people from entering Parliament by flagrantly dishonourable means. In theory, anyone with a reason-able-sized estate, a long purse, and utter unscrupulousness, could have won a county election; and if he was the sitting member, he would enjoy all the privileges of membership except the chore of sitting on election committees, until the petition against his return was disposed of (if, indeed, his opponent had not gone bankrupt in the meantime). The gentleman's code of honour was a necessary security, in view of the expense and uncertainty of election petitions; its effect on the representative system was purifying, not the reverse.

[2] J. A. Froude, *The English in Ireland in the Eighteenth Century* (3 vols., London, 1881), ii. 161 f.

[3] James Fortescue to Anthony Foster, 17 Sept. 1766, F.P. D.562/1760. Shortly after his withdrawal from the Louth election, in May 1761, Tipping was in fact returned for the borough of Kilbeggan, co. Westmeath—presumably by purchase, but with whose money is not clear.

But in September 1766, one became inevitable as a result of Anthony Foster's appointment as Lord Chief Baron of the Exchequer. The first candidate in the field was Blayney Balfour's son. So anxious was Balfour that Blayney Balfour Junior should represent Louth that he offered, as a quid pro quo for his son's election, to donate £500 towards the building of a county gaol, and to support the Foster and Fortescue candidates at the next general election. The Fortescues wanted to accept these terms. James Fortescue, William Henry's brother, thought they were handsome in view of the 'uncertain health of the King' and the strong possibility that a bill would be passed limiting the duration of Irish parliaments.[1] But they were not good enough for Anthony Foster. With the improving of his estate well under way, he must by now have been the biggest single political interest in the county, and he seems to have been determined to make one of its seats hereditary in his family (or perhaps the determination was John Foster's).[2] It was the Fosters' misfortune that they had no satisfactory candidate to put up in 1766. John Foster was already in Parliament for Dunleer and, as Irish electoral law stood until 1793, had no means of vacating his seat in order to stand for Louth; Anthony Foster's second son was absent at the Middle Temple; his brother, Dr. Thomas Foster, was in holy orders; and his other brother, William Foster, does not seem to have entered into consideration. This meant that in order to keep the seat for the county in his family, Anthony Foster had to resort to his elderly brother-in-law, Stephen Sibthorpe, whom Balfour Senior described as '. . . a Gentleman of seventy years of age . . . with one foot in the grave . . ., who has been heard to say he has no ambition for that honour. . . .'[3] The Fortescues were afraid that the gentlemen of Louth would form a general union to defeat him, and that their cousin, the 2nd Earl of Clanbrassill, the head of the Hamilton family, would declare for Balfour. One Foster supporter made tacit reference to Sibthorpe's unsuitability when he wrote to Anthony Foster: '. . . were you or your son in

[1] See p. 119, *n.* 3.
[2] In 1777, admittedly some years later, Anthony Foster was described as 'such a gentlemanlike old gentleman' that he was unfit for a negotiation in which hard bargaining was necessary—James Shiel to Lord Aldborough, 29 Oct. 1777, Stratford MSS., N.L.I.
[3] Blayney Balfour to Anthony Foster, 23 Sept. 1766, F.P. D.562/1765.

question, I do not think any one gentleman would have applied to me. But that not being the case, I am daily harassed . . .'[1] Even Balfour Senior had conceded that 'had your son been intended a candidate on this occasion mine should not have been a competitor . . .'

Undeterred, Foster began to prepare for the contest to come. Though his seat was vacated as soon as he accepted the office of Chief Baron, no by-election could be held before Parliament reassembled in October 1767. (The Irish Parliament met biennially until 1785, and until 1771 no election writ could issue unless Parliament was in session.[2]) Probably he welcomed the breathing space. A list of his freeholders in the central part of his estate, Collon, suggests that his registries were far from up to date. To be eligible to vote, a 40/– freeholder needed to have been registered at least six months before the test of the writ; which meant that Foster had plenty of time to make good the deficiencies in his registries in Collon and elsewhere.[3] Needless to say, the opposition were active in the same direction. In the autumn of 1766, Sibthorpe and Balfour were joined by two other candidates, Alan Bellingham of Castle Bellingham and Faithful Fortescue of Corderry. All four addressed the electors of Louth, and in May 1767 Fortescue addressed them again, this time raising the inevitable cry that he was standing in order to preserve the independence of the county and combat a monopoly. He also threw in for good measure a policy statement on the dominant issue in the national politics of the day, a limitation on the duration of parliaments, to which he pledged support, if elected.[4] This was an obvious ploy, in view of the Fosters' close association with the Government, which was assumed to be hostile to such a measure. Faithful Fortescue was the Fosters' most serious rival because of his family connections as well as the effectiveness of his propaganda. He was a brother-in-law of Thomas

[1] Revd. Richard Stewart to Anthony Foster, 20 Sept. 1766, F.P. D.562/1758.

[2] North to Northington, 7 Oct. 1783, Sydney MSS., N.L.I. MS. 51/8/11; Porritt, *Unreformed House*, ii. 207. The decision to hold annual sessions was taken in 1783, but it was not until January 1785 that the practice of biennial sessions was actually departed from. This was arguably the most important, and certainly the least publicized, off-shoot of the Constitution of 1782.

[3] List of registered and unregistered freeholders in Collon, Sept. 1766, F.P. D.562/2434; 1 Geo. II, c. 9, s. 6.

[4] *C.L.A.J.* i. 49 ff.

Tipping; he was also a cousin of William Henry and James Fortescue, and like them, a cousin of Lord Clanbrassill. In the event, the Fortescue brothers, and probably Clanbrassill,[1] held firm to the Fosters, but if anyone could have detached them it was Faithful Fortescue. This was probably why the various interests opposed to the Fosters held a meeting in August 1767 'to concert necessary measures to preserve the freedom of said county [Louth]',[2] and at this meeting decided that Balfour and Bellingham should stand down in favour of Faithful Fortescue. It was obvious that even Sibthorpe would easily defeat three separate opponents, and only common sense that the strongest of the three should be set up as the representative of the independent interest. This general union against Sibthorpe was what William Henry and James Fortescue had all along feared. But they were too deeply committed to the Fosters, too dependent on the Fosters' freeholders, and had made too many enemies at the time of the 1761 general election, to desert at this late stage.

The by-election took place in November 1767. Up to the last, the canvassing was furious on both sides. For example, out of thirty-four people whom Balfour and Faithful Fortescue entertained at an election dinner in Dundalk, five in the end turned their coats and voted for Sibthorpe.[3] There were defections on Sibthorpe's side as well. A total of thirty-seven people who were pledged to support him stayed away from the poll, the most important of them being, surprisingly enough, Attorney-General Tisdall, who was described as having 'hid' during the time of the election.[4] In spite of this, Sibthorpe won easily by 399 to 240.[5] Not content with this verdict, Faithful Fortescue on 12 December presented a petition against Sibthorpe's return, alleging that Sibthorpe had used improper influence; that the sheriff, Charles Craven, had shown gross partiality as returning officer; and that 200 of Sibthorpe's

---

[1] A list by John Foster of voters in the barony of Dundalk, [c. 1767], reckons Clanbrassill's agent, Isaac Read, as a supporter of Sibthorpe—F.P. D.562/2440.

[2] C.L.A.J. i. 49 ff.

[3] List of those who dined with Balfour and Fortescue at Dundalk, [Aug.–Nov. 1767], F.P. D.562/14653.

[4] List by John Foster of supporters of Sibthorpe who defected, [Nov. 1767], F.P. D.562/14649.

[5] Brief for Stephen Sibthorpe on a disputed election for co. Louth, 5 Feb. 1768, F.P. D.562/1214.

voters were disqualified on the usual grounds of being Papists, married to Papists, minors, unregistered, or not freeholders. The complaint about the sheriff, Craven, may have had some foundation, since Craven's family had been among the first to pledge support for Sibthorpe.[1] But Faithful Fortescue clearly can have had little hope of success, because he withdrew his petition at the beginning of February 1768, before any evidence had been heard.[2] In addition to the short-lived election petition, there was one other important sequel to the by-election of 1767. At the close of the poll, on 18 November, the Fosters got up a congratulatory address to Sibthorpe which, among other things, exhorted him to mark his gratitude for being elected by supporting '. . . the Bill now depending for Limiting the Duration of Parliament . . .: a law so essential to the Protestant interest, the support of our liberties, [and] the ancient, legal, and unrepealed right of all His Majesty's subjects of Ireland. . . .'[3] These stirring sentiments obviously harked back to Faithful Fortescue's address to the Louth electors in May 1767. In the meantime, a new Lord Lieutenant, Lord Townshend, had arrived in Ireland with instructions to support such a bill, as the price the British Government was prepared to pay for securing an augmentation of the army maintained on the Irish establishment. Privately, the Fosters no doubt disliked the bill—many of its supporters, particularly its supporters among the Opposition, privately did. But they knew that, if backed by the Government, it must pass, so that there was no point in making their private sentiments public or in missing a God-sent opportunity of knocking Faithful Fortescue's popular platform from under him. Having wrong-footed themselves in their county in 1755 through espousing the unpopular—and, what was worse, the losing—side in national politics, they had learnt the importance of the popular element in politics and the advisability of being, whenever this was compatible with their ambitions at national level, on the popular side. In 1767, with the Castle itself on the popular side,

---

[1] Arthur Craven to Anthony Foster, 20 Sept. 1766, F.P. D.562/1517; Walter Cope to Sir Archibald Acheson, 19 Nov. 1767, Gosford MSS., P.R.O.N.I. D.1606/1/48.

[2] *Commons' Journals* (Ireland), viii. 211, 220.

[3] Congratulatory address from the undersigned freeholders of Louth to Sibthorpe, 18 Nov. 1767, F.P. D.562/1809, 14650 A and B.

nothing was to be gained from pursuing a contrary course and much was to be gained by going over to that side with the maximum of propagandist éclat.

The Fosters had won an impressive victory at the 1767 by-election. They had retained their seat in spite of the poor quality of their candidate, and in the teeth of a general combination against them. What was more, they had succeeded at the last minute in coating their manœuvres with a veneer of political popularity by proclaiming their support for the Limitation Bill. In practical terms, however, their victory was short-lived, since the bill, in the form in which it was returned from Great Britain and in which it passed into law, included the provision that a general election should be held in the summer of 1768. Accordingly, the rival forces in Louth began to mobilize for another contest. This was what James and William Henry Fortescue had predicted would happen: if Sibthorpe was elected in 1767, they had argued, he 'may not enjoy it long, and then comes [*sic*] more disputes'. From the Fortescues' point of view, the by-election of 1767, like the general election of 1761, had been all loss and no gain. In September 1766, James Fortescue had been able to look forward to an unopposed return at the next general election, and had expressed himself as 'much indebted to every gentleman of this county for their kind support'.[1] All this was changed as a result of the part which his brother and he had been more or less forced into by the Fosters over the 1767 by-election. Now Fortescue, no less than the Foster candidate, was faced with the prospect of a stiff contest. Ranged against them were Blayney Balfour (presumably Junior) and, once again, Faithful Fortescue. Both sides formed a strict junction, which meant that each candidate was pledged to try to obtain the second votes of his supporters for his running partner. The Foster candidate this time was of course John Foster. As the Foster heir, he was obviously a much better candidate than an elderly brother-in-law who did not even bear the name. To this extent, therefore, the Fosters were in a stronger position now than they had been at the 1767 by-election. Moreover, with James Fortescue's fate indissolubly bound up with his own, John Foster could count this time on the wholehearted support of

---

[1] James Fortescue to Anthony Foster, 17 Sept. 1766, F.P. D.562/1760.

Lord Clanbrassill. All the same, the election was no walk-over. The best indication of this is the amount of money which the Fosters and Fortescues found it necessary to spend on it: between 19 and 20 July one only of the five pubs reserved for the entertainment, accommodation, and intoxication of their supporters, served 295 breakfasts, 492 dinners, and 39 suppers. The expenses in all five pubs came to £1,350, and the total expenses of the election to £3,000.[1] John Foster's calculations of numbers in advance of the election turned out to err significantly on the side of optimism; but in spite of this he was so far from regarding the result as a foregone conclusion that he took the precaution of having himself elected for Dunleer, and for another borough as well, in case he should come unstuck in Louth. In the event the precaution proved needless. He headed the poll with 437 votes, Fortescue came second with 397, and Balfour and Faithful Fortescue got 325 and 242 apiece.[2] The margin, though not as wide as Foster had forecast, was still comfortable.

Matters did not end there. When the result was declared and the victors were undergoing the compulsory rigours of being chaired, a not-very-serious riot broke out, instigated—according to the Fosters and Fortescues—by a relation of Balfour's, whom they proceeded to prosecute in the King's Bench. In the end, they dropped the prosecution, but their 'determined resolution to push this matter' (as Balfour Senior called it) enraged the independent interest and probably led to reprisals.[3] Charles Craven, the allegedly partial sheriff at the time of the 1767 by-election, was the next victim of a politically motivated prosecution in the King's Bench, this time sponsored by the independent interest and ostensibly relating to certain irregularities which he had committed when carrying out the unpopular job of baronial cess-collector. John Foster conducted his defence, and the proceedings were financed on both sides by subscription. Ultimately,

[1] Account of the expenses at Hatch's pub, Dundalk, 24 July 1768, F.P. D.562/14654; account of the expenses at all the public houses in Dundalk, [*c.* July 1768], F.P. D.562/4652A; account of the total expenses of the 1768 election, [*c.* July 1768], F.P. D.562/4654.

[2] Election calculations by John Foster, [pre-July 1768], F.P. D.562/14655A–E; *Dublin Journal*, 26–8 July 1768.

[3] Balfour to John Foster, 16 Dec. 1768, F.P. D.562/4528; George Adams to John Foster, 17 Jan. 1769, F.P. D.562/4527; [Henry Brabazon] to [George Adams?], [Jan. 1769], F.P. D.562/4531.

Craven appears to have been acquitted.[1] The third and final round of proceedings in the King's Bench was not inspired by Louth election politics, but was certainly intensified by them. This related to the borough of Ardee, whose patrons, the Ruxton family, were prominent members of the independent interest. At the 1768 election Attorney-General Tisdall had got up an unsuccessful opposition to the Ruxtons. Having been beaten at the election, he first presented a petition to the House of Commons, which he soon thought better of and withdrew, and then proceeded against the Ruxtons in the King's Bench on the ground of irregularities which he alleged they had committed in municipal elections in Ardee. The Fosters, apparently unmindful of Tisdall's desertion in 1767, joined in on his side, John Foster acting as leading counsel in the Ardee case, in which, after at least two trials, Tisdall was eventually worsted.[2] These three rounds of proceedings in the King's Bench illustrate the importance of the litigious, as well as the 'gladiatorial', element in Irish local politics. They also show that the election committee of the House of Commons was not the only—perhaps not even the most regular—place for the airing of grievances arising out of elections, and suggest that in other instances the silence of the *Commons' Journals* should not necessarily be taken as indicating the consent of the defeated candidates. Finally, they show that, in the sphere of local politics, a legal family like the Fosters were at a decided advantage, particularly if they had made a speciality of election law, as Anthony and possibly John Foster had done.

The expense of the contests and litigation of the 1760s, which ran on at least until 1771, probably had a considerable deterrent effect; for co. Louth was not again contested until 1826. John Foster sat for it from 1768 to 1821, his son, Thomas Foster, from 1821 to 1824, and his nephew, John Leslie Foster, from 1824 to 1830. The long period of calm is not comprehensible except in juxtaposition to the short period of storm which immediately preceded it. The expense incurred during the

---

[1] Case of Charles Craven, 22 Feb. 1769, F.P. D.562/5195A; *C.L.A.J.* i. 49 ff.; brief on behalf of defendant in the King *v.* Craven, [1770], F.P. D.562/5197.

[2] *Commons' Journals* (Ireland), viii. 293, 340; brief on behalf of defendant's motion in the King *v.* John and Charles Ruxton, [1769?], F.P. D.562/5210; brief on behalf of the relator in the King at the relation of Josias Ebbs *v.* John Ruxton, [1770?], F.P. D.562/5213.

decade 1761–71 was not, however, the only respect in which that decade proved decisive of the balance of power in co. Louth. It also saw two other developments, both of them redounding to the advantage of the Fosters. The first of these was the fragmentation of the old Beaulieu interest, on which William Aston had successfully stood in 1727 and his son-in-law, Thomas Tipping, as recently as 1755. Tipping's proprietary strength in 1755 had derived from two quarters: his own patrimonial property and that of his wife's family, the Astons. But in 1769, the Aston property passed into alien hands under the eccentric will of Mrs. Tipping's nephew, the last of the Astons in the male line.[1] Thereafter the Tipping and Aston interests went their separate ways. The second development, even more advantageous to the Fosters, was the change which the decade 1761–71 saw in the political standing of the Fortescue family, who by the end of it had slipped decisively into the position of junior partners to the Fosters. Being the biggest single interest in the county, the Fosters had been able to dictate terms, and the Fortescues had had to accede to those terms even at the cost of parting company with many of their former allies: in particular, the Bellinghams of Castle Bellingham and the Fortescues of Corderry, to whom they were no less closely related than to the Fosters, and against whom they were ranged by the Fosters in 1767 and again in 1768. What tended further to lessen their political importance in Louth was William Henry Fortescue's elevation to the barony of Clermont in 1770. This long-sought honour (especially after an earldom was added to it in 1777) had the effect of turning him into a semi-permanent absentee. A peerage had been the main object of his political activity, and once it had been achieved, he took less and less interest in Louth politics, and spent most of his time in London, or Paris, or on his Norfolk estate. His brother, James, and James's two sons, continued to reside in Louth and were its successive representatives in Parliament. But they were overshadowed by their colleague, John Foster, and one of them was described in the mid-1780s as Foster's dupe, tool, and partisan. No doubt

[1] Deed of covenant between Jane Rowan and Gavin Hamilton, 16 Mar. 1789, Rowan-Hamilton MSS., P.R.O.N.I. D.124. A decree in Wyatt and others *v.* Aston and others, 1767, ibid. D.151, and a deed of partition of the estate of Henry Tichborne, Lord Ferrard, 2 Jan. 1771, ibid. D.127, show that there was very little of the old Tichborne estate in Louth left at the time of Ferrard's death.

the description was exaggerated. But it gives a vivid impression of the state of political tutelage to which the Fortescues had been reduced.[1]

More important, probably, than the Fortescues in terms of the number of freeholders he could command was their cousin Lord Clanbrassill. However, he was in financial difficulties and was, moreover, an overbearing, unpopular man who, so far from being capable of heading a coalition against the Fosters, was not even capable of acting in concert with his own nearest relations.[2] In 1766, his cousin, James Fortescue, lamented that '. . . neither Billy [William Henry Fortescue] or I have the least power over him, and [there is] nothing he dreads so much as to have it thought that either of us govern him. . . .'[3] His foibles were an important element in Louth politics. Had he been able to work cordially with the Fortescues, they would have constituted a combined interest which was numerically the strongest in Louth, and which might in the vital decade 1761–71 have succeeded in stopping the Fosters in their tracks. By the end of that decade it was too late, though Clanbrassill's attitude towards the Fosters remained uncertain for some time to come. Then, in 1782, he became engrossed, to the exclusion of all other political concerns, in fighting off a take-over bid for his family borough of Dundalk. In spite of the fact that he had gone through all the Volunteer motions with considerable flamboyance (something which John Foster, characteristically, refrained from doing), the local Volunteer movement played a prominent part in this take-over bid, and among the local Volunteers involved, two of Foster's cousins, John William Foster and Robert Sibthorpe (son of Stephen Sibthorpe), were particularly prominent. Foster did not hesitate to denounce publicly the activities of his cousins; with the result that the Dundalk episode established a bond between Clanbrassill and him, as well as incapacitating Clanbrassill financially for political activity in co. Louth. Clanbrassill instructed his two M.P.s for Dundalk to vote for Foster when Foster made a preliminary canvass for the speakership in 1782,[4] and

---

[1] Malcomson, *Earl of Clermont*, pp. 37 f., 50 ff.   [2] *C.L.A.J.* xv. 40.
[3] James Fortescue to Anthony Foster, 17 Sept. 1766, F.P. D.562/1760. For Clanbrassill's character, see Malcomson, *Dundalk Borough*, pp. 23 f.
[4] Clanbrassill to William Conyngham, 10 Dec. 1782, Lenox-Conyngham MSS., P.R.O.N.I. D.1449/12/136.

Clanbrassill's co. Louth interest was almost certainly at Foster's disposal at the general elections of 1783, 1790, and 1797.

With the old Beaulieu interest eclipsed, the Fortescues subservient, and Clanbrassill propitiated, Foster had nothing left to fear except a coalition among a number of smallish interests which can collectively be described as the independent or popular interest in Louth. The leaders of this interest were, as before, the Balfours, Tippings, Fortescues of Corderry, Bellinghams, and Ruxtons. They had frequent opportunities to attack Foster on favourable ground, since his position in national politics by and large forced him to pursue a course of hostility, or at best indifference, to nearly all the popular questions of the period 1779–85; in this period there was much of the 'Ministerial' and little of the 'Patriotism' in his parliamentary conduct. Yet this conduct had no worse consequences in the sphere of local politics than to bring down upon him two sets of instructions from his Louth constituents, the first of which he secretly welcomed, and the second of which he dismissed with contempt.[1] He could afford to ignore the representations of the independent interest, because he well knew that it was not strong enough to topple him unless it allied itself with either the Fortescues or Clanbrassill. Such an alliance was hardly likely. The Fortescues and Clanbrassill were much more 'devoted courtiers' than Foster. James Fortescue was once described as 'the greatest jobber in Ireland'; his brother, Lord Clermont, as has been seen, rivalled Hely-Hutchinson in the number and success of his applications for patronage;[2] and Clanbrassill, a great sinecurist, on the rare occasions when he opposed government, did so out of pique, not principle. This, then, was the choice of allies open to the independent interst in Louth if they were to have a hope of ousting Foster.

Because his nearest rivals in Louth were politically more objectionable than he was, Foster was returned without opposition from the independent interest. This immunity even extended to the general election of 1783, when the Volunteer movement had still some steam left in it, and when his indifference to the Constitution of 1782, Renunciation, and Volunteering itself, were recent and live issues. He himself seems to

---

[1] See pp. 43 ff., 226 f.   [2] See p. 22.

have anticipated a contest in 1783, since he took the precaution
of having himself returned for his friend Owen Wynne's borough
of Sligo (although this may have been because Wynne wanted
him as a seat-warmer). The threat of a contest came from a
Mr. Tipping, who was probably Thomas Tipping's brother,
Edward; also, apparently, from Foster's own Volunteering
cousin, Robert Sibthorpe. Sibthorpe was a disreputable
character, who was in gaol for debt at the time, and for whom
the main attraction of being in Parliament was the immunity
which parliamentary privilege would afford him from his
creditors. In spite of the pension he enjoyed from the Crown,
he was an enthusiastic squib-writer in favour of parliamentary
reform, and he seems to have been a sufficiently influential
member of the independent interest in Louth for both Foster
and Lord Clermont to take seriously his aspirations to represent
the county, and to be at pains to keep him quiet.[1] They must
have been successful, as nothing more was heard of either Sibthorpe or Tipping. Foster was returned unopposed, along with
James Fortescue's eldest son, Thomas James.[2]

At this election Foster made his first and only concession to
the local Volunteer movement: he returned his other Volunteering cousin, John William Foster, for Dunleer (although this
may have been in accordance with some family arrangement
made years previously). The concession, if concession it was,
did not, however, avert a show-down between Foster and the
Volunteer element among his constituents, which was broadly
synonymous with the old independent interest. In January
1784, they presented him with an address instructing him to
support the plan of parliamentary reform which had been
drawn up at the Volunteer Convention in November of the
previous year. His reply showed plainly that he was not afraid
to defy them, especially at a time when the next general

---

[1] John Plunkett to Foster, 8 Mar. 1784, F.P. D.562/9468; Revd. William Foster
to Foster, 10 Sept. 1782, F.P. D.562/4647; unsigned 'tip-off' to the Castle about the
political activities of various people in the Marshalsea gaol, Pelham MSS., B.L.
Add. MS. 33101, fol. 37; list of the Irish Parliament at the time of the 1783 general
election, N.L.I. MS. 2098; photocopy in P.R.O.N.I. T. 3035; *Dublin Evening Post*,
12 July 1783.

[2] Another of John Foster's cousins, John Thomas Foster, M.P. for Dunleer,
1776–83, was the son-in-law of the Volunteering Earl-Bishop of Derry and to some
extent connected with him in politics (Bishop of Derry to J. T. Foster, 2 and 17 Apr.
1782, J. L. Foster MSS., P.R.O.N.I. T.2519/7/2/9–10.)

election could be assumed to be six or seven years away. He roundly denounced the plan as full of 'unnecessary and dangerous innovations', to which they retorted that his reply was 'highly disrespectful to this County and unbecoming Representatives to their Constituents'.[1] Strong language of this sort was untypical of Foster's relations with even the independent interest among his constituents, and the head-on collision of January 1784 is an isolated occurrence. He continued, it is true, to pursue a political course in national politics which must have displeased them—by opposing protecting duties, sponsoring his Libel Bill, and supporting without qualification the amended Commercial Propositions. Even his most popular measure of the years 1784–5, his Corn Law, was not universally popular in co. Louth; in February 1784 he actually had to present a petition to the House against his own bill, from the corn-dealers, maltsters, and brewers of the county, who feared that it would encourage oats at the expense of barley.[2] Yet, thanks to his approachability, his plain style of living, his country-gentleman ethos, it may be conjectured that, however politically unpopular he may at times have been with the independent interest, even with them he was never personally unpopular.

In any case, his election to the speakership in September 1785 removed him to a sphere in which he was unlikely to continue to excite their political hostility. The modern convention that a sitting speaker is not opposed in his constituency did not apply in the eighteenth century, so the speakership gave him no formal immunity from opposition.[3] However, the prestige of the office was such that opposing the speaker would probably have been regarded as an extreme step. Foster's behind-the-scenes opposition in the Irish cabinet to a variety of popular measures was well known; but he had no opportunity to oppose them publicly by voting against them in the House, except in the unlikely event of an equality of votes, and the only political matters on which he did in fact speak in committee throughout his tenure of the speakership were Catholic Relief and the Union—both of them issues on which his

---

[1] *Dublin Evening Post*, 27 and 29 Jan. and 19 Feb. 1784, quoted in *C.L.A.J.* vi. 121 ff.   [2] *Parl. Reg.* (Irish), ii. 384.
[3] Malcomson, *Foster and the Speakership*, p. 290, 1n.

sentiments were wholeheartedly echoed even by the independent interest. This being so, it is not surprising that Louth, which had returned him unopposed when he was almost at the height of his political unpopularity in 1783, should have continued to do so in 1790 and again 1797. Well in advance of the 1790 election, in February 1789, opposition was threatened by a body styling itself the Louth Constitution Club, and in 1790 Francis Tipping of Bellurgan Park, Edward Tipping's son, did in fact declare himself a candidate. However, he soon withdrew, alleging ill-health as his reason, and Foster and Thomas James Fortescue were again elected.[1] The 1797 general election passed off even more uneventfully. It was a quiet election all over Ireland because of the disturbed state of many parts of the country and the recent invasion scare; and co. Louth, as a particularly disturbed area, was no exception. Foster's unopposed colleague this time was James Fortescue's second son, William Charles, afterwards 2nd Viscount Clermont.

Foster's stands against Catholic Relief in 1793 and the Union in 1799–1800, were even more important than the speakership in reconciling him to the independent interest.[2] In 1805, he was told that there was 'nothing to prevent your general popularity but your opposition of the Catholic claims';[3] but even in 1805, the reverse was true in the sphere of local, as opposed to national, politics. The anti-Catholic address of the Louth Grand Jury in 1792 is symptomatic of local feeling on the issue, and in this feeling the independent interest participated to just the same extent as elements which by tradition supported the Fosters. Indeed, Balfour in 1793 was even more extreme than Foster in his opposition to the Relief Bill,[4] although he later became converted to Emancipation. The near-unanimity of the Protestant gentry of Louth on this issue at this stage meant, not only that Foster's local popularity received a fillip, but that there was no 'race for the Catholic'[5] on the part of the Protestant family interests. The absentee

---

[1] *Dublin Evening Post*, 17 Feb. 1789 and 4 Mar. 1790.
[2] See pp. 230 ff.   [3] Rochfort to Foster, 5 Feb. 1805, F.P. D.207/33/7.
[4] Revd. Edward Hudson to Lord Charlemont, 8 Sept. 1793, Charlemont MSS., R.I.A. 2nd ser., v. 60.
[5] Phrase used in Foster's speech on the Catholic Relief Bill of 1793 (*Parl. Reg.* (Irish), xiii. 343); the context was the 'race' between the British Government and the Irish Parliament for popularity in the eyes of the Catholic Committee.

Lord Clermont, it is true, was active in the period 1793–6 trying to ingratiate himself with the leading Catholic gentry family of the county, the Bellews of Barmeath, who, unlike their kinsmen, the Lords Bellew, had held on to their Louth estate (valued at £2,000 a year in 1806), and had never conformed to the Church of Ireland.[1] Nevertheless, no attempt seems to have been made in Louth for at least twenty-five years after 1793 to appeal to the Catholic vote. In this respect Louth was unusual—almost unique—among counties where Catholics constituted an overwhelming majority of the population. Lord Clermont's mild flirtation with the Bellews did not achieve its object, which presumably was to steal a march on Foster. Instead, Clermont wrong-footed himself badly early in 1799 by pledging his own and William Charles Fortescue's support for the Union. The Louth gentry were as unanimously and spontaneously anti-Unionist as they were anti-Emancipationist, and the independent interest no less than the rest of them. Very little of Foster's Union correspondence survives, and nothing survives of the correspondence he must have carried on over the first general election after the Union, that of 1802. However, the replies he received to his canvassing letters at the time of the next general election, that of 1806, show the new and altogether more favourable light in which he was regarded by the leading figures in the independent interest.[2] Clearly, Catholic Relief and the Union had made all the difference.

For his part, William Charles Fortescue, acting either from conviction or from fear of losing his seat, decided just before the start of the session in 1799 to go against Clermont's wishes and oppose the Union, and continued to oppose it through the session of 1800. As a result, he held on to the seat, but at the cost of placing himself more decisively than ever in a position of political tutelage to Foster. Both were returned unopposed in 1802, and Fortescue continued to be Foster's colleague and junior partner until just before the general election of 1806, when Clermont died. Under a special remainder, Fortescue then succeeded to the Viscountcy, though not to the Earldom,

---

[1] Clermont to Pelham, 10 Mar. 1796, S.P.O. 507/9/25; 'Notes as to Irish Catholics, 1806', Richmond MSS., N.L.I. MS. 60, fol. 204.
[2] For the 1806 election correspondence see F.P. D.562/4332–73.

of Clermont, and to his uncle's estates in Louth and Norfolk. He lived for most of the time in England, dying there childless in 1829, a year after Foster.[1] Because he was childless and without a close relative in the male line, his succession to the Clermont peerage brought to an end the long association of Fortescues and Fosters in the representation of Louth. It had lasted without a break since 1761. With the new Lord Clermont's strong approval,[2] the candidate chosen to stand in his place at the general election of 1806 was Viscount Jocelyn, the eldest son of the 2nd Earl of Roden. The Rodens were a new phenomenon in co. Louth politics. Lord Roden's mother was Clanbrassill's sister and heiress, and when Clanbrassill died childless in 1798, she had succeeded to his estates. Along with the estates went his proprietary interest in the borough of Dundalk, which he had ultimately been successful in re-establishing. A less welcome legacy was his debts, which Lady Roden increased by mismanaging the inheritance; so that when she died in 1802, her son and heir Lord Roden found her affairs in such confusion that he was forced to sell the seat for Dundalk for a term of six years.[3] The seat continued to be sold until 1832. This was something which Clanbrassill had seldom or never done, even though Dundalk had been a double-member constituency in the Irish Parliament. Instead, he had from the 1780s onwards given both seats to his heirs, the Jocelyns. Deprived by financial exigency of this mode of entry into Parliament, the Jocelyns now turned their attention to a seat for co. Louth, and they had their chance to secure one in 1806, when the Fortescues ran out of candidates for the county in the main branch of their family. Lord Jocelyn was accordingly set up on the old Fortescue/Clanbrassill interest, and John Foster did not hesitate to join forces with him. Any of the Foster supporters who were in doubt about the disposal of their second votes were told that 'the old interests went together'.[4]

[1] Malcomson, *Earl of Clermont*, p. 47.

[2] Clermont to Foster, 29 Oct. 1806, F.P. T.2519/4/434.

[3] Lord Roden (ed.), *The Diary of Anne, Countess Dowager of Roden* (Dublin, 1870), p. 166; Roden to Revd. Percy Jocelyn, 4 Jan. 1802, Roden MSS., P.R.O.N.I. Mic. 147/10, vol. 21, pp. 170; Sir Arthur to Henry Wellesley, 6 May 1807, *Wellington Supplementary Despatches*, v. 28.

[4] Michael Chester to Foster, 5 Nov. 1806, F.P. D.562/4345. Interestingly,

In spite of this, Jocelyn's election was very nearly opposed by the independent interest. Unlike Foster, and like the late Lord Clermont, the Jocelyns had been Unionists. Lord Jocelyn, moreover, was only eighteen in 1806, and because of minority would not be able to take his seat, if elected, for another three years. Lord Roden had hoped to have his brother, John Jocelyn, returned for Louth, but unluckily John Jocelyn happened to be a Commissioner of the Revenue, an office incompatible with a seat in Parliament. Roden then suggested that a seat-warmer of his nomination should be put into the revenue board, to allow John Jocelyn to sit for Louth until Lord Jocelyn came of age. But the Irish Administration refused to countenance such an egregious job. This left Roden no alternative but to inflict a greater indignity on the county than the Fosters had done by setting up Sibthorpe in 1767. Appropriately, it was Balfour, the quondam candidate of 1767, who raised objections to Lord Jocelyn's candidature, and threatened opposition. Since 1795 minors had been incapable of election to Parliament[1] and their return, as the Chief Secretary, William Elliot, pointed out, 'could not be sustained if challenged'.[2] In spite of this, Balfour eventually dropped the idea of opposition, and Foster and Lord Jocelyn were returned unopposed.[3] As things turned out, their tenure was short-lived, with another general election taking place only a few months later, in May 1807. This time, with a new Administration in power, Lord Roden was allowed to get away with a modified version of his proposal concerning the revenue board. John Jocelyn was accordingly elected for Louth along with Foster, and continued to represent it until Lord Jocelyn came of age.[4]

Thanks to the new political popularity which the Union brought him, and to the unbroken continuity of the old Foster/Fortescue/Clanbrassill alliance, Foster's interest in co. Louth can be said to have been at its high-water mark in the period 1799-1809. In 1809 recession began. Foster and the new Lord Clermont quarrelled over the patronage of the Carlingford

---

Chester belonged to a minor Catholic gentry family which was prominent in opposition to the Fosters in 1826.

[1] 35 Geo. III, c. 29, s. 81.
[2] William Elliot to Grenville, 4 Nov. 1806, *H.M.C. Dropmore MSS.*, viii. 422.
[3] Roger Twigg to Foster, 12 Nov. 1806, F.P. D.562/4368.
[4] Wellesley to Roden, 28 Apr. 1808, Apsley House MSS.

district, which each claimed as his right,[1] and the quarrel
ended by severing their long-standing political connection. The
Foster and Roden interests remained firmly united, but their
position was weakened by the defection of Lord Clermont, who
was at best neutral and at worst hostile. In spite of this, the
general elections of 1812 and 1818 passed off without opposition,
Foster and Lord Jocelyn being again returned. In any case,
by the latter year, Foster had more important things than Lord
Clermont's attitude to worry about. Up to 1815, the registered
electorate of Louth had stood at between 700 and 900; and
since the registered electorate in any county was always higher
than the numbers actually polled at an election, this suggests
that, in spite of the re-enfranchisement of the Catholics in
1793, the Louth electorate had risen little, if at all, since the
1760s: in other words, that the Louth gentry were very slow
to exploit the possibilities which the Act held out for the multiplication of their freeholders. The explanation lies presumably
in the popularity of Foster in the constituency, the solidarity
of the old alliance between the three leading interests in the
county (until 1809), the unanimity of the Protestant gentry
against Emancipation, the comparative fewness of the Catholic
gentry, the absence of contests since the 1760s, and so on.
All the same, although the phenomenon is not inexplicable in
the particular circumstances of Louth, this should not obscure
the very important point that, in 1815, Louth was much more
of a freak among Irish county constituencies than even its
smallness warranted. In almost all county constituencies the
electorate had at least trebled since 1793, and in some—notably
co. Mayo—the rise had been more spectacular still.[2] The Louth
electorate did not remain static much longer. From 1817
onwards, and particularly in the year 1820–1, it rose dramatically, until by the beginning of 1821 it totalled 2,830 freeholders.
It is some measure of the intensity of the activity in this period
that by 1824 the number had risen only slightly above the

---

[1] Clermont to Foster, and Foster to Clermont, Feb. 1809, F.P. D.562/12577-9.
[2] These figures for Louth and the other counties up to 1815 come from returns
made to the House of Commons, the deficiencies of which are discussed in Jupp,
'Parliamentary Representation', pp. 15 ff. I am very grateful to Dr. Jupp for
letting me see the abstracts he made for purposes of comparison, from these
returns; I have benefited greatly from his pioneering work on this aspect of the
subject.

1821 figure; probably the registered electorate remained pretty much the same between 1821 and the general election of 1826, after which it rose again, to 3,500 by 1828.[1]

The reasons for this sudden and dramatic multiplication of freeholders are not altogether clear. One must have been the alienation of Lord Clermont from the other two leading interests. Another must have been Foster's resignation from office in 1811, and his son, Thomas's, dismissal from office in 1813, which meant a loss of patronage and, more important, a loss of consequence. A third reason was a growing change of heart among the Protestant gentry of the county on the question of Emancipation. In 1813, for the first time, they proved to be insufficiently unanimous on the question to justify Foster in getting up an anti-Emancipationist address: Balfour, for one, had by this time been converted to the abortive doctrine of 'securities' and later became an out-and-out Emancipationist.[2] In general, Foster's influence in Louth was seen to be on the wane. The county was still unanimously behind him on a subject dear to the landed interest, the Corn Laws;[3] but this was small comfort. Even on a non-political question—his proposal in 1816 that a Peace Preservation force should continue to be stationed in Louth (and therefore paid for by the county)—he was easily out-voted by the local magistracy. Almost immediately afterwards, his view of the situation was triumphantly vindicated by events, the notorious Reaghstown murders of 1816. But that did not alter the fact that, on a matter vitally affecting the security of the county, he—its Governor—had failed to carry his point with a body of magistrates largely of his own nominating.[4] A final reason for the rise in the Louth electorate, and

[1] This last figure is taken from a letter from J. L. Foster to Peel of 16 December 1828 (Peel MSS., B.L. Add. MS. 40397, fols. 384–94); figures for the registered electorate of Louth at January 1821, January 1822, and January 1824, and for the electors registered between January 1824 and January 1825, January 1825 and January 1826, and January 1826 and January 1827, survive in the form in which they were printed under 1 Geo. IV, c. 11, s. 30 (Sir Henry Parnell's Election Act) in the co. Louth Library, Dundalk. They have been photocopied by P.R.O.N.I., ref. T.2519/14/1–6. I am most grateful to Miss Folan and Miss Ward of the Louth Library and to Mr. Trevor Parkhill, for drawing my attention to this invaluable source.   [2] Roden to Foster, 7 and 29 Jan. 1813, F.P. D.562/12892, 12820.
[3] Newspaper cutting reporting the Louth address in favour of protection, 17 Jan. 1815, F.P. D.562/81744; Balfour to Oriel, 25 May 1824 and 12 Apr. 1825, F.P. D.562/14187, 14333; Lord Norbury to Oriel, 15 Apr. 1825, F.P. D.207/51/31.
[4] Foster to Peel, 28 Oct., and Peel to Foster, 17 Nov. 1816, F.P. D.207/39/58, 60.

one more easily quantifiable than the foregoing, was a change in electoral law effected by an Election Act of 1820. This act simplified—some would have said nullified—the registration procedure for 40/– freeholders claiming either to own their freeholds outright or to lease them in perpetuity. According to its opponents, this provision admitted to the vote numerous squatters and introduced a novel abuse into the Irish electoral system, 'the fraudulent or fictitious franchise in fee'. It attracted the attention of Parliament in 1825, but nothing was actually done about it. By 1828 it was reckoned, on possibly biased authority, that fraudulent or fictitious freeholders in fee accounted for 500 of the then Louth electorate of 3,500.[1]

The effects of the increased electorate on Foster's interest in Louth are no more easily quantifiable than its causes. Foster, perforce, joined in the sudden move to multiply freeholders. By the beginning of 1821, his estate boasted some 420 free-holders out of the county total of 2,830 (and Lord Roden's some 320). This was no more than the potential number of which the Foster estate had been judged capable in 1806; but there is a world of difference between the potential and the actual. Foster was able to sustain the 420-figure until the beginning of 1822, and then it began to fall off. By the beginning of 1824, it was down to 335, and by the early summer of 1826, to 270. The reasons for the fall were probably economic. Certainly, there were no good political ones for it,[2] as Foster's voting strength, relative to that of other estates, was almost certain to decline once the opportunities created by the 1793 Act began to be exploited in Louth. On most other estates, the Catholic element in the tenantry must have been greater than on Foster's, and the opportunities of the 1793 Act greater in consequence. Foster had always had a preference for Protestant tenants. In his speech in 1793 he had denied that this was true of himself or any other Louth landowner, and his denial may have been honest to the extent that in his case the

---

[1] 1 Geo. IV, c. 11, s. 44; J. L. Foster to Oriel, 13 May 1825, F.P. D.207/74/155; J. L. Foster to Peel, 16 Dec. 1828, Peel MSS., B.L. Add. MS. 40397, fols. 384–94.

[2] Rochfort to Foster, 30 May 1806, F.P. D.207/33/95; *Louth Freeholders, 1821 and 1824*, P.R.O.N.I. T.2519/14/1, 3; statement of how Oriel's tenantry voted, [c. July 1826], F.P. D.562/14698. For the economic reasons for the fall, see pp. 306 ff., 326 ff.

preference for Protestant tenants was economically rather than politically motivated. However, the fact remains that the parish of Collon, most of which he owned, was the most Protestant in the county, with a ratio of 130 Protestants to 1,000 Catholics in 1812.[1] In these circumstances, the multiplication of freeholders from 1817 onwards was bound to redound to his disadvantage, even if he had been able to sustain the number of his freeholders at the 420-mark. As it was, he was unable to sustain it, and this made his position weaker still.

Its weakness was not exposed at the hustings for some years to come. Before the general election of 1820, Lord Clermont for the first time threatened opposition. He endeavoured to set up an English nephew as a candidate, and made an appeal to the Catholics of Louth to rally round him and 'relieve the county from the *thraldom* in which it has been so long kept'.[2] The appeal seems to have been oblique, in that it fell short of an avowal that Clermont's nephew would vote for Emancipation. Nevertheless, it was an important development in Louth politics. Nothing in the end came of Clermont's threatened opposition, and Foster and Lord Jocelyn were as usual returned without a contest. But shortly afterwards, a by-election occasioned by Lord Jocelyn's succession as 3rd Earl of Roden on the death of his father, exposed the Foster/Roden interest to attack from a new quarter, this time from Balfour. The Fosters exerted themselves warmly on behalf of the Roden candidate, John Jocelyn, and demonstrated to the new Lord Roden 'the value of your county friendship'; in any case, informed opinion held that it would be '. . . great madness in him [Balfour] to demand a poll. Upon an examination of the registries . . . it is obvious he could have no chance. . . .'[3] Balfour himself must have agreed with this estimate of his prospects, because he declined the poll, leaving John Jocelyn to be returned unopposed. This by-election was closely followed

[1] Revd. [Bramtfield?] to Foster, 3 Nov. 1807, F.P. D.562/12518; *Parl. Reg.* (Irish), xiii. 333; Edward Wakefield, *An Account of Ireland Statistical and Political* (2 vols., London, 1812), quoted in *C.L.A.J.* vii. 232.

[2] John Page to Foster, 15 Mar. 1819, F.P. D.562/13209. In his earlier days Clermont had been notable for his anti-Catholic prejudices—Wickham to Castlereagh, 14 Aug. 1803, Wickham MSS., P.R.O.N.I. T.2627/5/G/50.

[3] Lord Dufferin to Foster, 29 July 1820, F.P. T.2519/4/1733; James Johnston to Foster, 5 and 7 Aug. 1820, F.P. D.562/13484–5.

by another, made necessary by Foster's elevation to the peerage as Baron Oriel in July 1821. Once again there were rumblings of opposition from Balfour and the old independent interest, coupled with the threat that Lord Clermont would make common cause with them. Nothing however came of this. Foster's son, Thomas (who had assumed the name of Skeffington in 1816), was returned unopposed, Balfour's son commenting ruefully: '. . . Lord Clermont allows his friends to go as they please . . . I fear that Skeffington must come in, as our registry is hardly old enough . . .'[1] Skeffington held the seat until 1824 when, on the death of his mother, he succeeded to the viscountcy of Ferrard. This necessitated yet another by-election, at which his cousin, John Leslie Foster, was returned unopposed and probably without even a threat of opposition. One reason for this was that, since the previous by-election, the Foster interest had been strengthened by a reconciliation with Lord Clermont and a re-establishment of the 'old and long intimacy' between the two families.[2] John Leslie Foster accordingly had the advantage of Lord Clermont's support: a support which was not entirely disinterested, because Clermont hoped that the Fosters in return would back a candidate of his at some future election.[3]

His aspirations were ill-timed. The Fosters were already under strong pressure from the old independent interest to put an end to the aristocratic monopoly of the representation of Louth, and to throw open the second seat to an independent candidate. The candidate this time was not Balfour, but Sir William Bellingham of Castle Bellingham, who was so impatient for the seat that he even urged that John Jocelyn, whose health was failing, should resign at once in his favour. For the first time the Fosters and Jocelyns found themselves in no position to resist the demands of the independent interest. The reason was that, even with the help of Lord Clermont, they were no longer capable of carrying both seats without other allies, particularly when they had no suitable candidate for the second; John Jocelyn was too old and ill to think of standing again at

---

[1] Blayney Balfour Junior to his mother, [c. July 1821], Balfour MSS., N.L.I. MS. 10377.

[2] Oriel to Clermont, 19 Feb. 1824, F.P. D.562/14172.

[3] Clermont to Oriel, 4 Feb. 1824, F.P. D.562/14170.

the next general election, Lord Roden's half-brother was not yet of age, and there was no other Jocelyn available. In these circumstances, compromise with the independent interest was unavoidable. Accordingly, it was agreed early in 1825 that John Jocelyn should hold on to his seat until the dissolution (assuming that he did not die in the meantime), and that at the next general election John Leslie Foster should be re-elected unopposed in partnership with Bellingham.[1] This scheme had to be modified in the detail, when it was discovered that Bellingham was ineligible to sit in Parliament.[2] He was replaced by Matthew Fortescue of Stephenstown, who was in fact a better compromise candidate. Fortescue was not only a leading member of the independent interest with over 50 freeholders on his own estate,[3] he was also acceptable to the aristocratic interest, being a kinsman of Lord Clermont and a protégé of Lord Roden. Indeed, at the time of the 1826 general election he is generally referred to as Roden's nominee.[4] This however is misleading. In particular, it obscures the important point that the partnership between Foster and Fortescue was more broadly based, and for that very reason less close and compact, than the old Foster/Roden junction had been. As things turned out, the general election which took place in June 1826 was totally unlike anything which co. Louth had ever seen before, because of the revolt of the Catholic freeholders against their Protestant landlords. But this spectacular and sudden development should not be allowed completely to overshadow the significant events which preceded the election by a year and a half.

The 1826 Louth election has acquired subsequent celebrity as one of the dress rehearsals for the Clare election of 1828. But before the event, none of the leading interests in Louth seems to have anticipated the revolt of the Catholic freeholders. As has been seen, Lord Clermont as recently as 1819 had shown

[1] Oriel to J. L. Foster, 12 Feb. 1825, F.P. T.2519/4/2044.
[2] Foster to Oriel, 24 Aug. 1825, F.P. D.207/74/169. Presumably, his sinecure office of Receiver General of Land and Assessed Taxes for London was incompatible with a seat.
[3] List of freeholders on Fortescue's estate, [*c.* 1826?], Pyke-Fortescue MSS., P.R.O.I.
[4] John D'Alton, *A History of Dundalk* (Dundalk, 1864), p. 230; *Dublin Evening Post*, 29 June 1826.

that he regarded the Catholic vote as something which could safely be employed as a pawn in the old game between the Protestant proprietary interests. In the same year, Thomas Skeffington, writing to his father from Collon just after an Emancipation Bill had passed the Commons by a majority of three, reported that no '. . . feeling has been aroused among the commonalty here by the success of their Question. They are incompetent to it, or perhaps are too knowing to be deceived by a supposition that they can reap benefit from it.'[1] Lord Oriel, it is true, appears to have had some dim appreciation of the significance of the Catholic vote, because the argument he used against John Jocelyn's resigning his seat in favour of Bellingham in 1825 was that it would be dangerous to '. . . risk a contest while the Catholic Association existed, in the present uncertainty of what may be the discontents and party rage on their disappointment. . . .'[2] But this was only a momentary flash of vision. Since O'Connell himself failed at this stage to appreciate the importance of the Catholic 40/- freeholders,[3] it is no wonder that Oriel, an old man of eighty-six, who had never thought that political awareness existed below the level of the Catholic middle class, should have made the same mistake. So far was he from expecting trouble of any kind at the 1826 election, that he was absent from Louth on a private visit to Bangor, North Wales, when the election began, and only returned home in response to the urgent entreaties of his relations on the spot.[4]

The first warning that the Emancipation issue was likely to be prominent at the next Louth election had come in October 1825. It took the form of a printed circular letter from one Anthony Marmion, who described himself as 'Secretary to the Catholics of Louth', and called upon the freeholders of the county to unite in putting an end to the 'present unnatural state of the representation of this great (and should be independent) county'. To this end, Marmion urged that a meeting be held to nominate 'one or two liberal candidates, who will pledge themselves to support civil and religious liberty in

---

[1] Thomas Skeffington to Foster, 14 May 1819, F.P. D.562/3404.
[2] Oriel to J. L. Foster, 12 Feb. 1825, F.P. T.2519/4/2044.
[3] James A. Reynolds, *The Catholic Emancipation Crisis in Ireland, 1823–1829* (Yale, 1954), pp. 24, 29.
[4] Revd. W. H. Foster to Oriel, 14 June 1826, F.P. D.207/73/136.

parliament'.[1] His circular letter failed to elicit any response from the most important quarter to which it had been directed: the Catholic gentry of Louth, headed by Sir Edward Bellew of Barmeath. It also failed to elicit any response from the old Protestant independent interest, headed by the Balfours and the Bellinghams, which had already had its demands met with the nomination of Matthew Fortescue, and stood pledged to support Foster and Fortescue at the election. Though he supported Emancipation and was strongly pressed to stand on the Catholic interest, Balfour refused to do so.[2] This was about 10 June 1826, and the election was fixed for 21 June. At this late stage, the Catholic cause found a champion in the unpromising person of Alexander Dawson of Riverstown, Ardee. Dawson was a candidate of unimpeachable respectability, being a remote kinsman of Lord Cremorne. But he was an elderly man, with only a small property in the county, and, although credited with a certain amount of eloquence, had never sat or aspired to sit in Parliament before.[3] In the circumstances of 1826, however, all that mattered was his declared intention of standing 'on the present principles of independence and civil and religious freedom', or, as John Leslie Foster put it, 'on the Radical, Catholic interest'.[4]

At first Sir Edward Bellew and the Catholic gentry held aloof from Dawson. On 15 June, the Fosters still thought that Bellew would stay neutral.[5] But in the end, his hand was forced by the overwhelming support which Dawson had met with among the Catholic rank and file, amounting, it was reported, to promises of no less than 600 votes on his first canvass.[6] His campaign was financed out of a subscription raised among the Catholic tradesmen and merchants of Dundalk and the Catholics of almost every parish in Louth, and reaching in the end the remarkable total of £2,174 (which included £360 from

[1] *Circular letter from Marmion to the Louth freeholders*, 21 Oct. 1825, F.P. D.562/14689.

[2] *Letter from Alexander Dawson to Sir Edward Bellew and Others*, 14 June 1826, F.P. D.562/14690; *Saunders News Letter*, 5 July 1826.

[3] *C.L.A.J.* viii. 26; D'Alton, *Dundalk*, p. 229; Reynolds, *Catholic Emancipation*, p. 97.

[4] *Dawson to Bellew and Others*, 14 June 1826, F.P. D.562/14690; Foster to Oriel, 13 June 1826, F.P. D.207/74/203.

[5] R. B. McDowell, *Public Opinion and Government Policy in Ireland, 1801–46* (London, 1952), p. 105; Revd. W. H. Foster to Oriel, 15 June 1826, F.P. D.207/73/51.

[6] Revd. W. H. Foster to Oriel, 13 June 1826, F.P. D.207/73/64.

Dawson himself, who had declared in his election address that he would not spend a penny on the contest).[1] The local priests took the lead in whipping up popular enthusiasm for Dawson, and on 15 June the Fosters learned that the Catholic Association intended to take up the Louth election, and that O'Connell was to come to Louth in person to help in Dawson's campaign.[2] It was, in fact, Sheil who came, and after mass on Sunday 25 June, when the election had already begun, made an inflammatory speech outside Dundalk church, in which he compared the landlords' claim to direct the votes of their tenants to their claim in feudal times to sleep with every newly married bride on their estates; '. . . I tell you', he concluded, 'that your landlords have no more right to ask you to vote against your religion and your conscience than they have to ask you for the virginity of your children . . .' (On the actual hustings, however, his language had been more moderate; he paid tribute to John Leslie Foster's personal and political character and to the record of the Fosters as landlords, and stated that the only objection to Foster as a candidate for Louth was that he opposed the Emancipation of the religion to which the majority of his constituents belonged.)[3] Overwhelmed by the popular upsurge in Dawson's favour, the Bellews and the Catholic gentry contributed heavily to his subscription fund and, casting aside their scruples as members of the landed class, joined in the movement 'to separate the tenantries from their landlord'.[4] From the Fosters' point of view, the only consolation was that the popular upsurge so frightened Balfour that, instead of being neutral as he had intended, he threw in his lot with Foster and Fortescue. Unfortunately, this proved an empty advantage, since Balfour's tenants disobeyed him almost to man.[5]

Fortescue, too, was frightened by what was going on. On 17 June, he wrote urgently to Lord Oriel, asking point-blank

[1] Revd. W. H. Foster to Oriel, 14 and 15 June 1826, F.P. D.207/73/136, 151; copy of Dawson's subscription list, Ross MSS., P.R.O.N.I. T.2519/11/2.

[2] J. L. Foster to Oriel, 15 June 1826, F.P. D.207/74/205.

[3] *Copy of Sheil's Speech*, [25] June 1826, F.P. D.562/14691; *Freeman's Journal*, 28 June 1826; *Drogheda Morning Post*, 26 July 1826. I am indebted for this last reference to Mr. Noel Ross.

[4] Revd. W. H. Foster to Oriel, 19 June 1826, F.P. D.207/74/206.

[5] Revd. W. H. Foster to Oriel, 27 June 1826, F.P. D.207/73/65.

for a promise of Oriel's second votes.[1] Oriel was still absent from Louth, but he had been warned already by John Leslie Foster that '. . . the first laws of self-preservation make it absolutely necessary that you should say or write nothing about your second vote until you have had full communication with me in person'.[2] When this communication took place, Foster must have convinced his uncle that he would be lucky if his tenants and dependants used one of their votes according to his directions, and that to demand both would be suicidal. Matthew Fortescue was accordingly told that there would be no junction. On the first day of polling, 24 June, and possibly on the second, 26 June, Foster and he gave each other some assistance. Thereafter, when it had become apparent that Dawson was going to win and that the only contest was for second place, Foster and Fortescue began to throw every possible impediment in each other's way.[3] Only six of Oriel's tenants gave their second votes to Fortescue, and only ten of Lord Roden's gave theirs to Foster.[4] Probably these were men who polled on the first or second day. After that it looks as if Oriel's tenantry were instructed to give their first vote to Foster and sink their second, and Roden's were no doubt told to do the same for Fortescue. This open rupture between the two anti-Emancipationist candidates gave the Dawsonites an opportunity which, fortunately for Foster, they were slow to exploit. The importance of the Foster family's consistent opposition to Emancipation in national politics meant that Foster, not the obscure and unimportant Fortescue, should have been the first object of their attack; not only had Oriel been one of the most distinguished and consistent opponents of all concessions to

---

[1] Matthew Fortescue to Oriel, 17 June 1826, F.P. D.562/14481.

[2] J. L. Foster to Oriel, 15 June 1826, F.P. D.207/74/204.

[3] *Dublin Evening Post*, 29 June 1826; *Drogheda Morning Post*, 26 July 1826.

[4] Statement of how Oriel's tenantry voted, [*c.* July 1826], F.P. D.562/14698; J. L. Foster to Peel, 8 July 1826, Peel MSS., B.L. Add. MS. 40388, fols. 7–10. Foster in this letter claimed that Lord Roden was 'heartily' with him in the election: a statement which does not square with the rest of the evidence. Perhaps Foster was reluctant to admit to Peel the extent of the divisions between the two anti-Emancipationist candidates. If so, this is an example of the danger of relying exclusively on central-government sources. At the next election, in 1830, Roden may in the end have supported the Foster candidate, but at one point in the canvass he seems to have withdrawn his support from him—John McClintock to Anglesey, 30 Apr. 1830, and Anglesey to McClintock, 16 May 1830, Anglesey MSS., P.R.O.N.I. D.619/32L/3, 7.

the Catholics since 1782, but Foster himself was at the present moment the ablest Irish opponent of Emancipation in the House of Commons. On both counts his defeat in Louth would have been a great moral victory for the Catholic cause. However, it was not until the second-last day of the poll that the Dawsonites resorted to the fairly obvious tactic of giving what second votes they had left to Fortescue, in the hope of keeping Foster out. Foster was horrified to learn that they had 'resurrected' fifty such votes,[1] and in fact they seem to have polled about forty. It was nearly sufficient to defeat him. The result of the election was Dawson, 862; Foster, 552; and Fortescue, 547.[2] Foster would certainly have been beaten if the Dawsonites had hit upon this ploy earlier in the poll, or if Roden's Orange leanings had not prevented Fortescue from forming a junction with Dawson.

Special and non-recurrent circumstances contributed to the near-defeat of the Fosters in 1826. There were one or two muddles and misunderstandings, which had the effect of disheartening their supporters.[3] More important, 105 freeholders out of their reduced total of 270 turned out to be improperly registered, and had their votes disallowed on a technicality.[4] As John Leslie Foster put it, 'never was anything more vexatious than to see such great interest compromised by such trifles. . . .'[5] The trifles were eagerly seized on by Oriel, who was too old a man to come to grips with the realities of the situation, as providing the full explanation for his family's near-defeat. He busied himself planning reprisals against such of his tenantry as had gone against him, though it seems that the more extreme of these reprisals were never actually carried into effect.[6] (If they had been, the tenants' losses would have been made

---

[1] J. L. Foster to Oriel, 27 June 1826, F.P. D.207/74/207.

[2] *Saunders News Letter*, 3 July 1826. Sheil had apparently advocated a concentrated effort against J. L. Foster, but Anthony Marmion, who seems to have been the most important local organizer of the Catholic vote, preferred anyone to Fortescue—*Drogheda Morning Post*, 26 July 1826.

[3] W. H. Griffith to Oriel, and Oriel to Griffith, 1, 4, and 5 July 1826, F.P. D.562/5076–8; information sworn by John Campbell of Shamrock Hill, July 1826, F.P. D.562/3934; Revd. W. H. Foster to Oriel, 15 June 1826, F.P. D.207/73/51.

[4] Statement of how Lord Oriel's tenantry voted, [*c.* July 1826], F.P. D.562/14698.

[5] J. L. Foster to Oriel, 28 June 1826, F.P. D.207/74/208.

[6] W. H. Griffith to Oriel, 5 July 1826, F.P. D.562/5078; Oriel to W. P. Greene, 3 Dec. 1826, F.P. T.2519/4/1609.

good by the Catholic Association, as were the losses actually inflicted on tenants by other vengeful landlords.[1]) Drawing on Foster's expertise as a lawyer, Oriel set about repairing the defects in his registries, and in particular about producing a new and unexceptionable form of freeholder's affidavit which would obviate for the future the 'distressing casualties'[2] of the 1826 election. In addition to this, he resorted to the characteristic tactic of the Fosters, which had served them well in the decade 1761–71, and began a prosecution against two Catholic landowners called Chester, who had apparently forgotten their duty as magistrates in their anxiety for Dawson's success. He also collected evidence for a petition against Dawson's return, but never actually presented one.[3]

His advanced age and understandable inability to draw the correct conclusions from the 1826 election meant that the effective political headship of the Foster family devolved from then onwards on John Leslie Foster. The actual headship devolved, of course, on Lord Ferrard when Oriel died in September 1828; however, just as the nature and basis of Oriel's political influence in Louth cannot be understood except by reference to events prior to his first return for the county in 1768, neither can they be understood except by reference to events after the effective and the actual headship of the family had passed from him. John Leslie Foster, though he exerted himself to make sure that the trifles which had compromised the Foster interest at the 1826 election should not recur, was too astute a man to regard them as anything more than a contributory factor to his near-defeat. To his friend, Peel, the Home Secretary, he foretold an Emancipation-ist landslide at the next general election in Ireland, unless the monetary qualification for the freehold franchise was at once raised from 40/– to £20; and if it became necessary to grant Emancipation, he went on, sixty Irish constituencies would return Roman Catholics on the present franchise, and Louth would return Sheil if he cared to stand there.[4] Peel was not so

---

[1] [Anon.], *The Book of Dundalk* (1946), p. 17.

[2] J. L. Foster to Oriel, 27 June and 9 Aug. 1826, F.P. D.207/74/207, 218.

[3] Foster to Oriel, 8 July 1826, F.P. D.207/74/212; note by Oriel of the evidence showing that the son of Dawson's agent carried a flag, [*c*. July 1826], F.P. D.562/14694.

[4] Foster to Peel, 6 Nov. 1826, Peel MSS., B.L. Add. MS. 40389, fol. 266.

pessimistic. He was '. . . not at all clear that the late triumph
of the priesthood will be a lasting one, or will add to their
permanent influence...'; and he still pinned faith on the ability
of the Protestant landlords to remedy the situation by refusing
to renew the freehold leases of their Catholic tenantry when the
present ones expired.[1] In reply Foster pointed out that this was
too long-term a cure for a pressing and immediate ill. In any
case, he did not accept that it was a cure at all; how was it
ever going to be possible for the Protestant landlords to find a
large enough number of trustworthy tenants to out-vote the
Catholic 40/– freeholders of the Catholic landlords? The only
solution in Foster's eyes was to wipe out the 40/– freehold
franchise altogether; nor would it be any good raising the
qualification to only £5 or £10, since this measure would be
counteracted by the allegedly notorious perjury of the lower
orders of the Catholics; a £20 freehold franchise was the
lowest which could safely be adopted. Drastic though this
increase was, it is significant that Foster did not include Louth
among the counties in which it would produce 'a decided
majority' of Protestant voters; there would be a majority,
but not a 'decided' one.[2]

The reason for his pessimism where Louth was concerned
was that, at the 1826 election, 'the Radical, Catholic interest'
had been much more seriously under potential strength than
the Fosters had been. The Catholics' great weakness had
been lack of organization. They had had no candidate until
ten days before the poll began, and their intervention in the
election had largely been inspired from the bottom upwards
instead of from the top downwards. Apart from the last-
minute assistance of the Catholic Association and a last-
minute circular letter from the Catholic Primate, Dr. Curtis,
the revolt of the Louth freeholders had been engineered by the
rank-and-file themselves and by their clerical counterparts, the
parish priests. The Catholic gentry had played no part in
the movement, and only joined it belatedly to save themselves
from complete discredit among their co-religionists. In fact,
it was not until 1831 that the Bellew family regained the position
of authority which they had lost as a result of their faint-

---

[1] Peel to Foster, 12 Dec. 1828, ibid. 40397, fols. 372–6.
[2] Foster to Peel, 16 Dec. 1828, ibid. fols. 384–94.

heartedness in 1826. This lack of organization from the top contrasts sharply with the high degree of organization and the lengthy preparations which lay behind the spectacular Catholic victory in the co. Waterford election of 1826. This contrast is manifest in the way in which the Louth and Waterford polls were conducted. In Waterford the most striking feature of the election was the sobriety, good order, and discipline of the Catholic freeholders: in Louth, on the other hand, as in most of the other half-dozen constituencies in which the Catholic vote played a decisive role in 1826, the characteristic Irish shortcomings of drunkenness and violence predominated.[1] Foster complained bitterly to Peel of the prevalence of intimidation, and claimed that Oriel's tenantry had been assaulted on their way from the hustings by a mob of a thousand people.[2] This and many other instances of violence and disorder were symptomatic of the spontaneity of the Catholic opposition in Louth. No doubt they raised in Foster's mind the obvious question, if an unorganized Catholic opposition could achieve so much, what could an organized one not achieve at the next election?

He could certainly be sure that at the next general election there would be two Emancipationist candidates in the field. Archbishop Curtis, for one, was convinced that if a second had offered himself at the 1826 election, Foster as well as Fortescue would have been defeated.[3] No doubt he was right. In such circumstances the only hope for the Protestant, landlord cause would have been that either Foster or Fortescue should have stood down in favour of the other: an eventuality which, in view of the strained relations between them, was hardly likely. As it was, the presence of only one Emancipationist candidate meant that the Catholic freeholders could compromise between 'the distress warrant and the Cross'. Most of them showed themselves to be more in awe of the Cross; but even Foster, writing just after the event, when his shock and humiliation were at their height, pointed out that the revolt of the tenants, though almost universal as far as their first votes were concerned, was only 'very general' in the case of their

---

[1] Reynolds, *Catholic Emancipation*, pp. 94 ff.
[2] Foster to Peel, 8 July 1826, Peel MSS., B.L. Add. MS. 40388, fols. 7–10.
[3] Reynolds, *Catholic Emancipation*, p. 98.

second.[1] This distinction, fine though it was, between first and second votes was the life-line of the Protestant, landlord interest in Louth. It was almost certain that it would be severed as soon as the Catholic freeholders had something more constructive to do with their second votes than sink them or pour them into the scale of the less objectionable of two anti-Emancipationist candidates. Another thing which was almost certain to happen at the next election was a much bigger turn-out of Catholic voters. While actual polls were always lower than the registered electorate in any county, the Louth poll of 930 in 1826 on a registered electorate of at least 2,800 was very low indeed. Presumably, many voters had avoided the sudden choice between the distress warrant and the Cross by staying away. The choice would not be sudden next time, and the propaganda of the Catholic Association would have ample opportunity to take effect. Protestant landlords might now be chary of registering Catholic freeholders, but the Association would provide the Catholic freeholders with the financial means and the legal know-how to enable them to register themselves. Significantly, no less than 170 40/- freeholders registered or re-registered themselves just after the election, in September 1826, all under the controversial section of the 1820 Election Act simplifying the procedure for freeholders who claimed to own their freehold outright or to lease it in perpetuity. By the end of 1828, the registered electorate had once again risen markedly, to 3,500. The Foster estate's share of the electorate had risen also, from 270 to 360.[2] But granted a heavy poll and good organization on the Emancipationist side, this would make no difference to the Fosters' chances.

In fact, a direct confrontation on the hustings never took place. This was, firstly, because by the beginning of 1827 even Oriel had become convinced of the need to concede Emancipation;[3] secondly, because by the middle of 1828 Foster had decided that it would be futile for him to contest the seat again, and so, when the next general election took place, in 1830, stood down in favour of his kinsman by marriage, John McClin-

---

[1] Foster to Peel, 8 July 1826, Peel MSS., B.L. Add. MS. 40388, fols. 7–10.
[2] *Louth freeholders, Jan. 1826–Jan. 1827*, P.R.O.N.I. T.2519/14/6; Foster to Peel, 16 Dec. 1828, Peel MSS., B.L. Add. MS. 40397, fols. 384–94.
[3] F. T. Foster to Oriel, 20 Feb. 1827, F.P. D.207/73/199.

tock of Drumcar;[1] and thirdly, because by the time of the
1830 general election the Catholic cohorts had been decimated
by the raising of the qualification for the franchise from 40/–
to £10. This measure of disfranchisement was the sequel to
the concession of Emancipation in April 1829 and was the
sting in its tail. It went into immediate operation,[2] and in Louth
its effect was dramatic. In 1830 only 894 voters went to the
polls[3] as compared with the 3,500 registered voters of 1828
(the effect is of course less dramatic if the comparison lies
between the 894 of 1830 and the 930 of 1826). At first Foster,
sounding an uncharacteristic note of optimism, was hopeful
that the raising of the qualification would produce a favourable
change in the composition of the electorate. To Peel, he reported
that in Louth £10 freeholders who had been induced by their
priests to register under the new Act, were giving secret
assurances of support to their landlords, and this phenomenon
he believed was general except perhaps in Clare.[4] Even as
late as 1832, during the discussion of the terms of the Reform
Bill, he retained his belief in the fundamentally good disposition
of tenants towards their landlords, and was of opinion that a
secret ballot 'would certainly give great protection in Ireland to
tenants and assistance to the interest of landlords'.[5] Perhaps
he was deceived by the fact that his own family had always
been exceptionally good landlords, and were in consequence
blessed with an exceptionally faithful tenantry. The experience
of 1826 had proved this, in spite of Oriel's assertions to the
contrary: of 165 tenants whose votes had not been disallowed,
139 had cast one of them for Foster, and 109 of these had sunk
their second. It is most unlikely that any other Protestant-
owned estate in Louth could have boasted a similar record of
fidelity. Certainly, the 1830 election demonstrated that the £10
freeholders of the county as a whole were even less amenable
to landlord control than their 40/– predecessors had been. As
things turned out, Foster's original prediction that a £10
qualification would be too low, proved to be correct.

On paper, however, the result of the 1830 election was much

---

[1] Augustus Foster to Lord Ferrard, 9 July 1828, F.P. D.562/3378.
[2] 10 Geo. IV, c. 8, s. 2.   [3] *Saunders News Letter*, 12 Aug. 1830.
[4] Foster to Peel, 12 Sept. 1829, Peel MSS., B.L. Add. MS. 40399, fol. 328.
[5] Foster to Ferrard, 30 May 1832, F.P. T.2519/4/2140.

the same as that of the 1826. Once again the representation of the county was divided between the Protestant, landlord interest on the one hand and 'the Radical, Catholic interest' on the other; and once again Alexander Dawson headed the poll. His opponent, John McClintock of Drumcar, was particularly unpopular among the Catholics because he was a proselytizer,[1] but in fact he fared better than Foster had done in 1826, coming second by the narrow margin of only thirty-eight votes. The reason for his comparative success was however that 'the Radical, Catholic interest', which had been merely unorganized in 1826, was in 1830 divided against itself. Instead of two 'Radical' candidates, three appeared. Dawson's claim to a seat, after his triumph in 1826, was incontestable. But Sheil, who had acquired a considerable personal following during that election campaign, was also ambitious to represent Louth; and so too was Sir Edward Bellew's younger son, Richard Montesquieu Bellew, who felt that his family's sizeable estate and ancient standing in the county entitled them to a seat now that the political disabilities of the Catholics no longer barred them from it. Since neither Sheil nor Bellew would withdraw, the Catholic vote was split. Sheil accused Bellew of stabbing him in the back, and his partisans attempted to burn Bellew in effigy. The result was broken heads all round. The 1830 election was once more a scene of bloodshed and violence, not only on account of the conflict between the Sheil and Bellew factions, but also on account of the more traditional conflict along religious lines. One Protestant landlord, whose family were time-honoured supporters of the Foster interest, was nearly killed in an affray, and two troops of hussars were required to keep the peace throughout the duration of the poll. When it was over, neither McClintock nor his backers could derive much satisfaction from the result. McClintock had come second by only a small margin; but the combined votes cast for Sheil and Bellew, who came third and fourth respectively, easily outnumbered those cast for McClintock.[2] His success was therefore to be attributed, not to his own strength, but to the disunion of his opponents.

---

[1] *Dublin Evening Post*, 29 June 1826.
[2] *Saunders News Letter*, 12 Aug. 1830; Edward Lucas to Henry R. Westenra, 4 May [1830], Rossmore MSS., Rossmore Park, Monaghan, 4/27.

This was made clear by the events of the next general election, which took place soon afterwards, in May 1831. On this occasion it seemed once again that the Catholic vote might be split. But at the last minute, one of the three 'Radical' candidates, Sir Patrick Bellew, the son and successor of Sir Edward, announced that for the sake of the cause of parliamentary reform he was going to withdraw from the election. This announcement dashed the hopes of the landlord interest's only candidate, who also withdrew, leaving the two remaining 'Radicals' to be returned unopposed.[1] Thereafter, unanimity prevailed in the 'Radical' ranks. When Dawson died later in 1831, Sir Patrick Bellew, his prestige re-established by his high-minded withdrawal at the general election, was elected in his place. At the next general election, that of 1832, Sheil bowed himself out of Louth and stood instead (successfully) for Tipperary. The Bellews now reigned supreme. Sir Patrick seems to have been cautious and Whiggish in his politics: in 1828, for example, he had sighed for a raising of the qualification so that the Catholic gentry would be rescued from Catholic demagogues like Sheil.[2] However, his brother, Richard Bellew, was a member of O'Connell's Repeal party; and this undoubtedly saved the Bellew family from being out-flanked by candidates more 'Radical' than themselves. At the general election of 1832, when the Repeal issue was uppermost, Richard Bellew rather than Sir Patrick stood for Louth; but Sir Patrick joined his brother in the representation of the county at a by-election in December 1834. At the general election of 1835, the Fosters made a last effort to recapture a seat for Louth by setting up Lord Ferrard's second son, who stood as a Tory.[3] The attempt was unsuccessful, and the expense of it contributed to a crisis in the family finances which was severe even by Foster standards. For many years after 1835, even if they had had any hope of success, they would not have had the financial resources to stand another contest.[4]

Viewed from a distance, the Foster interest in Louth looks like a great monolith, suddenly toppled (or nearly so) in 1826:

[1] *Dublin Evening Post*, 19 and 21 May 1831.
[2] Augustus Foster to Lord Ferrard, 9 July 1828, F.P. D.562/3378.
[3] Brief in Lord Massereene *v.* Lord Ferrard, 1838, F.P. D.1739/3/15; *The Book of Dundalk*, p. 17.
[4] Brief in Lord Massereene *v.* Lord Ferrard, 1838, F.P. D.1739/3/15.

viewed from close up, variations in its strength and in the basis of its strength, can easily be discerned over the whole period of its existence. The one virtual constant is that issues in national politics were never allowed to upset the alliance between the Fosters and their county partners. These issues were important from the earliest days of the Foster interest— probably decisive in 1755, and at least significant in 1767. But 'the old interests' were always either on the same side of them or else agreed to differ. The only, unimportant exceptions were Lord Clanbrassill's brief flirtation with the Volunteers in 1780–1, and the Clermonts' brief flirtations with the Catholics in the early to mid-1790s and, more seriously, in 1819. However, the second and more serious flirtation of the Clermonts derived from an existing breach in the old interests, which in turn derived from an eighteenth-century style dispute over patronage; and what is surprising is that the Clermonts did no more than flirt. By 1820 there existed in eighteen of the twenty-three counties outside Ulster distinct 'Catholic interests' who gave their support to the candidate or candidates who promised to vote for Emancipation; and in that year forty-five of the fifty-two M.P.s who represented constituencies, including borough constituencies, where Catholic interests existed, did in fact vote for Emancipation.[1] Since Louth was a predominantly Catholic constituency, and yet apparently had no Catholic interest and certainly no Emancipationist M.P., it was a decided rarity by 1820. The explanation was, presumably, the absence of contests and the fact that no 'timid, ill-judging' candidate had so far played to the Catholic vote, as Foster had recognized since 1795 that candidates would be tempted to do.[2] Lord Roden had been inhibited from so doing by his own anti-Emancipationist views, Lord Clermont by his absenteeism and general loss of contact with the constituency, and the Emancipationists among the old independent interest by their respect, either for John Foster personally, or for the combined strength of Foster's and Roden's registries.

---

[1] Jupp, 'Parliamentary Representation', p. 40; Jupp, 'Irish Parliamentary Elections and the Influence of the Catholic Vote, 1801–20', *Historical Journal*, x (1967), 194.
[2] Foster to Sheffield, 26 Mar. 1795, *Anglo-Irish Dialogue*, p. 13.

However, it was a mutual determination to stick to eighteenth-century style politics, not the community of their sentiments on Emancipation, which really held Foster and the Rodens together. After all, they had held together after the Union, in spite of the fact that Foster had been on one side of the issue, and the Rodens and Clermont on the other; had an election been held during the crisis, it is hard to imagine Foster preferring Balfour, who was a diehard anti-Unionist, to the lukewarm anti-Unionist, Fortescue. Interestingly, at a co. Roscommon by-election in May 1799, the successful canvass of the Mahon family of Strokestown was conducted without reference to the Union, and only three out of some ninety replies adverted to it: one made the assumption that Thomas Mahon would vote for the Union and the other two the assumption that he would vote against it.[1] As the Hon. H. R. Westenra observed in 1824, apropos of his family's alliance with Lord Cremorne in co. Monaghan, 'general politics had nothing to do with our engagement: county politics had'.[2] The county engagement was under strain in Monaghan in 1824 because Cremorne was an Emancipationist and Westenra was still undecided. In Louth, it came under strain in 1825, when it became clear that Foster and Roden had to widen the basis of their alliance; and it broke in 1826, when it became clear that two anti-Emancipationists, indeed two landlord candidates, had no hope of being returned. Once that stage had been reached, community of sentiment on Emancipation proved to be no bond between the old interests, and Foster and Roden each concentrated on getting his own man returned. The old interests held together because, and for as long as, they could carry both seats.

The eighteenth-century ring of H. R. Westenra's remark is

[1] Francis Blake to Maurice Mahon, 19 Apr. 1799, Ross Mahon to Mahon, 8 May 1799, and Edmond Kelly to Mahon, 18 May 1799, Pakenham-Mahon MSS., N.L.I. MS. 10087/2, 5, 7. Another reply was a marvel of perhaps deliberate ambiguity: '. . . I am extremely happy to have had an opportunity of showing my respect for a family whose character, property, and residence in the country [*sic*] give them so good a claim for the support of the County of Roscommon. At such a crisis as this, it is the peculiar duty of every man to send men of integrity and independence into Parliament, and I am confident the County will find its expectations fulfilled in a representative of the House of Strokestown. . . .'—John Geoghegan to Mahon, 18 May 1799, MS. 10087/7.
[2] Westenra to his father, Lord Rossmore, 31 Oct. 1824, Rossmore MSS., 3/87.

deceptive; among Ascendancy families, the Westenras were the supreme political opportunists of early- to mid-nineteenth-century Ireland, and are the best example of a Protestant proprietary interest which, having supported Emancipation and reform, succeeded in riding the ensuing whirlwind. Monaghan was a very different county from Louth. The religious balance within the Monaghan electorate was fairly even, and Westenra wanted to keep his options open on the Emancipation issue for as long as possible, and if possible until the fate of the 40/- freehold franchise had been decided.[1] This form of constituency-inspired trimming on the issue was unusual and derived from the unusual circumstances of Monaghan: the usual form was playing to the Catholic vote. Foster was not alone in denouncing this pernicious practice. In 1812, the anti-Emancipationist Lord Lieutenant, Richmond, asserted that, but for the 1793 Act, there would not be six Irish M.P.s who supported Emancipation, and that there were not three who sincerely wanted to see Catholics sitting in Parliament.[2] In Louth, no electoral advantage was to be gained from playing to the Protestant vote (as, for example, Foster's anti-Emancipationist nephew, John Maxwell Barry, did in Cavan[3])—quite the reverse; and Foster's anti-Emancipationist principles precluded him from playing to the Catholic vote. It may well also have been a principle with him not to play to any vote and, as far as possible, to keep politics out of elections. This question cannot be resolved, because of the absence of contests and even

[1] Westenra to Rossmore, 5 Apr. 1823, Rossmore MSS., 3/27. Westenra's extremely uninhibited (and extremely long) letters to his father give a vivid impression of the effortlessness with which, in his case, eighteenth-century style politics merged into party, or at any rate partisan, politics during the 1820s and early 1830s. An earlier example of an M.P. for a county with a 'mixed' electorate, and of an attempt to keep options open, is Charles O'Hara, M.P. for co. Sligo, in the period 1807–10 (and possibly for longer). O'Hara was an anti-Emancipationist Whig, so party loyalty as well as electoral trimming influenced his ambiguous conduct. See O'Hara to his son, 27 May and 1 June 1807, O'Hara to a local Catholic, J. Everard, 16 Oct. 1810, and O'Hara to George Ponsonby ('not sent'), [early 1810?], O'Hara MSS., N.L.I.

[2] Jupp, *Influence of the Catholic Vote*, p. 193. For a vigorous attack on insincere Emancipationists and defence of anti-Emancipationist paternalists, see Jeremiah Fitz-Henry to Viscount Stopford, 27 Sept. 1824, Courtown MSS., Marlfield, Courtown, co. Wexford. See also pp. 342 ff.

[3] Michael Babington to Henry Maxwell, 2 Sept. 1825, William Gibson to Maxwell, 13 June 1826, and William Graham to Maxwell, 15 June 1826, Farnham MSS., N.L.I., unsorted section.

of election addresses in Louth, particularly during the period when Foster was politically popular among his constituents and would have been tempted to make capital out of that popularity. It may be significant that at the general election of 1830 the Foster candidate, John McClintock, struck a purely paternalist note in his canvassing letters: he pointed out that neither Sheil nor Richard Bellew possessed 'any property or even a residence in the county of Louth', while he was 'a constant resident in the county . . ., where my ancestors had [*sic*] been long established.'[1] In the circumstances of 1830, the words have a hollow and ironical ring (although they may perhaps have been tailored to suit the recipient of the letter, the Emancipationist ex-Lord Lieutenant, Lord Anglesey, who not surprisingly supported Sheil). From about this time on, appeals to the residence-record and quality of landlordism of a candidate, carried weight mainly in the rarefied sphere of elections to the Irish Representative Peerage.

It is easy to dismiss Foster's paternalist politics as 'old style' or even as 'old hat'. But in the period 1826–32, there was no 'new' alternative for an anti-Emancipationist and anti-reform proprietary interest in a 'Radical, Catholic' county like Louth. Even if Foster had been prepared to play to the Catholic vote, he would probably have gone the way of Vesey FitzGerald in Clare in 1828 or of Maurice FitzGerald, Knight of Kerry, in Kerry in 1831. With the passing of the Irish Reform Act in 1832, the day of landlord M.P.s was far from done,[2] partly because of the difficulty of finding sufficiently affluent candidates for the counties who came from any other background, and partly because the heterogeneous social composition of the new electorate circumscribed the impact of 'popular' electoral politics.[3] Indeed, some of the old proprietary interests were to show remarkable resilience in resisting the assaults of Repeal and later those of tenant right. However, this could not have been foreseen during the apparent cataclysm of Foster's last years. Nor does it mean that the idioms of politics remained

[1] McClintock to Anglesey, 30 Apr. 1830, and Anglesey to McClintock, 3 May 1830, Anglesey MSS., P.R.O.N.I. D.619/32L/3, 4.

[2] B. M. Walker, 'Irish Parliamentary Election Results, 1801–1922' (volume at present in draft, to be published as an ancillary to the *New History of Ireland*).

[3] K. T. Hoppen, 'Politics, the Law, and the Nature of the Irish Electorate, 1832–1850', *E.H.R.*, xcii (1977), pp. 746 ff.

unchanged (although it does mean that the changes were complex and subtle and uneven in their impact). Outside Ulster, the landlord M.P.s of the post-1832 era were often not representatives of the old proprietary interests, and often were small landlords by pre-1832 standards. Even in Ulster, the political survival of certain of the old proprietary interests, one or two of them almost down to the present day, should not be taken as proof of an unchanged style of politics.[1] After 1832, all over Ireland, the proprietary strength of the landlord candidates still counted to a surprising degree. It had never been alone decisive of electoral success: the great difference after 1832 was that it sank to merely co-equal importance with skilful navigation of the political issues.

[1] At the co. Tyrone by-election of 1873, when Capt. the Hon. Henry Lowry Corry was elected *vice* his late uncle, the Rt. Hon. H. T. Lowry Corry, the Conservative Chief Whip thought that 'the family name in part carried the election . . .' But the decisive factor was the family's record as landlords who respected tenant right, and the skill with which they handled tenant right as an election issue. The opposition had so little respect for the family name that they penned the unkind verse:

> Then, vote for Corry be the word;
> His uncle was your member.
> His other claims, upon my word,
> I cannot well remember.

See Col. Thomas Taylor to Earl Belmore, [*c.* 11 Apr. 1873], and anti-Belmore election poem, [Feb.–Apr. 1873], Belmore MSS., P.R.O.N.I. D.3007/P/118, 128.

CHAPTER FOUR

'The Speaker's Town of Drogheda'
1796–1812

PRIOR to his intervention in the politics of Drogheda in 1796, Foster's only experience of borough electioneering derived from sleepy Dunleer, an extreme form of pocket borough, where the few electors were all his relations or friends.[1] Drogheda was a far cry from Dunleer. Its dominant features were venality, a plethora of competing political interests, and unpredictable election results. Nevertheless, Foster's political approach to Drogheda was characteristically old-style and paternalist. In contrast to the situation in co. Louth, the Emancipation issue was extremely important in Drogheda elections, certainly by 1807; but in the general election of that year, when Thomas Foster was the successful candidate, the Foster canvass scrupulously avoided the 'no Popery' cry, in spite of the fact that 'no Popery' was such a vote-spinner in this election that Thomas Foster's opponent was equally scrupulous in avoiding an avowal of his Emancipationist sentiments.[2] Many—perhaps most—people who voted for Thomas Foster did so because he was an anti-Emancipationist, and vice versa for his opponent; but each candidate concentrated on trying to obtain support from those with whom he differed on this issue, instead of overtly soliciting the support of those with whom he agreed. Thomas Foster's pretensions to represent Drogheda were left implicit, and were largely paternalist: in effect, that he was his father's son; that his father had been the hero of the Union crisis; that he was now a prominent man in the Government, and particularly influential on the linen board; that he was a well-known and justly esteemed local resident; and that Thomas Foster himself was Colonel of the Louth Militia, in which the Drogheda was incorporated,[3] and along with his father was Joint Governor of co. Louth.

[1] See p. 289.   [2] See pp. 176, 188.   [3] See p. 254, n. 3.

The Fosters' interest in Drogheda was of a personal kind, not just because the Fosters declined to give prominence to the one political issue which mattered; their interest was necessarily personal because, in contrast to their interest in Louth, it had no real or territorial basis. Jobs and hard cash were powerful factors in the Fosters' interest in Drogheda— and not just jobs and hard cash for individuals, but the Fosters' ability or presumed ability to obtain parliamentary grants for the Boyne Canal or Drogheda harbour, and to obtain concessions from the linen board on behalf of the Drogheda linen market. However, real political estate in the form of freeholders was largely absent. John Foster owned a couple of houses in the town (which were in any case let in perpetuity) and a small tract of land called Manimore, capable of being stocked with a handful of freeholders.[1] However, many other families had a much greater territorial stake in the 3,500-odd acres comprising the county borough of Drogheda.[2] Besides, political interest in such a constituency did not necessarily derive from ownership of land; the Hely-Hutchinson family, for example, who enjoyed a long-lived ascendancy in Cork City, seem to have owned no land there, and lived miles away, at Knocklofty, near Clonmel, co. Tipperary. Instead, political interest derived from membership of, and influence in, the corporation. The seven county boroughs (Cork and Drogheda included) possessed a composite franchise of freeholders and freemen, the former by and large resident, the latter resident in theory but in practice often not. The corporation had some indirect influence over the freeholders, but its strength lay in its influence, amounting almost to control, over the composition and size of the freeman body, which if necessary it could swell to such an extent that the votes of the freeholders became irrelevant. To this extent the territorial element in Drogheda politics was subordinate to the personal, and any influence in the constituency was primarily personal in character. But Foster's was a personal influence of the most tenuous kind, since neither he nor his son, Thomas, was a member of the corporation. The main basis for his

[1] Statement of Lord Ferrard's title to his unsettled estates, [c. 1836], Kirk MSS., P.R.O.N.I. D.2121/7/33.

[2] *Municipal Corporations (Ireland); Appendix to the First Report of the Commissioners (part ii)*, [28], H.C., 1835, 805. 1835 [28], xxviii. 805.

influence was therefore his position in national politics: his personal and political popularity among many of the electors which, in the case of Drogheda though not of Louth, was virtually indistinguishable from the real estate factor of the patronage he could command.

No one knew better than Foster the limitations and drawbacks of this precarious kind of interest in a constituency. Because he knew them so well, he declined in 1797 (ironically the year after he became politically active in Drogheda) an invitation to stand for Dublin City, where any interest he could have established would have been more precarious still. Years later, in 1820, he explained the grounds of his decision to his nephew, John Leslie Foster, who had just received the same invitation from the city fathers of Dublin:

> . . . I am confident no success could make up the worryings, the expenses and waste of Government favours and eleemosynary law advices which would attend it. When the City and many of the Corporations pressed me by formal Addresses and assurances of no opposition in Lord Camden's time, I declined it; and they went from me to Arthur Wolfe, then Attorney General, and he accepted. Next day, however, he called on me to know why I refused. I told him what I now say to you; but he had embarked, and he afterwards lamented he had not spoken to me in time. Though no contest, it cost him in hard cash lent in small sums £2,000, and much more all the time he sat for it. His house was ever filled with hungry visitors, and he never ceased to applaud my foresight and lament his own indiscretion . . .[1]

In view of these remarks, it may at first sight seem strange that Foster should have allowed himself to be sucked into the politics of Drogheda at the very time he was steering well clear of the politics of Dublin City. However, there were important differences between the two. As a local man whose seat was only seven miles from the town, Foster could claim to have some natural connection with Drogheda, the more so as he had been presented with its freedom in a gold box in 1786.[2] Again, it was consistent with the political tradition of Drogheda that local landowners should play a part in its affairs; several

---

[1] Foster to J. L. Foster, 7 May 1820, F.P. D.562/4043.
[2] *Belfast Evening News*, 24 July 1786. I am indebted for this reference to Mr. S. C. McMenamin.

such landowners were members of the corporation (though, admittedly, some of them belonged to families who had formerly been merchants in the town), and in the years after 1796 Foster was not the only local landowner to concern himself with Drogheda politics—the 1st Earl Conyngham, who lived at nearby Slane Castle, and Blayney Balfour, whose seat, Townley Hall, was also nearby, were active in the same direction.[1] Besides, in view of the overlap which existed between the electorates of Louth and Drogheda,[2] Foster already had some sort of interest in the latter, and could hope to be able to build it up with a greater economy of government patronage than would have been possible for anyone else. In any case, at the start of his political association with Drogheda, he was not even trying to build up an interest in the constituency for himself: rather, he was throwing the weight of his prestige and patronage into the scale of one of the existing interests in the corporation, his old friend and confidant in commercial matters, Edward Hardman. It was only in the years after the Union, when he wanted the Drogheda seat to re-establish the electoral strength he had enjoyed in the old Irish Parliament and to enhance his consequence in national politics, that he tried to win it, and succeeded in winning it, for a member of his own family.

In 1796 Drogheda, with a population of about 15,000, was roughly the fifth-largest town in Ireland.[3] It was also, by Irish standards, exceptionally industrialized, the main industry being linen. The importance of linen in the economy of Drogheda, and the importance of Foster on the linen board, were very significant elements in his subsequent influence in the constituency. In the period 1785–1808 Drogheda was enjoying a boom in prosperity, one of the effects of which was to make its corporation increasingly unrepresentative of its merchant

[1] For one instance of Conyngham's activities, see Cornwallis to Portland, 22 Oct. 1799, *Cornwallis Correspondence*, iii. 140. Conyngham had been Colonel of the Drogheda Militia before it was amalgamated with the Louth.

[2] See pp. 189 f.

[3] Unless otherwise attributed, the information in this paragraph is drawn from J. Fitzgerald, 'The Organisation of the Drogheda Economy, 1780–1820', U.C.D. M.A. thesis, 1974, *passim*. I am extremely grateful to Mr. Fitzgerald for making available to me one of his own copies of the thesis. It has led me to modify considerably earlier views I had formed on the Fosters' influence in Drogheda, and of course has helped me to fill in the economic and social background to Drogheda politics.

community. In 1780, its trade had been in the hands of no more than five merchants, including Edward Hardman, all of them Protestant. Thereafter, the number of merchants rose, in spite of fluctuations caused primarily by bankruptcies, and by 1820 there were roughly three times the number of merchants there had been in 1785, and most of them were Catholic. Up to 1793, Catholics were excluded from the corporation and the freeman body by law: after 1793 they continued, with a few exceptions (including, interestingly, the Catholic Bishop of Cork) to be excluded from both by agreement among the Protestant members of the corporation. This gave them an economic as well as a political grievance, since only freemen were exempt from tolls and various other dues, and were eligible to bid for the corporation property as and when it came up for re-letting (several members of the corporation, including Hardman, held leases of corporation property on suspiciously advantageous terms). This economic grievance rankled the more because of the increasing number of Catholics who had the capital as well as the inclination to acquire such leases. From 1813, or before, the Drogheda Catholics began to agitate for admission at least to the freeman body. But still the corporation refused to yield. As late as 1823, Sir Edward Bellew, who was used by the Catholics as a test case because of his unimpeachable respectability and political moderation, was denied admission to the freeman body; and this denial led to a petition to Parliament, presented on behalf of the Catholics of Drogheda by Stephen Lushington, and backed by Newport, Brougham, Althorp, and Lord John Russell.[1]

The corporation of Drogheda was the Assembly, or Common Council, whose members held office for life, and the majority of which was, in effect, self-electing. The Assembly was composed of 24 aldermen (including the mayor), 14 elected representatives of the guilds, two sheriffs, and a fluctuating number of 'sheriffs' peers' (people who had previously filled the office of sheriff); somewhere around 1807 it consisted of 66 members. In practice, however, power was more narrowly based than this, because the 24 aldermen could always out-vote the 14

<hr />

[1] Copy letters from Thomas Brodigan to Lushington and others, Apr. 1824, Aylmer [Brodigan] MSS., N.L.I. Again, I am grateful to Mr. Fitzgerald for drawing my attention to this source.

elected representatives of the guilds, and so ensure that the two men chosen each year to fill the offices of sheriffs were their own nominees; these sheriffs in due course took their place in the Assembly as sheriffs' peers. In addition to their control over the election of sheriffs, the 24 aldermen also had the right to 'cushion' (i.e. suppress) applications for the freedom before they ever reached the main body of the Assembly, which in theory was responsible for accepting or rejecting all such applications.[1] In 1770, a decision of the Irish Court of King's Bench that anyone qualified by birth or service for the freedom of Drogheda could not be denied the right by the Assembly, somewhat contracted the aldermen's power. However, they counter-attacked in the course of the 1770s and 1780s by repealing corporation by-laws which on the one hand had forbidden freemen to be non-resident and on the other had obliged all Protestant traders in the town to take out their freedom at no cost to the traders concerned.[2] What the collective effect of these conflicting developments was, is not clear. In any case, by 1796, when Foster first intervened in the politics of the town, the situation had completely changed. As has been seen, Drogheda, like the seven other county boroughs, had a composite electorate of freemen and freeholders; and since its population was overwhelmingly Catholic (80% to 90%), the great majority of its freeholders were bound to be Catholic too. In the years immediately after the re-enfranchisement of the Catholics in 1793, the corporation's main preoccupation seems to have been to increase the Protestant freemen as a counterpoise to the Catholic freeholders. By about 1796, it appears that nearly every resident Protestant was a freeman, and that there were many non-resident Protestant freemen besides.[3] This juxtapositioning of Protestant freemen and Catholic freeholders was typical of the county boroughs after 1793, with the exception of Carrickfergus, the only county borough in predominantly Protestant Ulster.

Narrowly based though political power in Drogheda was, two or three families never came to dominate it, in the way that

[1] *Municipal Corporations*, App. ii., p. 812; list of the Drogheda corporation, [*c*. 1807], F.P. D.207/24/9; Porrit, *Unreformed House*, ii. 331.

[2] *Commons' Journals* (Ireland), viii. 345 ff.; *Municipal Corporations*, App., ii., p. 814.

[3] Fitzgerald, 'Drogheda Economy', p. 100; election calculations by Edward Hardman, 20 Sept. [1796], F.P. D.207/24/4.

two or three families came to dominate co. Louth. Instead, Drogheda remained an oligarchy, though a fairly venal one. The oligarchical nature of the corporation is clearly illustrated by the findings of the Municipal Corporations Commissioners of 1835 about how two of the most lucrative offices in the corporation's gift had been disposed of years previously. Clearly, there had been a likelihood of deadlock among the leading interests in the corporation over the disposal of these offices, and this had been averted by a dubious arrangement whereby each was given to one aspirant on condition that he paid a stated proportion of the salary to the other.[1] The oligarchical nature of the corporation is also illustrated, though less clearly, by the way in which family interest succeeded family interest in the parliamentary representation of Drogheda, without any one family establishing what could reasonably be called a permanent hold on either seat. Up to 1796, the prominent family interests were the Singletons, the Grahams, the Leighs, and the Meade Ogles. The Singletons' position in the constituency depended very much on the personal prestige of Lord Chief Justice Henry Singleton, M.P. for Drogheda, 1713–40, and only one of them ever sat for it after his death. The Grahams had faded out of the picture by the 1770s due to the loss of their fortune. The Leighs were prominent by the 1720s and paramount by the 1770s, but thereafter they too faded out. The Meade Ogles, who started off in the late 1760s by leaning heavily on the Leighs, their relations, ultimately enjoyed the longest run of all—though not an uninterrupted run—and ceased to represent Drogheda only in 1820.[2] During the 1807 Parliament, when Thomas Foster sat for Drogheda, its parliamentary representation was obviously only an indirect reflection of the balance of power in the corporation, since the Fosters did not have even a foothold in that vital quarter. However, in the eighteenth century also the reflection had probably been indirect. There were perhaps two reasons for this. In the first place, the existence of freeholders meant that there was an element in the parliamentary electorate of Drogheda which was not amenable to the corporation's control, except in the sense that some of the freeholders might be the tenants of individual members of the corporation (the

[1] *Municipal Corporations*, App., ii, pp. 818 f.   [2] Bodkin, *Notes*, p. 190.

corporation's own property, amounting to roughly 1,200 out of the 3,500 acres, was let largely on non-freehold leases[1]). This was not a particularly important factor prior to 1793, as the freeholders prior to then were not numerous. The more important factor was that Drogheda seems to have been an expensive constituency to contest and represent. It had a reputation for venality which, though exaggerated, was not altogether undeserved. One person who exaggerated it was Foster's snobbish and silly niece, the Countess De Salis, who referred in 1822 to the probability that Drogheda would incur 'the disgrace of being a second time bought by an attorney'.[2] This was an exaggeration, because both attorneys in question came from aldermanic families, as did virtually all the M.P.s for Drogheda from 1700 to 1830—with the exception of her cousin, Thomas Foster. All the same, with its comparatively large electorate of roughly 500 in 1800, virtually none of it tenurially dependent on the candidates, it is not surprising that Drogheda should have been an expensive constituency, and that the expense should have deterred several aldermanic families from attempting to represent it, and opened the door to others who were not among the foremost interests in the corporation. A case in point was the Forbes family, one of whom, John Forbes, sat for Drogheda from 1783 to 1796.

The most important thing about Forbes was that he was an excellent candidate, particularly in the political circumstances of 1783.[3] He was an intimate of Grattan's, personally and politically, and a prominent Irish Whig, who had distinguished himself in support of all the popular measures of the late 1770s and early 1780s, and was later to distinguish himself as the promoter of the Irish Place Act of 1793. He was not devoid of family interest in the Drogheda corporation, as his uncle was an alderman.[4] But his successive elections as Recorder in April 1782 and as an alderman in January 1783, seem to have been in recognition of his 'patriotic conduct' in Parliament,

---

[1] *Municipal Corporations*, App., ii, pp. 849 ff. This was the corporation's rural property only; it also owned many houses and tenements. For a discussion of what did and did not constitute a freehold lease, see pp. 282 ff.

[2] Countess De Salis to Lord Oriel, 1 Mar. 1822, F.P. D.562/4621.

[3] Fitzgerald, 'Drogheda Economy', pp. 102 f. For Forbes, see also pp. 396 ff.

[4] Alderman William Forbes to John Forbes, 7 Mar. 1775, Forbes MSS., N.L.I. MS. 978.

for which he had previously received the freedom of the town. His personal attributes were thus more important than his family interest in placing him in the corporation and in securing his election as M.P. for Drogheda at the general election later in 1783. His willingness to spend money was also very important. In 1796, the year of his retirement from the seat, he reckoned that Drogheda had cost him £7,000 (although neither in 1783 nor in 1790 had his return been contested), plus £6,500 lost in forfeited securities and other bad debts, which he implied that he had only involved himself in for electioneering reasons. These figures were probably an exaggeration, since he was trying at the time to adduce his losses in the Whig cause as an entitlement to receive some form of lucrative office.[1] However, the need for expenditure on anything like this scale, combined with his political popularity in Drogheda, would explain why he had not been challenged by one of the more powerful family interests in the corporation, and indeed why the representation of Drogheda had been uncontested during the years 1783–96. Under Forbes's auspices, Drogheda took up an apparently unanimous opposition posture. In July 1785, it petitioned against the amended commercial propositions (which Foster, as Chancellor of the Exchequer, was to second in the House), and in September 1789, well after the Regency crisis, it conferred its freedom on the Prince of Wales '. . . at a time when no other public body in this kingdom could be prevailed on to pay him that tribute of respect. . . .'[2] These political gestures were made under Forbes's auspices, rather than at his instigation; for the popular, opposition politics of Drogheda seem to have been too broadly based to be conjured up by any one individual. They had their effect on even the conservative Hardman, and were espoused by Forbes's successive colleagues in the representation of Drogheda, the Meade Ogles, who were written off by the Castle as independent, inclined to opposition, and attached to Forbes's political Nestor, the Duke of Portland. Although the

[1] Forbes to James Adair, 12 Jan. 1796, Adair MSS., B.L. Add. MS. 53802—unfoliated. I am indebted to Professor R. B. McDowell for drawing the Forbes–Adair letters to my attention.

[2] Forbes to Charlemont, 10 July 1785, *H.M.C. Charlemont MSS.*, ii. 21; Forbes to J. W. Payne, 24 July 1794, printed in A. Aspinall (ed.), *The Correspondence of George Prince of Wales, 1770–1812*, ii (London, 1964), 447.

Meade Ogles occupied a much stronger and more durable position in the corporation oligarchy than Forbes, they were still deemed by the Castle to have been 'returned on [the] popular interest'.[1]

The strength of the 'popular interest' in Drogheda was initially a great obstacle to Foster's designs on the constituency, until of course his opposition to the Union enabled him to cash in on it. In 1796 it probably swung the election against Hardman, the candidate whom he supported. A by-election became necessary in that year because Forbes had at last succeeded in obtaining an office—the governorship of the Bahamas—which under the terms of his own Place Act vacated his seat in Parliament, and which, unfortunately for him, came too late to repair either his shattered health or his shattered finances.[2] In 1796 the unanimity which had characterized Drogheda elections over the preceding period came to an end. This time there were two contestants for the seat, Hardman and a Dublin barrister called John Ball. Ball was a native of Drogheda and had been a freeman since 1786 (the same year as Foster). But he lacked influence in the corporation, and stood on the popular or independent interest (which did not mean the same thing in Drogheda as it did in Louth, though what it meant in Drogheda is not quite clear). Hardman, on the other hand, was one of the leading aldermen of the corporation. His family had never represented Drogheda in Parliament, but his grandfather, father and he had been mayors of the town and had been engaged in trade there for nearly a century. In 1796, Hardman was the wealthiest and most important of the Protestant merchants. It is a good indication of the scale of his commercial activities that in the late 1780s he had been exporting £20,000 worth of grain a year, that the turnover of

[1] Fitzgerald, 'Drogheda Economy', pp. 103 f.; G. O. Sayles (ed.), 'Contemporary Sketches of the Irish House of Commons in 1782', *Proc. R.I.A.*, vol. 56, Sec. C, No. 3 (1954), 245; Johnston, *Irish House of Commons in 1791*, p. 27; list of the Irish Parliament, [mid-January 1788], Buckinghamshire MSS., Buckinghamshire R.O.; photocopies in P.R.O.N.I., ref. T.2627/1/1. Popular, opposition politics must have been a new departure for Drogheda, as one of its recent M.P.s, Francis Leigh, who had represented it from 1741 to 1776, was described as having supported the government on every question for thirty years—Philip Tisdall to Heron, 28 Aug. 1777, Heron MSS., N.L.I. MS. 13035/9.

[2] This slightly waspish comment was made by Dr. Alexander Halliday in a letter to Charlemont of 17 August 1797, Charlemont MSS., R.I.A. 2nd ser., viii. 63.

his wine business (his principal line) was between £3,000 and
£5,000 a year, and that his total gross income from trade over
the period 1779–1809 was £36,000. He also owned, or leased
from the corporation, considerable property in Drogheda.[1]
Although supported by Foster and bound to him by many
ties of obligation and friendship, Hardman was thus a very
strong candidate in his own right. Nevertheless all his political
assets, even when supplemented by Foster's '. . . jobs of all
sorts—Militia jobs, Revenue jobs, road jobs, Yeomanry jobs
. . . proved too weak . . .'[2] The 1796 by-election was won by
John Ball.

Foster and Hardman were not deterred by this reverse, and
began to muster forces for the forthcoming general election. The
decisive alignment, or rather re-alignment, which took place
in the interval between the by-election and the general election
of 1797, and which was presumably the result of their activities,
was a junction of interests between Hardman and his previous
opponent, Ball. A broadsheet hostile to Foster and Hardman,
and obviously anxious to conciliate Ball, endeavoured to
explain away Ball's action on the ground that he had mis-
takenly come to the conclusion that a junction with Hardman was the only way to preserve one seat to 'the independent
interest'. This explanation almost certainly did Ball too much
justice. His weakness as the spearhead of 'the independent
interest' was that he was ambitious for professional advancement. It is therefore no coincidence that, soon after the general
election, in November 1797, Foster is to be found pressing
the Castle to give Ball Chief Baron Anthony Foster's former
office of Counsel to the Revenue Commissioners, and to bear
him in mind as a candidate for promotion to the judicial
bench.[3] The application was not in fact successful, but presumably the price of Ball's junction with Hardman was that Foster
should make it. The effect of the junction was to threaten the
position of the other sitting member, William Meade Ogle.
In any case, Ogle was a friend and kinsman of Hardman, and
later (in 1802) refused to commit himself against him, even

[1] Fitzgerald, 'Drogheda Economy', pp. 48, 52, 74, 81, 93.
[2] *Address to the Electors of Drogheda*, [early 1798], F.P. D.207/24/1.
[3] Entry in the Lord Lieutenant's audience book for 30 Nov. 1797, Pratt MSS.,
K.A.O. U.840/O.129.

though Hardman's opponent on that occasion was Ogle's own son, Henry. In view of this, it is not surprising that Ogle decided not to oppose Hardman in 1797. Instead, the opposition came from another alderman, Ralph Smyth. From 1797 until 1812, indeed until at least 1822, Drogheda politics were to be dominated by the bitter rivalry of two fairly equally balanced factions in the corporation, one the Foster/Hardman faction and the other the Smyth, later the Henry Meade Ogle/Smyth faction.[1] The balance, however, was not nearly so equal in the constituency at large as it was in the corporation. At the 1797 election Smyth, having somehow or other deluded himself into thinking that the Government would support him against Foster's candidate, pressed matters to a poll, and came third. Ball, in spite of the popularity he must have lost through his junction with Hardman, headed the poll, with a majority of 67 over Smyth, and Hardman came second. Smyth then lodged a petition against Hardman's return, and succeeded in getting him unseated on grounds of bribery and undue influence (an embarrassing success from Foster's point of view, as Speaker of the House of Commons). This made a new election necessary. It took place in March 1798, and Hardman again beat Smyth, this time by the convincing majority of 203 to 155.[2]

His declared opposition on the hustings to the very idea of a Union was one element in Hardman's success.[3] Drogheda was vehemently anti-Unionist. Although Lord Cornwallis endeavoured to pass this off later, in 1799, by referring disparagingly to Drogheda as 'the Speaker's town',[4] he was only deceiving himself (and the British Government) as to the spontaneity and unanimity of local feeling against the measure. The fact of the matter was that if Foster had been a supporter of the Union he would have been unable to extract a Unionist address from *his* town of Drogheda. By opposing it, however, he greatly augmented his standing there. The Union crisis

[1] Fitzgerald, 'Drogheda Economy', pp. 107 f.

[2] Smyth to Castlereagh, 10 Jan. 1799, Castlereagh MSS., P.R.O.N.I. D.3030/473; *Address to the Electors of Drogheda*, [early 1798], F.P. D.207/24/1.

[3] Hardman to Castlereagh, 15 Jan. 1799, Castlereagh MSS., P.R.O.N.I. D.3030/512.

[4] Cornwallis to Portland, 22 Oct. 1799, *Cornwallis Correspondence*, iii. 140. This was a common form of myopia; many years earlier, it had been assumed that Drogheda belonged to Henry Singleton (Baron Wainwright to George Dodington, 2 Jan. 1733/4, *H.M.C. Various MSS.*, vi. 57).

provided for the first time a natural basis for the junction between Hardman and Ball, who was a strong anti-Unionist and a brother of the prominent anti-Unionist pamphleteer, Charles Ball. Ball's new-found enthusiasm for Foster was reflected in the fact that he was prominent in the move to get up the subscription for the payment of Foster's debts.[1] The Union crisis further strengthened Foster's and Hardman's position by discrediting their most prominent opponent, Smyth who, in an unlucky moment for himself, was cajoled by the Government into making an unsuccessful attempt to get up a Unionist address from the town.[2]

By the terms of the Act of Union, Drogheda in common with thirty other boroughs was reduced to a single-member constituency. This meant that Hardman and Ball had to decide, either by private agreement or by public ballot, which of them should represent it for the remainder of the current British Parliament. Fortunately for Foster, the decision was in Hardman's favour. Once arrived at Westminster, he showed himself well-disposed to the Addington Administration, and was in consequence rewarded with the lion's share of the patronage of Drogheda. Even when Foster arrived over to take his seat at the beginning of 1802, Hardman continued to vote steadily with the Government, and by his parliamentary conduct gave the impression that he would not follow Foster, should Foster go into decided opposition.[3] Hardman, if not in actual financial difficulties, was beginning at this time to feel the pinch of insufficient capital, and it may be that he was trying to hedge his bets; more probably he was only acting on a plan previously concerted with Foster, the object of which was to secure for Hardman the 'pretty considerable' government influence in Drogheda at the next general election.[4] Abbot, the Chief

[1] John Patrickson to Downshire, 14 Jan. 1799, Downshire MSS., P.R.O.N.I. D.607/G/18. For this subscription, see also pp. 81 f., 326, 386.

[2] Henry Alexander to Castlereagh, 12 Jan. 1799, Castlereagh MSS., P.R.O.N.I. D.3030/496.

[3] Hardman to Wickham, 6 July 1802, Wickham MSS., P.R.O.N.I. T.2627/5/Q/30; Hardwicke to Pelham, 26 May 1802, Hardwicke MSS., B.L. Add. MS. 35772, fol. 19.

[4] Alexander Knox to Marsden, 6 Aug. 1802, S.P.O. 620/62/56; Fitzgerald, 'Drogheda Economy', pp. 70 f.; Marsden to Hardwicke, 3 June 1804, Hardwicke MSS., B.L. Add. MS. 35724, fol. 144; Hardman to Abbot, 13 Nov. 1801, Colchester MSS., P.R.O. 30/9/2/1/4. In Drogheda, there was something identifiable as

Secretary, inclined to this latter interpretation. Consequently, he was put on the spot when Hardman wrote to him in November 1801 asking point-blank for a promise of government support when the election took place. For the moment Abbot was able to fob him off with an evasive reply. But this became increasingly difficult when a rival candidate appeared in the person of Ogle's son, Henry Meade Ogle, who was backed by the Smyth faction in the corporation and by roughly the same people as had supported Smyth in 1798. Like Hardman he, too, asked for the assistance of the Government. In May 1802 a discussion on the subject of Drogheda took place in London among Addington, Abbot, Isaac Corry, and Wickham, the new Chief Secretary. It was then decided (or at least Wickham thought it had been decided) that Hardman's attachment to Foster was 'unquestionable' and that the government interest should therefore be given to Henry Meade Ogle.[1]

The Drogheda election of 1802 is one of the best examples of the shortcomings of central-government sources as a guide to politics at local level. No candidate angling for the support of the government at an election ever understated the support he already possessed in his own right, and Ogle was no exception. Isaac Corry was the only person present at the meeting in May who had expressed doubts about his prospects; as a Newry man, Corry had the advantage of local knowledge, and his suggestion was that the Government should offer to support John Ball, if Ball would agree to stand against Hardman. The other members of the Irish Administration, however, were convinced that Henry Meade Ogle had the 'natural interest' in Drogheda, and that his success was certain if they gave him their support. They failed to appreciate that in an oligarchy like the Drogheda corporation, Ogle's position was very much that of *primus inter pares*, and that there was more to winning Drogheda elections than possessing the natural interest in the corporation. In particular, they failed to recognize that

the government interest because, in the recent past, the Drogheda M.P.s had been in opposition. In co. Louth, by contrast, where all the M.P.s had been government supporters since at least 1761, the government interest was virtually indistinguishable from the Foster interest and, to a lesser extent, from the Clermont and Roden interests.

[1] Hardwicke to Pelham, 26 May 1802, Hardwicke MSS., B.L. Add. MS. 35772, fol. 19.

Hardman, too, had influence in that quarter, when they wrote him off as '. . . the agent and mere creature of Mr. Foster, brought in by him . . . by means of the Government interest . . . [with] no shadow of pretensions but in his connection with Mr. Foster...'[1] This also took no account of Hardman's position in the commercial life of the town, which even if it was no longer as commanding as it had been in 1796, was still a factor to be reckoned with. Certainly, Ogle could not rival him in this respect as the Ogle family had long since abandoned active trading and drew their income (of roughly £3,000 a year) from land and property in Louth and Drogheda.[2] The Castle's misreading of the situation in Drogheda was in fact so glaring that it is probable that it was the result of self-deception, as well as of misinformation—like Cornwallis's exaggeration of the extent of Foster's influence there in 1799. Hardwicke, Abbot, Wickham, and Under-Secretary Marsden were all, to a greater or lesser extent, personally hostile to Foster, and this personal hostility seems to have coloured their views. Nothing else can explain Marsden's remarkable assertion that Ogle's family had been 'always attached to Government':[3] an assertion which the Castle lists of the late eighteenth-century Irish Parliament contradict. In 1802, the Castle seems to have been misled by its own prejudices, as well as by the defective or slanted information on which at the best of times it had to rely.

As a result of the meeting in May 1802, Ogle was told that the government interest in Drogheda would be exerted on his behalf. He was therefore understandably indignant to learn, only four days before the election, that Addington had written to Hardman promising Hardman the government interest.[4] At the same time, or shortly afterwards, the Prime Minister's brother, Hiley Addington, also wrote to Hardman endorsing Addington's sentiments. This news caused the utmost concern in the Castle. But it was too late for the Irish Administration to do anything except re-affirm their support for Ogle and write to Addington regretting the misunderstanding, and pointing out that they were too deeply committed to Ogle

[1] Marsden to Abbot, 18 July 1802, S.P.O. 620/18/18.
[2] Fitzgerald, 'Drogheda Economy', p. 118n.
[3] Marsden to Abbot, 18 July 1802, S.P.O. 620/18/18.
[4] Ogle to Marsden, 16 July 1802, S.P.O. 521/131/8.

to desert him at the eleventh hour. Addington, whose reply cannot have reached Dublin till after the election was over, agreed that under the circumstances they could not have acted otherwise. He stressed, however, that in his own view Hardman's connection with Foster 'cannot be a just or colourable ground for prosecuting him', and was emphatic that Wickham had misunderstood the decision taken at the meeting in May. He also made the unstatesmanlike suggestion that the Irish Administration should let it be known that the objections to Hardman were on Irish grounds alone, and came, not from London, but from the Castle.[1] Clearly, he was more concerned about his personal honour than about the coherence of his Government. The result of this misunderstanding was that the Irish Administration, conscious of the ridicule which would attach to it if Hardman won, strove harder on Ogle's behalf than it otherwise would have done. Marsden ransacked Dublin for Drogheda voters, and tried unsuccessfully to get a patient released from Simpson's Hospital so that he could go to Drogheda and give his vote for Ogle.[2] But gloomy reports kept coming in about the reluctance of 'the Revenue gentry' to support Ogle, and about the advantage which Hardman had derived from Hiley Addington's letter.[3] Two years later Marsden was to recall how '. . . a foolish letter from Hiley Addington produced by Mr. Foster on the hustings overset all our plans and we were laughed at. . . .'[4] This was an exaggeration. In spite of the confusion caused by the letter, the government interest seems to have gone chiefly to Ogle. A Castle list of forty-four Drogheda voters 'connected with Government', reckoned that only ten would support Hardman against the wishes of the Irish Administration. The list is undated; but since it makes an exaggerated estimate of Hardman's strength—two of the ten in the event abstained—the likelihood is that it was compiled after, rather than before, the receipt of Hiley Addington's letter. No doubt Marsden afterwards exaggerated the importance of the letter in order to cover up the fact that the Irish

    [1] Addington to Hardwicke, 22 July 1802, Hardwicke MSS., B.L. Add. MS. 35708, fol. 39; Abbot to Marsden, 22 July 1802, S.P.O. 521/136/2.
    [2] Singleton Harpur to Marsden, 24 July 1802, S.P.O. 521/131/8.
    [3] Major W. Swan to Marsden, 20 and 22 July 1802, S.P.O. 521/131/8.
    [4] Marsden to Hardwicke, 3 June 1804, Hardwicke MSS., B.L. Add. MS. 35724, fol. 144.

Administration had miscalculated the strength of Ogle's influence in the first place. It is true that Hardman would in all probability have been beaten if the government interest had been solidly behind Ogle, since, as things were, he only won by the very narrow margin of five votes.[1] Yet, for all the fuss about it, the split in the government interest was not the decisive factor in the election. The decisive factor, almost certainly, was the rivalry between the Foster/Hardman and Smyth/Ogle factions in the corporation, a rivalry which the events of the Union crisis seem to have intensified. Significantly, Ogle was proposed as a candidate in 1802 by the Unionist Smyth, and Hardman by the anti-Unionist Ball.[2] Perhaps the result would have been different if the Irish Administration had followed Corry's advice and had tried to split the old anti-Unionist axis by offering the government interest to Ball.

Ogle was prevailed upon by his more violent partisans to challenge the result by lodging an election petition. The petition was proceeded on listlessly by both sides, perhaps because the Irish Administration, chastened by the experience of 1802, refused to guarantee its support to either in the event of Hardman's being unseated and a new election taking place. In the end the petition fell down on a technicality early in 1803, and its failure was probably no accident. The likelihood is that Ogle was bought off with a promise that he would be returned unopposed at the next election; which was what happened at the general election of 1806.[3] Unfortunately for Ogle, the 1806 Parliament lasted for only five months, and its dissolution in April 1807 left him with a sense of grievance, and spoiling for a fight. As a result, Drogheda went once again to the polls at the end of May, and was the scene of a contest no less sharp though much less confused than that of 1802. There was this time no question of the government interest being split, since Foster, as Chancellor of the Irish Exchequer in the new Government, had the unqualified disposal of it (it had of

[1] List of Drogheda voters, [July 1802], S.P.O. 521/131/8; John Pollock and William Riddocks to Marsden, 24 July 1802 (ibid.).

[2] *Voters' List for the 1802 Drogheda Election*, F.P. D.207/24/5.

[3] Hardman to Wickham, 7 and 18 Oct. 1802, Wickham MSS., P.R.O.N.I. T.2627/5/Q/74, 80; Messrs. Debary & Cope to Hardman, Jan. 1803, F.P. D.207/24/ 7B; Knox to Marsden, 6 Aug. 1802, S.P.O. 620/62/56; Beresford to Auckland, 12 Aug. 1802, Sneyd MSS., Keele University Library, photocopies in P.R.O.N.I., ref. T.3229/2/72.

course been considerably reduced by the disfranchisement of revenue officers in 1803). Moreover, party alignments and differences of political principle were in 1807 more clear-cut at national level than they had been in 1802, or were to be again for many years, and this inevitably made its mark on the constituencies. Drogheda was no exception to the general rule. Ogle, as its M.P. during the Talents' last months in office, had attached himself to them—perhaps for no better reason than that Foster was in opposition. By the time of the 1807 election he was so closely identified with their political principles that his opponents were able to accuse him of cribbing his election address from the election address of the Talents' candidate for co. Durham.[1] The Talents had been dismissed over a side-issue of the Emancipation question. In these circumstances, it was inevitable that the election of 1807 should give a degree of articulation and direction to the Catholic vote in Drogheda which it had never possessed before, although Foster probably exaggerated this element in the situation when he reported to the Chief Secretary: 'the Catholics are working priests and nuns and every engine', and 'are all in party, which we have broke in upon a little'.[2] No doubt he exaggerated it because he wanted to depict the struggle as one in which the new, 'no Popery' Administration was vitally interested, and not just as a continuation of the old faction-fight within the Drogheda oligarchy.

One other new feature of the 1807 election was that the Foster/Hardman candidate was for the first time a member of the Foster family, Thomas Foster. As Hardman since 1802 had faithfully followed John Foster's lead in national politics—most notably by going over to Pitt in March 1804[3]—there is no reason for thinking that Foster wanted to be rid of him in 1807, and it was probably his own increasing financial difficulties which decided him not to stand. The Fosters were very cautious about setting up Thomas Foster. His candidature seems to have been kept secret, and probably had not been finally decided upon until the very eve of the election.[4] Presumably, they hesitated to obtrude themselves too prominently on a con-

[1] Printed election squib known as 'Ogle's Plagiarism', [late May 1807], F.P. D.207/24/14.

[2] Foster to Wellesley, 24 and 10 May 1807, Apsley House MSS. and F.P. D.207/35/2.   [3] Parl. Debs. i. 927.

[4] Bishop of Meath to Foster, 18 May 1807, F.P. D.207/50/32.

stituency where they were outsiders and where there was no solid, permanent basis for their influence. Certainly, they were worried about whether 'the old interests'[1] on which Hardman had successfully stood, still held together, and in particular about the line which Ball would take in 1807. Ball had been favourably noticed by the Talents and promoted by them to the office of Second Serjeant-at-Law. Now, while denying the existence of any political connection between the Talents and himself, he was anxious for assurances that the new Administration would be equally generous.[2] The Smyth/ Ogle party cleverly directed part of their propaganda at him, and took pains to remind him of the glorious spirit he had displayed in 1796, when he had successfully resisted 'the influence of a great, wholesale parliamentary jobber'.[3] But in spite of this appeal, Ball stood firm, relying on assurances of preferment which John Foster did not live up to.[4] Thomas Foster was accordingly set up on 'the old interests', and beat Ogle by the comfortable margin of 217 to 174.[5] Nonetheless, the contest was stiff and fairly expensive. One man was offered no less than seventy guineas by the Ogle party for a single vote.[6] On their side, the Fosters were involved in at least one egregious job: a promise that John Foster would use his influence as a Governor of the Erasmus Smith Schools to get an influential voter appointed headmaster of the Drogheda school next time the post fell vacant.[7] The election cost Thomas Foster in hard cash £2,441. This included some interesting items, like £17 for ribbons and a chair, £5 13s. 9d. to get one Hugh McVeigh out of gaol, and £12 worth of silver for Thomas Foster to throw to the mob.[8] It also included hypocritical donations to Catholic charities: donations which Thomas Foster made sure were more generous than Ogle's.[9]

[1] Revd. George Lambert to Foster, 28 Apr. 1807, F.P. D.562/12449.

[2] Charles Ball to Foster, 17 Apr. 1807, F.P. D.562/12445.

[3] *Address to the Electors of Drogheda*, 3 May 1807, F.P. D.207/24/10.

[4] Foster to John Ball, 1 Apr. 1807, F.P. D.562/12443.

[5] Jupp, 'Parliamentary Representation', article on Drogheda.

[6] Sir John Macartney to Foster, 27 Aug. 1807, F.P. D.207/73/207.

[7] Revd. George Lambert to Foster, 3 May 1807, F.P. D.562/12450; Foster to Revd. Henry Ashe, 5 Feb. 1811, F.P. D.562/12681.

[8] Thomas Foster's account with George Pentland, [post-May 1807], F.P. T. 2519/4/1888.

[9] Edward Carolan Junior to Thomas Foster, 25 July 1809, F.P. T.2519/4/1926.

Yet this jobbing and expense only secured the seat to Thomas Foster for one Parliament. At first the Fosters hoped that Ogle would at last 'make his bow to Drogheda';[1] but Ogle did no such thing. By February 1811, he had started to canvass the town,[2] and in September he made an attempt to detach Edward Hardman from the Foster ranks by appealing to the close connection which had once subsisted between the Ogles and the Hardmans, and by holding out more concrete, monetary inducements. Hardman, however, was proof against temptation, though resentful that Thomas Foster would come to no decision with regard to his future intentions towards Drogheda. The next general election did not in fact take place until mid-October 1812, but even at the end of September Thomas Foster seems still to have been undecided.[3] At this point one of his supporters in the corporation had an interview with Ogle, from which he gathered that '. . . Ogle feels that the Colonel [Thomas Foster] would beat him, and that the want of money makes even his [Ogle's] trying a contest doubtful. . . .' The more significant feature of the interview was that Ogle in the course of it '. . . offered in case of a resignation [in his favour] to forward his [Thomas Foster's] views in Parliament . . . upon every question but the Catholic . . .'[4] This suggestion Thomas Foster seized upon eagerly, although his father some years later claimed to the Chief Secretary that, if Thomas Foster had stood, there would have been only a nominal opposition.[5] Whether John Foster believed this himself is problematical; probably he was anxious to inflate the strength of his family's influence in Drogheda, so that the Castle would continue (as they did) to entrust to the Fosters the disposal of the government interest there, and to use the Fosters as their main channel of communication with the Drogheda corporation. In any case, Thomas Foster did not stand, and Ogle was accordingly elected on the terms proposed by himself and with the support of the Fosters.

Thomas Foster's tame withdrawal in 1812 is perhaps the

[1] Lambert to Foster, 18 Nov. 1807, F.P. D.562/12529.

[2] Edward Hardman Junior to Foster, 4 Feb. 1811, F.P. D.562/11708.

[3] Hardman Senior to Foster, 1, 2, and 27 Sept. 1811, F.P. D.562/12738, 12740, 12759.

[4] George Pentland to Foster, 28 Sept. 1812, F.P. T. 2519/4/1398.

[5] Foster to Peel, 3 June 1818, Peel MSS., B.L. Add. MS. 40278, fol. 44.

best single illustration of the nature and limitations of the Fosters' influence in Drogheda. His father's retirement had a good deal to do with his decision. This did not mean that the government interest would have been withdrawn from him at the 1812 election: on the contrary, the Government expected him to stand, were highly displeased when he did not, and frowned upon the compromise agreement with Ogle.[1] Even in 1818, after a long period of coolness between the Fosters and the Castle, the Fosters were still assured by Peel, the then Chief Secretary, that the government interest would be disposed of on their recommendation.[2] In 1812, therefore, it was not the loss of the government interest but the loss of John Foster's official patronage, which discouraged Thomas Foster from standing. He knew too well the volume of patronage which was required to keep his Drogheda supporters faithful, and he was not prepared to embark on a contest without his former official resources to support him. His financial resources, too, had diminished since 1807: in 1812 he was no longer a bachelor, had a wife and child to support, and was strictly limited in his borrowing power by the family settlement made on the occasion of his marriage in 1810. This same settlement pegged his income from the Foster estate at only £1,680 a year during his father's lifetime,[3] and although he enjoyed another £1,000 a year as a Lord of the Irish Treasury, he lost this early in 1813. The Drogheda voters, particularly the Protestant freemen, were not accustomed to voting 'on a drink of water',[4] and in these circumstances it is not surprising that he fought shy of election expenditure, particularly since election expenditure on Drogheda was bound to be a continuous process. The Fosters had spent £1,500 on the Louth election of 1768, but this expenditure had secured them an uncontested return for the next fifty-eight years: in Drogheda, with a not-much-smaller electorate, virtually none of it tenants of the Fosters, there was no hope of their being able to achieve a hegemony of anything like this duration.

---

[1] Peel to Lord Liverpool, 27 Oct. 1812, ibid. 40280, fol. 72.

[2] Peel to Foster, 30 May 1818, F.P. D.207/39/27.

[3] J. L. Foster to Thomas Foster, 19 Oct. 1810, F.P. D.562/2237. For the change in the Fosters' financial situation, see pp. 324ff., 333f.

[4] Revd. W. H. Foster to Oriel, 14 and 15 June 1826, F.P. D.207/73/136 and /73/51; *Municipal Corporations*, App., ii. 824.

The plain fact was that between 1807 and 1812 Thomas Foster had been unable to entrench his position in the constituency, or indeed to achieve anything which would have helped to prevent a repetition of the expenses of the 1807 election. In particular, he had failed to get himself elected an alderman, which George Pentland, his leading aldermanic ally, had warned him he must, 'if you are to have a permanent interest in Drogheda'.[1] Election to the aldermanic body was by the aldermen themselves; so Thomas Foster's failure is a good indication of the state of near-deadlock to which the faction-fight had reduced the corporation. Nor was this the only failure to which he was subjected by the Smyth/Ogle faction. In 1808 and again in 1809, he projected a private Act of Parliament to increase the river tolls in Drogheda and divert part of them to the erection of a gaol and a hospital.[2] But his plan was defeated in both years by his opponents, among whom party feeling allegedly ran so high that they 'would refuse a boon from Heaven if it was offered by the hands or at the instance of Colonel Foster'.[3] Thomas Foster was not by nature or inclination a politician, nor was he the sort of man who could patiently endure the crosses which had to be carried by the M.P. for a noisy, venal, and troublesome constituency like Drogheda. This unsuitability of temperament was of importance in dictating his conduct, and helps to explain Hardman's reference in September 1811 to '. . . the very general opinion . . . which had gone forth that he had relinquished all ideas of representing the town in future, founded upon the little intercourse he had had with it or with the people for a considerable length of time. . . .'[4]

Without a working majority in the corporation, the Fosters were bound to remain 'a foreign influence'[5] in Drogheda, liable to never-ending election expenditure. In fact, their foreignness was a point of decreasing significance. The fear that 'Collon will become the tyrant of Drogheda'[6] had been employed to considerable propagandist effect in the elections of

[1] Pentland to Thomas Foster, 21 Apr. and 9 May 1809, F.P. T.2519/4/1918–9.
[2] Thomas Foster to George McEntagart, 21 Apr. 1809, F.P. D.562/4604.
[3] McEntagart to Thomas Foster, 17 Apr. 1809, F.P. D.562/4602.
[4] Hardman to Foster, 1 Sept. 1811, F.P. D.562/12738.
[5] Address to the Electors of Drogheda, Sept. 1816, F.P. D.562/4614.
[6] Address to the Electors of Drogheda, [early 1798], F.P. D.207/24/1.

the late 1790s, but in the circumstances of the early nineteenth century, it was increasingly unreal. As the number of Catholic merchants rose, the number of Protestant merchants remained static (although there were changes in their identity). This made it harder and harder for the leading interests in the corporation to produce a candidate capable of bearing the election expenditure necessary in Drogheda, especially in view of the continuing faction-fight within the corporation, which was sometimes submerged by more important issues, but which re-emerged with most of its old bitterness at a by-election as late as 1822. On the Foster/Hardman side, Hardman himself died in 1814, and his son was unable to continue the family business. On the Smyth/Ogle side there were still some active merchants: Ralph Smyth's son and namesake, Ralph Smyth Junior; St. George Smith (Ralph Smyth Senior's son-in-law); James Schoales; and John Tandy.¹ But these men, simply because they were active merchants, had better uses for their capital than pouring it into election contests for Drogheda. Even Ogle, who was probably still the leading interest in the corporation, and certainly bore the brunt of the expenditure from 1812 until his retirement from the seat in 1820, was in a sense 'a foreign influence'. At the time of the 1807 election his propaganda stressed that, in contrast to his opponent, Thomas Foster, he was a resident in Drogheda, and the scion of a respected, independent, native family;² but, as has been seen, he played no part in the commercial life of the town and his sources of income were partly external to it. After 1820, the majority of the candidates for Drogheda were outsiders, and of necessity had to be. This included the successful candidate in 1820, Henry Metcalfe who, though of an aldermanic family, had himself moved to England; and it also included the successful candidate in 1830 and 1831, John Henry North, a Dublin barrister married to Thomas Foster's cousin, who had been dissuaded by Thomas Foster from standing against Metcalfe in 1820 on the ground that 'one so perfectly a stranger would [not] be approved of'.³ In 1826, it is true, two out of the three candidates were natives, but that election was characterized by the,

---

¹ Fitzgerald, 'Drogheda Economy', App. 1.
² *Address to the Electors of Drogheda*, 3 May 1807, F.P. D.207/24/10.
³ Thomas Skeffington to Foster, 23 May 1819, F.P. D.562/3404.

for Drogheda, unusual feature that no money was going for votes. It was inability to finance a contest, therefore, rather than their foreignness, which kept the Fosters out of Drogheda elections (except in a minor, contributory capacity) after 1812.

On his side, Ogle's ability to finance contests was soon exhausted. Already, during the negotiations in advance of the 1812 election, it had been clear that the expense likely to be involved was a source of anxiety to him; and subsequent events proved that his anxiety was justified, and that Thomas Foster had been right to extricate the Fosters from Drogheda under the lame pretext that, on all questions but the Catholic, they were represented there by deputy. It was not long before the inglorious compromise by which Ogle had secured his return in 1812 became common knowledge. In 1816 a broadsheet directed at the Catholic freeholders drew attention to the fact that Foster influence in Drogheda was still present, and that Ogle 'seldom or never votes on the popular side, except on the Catholic Question'.[1] By at least April 1817, the Emancipationist cause had found a more radical candidate than Ogle, in the person of Thomas Wallace, a Dublin barrister with no property or connections in the town. In these circumstances, John Leslie Foster approached Ogle, and formed the impression that he did '. . . not intend to decline if he finds he can come in easily, but that he would have not much stomach for a sharp contest. . . .'[2] Thomas Foster (now Thomas Skeffington) was even less decisive about his intentions. Although the election was fixed for the beginning of July 1818, he had not made up his mind by 3 June, and his father was still telling the Castle that he had hopes that Skeffington would stand.[3] The situation was further complicated when the Prince Regent's confidant, Sir Benjamin Bloomfield (a co. Meath man), made an imprudent declaration in favour of Wallace; and still further complicated when another candidate appeared in the person of the anti-Emancipationist Lord Henry Moore, a younger son of the 1st Marquess of Drogheda. Lord Drogheda's family had not sat for Drogheda since the 1703 Parliament, and apart from their title had no longer any connection

[1] *Address to the Electors of Drogheda*, Sept. 1816, F.P. D.562/4614.
[2] J. L. Foster to Pentland, 30 Apr. 1817, F.P. D.207/74/24.
[3] John Foster to Peel, 3 June 1818, Peel MSS., B.L. Add. MS. 40278, fol. 44.

with the place. Peel was therefore afraid that, if Moore persisted, he would only split the Protestant vote and let Wallace in.[1] The upshot was that Moore, under pressure from Peel, withdrew his pretensions, and Ogle was again set up by consensus among the two factions in the corporation. The ensuing contest nearly lived up to Peel's worst fears. The corporation books had been so confusedly kept that Wallace was able to knock many of Ogle's voters off on a scrutiny, and Ogle only just beat him by a majority of 201 to 191.[2] Wallace then went on to lodge a petition. This immediately exposed Ogle's lack of stomach for a fight and lack of means to support one. Due to the cumbrous procedure for trying Irish election petitions, the hearing of Wallace's dragged on and on. In May 1819 an Ogle supporter reported that '. . . Wallace must be almost at the bottom of his purse; but he is desperate and the seat is the only thing which can repay him. The expense on Ogle has been and must continue enormous. . . .'[3] Ogle was successful in the end. But his victory was as short-lived as it had been costly, because Parliament was dissolved early in 1820 on the death of George III. Not surprisingly, he did not offer himself for re-election, and Henry Metcalfe was elected in 1820, again by consensus among the two factions in the corporation, and after a contest against Wallace which was decidedly less sharp than that of 1818.

The importance of the Emancipation issue in Drogheda elections, and the strength of the Catholic vote, must also have contributed greatly to Thomas Foster's decision to withdraw in 1812: Ogle presumably enjoyed some support among moderate Catholics, but Thomas Foster would have enjoyed none. The Catholic vote had been able to assume this strength for two reasons. First, the increasing affluence of the Catholic community, or at least of its leaders, meant that more and more Catholics were in a position to buy or, more commonly, to lease freehold property in the town; and the community's increasing political consciousness, heightened by its local,

---

[1] Peel to J. L. Foster, 13 June 1818, J. L. Foster MSS., P.R.O.N.I. T.2519/7/1; Peel to John Foster, 30 May 1818, F.P. D.207/39/27.

[2] Jupp, 'Parliamentary Representation', article on Drogheda.

[3] Letter from someone with an illegible signature (possibly 'T. Wade') to Blayney Balfour, 11 May 1819, Balfour MSS., N.L.I. MS. 10368; Pentland to Foster, 29 Jan. 1819, F.P. D.562/13226.

economic disabilities, meant that freeholder votes arising out of such property were unlikely to remain unregistered. Typical leaders of the Catholic community in this period were the Brodigans, father and son, who had set up in business in the 1780s and by 1815 were among the largest merchants in the town; Thomas Brodigan, the son, was the Secretary to the Catholic Committee of Drogheda.[1] It is easy to trace the varying ratio of freeholder to freeman votes because of the number of contests in the period; and it may be assumed that virtually all the freeholders were Catholic and virtually all the freemen Protestant. In 1796 there seem to have been only 85 freeholders in existence, as compared with nearly 400 freemen (these figures are maxima, not actual voters polled); 115 freeholders voted in 1798, as compared with 243 freemen, and the same number of freeholders in 1802, as compared with 305 freemen. The number of freeholders who voted in 1807 dropped to 80, and the freemen rose slightly to 311, but thereafter the number of freeholders rose and that of freemen fell away: the corresponding figures in 1820 were 251 and 207, and 320 and 188 in 1826. The process was then reversed: in 1831 the number of freeholders who voted dropped to 204 and the freemen rose to 313; by 1832, though no figure is available for the number of freeholders in existence, the number of freemen in existence was over 400.[2] The fluctuations in the number of freeholders must to some extent have been caused by the necessity for them, though not for freemen, to be registered; and defective registry may explain the drop in freeholders in 1807 and possibly in 1831. Otherwise, the overall rise in the number of freeholders can be attributed to the rising affluence and political consciousness of the Catholic community, and the fluctuations in the number of freemen to the faction-fight within the corporation.

This faction-fight was the second reason for the strength of the Catholic vote in Drogheda. There can be little doubt that, had the corporation been united, it could have dealt with

[1] Fitzgerald, 'Drogheda Economy', p. 234; see, for example, Thomas Flanagan to Thomas Brodigan, 1 Apr. 1824, Aylmer MSS., N.L.I.

[2] Hardman's election calculations, 20 Sept. [1796], F.P. D.207/24/4; Fitzgerald, 'Drogheda Economy', pp. 101 f., 122; Jupp, 'Parliamentary Representation', article on Drogheda; *Drogheda Polls at the 1798 and 1802 Eelections*, F.P. D.207/24/3, 5; *Saunders Dublin News Letter*, 21 June 1826; *Municipal Corporations*, App., ii. 813.

the danger arising from the Catholic freeholders with much more effect and much less expense. But, granted the even balance of power between the two factions, it must have been very difficult for the corporation to agree. Although consensus candidates were put up in 1812, 1818, and 1820, and although after the near-disaster of the 1818 election, agreement to admit nearly 100 freemen was reached, the two factions continued to eye each other suspiciously, and the ratio of freemen to freeholders was still unsatisfactory from the corporation's point of view. The last clash between the factions came at the 1822 by-election.[1] On that occasion the old Foster/Hardman faction (in which Fosters and Hardmans were probably no longer dominant) was decisively beaten. But its defeat did not restore harmony to the corporation or bring about a closing of ranks against the Catholic freeholders. Instead, the old Smyth/Ogle faction split, with two of its members out-bidding each other for the support of the Catholics at the election of 1826.[2] It was not until after this election that the corporation closed ranks and admitted a large enough number of freemen to ensure an easy victory for Thomas Skeffington's cousin, John Henry North, the consensus candidate of 1830 and 1831. It was probably financial exhaustion among the leading interests in the corporation which brought about this closing of ranks. It can only have been their financial exhaustion which let Wallace in at last at a by-election later in 1831.[3]

Wallace's victory on the eve of the passing of the Reform Act should not be allowed to obscure the important fact that, granted consensus among the leading interests in the corporation, and a candidate with the necessary financial resources, the corporation's control of the constituency was good for the duration of the unreformed electoral system. In spite of the Catholic petition of 1824 and a further determined Catholic effort in 1830, the freeman body was still almost exclusively Protestant,

---

[1] Countess De Salis to Oriel, 30 Feb. and 1 Mar. 1822, and J. L. Foster to Oriel, 3 Mar. 1822, F.P. D.562/4620–2.

[2] *Saunders Dublin News Letter*, 21 June 1826.

[3] Ibid. 18 Aug. 1830, 14 May and 21 Oct. 1831; Lord Anglesey to Earl Grey, 30 Apr. 1831, Anglesey MSS., P.R.O.N.I. D.619/28A, p. 105. A letter from Sir Frederick Shaw to Lord Ferrard of 6 October 1831 (F.P. T.2519/4/2130) suggests that no anti-reform candidate could be found to oppose Wallace except for a complete stranger to the constituency, who in the end was not put up.

and remained so until at least the mid-1830s. In view of the increasing Catholic dominance of the commercial life of the town, the corporation had been able to keep the freeman body Protestant only by resorting to non-resident freemen on a very large scale. This was an expensive business. Although the corporation had waived its own fines on the admission of all types of freemen, probably in 1818, the stamp duty on the admission of freemen 'by grace' (the category into which almost all non-residents would fall) was £3 a time, as compared with £1 for freemen by birth or apprenticeship (and only a few shillings for the registration of a freehold). In spite of the expense, there was no alternative to non-residents, and only 153 out of the 400 freemen in existence in 1832 were in fact resident.[1] This was because freemen by birth or apprenticeship, though not necessarily resident, were very likely to be, and so would fall an easy prey to boycotting and intimidation on the part of the Catholic population. In the years when Thomas Foster represented Drogheda, residents must have constituted the great majority of the freeman body and, exposed as they were to the economic resentment of their Catholic neighbours, it is not surprising that they should have been very costly in cash and patronage. The Foster/Massereene MSS. abound in hard-luck stories such as that of a Foster supporter at the 1807 election who lamented ungrammatically that he had '. . . been severely handled by the friends of Mr. Ogle in the Catholic interest since me and my family so warmly supported your son. . . .'[2] Years later, in 1827, such retaliatory tactics assumed particularly alarming proportions under the auspices of the Catholic Association.[3] Nevertheless, with its unbroken power of creating non-resident freemen, the corporation was able to counter even these tactics, and the election victories of 1830 and 1831 are a testimony to the effectiveness of its reaction. Moreover, these victories owed nothing to the interposition of Parliament, as John McClintock's victory in co. Louth in 1830 certainly did: the Act of 1829 disfranchising the 40/- freeholders

[1] Jupp, 'Parliamentary Representation', article on Drogheda; *Municipal Corporations*, App., ii, pp. 815 ff.; Richard Nevill to Vesey FitzGerald, Vesey FitzGerald MSS., N.L.I. MS. 7820, p. 85.

[2] John Coulter to Foster, 17 Nov. 1807, F.P. T.2519/4/442.

[3] Letter from nineteen undersigned Protestants of Drogheda to Lord Manners, 28 Mar. 1827, F.P. D.562/14321A.

did not extend to county boroughs like Drogheda. Indeed, one essential difference between Louth and Drogheda was that the power of the old family interests in the former was as good as broken before the passing of the Reform Act, while in the latter it was the Reform Act which broke it.[1]

In 1812, when Thomas Foster had retired from the Drogheda seat, there had been no sign of the corporation's uniting to exercise its undoubted power to swamp the Catholic free-holders. Indeed, the signs pointed in the opposite direction. Over the years the Smyth/Ogle faction had become increasingly overt in its courting of the Catholic vote, and at this stage it was extremely unlikely that they would have thrown away the electoral gains they had made in that quarter in order to accommodate Thomas Foster. This courting of the Catholic vote dates probably from the 1802 election. Forbes had been a prominent Emancipationist; but in the elections of the late 1790s, Ralph Smyth, no less than John Foster and Hardman, was hostile to the Catholic claims, and the only sense in which either side appealed to the Catholic vote was that Foster and Hardman accused Smyth of being an Orangeman, and Smyth held up Foster as the foremost and most resolute opponent of Emancipation in the sphere of national politics. The most that can be said about the Catholic vote in the late 1790s is that the Catholics tended to vote for the same candidate, Ball in 1796 and, interestingly, Hardman in 1798.[2] At the 1802 election, the circumstances were a little different. Ogle did not share Smyth's anti-Emancipationist views (and lost some support in the corporation as a consequence). When he found that the Catholics seemed to be on his side, he suggested to the Castle that it might be a good idea for him to employ an

[1] The Reform Act broke it by disfranchising the 247 out of 400 freemen who were non-resident. This was balanced by no accompanying disfranchisement of the freeholders, since the Act retained the 40/- freehold franchise in county boroughs for as long as those in present enjoyment of it held on to the same piece of property. The further effect of the Act was to enfranchise £20 leaseholders and £10 householders. The second category did not in fact come into play in time for the general election of 1832; but their presence was not necessary, as the aldermanic interest was outgunned without them. See 1 & 2 William IV, c. 88, ss. 5 and 6, and *Municipal Corporations*, App., ii, pp. 813 ff.

[2] Fitzgerald, 'Drogheda Economy', pp. 108, 120; *Address to the Electors of Drogheda*, [early 1798], F.P. D.207/24/1. A turgid pro-Foster ballad of 1796 attributed Hardman's defeat in the election of that year to the activity of 'the Papists' in creating freeholders (F.P. D.562/4612).

agent among them, to stimulate them to greater exertions.[1] The Castle's reaction is not recorded. In any case, although a majority of the Catholic voters (84) supported him, a substantial number (31) voted for Hardman. Ogle's defeat in 1802 taught him to look for new allies, and made him less coy about courting the Catholics. In 1807 the rumour went abroad that he 'turned Papist and went to mass on Sunday the 24th of last month [May—the day before the Drogheda election started]'.[2] The circumstances under which the Talents had been dismissed gave him his cue, although, as has been seen, he did not admit in his election address that he was an Emancipationist; he also denied that Emancipation was an issue at the election, and claimed that the real issue was whether the King was constitutionally entitled to demand a pledge from his Ministers that they would never, whatever the circumstances, introduce a particular measure.[3] But these constitutional niceties were lost on the voters of Drogheda, and his address, as the Fosters were quick to show, was only a piece of party common form. The extent to which he had committed himself on the Emancipation issue was made clear by the events leading up to the 1812 election, when he was prepared to do anything to secure an uncontested return, except agree to vote against Emancipation. Soon after came disillusionment. The Catholics lost interest in him and turned to Wallace, a man for whom Emancipation was only one plank in a platform of radical reform. The events of the 1818 election and the ensuing petition showed how near the Catholic vote in Drogheda had been to becoming a Pandora's box. But even then, although steps were taken which gave Metcalfe an easier passage in 1820 than Ogle had had in 1818, the lesson was learned only imperfectly: at the 1826 election the two rival candidates from the old Smyth/Ogle faction ran a more furious 'race for the Catholic' than ever the unfortunate Ogle had done.

The 'race for the Catholic' run in Drogheda from at least 1807, contrasts strikingly with the reluctance of the Fosters' rivals in Louth to adopt such electioneering tactics. To some extent the contrast is explained by the fact that, to appeal to the

---

[1] Ogle to Marsden, 11 July 1802, S.P.O. 521/131/8.
[2] George Murphy to Foster, 18 June 1807, F.P. D.562/12458B.
[3] 'Ogle's Plagiarism', [late May 1807], F.P. D.207/24/14.

Catholic vote in Louth, would have been to attempt to 'separate the tenantries from their landlord'; which was not the case in Drogheda, where influence was personal rather than proprietary. It is significant that Sir Edward Bellew, who had gladly lent his name to the campaign of the Drogheda Catholics, continued to behave in co. Louth as a landlord first and a Catholic leader second, until stampeded out of his conservatism by the 1826 election. It may be that the Fosters were frightened out of Drogheda in 1812 by the unwelcome prominence which Drogheda politics had given to the Emancipation issue locally, and by the fear that their unpopularity among the Catholics of Drogheda (whose grievances were of course greater than those of the Catholics of Louth, because they were economic as well as political)[1] would invite attack in Louth, the constituency which was the Fosters' primary concern. There seems to have been a considerable interaction between the politics of the two constituencies: in 1822 Balfour, who was thinking of setting up his son, an alderman of Drogheda, as a candidate for the town, was reminded by a friend that, '. . . if Blayney [Balfour Junior] is member for Drogheda, *your own* objects in Louth will be advanced in full proportion to any trouble or expense he may have encountered there. . . .'[2] This interaction derived presumably from the fact that the two constituencies overlapped, not territorially, but in terms of electorates and personnel. No Drogheda freeholder, unless he happened to have a separate qualification in co. Louth, could vote in co. Louth elections; but in practice many Drogheda freeholders, and freemen, did have such a qualification in co. Louth, just as many co. Louth freeholders were either freeholders or freemen of Drogheda. At the time of the 1767 Louth by-election, for example, a canvass of Drogheda turned up 'near forty votes' which the Fosters 'had no idea of';[3] since the total number of votes cast for the Foster candidate, Sibthorpe, at that by-election was only 399, the 'near forty' unexpected votes, plus

---

[1] Mr. Fitzgerald notes that their '. . . chief concern was membership of the corporation. Even in the early 1820s, when the question of Catholics sitting in Parliament was becoming a major national issue, they did not allude to it in their petitions, but concentrated on seeking membership of the corporation. . . .' ('Drogheda Economy', p. 122).

[2] Wallop Brabazon to Balfour, 9 Feb. 1822, Balfour MSS., N.L.I. MS. 10360.

[3] W. H. Fortescue to Anthony Foster, [October? 1767?], F.P. D.562/4629.

whatever votes had been expected from Drogheda, constituted a considerable proportion of the then Foster interest in Louth. This must have been a factor of decreasing importance. By 1821, remarkably few Louth freeholders (less than 20 out of the registered total of 2,830) lived in Drogheda.[1] More Louth votes were controlled from Drogheda, even in 1821, than these figures would suggest, because some of the family interests in the Drogheda corporation owned land and possessed free-holders in Louth—the Fosters' support of Metcalfe in 1820 won them the support of Metcalfe's Louth freeholders, and the same seems to have happened with Ogle in 1806.[2] On the whole, however, the family interests in the Drogheda corporation—apart from the Balfours—were not large landowners in Louth, and neither were the substantial Catholic merchants of the town.[3] This would suggest that it may have been subscriptions from the Catholic merchants of Drogheda which Balfour's correspondent in 1822 had in mind; and the importance of Catholic subscriptions from Dundalk to Dawson's campaign in Louth in 1826 gives some colour to the suggestion. Granted his diffidence about playing to the Catholics, Balfour Senior was hardly the man to attract this very practical form of Catholic support. But the Fosters, in their parlous financial situation, must have dreaded a Catholic-sponsored run on them, and this may well have been a factor in their withdrawal from Drogheda.

In theory the issue of Emancipation should not have loomed so large in Drogheda: paternalism should have been a successful formula for winning Drogheda elections up to the passing of the Reform Act, and the only problem should have been the cost in terms of patronage and hard cash. In practice, however, because of the bitter divisions within the corporation, and because the contestants for Drogheda lacked the *esprit de corps* which restrained even the Catholic landlords of Louth, Drogheda elections turned into a 'race for the Catholic': all the contestants between 1812 and 1829 were in fact avowed

[1] *Louth Freeholders, 1821*, P.R.O.N.I. T.2519/14/1.

[2] List of unregistered Louth voters, including some whose landlord was Ogle, [pre-1806 election?], F.P. D.562/14661; George Ball to Foster, 22 Dec. 1809, Pentland to Foster, 18 Aug. 1819, and James Johnston to Foster, 5 Aug. 1820, F.P. D.562/12627, 13329, 13845.

[3] Fitzgerald, 'Drogheda Economy', App. Three.

Emancipationists of varying degrees of radicalism. Had the Fosters persevered with Drogheda, their prominence as anti-Emancipationists in national politics would have been grist to their opponents' mill, and the adverse publicity might have had disastrous consequences in Louth. In Drogheda, the day of paternalism was almost done in 1807, and was definitely done by 1812. Aggressive anti-Emancipationism and a plentiful expenditure of cash were the most promising expedients for the Fosters, and they could afford neither.

CHAPTER FIVE

'A Pretty Strong Phalanx': Command of Seats

THANKS to Drogheda, Foster commanded three seats during the last three years of the Irish Parliament, and without Drogheda had commanded two in the years up to 1797. It is axiomatic that in Great Britain possession of electoral interest was not a necessary qualification for top political office or top political influence: thus, while the Duke of Newcastle was one of the foremost borough proprietors in England, another Prime Minister, Lord North, could do no more than guarantee his own return (via his father); and two others, the Elder and the Younger Pitt, could not do even that, as they did not belong to the borough-owning branch of their family.[1] The same was even truer of Ireland. In Ireland, there was always, except in moments of political crisis, so much real political estate, in the form of seats and votes, at the disposal of the government that such influence as was accorded to 'natives' over the shaping of policy was accorded on quite different grounds, and usually only to 'efficient men', 'men of business', and good parliamentarians. The government was almost always weaker in oratory and argument than in numbers. Chief Secretary Eden reported in 1781:

... Our debate on the Mutiny Bill was carried triumphantly by the prevalence of Members against abilities. Almost the whole strength of speaking, and perhaps, too, the strength of the argument, was with the minority. However, we did as well as we could; and partly by exertion, but chiefly by management, the business is for the present well closed ...[2]

Oratory and argument were necessary, to mask the presence of 'management' and, hopefully, to win converts among the

---

[1] Namier, *Structure of Politics*, pp. 12 ff.; Ian Christie, *The End of North's Ministry, 1780–2* (London, 1958), p. 89.

[2] Quoted in Johnston, *Great Britain and Ireland*, p. 282.

independent members: in the absence of oratory and argument, the bought might be ashamed to stay bought, and management might lose its binding power. For governments, as for individuals, success derived from a combination of personal and real interest.

The *caveat* entered above—such influence as was accorded to natives over the shaping of policy—is important. The principle on which the whole government of Ireland was based from the early 1770s onwards was that formal authority and actual power should be concentrated in the hands of the lord lieutenant and, under him, the chief secretary.[1] In practice, the burden thus imposed on these two men was too great, particularly since they were usually strangers to Ireland, sometimes politically inexperienced, and sometimes politically obtuse. Part of the burden was passed on to the successive private secretaries to each lord lieutenant—men like John Lees and Edward Cooke (both of whom subsequently became Under-Secretaries), and a greater part to the two under-secretaries at the Castle, who like the private secretaries were usually not natives (in this respect, Sackville Hamilton is a very important exception). Lord Fitzwilliam was not correct in saying that the Under-Secretaries had been 'clerks' in 1781–2. But he was not far wrong in saying that they were 'Ministers' by 1795. Indeed, another English Whig, Lord Wycombe, when visiting Ireland in 1797, heard on all sides 'that the man who really governs this Kingdom is a Mr. [Under-]Secretary Cooke . . . —a youngish man, too'.[2] The rest of the burden of government was distributed among the natives, but on a very pragmatic, informal basis. There were a number, though not a large number, of offices in Ireland whose holders were guaranteed a say in the shaping of measures —the lord chancellorship, the first or chief commissionership of the revenue, the attorneyship-general, and the speakership,

---

[1] Thomas Bartlett, 'The Townshend Administration in Ireland, 1767–72', Q.U.B., Ph.D. thesis, 1970, *passim*. I am grateful to Dr. Bartlett for allowing me to read one chapter of his thesis in draft form, for several illuminating papers which he has read on the subject, and for numerous informal discussions of various points.

[2] Fitzwilliam to Lord Carlisle, 6 Mar. 1795, *Beresford Correspondence*, ii. 79; Wycombe to Lady Holland, 28 Nov. 1797, Holland MSS., B.L. Add. MS. 51682— folio numbers provisional. For the role of the under-secretaries, see Johnston, *Great Britain and Ireland*, pp. 45 ff.

for example. But the extent of the say depended very much on who the holder was. Other offices (like the secretaryship of state and the chancellorship of the exchequer) could mean something or nothing, depending on circumstances; and even as late as the 1790s there was still room in the Irish Cabinet for Archbishop Agar, who held no office at all in the executive and was not even the Primate. Apart from the chancellorship of the exchequer in 1784, no new or as-good-as-new office, of the 'efficient' and 'responsible' type, was created during the existence of the Constitution of 1782. The number of such offices remained as small as before, and—much more important —so did the number of native politicians who, regardless of the offices they held, really played some part in the shaping of measures. The government took on few passengers; ability and efficiency were the main criteria on which the Irish cabinet was hired.

In 1806, the borough-owning Earl of Caledon cynically reminded his brother-in-law, Lord Blayney, that shortage of votes on the Government's part, not 'parliamentary harangues' on Blayney's, would be 'the means by which your success will be ensured.'[1] Blayney's ambition was the modest one of being elected an Irish Representative Peer: where top political office or top political influence was the object, 'parliamentary harangues' were obviously a much more important factor. However, they were not alone decisive. By the time Hely-Hutchinson obtained the secretaryship of state for Ireland, in 1777, he had forfeited his character; his old capacity for 'parliamentary harangues' was still there, but he was considered a 'profligate',[2] and was not much listened to or confided in;

---

[1] Caledon to Blayney, March 1806, Caledon MSS., P.R.O.N.I. D.2433/C/9/4. Lord Caledon was probably unique among Irish borough proprietors in that he purchased a British borough, the notorious Old Sarum, to make up (in fact, more than make up) for the Irish borough he had lost through disfranchisement at the Union. Lord Waterford acquired one seat for Berwick after the Union, but this was by inheritance from the Delaval family, not by purchase.

[2] Hussey Burgh to Foster, June 1779, F.P. D.562/4569; Heron to Robinson, 20 Aug. 1779, *Beresford Correspondence*, i. 47. Tisdall and Hely-Hutchinson, like Sir Robert and Edward Southwell before them, held the secretaryship of state for life; like Tisdall, the Southwells (at times) filled the position of parliamentary pre-eminence which the name of the office implied; under Hely-Hutchinson the office was nominal only, in spite of his efforts to have it made 'efficient' (memo. by Hely-Hutchinson, [1787?], Melville MSS., N.L.I. MS. 54A/68); it was later attached to the chief secretaryship.

he thus succeeded to one of Tisdall's offices, but not, as he had hoped, to Tisdall's political influence. Also, with the Constitution of 1782 came a greater emphasis on recruiting for the government men of business and experience rather than 'parliamentary haranguers'—men to whom the detailed drafting of legislation could be safely entrusted.[1] The list of those native politicians who definitely attained top political influence in the cabinets of the period 1777–1800 is therefore not exclusively composed of orators: Tisdall, Pery, Hussey Burgh, Foster, Scott, Beresford, Yelverton, Fitzgibbon, Archbishop Agar, Parnell, William and George Ponsonby, Grattan, Castlereagh, and Corry; to these names might be added, though more questionably, Hely-Hutchinson, Conolly, the Duke of Leinster, Lord Charlemont, Forbes, Arthur Wolfe, and John Toler. (Flood is excluded, though he retained his vice-treasurership until 1781, because in this period and throughout his career his influence over measures derived, not from office or participation in cabinets, but from parliamentary opposition and extraparliamentary agitation: Grattan is included because of his participation in the Portland, Temple, Northington, and Fitzwilliam Cabinets, and his independent support in the early days of the Rutland Administration.) Obviously, several 'sublime orators'[2] are on the list; but also there are 'sensible reasoners' like Foster, and even not-so-sensible reasoners like Parnell.

Regardless of whether these politicians were parliamentary performers or backroom boys, if command of seats had been a recommendation for top political influence, most of them would not have qualified and some very different people would. The only ones who had a reasonably effective control over three or more seats were Foster (between 1797 and 1800 only), Beresford (through his brother, the 1st Marquess of Waterford), Agar (through his brother, the 1st Viscount Clifden), William Ponsonby, Castlereagh (through his father, 1796–1800, and previously through his grandfather, Lord Hertford), Conolly, and the Duke of Leinster. Of the rest, Lord Charlemont controlled two seats; Parnell and Hely-Hutchinson each had a reasonably firm hold on their own seat and a shaky hold on another; Pery, George Ponsonby (the latter through his

---

[1] Sydney to Rutland, 6 May 1784, *H.M.C. Rutland MSS.*, iii. 93.
[2] For the significance of this quotation see p. 413.

brother William or other relations), Forbes, and Corry could more or less guarantee their own return to the House; and the rest could not do that, but came in under the auspices of a patron, by purchase, or as M.P.s for a precarious open constituency such as Dublin University. Furthermore, the top political influence attained by the six people enjoying the command of three or more seats, can easily be explained on grounds other than their electoral influence. The faintest praise bestowed on Beresford was that he was 'remarkably intelligent in his immediate department', and most people, particularly British politicians, rated his ability and utility far higher than that; Agar was described in 1789 as having spoken 'wonderfully well' in debate, and in 1791 as 'a political character of great consideration'; William Ponsonby was of sufficient personal calibre to be twice the Opposition's candidate against Foster for the speakership; Conolly owed his brief period of influence to his family connection with Lord Buckinghamshire and, more generally, to his standing as 'the head of the landed interest of Ireland'; Leinster owed his brief period of influence to the same family connection, to the uniqueness of his rank in the Irish Peerage, and to his tawdry popularity with the Dublin mob; and Castlereagh owed his unprecedented influence (for an Irish politician) to his personal ability and to his English family connections, one of them with the reigning Lord Lieutenant.[1]

In 1790 Lord Westmorland, in a phrase already quoted, described Foster as 'a very able man and considerable connection'.[2] But it is clear that in this context 'connection' did not refer to real political estate, but to something much less definable and much more creditable. If Foster's electoral influence prior to the Union (and the post-Union period is a very different matter, which will be dealt with separately) is given the widest possible definition, it still amounts to no more than three

---

[1] Buckinghamshire to Heron, 12 Apr. 1779, Heron MSS., N.L.I. MS. 13037/8; Buckingham to Grenville, 31 Mar. 1789, *H.M.C. Dropmore MSS.*, i. 441; Johnston, *Irish House of Commons in 1791*, p. 48; Malcomson, *Foster and the Speakership*, pp. 278 f., 302; 'Falkland', *Parliamentary Representation*, p. 59; Scott to Robinson, 26 Oct. 1780, *Beresford Correspondence*, i. 148. In the last source cited, Scott described Leinster as '. . . the most noble and puissant Patriot, His Grace Cromeboo of Leinster . . ., a very high and very variable weathercock, whose face turns the City of Dublin, and some other interesting parts of this Kingdom, almost to peace or war. . . .'

[2] See p. 64.

seats, with some influence over two others. This excludes his influence in Clogher borough (a doubtful case),[1] but it assumes that from 1797 to 1800 he controlled the parliamentary conduct of Edward Hardman, and that he had some influence over the return and parliamentary conduct of the second members for Louth and Drogheda, William Charles Fortescue and John Ball, particularly the former. Fortescue followed Foster's lead, not only at the time of the Union, but also during the ministerial crisis of late April 1804, when he deserted Addington for Pitt;[2] the weight of Foster's authority and the numerical preponderance of his freeholders probably had much to do with this. Nevertheless, three and a bit members does not amount to much in terms of real political estate—although it must be remembered that in Ireland, as in Great Britain, the great borough proprietors returned fewer members to Parliament than might be supposed. It is reasonable to regard as a great borough proprietor anyone who controlled five or more seats in his own right (including, where it existed, strong influence over county or other open seats). This may seem to be pitching the level of great borough proprietorship rather low. But, in fact, though inflated guesses to the contrary were and are frequently made, no single individual actually *returned* more than nine members to the Irish Parliament in the period 1777–1800—a period when electoral influence was concentrated in the hands of a smaller number of individuals than at any other time in the eighteenth century. Moreover, the two greatest proprietors of the period, the 1st and 2nd Marquesses of Downshire and the 2nd Earl of Shannon, could only return nine members when they exerted themselves to the maximum and everything went right for them.[3] Nine well-disciplined

[1] See pp. 269 f.

[2] Nepean to John King, 29 Apr. 1804, H.O. MSS., P.R.O. H.O. 100/122, fols. 204–5.

[3] Lord Downshire controlled Blessington, Fore, and Hillsborough boroughs, one seat for Carlingford, a parlous seat for Newry, and a safe seat for co. Down. He also had some influence in Carrickfergus, which the family increased and began to exploit after the Union. Lord Shannon controlled Castlemartyr, Clonakilty, and Youghal boroughs, one seat for Charleville, and two parlous seats for Cork City and County. By the early 1790s, his influence in Cork City had been eclipsed by that of Richard Longfield, an erstwhile satellite. Likewise, Lord Downshire controlled the three seats for Carlingford and Fore only during the last few years of the eighteenth century. In both cases, the estimate of nine seats is therefore on the generous side, and does not apply to the whole period 1777–1800.

members, or a difference of eighteen on a division, was of course a sizeable following in a House of Commons of 300, where party discipline was undreamt of and the quorum of forty sometimes difficult to obtain. Foster's three and a bit members do not look impressive against the nine of Lords Downshire and Shannon; yet he wielded much greater political influence than either of them, and had a much wider political 'connection'. This 'connection', or personal interest, extended far more widely than his electoral or real interest; it embraced members who shared his 'Ascendancy' views, members for some of the linen counties and towns, and numerous relations and friends who looked to him for leadership, not primarily because of relationship and friendship, but because of his commanding ability. Naturally, it was the kind of 'connection' which tended to evaporate under the heat of ministerial displeasure. It is impossible to be precise about the number of members who opposed the Union out of loyalty to Foster, because it is impossible to know how many of his 'connection' would have opposed it anyway. Probably he carried with him into opposition some half dozen members who were in no way dependent on him for their return.[1] He certainly failed to carry with him into opposition some leading members of the 'connection' who were not prepared for massacre as Fosterite innocents: notably Richard Nevill, who returned himself to the House, and Foster's own brother-in-law, Thomas Burgh, who sat for a government seat.[2]

The Irish Cabinet of the 1790s, of which Foster was a member, constitutes the clearest example of native influence

[1] Possible cases in point were John Maxwell Barry, Henry Coddington, Sir John Macartney, John S. Rochfort, and John Wolfe. Coddington is a doubtful case, because he tried initially to do a deal with the Government for his vote; however, when he failed, he opposed the Union in 1799, and in 1800 vacated his seat in favour of an anti-Unionist protégé of Foster, Quintin Dick. Parnell, his son, Henry, and other connections of the Parnell family are probably too important in their own right to be placed to Foster's credit. Four other M.P.s connected politically with Foster would almost certainly have opposed the Union anyway— Jonah Barrington, Richard Lovell Edgworth, Nathaniel Sneyd, and Owen Wynne —and two others over whom he had influence opposed it in 1799 and then changed sides—Gustavus Rochfort and Thomas Stannus. The anti-Unionists whose return Foster either influenced or controlled were Thomas Foster, Edward Hardman, John Ball, William Charles Fortescue, and himself.

[2] Bolton, Union, p. 171; Cornwallis to Portland, 26 June 1799, Cornwallis Correspondence, iii. 107.

over the shaping of measures; in 1792 a knowledgeable commentator referred to 'the Beresfords, the Chancellor, the Speaker and Hobart—that is to say, the Government', and in 1798 Lord Wycombe described Fitzgibbon as 'the lord and master of this Country by the grace of the Beresfords and the Speaker'.[1] Both commentators omitted Agar and Parnell, who almost certainly should be included. Thus, of the Irish Cabinet of the 1790s, consisting of Foster, Fitzgibbon, Beresford, Agar, and Parnell, only two members, Beresford and Agar, came from families who count as great borough proprietors, as already defined. This point could be more strikingly made if the Attorney- and Solicitor-General, Wolfe and Toler, and the Under-Secretaries at the Castle, Hamilton and Cooke, were counted as members of the Irish Cabinet, since none of them could command a single seat; however, Wolfe was too timid and Toler too burlesque to carry much weight, and Hamilton and Cooke are best regarded as of the civil servant type. As has been seen, Beresford's and Agar's presence in the Cabinet can easily be explained on the ground of their ability; but since so much publicity was given, during and after the Fitzwilliam débâcle, to the extent of Beresford's influence, it is profitable to examine how far it (and Agar's) was electorally based.

In 1791, the Marquess of Abercorn asked his political manager, Thomas Knox, to draw up for him a statement of the Beresford family's '. . . interest as it stands: how much their own; how much by the support of Government; how much lent them by others; how much secure; how much liable to be shaken. . . .' Knox failed to provide satisfactory answers to these questions. What he came up with was a total parliamentary 'connection' of eight, to which he probably ought to have added Theophilus Jones, M.P. for co. Leitrim, a Beresford kinsman who was in no way indebted to the Beresfords for his return to Parliament. However, Knox's eight included John Beresford's colleague as M.P. for co. Waterford—a doubtful case; they also included one Beresford who sat for a government borough and therefore should have been placed to the credit of the Government, not the Beresfords; and they included the

[1] George Knox to Lord Abercorn, 13 Dec. [1792], Abercorn MSS., P.R.O.N.I. T.2541/IB1/3/35; Wycombe to Lady Holland, 8 May 1798, Holland MSS., B.L. Add. MS. 51682.

Beresford M.P.s for Dungarvan and Swords, two shaky seats almost entirely dependent on John Beresford's Revenue patronage, and Sir Hugh Hill, M.P. for Derry City, who had a considerable interest in the constituency independent of the Beresfords. At about this time, John Beresford's elder brother, Lord Waterford, purchased the second seat for Coleraine borough (he already controlled the first), thus adding one M.P. to the number whom he could definitely return. But even with the addition of this one member, Lord Waterford and John Beresford combined could only return with reasonable certainty seven people, including the M.P.s for Derry, Dungarvan, and Swords, but excluding the second M.P. for co. Waterford and the M.P. for the government borough.[1] This was not a spectacular amount of electoral interest, considering that the Beresfords enjoyed the Revenue and other patronage of cos. Londonderry and Waterford, Derry, Dungarvan, and Swords. Without this patronage they would have been reduced to four, or at most five, seats. In other words, in their own right they were barely a major parliamentary interest; the twenty votes which Beresford claimed to influence in 1779 were mostly his 'connection' rather than his members; and his influence at constituency level and in Parliament 'derived the essence of its strength from office' (as Lord Carlisle reminded Lord Fitzwilliam in 1795).[2] Certainly, his high official station did not derive from his or Lord Waterford's electoral interest.

The Agar family possessed a more extensive command of seats in their own right. The Archbishop's elder brother, Lord Clifden, was sometimes able to return a county member for Kilkenny, and controlled four borough seats in that county; also, an Agar cousin controlled two more borough seats in Kilkenny. This means that the Agars possessed an absolute maximum of seven seats. However, a Castle list of 1785 noted that '. . . This is the first time Lord Clifden ever pretended to a following in Parliament, as he constantly sold his five [sic—four?] seats . . . His fortune is not equal to such an exertion as he has now made, and therefore it is impossible for him to continue

---

[1] Johnston, *Irish House of Commons in 1791*, pp. 3, 47 f.; Trainor and Crawford, *Aspects*, No. 56.
[2] Beresford to Thomas Allan, 14 Oct. 1777, and Carlisle to Fitzwilliam, 17 Apr. 1795, *Beresford Correspondence*, i. 20, and ii. 96.

it. The two last Members on his list are very precarious. . . .'[1] 'The two last members' were those returned by the Agar cousin, over whom Lord Clifden's and the Archbishop's influence was parlous; he had earlier declared his independence of them, and he later supported the Government during the Regency crisis, when they were in opposition.[2] In short, he was a supporter of the government rather than a follower of Lord Clifden. The only conclusion which can be drawn from these facts and figures is that, if the government had accorded influence over the shaping of measures on the basis of which native politician could provide in return the greatest electoral support, it would not have included even Agar and Beresford in the Irish Cabinet of the 1790s.

Those on the opposition side during the 1790s did not attain office or influence in cabinet, except during the short-lived Fitzwilliam Administration; after that, they ceased to want to do so, except as a consequence of a change of government in Great Britain.[3] However, important developments went on internally within the Opposition during the decade. What in effect happened was that those opposition groups who were primarily dependent on command of seats either returned to the government fold or began to go to the wall politically. Lord Shannon, for the second time in his career, found opposition incompatible with both his interest and his instinct, and returned to the government fold (as First Lord of the Treasury) in 1793. Conolly sold his two boroughs in the mid-1790s, and was left with only his own county seat for Londonderry; and the Duke of Leinster sold one borough, began to sell seats, and found his political position in co. Kildare increasingly under challenge. Two lesser opposition borough proprietors also sold their boroughs—William Burton and the Earl of Mount Cashell.[4] The government was the gainer from these developments,

---

[1] Typescript made by Miss Patricia Mary Simpson of a list of the Irish Parliament in 1785 among the Stowe (Marquess of Buckingham) MSS., in the Huntington Library, California. I was ignorant of this source, and am very grateful to Miss Simpson for allowing me to see a copy of her typescript. The same list comments: 'the real Parliamentary interest of the Beresford family is but small'.

[2] E. M. Johnston (ed.), 'Members of the Irish Parliament, 1784–7', *Proc. R.I.A.* vol. 71, Sec. C, No. 5 (1971), 169.

[3] Bolton, *Union*, p. 26.

[4] Ibid. 22; Thomas Tickell to Leinster, 4 Dec. 1801, and Leinster to Tickell, 7 Jan. 1802, Tickell MSS., by permission of the late Major-General Sir Eustace

obviously from the return of Lord Shannon to his allegiance, and also from the sales of seats and boroughs, since all the purchasers were people who were prepared to support the government—at a price. The other gainers were William and George Ponsonby. In the course of the 1790s, the Ponsonbys converted the Irish Whigs from a small number of separate groups, each liable to make its separate bargain with the Castle, into a reasonably well-disciplined party under their own leadership: a party reduced numerically by the decline of Conolly and Leinster, but probably the more cohesive because of their decline. This party the Ponsonbys held together, with one or two defections,[1] and with the loss of William Burton's and Lord Mount Cashell's boroughs, in spite of the fact that it was in constant opposition except under Fitzwilliam. A variety of factors enabled them to hold it together. They were connected, via a complex 'cousinhood', with many of its members; they derived ideological sustenance, or rather, party common form, from the British Whig Opposition, and electoral strength from two of their connections among the English Whigs, the Duke of Devonshire and Fitzwilliam; and finally, they were able parliamentarians and party leaders, to whom family connections with electoral influence naturally and willingly deferred.[2] Certainly, their own direct command of seats was minimal—even smaller than that of their traditional rivals, the Beresfords. In 1782, their father had been credited with control of eleven seats and influence over twenty-seven others.[3] But, in fact, he and they controlled no more than one borough (Newtownards, swapped in 1788 for Banagher), and could be fairly confident of holding one seat for their native county of Kilkenny. As Thomas Knox informed Lord Abercorn in 1791, '. . . This party is made up entirely of connections, Mr.

Tickell, Wood End, Silvermere, Cobham, Surrey, D./2 and /4; T. U. Sadleir (ed.), *An Irish Peer on the Continent, 1801–3* (London, 1920), p. vi. The Irish peer was Lord Mount Cashell.

[1] The most prominent defectors were Sir Henry Cavendish and Lodge Morres— see Lismore election committee minutes, 1791, B.L. Egerton MS. 264; Bolton, *Union*, p. 21.

[2] In this paragraph I have drawn on P. J. Jupp, 'Politics and Parties in Great Britain and Ireland, 1782–1820' (unpublished paper read to the U.C.D. Historical Society in 1969). I am grateful to Dr. Jupp for lending me his typescript of this paper.

[3] Quoted in Malcomson, *Foster and the Speakership*, p. 290.

[William] Ponsonby having but two seats that he can *actually* rely upon, exclusive of his seat for the county of Kilkenny . . .'[1] Again, it was a case of 'connection' or personal interest rather than electoral or real interest. Obviously, without a foundation on electoral interest, the Ponsonby party could not have existed except by purchasing seats. But the important point is that, on the opposition as on the government side in the 1790s, ability and not command of seats determined who got to the top.

Had it been otherwise, the Irish cabinet would have been composed of the great borough proprietors. Inevitably, such magnates exercised some slight degree of influence over measures. Unless they were in declared opposition, and sometimes even then, they were sure to receive a letter of fulsome compliment from each in-coming lord lieutenant, and were sure to be specially summoned to attend meetings of the Privy Council at which any measure likely to give rise to parliamentary criticism—for example, the embargo on the export of corn from Ireland in November 1782[2]—was going to come under discussion. However, the spirit in which they were thus summoned varied with the personalities concerned. For example, the 1st Marquess of Ely was a political prostitute who used his seven borough votes in the 1780s and 1790s to make up in financial terms what he lacked in landed income; Lord Abercorn must have been extremely difficult for the viceroys of the 1790s to handle, as he considered himself a kind of unofficial viceroy, on the strength of his personal friendship with Pitt (which he much exaggerated); and the 2nd Duke of Leinster during the 1770s and 1780s was usually in a huff about some point of protocol, precedence, or emolument, and pursued an extremely erratic political course dictated by his huffs rather than the popular political causes which they led him to espouse.[3]

---

[1] Johnston, *Irish House of Commons in 1791*, p. 51.

[2] Bundle of letters to Lord Temple on this subject, 11–19 Nov. 1782, Additiona Dropmore MSS.

[3] Bolton, *Union*, pp. 95 f.; Leinster to Temple, 24 Sept. 1782, Leinster MSS., P.R.O.N.I. D.3078/3/4. In this letter Leinster declared that he would not attend council meetings until a host of jobs had been conferred on his dependants and himself. His own object was a vice-treasurership for Ireland, of which he observed modestly: '. . . I confess I do not think it quite so honourable an employment as my rank ought to expect. Yet I see no other employment in this country, and by giving it to me, it would in fact be giving it to the country . . .' Temple nicknamed him

None of these borough proprietors can have been summoned to the Privy Council for the benefit of his advice, but merely with a view to making him a party to the policy decision, and so making it difficult for him to oppose it subsequently in Parliament. Others, however, must have been more welcome and more useful visitors to the Castle. The 1st Marquess of Downshire had held British cabinet office (at one time with responsibility for Ireland), although this very fact, combined with his unconcealed ambition to be Lord Lieutenant himself, probably made him liable to some of the objections which attached to Lord Abercorn.[1] No such objections attached to the 2nd Earl of Shannon. A worthy son and successor of Henry Boyle, Lord Shannon stood deservedly high in his native Munster, and lent a certain moral authority to the government in addition to a 'connection' which was almost double his command of seats. Lord Shannon himself possessed some awareness of the moral authority he conferred. When he was making up his mind about returning to the government fold in 1793, he asked the Lord Lieutenant, Lord Westmorland, what Place, Pension, and Responsibility measures the Government intended to carry, because '. . . he thought it impossible for him to be of any use to Government, unless by taking some conciliatory steps we should give him sufficient justification for his character, as well as to stem the popular run [against him] . . .' Because of his 'character' and sound sense, Lord Shannon was in fact of some practical 'use to Government', and was not just made a party to measures in a token way. During the rebellion, for example, he was a member of 'a sort of Cabinet' which met every day at twelve 'to compare notes and hear the contents of the express and post dispatches', although he was not a member of what he called the 'interior' Cabinet, which dealt with

'Nolo Privy Councillari' and described him as 'this blockhead of a Duke'—Temple to Grenville, 13 Jan. 1783 and 21 Dec. 1782, *H.M.C. Dropmore MSS.*, i. 180, 172. For Lord Abercorn's role, see pp. 404 ff.

[1] For the influence of Downshire (then Earl of Hillsborough) over the shaping of measures, see Rutland to Sydney, 29 Jan. 1786, *H.M.C. Rutland MSS.*, iii. 279: for his ambition to be Lord Lieutenant, see Allan to Beresford, 16 Dec. 1779, *Beresford Correspondence*, i. 119. The Stowe list of 1785 (see p. 201, *n.* 1) describes Downshire as '. . . of the first consequence in the Kingdom, abstracted from his Parliamentary following. This is principally owing to his residence in the North, in the centre of estates which are remitted to absentee landlords. He is also a great check upon the Dissenters and Volunteers, who swarm in that part of the North . . .'

high military policy.[1] The significant thing, which the case of Lord Shannon demonstrates, is that the government drew a qualitative distinction between one great borough proprietor and another, not just a quantitative distinction between the sizes of their parliamentary followings. No government went out of its way to huckster for the 'rotten' support of Lord Ely, if it could reach a gentleman's agreement with Lord Shannon, or partake of the Duke of Leinster's prestige; even the Duke of Leinster, because of his stupidity and waywardness, was a doubtful asset; in 1788 the Lord Lieutenant, Lord Buckingham, observed: '. . . I . . . hardly think it worthwhile to continue our negotiation, for the impression of weakness which it will give, will injure me more than can be repaid by the accession of his votes.'[2]

There was, thus, more to the influence of the great borough proprietors than simply the number of seats they could command. When some of them exercised significant influence over measures—for example, Conolly and Leinster in the late 1770s, and possibly Abercorn in the early 1790s—this resulted not just from their command of seats but from other factors (including Conolly's and Leinster's connection with Buckinghamshire and Abercorn's with Pitt). More often, the great borough proprietors were not so much interested in shaping measures as in obtaining honours and emoluments for their dependants and themselves. The fact that all of them but Conolly were peers, in itself set limits to their personal political ambition (a scheme under consideration in 1784 for setting up a couple of offices of parliamentary responsibility in the Irish House of Lords was designed to pander to that limited ambition[3]); all of them, Conolly included, were inevitable

[1] Johnston, *Irish Parliament, 1784–7*, p. 232; Westmorland to Pitt, [pre-18 Feb.? 1793], Chatham MSS., P.R.O. 30/8/331, fol. 191; Shannon to Lord Boyle, 6 and 15 June 1798, Shannon MSS., P.R.O.N.I. D.2707/A3/3/79, 88. In 1777, Shannon was told by Lord Harcourt, the out-going Lord Lieutenant, that Harcourt had fully apprised the in-coming Lord Lieutenant, Lord Buckinghamshire, '. . . of my consequence and character; . . . that he considered me both with respect of my influence, steadiness, and abilities, as the first object of Government; and that he had never, in this or any other Kingdom, experienced more honour than in his connection with me . . .' (Memo. by Shannon, [*c.* 28 Jan. 1777], Shannon MSS., P.R.O.N.I. D.2707/A/2/2/21).

[2] Buckingham to Grenville, 16 Mar. 1788 and 3 Apr. 1789, *H.M.C. Dropmore MSS.*, i. 310, 443.

[3] Rutland to Pitt, 13 Sept. 1784, *H.M.C. Rutland MSS.*, iii. 136.

politicians rather than politicians by choice, and part-time politicians even by late eighteenth-century standards. Moreover, what is also striking is the absence of political ambition among those whom they returned to Parliament, and the on-the-whole low political calibre of these people. Of the politicians already listed as attaining top political influence during the period of Foster's official career up to 1800, only three ever sat in Parliament as the nominees of borough proprietors, great or small. Grattan sat on an unusual footing of independence as one of Lord Charlemont's members for Charlemont; Yelverton sat for Carrickfergus and was politically connected with the absentee Earl of Donegall in some indistinct way; and Hussey Burgh alone sat as the nominee of a great borough proprietor, the Duke of Leinster (but either returned himself or else was out of Parliament during the period of his greatest influence, the years 1777–9 and 1782–3).[1] When Lord Ely (the 1st Earl of the second creation) got his political manager, Robert Hellen, appointed Solicitor-General, the consequences were disastrous; and Ely himself was the first to admit that 'a man of more volubility' was needed.[2] In fact, the only career politicians of anything like front-rank calibre who were satellites of the great borough proprietors, were James Dennis (Lord Tracton), who was Lord Shannon's political manager, and the Hon. George Knox, who was connected with, though not returned by, Lord Abercorn. Interestingly, Lord Abercorn's political connection came to grief partly because it included too many people of some calibre and political ambition: Knox; his eldest brother, Thomas Knox; and their kinsman,

[1] For Grattan's relationship with Charlemont, see Grattan, *Life*, iii. 89 ff.: for Yelverton's with Donegall, see Lord Hertford to Hely-Hutchinson, 26 Mar. 1776, *H.M.C. Donoughmore MSS.*, p. 286; Scott to Robinson, 15 Oct. 1779, *Beresford Correspondence*, i. 63 f.; Sayles, *Contemporary Sketches*, p. 236; Mrs. McTier to Dr. William Drennan, [pre-July 1782?], [Jan.? 1784], [Jan.? 1784], and [1785?], Drennan MSS., P.R.O.N.I. D.591/160, 110, 116, 172; *Commons' Journals* (Ireland), xi. 212. Fitzgibbon sat for the close co. Limerick borough of Kilmallock, 1783–9, but almost certainly as a free agent, and probably without purchase—see Fitzgibbon to Eden, 11 Oct. 1783 and 10 Jan. 1786, printed in H. L. Falkiner, 'Lord Clare', in *Studies in Irish History and Biography* (London, 1902), pp. 141, 145.

[2] Ely to Buckinghamshire, 6 Apr. 1779, Heron MSS., N.L.I. MS. 13037/7. Lord Shannon urged the claims of *his* leading satellite in the House of Commons, Attiwell Wood, to succeed Hellen as Solicitor-General, but the Government had learned their lesson and did not appoint Wood, who was 'dull to a proverb'— Buckinghamshire to North, 31 Dec. 1779, *Beresford Correspondence*, i. 124.

the Hon. Edmond Henry Pery (the last two of whom, like the first, did not owe their return to Lord Abercorn).[1] It was more usual for the followers, and certainly the nominees, of the great borough proprietors to be unambitious yes-men, who were content to draw the wages of silent support, and were not capable of giving their patrons an indirect influence on the shaping of measures.

Significantly, all the politicians listed as attaining top political influence, with the exception of Scott and Toler, at one time or another established a precarious interest in an open constituency like the University, if they did not have a family interest in either a county or a borough. Scott and Toler were content to continue to purchase their way into Parliament; the others who had no inherited electoral interest—Tisdall, Hussey Burgh, Yelverton, Fitzgibbon, Grattan, and Wolfe—preferred to return themselves than to be returned by purchase or by a patron (here again the peculiar relationship between Yelverton and Lord Donegall is a complicating factor). The reason lay partly in the prestige of representing an open constituency, particularly the University. But it lay also in the fact that purchase often had political strings attached—usually strings which attached the member to the Castle, but sometimes to the opposition—and it was not always easy to find a seat for sale. Being returned free of charge by a borough proprietor obviously had strings attached. Equally obviously, career politicians ambitious for political office had to be in Parliament, or they would go unobserved by the government, and had to be there, if possible, on a footing which gave them complete freedom of manœuvre. The Castle, of course, had seats at its disposal in the form of the four bishops' boroughs of Armagh, Clogher, Old Leighlin, and St. Canice, and a fluctuating number of other seats besides. But most career politicians did not want to be returned directly by the Castle, any more than they wanted to be returned by a borough proprietor. Apart from the chief secretary, who was very seldom an Irish politician, the people brought in for the bishops' boroughs were Castle make-weights like Foster's brother-in-law, Thomas Burgh, who were bound by their offices to support the government, and who were

---

[1] Johnston, *Irish House of Commons in 1791*, p. 35. It came to grief for other reasons too, notably a cooling in Abercorn's relations with Pitt.

returned to Parliament to vote rather than to speechify. In any case, the bishops could not always be relied upon to return government nominees—two did not in 1783 and one in 1761; one of the bishops' boroughs, Clogher, was far from being close; and prior to the Place Act of 1793, the government had enough trouble finding a seat for the chief secretary without worrying about anyone else. (The absence of a Place Act until then also meant that some government seats were liable to be cluttered with the deadwood of departed chief secretaries until the next general election.)[1] For a variety of reasons, therefore, career politicians ambitious for political office did not sit for government seats. The exception was Tisdall, who was brought in for Armagh in 1776 after being driven out of the University, which he had represented since 1739, by Hely-Hutchinson; but this was long after his political ambitions had been realized. Another unimportant exception was Foster's successor as Chairman of Committees, John Monck Mason, who sat for St. Canice.[2] In general, however, career politicians wanted to return themselves, as it was a great help to them if they were in Parliament without purchase, or at least without political tutelage.

If this was true of Irish career politicians in general, it was especially true of Foster, whose particular ambition was the speakership. He could not have been elected Speaker if he had not had a safe seat of his own, for Louth or, if Louth rejected him, for Dunleer. It was desirable that the speaker should sit for an open constituency, and most speakers did; but two had sat for close family boroughs without provoking adverse comment.[3] What would have provoked adverse comment, and probably made his election an impossibility, was the candidature

---

[1] Bishop of Ferns to Bedford, 28 Mar. 1761, Bedford MSS., P.R.O.N.I. T.2915/11/52; Johnston, *Great Britain and Ireland*, pp. 190 ff. For further details about Clogher borough, see pp. 269 f. In May 1796 there were still three ex-chief secretaries holding down government seats, in spite of the Place Act. One of them was Lord Fitzwilliam's Chief Secretary, so perhaps he stayed on to inconvenience the Camden Administration: also acceptance of office in Ireland vacated a man's English seat. See Camden to Pelham, 23 May 1796, Pelham MSS., B.L. Add. MS. 33102, fols. 16–18.

[2] Monck Mason was also 'strongly connected with the interests of the borough in question'—Eden to Northington, 30 Aug. 1783, ibid. Add. MS. 33118, fols. 298–9.

[3] Malcomson, *Foster and the Speakership*, pp. 290 f., n. 100.

of a man who sat for a government borough, for a purchased seat, or for a seat which had been obtained for him as a result of a non-cash transaction between the government and some borough proprietor. The spokesman of the House of Commons in its dealings with the executive, could not have sat in the House on such terms. In this special sense, Foster owed his rise to the top to the fact that he could guarantee his own return to the House.

With the Union and the abolition of the speakership, Foster's special dependence on his command of at least one seat ceased to apply. However, the Union made a sweeping change in the Irish representative system, in the value of electoral influence in Ireland, and in particular in its value to a career politician. It had the obvious effect of drastically reducing the number of Irish seats which any one individual could command, by disfranchising no less than 85 boroughs outright, and converting a further 31 and the University to the status of single-member constituencies. It is an indication of the change it wrought that Lord Downshire lost seven seats and Lord Shannon six.[1] In effect, it was an Irish Re-Distribution Act, passed thirty-two years before the first English Re-Distribution Act, and so sweeping in its results that a further Re-Distribution Act was not deemed necessary for Ireland until 1885. It affected Drogheda, and did not affect Louth, in the obvious sense that Drogheda, like all the county boroughs except Dublin and Cork, lost one of its seats, and Louth, like all the counties, retained both. However, many counties were still affected by it in the subtler sense that it upset the balance of power within them, by disfranchising or reducing to single-member constituencies the double-member boroughs which they had hitherto contained. Monaghan and Queen's County are the simplest and clearest examples of this. In both, all the boroughs (Monaghan had only one, Queen's County three) had been under the patronage of families who were leading interests in the county as well, and the representation enjoyed by the boroughs had thus been an important element in keeping the county representation uncontested. The Union largely removed this safety valve by disfranchising Monaghan's one borough and two of Queen's County's three. The effect

---

[1] Jupp, *Irish M.P.s at Westminster*, p. 74; *Cornwallis Correspondence*, iii. 321 ff.

was of course to intensify pressure on the county seats. In Monaghan, especially, the family interest which controlled the one borough and which, probably in consequence of this, had stayed out of the county, successfully contested a by-election for the county as soon as the Union had passed and before it had even come into operation.[1]

The effect of the Union on Louth was by no means so dramatic. In Louth the patrons of two out of the three disfranchised boroughs, Ardee and Carlingford, were extremely unimportant in county terms, and in no position to increase the pressure on the county seats. The part-patron of the other disfranchised borough, Dunleer, was in the same position. The other part-patron of Dunleer was of course Foster, who already held one county seat. The patron of the remaining borough in the county, Dundalk, which was reduced to a single-member constituency, was Lord Roden. Roden had no reason to press for one of the county seats at this stage, because his obvious candidate for it, his eldest son, was not nearly of age; he did not even use his remaining seat for Dundalk to return another member of his family to Parliament, preferring instead to go to market with it. So there was no pressure from Roden on the county seats for Louth until 1809, when his son at last came of age; and well before then the occupant of the second county seat, Lord Clermont, had run out of candidates for it and had been happy to see it go to Roden. As a result of these purely fortuitous circumstances, therefore, the Union had no effect on the balance of power in Louth.

Drogheda was quite different. The fact that it had been a double-member constituency in the Irish Parliament had made possible the compromise arrangement between Hardman and Ball in 1797. The Union did not upset this compromise arrangement, because Ball, whose ambitions were professional rather than parliamentary, found that his profession required that he stay in Dublin, while Parliament would have required that he move to London. Under these circumstances a ballot may not even have been necessary between Hardman and him in 1800; Ball may have been happy to concede the one post-Union seat to Hardman, no doubt for a consideration. However, the Union did have the important and unfortunate effect on

[1] Malcomson, *Earl of Clermont*, pp. 36 f.

Drogheda that it made it impossible for the embattled Foster/Hardman and Smyth/Ogle factions in the corporation to compromise and share the representation in the way that Hardman and Ball had done, because now there was only the one seat. A compromise arrangement based on alternate representation, such as appears to have been agreed upon in 1803, was always liable to break down, and for the reason that the Drogheda arrangement broke down: the unexpectedly short duration of the 1806 Parliament. When it was dissolved in 1807, John Foster was certainly not disposed to give Ogle a second term. Foster, after all, had been accustomed to commanding two seats in Parliament, and wanted to make up in Drogheda what he had lost in Dunleer. In purely financial terms, one seat in the United Parliament was worth two in the old Irish. However, he was not thinking in financial terms, but in terms of his parliamentary following and of his parliamentary consequence, relative to English family interests which had not been the victims of a measure of re-distribution and concealed parliamentary reform. The Union, while increasing the pressure on Drogheda's one remaining seat, made winning a Drogheda election more desirable, especially to a career politician like Foster. Without the advantage of his official position, he could not have secured the Drogheda seat in 1807; but if he had not had an official position to maintain, he might well not have wanted to.

After the Union, Irish career politicians had much greater need of electoral interest or any other asset they could lay claim to than before, because the government now had much less need of the services of Irish politicians. The abolition of the Irish Parliament ended the necessity for an Irish cabinet. With the exception of the chancellorship of the Irish exchequer, which survived until 1817, and the vice-treasurership for Ireland thereafter,[1] there ceased to be offices of parliamentary business in the Irish administration for Irish politicians to fill. The precedents of appointing Irish politicians to the chief secretaryship and the lord chancellorship were not followed,

---

[1] Kiernan, *Financial Administration*, pp. 323 f. The Vice-Treasurers were Sir George F. Hill, 1817–30 (when he had to take a colonial governorship in order to escape from his creditors) and the Knight of Kerry, 1830. The office was abolished by the Whigs (FitzGerald MSS., 13/42–113, 18/39–52). Hill's papers, among other things as Vice-Treasurer, are in P.R.O.N.I., ref. D.642.

unless the Wellesley brothers are counted as Irishmen, and except in the case of George Ponsonby, who was not a member of the House of Commons while Lord Chancellor, 1806–7. In any case, Ponsonby, like Castlereagh on the other side of the House, was a successful transplant from Irish to British politics, and both became leaders of their respective parties in the House of Commons. Commissionerships of the revenue in Ireland became incompatible with a seat in Parliament in 1801;[1] commissionerships of the treasury continued to be so compatible, but as has been seen the Irish treasury did not develop as a political or even administrative institution, and most of the commissioners, with notable exceptions like Parnell's son and successor, Sir Henry Parnell, and Vesey FitzGerald, were nonentities with electoral interest. The Irish law offices remained, and their early holders were people who had distinguished themselves in the Irish Parliament (or, in the case of the Unionist appointees, had at least belonged to it); but the duties of these offices were barely compatible with attendance at a distant Parliament at Westminster, and the Law Officers, including even first-rate parliamentarians like W. C. Plunket, were seldom M.P.s.[2] A few Irish politicians of younger vintage than Ponsonby and Castlereagh followed them into the mainstream of British politics—Vesey FitzGerald, Sir Henry Parnell, and younger still, Thomas Spring-Rice. But those who failed, or did not want, to enter the mainstream usually sank without trace—John Leslie Foster, for example: his highest office while he sat in Parliament was that of First Counsel to the Revenue Commissioners in Ireland, and he died a mere Judge of the Common Pleas.

In 1803 Chief Secretary Wickham pointed out that there was a greater shortage of 'efficient men' among the Irish members than of 'leading interests'.[3] The government, however, did nothing to improve this situation. They did not go talent-

[1] Beresford to Abbot, 15 Nov. 1801, Colchester MSS., P.R.O. 30/9/1, part 1/2; 41 Geo. III c. 52, s. 4.
[2] Plunket, while Solicitor- and then Attorney-General, 1803–7, sat in Parliament for only a couple of months at the beginning of 1807, when the Talents returned him for an English borough; his successor in both offices, William Saurin, never sat in Parliament.
[3] Wickham to Addington, 29 Aug. 1803, Wickham MSS., P.R.O.N.I. T.2627 5/D/69.

spotting among the Irish members—or rather, they spotted the untalented Henry Alexander, who had already made an exhibition of himself as Chairman of Committees in the Irish Parliament,[1] and made him Chairman of Committees in the first session of the Parliament of the United Kingdom, as a gesture towards the Irish members. At the general election of 1802, it is true, the Addington Administration returned to Parliament, apparently at no cost to the candidates, two Irish politicians who would not otherwise have been able to secure seats: C. M. Ormsby, First Counsel to the Revenue Commissioners and a friend of Isaac Corry's, who was to assist with the Irish parliamentary business; and Richard Archdall, in whom Addington himself had spotted talent which never materialized.[2] With these exceptions, and a few others— Corry in 1806–7, Plunket in 1807, and John Leslie Foster from 1816 to 1824—the government did not find seats for 'efficient men' among the Irish members; and in the case of Corry the seat was merely found, not paid for, by the Government.[3] Otherwise, the government continued to regard Ireland as a land of close boroughs, ignoring the Union disfranchisements, and even quartered British politicians on the remaining close Irish seats which fell to its disposal.[4] Generally speaking, the Irish politicians were left to return themselves, or go to the wall; and aspirants to the few Irish offices compatible with a seat in Parliament were expected to earn them by returning themselves or nominees. Thus, in 1806, it was assumed by J. S. Rochfort that one particular Lord of the Irish Treasury

[1] Bishop of Killaloe to Abercorn, 19 Mar. [1799], Abercorn MSS., P.R.O.N.I. T.2541/IB3/7/7.

[2] John Stewart to Abercorn, 21 Jan. 1803, ibid. IB2/4/1; Jupp, 'Parliamentary Representation', article on Archdall.

[3] Corry was returned through the agency of the Talents, but his seat was in fact paid for by the Dowager Lady Downshire, as part of an election pact over Newry borough—Buckingham to Grenville, 14 Oct. 1806, *H.M.C. Dropmore MSS.*, viii. 387. J. L. Foster was returned free of charge in 1816, and probably in 1818— Vesey FitzGerald to J. L. Foster, 24 Feb. 1816, Vesey FitzGerald MSS., N.L.I. MS. 7846, p. 112; Peel to J. L. Foster, 19 June [1818], and Liverpool to J. L. Foster, 20 Dec. 1818, J. L. Foster MSS., P.R.O.N.I. T.2519/7/1, 3.

[4] Canning sat for Tralee, 1802–6, and 'Prosperity' Robinson for Carlow borough, 1806–18. For four Englishmen or Scots, none of whom had any connection with the Irish Administration, whom the Talents returned (not free of charge) for Irish borough seats in 1806, see William Fremantle to Elliot, 10 Nov. 1806, Elliot of Wells MSS., N.L.S. E.W. 31. Fremantle, the Joint Secretary to the British Treasury, himself sat for Enniskillen at the time.

would be removed by the in-coming Talents Administration, '. . . as he once [in 1795] deserted that party and has no parliamentary interest to support him . . .'[1] His lack of parliamentary interest must have tipped the scale against him, for he was in fact removed. Likewise, in 1807 John Foster was told that he could have a lordship of the Irish treasury for Thomas Foster only if Thomas Foster was able to bring himself into Parliament, and when Thomas Foster did not even stand for re-election in 1812, he was punished by being dismissed from the treasury early in the following year: lordships of the treasury being among the few offices compatible with a seat in Parliament, administrations tended to use them to induce supporters to contest seats which might otherwise go to the opposition.[2] Even in the case of the chancellorship of the Irish exchequer, the only really important Irish political office to survive the Union (apart from those normally reserved for British politicians), a man's ability to return himself to Parliament was a corroborative qualification: when the Liverpool Administration was considering whom to appoint to the resuscitated chancellorship in 1812, one of the arguments used against John Leslie Foster (besides his relationship and resemblance to his uncle) was that he was unlikely to hold his seat at the next election and thus, if appointed, would have to be brought into Parliament by the Government. Once again, lack of parliamentary interest tipped the scale; John Leslie Foster was passed over in favour of Vesey FitzGerald, who controlled at least an alternate return for Ennis borough, and later returned himself for co. Clare.[3]

[1] Rochfort to Foster, 3 Feb. 1806, F.P. D.207/33/67. This was Lord Frankfort, formerly Lodge Morres.

[2] Hawkesbury to Wellesley, 27 Apr. 1807, *Wellington Supplementary Despatches*, v. 23. Thomas Foster was able to cite two precedents for post-Union lords of the treasury being seatless—Thomas Foster to Peel, 24 Jan. 1813, Peel MSS., B.L. Add. MS. 40224, fols. 206–8.

[3] Vesey FitzGerald to Vansittart, 23 Feb. [1814], and Sir Edward O'Brien [who seems to have been the co-patron] to Vesey FitzGerald, 6 Mar. 1814, Vesey FitzGerald MSS., N.L.I. MS. 7828, pp. 52–5, 184; Richmond to Peel, 5 Aug. 1812, Peel MSS., B.L. Add. MS. 40185, fols. 11–14. Between the Great Reform Act and 1867, when the provision of the Place Act obliging politicians to vacate their seats on acceptance of office was repealed, having a safe seat of one's own became an almost essential qualification for office, as the government in that period had very few seats at its disposal—see N. Gash, *Politics in the Age of Peel: a Study in the Technique of Parliamentary Representation, 1830–1850* (London, 1953), pp.

Under post-Union circumstances, therefore, Foster's safe seat for co. Louth was arguably vital to his political come-back, especially in view of his embarrassed personal finances; if he had not been able to return himself inexpensively at the general election of 1802, the come-back might never have taken place. The Union disfranchisements had gravely restricted an Irish politician's chances of being able to purchase his way into Parliament—at least for an Irish constituency. This restriction applied particularly to those Irish politicians who were either uncommitted or in opposition, since the remaining Irish seats which were close and for sale were usually sold through the medium of the government, and only to government supporters.[1] It would not have suited Foster in 1802 to have lost his freedom of action, because, by holding aloof from the Addington Administration and playing a waiting game, he was later able to secure much better terms from Pitt. No doubt somewhere in Great Britain he could have found a seat without strings attached. But, in his then financial situation, it is doubtful if he could have raised the money to pay for it: seats in the United Parliament of 1802 cost £5,000 or more—as compared to £2,000 or £2,500 in the Irish Parliament of the 1790s.[2] This was another significant change effected by the Union. Whatever the disadvantages of purchase, it was probably in the long run a cheaper way of entering successive Irish Parliaments, than nursing an interest in an open constituency with patronage and cash: after the Union, this generally speaking ceased to be the case, and certainly was not the case when the open constituency was uncontested and comparatively inexpensive to nurse. Even in Drogheda in 1807, Thomas Foster did not have to go to immoderate expense in order to win a contested election. However, the all-important consideration was John Foster's safe seat for Louth. His return to office in 1804 was in large measure due to the impression he had made

---

224 ff. However, this should not have been a factor prior to 1832, even in Ireland. For further discussion of the situation of Irish career politicians after the Union, see pp. 446 ff.

[1] See p. 334.

[2] James Stewart to Lord Alexander, 14 Mar. [1802], Caledon MSS., P.R.O.N.I. D.2433/C/3/52; Wickham to Addington, 5 Nov. 1802, Wickham MSS., P.R.O.N.I. T.2627/5/D/29; Knox to Abercorn, 21 Apr. 1790, Abercorn MSS., P.R.O.N.I. T.2541/IB/1/1/8; Bolton, *Union*, p. 33.

on the United Parliament, particularly on the English country gentlemen, and without the Louth seat it is unlikely that he would have had a chance to make this impression.

Nor did the advantages he derived from the safety of his seat end there. His successive rivals for the chancellorship of the Irish exchequer at Westminster, Corry and Newport, both sat for constituencies where their interest was precarious, and like him neither of them could readily have found the means to buy their way into Parliament—certainly into parliament after parliament. The result was that the necessity for nursing their ailing interests interfered with their official duties and, in the eyes of their English colleagues, compromised their political credibility. They sat for the voracious mercantile constituencies of Newry and Waterford City respectively, which in character resembled Drogheda rather than Louth, and were two of the most difficult places in Ireland for a chancellor of the exchequer to represent. Corry was M.P. for Newry, 1776–1806 (with a short break from 1800 to 1802, after he had been unlucky in the Union ballot); but in fact his interest there was not nearly as strong as this lengthy run would suggest, because it depended very much on the apathy of the leading interest in the borough, the Needham family. His hold was weakened when Newry became a single-member constituency in 1800, and it broke altogether when the Needhams became for the first time politically active.[1] But even before the Union, in 1798, he had been accused of neglecting his duties as Chairman of Committees in the Irish Parliament, 'in order to intrigue with the United Irishmen about Newry'.[2] His dependence on revenue and other jobs to maintain his position in Newry was a major source of friction between the Irish Administration and himself, causing Wickham to exclaim in 1802: 'It were better he had been an Englishman, or that the borough of Newry had never existed!'[3] To a lesser extent, Newport's conduct was similarly objectionable. Though a tenacious and vociferous reformer, he showed something less than reforming

[1] Johnston, *Great Britain and Ireland*, p. 163; Elliot to Grenville, 4 June 1806, *H.M.C. Dropmore MSS.*, viii. 175.

[2] Robert Johnson to Downshire, 20 Oct. 1798, Downshire MSS., P.R.O.N.I. D.607/F/475.

[3] Wickham to Addington, 18 Dec. 1802, Wickham MSS., P.R.O.N.I. T.2627/5/D/33.

purity in his disposal of revenue jobs in Waterford; which dismayed his ministerial colleagues, the Talents, and exposed him to the charge that 'his [Waterford] City politics . . . are too much influenced by Party under pretence of patriotism'.[1] In fact, like Foster in Drogheda, he could ill afford to be squeamish about the methods he resorted to. He first won the seat for Waterford after a disputed election in 1802; he held on to it at an uncontested by-election in 1806, made necessary by his appointment as Chancellor of the Irish Exchequer, but informality in the manner of his appointment had subsequently to be hushed up, as it was 'peculiarly desirable' to him to avoid a second re-election;[2] he fought two sharp contests at the general elections of 1806 and 1807; and by 1812 he was so hard-hit by the effects of electioneering that he confessed that another contest would force him to sell New Park, his residence outside Waterford. In the event, however, the 1812 election passed off without a contest, and in 1818 an agreement was reached among the local interests guaranteeing him the seat for the rest of his life.[3] Not until then did he acquire the advantage of a safe seat, which Foster had enjoyed throughout his political, or at any rate his official, career.

Foster was thus an 'efficient man', whose efficiency was on display because he could return himself to Parliament, and whose efficiency was not impaired by electioneering jobbery (at any rate in Louth—Drogheda was a rather different story). He was also, by post-Union Irish standards, a 'leading interest'. In the state of parties in the spring of 1804, Foster's influence over Hardman and William Charles Fortescue must have strengthened his claims to office, as must the more nebulous influence he possessed over the survivors of the Foster 'connection'.

[1] Elliot to Grenville, 23 June 1806, *H.M.C. Dropmore MSS.*, viii. 195; Newport to Elliot, 11 and 19 June 1806, Elliot of Wells MSS., N.L.S. E.W. 30; Cornelius Bolton to Foster, June 1809, F.P. D.562/11173; Pollock to Hobart, 4 Mar. 1807, Hobart MSS., P.R.O.N.I. T.2627/1/7; Cornelius Bolton to Foster, 29 Apr. 1807, F.P. D.562/12139. Newport's zeal for ferreting out cases of corruption and malversation is neatly held up to ridicule in [Lord Palmerston], *The New Whig Guide* (London, 1819), pp. 15 ff.

[2] J. Beckett to Marsden, 21 Feb. 1806, S.P.O. 531/225/3. I am indebted for this reference to Dr. P. J. Jupp.

[3] Jupp, 'Parliamentary Representation', article on Newport; articles of agreement between Newport, William Newport, Henry Alcock, and James Wallace about the Waterford representation, 10 Jan. 1818, Howard Bury MSS., Longford-Westmeath Library, Mullingar; photocopies in P.R.O.N.I., ref. T.3069/D.34, p. 73.

The importance of this latter species of influence under post-Union conditions should not be over-stressed. The Irish members at Westminster in the early nineteenth century usually succumbed to baser pressures than those of loyalty and friendship. It is significant that in May 1804 Pitt's intermediary with Foster's old friend and fellow anti-Unionist, Owen Wynne, M.P. for Sligo borough, was not Foster but Lord Camden, whose contacts among the Irish members dating from his viceregal days were of considerable service to Pitt; also that Wynne's support seems to have been secured by the promise of a living for his brother.[1]

Between October 1806 and April 1807, when Henry Meade Ogle was M.P. for Drogheda, and Foster could command no vote but his own, he was in opposition and in any case was absent from Westminster. In April 1807, however, when he was once again a candidate for office, his electoral interest looked like reaching a new peak of three votes, including his own, and in the event did so. At the general election of that year he got, not a Hardman, but a Foster, returned for Drogheda, and was also successful in gaining another seat which he had probably had his eye on since the 1790s, the University.[2] His interest in the University was distinct from the government interest there (although it undoubtedly derived strength from his high position in national politics). Indeed, on one occasion his interest had actually been exerted against the Government—admittedly without success. The occasion was the University by-election of 1805 when Foster, though Chancellor of the Exchequer at the time, had set up John Leslie Foster against the government candidate, George Knox (Lord Abercorn's protégé).[3] John Leslie Foster had been easily defeated at this election, but he came near to turning the tables on Knox at the general election of 1806, when the Talents stood neutral, regarding both candidates as 'hostile'.[4] In 1807, the

---

[1] Camden to Wynne, 31 May 1804, Pratt MSS., K.A.O. U.840/C.270/2.

[2] Hobart to Pitt, 31 Jan. 1794, Chatham MSS., P.R.O. 30/8/328, fols. 187–8. In this letter Hobart refers to John Wolfe's interest among the Fellows, and Wolfe was a relation and protégé of Foster.

[3] J. L. Foster to Foster, 3 Mar. 1805, F.P. T.2519/4/821; Hardwicke to Hawkesbury, 7 Mar. 1805, Hardwicke MSS., B.L. Add. MS. 35710, fol. 38.

[4] Rochfort to Foster, 29 Mar. 1805, F.P. D.207/33/19; Elliot to Grenville, 6 Nov. 1806, *H.M.C. Dropmore MSS.*, viii. 429.

new 'no Popery' Ministry, which succeeded the Talents, threw its weight behind John Leslie Foster, who was returned after only a token opposition.[1] With his nephew as M.P. for the University, his son for Drogheda, and himself for Louth, Foster had 'a pretty strong phalanx', as another nephew, John Maxwell Barry, put it.[2] Although his appointment as Chancellor of the Exchequer had come through several weeks before the election, the probability of his being able to return three members—two of them of course with much help from the Government—may have given him the advantage over his rivals for the office, Lord Clancarty, Sir Laurence Parsons, and Barry himself,[3] each of whom could decisively influence no more than one seat, if even that. Command of three put Foster back to his pre-Union strength: a very rare feat among Irish electoral interests. It also strengthened his bargaining power with the 'no Popery' and Perceval Ministries (both of which were weaker in Irish support than any of the other ministries between 1800 and 1820)[4]—the more so as the defeated sitting members for the University and Drogheda in 1807 were both Emancipationists.

The general election of 1812 put paid to Foster's electoral interest, except as regards his own seat for Louth; John Leslie Foster had to retire from the University[5] and Thomas Foster from Drogheda. After the election, the Prime Minister, Lord Liverpool, expressed some anxiety about offending 'the Foster connection', which he pointed out in the then state of parties was 'of some consequence'.[6] However, by this stage the 'connection' was more nebulous than ever; its only surviving member, apart from Barry, was Foster's son-in-law, Lord Dufferin, who was in the habit of purchasing an English seat through the

[1] Jupp, 'Parliamentary Representation', article on Dublin University.

[2] Barry to Foster, 1 May 1807, F.P. D.207/52/17.

[3] Barry's subsequent comments on Foster show that he was not a very loyal, or at any rate not an uncritical, member of the Foster 'connection'—see Barry to Vesey FitzGerald, 30 Aug. 1812, Vesey FitzGerald MSS., N.L.I. MS. 7821, pp. 64–5.

[4] Jupp, *Irish M.P.s at Westminster*, p. 71.

[5] J. L. Foster to Thomas Foster, 20 June 1812, J. L. Foster MSS., P.R.O.N.I. T.2519/7/3; Richmond to Liverpool, 5 May 1813, Richmond MSS., N.L.I. MS. 62/475. The first letter shows that J. L. Foster wanted to give up the seat, on professional grounds; the second that he would almost certainly not have been re-elected anyway.

[6] Liverpool to Peel, 1 Nov. 1812, Peel MSS., B.L. Add. MS. 40181, fols. 25–6.

agency of the government, and who was primarily concerned with obtaining favours and jobs for members of his own family and himself.[1] In spite of 'the Foster connection', Thomas Foster lost his lordship of the treasury, and no seat or suitable office was found for John Leslie Foster. The principal supporter of the Fosters in their various claims and objects in the years after 1812 was in fact John Leslie Foster's successful rival for the chancellorship of the Irish exchequer, Vesey FitzGerald; he had come to the fore under John Foster's auspices and his sister later married John Leslie Foster. Vesey FitzGerald laboured under the unfortunate imputation of being an Irish adventurer on the make—largely on account of a scurrilous pamphlet written against him by the Duke of York's ex-mistress, Mrs. Clarke. However, the loyalty and gratitude he showed to the Fosters did him credit and should be placed to his account.[2]

Over his whole official career, John Foster had depended on the command of at least one safe seat to a perhaps unusual extent among Irish career politicians: in the period up to the Union because of the special circumstance of the type of constituency which the speaker had to represent, and in the period after the Union because of circumstances common to all Irish politicians, combined with another special circumstance, his shortage of ready cash. Also, over his whole official career—and the Union in this respect made no difference—he had derived some subsidiary, tactical advantage from the fact that he represented an open constituency, possessed considerable influence in another, Drogheda, and some for a time in a third, the University. Representing an open constituency could well be a disadvantage to a career politician, particularly after the passing of the Place Act. It has already been suggested that, on balance, Corry's and Newport's local

---

[1] Dufferin to Foster, 12 May and 25 June 1807, 23 July 1809, and 12 Aug. [1810], F.P. T.2519/4/1627, 1628, 1635, 1654.

[2] Vesey FitzGerald to Peel, 3 Feb. [1813], Vesey FitzGerald MSS., N.L.I. MS. 7818, p. 22; *A Letter Addressed to the Rt. Hon. William FitzGerald . . . by Mrs. M. A. Clarke* (London, 1813). This latter extraordinary production includes the following apostrophe: '. . . You, whose grandfather, roguish Billy FitzGerald of Ennis, was a poor, pettifogging attorney; whose father owes his advancement in life, not to merit, but to the dirty arts of political intrigue; whose aunt is a common street-walker; and whose cousin was hanged for horse-stealing—you whose whole conduct since your first entrance into the world has been a tissue of infamy and complicated guilt. . . .' (pp. 56–7).

interests were encumbrances to their political careers. The balance is less easy to strike in other cases, for example the case of the Hely-Hutchinson interest in Cork City. At times it gave the Hely-Hutchinsons bargaining power *vis à vis* the government (as in 1779):[1] at times it did the reverse; in 1802, for example, Hardwicke thought that Lord Donoughmore, Hely-Hutchinson's son, would not oppose the Government, because such conduct '. . . would endanger his interest at Cork, where the merchants would not find their own interest, either public or private, advanced by supporting him in opposition. . . .'[2] The balance is also not easy to strike in the case of Castlereagh's interest in co. Down. Until 1812, when it was secured by an election pact with the Downshires, co. Down was probably an encumbrance to him, to say nothing of its expense. The popular posturings of his early days as M.P. for co. Down, including moderate support of the French Revolution, were not a help to his future career (perhaps George III was thinking of them when he described Castlereagh's advocacy of Catholic Emancipation in 1801 as 'Jacobinical'), and when he was a candidate for the chief secretaryship in 1797–8, these earlier popular posturings were only effaced by his exceptionally good English connections. When eventually appointed Chief Secretary in 1798, he evaded the provisions of the Place Act (presumably because of the precariousness of his seat);[3] at the general election of 1802 he was saved from defeat only by the intervention of Addington himself; and at the by-election occasioned by his appointment as Secretary of State for War and the Colonies in 1805, he was in fact defeated and kept out of co. Down until 1812.[4] Co. Down, in other words, strained his credit in national politics, at a time when his political future was far from assured.

Because Louth, too, was an open constituency, its M.P. was not entirely absolved from the worries and distractions which went with Newry, Waterford, Cork City, and co. Down.

[1] See p. 227.

[2] Hardwicke to Addington, 29 Nov. 1802, quoted in Jupp, 'Parliamentary Representation', article on Cork City.

[3] Beresford to Auckland, 19 Mar. 1800, Sneyd MSS., P.R.O.N.I. T. 3229/2/60; commonplace book kept by Foster as Speaker, 1786–98, F.P. D.562/7564; Percy to his wife, 6 Feb. 1799, Percy MSS., B.L. Add. MS. 32335, fol. 133. The chief secretaryship was not, strictly speaking, an office under the Crown.

[4] Jupp, *Co. Down Elections*, p. 185; Hyde, *Castlereagh, passim*: Bolton, *Union*, p. 211.

In the years before Foster's entry into office in 1777, he had been described as occasionally deserting the government on popular issues because he was M.P. for a county,[1] although these occasional desertions were perhaps inspired by diplomacy as much as necessity: not only did they help to mollify the independent interest, they also raised his market value in the eyes of the government, who would be unlikely to bid high for a man who it thought would support it for nothing. In the years after 1777, once it had acquired his support, the fact that he was M.P. for a county did not prevent him from pursuing a politically unpopular course on most of the popular issues of the period between then and his election to the speakership in 1785. In September 1780, for example, he was prepared to go even further than Scott in opposing a motion of Grattan's declaratory of the independence of the Irish Parliament:[2] an episode which in itself gives a good idea of the strength of his hold on Louth, because Scott sat, as always, for a purchased seat and had no constituents to worry about. The political unpopularity of Foster's conduct in these years contrasts strongly with the popularity, locally, of his conduct in the 1790s, at least on the two most important political issues of the decade. On these, Foster and nearly all his constituents were agreed, and he paraded their sentiments as 'confirmation' of his own, and on at least one occasion—the debate on the Catholic Relief Bill of 1793—paid lip-service to the radical doctrine that M.P.s were trustees for their constituents.[3] It was not all parade and lip-service: their mutual opposition to Catholic Relief and the Union established a bond between Foster and even the more radical of the Protestant gentry of Louth. In addition, then, to the safety of his seat, and contributing materially to its safety, Foster enjoyed the further advantage that there was at this time a genuinely popular element— political as well as personal and paternalist—in his interest in Louth. This gave him, from the point of view of the government, a superior value to the man whose safe seat was for a close borough like Dunleer.

[1] Hunt, *Irish Parliament*, p. 22.

[2] O'Connell, *Irish Politics and Social Conflict*, p. 231.

[3] Foster's reply of 15 Jan. 1799 to an anti-Unionist address from the freeholders of Louth, *Dublin Evening Post*, 22 Jan. 1799; *Parl. Reg.* (Irish), xiii. 342.

The government could of course have ignored the open constituencies and controlled the Irish Parliament, which was after all a 'Borough Parliament', through the votes of members for close constituencies alone. But this was a course which would have given no veneer of popularity to its proceedings and would have been grist to the mill of the parliamentary reformers. Hence the interesting reaction of one of Lord Abercorn's members to the Place Act of 1793:

> . . . It seems to me that the imitation of the English Place Bill, so far as making placemen vacate their seats on their appointment to office, does not suit this Country. No Administration will ever be able to get a country gentleman whose County or City is contested, and yet that is very necessary for the tranquillity of the Kingdom; and the power of borough holders will be much increased, and consequently the state of the representation more questioned and condemned. . . .[1]

Just as there was a qualitative as well as quantitative distinction between the support of one borough proprietor and that of another, so there was a qualitative element in the support of M.P.s for the open constituencies, which was of much more than quantitative value. For this reason, the government, in Ireland as in Great Britain, gloried, when it could, in the fact that '. . . much of our strength depends on county members, of whom we divided 26 against 23, a sort of division never known before, particularly upon such a question . . .'; and the government endeavoured to demonstrate that what Foster called 'the real, uninfluenced sense of the country' was to some extent behind what it was doing.[2] The best example of this is the Union, when the Cornwallis Administration spent as much time trying to obtain Unionist addresses from the country as building up a Unionist majority in Parliament. Foster's own opposition to the Union would have come with much less effect from a man who sat for a close constituency: sitting as he did for an open constituency, he was able to appeal convincingly to '. . . the determined sense of the 120 members who compose it [the minority on the question], two-thirds of the county

[1] George Knox to Abercorn, 13 June 1793, Abercorn MSS., P.R.O.N.I. T. 2541/IB1/4/21.

[2] Buckingham to Grenville, 22 Apr. 1789, *H.M.C. Dropmore MSS.*, i. 458; the 'question' was an opposition bill for disfranchising revenue officers. For the remark about 'the real, uninfluenced sense of the country', and its context, see p. 79.

members among them, and supported by the voice of the
nation. Look on your table', he continued in his speech in
February 1800, 'at the petitions from 25 counties, from 8
principal cities and towns, and from Dublin; 23 of the counties
convened by legal notice have from time to time declared
against it, and 20 of them unanimously. . . .'[1] In his private,
or rather his semi-public, correspondence with Lord Sheffield,
he made even greater play with the Administration's failure to
carry a majority of the open constituencies:

. . . The little success which attended the efforts of a Lord Lieutenant
travelling through the Kingdom in obtaining addresses, shows
how little the real sentiment of the country is with the Union.
In Dundalk, eleven Corporators only joined, and it is a close borough
of Lord Roden's: the inhabitants refused. In Newry, no address.
Down, Armagh, Antrim, Tyrone, Monaghan, Fermanagh, Cavan,
none from the counties. Coleraine Corporation, lately purchased
by Lord Waterford, Newtown[ards], whose Corporators were lately
sold to Lord Londonderry,[2] Strabane and Lifford, the close boroughs
of Lord[s] Abercorn and Erne, did address. Belfast Corporation
belongs to Lord Donegall; it addressed, but not the inhabitants,
yet so sure was he of their joining that his answer went equally
to them, and he forgot to strike out their names. Drogheda refused,
though every effort, even for a common, simple address without
Union, was exerted. Even the great and populous village of Monknewtown, the property of Lord Sheffield [on the Louth/Meath
border], was tried in vain: the priest summonded the people for
the purpose after prayers, with the resolution in his pocket; they
professed ignorance; he could not explain; and they went away.
Castlefinn, a town very little larger than Monknewtown, did address,
signed as the paper says by 128 merchants. Such attempts are
a burlesque on History. And believe me, that I have as good reason
at least to say the real sense of the Kingdom is against the measure,
as I ever had to judge of any general question by. . . .[3]

The real sense of the kingdom, or of any open constituency,
was never of course entirely uninfluenced; which placed a

---

[1] *Foster's Speech of 17 February 1800*, p. 42; Bolton, *Union*, pp. 126 ff.

[2] This must be a mistake—or at any rate premature. The then patron of Newtownards was the 1st Lord Caledon, whose son swapped it for Lord Londonderry's
close borough of Limavady, co. Londonderry, in 1803, after the disfranchisement
of both boroughs in 1800. On the question of swaps and sales of boroughs, see
A. P. W. Malcomson, 'The Newtown Act: Revision and Reconstruction', *I.H.S.*
xviii (1973), 313 ff.

[3] Foster to Sheffield, 8 Dec. 1799, *Anglo-Irish Dialogue*, p. 32.

premium, from the government's point of view, on people who could influence it in a desirable direction. After the grand jury resolutions of 1792, Grattan had protested at the Irish Cabinet's acting in the 'mongrel capacity' of Ministers and country gentlemen;[1] but ability to act in such a capacity lent weight to a Minister's advice, and Foster was one who possessed that ability. Of the four constituencies where, at one time or other, he had influence, three counted qualitatively as well as quantitatively; they commanded prestige as well as votes.

The value which the government set on his influence at local level, and the success he had in exploiting it to strengthen his position in national politics, are well illustrated by the events of February and March 1780. At the beginning of February Foster wrote, apropos of the forthcoming assizes, 'the friends of Government and moderation may be of most essential service in the country at a time of such general meetings'.[2] Notwithstanding that he was at this time the Lord Lieutenant's Minister in the House of Commons, the country was the place where he considered that he himself could be 'of most essential service'. There, he exerted himself to prevent Louth from petitioning against Poynings's Law (it was only four months since the Louth resolutions in favour of the Short Money Bill), and also devoted his attention to Drogheda and, further afield, to Newry.[3] On 10 March, he was able to report with satisfaction to the Lord Lieutenant that Louth had '. . . just agreed to a very loyal address to His Majesty. Newry did the same last Wednesday and Drogheda last Tuesday. Not a word of instructions, Poynings or Declaration of Rights here, and I do not understand that any measure relative to them has been spoke of by any man in this county; but there is no being sure till our Assizes are over . . .'[4] The note of caution was justified; for although Louth remained silent, Drogheda and Newry did

---

[1] Quoted in Harlow, *British Empire*, i. 638. It must be said, in fairness to Grattan's attitude on this issue, that he had always disapproved in principle of signing grand jury or even county addresses on political topics, even when he approved of their contents, because he thought it detracted from the weight of his conduct and declarations in his higher capacity of M.P. (Grattan to Orde, 20 Sept. 1784, Bolton MSS., N.L.I. MS. 16350/11).

[2] Foster to Sackville Hamilton, 8 Feb. 1780, F.P. D.562/8356. It was customary for Parliament to be adjourned during the assizes.

[3] James Davis to Foster, 6 Mar. 1780, F.P. D.207/28/551.

[4] Foster to Buckinghamshire, 10 Mar. 1780, Heron MSS., N.L.I. MS. 13039/5.

in fact send up resolutions against Poynings's Law.[1] Still, Foster's influence in both had at least helped to obtain counteracting resolutions expressive purely of gratitude for the recently conceded Free Trade.

In this instance Foster was using his local interest to back up the policy of the government: in other instances he tried, with varying degrees of success, to use it to influence that policy. Obvious cases in point are the grand jury resolutions of 1792, which were part of the widespread plan of the Irish Cabinet to demonstrate the extent of popular hostility to Catholic Relief at constituency level, and the county petitions of 1799 and 1800, which were likewise part of a widespread plan to demonstrate that the force of popular opinion was hostile to the Union. A less obvious case occurred at the time of the Free Trade crisis late in 1779. At that time, it will be remembered, Foster, though the acting Chancellor of the Exchequer and the most important remaining supporter of the Government in the House of Commons, was privately convinced that Free Trade must be granted, and though prepared to do all in his power to prevent the Government from being 'distressed', was not prepared to compromise on the principle of Free Trade. In these circumstances he cannot have been unduly disconcerted when the popular, independent interest in Louth sent up in November 1779 an address instructing their M.P.s to vote for a Short Money Bill as the most effective means of securing Free Trade. He replied in conciliatory terms, pointing out that part of the supplies would have to be granted for the term to which the public faith was already pledged, but adding that, although he did not wish to 'predetermine' about the rest, he hoped and expected that his conduct where they were concerned would be consonant with the wishes expressed in the Louth address.[2] In the event he lived up to these expectations. After an attempt to move for the whole of the supplies for the usual term, he fell back on the distinction which he had made in his reply, and moved only for that portion of them which was necessary to cover the existing arrear and the loans already contracted for.[3]

[1] O'Connell, Politics and Social Conflict, p. 226.

[2] Address of the Louth freeholders to their M.P.s, 8 Nov. 1779, F.P. D.562/14657; Foster's reply, Dublin Evening Post, 22 Nov. 1779.

[3] Buckinghamshire to Weymouth, 25 Nov. 1779, Grattan, Life, ii. 8 f.

This on-the-whole submissive reaction is in marked contrast to his defiance of his constituents on the issue of parliamentary reform in 1784. Even his undistinguished colleague, James Fortescue, was not afraid to adopt a firmer tone in replying to the 1779 address; Fortescue pointedly assured his constituents that he would do everything he *ought* to secure a Free Trade, the implication being that voting for a Short Money Bill was something he ought not to do.[1] The contrast between Foster's and Fortescue's conduct, and between Foster's conduct in 1779 and 1784, can best be explained on the ground that it suited Foster's book in November 1779 to have his hands partially tied on the issue of Free Trade. He wanted, in other words, to be able to adduce the Louth address in the Lord Lieutenant's cabinet as an additional reason for his inability to oppose the measure. Significantly, Hely-Hutchinson was at the same time making identical use of an address he had received from his Cork City constituents,[2] though in Hely-Hutchinson's case the object probably was, as usual, to extort higher bounty. Nevertheless, it is clear that Foster had not inspired the Louth address, since none of its signatories were, as far as is known, supporters of his, and many were his opponents—Balfour, Faithful Fortescue, John Ruxton, Bellinghams, Tippings, Brabazons, and so on. But even though he had not inspired it, he was quick to exploit its potential.

On the great issues of Catholic Relief and the Union, Foster's position in national politics was considerably strengthened by his local interest. However, even after the Union his local interest continued to be of some tactical value to him in his relations with the government. Because he was Governor of Louth, one of its M.P.s, and his son the colonel of its militia, he had an ever-open channel of communication with the Castle even when he was in opposition (as was the case during much of 1802 and 1803). In a recent, pre-Union instance, in January 1796, Lord Camden had availed himself of precisely this channel of communication to put out a feeler to Foster's rival, William Ponsonby, then in such determined opposition to the Government that Camden approached him through

---

[1] Fortescue's reply to the Louth address, *Dublin Evening Post*, 16 Nov. 1779.
[2] Buckinghamshire to Weymouth, Nov. 1779, Heron MSS., N.L.I. MS. 13038/16.

Ponsonby's brother-in-law, Lord Shannon; the pretext was the governorship of co. Kilkenny, and although Ponsonby was not prepared to play, the correspondence at least terminated in mutual civilities.[1] The necessary discussion of military recruitment in Louth and of local law and order matters, greatly facilitated the negotiations between the Government and Foster for Foster's return to office in the early summer of 1803, which, thanks to the Government's increasing disenchantment with Corry, would probably have borne fruit, had Foster not pitched his terms unacceptably high. When, shortly afterwards, Foster decided to declare war on the Hardwicke Administration, his Louth interest gave him the chance to stage a demonstration which made an impact even on Whitehall, and caused Hardwicke to redouble his efforts to muzzle him with office. At the end of July the Louth Grand Jury passed resolutions which implied a censure on the Irish Administration's handling of Emmet's insurrection, and at the beginning of August a meeting of the gentlemen and freeholders of the county voted an address to the King which was a direct and pointed censure.[2] Hardwicke, through whom the address had as a matter of course to be transmitted, contemplated suppressing it. But Foster had already out-manœuvred him by sending a copy to the Home Secretary, Lord Pelham (the former Chief Secretary), who he knew was at loggerheads with Hardwicke at the time.[3] The effect of this episode was to send Foster's political stocks soaring. Initially, Wickham took the view that his conduct had been so 'hostile, mischievous, and malicious . . . as to put an end to all communication with him on the part of Government'.[4] But by the end of the month Wickham had eaten his words, and was not only communicating with Foster, but was negotiating for Foster's return to office on rather more handsome terms than had hitherto been offered him.[5]

[1] Camden to Shannon, 16 Jan. 1796, and Ponsonby to Shannon, 20 Jan. 1796, Pratt MSS., K.A.O. U.840/O.175/1, 4/2.

[2] Foster to Hardwicke, 25 July 1803, Hardwicke MSS., B.L. Add. MS. 35741, fol. 22; Baron James McClelland to Redesdale, 1 Aug. 1803, Redesdale MSS., P.R.O.N.I. T.3030/9/8.

[3] Hardwicke to Addington, 3 Aug. 1803, Hardwicke MSS., B.L. Add. MS. 35772, fol. 218.

[4] Wickham to Addington, 12 Aug. 1803, Wickham MSS., P.R.O.N.I. T.2627/5/D/65.

[5] Wickham to Addington, 29 Aug. 1803, ibid. /69.

In the event, the tactical advantages which he derived from his interest in an open constituency had no bearing on his return to office, because he returned, not under the auspices of Addington, but of Pitt. However, these tactical advantages continued, even after his final retirement from office in 1811, to be of some relevance to his role, such as it then was, in national politics. After 1813, Louth would no longer sign anti-Emancipationist addresses with suitable unanimity, but as late as 1821, Foster's county interest probably played some part in securing what he had been pressing for since 1811, a United Kingdom peerage. At the beginning of January 1821, a meeting of the gentlemen of the county was held, largely at his instigation, to vote an address to the King deploring 'the desperate attempts made in Great Britain to alienate the affections of the people from the Constitution . . .'[1] Coming, as it did, hot on the heels of the Queen's trial, this address was bound to be considered as referring to that delicate and controversial topic. Because of this, several of the Louth gentlemen (including, predictably, Bellew, Balfour, Ruxton, and Dawson) refused to sign it.[2] However, it was transmitted to the King without their signatures, and must have proved consolatory to wounded royal pride; six months later Foster was gazetted one of George IV's coronation peers: an honour which he had last solicited in April 1820 and which on that occasion he had been given no reason to expect. It may have been the Louth address of January 1821 which tipped the scale in his favour.[3]

Several politicians who attained top political influence in the period of Foster's official career like him enjoyed the tactical advantages of interest in open constituencies. The criterion of whether a politician could or could not guarantee his own return to the House, is fairly easy to apply: it is very hard even to devise criteria by which the relative strengths of politicians' interests in open constituencies are to be assessed. What is

---

[1] Foster's draft for the Louth address, 8 Jan. 1821, F.P. D.562/3734.

[2] List of those who refused to sign the Louth address, 2–6 Jan. 1821, F.P. D.562/3730.

[3] Camden to Foster, 7 May 1820, F.P. D.562/3528. Another factor which was probably important was that two of Foster's neighbours, Lords Roden and Conyngham, were given subsidiary U.K. baronies in the same creation. Under these circumstances, it would have been very invidious for Foster to have been omitted, especially in view of the age and strength of his claim.

quite clear is that all the members of the Irish Cabinet of the 1790s—Beresford, Agar, Fitzgibbon, and Parnell—were sufficiently influential in this sphere to be able to stimulate grand jury resolutions in 1792 like those of co. Louth. Foster was certainly not unique. The guess may be hazarded that the Beresford family's interest in co. Waterford was similar in strength to Foster's in Louth,[1] and their interest in co. Londonderry somewhat weaker; and that the Agar family's interest in co. Kilkenny and Fitzgibbon's and Parnell's in co. Limerick and Queen's County respectively, were considerably weaker than Foster's in Louth.[2] However, the very strength of his interest in Louth, and the very smallness of Louth geographically, were in one sense disadvantages; they gave plausibility to the illusion that the whole county was Foster's bailiwick, and deprived the Louth Grand Jury of credibility as an organ of popular opinion.

At the best of times the Castle was apt to assume that the only interests in any open constituency which were prominent enough to come to its notice, were the only interests there; and the Castle (and other commentators[3]) were especially apt to make this assumption when it accorded with their own political bias. Thus, Cornwallis called Drogheda 'the Speaker's town', and Burke had made much the same mistake about Louth when he called the resolutions of the Louth Grand Jury in 1792 'Mr. Foster's declaration of war'. This was a wild oversimplification of the nature and strength of Foster's hold on his constituency. For one thing, the grand jury of any county—

---

[1] It was not above challenge; see Beresford and Lord Tyrone to Buckingham, 9 Nov. and 10 Dec. 1788, Buckingham MSS., B.L. Add. MS. 40180, fols. 63, 124. In the second half of the eighteenth century the Beresford interest in co. Londonderry was usually represented by their kinsmen, the Carys of Dungiven.

[2] For Fitzgibbon's interest in co. Limerick, see Fitzgibbon to Eden, 11 Oct. 1783 (p. 206, *n.* 1); Johnston, *Irish House of Commons in 1791*, p. 33. For Parnell's interest in Queen's County, see R. F. Foster, *Charles Stewart Parnell: the Man and his Family* (Brighton, 1976), p. 11; Charles Henry Coote to Scrope Bernard, 25 Feb., 5 Mar., and 2 Dec. 1790, calendared in *Irish Official Papers*, pp. 228 f.; [name illegible] to [Sir John Parnell], 29 Apr. [1783?], and George Evans to his wife, *née* Parnell, [11? and 29?] June 1818, Congleton MSS., Ebbesbourne Wake, near Salisbury, Wiltshire. I have no better information on the Agars in co. Kilkenny than what may be gleaned from the various lists of the Irish Parliament and from the returns of members.

[3] See, for example, James Bird to Thomas Braughall, 19 Oct. 1792, F.P. D.207/ 5/75A; George Knox to Abercorn, 24 Apr. 1793, Abercorn MSS., P.R.O.N.I. T.2541/IB1/1/4.

even though there was doubt about the constitutional propriety of its passing resolutions on political subjects[1]—was still the body most fairly representative of the landed property of the county. In an age when landed property was political power, no body could be expected to be more representative than that. Addresses of the gentlemen, clergy, and freeholders of a county could be heavily influenced by one or two leading magnates, and petitions signed by hordes of obscure and dependent freeholders were even more susceptible to the same influence; but in general resolutions of the grand jury were not. Sometimes, of course, the magnates were successful in packing even the grand jury. But this was only easy when a high proportion of the local landowners were absentees, and very hard in a county like Louth where a high proportion of them were resident.[2] In any case, the composition of the Louth Grand Jury of 1792 shows that it had not been packed—not at least by Foster, its foreman. Of the twenty-three grand jurors who signed the resolutions, no less that eleven can be designated as belonging to the popular, independent interest.[3] These include Francis Tipping (the short-lived opposition candidate for the 1790 general election), O'Brien Bellingham (a former secretary of the 'Louth Constitution Club'), and Richard Dawson (a former chairman of the club, a regular opponent of the government, and a kinsman of Alexander Dawson).[4] Not one of these men, or of the whole eleven, was amenable to Foster's political influence.

The popular, independent interest was likewise prominent in the co. Louth opposition to the Union. Just as Cornwallis tried to minimize the extent and spontaneity of anti-Unionist feeling in Drogheda, so he tried to give the impression that

[1] Dr. William Drennan to Samuel McTier, 13 Sept. 1792, *Drennan Letters*, p. 91. It is probable that Fitzgibbon entertained such a doubt; co. Limerick may loosely be said to have participated in the grand jury movement, but the Limerick resolutions actually came, not from the grand jury, but from the freeholders of the county.

[2] Draft of a reward notice in Lord Ferrard's handwriting, [*c.* 1828], F.P. T.2519/4/2112.

[3] The resolutions and the names of the grand jury are printed in Francis Plowden, *A History of Ireland from Henry II to the Union* (2 vols., London, 1812), App., pp. 187 f. The names should be compared with the signatories of the Louth address of January 1784, *Dublin Evening Post*, 27 Jan. 1784, quoted in *C.L.A.J.* vi. 122.

[4] Bellingham to Napper Tandy, 7 Oct. 1784, Chatham MSS., P.R.O. 30/8/330, fol. 278; *C.L.A.J.* viii. 26; *Dublin Evening Post*, 17 Feb. 1789.

anti-Unionist feeling in Louth also was to be attributed to the intrigues and influence of Foster.[1] Yet once again this was an oversimplification. On Cornwallis's own testimony, one of the most vociferous of the Louth anti-Unionists was Balfour:[2] an unlikely person to have taken his political cue from Foster. And although Louth's two declarations against the Union in 1799 and 1800 took the suspect form of petitions from the freeholders of the county, there is every reason for thinking that these were petitions representative of the opinions of an overwhelming proportion of its landowners. Obviously, no petition was spontaneous in the sense that it came into being without organization on someone's part. In the case of the Louth petitions, the Fosters seem to have done much of the organizing, sending agents round the county with blank pieces of paper to get filled up with signatures, and with instructions to write the names of 'marksmen', or illiterates, for them, 'no two in the same hand'.[3] Yet, in spite of the fact that many of the signatories put their names to the blank pieces of paper without ever seeing a copy of the petition, and in spite of the Fosters' unscrupulous methods of making some of them appear more literate and respectable than they actually were, there can be little doubt that the petitions fairly represented landed opinion in Louth. That of 1800, in particular, was signed by no less than 1,240 freeholders:[4] 400 more than the probable registered electorate of the county at that time. This is a fairly impressive figure, considering that the largest and third-largest landowners in Louth, Lords Clermont and Roden, were Unionists and presumably prevented their tenantry from signing. Had the anti-Unionist petitions been no more than trumped-up devices of Foster's, these two magnates would have been able to do something to counteract them. The fact that they were unable to do anything except procure a Unionist address from the corporation of Roden's close borough of Dundalk, shows that the opposition to the Union in co. Louth was far from being trumped-up.[5]

[1] Cornwallis to Ross, 26 Dec. 1798, *Cornwallis Correspondence*, iii. 24.
[2] Cornwallis to Portland, 19 May 1799, ibid. iii. 99.
[3] Instructions in Thomas Foster's handwriting to those collecting signatures for the Louth petition of 1799 or 1800, F.P. D.207/10/22B.
[4] List of petitions against the Union, 1 Mar. 1800, F.P. D.207/10/27.
[5] Cornwallis to Ross, 24 Oct. 1799, *Cornwallis Correspondence*, iii. 140 f.

In conclusion, it must again be stressed that ability to influence opinion in an open constituency was of no more than subsidiary, tactical advantage to the career politician in his relations with the government. It was an undoubted asset to him to be able to influence an open constituency in the direction the government desired; but if he contributed to influencing an open constituency in the direction in which he desired the government to go, the government was apt to mistake his influence for control, and to dismiss the constituency as close, not open. With this reservation, interest in open constituencies was a help to the career politicians, and in fact, a considerable majority of those who attained top political influence in Ireland throughout the eighteenth century did represent open constituencies—in marked contrast to the situation in contemporary Great Britain. This contrast, however, cannot be explained on the ground that interest in open constituencies was a more important recommendation to top political influence in Ireland than it was in Great Britain. Instead, it is to be explained on other grounds: in Ireland there was no Place Act until 1793 and many fewer general elections than in Great Britain throughout the eighteenth century, with the result that winning a seat for an open constituency was a much more attractive proposition for an Irish career politician than it was for a British.[1] In Ireland, it is true, the government was several degrees less 'popular' than the government in Great Britain, simply because it was 'alien', and as a result was probably more concerned to acquire the high-quality support of members for the prestigious open constituencies (which were also pro- portionately fewer in the Irish Parliament than they were in the British): in other words, to build up its personal as well as its real interest. But this greater concern for high-quality support did not lead the government to accord top political influence to such supporters. In this respect, Conolly was a short-lived

[1] Before the Place Act had time to influence the conduct of the Irish career politicians in this respect, the Union wiped out most of the close constituencies and so left them with few Irish alternatives to the open ones. Of the politicians listed as attaining top political influence in the period 1777–1800, all those who sat in the House of Commons at one time or another sat for open constituencies, except for Scott, Toler, and George Ponsonby. The only one who first sat for an open con- stituency *after* the passing of the Place Act was Wolfe, who had already attained the highest office open to him which was compatible with a seat in Parliament.

exception. Independent country gentlemen of Conolly's type were attended to and sought after by the government to a quite remarkable extent: obvious examples in the period 1777–1800 are Denis Daly, M.P. for co. Galway, Luke Gardiner, M.P. for co. Dublin, George Ogle, M.P. for co. Wexford, and John O'Neill, M.P. for co. Antrim. But when they proved amenable to the blandishments of the government (and all four of these at one time or another did), the blandishments took the form of peerages, non-political offices, and pensions: top political offices and top political influence (in so far as any Irishmen enjoyed them) were reserved for the able career politicians, the men of business perhaps more than the parliamentarians. For these career politicians, the only aspect of electoral interest which really mattered was the ability to return themselves to Parliament, without political tutelage and without the impediment of a troublesome and voracious constituency. In Foster's case, this mattered particularly: before the Union, he wanted to be Speaker; after the Union, he wanted an office which was the object of keen Irish competition because it was the only Irish office of parliamentary business which still survived and was still open to the Irish politicians.

CHAPTER SIX

'Jobs of All Sorts': Command of Patronage

COMMAND of patronage, like command of seats, was an important aspect of political real estate. However, historians have probably exaggerated its importance. In the absence of parties and party discipline, patronage has been seen as the dough which bound people together, from the top of the political spectrum down to the bottom; and in the virtual absence of political issues, patronage has been seen as the yeast which kept up some degree of fermentation among the political élite, who would have had little to quarrel about if they had not quarrelled about jobs. This view is suspect, as it attributes to patronage alone the omnicompetent role of keeping people together and keeping them apart. Patronage was probably less effective in the former role than in the latter. For example, ex-Chief Secretary Eden warned one of his successors, Grenville, in 1782 not '. . . to make any promise or to confer any favours till after the close of the first session. Every new favour granted by a Lord Lieutenant operates against the future strength of his Government by creating both expectancies and resentments . . .'; and in 1785, Beresford—supposedly a great jobber—remarked: '. . . if hereafter a system should be taken up of adhering to the real interest of the Revenue in its collection, and that the whole be not guided by Parliamentary influence, . . . Government here will find that their influence will not diminish in Parliament, for at present they offend more people than the [*sic*] please. . . .'[1] In other words, patronage was an encumbrance as well as an asset, because no matter how extensive it was, demand always exceeded supply. Hence its greater effectiveness as yeast than as dough. For example,

[1] Eden to Grenville, 21 Sept. 1782, Additional Dropmore MSS.; Beresford to [Rose], 1 Apr. 1785, Chatham MSS., P.R.O. 30/8/325, fol. 90. See also Beresford to Robinson, 8 Jan. 1781, *Beresford Correspondence*, i. 50.

the Beresford family in 1806 saw no political inconsistency in
supporting an Administration headed by Grenville, and Grenville on his side saw no point in allowing Fox to make Orange
martyrs of people who were willing to give the Administration
parliamentary support; in the end, this mutually convenient
rapprochement was wrecked, not by a political issue, but by the
conflicting patronage claims of the Beresfords and Newport
in Waterford City, and of the Beresfords and the Ponsonbys in
Londonderry City and County.[1] However, what really kept
up fermentation among the political élite was not patronage,
but personal rivalries like those between the Beresfords and the
Ponsonbys (with which patronage often had much to do). It was
such personal rivalries rather than jobs *per se*, which supplied
the place of issues.

The omnicompetence of patronage is one assumption which
needs to be challenged: another assumption which needs to be
challenged is that jobbery was a peculiarly Irish vice. This
assumption was commonly made by the British politicians who
saw political service in Ireland or had responsibility for Irish
affairs, and they made it about the Anglo-Irish Ascendancy as a
whole. To some extent it was justified. In England the ruling,
or landed, class was numerically so large that many influential
local worthies must have been excluded by sheer pressure of
numbers from participation in the patronage of the Crown: in
Ireland, the Ascendancy was numerically sufficiently small
to become in some sense parasitical, looking to the Castle and,
more remotely, to the British connection, not only for defence
against the Catholic majority, but also for supplementation of
its income through the patronage of the Crown. In spite of
Henry Grattan Junior's persistent use of that old-fashioned
Whig term 'the Court', there must surely have been very
little court-and-country distinction in Ireland, particularly
after the fall of the Undertakers, which had the effect of
bringing a high proportion of the Ascendancy into direct
contact with the Court or Castle? The Irish politicians who
at any given moment made up the Irish cabinet, participated
in this parasitical 'Ascendancy' attitude; and their opportunities for obtaining patronage were greater than those of most

---

[1] See, for example, Elliot to Grenville, 14 July and 15 and 21 Aug. 1806, and
Grenville to Elliot, 21 Aug. 1806, *H.M.C. Dropmore MSS.*, viii. 235, 282, 290 f.

Irishmen, as of course were their services to the Crown. The British politicians tended to begrudge the opportunities and undervalue the services. They thus came to regard the members of the Irish cabinet as extreme and particularly unsavoury exemplars of Irish jobbery. It was said of Hely-Hutchinson (with some justification) that, if he were granted the whole of Great Britain as his estate, he would still ask for the Isle of Man as his potato garden. Flood's huckstering over the terms on which he came into office in 1775 was deemed to be base and ungentlemanly, although the real cause of British indignation at Flood was that he was determined to be provided for at the expense of English sinecurists on the Irish establishment. Beresford was nicknamed, most unfairly and inaptly, the uncrowned King of Ireland. Foster, too, although he has not passed into unflattering legend in the way that Hely-Hutchinson, Flood, and Beresford have done, caused Chief Secretary Pelham to exclaim in 1795 that he would '. . . rather work at the plough all the rest of my days than engage in that dirty traffic of patronage, which must in . . . [Ireland] always remain upon a shabby footing while men like the Speaker act in the manner they do. . . .'[1] The most extreme castigators of Irish jobbery were the Englishmen who came to rule Ireland immediately after the Union—Hardwicke, Abbot, Wickham, and Redesdale: Redesdale, in particular, was not long in discovering (on the basis of evidence which he did not cite) that the Irish in their hearts preferred to be ruled by Englishmen than by jobbers of their own nationality, and that 'even the tenants prefer an English to an Irish steward'.[2] Earlier, the expatriate Irishman, Edmund Burke, who ought to have been better informed, had written off the Irish Cabinet of the 1790s as a 'Junto of Jobbers'.[3]

Of the 'Junto of Jobbers', the only one who would seem to have been personally rewarded beyond his deserts, was Agar, who ended his days as Archbishop of Dublin and an earl. Beresford, too, did well for his family and himself, but no better than he was surely entitled to do, in view of the great

---

[1] Pelham to Camden, 1 Dec. 1795, Pratt MSS., K.A.O. U.840/C.122/6. The preceding comments require no citation.
[2] Redesdale to Abbot, 15 Aug. 1802, Colchester Diary, i. 407.
[3] Burke to Richard Burke, [18 Nov. 1792], Burke Correspondence, vii. 290.

savings he made in the revenue by his administrative reforms?[1] Also, it is important not to confuse Beresford's claims to patronage, arising out of his services to the Crown, with the claims of his brother, Lord Waterford, as a great borough proprietor and a leading interest in two counties. Parnell, because of his dismissal in 1799 and his premature death too soon for reparation to be made, did badly out of politics and office.[2] Fitzgibbon did much worse than he might have done, and than his predecessor and successor did. Much more than Pelham, he was wont to apply the adjective 'shabby' to matters of patronage; his salary as Lord Chancellor was no more than he would have earned at the bar, and must have been largely consumed in keeping up his idea of the dignity of the office; and after his death, when his widow disgraced his memory by applying for all sorts of emoluments, British politicians deemed it almost a matter of reproach against Fitzgibbon that he had done so little for his relations while he had the chance.[3] Foster was even more careless of his personal financial situation than Fitzgibbon. Fitzgibbon at least secured for his own life and the life of his second son a sinecure worth the not-enormous sum of £1,500 a year:[4] Foster secured no life provision for himself or his son. Yet there was only one clear Irish precedent for a retiring speaker's receiving a pension, Foster would almost certainly not have received a pension if there had been a change of government in 1789 and William Ponsonby had defeated him at the speakership election of 1790,[5] and since the speakership was an elective office, not an office held for life, there would have been grounds for withholding compensation from him in 1801. Foster's demands for patronage on behalf of his relations and dependants may have been 'shabby'—nepotic

---

[1] See, for example, Beresford to Buckinghamshire, 2 Sept., and Buckinghamshire to Beresford, 17 Sept., 1782, *Beresford Correspondence*, i. 226 ff.

[2] Henry Parnell to Wickham, 17 Mar. 1803, Wickham MSS., P.R.O.N.I. T. 2627/5/K/82. In this letter, Parnell solicits the chancellorship of the Irish exchequer, by way of reparation: a request which caused much merriment to the Irish Administration.

[3] Clare to Castlereagh, 14 Nov. 1800, *Cornwallis Correspondence*, iii. 302; Earl of Rosslyn to Aukland, 1 Feb. 1802, Sneyd MSS., P.R.O.N.I. T.3229/2/70.

[4] Shannon to Boyle, [4 Feb.] 1802, Shannon MSS., P.R.O.N.I. D.2707/A/3/3/185.

[5] Malcomson, *Foster and the Speakership*, p. 274; Westmorland to Grenville, 20 Mar. 1790, *H.M.C. Dropmore MSS.*, ii. 158.

he may have been: mercenary he was not. Perhaps the justest contemporary view of the matter was that expressed by the Dowager Lady Moira, a fairly impartial commentator, as her connections lay equally in government and opposition circles; writing to Camden's sister in 1796, she described Foster as

... a man who I am convinced has the most sense and, in most instances, the best judgement in the Kingdom. But his pecuniary distresses (not originating from himself, but from his father), a hospitable and generous disposition, with a wife who in no degree attends to *that* regulation and economy which he has not leisure to preside over, not only renders [*sic*] his situation uncomfortable, but obliges him to look to the loaves and fishes with avidity; and one can scarcely blame him for taking care of himself and his connections whilst he has power to do so . . . ; if he acts with skill and integrity in your brother's cause, you must *feel* that emoluments are as duly as gratefully bestowed in that quarter, and after he is satisfied, I should think the Speaker would recommend judiciously those others who ought to be gratified. . . .[1]

Even Lady Moira, however, exaggerated the extent to which Foster took care, or tried to take care, of himself.

The jobbery of the 'Junto of Jobbers' cannot be considered in a vacuum; some contemporary yardstick by which to assess it must be found. The most convenient yardstick is that provided by the conduct of the Irish Cabinet's principal detractors, the British politicians who saw short-term service in Ireland. In the last quarter of the eighteenth century, the patronage of Ireland was by and large confined to Ireland, in the sense that English politicians with no connection whatsoever with the country (like Fox, later a greater scourger of Irish jobbery) were no longer allowed a lien on it. But many such English grantees of a former era remained as sitting tenants on the Irish establishment. In December 1782 the Lord Lieutenant, Temple, though of course an Englishman himself, did justice to Ireland and the Irish politicians in this respect; writing to his brother and Chief Secretary, Grenville, he observed caustically:

... If Lord Shelburne [the Prime Minister] presses you again about Ireland giving a portion of Civil List to the King, you will let him

<hr />

[1] Lady Moira to Lady Castlereagh, [?14] Jan. 1796, Pratt MSS., K.A.O. U.840/ C.584/3.

know that I am preparing a state to convince him that, after striking out pensions to Irish [Chief] Secretaries or dependants, or to Irish resident in England, it appears that above half the pension list is for English jobs and to English connections, exclusive of Vice-Treasurers, Clerks of Pells, Chancellors of Exchequer, Masters of Rolls, Conways without end, Clerks of Quit Rents, *cum multis aliis*. . . .[1]

Ironically, in view of this letter, Temple spent much time during his second viceroyalty negotiating to obtain the Irish mastership of the rolls for Grenville, who no longer had anything to do with Irish affairs, and ultimately obtained for him the reversion of the chief remembrancership of the Irish exchequer. Hobart, who was Chief Secretary for four and a half years (1789–93), secured for himself the clerkship of the pleas in the same court, which was netting to him in the early nineteenth century the vast sum of £8,000 a year.[2] His successor, Sylvester Douglas, served for less than a year; yet Pitt jeopardized not only the formation of the Fitzwilliam Administration but his coalition in Great Britain with the Portland Whigs, by stipulating that Douglas should be given the secretaryship of state for Ireland recently vacated by the death of Hely-Hutchinson.[3] Similar jobbery can be imputed even to the self-consciously virtuous Englishmen who came to rule Ireland after the Union. Before accepting the lord chancellorship, Redesdale held out, among other things, for a pension of £4,000 a year,[4] as compared to Fitzgibbon's two-life sinecure of £1,500. Thus entrenched, Redesdale was quick to attack his colleagues. He sharply criticized Abbot, who after less than a year's service in Ireland went off with 'the brightest jewel in the casket of the Chief Secretary [the keepership of the privy seal], at which Ireland is not a little jealous'. Privately, Redesdale was also of the opinion that Hardwicke remained as Lord Lieutenant, in spite of many provocations to quit, because 'the appointment is convenient and he does not think it advisable to quarrel

[1] Quoted in Johnston, *Great Britain and Ireland*, p. 293.

[2] Accounts relating to the clerkship of the pleas, 1793–1813, Buckinghamshire MSS., P.R.O.N.I. T.2627/1/8.

[3] William Elliot to Sir Gilbert Elliot, 1 Nov. 1794, Aspinall transcript from the Minto MSS., kindly placed at my disposal by Dr. P. J. Jupp.

[4] Redesdale to Hardwicke, 8 Mar. 1802, Redesdale MSS., P.R.O.N.I. T.3030/5/1.

with his bread and butter'.[1] Certainly, Hardwicke laid himself
open to attack, because he was probably unique among the
lords lieutenant of the late eighteenth century and early
nineteenth century in obtaining a sinecure (in reversion) for
himself. This was sneeringly described by one of Foster's
adherents as 'the sop to the dog'.[2]

Hardwicke is an extreme case. The purpose of the examples
quoted—and many more could have been quoted—is only to
demonstrate that it would have been as easy for the Irish
Cabinet to develop a myth of English jobbery out of the conduct of the British politicians serving in Ireland, as it was for the
British politicians to develop the myth of Irish jobbery out of
the conduct of the Irish Cabinet. Much can be said in extenuation of the conduct of the British politicians (as of that of
the Irish Cabinet). For one thing, the chief secretaryship was
a notoriously expensive office to hold (though perhaps no
more expensive than the speakership), and was greatly under-
remunerated until Pelham's appointment in 1795: since chief
secretaries were usually young politicians at the bottom of the
ladder, it was unreasonable to expect that they should fulfil
the expensive social responsibilities of the office without some
expectation, at least, that the in-roads into their private
fortunes would be made good.[3] In more general terms, British
career politicians who were younger sons (like Grenville and
Redesdale), or for other reasons had their own way to make
in the world (like Douglas), expected to secure some permanent provision for themselves, to compensate them for
what they had lost by not pursuing a profession, to supplement
the inadequate remuneration of political offices, and to cushion
them against a fall from power. This was a norm of late-
eighteenth-century and early-nineteenth-century British politics;[4] and, if the British politicians concerned saw service in
Ireland, they naturally looked to Ireland as well as Great
Britain as a possible source for their permanent provision.
If only their service in Ireland is reckoned, they appear to
have been rewarded out of all proportion to the Irish Cabinet,

---

[1] Redesdale to Perceval, 5 Nov. 1804, ibid. /7/27.

[2] J. S. Rochfort to Foster, 23 Sept. 1805, F.P. D.207/33/53.

[3] See, for example, Eden to North, 23 Sept. 1780 and 27 Aug. 1781, *Beresford
Correspondence*, i. 145 ff., 169 f.

[4] Pares, *George III and the Politicians*, pp. 27 f.

on whom they were heavily dependent during their short sojourn in Dublin Castle; but the disproportion may not be so great if their total political service, in Great Britain as well as Ireland, is brought into the reckoning. The Irish Cabinet were certainly not the least deserving or the best-rewarded beneficiaries of the political system in late eighteenth-century Ireland. No doubt they felt they had a grievance against their fleeting English superiors. But their more serious grievance was against some of their fellow-Irishmen—the great, and even the small, borough proprietors in particular—the men who responded to the call of the division bell, but bore neither the administrative nor the parliamentary brunt.

It was because the political system in late eighteenth-century Ireland was defective, not because Irish political man was particularly corrupt, that the myth of Irish jobbery gained currency. In July 1793, Henry Dundas, conveniently forgetful of the many Indian and Scottish jobs which could be laid to his own charge, declared 'that it was the wish of Great Britain to govern Ireland on a less corrupt system than formerly'.[1] He did not explain how this was to be accomplished in a situation where there was no constitutional safety-valve for a defeat of the Irish administration in the Irish House of Commons.[2] Fitzgibbon, who was a sterner critic of his countrymen than any Englishman, and castigated 'our strong national love of Jobbing',[3] saw clearly that it was the political system rather than the national character which was at fault:

... [Ireland's] must be a provincial government, and of the worst description—a government maintained, not by the avowed exercise of legitimate authority, but by a permanent and commanding influence of the English executive in the councils of Ireland, as a necessary substitute for it. . . . The first obvious disadvantage to Ireland is that in every department of the state, every other consideration must yield to parliamentary power; let the misconduct of any public officer be what it may, if he is supported by a powerful parliamentary interest, he is too strong for the King's representative. A majority in the parliament of Great Britain will defeat the Minister of the day; but a majority in the parliament of Ireland against the

[1] Sir Gilbert Elliot to Lady Elliot, 1 July 1793, Aspinall transcript from the Minto MSS, now N.L.S. MS. 11048, fols. 297–301.
[2] See pp. 38, 373 ff.
[3] Clare to Auckland, 3 July 1798, Falkiner, *Lord Clare*, p. 151.

King's government, goes directly to separate this kingdom from the British Crown. . . . And it is vain to expect, so long as man continues to be a creature of passion and interest, that he will not avail himself of the critical and dangerous situation in which the executive government of this kingdom must ever remain under its present constitution, to demand the favour of the Crown, not as the reward of loyalty and service, but as the stipulated price, to be paid in advance, for the discharge of a public duty. . . .[1]

Thus, in Fitzgibbon's view, man, in general, was 'a creature of passion and interest', and Irish political man only seemed worse because the defective political system in Ireland obliged the government to capitulate more regularly to 'passion and interest' than it had to do in, say, Great Britain.

To the extent already discussed, the Irish Cabinet were creatures of 'passion and interest', who exploited the system for the advantage of their connections and themselves: after recommending Foster's brother for a bishopric in 1795, Camden commented listlessly: '. . . I am certain, under all the circumstances, that the Speaker's importance in the country deserves this consideration . . .; and if ever there was a recommendation sent over from the pure principle of being useful to the Government of Ireland, it is the one I have now sent, for my private wishes all lean the other way.'[2] However, the Irish Cabinet, quite obviously, were not responsible for the system, nor were they even responsible for operating it, except as the mere agents of the lord lieutenant and chief secretary. As a result of the events of the Townshend Administration, the principle of direct Castle management of the Irish Parliament had been established, and—more important—the whole patronage of the revenue departments had come to be vested in the lord lieutenant, who had previously had to concede the lion's share to the commissioners of the revenue, as a matter of right.[3] For this crucial reason, the Irish Cabinet of the 1790s were not new-style Undertakers; for this crucial reason, Foster's personal following was as small as it was at the time of the Union—and Lord Waterford's and the un-crowned King of Ireland's would have been not much larger

---

[1] *The Speech of the Right Honourable John, Earl of Clare, . . . on a Motion Made by him on Monday, February 10, 1800* (Dublin, 1800), pp. 45 f.

[2] Camden to Pelham, 19 Sept. 1795, Pelham MSS., B.L. Add. MS. 33101, fol. 354.   [3] Bartlett, 'Townshend Administration', p. 334.

if they had ever gone into opposition. Beresford's private criticism of the exploitation of revenue patronage for political purposes, has been quoted. What is even more significant, is that he criticized it publicly in Parliament (in 1784):

... As to the [revenue] pensions granted ..., I confess I agree with the right honourable gentleman [Grattan], that many of them are very great abuses. .... I agree ... as to the period of service which should entitle a man to be superannuated on his full salary: forty years was fixed by Sir William Osborne [one of the former Commissioners] when first I went into the revenue, but soon after, that rule was broken through, and men of all standings allowed to enjoy their otium. However, I must say that, if the board had not frequently remonstrated with government against this practice, the number on the list would have been double at this day. ....[1]

These observations cannot have endeared Beresford to the Rutland Administration. Foster's efforts in 1804–6 to reform the revenue departments and reduce the cost of the collection of the revenue, were the continuation of Beresford's pre-Union efforts in the same direction, and like them hardly compatible with the continuing political exploitation of revenue patronage. Such exploitation, and indeed the whole Irish patronage system, went on long after the Union, and long after the deaths of all the old Irish Cabinet except Foster. If there was a difference, it was that after the Union patronage was even more tightly concentrated in the hands of the lord lieutenant and chief secretary than it had been before.

Thus, the volume of patronage which had been dispensed to keep docile an Irish Parliament of 300 members and, basically, to maintain the British connection, survived to corrupt the 100 Irish members at Westminster, when the threat to the British connection could no longer be adduced in extenuation.[2] It would be unhistorical to indict post-Union British governments of machiavellianism in thus treating the Irish members as division-fodder; several of the post-Union British governments were too hard-pressed for votes to worry over-much how their support was obtained. There was perhaps more cynicism than machiavellianism in their attitude: until

[1] Quoted in Plowden, *Historical Review*, App. 40. See also Beresford to Aukland, 5 Sept. 1801, Sneyd MSS., P.R.O.N.I. T.3229/2/63.
[2] Cooke to Aukland, 25 Sept. 1801, ibid, 164; Jupp, 'Parliamentary Representation', p. 217.

financial amalgamation in 1817—and, as has been seen, the British Government of the day was extremely slow to recognize the necessity for financial amalgamation—British governments could deceive themselves that the Irish members were being corrupted at the expense of Ireland, not of the United Kingdom. It is surely no coincidence that economical reform hit Ireland *after*, not before, financial amalgamation. Where post-Union British governments are not excusable, is in their perpetuation of the myth of Irish jobbery: Fox, for example, warned the Talents' Lord Lieutenant never to '. . . forget that you have to do with the most rapacious and unreasonable people on the face of the Earth, the Scotch themselves not excepted; to be importunate and successful in jobs is not their shame, but their glory. . . .'[1] No doubt 'the Scotch' can be defended on similar grounds to the Irish. However, the important point is that there are two sides to a bargain, not to say a corrupt transaction; and post-Union British governments had no right to moralize unless they dismantled the Irish patronage system. Like Maria Theresa, they wept, but they pocketed the advantages all the same.

Conclusions about patronage across the broad front of national politics must of necessity be tentative: the rest of this chapter is devoted to a consideration of patronage in the narrower, local sphere, as exemplified by the Foster interest in Louth and Drogheda. In 1777, the great co. Down magnate, the Earl of Hillsborough, later 1st Marquess of Downshire, reminded the Lord Lieutenant 'how useful, and indeed necessary, to one's importance in one's County the favour and countenance of Government are'.[2] The question is, was patronage merely useful or positively necessary? The main difficulty in answering it is that Foster was not just a local interest, but a major figure in national politics (as indeed was Hillsborough); the difficulty lies in determining to what extent the local patronage which men like Foster and Hillsborough received was a recognition of their position in national politics, and to what extent it was simply a recognition of their position in

[1] Fox to Bedford, 9 June [1806], Aspinall transcript from the Holland MSS.
[2] Hillsborough to Buckinghamshire, 9 Aug. 1777, *H.M.C. Lothian MSS.*, p. 314. Professor E. M. Johnston informs me that this was a heavily ironical remark, as Buckinghamshire had recently been discomfited in his own county of Norfolk through failure to obtain 'the favour and countenance of Government'.

their respective localities. Annexed to this is the subsidiary difficulty of determining to what extent such patronage as they received in recognition of their position in national politics was applicable to local uses.

If prominence in national politics conferred special advantages in the sphere of local patronage, nobody was more likely to have profited from them than Foster. His attitude to patronage was reputedly 'shabby', and he enjoyed a remarkable continuity of government favour and countenance, particularly when it is remembered that all his offices, even the speakership, were in 'the hurricane sphere'. As one lord lieutenant put it, he was 'of consequence to us' (indeed, to a long series of administrations), and so was entitled to expect patronage which was 'of consequence to his interest'.[1] Indeed, Foster once boasted that he 'had done more for . . . [his] friends with Government than any Member of the House'.[2] The only sustained period for which he was, by and large, out of favour and for most of it out of office, was the period 1799–1804. Yet it is probable that during these years his local influence came to little harm. What he lost in patronage he made up in prestige, because of the popularity among the voters of anti-Unionist Louth and Drogheda of his stand against the Union. In any case, for much of the period 1801–4 he was being courted by the Government, who wanted either to muzzle his opposition or to cajole him back into office. In these circumstances, it is unlikely that his more modest requests for patronage were turned down; even in March 1799 he was able to obtain a living for the son of his fellow anti-Unionist, Edward Hardman.[3] More important still, the period when he was out of favour was a bleak one even for those who had been prominent in support of the Union. This was because Union engagements had mortgaged the patronage of the government and temporarily diverted it into unaccustomed channels. In 1801, Lord Abercorn—an important Unionist and a most self-important man—was lamenting that these engagements were interfering with 'the common patronage of Tyrone and Donegal' and even with

[1] Northington to Pelham, 7 Sept. [1783], Pelham MSS., B.L. Add. MS. 33100, fol. 304.
[2] Revd. Francis Ennis to Foster, 25 June 1821, F.P. D.562/13666A.
[3] Revd. Brinsley Nixon to Downshire, 24 Mar. 1799, Downshire MSS., P.R.O.N.I. D.607/G/134.

'my own town of Strabane';[1] and in the same year the Unionist Lord Roden was meeting with similar difficulties in *his* town of Dundalk.[2] To the remonstrances of such magnates, the harassed Lord Lieutenant had the standard reply that all local claims to patronage 'must give way to positive and specified Union engagements'.[3] Even if he had still been in office and favour, Foster could have been given no other reply.

The period 1799–1804 did not, therefore, see any serious or avoidable interruption in the flow of patronage with which Foster's local influence was accustomed to be irrigated. Continuity was of the essence where patronage was concerned. The recipients of government favours, like the Duke of Newcastle's bishops, would remember their maker for as long as he remained in power; and if patronage in their locality had been flowing for long enough through the channel of one family, they would come to regard that family, not as its channel, but as its source. This is what had happened in co. Wexford by 1806, when the Chief Secretary admitted ruefully that '. . . the influence of Government is very little in that County, for Lord Ely had for a series of years almost the entire management of it . . .'[4] The Waterford City election of 1802 shows, even more clearly than the confused Drogheda election of the same year, how hard it was for the government suddenly to divert the course of patronage; in Waterford the channel of patronage had for years been Beresford, who had been Chief Commissioner of the Revenue since 1780. In 1801 he resigned his office, but his influence was still so strong among the revenue officers of the town that he was able to prevail upon most of them to vote against Newport, the government candidate at the 1802 election.[5] For the revenue officers of Waterford and Drogheda, the problem was to decide who their maker was. In the following year the Irish Administration put them out of their dilemma by disfranchising revenue officers

---

[1] Abercorn to Hardwicke, 25 Nov. 1801, Abercorn MSS., P.R.O.N.I. T.2541/IK/17/24.
[2] Hardwicke to Roden, 23 Nov. 1801, Roden MSS., P.R.O.N.I. Mic.147/10, vol. 20, p. 279.
[3] Wickham to Addington, 25 Apr. 1802, MacDonagh, *Viceroy's Post-Bag*, p. 19.
[4] W. Elliot to Lord Grenville, 6 Apr. 1806, *H.M.C. Dropmore MSS.*, viii. 81.
[5] Newport to Wickham, 21 July 1802, Wickham MSS., P.R.O.N.I. T.2627/5/K/50.

everywhere.[1] The Fosters in co. Louth enjoyed, to an even higher degree than the Beresfords in Waterford City, the advantage of continuity of government patronage. This they owed not only to the continuity of John Foster's official career, but also to the smooth and easy manner—reminiscent of a baton-change—in which his official career had followed on that of his father, the Chief Baron.

While it is true that Foster was no ordinary county interest, because of his prominence in national politics, it is equally true that he played a role in his county which transcended political considerations. His role was that of a very necessary agent of civilization and good order in his locality, and in this role there was no obvious substitute for him. John Pollock, the ultra-loyalist protégé of Hillsborough's son, the 2nd Marquess of Downshire, made this point with some exaggeration and ultra-loyalist bias in a letter to the former Chief Secretary, Lord Hobart, written in 1803, at a time when Pollock was fearful that the Union had weakened the power of local magnates like Downshire and Foster:

. . . Heretofore, one or two or three great men have kept their respective Counties or Provinces loyal and attached. How? By dispensing the patronage of the Crown amongst the people. But if these great men have lost their power, if they follow the Court to Westminster, if they cease to reside or, being resident, are fallen from their station, their adherents will drop off as rats do from a sinking ship, and every man of them becomes, from his disappointments in his views and expectations, an instrument half-formed for the seditious and rebellious emissary to work upon. . . .[2]

While there was some bias, there was also substantial truth in what Pollock said. Patronage was not distributed merely for electioneering purposes; it was distributed also as a reward and encouragement to the loyal and well-affected. Those local magnates who had the distribution of it, were not merely electoral interests; they were the unpaid representatives of the

[1] 43 Geo. III, c. 25, s. 1. One factor in the Government's decision to pass this act was that, when a conflict of loyalties occurred, the Government could not 'punish its own officers for disobedience to its orders', because the disobedience was of a delicate, political nature—Wickham to Marsden, 4 Mar. 1803, Wickham MSS., P.R.O.N.I. T.2627/5/K/60.

[2] Pollock to Hobart, 17 Sept. 1803, Buckinghamshire MSS., P.R.O.N.I. T. 2627/1/17. The same point is made in a letter from Denis Browne to Peel, 6 Mar. 1815, quoted in McDowell, *Public Opinion and Government Policy*, p. 47.

government in the provinces, and as such were entitled to
expect that the patronage as well as the authority of the
government would be delegated to them. As the Lord Lieutenant had remarked to Hillsborough in 1784: '... I should be not
only very inattentive to your wishes, but careless of the interest
of my Government, if I put into an avoidable risk the full
strength of your credit and influence in your neighbourhood.'[1]

For this reason, patronage at local level was to a considerable extent withdrawn from 'the hurricane sphere'. Professor
Pares has suggested that in Great Britain most magnates
could expect a fair share of such patronage, provided they
were not in systematic opposition to the government;[2] and the
same was true of Ireland. The treatment accorded by the
Irish Administration to the 2nd Marquess of Downshire during
the Union crisis illustrates this well. In July 1799, when it was
tolerably clear that Downshire was going to oppose the Union,
the Administration were still granting him all sorts of favours
which were not 'of that magnitude which renders it necessary or
polite to bring him to a decided explanation';[3] and in the following year, when his opposition had taken too violent and
factious a form to be overlooked, the Administration, though
they dismissed him as Governor of co. Down, were careful to
keep the office open until he died in 1801, and probably would
have kept it open still longer had his successor in the Marquessate not been a minor.[4] Foster, it is true, was dismissed early
in 1801 as *Custos Rotulorum* of co. Louth, an office which he
had held conjointly with the governorship of the county since
1798. (The relationship between the *custodia* and the governorship is hard to determine, the more so as the two were often
combined; the *custos* was, technically, appointed by the lord
chancellor, not the lord lieutenant, and to the *custos* 'more
properly belongs the superintendency of the Magistracy',
even though the governor seems to have had a considerable
say in such matters.)[5] Foster's dismissal as *Custos* was probably

[1] Rutland to Hillsborough, 25 Sept. 1784, *H.M.C. Rutland MSS.*, iii. 140.

[2] Richard Pares, *King George III and the Politicians* (Oxford, 1963), p. 11.

[3] Castlereagh to Camden, 17 July 1799, Pratt MSS., K.A.O. U.840/C.98/6.

[4] Hardwicke to Pelham, 18 Sept. 1801, Pelham MSS., B.L. Add. MS. 33114,
fol. 51.

[5] Glandore to the Lord Chancellor, George Ponsonby, 7 Jan. 1807, Talbot-
Crosbie MSS., N.L.I. In 1793 Capt. Bellew of the Louth Militia, Sir Edward

provoked by his refusal to recommend Catholics for the bench. But coming immediately in the wake of the Union, it was ill-timed—indeed, a typical piece of over-reaction on the part of Lord Clare. Foster's comment was: '. . . Although I cannot impute it to Administration [as distinct from the Chancellor], I cannot wholly clear them of it. It was a pitiful [?effort] of resentment, if it was so . . .'¹ It was the sort of resentment in which administrations usually did not indulge. In Ireland, as in Great Britain, the dismissal of magnates from their local offices because of political opposition, was usually regarded as a harsh measure, to be reserved only for the most flagrant forms of opposition. Moreover, in Ireland the endemic lawlessness of much of the country made it a dangerous as well as a harsh measure, since the dismissal of a man who had long represented the authority of government in a particular county might deal a severe blow to the authority of government itself. Lord Townshend was perhaps insufficiently alive to this danger: in 1769 he reported to London that 'neither Lord Shannon nor Mr. [John] Ponsonby [the leading Undertakers] could preserve even their common Provincial influence without their offices.'² He may have been correct in his assessment, as neither Shannon nor the Ponsonbys enjoyed, proportionately, the strength of Foster's position in Louth. However, the more important consideration was, could Townshend preserve order in cos. Cork and Kilkenny, Shannon's and the Ponsonbys' provincial strongholds, without the agency of Shannon and the Ponsonbys?

The dismissal of local magnates was obviously a particularly sensitive matter; but even in the less sensitive matter of appoint-

---

Bellew's brother, asked Foster to recommend him as a J.P. for Louth; Foster refused, and Bellew was subsequently appointed on the recommendation of the Earl of Clermont (Revd. E. Hudson to Charlemont, 8 Sept. 1793, Charlemont MSS., R.I.A. 2nd ser., vi. 60). The interesting feature of this episode is that at that time neither Foster nor Clermont was Governor or *Custos*, both offices being held by Lord Clanbrassill. In 1827 it was, according to the Lord Chancellor's office, 'normal' for recommendations to the magistracy to come from the governor; but when Alexander Dawson asked Foster, now Lord Oriel, to recommend two people, Oriel bluntly took 'leave to decline so doing' (Dawson to Oriel, 28 Jan. 1827, and Oriel to Dawson, 31 Jan. 1827, F.P. D.562/3948–9).

¹ Foster to Sheffield, 5 Feb. 1801, *Anglo-Irish Dialogue*, p. 36.
² Townshend to Weymouth, 18 Aug. 1769, quoted in Froude, *English in Ireland*, ii. 81 f.

ment, political considerations did not prevail unless other things—notably record of residence, size of property, and personal respectability—were equal or nearly equal. This is demonstrated by the storm of protest which was raised by the Whigs' supposedly reforming measure of 1831, by which they abolished the system of county governorships unique to Ireland, and created lieutenancies on the English model. Unfortunately, they took the opportunity which this reform afforded them to replace governors who were their political opponents with lieutenants who were their political supporters—often without regard to residence, property, or personal capacity to carry out the duties of the office (they did have regard to respectability). In the case of Louth, the Prime Minister, Lord Grey, wrote to the Lord Lieutenant, Lord Anglesey: 'If you are sure that Lord Ferrard [formerly Thomas Foster] is an enemy, might not Lord Caledon do for Louth, if he resides in or sufficiently near the county?'[1] Lord Caledon, as Grey subsequently discovered, did not live in or near the county, and moreover owned not an inch of property in it; Sir Patrick Bellew was in the end appointed. The flagrant political motivation behind most of the appointments gave the Irish Tories a field-day in the House of Commons. Among numerous embarrassing questions, they asked: if a Tory who was the obvious choice had not been appointed to Waterford, because he would not be of age for a few months and consequently could not immediately act, why had a Whig been appointed to Tipperary who '... suffered under paralysis, was bed-ridden, unable to walk or to attend to public business.... Was this appointment to be an exception because Tipperary was the Arcadia of Ireland, remarkable for its internal peace and tranquillity? . . .'[2] In fairness, it must be added that the Grey–Anglesey correspondence reveals, not just political bias and sheer ignorance of the country, but a sincere, though

[1] Grey to Anglesey, 22 Aug. 1831, Anglesey MSS., P.R.O.N.I. D.619/28F, p. 137.

[2] Newspaper cutting reporting this debate, [autumn/early winter 1831], Howard Bury MSS., P.R.O.N.I. T.3069/D34, p. 25. This remark was made by the Bury heir, Viscount Tullamore, who proposed a motion of censure in the House of Commons. For the grievances of the Earl of Courtown, who was passed over, probably unjustly, as Lieutenant of co. Wexford, see Viscount Stopford [his son] to Capt. Robert Owen, 3 Oct. 1831, Courtown MSS., Marlfield, Courtown, co. Wexford; now (1978) in the T.C.D. Department of MSS.

probably misguided, belief that magnates of a high Tory or Orange complexion could not be trusted to administer justice impartially between Protestants and Catholics. To this extent, then, even the appointments of 1831 were not a complete departure from the previous practice. The previous practice had been, generally speaking, to give the political no greater weight than other considerations; and this often applied to even the politically very important office of sheriff.[1] There is some evidence that the government genuinely wanted to get appointments to the shrievalty reduced to some system which would prevent its being constantly pestered by the local magnates.[2] In 1760, even the Undertaker Lords Justices, who were probably less virtuous in this respect than English lords lieutenant and chief secretaries, were very anxious to have the forthcoming general election held within the term of office of the existing sheriffs, 'that they might stand clear of all importunities for new sheriffs and of all suspicion of partiality'.[3] In a known election year, the government usually yielded to the wishes of local magnates who were government supporters and who expected reciprocal support in the matter of the sheriff.[4] But it is important to remember that government supporters did not expect—or at least they never wrote saying that this was what they expected—that someone biased in their favour

[1] For examples of strong and almost certainly sincere disclaimers of political motivation in the recommendation or appointment of sheriffs, see Lord Bessborough to Luke Gardiner, 19 and 26 Nov. 1746, Domvile MSS., N.L.I. MS. 9399; Lord Llandaff to Buckingham, 29 Jan. 1789, Joly MSS., N.L.I. MSS. 39–40, fol. 155.

[2] Arthur Pomeroy to Abercorn, 7 Dec. 1756, Abercorn MSS., P.R.O.N.I. T. 2541/IA1/4/46. The 'system', such as it was, was that the out-going sheriff submitted five names of suitable people to the assize judge, who selected three from the list and submitted the three to the government for the final selection. The government could go outside the three, but in this letter Pomeroy quotes Lord Kildare, one of the Lords Justices, as expressing strong disinclination, apparently on grounds of principle, so to do.

[3] Memorandum by Anthony Foster about the Money Bill dispute of 1760–1, F.P. D.562/5182; Lords Justices to Bedford, 7 Nov. 1760, Shannon MSS., P.R.O.N.I. D.2707/A/1/6/1.

[4] Nathaniel Sneyd to Hardwicke, 6 Feb. 1802, Hardwicke MSS., B.L. Add. MS. 35733, fol. 15; C. H. Coote to Abbot, 9 Jan. 1802, Colchester MSS., P.R.O. 30/9, 1 part 1/3. However, in a non-election year, 1800, Lord Clanricarde, the Governor of co. Galway, refused to take account of the views of the M.P.s—Clanricarde to Castlereagh, 3 Aug. 1800, S.P.O. 515/83/28. It is probable that at no time was there any hard and fast rule for deciding between the conflicting claims of governors and M.P.s, if and when conflict arose.

should be appointed: their request was always for 'impartiality', and that the appointment of someone biased against them should be blocked.[1] In any case, much more of the correspondence generated by the matter of sheriffs relates to people who wanted out of the office than people who wanted into it;[2] much more of it (although this is often hard to recognize) relates to the debt-collecting and law-enforcing role of the sheriffs than to the political role;[3] and the vast majority of sheriffs never had to act as returning officers in elections.

There was thus an ill-defined, but substantial, area of local patronage which was awarded not solely on political grounds and not necessarily to government supporters. Perhaps the clearest example of this kind of patronage in the Fosters' case is the colonelcy of the Louth Militia, which was given to Thomas Foster when the Irish militia was established in 1793. John Foster's position in national politics was irrelevant to this appointment. The colonelcy went to Thomas Foster because his father was M.P. for the county and the leading figure in it, just as the colonelcy of the co. Londonderry Militia went to Conolly, the M.P. for the county, and the colonelcy of the co. Kildare to the Duke of Leinster, even though both were in opposition at the time. The case of Conolly is particularly instructive, as his junior colleague in the representation of co. Londonderry—in years and in length of service—was Lord Tyrone, the Beresford heir; yet the colonelcy was still given to Conolly. The patronage of a militia colonel was extensive. He had the choosing of the regiment's officers (subject to the lord lieutenant's veto), and if and when it was disembodied, he had the choosing of those N.C.O.s who were to remain on the permanent peace-time establishment. The Irish practice differed markedly from the English in this respect, as in England all such patronage was in the hands of the lord

[1] Gardiner to Bessborough, *c.* 20 Nov. 1746, Domvile MSS., N.L.I. MS. 11848; Henry Flood to [?], [late 1760s?], Burrowes MSS., R.I.A. MS. 23 K. 53, fol. 10; Sir Lucius O'Brien to Sackville Hamilton, 7 Nov. 1782, Additional Dropmore MSS.

[2] See, for example, Shannon to Hon. William Crosbie, 26 Feb. 1761, Talbot-Crosbie MSS., N.L.I.

[3] Edmond Hogan to Robert French, 6 Nov. 1742 and 7 Oct. 1747, Petworth House MSS., M.C. 7/35; Nathaniel Nisbitt to Abercorn, 23 Jan. 1757, Abercorn MSS., P.R.O.N.I. T.2541/IA1/4/55; John Eyre to Shannon, 15 Dec. 1764, Shannon MSS., P.R.O.N.I. D.2707/A/1/5/56.

lieutenant of the county.[1] Yet, just as the colonelcy was not a political appointment, so the best of the colonels did not put it to political use, in spite of the extensive patronage it commanded. As Lord Abercorn observed loftily, when writing to offer the command of the Tyrone Militia to a political adversary: 'Upon all really national points, party is always out of the question with me.'[2] When the 2nd Marquess of Downshire put the colonelcy of the Down Militia to flagrantly political use during the Union crisis, he transgressed against a convention which was no less strong for being unwritten, and was deservedly dismissed and disgraced. Thomas Foster, scion though he was of one of the most ambitious and politically-minded families in Ireland, did not transgress against this convention.

The propriety of his conduct is gainsaid by a considerable volume of contemporary evidence. He was accused, as has been seen, of employing 'Militia jobs' to further Foster influence in Drogheda.[3] More seriously, he was accused of deliberately using the regiment in Drogheda, Belfast, and elsewhere 'to gratify a wicked and destructive policy' and 'Foster' discord between Protestant and Catholic; hence the Louth Militia became known as 'the Speaker's bloodhounds'. Even a well-informed contemporary like George Knox accused John Foster of '. . . endeavouring to raise a Protestant Militia in his county, and to keep alive the suspicions and animosity of the Louth gentlemen against the Catholics. . . .'[4] In fact, this was nonsense. The Dublin Evening Post in September 1793 commended Thomas Foster for not allowing his own and

---

[1] Sir Henry McAnally, The Irish Militia, 1793–1816: a Social and Military Study (London, 1949), pp. 70, 169; Foster to Sheffield, 22 Mar. 1793, Anglo-Irish Dialogue, p. 12.

[2] Abercorn to James Stewart, 25 Feb. 1793, Abercorn MSS., P.R.O.N.I. T.2541/IK/13/28.

[3] Until 1797 there was a separate Drogheda Militia, under the colonelcy of Lord Conyngham, which was merged with the Louth in that year. The merger coincided roughly with the Fosters' political intervention in Drogheda, but there were sound administrative reasons for it: Louth was the smallest county, and the Drogheda regiment, while it existed as a separate entity, the smallest regiment, in Ireland—McAnally, Irish Militia, pp. 59, 67.

[4] 'Amicus' to the printer of the Drogheda Journal, Oct. 1794, F.P. D.562/3745; Mrs. McTier to Dr. William Drennan, [1793?], Drennan MSS., P.R.O.N.I. D.591/397; George Knox to Abercorn, 21 Apr. 1793, Abercorn MSS., P.R.O.N.I. T.2541/IB1/4/19.

his family's views on Emancipation to interfere with his recruiting policy as Colonel of the Louth. In that month he
appointed Sir Edward Bellew's brother a captain in the regiment (causing Balfour to resign as major in protest); and
Wakefield later recorded that any reluctance there was to
enlist in the other ranks was all on the Catholic side, and was
not effaced until the brother of the parish priest of Collon,
prompted by the Fosters, joined up.[1] The only occasion on
which the Louth Militia may have been used to further the
Fosters' political views was during the Drogheda election of
1807, when the regiment as a whole, and individual officers
in it, are mentioned suspiciously often in the inventory of
Thomas Foster's election expenditure. With this possibly
innocent exception, the Louth seems to have been above
politics. Thomas Foster's correspondence as its Colonel
shows him to have been a ponderously earnest young man,
who if anything went too far in his anxiety to maintain high
standards in his regiment.[2] His father had been one of the
keenest advocates of an Irish militia, and was the most influential of the 'militia purists' who believed that the system
of recruitment by parochial ballot, as envisaged by the 1793
Act, should be rigorously implemented.[3] Naturally, the alternative—recruitment by means of paid substitutes—was more
popular among the parishioners themselves. But Foster did
not let the murmurings of his Louth constituents deter him,
and Louth was one of the few counties which was balloted
when the Irish militia was re-embodied in 1803. In 1799,

---

[1] Quoted in McAnally, *Irish Militia*, p. 59; Wakefield, *Account of Ireland*, quoted
in *C.L.A.J.* vii. 232. The 1794 *Almanack* says that it was Edward Bellew himself (he
did not succeed to the family baronetcy until 1795) who was appointed, but this
must be a mistake. The Fosters later had cause to regret the appointment of his
brother, who in 1796 made an allegation to a general on the Irish staff that Roman
Catholics in the Louth were forced to worship in Protestant churches; this Thomas
Foster formally denied in a letter to the Chief Secretary—Thomas Foster to Pelham
[5 Oct. 1796], Pelham MSS., B.L. Add. MS. 33102, fol. 228. It is symptomatic of
the Fosters' attitude towards the military role of the Catholics that John Foster's
own Collon corps of yeomanry contained Catholics, including one prominent
Catholic tenant of his, whose son turned out to be one of the ringleaders of the
3,500 or so United Irishmen sworn in Louth—Grattan, *Life*, iv. 280; *C.L.A.J.* xiii.
266 ff.

[2] See, for example, Thomas Foster to Pole, 17 Feb. 1810, F.P. D.562/3635A and
B; John Foster to Sheffield, 22 Mar. 1794, *Anglo-Irish Dialogue*, p. 12.

[3] McAnally, *Irish Militia*, p. 103.

Cornwallis paid tribute to the zeal of both father and son when
he declared that the Louth Militia was 'the best disciplined
of the whole'.[1] This judgement, coming as it did from a man
who was a professional soldier, who sympathized with the
Catholic cause, and who had a strong bias against the Fosters,
can be regarded as the best possible refutation of the charge
that they used the regiment to serve their own political ends.

The Louth Militia is therefore a clear-cut example of the
sort of local patronage which was above politics and which
was entrusted to the Fosters in recognition of their 'provincial
influence', and not of John Foster's political influence at
national level.[2] An example of local patronage which, though
not above politics, came his way purely because of his position
in the local context of Louth, was the nomination to the clerkship of the peace for the county. This was the *Custos Rotulorum's* right,[3] and the clerkship happened to fall vacant in the
period 1798–1801, when he was *Custos*. By nominating one
John Bourne to it, he performed what was, in terms of his
political interest in Louth, the most significant, single exercise
of patronage in his career. A friendly clerk of the peace was a
vital ally in the period after 1795, when the registration system
was at its most exacting. Bourne acted as a kind of unpaid
election agent for him, not only checking that his registries
were correct in point of form, but advising on their timing as
well:[4] a most important contribution in view of Foster's

---

[1] Cornwallis to Dundas, 1 July 1799, *Cornwallis Correspondence*, iii. 110.

[2] Dr. P. J. Jupp has made the important point that, after the Union, even the
patronage which *was* distributed to local magnates on political grounds, was
used not so much for the purpose of getting supporters of the government elected
as for the purpose of winning over to the government the M.P.s who had already
been elected. Dr. Jupp calculates that the government took a direct part in 20
elections between 1800 and 1820, successfully in seven instances and unsuccessfully in thirteen. Drogheda in 1802 was of course one of its failures. These figures
endorse what I have said about the poorness of the Castle's intelligence service
and the unreliability of central-government sources. (Jupp, 'Parliamentary
Representation', pp. 35 ff.) Patronage was virtually the only weapon at the Castle's
disposal, because the Crown lands were of limited extent; just as there was no Irish
equivalent of the Cinque Ports (except the parlous bishops' boroughs, only one of
which survived the Union), so there was none of the Duchy of Lancaster.

[3] It seems to have been a fairly recently established right, as the co. Tipperary
clerk was appointed by the Crown in 1796, and was finally ousted in favour of the
Custos's nominee after lengthy litigation—Fred. Falkiner to John Bagwell, 8 Dec.
1801, Hardwicke MSS., B.L. Add. MS. 35731, fol. 324.

[4] Anthony Sillery to Foster, 7 Feb. 1809, F.P. T.2519/4/525.

absences from Louth during his years of office at Westminster, and in view of the fact that he was not a large or wealthy enough landowner to employ in the normal running of his estate the sophisticated type of person who looked after the registries of great magnates like the Downshires and the Abercorns. Bourne was such an important component of Foster's interest in Louth that it was probably due to some kind of nervous breakdown which he suffered in 1820 that the Foster registries got into the confusion that was exposed with unhappy consequences in 1826. By that time Bourne had partially recovered, and it was a measure of the importance which the opposition attached to his services that they poisoned three of his horses in succession in a vain attempt to keep him away from the hustings.[1] In justice to Bourne's integrity as a county official, it should be said that he gave the benefit of his advice to other county interests also, notably Balfour; but his first loyalty was to Foster.[2] It is important to remember that Foster had won this strategically vital loyalty because he was a local magnate and *Custos Rotulorum*, not because he was a prominent figure in national politics.

At the same time it would be an oversimplification to say that prominence in national politics had no bearing on local patronage and the way it was distributed. Obviously, a man who was important in national terms had the advantage, even in the sphere of local patronage, over a rival who was not. In co. Limerick, for example, Lord Clare seems to have been able to monopolize the nomination to the shrievalty during the time that he was Lord Chancellor; but after his death in 1802 the same monopoly was not granted to his family. Ironically, the nomination was given in 1812 to a local magnate who happened to be Lord Chief Baron of the Exchequer—to the

[1] Bourne to Oriel, 25 Aug. 1827, F.P. D.562/14544.
[2] Bourne to Balfour, 29 Nov. 1803, Balfour MSS., N.L.I. MS. 10368; Bourne to Foster, 6 Mar. 1807, F.P. D.562/12439. In 1819, there was a series of debates in the House of Commons about the co. Limerick clerkship of the peace, at the end of which Newport proposed that, instead of holding their offices during the pleasure of the *custos*, the Irish clerks of the peace should be appointed during good behaviour, as was the system in England—nine issues of the *Courier* recording these debates, 5 Feb.–30 Mar. 1819, Dunraven MSS., P.R.O.N.I. D.3196/C/5. The tenure of the Irish clerks was changed accordingly by 1 Geo. IV, c. 27. Because of Foster's dismissal as *Custos* in 1801, the nature of Bourne's tenure was not of course a factor in their relationship.

indignation of Clare's widow, who did not like to see the argument that national prominence entitled a man to special consideration, used against her family's interest.[1] The same argument was used against that most indignant of dowagers, Lady Downshire, widow of the 2nd Marquess, who was told in 1803 that she could not recommend to two revenue jobs in Newry because her claims conflicted with those of Isaac Corry, who was '. . . intimately connected with the King's Government in this country by his office of Chancellor of the Exchequer . . .'[2] Some years later, in 1815, Sir Edward O'Brien, M.P. for co. Clare, found himself deprived of what he considered his fair share of the local patronage of Clare, because his claims conflicted with those of Vesey FitzGerald: '. . . County Members', lamented O'Brien, 'while they act with and support an Administration, think that they have claims for reciprocal support . . .'[3] His lamentation can be regarded as typical of the run-of-the-mill government supporter who found his slice of local patronage being eaten into by the claims of a man whose support was of greater consequence. In co. Louth, Foster was not only the most important figure, in purely local terms; he was also, in national terms, a man whose support of the government was of the greatest consequence. On both counts, he was head-and-shoulders above his nearest county competitors, the Clermonts and Clanbrassill/Rodens, so there was no conflict in co. Louth between local and national claims, such as O'Brien complained of in Clare. Certainly, the Clermonts and Clanbrassill/Rodens had nothing to complain of, since (as has been seen) they received more, in terms of emoluments for themselves, for their undistinguished and on the whole silent support of 'His Majesty's Ministers . . . on every occasion', than Foster did for being one of the most important figures in the national politics of his day.

On local, reinforced by national, grounds Foster was thus accorded what was called 'the patronage of Louth'.[4] What

---

[1] Hardwicke to Wickham, 9 Nov. 1803, Wickham MSS., P.R.O.N.I. T.2627/5/E/262; Norman Gash, *Mr. Secretary Peel: the Life of Sir Robert Peel to 1830* (London, 1964), p. 122.

[2] Hardwicke to Lady Downshire, 25 May 1803, Wickham MSS., P.R.O.N.I. T.2627/5/E/175.

[3] O'Brien to Peel, 18 Jan. 1815, quoted in Jupp, 'Parliamentary Representation', article on O'Brien.   [4] Richmond to Pole, 22 May 1811, F.P. D.207/38/62.

this meant in practical terms is not easy to define. It obviously meant that he had a lien on the highest county offices, although or many years the very highest, the governorship of the county, eluded him. This had been conferred on the 2nd Earl of Clanbrassill in 1758 on the death of the 1st Earl, the previous Governor, and it did not fall vacant until Clanbrassill's death in 1798. Lord Camden's Administration was only recognizing the shift in the balance of political power and proprietary strength which had taken place in co. Louth since 1758, when it by-passed Clanbrassill's successor, Lord Roden, and made Foster both Governor and *Custos* (as Clanbrassill had been): there is no reason to suppose that Cornwallis's Administration would have acted any differently if the vacancy had occurred later in the year. In 1801, as has been seen, Foster lost the *custodia*, which was given to Lord Roden, and descended to Roden's son, the 3rd Earl, in 1820. It is tempting to regard this as a political appointment, designed to exalt the Unionist Roden at the expense of the anti-Unionist Foster. However, Roden's contribution to the Union had already been more than generously rewarded, and as a frequent resident and the owner of property in the county which, although less extensive, was more valuable than Foster's, Roden had strong claims on local grounds. The objectionable feature of the transaction was, not the appointment of Roden, but the dismissal of Foster. As has been suggested, this was probably a step taken on Clare's own hasty initiative; certainly, it does not accord with the Government's policy towards Foster and towards most anti-Unionists at the time. Soon afterwards, however, Foster had the consolation of having his son, Thomas, associated with him in the governorship. This was an unusual arrangement, but it did not derive from the unusual strength of the Foster family's position in their county; it was the automatic consequence of the 1803 Militia Act, which made all militia colonels governors of their respective counties, if they were not so already. This is a further example of the low priority which political considerations held in local appointments. In many counties—Louth indeed is an example —the establishment of the militia had in practice enabled the government to vary the county honours by giving the colonelcy to a family interest which did not hold the governorship, but the 1803 Act, inspired purely by a desire to facilitate recruitment, upset the precarious balance thus established—with especially awkward consequences in Kerry.[1] Another unusual feature of the arrangement of the county offices in Louth, is that John Foster between 1798 and 1821, and Thomas Foster between 1821 and 1824, were Governors and county M.P.s at the same time. This was apparently illegal in England (according to the Irish Solicitor-General, who protested in 1831 against the Whigs' appointment of one of the M.P.s for King's County as Lieutenant).[2] It was not illegal in Ireland, but it was unusual, simply because most of the governors prior to the 1803 Act were peers. The Fosters remained joint Governors until 1828, when Thomas Foster, by then Lord Ferrard, became sole Governor on his father's death. On the establishment of county lieutenancies in Ireland in 1831 he was, as has been seen, replaced by Sir Patrick Bellew.

In practical terms, then, this was what the enjoyment of the patronage of Louth meant to Foster, where the highest county offices were concerned. Lower down the scale, it is not so easy to define what it meant. Up to 1798, Clanbrassill because he was Governor, Foster because he was the senior county M.P., and Clermont because he claimed to return the second county M.P., all enjoyed a share in the patronage of Louth when it came to minor revenue jobs and even recommendations to the magistracy. Although the three were in political alliance at election time, at other times they did not always speak with one voice and, indeed, were so discordant on one occasion in 1795–6, that they seriously embarrassed the Castle. The occasion was the institution of chairmen of quarter sessions (assistant barristers) for the thirteen counties which did not already have one. Clanbrassill, Foster, and Clermont each recommended a different person for Louth. Foster's and Clermont's nominees, and possibly Clanbrassill's, were local men, and it was probably government policy that assistant barristers, like militia regiments, should not be stationed in their county of origin. The Castle was therefore placed in an awkward predicament by Foster's 'eagerness' on behalf of his nominee, T. P. Filgate, a member of a family which had always

---

[1] Glandore to George Ponsonby, 7 Jan. 1807, Talbot-Crosbie MSS., N.L.I.
[2] See p. 251 n. 2.

been warm adherents of the Fosters in county politics. In the end, he was obliged to accept the chairmanship of not-too-distant co. Wicklow for Filgate, and Clanbrassill and Clermont got no satisfaction at all.[1] After 1798, when Foster was Governor of Louth as well as its M.P., the situation became a little less complicated. But Lords Roden and Clermont could still not be excluded altogether from the patronage of Louth—particularly Clermont, who did not enjoy the patronage of any borough, as Roden did of Dundalk.[2] So, even after 1798, it is not possible to define what was meant by the patronage of Louth, and it would be unrealistic and unhistorical to try; after all, if a clear definition had existed there would have been no room for the bitter dispute between Foster and the 2nd Lord Clermont between 1809 and 1824 over the patronage of the Carlingford district.

A constantly confusing element in the patronage of Louth, and probably in the patronage of most counties, was that, although most of it took the form of revenue jobs, the county boundaries did not coincide with any revenue district. There were four revenue stations in Louth. One—the Carlingford—was administratively under the control of the Collector of the Revenue at Newry, and the other three under the Collector of Drogheda.[3] This means that when mention is made of Foster's successfully recommending to a revenue post 'in the Drogheda district', it is not clear whether the post falls within his Louth or his Drogheda patronage. Because of this and the other confusing elements in the patronage of Louth, he was involved in more disputes than the one with Lord Clermont: in 1811, for example, over the nomination to the revenue post of coast officer of Louth. Since this post was administratively within the Newry district, General Francis Needham claimed it as his perquisite as M.P. for Newry; since it was located in Dundalk Bay, Lord Roden claimed it as his perquisite as proprietor of Dundalk borough; and since it was

[1] Entries in Camden's audience book, 28 Nov. 1795 and 18 June 1796, Pratt MSS., K.A.O. U.840/O.130A; Clermont to Pelham, 10 Mar. 1796, and Foster to Pelham, 17 Mar. 1796, S.P.O. 507/9/25; Camden to Pelham, 23 May 1796, Pelham MSS., B.L. Add. MS. 33102, fols. 16–18.

[2] For some discussion of what was and was not included in the patronage of Dundalk, see Malcomson, *Dundalk Borough*, pp. 30 f.

[3] Oriel to Lord Talbot, the Lord Lieutenant, 19 Oct. 1821, F.P. D.562/16063.

called coast officer of Louth, rather than of Newry or Dundalk, Foster claimed it as his perquisite as M.P. for Louth. Foster won in the end, largely because he could show that he had successfully nominated to the post since 1768.[1] But he had other battles to fight, on similar ground, in 1819 and again in 1821.[2] In all such battles a man who was important at national level had the advantage of superior bargaining, indeed blackmailing, power *vis à vis* the government, because in the last resort he could always threaten to withdraw his support unless he was allowed to have his way. This Foster did over the Collectorship of Drogheda (as well as the Bishopric of Clogher) in 1795.[3]

Prominence in national politics, therefore, was useful rather than necessary in the sphere of local patronage. All patronage, however, was not distributed along local lines; and it was in the case of patronage which lay outside the sphere of local nomination that the national figure came into his own. It is not always easy to see where this non-local sphere began and ended. Obviously, it included all jobs in Dublin Castle, the Dublin Customs House, the Four Courts, and the Irish Parliament House. But it also included certain jobs which were ostensibly local in character; for example, all sinecure offices, newly-created offices, and offices under the stamp board, were reserved by convention to the nomination of the lord lieutenant, no matter where they were situated.[4] The same must have been true of chairmanships of quarter sessions. In general, the more important and valuable local offices were reserved for the lord lieutenant's nomination. Lord Hardwicke, weighed down by the burden of the Union engagements he had inherited, felt particularly strongly on this point. He refused to allow 'what is called the patronage of a place to be construed to extend to situations of £700 a year [e.g. collectorships

---

[1] Richmond to Pole, 7 May 1811, Whitworth MSS., K.A.O. U.269/O.214/5; Foster to Pole, Feb. 1811, F.P. D.207/38/43.

[2] Memorial of George Read to Talbot, 5 Jan. 1819, F.P. D.562/15726; Oriel to Talbot, 19 Oct. 1821, F.P. D 562/16063.

[3] Pelham to Camden, 20 Dec. 1795, Pratt MSS., K.A.O. U.840/O.189/5. For an example of a bluff of this kind which was called, see Gash, *Secretary Peel*, p. 122.

[4] Marsden to Hardwicke, 1802, Hardwicke MSS., B.L. Add. MS. 35723, fol. 65; Saxton to Robert Dundas, 4 May 1809, Melville MSS., N.L.I. MS. 55/244; Foster to Lord Courtown, 30 June 1810, F.P. T. 2519/4/999.

of the revenue]', and maintained that the two most important classes of revenue jobs, collectorships and surveyorships, should lie outside the scope of local nomination, 'as a measure equally necessary for securing the due collection of the Revenue and the just and effective patronage of the Crown'.[1] There is no reason to think that this principle was new and inspired by the burden of Union engagements. In the late eighteenth century, for example, the Marquesses of Downshire were in the habit of recommending—in at least one case successfully— to surveyorships in Louth and Drogheda, although they had no pretensions on local grounds to do so.[2] Nor is there any reason to think that the principle was relaxed after 1804, when most of the Union engagements had been satisfied. In 1807, for example, surveyorships in the excise department were being filled by nomination of the Commissioners of Excise in rotation, except in the case of particularly meritorious officers, whose promotion to surveyorships could be made 'a general business of the board'.[3] In general, the most valuable revenue offices were still withdrawn from the sphere of local nomination, since in 1808 Thomas Foster had to point out to one applicant that 'it does not fall to the lot of any one individual to command the obtaining of' jobs worth upwards of £600 a year; however, he added more hopefully that his father might be able to do something.[4] As a prominent national figure and high office-holder, John Foster could do things which would have been impossible for a local magnate.

His non-local patronage fell into two classes. The first was his departmental patronage: the patronage of his own office. The second may for brevity's sake be called his residual patronage; this was the miscellaneous non-local patronage which his general importance to the government entitled him to expect, but which was not specifically annexed to his own department. The first class applied to office-holders only, and was something

[1] Wickham to Addington, 25 Apr. 1802, MacDonagh, *Viceroy's Post-Bag*, p. 19; Wickham to Castlereagh, 30 Oct. 1802, Wickham MSS., P.R.O.N.I. T. 2627/5/G/21.
[2] John Reilly to Downshire, Nov. 1797, Downshire MSS., P.R.O.N.I. D. 607/Nov. 1797. The 2nd Marquess had bought half of Carlingford borough in 1796, but this would hardly have given him a claim on such valuable patronage.
[3] John McCollum to Foster, 14 June 1807, F.P. D.562/10161.
[4] Thomas Foster to Lord Montfort, 27 Apr. 1808, F.P. D.562/3336.

which they could claim as a right: the second applied to prominent supporters of government as well as to office-holders, and was something which they could only ask as a favour. Obviously, the two overlapped at many points, both with each other and with local patronage. But all three could be used to strengthen interest at constituency level; Foster's departmental and residual patronage was useful in gratifying important individuals like Edward Hardman, the local in gratifying the smaller fry. In general his departmental and residual patronage took the form of jobs outside the confines of Louth and Drogheda, and the local of jobs within them. But this was not always so. For example, it was as part of his residual patronage that he was allowed twice to nominate to the Collectorship of Drogheda:[1] a job which was too valuable and influential to be included in his local patronage, and which was a vital factor in his influence in Drogheda. Moreover, many of the smaller jobs which were within the sphere of local nomination were allocated on a national rather than a local basis. In the case of customs tidewaiterships and collector-ships of hearth-money, for instance, allocation was by means of a waiting-list; Foster, as a local magnate, could get his nominees placed on the list, but could exercise no say over where they were posted once their names reached the top.[2] With these exceptions, however, it is true to say that there was a geographical demarcation between his departmental and residual patronage, on the one hand, and his local on the other.

Political considerations were not the only ones which weighed with Foster in the use he made of his local patronage; and in the use he made of his departmental patronage they must have been low down in his list of priorities. He was not the man to impair the efficiency of a department under him by stocking it with incompetent Louth freeholders. To maintain efficiency and continuity he must often have had to retain the services of people appointed by a predecessor; certainly, when he himself retired in 1811 he managed to quarter all his staff on his successor, so perhaps this was one unwritten rule

---

[1] Rochfort to John Foster, Oct. 1807, F.P. D.207/34/19; Wellesley to Foster, 11 Jan. 1809, F.P. D.207/35/84.

[2] Allan McLean to Foster, 9 Sept. 1811, F.P. D.207/38/84; Foster to John Christy, 2 Apr. 1811, F.P. D.562/6237.

by which the game of departmental patronage was cus-
tomarily played.[1] In any case, the successive offices he held
did not, with the exception of the speakership, possess large
staffs. As Chairman of Committees from 1777 to 1784, he
probably had no staff at all, apart from a clerk or two; and a
few clerkships seem to have been the extent of his patronage as
Customer of Dublin Port from 1779 to 1784.[2] Even the
chancellorship of the exchequer, because it had ceased to be an
efficient office, probably had only a small staff when Foster
came to it in 1784. No doubt the staff increased greatly,
especially after he set up an Irish Exchequer Office in London
in 1805;[3] but it is unlikely to have increased so much that there
was room for any passengers. The only place where there was
room for passengers was on the judicial side of the exchequer,
where even as late as the early nineteenth century the chancellor
of the exchequer still retained some patronage, even though
he had long since ceased himself to exercise any judicial
functions.[4] Like the chancellorship of the exchequer, the
treasury carried a comparatively small working staff. The
sinecure or semi-sinecure offices under it are likely to have
been in the gift of the lord lieutenant, not of the vice-treasurers
or of the treasury board which succeeded them in 1793.
Foster, as First Lord of the Treasury from 1804 to 1806,
had some success in expanding the board's patronage, but
much of his work in this direction was undone by the Talents.
Both as Chancellor of the Exchequer and as First or Second
Lord of the Treasury, he had some presumably stipulated
share in the nomination of the treasury clerks (although even
this limited sphere of patronage was being eyed jealously by the
Lord Lieutenant in 1811).[5] But in none of these capacities

---

[1] Foster to Pole, [late June 1811], and Pole to Foster, 8 July 1811, F.P. D.207/
38/99, 167; ex-Chief Baron Edward Willes to Chief Baron Anthony Foster, 15
Sept. and 15 Oct. 1766, F.P. D. 562/1527, 1523.

[2] John Foster to Sackville Hamilton, 16 Jan. 1780, F.P. D. 562/8346.

[3] Rochfort to Foster, 1 Jan. 1805, F.P. D.207/33/2; Sir Charles Flint to Marsden,
6 Feb. 1806, S.P.O. 530/213/2.

[4] David Courtnay to Oriel, 6 Nov. 1822, F.P. D.562/14037. In 1819 it appears
that the staff of the Court of Exchequer numbered sixty-nine—V. T. H. Delany,
Christopher Palles (Dublin, 1960), p. 95.

[5] Elliot to Under-Secretary James Traill, 10 Oct. 1806, Elliot of Wells MSS.,
N.L.S. E.W.26; Pole to Richmond, 31 Jan. 1811, Richmond MSS., N.L.I. M.S.
65, fol. 742.

does he seem to have had any stipulated share in revenue employments: in this much more extensive sphere, his successful recommendations must be attributed, not to his departmental, but to either his local or residual, patronage.

The best testimony to the limited nature of his departmental patronage is to be found in the papers of his not-quite-immediate successor as Chancellor of the Exchequer and Second Lord of the Treasury, Vesey FitzGerald. Writing early in 1813, and early in his official career, FitzGerald expressed his willingness to oblige someone, if only he '. . . had any patronage within my own office, or power of placing him . . . in any of the Public Departments. But I assure you that I have not the means of providing in any of the Departments, even for those immediately connected with my own office or with the financial branches of the public service, even in cases where I might wish to bring forward any such individuals and reward them, I am in these respects miserably hampered. . . .' Later in that year, he observed (more intelligibly) to another suppliant: '. . . I believe you are not aware that the promotion of Offices [sic] in the Excise Department does not at all rest with me, and since I have been in Ireland, though I have recommended two persons to Mr. Marsden [the Chief Commissioner of Excise] . . . , I have been unable to succeed. . . .' A year later, in September 1814, he complained: 'Our Revenue patronage . . . rests entirely with the Lord Lieutenant'; and added that only one small situation had fallen within his patronage since he came to preside at the treasury two years earlier—possibly a treasury clerkship.[1] There is no reason for imagining that the situation was any different in Foster's day, even when he was First Lord of the Treasury from 1804 to 1806. It might be argued that FitzGerald, in refusing a favour, was likely to underestimate the extent of his patronage in order to sweeten the refusal; but his first two correspondents were highly placed individuals, with their own means of obtaining accurate information on this subject, and the last he referred for confirmation of what he had said to an experienced revenue officer, who was bound to know the true position. In any case, it was, as has been seen, a

[1] Vesey FitzGerald to Lord Kingston, 7 Feb. 1813, to Richard Martin, 19 Sept. 1813, and to J. G. Street, 27 Sept. 1814, Vesey FitzGerald MSS., N.L.I. MS. 7817, p. 115, MS. 7813, p. 214, and MS. 7827, p. 159.

principle of government that the patronage of Ireland should be almost entirely confined to the lord lieutenant, to the virtual exclusion of Irish politicians and bureaucrats at the heads of the various departments.

The only office which Foster held and which enjoyed an extensive and well-defined sphere of departmental patronage, was the speakership. The offices under it are itemized in the *Commons' Journals*, and all told the salaries amount to almost £4,000 a year, exclusive of fees—which in most cases were considerable.[1] This figure also excludes the salaries for the clerkship and assistant-clerkship of the House, because these offices were almost certainly reserved to the nomination of the lord lieutenant. It includes, however, the salary of the Serjeant and Deputy-Serjeant at Arms. Both of these were patentee offices, held for a life or lives; but they seem to have been in the gift of the speaker within whose term of office they fell vacant. Both fell vacant during Foster's term of office, and he gave them to his cousins, John McClintock Senior and Junior, of Drumcar, co. Louth.[2] These are the only two co. Louth men whom he is definitely known to have obliged with offices in the speaker's department. No doubt there were others concealed among the messengers, doormen, and clerks; but even in the case of the most menial employees he was strict in applying the criterion of efficiency, and at the end of his first session was able to boast that '. . . a better set could not have been collected. During the whole of the session I never heard of one messenger being off his station or drunk or negligent. . . .'[3] The patronage of the speakership was not however confined to the staff of the House of Commons. During Foster's term as Speaker two major reconstructions of the Parliament House were undertaken under his direction, and the contracts for this work were his to dispose of, subject of

[1] *Commons' Journals* (Ireland), xi, Index, Table of Supply.
[2] Oriel to McClintock Junior, 24 Nov. 1824, F.P. D.562/14279. The previous grantees, the Coddingtons, although connected with Foster, had been made Serjeant and Deputy-Serjeant by Speaker Ponsonby—Hughes, *Patentee Officers*, p. 29; Hunt, *Irish Parliament*, p. 13. The most that Foster can have done for them was to arrange for the elderly Dixie Coddington to retire on pension from the serjeantcy-at-arms in 1792, thus obliging the McClintocks and him at one stroke—list of the Irish Parliament, [mid-January 1788], Buckinghamshire MSS., P.R.O.N.I. T.2627/1/1; *Commons' Journals* (Ireland), xv. 24.
[3] Commonplace book kept by Foster as Speaker, 1786–98, F.P. D.562/7564.

course to the overriding supervision of the House.[1] Foster, as Lord Westmorland observed satirically, was 'a great architect', and took an active interest in these operations. Perhaps his interest was too active, since the heating system he installed was widely blamed for causing the fire in the House of Commons in 1792. He himself indignantly rejected 'the imputation on his flues'.[2] In addition to his heating schemes and building projects, he had a further, more traditional source of patronage: the speaker's money. This took the form of an annual parliamentary grant which the speaker applied as he thought fit for the relief of distressed work-people. Even in the early 1780s, Foster had been active in obtaining from Speaker Pery some share of this money for Hardman to employ in Drogheda; and no doubt Drogheda's share increased after Foster became Speaker himself.[3] In all these ways the speakership was a valuable source of patronage. It was moreover the only office which Foster ever held whose patronage is at all definable.

The second class of his official patronage—the residual—is impossible to define. More often than not it took the form of places on the revenue board, the treasury board, or his own enquiry board: in other words, the form most difficult to distinguish from his departmental patronage as Chancellor of the Exchequer and First or Second Lord of the Treasury.[4] The career of his brother, the Revd. William Foster, however, is one clear-cut illustration of his residual patronage in operation. As one of his correspondents bluntly put it, 'the road to preferment in the Established Church is the road of interest';[5] and the career of William Foster not only shows how powerful John Foster's interest was, but also how it might be exploited to extend the Foster interest at constituency level. William

[1] D. J. T. Englefield, 'The Irish House of Parliament in the Eighteenth Century', *Parliamentary Affairs*, ix (1956), 58; *Parl. Reg.* (Irish), xx, 35 ff.; Malcomson, *Foster and the Speakership*, pp. 280, 297.

[2] Westmorland to Pitt, 3 Mar. 1792, Westmorland MSS., S.P.O. fol. 49.

[3] Hardman to Foster, 28 Jan. 1781, F.P. D.562/8823. I have been unable to find a reference to this source of patronage in the *Commons' Journals*. The grant to Drogheda in 1780 was for only £50—draft from Speaker Pery to Foster and others, Dec. 1780, F.P. D.562/8821.

[4] Nepean to Hardwicke, 12 July 1804, Hardwicke MSS., B.L. Add. MS. 35715, fol. 112; Bedford to Grenville, 3 July 1806, *H.M.C. Dropmore MSS.*, viii. 215.

[5] Revd. Francis Ennis to Foster, 25 June 1821, F.P. D.562/13666A.

Foster's first important preferment was the chaplaincy to the Irish House of Commons, which was obtained for him in 1780 by the joint solicitation of his brother and the Duke of Leinster, and was followed in 1781 by a very valuable living worth £1,000 a year.[1] The chaplaincy to the House was regarded as a sure stepping-stone to a bishopric, and this was the destination which John Foster had in mind for him. In 1787, by dealing 'very much *en juif*' with the Lord Lieutenant, John Foster obtained a promise of the next vacant bishopric, and in 1789 William Foster duly succeeded to the Bishopric of Cork.[2] This too was regarded by John Foster as a stepping-stone to better things: to the Bishopric of Clogher in particular. Clogher had the great attraction that it was one of the bishoprics with a parliamentary borough attached; and in 1783 the then Bishop of Clogher had been one of the recalcitrants who had refused to return government nominees for both seats.[3] No doubt this was the precedent which Foster had in mind when he first applied at the beginning of 1790 for his brother to be translated to Clogher: no doubt it was the precedent which the Government had in mind when they refused him, and translated William Foster to harmless Kilmore instead.[4] In 1794 the application was renewed, and again refused.[5] Not in fact until the end of 1795 did John Foster get his way; and then only after his brother had made 'a most unequivocal declaration' about Clogher borough.[6] William Foster did not hold Clogher for long, because he died in November 1797; but he was in possession of it at the time of the general election of that year. The M.P.s returned in 1797 on the Bishop's interest in Clogher were Thomas Burgh, the Secretary to the Treasury, and the celebrated Jonah Barrington. Both were government supporters, but both were also closely attached to John Foster, Burgh being his brother-in-law and

[1] Leinster to Pery, 21 Dec. 1780, *H.M.C. Emly MSS.*, part ii, 161; Carlisle to Lord Gower, 30 June 1781, *H.M.C. Carlisle MSS.*, 510.

[2] Buckingham to Grenville, 16 Nov. 1787, *H.M.C. Dropmore MSS.*, i. 290.

[3] Northington to North, 4 July 1783, and Bishop of Clogher to Windham, 4 July 1783, H.O. MSS., P.R.O. H.O. 100/9, fols. 207–9, 221–2.

[4] Westmorland to Grenville, 20 Mar. and 12 Apr. 1790, *H.M.C. Dropmore MSS.*, i. 568, 571.

[5] Westmorland to Pitt, 1794, Chatham MSS., P.R.O. 30/8/331, fols. 310–12.

[6] Camden to Pelham, [Dec. 1795/Jan. 1796], Pelham MSS., B.L. Add. MS. 33101, fol. 371.

Barrington one of his protégés. It was probably a serious
mistake on the Government's part to return two of Foster's
political connections for Clogher, because when he went into
opposition in 1799, Barrington followed him, even though
Burgh in the end did not. The Government, anxious to muzzle
Barrington and to replace Burgh with a more reliable supporter, called on both to resign their seats at the beginning of
1800; and both complied, although Barrington was urged by
Foster to refuse.[1] In the event, their resignation only did the
government cause harm. At the ensuing by-election two anti-
Unionists, John King and Charles Ball (John Ball's brother)
opposed the government nominees put up for Clogher by
William Foster's successor, and were victorious after a disputed election. There had been a party among the local
inhabitants opposed to the Bishop's interest at the election of
1783, and it may be that they showed their teeth again in 1800.[2]
But it is not fanciful to suspect that Foster was behind the successful opposition of 1800, and that this opposition was the
culmination of a well-thought-out plan for carving an interest
of his own out of the government interest in Clogher borough.
John Stewart, one of Lord Abercorn's followers, may have
had this in mind, and certainly had the patronage of the see of
Clogher in mind, when he wrote to Abercorn in November
1797: '. . . Your interest will stand nearly the first in Ireland
in this Parliament. I consider that of the Speaker . . . grossly
injured by the death of Foster of Clogher . . .'[3]

The Louth Militia and clerkship of the peace serve as
clear-cut examples of Foster's local patronage, the speakership
of his departmental, and his brother's career in the Church
of his residual. There remains, however, one very important
vehicle of patronage which does not properly belong to any of
these three classes: his patronage as a member of the linen
board. It was a species of local patronage in the sense that the

[1] Barrington, *Personal Sketches of His Own Times* (3 vols., London, 1827), ii. 267.
Barrington had not in fact been returned for Clogher until a by-election at the
beginning of 1798, but his return had almost certainly been arranged before
William Foster's death.

[2] *Common's Journals* (Ireland), xix. 123 ff.; Crawford and Trainor, *Aspects of
Irish Social History*, No. 59.

[3] Stewart to Abercorn, 15 Nov. 1797, Abercorn MSS., P.R.O.N.I. T. 2541/
IB2/2/32. Abercorn had wanted to obtain Clogher for a protégé in 1795, and was
disappointed again in 1797.

seventy-two members of the board were appointed by the lord lieutenant on a provincial basis, eighteen for each province, and usually included the leading landowners in each; it was departmental in the sense that Foster's successive offices, particularly the chancellorship of the exchequer, entitled him to speak with greater authority as a member of the board than he otherwise would have done, and also gave him opportunities to extend the board's patronage; it was residual in the sense that his influence with the government was necessary to get his connections appointed members and so keep up his voting strength on the board.[1] The three elements combined to give Foster an even more commanding position on the board than his father had enjoyed. Although no such office existed, he was sometimes called the 'Chief Trustee of the Linen Manufacture'; and one candidate for an office under the board, writing to Thomas Foster in 1810, reported that he had '. . . promises from several Noblemen and Gentlemen . . . , but without the aid of Mr. Foster and his interest I have little to hope for. . . .'[2] John Foster's strongest card was that he could count on the unswerving loyalty of the secretary to the board, James Corry. Corry and his father before him had been appointed secretary through Foster's influence, and both had served under him as clerks in the Irish House of Commons and in other key situations.[3] The Corrys' loyalty was personal to Foster, as their patron, rather than a general loyalty to the government or the body in whose service he had enlisted them.[4] This was of great importance, because the secretaryship to the linen board was in practice a very powerful office, due to the in-attention and bad attendance of almost all the members. In 1823, for example, Corry Junior reported caustically to Foster (now Lord Oriel) that there had been an unusually high attendance of nine members on one particular day because there was an office to be given away.[5] In 1802 a member

---

[1] Marsden to Hardwicke, [1803?], Hardwicke MSS., B.L. Add. MS. 35724, fol. 67; Wellesley to Richmond, 29 Mar. 1808, Apsley House MSS.; Rochfort to Foster, 7 Mar. 1809, F.P. D.207/34/66.

[2] Memorial of various Drogheda weavers to Foster, [c. 1800], F.P. D.562/5618; Charles Duffin to Thomas Foster, 28 July 1810, F.P. D.562/6209.

[3] Case of James Corry Senior, 15 July 1782, F.P. D.562/7538; account of money distributed to clerks, 1794, F.P. D.562/7531.

[4] See, for example, James Corry Junior to John Foster, 11 Feb. 1809, F.P. D.562/6352.   [5] Corry to Oriel, 5 Feb. 1823, F.P. D.562/6723.

hostile to Foster complained to the Castle that '. . . the Trustees don't attend properly and there is no uniformity in the proceedings. It might be thrown out that a regular Board should be constituted to manage so extensive an Establishment. The very mention of such a thing would give an electric shock to Mr. Foster, for he is at present sole manager of every part of the Establishment; and I can positively assure you, if some bounds are not put to his ambitious views, he will be soon too powerful for Administration. . . .'[1] This is an exaggerated picture of the state of affairs. It is, however, interesting to note that it was painted at a time when Foster was not only out of office, but in open opposition: one important aspect of his situation at the linen board was that it was held for life, was not at the mercy of the government, and was not greatly affected by his fall from power and favour.

The Chief Secretary, writing to the Lord Lieutenant in 1808, observed: 'It is inconceivable how much these Offices [trusteeships] at the Linen Board are sought after.'[2] Many of the Trustees, like Foster himself and his friends, Lords Sligo and Norbury (as John Toler had become), served on the board because they were genuinely interested in promoting the well-being of the linen industry; for them the patronage was only a contributory factor. But in the case of some Trustees it was the only one. The incorrigible Hely-Hutchinson, writing to his son in 1794, urged him to get himself made a Trustee '. . . for which your connection with Cork is a just pretension, and which may be successfully used for a more useful purpose—the establishment of a small village of manufacturers on the Knocklofty estate [co. Tipperary]. This would be the means of getting you a Seat in Parliament upon moderate terms . . .'[3] Collon, needless to say, was a 'small village of manufacturers'. A bleach-green was established there by the 1780s, and in 1790 there is mention of a 'factory'. At some point Anthony or John Foster imported a small colony of foreign Protestant weavers to Collon, and built an octagonal meeting-house for their religious observances, which still stands in the main

[1] Lord Frankfort to Marsden, 20 Mar. 1802, Hardwicke MSS., B.L. Add. MS. 35771, fol. 210.

[2] Wellesley to Richmond, 29 Mar. 1808, Apsley House MSS.

[3] Hely-Hutchinson to Donoughmore, 2 July 1794, *H.M.C. Donoughmore MSS.*, p. 332.

street today. A bleach-green and spinning works were still in operation at Collon at the time of John Foster's death, and other more experimental spinning-mills had been tried in the intervening period.[1] No doubt these various schemes were financed by the linen board. Their usefulness in political terms was that they provided the tenants of an estate with enough supplementary earnings to enable them to subsist comfortably on a 40/– freehold. Indeed, such tenants would not have time or inclination for a larger holding.[2] In this way the establishing of 'a small village of manufacturers' helped a local magnate to exploit the political potential of his estate without damaging it economically.

In other respects, too, membership of the linen board strengthened Foster's political interest at local level. Every year (at least during the early nineteenth century) the board used £3,000 out of its grant of £21,000 to purchase spinning-wheels, costing ten shillings each, which were then lent out by individual Trustees to applicants in their neighbourhood whom they considered deserving.[3] This was a valuable species of minor, recurrent patronage for the Trustees (one of them had remarked cynically in 1748, 'we begin to scramble for wheels and reels tomorrow');[4] it was not of course a species of patronage of which Foster had the local monopoly, as other leading interests in Louth and Drogheda were well represented on the board. However, when it came to a matter of real importance to his influence at local level, his commanding position among the Trustees could be employed to good effect. It was, for example, a matter of real importance to him that a candidate of his nomination should be appointed to the Seal-Mastership of Drogheda when it fell vacant in

[1] Hardman to Foster, 5 Nov. 1783, F.P. D.562/8829; Shekleton's bill for the entertainments at Collon on the occasion of John Foster Junior's coming-of-age, July/Aug. 1790, F.P. D.562/9204; oral information given me by Fr. Colmcille of Mellifont Abbey; petition of the Collon weavers to Foster, 1809, F.P. D.562/12634; William Pollock to Peter Besnard, 19 Aug. 1819, F.P. D.562/7485; brief in Lord Massereene *v.* Lord Ferrard, 1838, F.P. D. 1739/3/15.

[2] See Foster's speech on the Catholic Relief Bill of 1793, *Parl. Reg.* (Irish), xiii. 342.

[3] Corry to Foster, 13 Dec. 1810, F.P. T.2519/4/1199; *Proceedings of the Trustees of the Linen and Hempen Manufactures of Ireland from the 5 January to the 5 July 1809* (Dublin, 1809?), App., xxxiv.

[4] Charles Coote to Abercorn, 31 Mar. 1748, Abercorn MSS., P.R.O.N.I. T.2541/IA1/1D. I am indebted for this reference to Mr. W. H. Crawford.

1809. Ralph Smyth got up a petition to the board among most of the linen merchants of the town in favour of a rival candidate; but Foster's supporters among the Trustees, 'assembled by a previous canvass', were easily able to out-vote the opposition.[1] In 1809 Thomas Foster had 'the patronage of Drogheda'; yet this availed him nothing when it came to linen board appointments, since they were something with which the government did not interfere. In the same year General Needham, who had been given the patronage of Newry, had to come cap in hand to John Foster requesting his support at the linen board for Needham's candidate for the flaxseed inspectorship of that port.[2] In other words, no one could feel that his local patronage was complete unless he belonged to or had influence on the linen board. In the case of a constituency like Drogheda, where linen was easily the major industry and which had the most extensive linen market in Ireland, it was desirable that this influence should extend beyond the mere appointment of the linen board officials in the town. Whenever, as was frequent, disputes broke out about the quality or measurement of linen in the Drogheda market, Foster was inundated with memorials and begging letters from the Drogheda weavers, calling upon him to fight their case before the linen board.[3] His effectiveness in doing so played no small part in making Collon the short-lived 'tyrant of Drogheda'.

It does seem that, in general, he exploited his opportunities to command patronage lying outside the sphere of local nomination with little scrupulousness where Drogheda was concerned. His nominee for the seal-mastership in 1809 appears not to have been favoured by the Drogheda linen merchants (though that in itself could be a recommendation), and his first nominee as collector of the port, his cousin John William Foster (the Volunteering cousin of the 1780s) definitely proved to be an improper person, by reason of either incapability or plain dishonesty.[4] However, it may be that Drogheda was an exception, and that he fell short of his usual standards in Drogheda's case, as even the reforming Newport did in

[1] Corry to Foster, 6 and 8 Mar. 1809, F.P. D.562/6436, 6440.
[2] Needham to Foster, 26 May 1809, F.P. D.562/7416.
[3] Memorials to Foster concerning the Drogheda linen market, 30 May 1799, late 1811 and [c. 1820], F.P. D.562/5619, 5623, 7390.
[4] Rochfort to Foster, Oct. 1807, F.P. D.207/34/19.

Waterford, because his influence there was so tenuous that he could not afford to be squeamish. This conjecture is hard to substantiate (or refute) because so much of the contemporary evidence about his use or abuse of his non-local patronage comes from English politicians in the Castle, who suspected jobbery in every Irish recommendation made to them.

The Castle's suspicions of Foster are best illustrated by the cool reception it gave his proposal, first made in 1803, that the Farming Society of Ireland should be given a charter of incorporation and be maintained out of public funds, like the Dublin Society, instead of by private subscription, as heretofore. The Farming Society of England, of which Foster was a member and Lord Sheffield one of the founders, had been transformed into a government-financed Board of Agriculture; and this had inspired his plan for the Farming Society of Ireland, of which he was the first President. The society accordingly petitioned the Lord Lieutenant to that effect.[1] Hardwicke, however, regarded the spread of local farming societies like that founded by Foster at Collon (which were affiliated to the central body) with increasing alarm, and feared that they might assume a political character.[2] Redesdale, ever hostile to anything which originated with Foster, was emphatic that it was '. . . the plan of Mr. Foster . . . indirectly to put himself in the management of everything in this Country. The Linen Board he will now [since his return to office in 1804] rule despotically, and if he should get his Farming Society incorporated, he will make that a new engine of power. . . .'[3] Because of these fears, a charter for the Farming Society was long delayed; and when it was at last granted in 1815, Foster complained that its terms excluded him, as President, '. . . from any voice or interference in the concerns of the Society. . . .'[4] No doubt it would not have been granted on any other terms. The Farming Society episode shows how the Castle was apt to put a sinister and political construction on even an innocent-sounding project which bore Foster's name.

[1] Thomas Burgh to Foster, July 1807, F.P. D.562/12112.
[2] R. S. Tighe to Foster, 7 Aug. 1801, F.P. D.1739/3/7; Wickham to Addington 3 Jan. 1803, Wickham MSS., P.R.O.N.I. T.2627/5/D/38.
[3] Redesdale to Hardwicke, 4 July 1804, Hardwicke MSS., B.L. Add. MS. 35718, fol. 14.
[4] Foster to Revd. Thomas Radcliffe, 13 Oct. 1819, F.P. D.562/7946.

Its suspicions were probably exaggerated. Certainly, Foster himself professed to be ignorant of the 'latent cause' which lay behind the continued resistance to the charter.[1] As the case of the Louth Militia demonstrates, not everything which he touched was turned by him to political advantage. Moreover, his non-local patronage, whether departmental, residual, or derived from the linen board, the Farming Society, or the Dublin Society (another institution in which he was extremely prominent), tended to consist of important, well-remunerated, and reasonably prestigious posts: the sort of posts which were far above the pretensions of the ordinary Louth or Drogheda voter, and were suitable for gentlemen only. Foster used some of this non-local patronage in favour of politically influential gentry families in co. Louth—the McClintocks (who were relations anyway), the Sibthorpes (also relations), the Coddingtons (more relations, and the co-patrons of Dunleer), the Pages (wine merchants in Dundalk and landowners in Louth[2]), the Filgates, and so on. The various cadet Fosters whom he advanced, for example the undeserving John William, were most of them Louth gentry, but because their land was largely non-freehold[3] he can be accused of nepotism, but hardly of political motivation, in advancing them. Almost certainly, he used much more of his non-local patronage on Drogheda than on Louth; in Drogheda it was vital to his interest in two respects: it gave him some influence over the commercial and industrial life of the town, and it enabled him to win the adherence of a number of leading interests in the corporation or the constituency who, if he had not been able at least to hold out the promise of such patronage to them, would have had no reason to make themselves subservient to his designs. These leading interests included, obviously, Edward Hardman and his family; George Pentland (Foster's attorney, his second-most-important aldermanic ally in Drogheda, and the father of the defeated candidate at the 1822 by-election); John Ball and at least one of Ball's principal supporters in the corporation; George Ball of Ball's Grove (a bombastic individual who controlled several freeholder votes and wanted a baronetcy);

---

[1] Foster to Revd. Robert Wynne, 9 Sept. 1809, F.P. D.207/29/88.
[2] John Page to Foster, 15 Jan. 1804 and 15 July 1810, F.P. D.562/4818, 11439. [3] See p. 286.

and so on.[1] This list of Drogheda gentlemen, drawn to him because of his command of non-local patronage, is not exhaustive. But an exhaustive list would not be very much longer, simply because there was a limit to the volume of patronage of this quality which any one individual, no matter how prominent in national politics, could obtain or colourably promise. In any case, Foster put most of his share of such patronage to other uses besides strengthening his local interest, even in the vulnerable quarter of Drogheda.

One use he put it to was appeasing his creditors.[2] Some of these, especially the Pages, Hardmans, and Pentlands, were politically as well as financially necessary to him: others were not. This latter category includes a dubious family called Byrne, who were money-lenders in Dundalk, whom Foster at one point owed £7,000 and whose sons he seems to have provided for in some way; the Revd. Francis Saunderson, a collateral of a well-known co. Cavan family, whose sons he advanced in the army and navy; Thomas Kemmis, his Dublin attorney, to whom he gave a valuable place in the Court of Exchequer in 1804; and George Grierson, for whom he helped to obtain a renewal of Grierson's patent as King's Printer for Ireland.[3] This too is not an exhaustive list, but is not far off it. Much the most voracious consumers of his non-local patronage, however, were not his creditors, but his relations. Apart from his nephew, John Maxwell Barry, most of the relations on the Foster side whom he advanced have already been mentioned. Most of them had some political influence in Louth or Drogheda, but with most of them this was only a contributory inducement to Foster to advance them. In the case of the much more numerous category of his wife's relations, it was not even a contributory inducement, since they all came from the Kildare/Carlow area, and could not muster

[1] Wellesley to Foster, 28 Oct. 1807, F.P. D.207/35/24; Hardman to Foster, 18 Feb. 1811, F.P. D.562/12684; Pentland to Foster, 19 Sept. 1810, F.P. D.562/11465; Foster to John Ball, 4 Aug. 1808, F.P. D.562/12799; Wellesley to Foster, 11 Jan. 1809, F.P. D.207/35/86; George Ball to Foster, 22 Dec. 1809, F.P. D.562/12627.

[2] See also pp. 325 f.

[3] Mrs. M. Byrne to Foster, 21 Oct. 1798, F.P. D.562/4904; Revd. Francis Saunderson to Foster, 21 Oct. 1805 and 7 June 1807, F.P. D.562/5103–4; William Kemmis to Oriel, 12 Nov. 1823, F.P. D.562/5068; Grierson to Foster, 3 May 1811 and [1813?], F.P. D.207/6/73, 75.

a vote in Louth or Drogheda, and very few votes anywhere else. Like Mrs. Foster herself, the Burghs were blue-blooded and poor, and unlike her they married more or less according to their parlous economic position. Foster provided for them generously, and where the names Burgh—obviously, and less obviously—Rochfort, Macartney, Wolfe, Keatinge, McCarthy, and Griffith (including Richard Griffith, the celebrated Commissioner of Valuation), occur in the *Almanacks* of the day, there it can be assumed that his influence has been at work, using his non-local patronage for the benefit of his wife's poor relations.[1]

Their poverty was not of course his only criterion; he also advanced, by and large, only those of them who were likely to make efficient officers. His Burgh, much more than his Foster, relations provided the administrative backbone for the various schemes, boards, and institutions with which he was prominently associated, and took their places there beside people whom he had advanced on merit alone, without the added inducement of kinship, notably James Corry Senior and Junior, John Croker (father of John Wilson Croker),[2] and a great many others. Indeed the biggest single use to which, probably, he put his non-local patronage was the building up of a strong personal following within the Irish bureaucracy and in the less political offices in the executive (notably the enquiry board), and his object in building up such a following was to ensure that his measures were not sabotaged in their detailed implementation. By modern standards, this was not a laudable object. However, it was not so very reprehensible at a time when the distinction between civil servants and politicians, between safe berths and 'the hurricane sphere', was fine, and when most bureaucrats had political patrons. Foster was not the only politician who was guilty in this respect, nor was it a particularly Irish failing. For example, after the fall of the Talents in 1807, their departed Chief Secretary, William Elliot, who had formerly served as an Under-Secretary in the Castle and should have known better,

---

[1] See, for example, Foster to J. L. Foster, 10 May 1810, F.P. D.562/2197; Foster to Mrs. Richard Griffith, 19 Sept. 1810, F.P. T.2519/4/1099; Lady Macartney to Lady Dufferin, 1 May [1824], F.P. D.207/73/232.

[2] For Foster's relations with the Croker family, see F.P. D.207/71.

did not scruple to exploit his personal relationship with one
of the then Under-Secretaries, James Traill, to get information
out of the Castle for use in Parliament against Foster as Chancellor of the Exchequer in the new Government (Traill had
been appointed by the Talents and was continued by their
successors).[1] Foster can hardly be blamed for using methods
which his political opponents did not scruple to use against
him. Nevertheless, it was the building up of a personal following in the bureaucracy which gave rise to most of the contemporary complaints of his rapacity, made by political
opponents and political allies alike, and caused his official
colleague, Pole, the Chief Secretary, to accuse him in 1811 of
grasping 'at everything'.[2] It was the use or abuse of his non-
local patronage for this purpose, and not for the purpose of
building up his interest in Louth and Drogheda, which made
him a constant object of suspicion to the Castle.

All this suggests that, in the local context of Louth, though
not of Drogheda, the patronage aspect of his prominence in
national politics was very much less important than might at
first be assumed. Undoubtedly, it enabled him to gratify
some influential Louth constituents in a way that most M.P.s
could not emulate; but basically the patronage which nourished
his interest in Louth was of the local kind which any leading
county interest not in systematic opposition to the government
enjoyed. Prominence in national politics was certainly a help
in reinforcing his local claims and in preserving him from
notorious local predators like the Earl of Clermont and the
Rodens. Moreover, it enabled him to nominate to local offices
which, except in the case of politically important people
or people with a specified claim on the government, were too
valuable to be included in the sphere of local nomination.
His position on the linen board was also important; the flow
of linen board patronage was directed by the board, not by
the government, and influence on the board was necessary to
obtain the more valuable patronage at least. In these various
ways command of patronage outside the sphere of local
nomination, rounded off what Foster already enjoyed, the

---

[1] See, for example, Elliot to Traill, 18 June 1807, Elliot of Wells MSS., N.L.S.
E.W.26.

[2] Pole to Richmond, 27 Mar. 1811, Richmond MSS., N.L.I. MS. 60, fol. 760.

patronage of Louth. But the difference it made was not enormous. In the case of offices outside the Louth area it made very little difference at all. Such offices were usually too valuable for local use and too important to be disposed of to duffers primarily on electioneering grounds. In any case, Foster generally had plans and priorities for them which were more important to him than the strengthening of his local interest, certainly than the strengthening of his interest in Louth.

CHAPTER SEVEN

Real Estate, Personalty, and Personality

FOSTER'S interest in Louth, unlike his interest in Drogheda, was not dependent on his special opportunities in the sphere of patronage, because it rested firmly on the secure basis of landed property. This was the basis on which the county representation of Ireland, as of England (not Scotland), rested in the days of the unreformed Parliament. In 1779, Conolly reminded the Irish House of Commons that they represented 'property, not numbers'; and earlier, at the time of the 1761 general election, the co. Wicklow magnate, Lord Carysfort, had remarked quaintly, '. . . I beg to be understood that no part of my property shall give their consent to Mr. Whaley's election. I beg that he may not have the disposal of any part of my interest or property. . . .'[1] The use of the favourite eighteenth-century term, 'interest', as something distinct from 'property', is significant. 'Interest' strikes twentieth-century ears as meaning something more real and territorial than the neutral modern equivalent, 'influence'; thus, the promise of a man's interest to a candidate is usually interpreted as meaning the promise of a bloc of very countable heads. In fact, interest and influence are synonymous. For example, that politically most advanced of Irish landlords, Lord Anglesey, was still talking about his interest as late as 1830. By this he meant, not just the votes of his tenants but, in the words of his agent, the votes of '. . . all those freeholders over whom your Lordship possessed influence . . ., as well as . . . those who from other motives were disposed to oblige your Lordship'; and a candidate who applied to Lord Anglesey for his interest did so because of 'the great popularity enjoyed by your Lordship, as well

[1] Quoted in O'Connell, *Politics and Social Conflict*, p. 186; Carysfort to Ralph Howard, 12 Apr. 1761, Wicklow MSS., N.L.I., unsorted section; photocopies in P.R.O.N.I., ref. Mic.146.

as the considerable property you possess in Louth . . .'¹ In 1807, the 2nd Lord Rossmore expressed the point very clearly when he described himself as possessing 'near 500 voices [i.e. votes on his estate] and a large personal interest' in co. Monaghan.² The word interest is thus in no degree more pejorative than influence, and though it is often used to denote that combination of property and personal influence which made for electoral success (for example, 'the Foster interest'), it is never used to denote property *per se*. Property *per se* did not determine who was elected for a county: it only determined who was eligible for election. In practice, nobody was elected who could not field from his own property or from the property of his chief backer, something between one-tenth and one-quarter of the registered electorate or, in the case of a contest, of the votes polled.³ The difference between this fraction and the fraction of more than one-half which was necessary to secure the candidate's return, was made up by interest.

Strictly speaking, the county representation of Ireland and England in the days of the unreformed Parliament rested, not on landed property as a whole, but specifically on freehold property, which alone conferred the right to vote. Freehold was the highest form of property and was to be distinguished from lower forms by the fact that it was owned or held for an indeterminate period. In other words, it was property either owned in fee simple or leased for a term of life. The anomalous feature of this distinction was that a lease for one life was a freehold, while a lease for 999 years was not. Foster, in his speech on the Catholic Relief Bill of 1793, made great play with this and other anomalies, using them to demonstrate that there was no such thing as an inherent right to the franchise. He pointed out that '. . . copyholders . . . constitute a great body

¹ Col. W. Armstrong to Anglesey, 6 May 1830, and Sir Patrick Bellew to Anglesey, 6 June 1829, Anglesey MSS., P.R.O.N.I. D.619/32L/5, 1.

² Rossmore to Wellesley, [Nov.] 1807, Apsley House MSS.

³ The classic, and probably unique, case of a landless man being elected for a county without the backing of any large landed interest, is James Willson's election for co. Antrim at the general election of 1776. However, the political discipline of landlords in co. Antrim was very weak at this time and the circumstances of the election were highly unusual. Willson proved to be such a venal member that he was not re-elected. Interestingly, though he himself was a landless half-pay sea-captain, his brother was a minor landlord at Purdysburn, near Belfast. I am indebted for this last point to Dr. D. H. Smyth.

of the landholders of England, and the tenure is in fact perpetual; but by very little better than a fiction they are excluded, upon the idea that nominally they hold at will. Lessees for years are a numerous class, and there seems a great stretch of speculative reason to say that a man possessed of land for 999 years is not as independent a voter as he whose interest depends on a decayed life. Almost all the Bishops' land and much Corporation land can produce no voters on the same principle, being all demised for years. . . .'[1] The point about non-freehold property producing no voters is important; a man with a lease for years was not only himself excluded from the franchise, he was also precluded from granting leases for lives, which would confer the franchise on his tenants. Even though a lease for, say, 999 years would obviously run for longer than one life, it was not possible for a man with a 999-year lease to sub-let even in one-life leases, since that would have been creating a freehold interest out of a chattel one.

The chief casualties of the system, in terms of the political influence of which it deprived them, were, as Foster mentioned, the bishops of the Church of Ireland. They were empowered to let land for a maximum of only 21 years, and were not empowered to grant leases for a life or for lives. In 1713, the transgressions of the Bishop of Derry in this respect created a great stir. '. . . I hear the Bishop of Derry is mad,' one lay landlord of the county wrote, 'or else he would not have done what he has . . ., which I am afraid will make a great hurly-burly in the County of Derry; for certainly never was a freehold made by a Bishop, which I am sorry for. . . .'[2] The effect of this restriction was most important. The Church was the biggest landlord in Ireland, owning an estimated quarter of the country, and in most counties (though not in Louth), the Church was the biggest landlord: Armagh's see lands numbered 100,000 acres (not all in the one county, of course), Derry's 70,000, Clogher's 80,000, and even humble and uncoveted Elphin's 24,000.[3] As things were, the bishops were fairly influential in

---

[1] *Parl. Reg.* (Irish), xiii. 336 f. The land of the Drogheda corporation is a case in point.

[2] Viscount Massereene to Clotworthy Skeffington, 31 Oct. 1713, F.P. D.562/195.

[3] John Stewart to Abercorn, 21 Apr. 1795, Abercorn MSS., P.R.O.N.I. T.2541/IB2/1/16; memo. [by Edward Cooke] on the see lands of Ireland, [1799?], Castlereagh MSS., P.R.O.N.I. D.3030/592; Maxwell, *Country and Town*, p. 327. At

county elections, among other reasons because the clergy, though not the lay tenants of the bishops, were freeholders in right of their benefices. In 1790, for example, at the time of William Foster's translation to that see, the Bishop of Kilmore was described as deciding the co. Cavan election in favour of a government supporter,[1] and earlier in the eighteenth century the bishops' influence was, relatively speaking, far greater. It is not going too far to say that, if the bishops could have granted freehold leases, the balance of power in most counties would have been tilted in the direction of government supporters (the bishops' subservience to the government was notorious). Yet, whenever it was proposed, on purely economic grounds, that the bishops should be empowered to grant longer leases, including leases for lives, the government always resisted the proposal; in 1737, for example, it threw all its influence against a private member's bill to that effect.[2] The government would no doubt have welcomed an increase of influence in the open constituencies. But the 21-year restriction was considered inviolable, as it prevented bishops from impairing the future income of their sees by levying and pocketing large fines on long leases. Even under the 21-year restriction, the bishops commonly levied and pocketed more fines than was their due, by renewing leases before the 21-year term had expired; and they were particularly likely to do this if they thought they were not going to hold the see for long. Indeed, thoroughly unscrupulous manipulators like the Earl-Bishop of Derry and Archbishop Agar[3] actually contrived to alienate see lands outright.

The distinction between lives and years is clear-cut. However, it was a common practice to grant leases for terms of life with the alternative of terms of years, and this practice leads to a good deal of conflicting contemporary evidence as to what

the conclusion of his memo., Cooke proposed that the bishops should be allowed to lease their lands for 31 years or three lives.

[1] Westmorland to Grenville, 12 Apr. 1790, *H.M.C. Dropmore MSS.*, i. 571.

[2] Duke of Devonshire to Duke of Newcastle, 'Received 18 Nov. 1737' and 22 Nov. 1737, Newcastle MSS., B.L. Add. MS. 32690, fols. 433, 441.

[3] For Agar's expropriation, see two lists of lands in co. Tipperary, 1802 and [c. 1805], with endorsements on the back in Agar's handwriting that these had been see lands and were now 'my own', Normanton MSS., Hampshire R.O. 21 M, 57, box 18/243. Agar was created Earl of Normanton after the Union.

constituted a freehold. In 1792, for example, Lord Abercorn was told about twelve houses in Strabane, 'all granted in freeholds but one, and that is for a lease of lives or years'.[1] His correspondent either did not understand the law, or else was using a shorthand unintelligible to all but Abercorn. The fact that a lease for lives offered an alternative of years did not necessarily invalidate it as a freehold. Jacob's *New Law Dictionary* instanced one such lease which was not freehold: '. . . A lease for 99 years etc., determinable upon a life or lives, is not a lease for life to make a freehold, but a lease for years, or chattel, determinable upon life or lives.'[2] Presumably, on an extension of the same argument, a lease for a life or lives, determinable on a term of years, would also not constitute a freehold. However, if it was desired to specify a fixed term of years (and this would be necessary in a building lease, or on an estate where leases for years were the custom), and at the same time to create a freehold, the lease could be worded so as to satisfy both requirements. In 1802, for example, the 2nd Marquess of Donegall's attorney wrote, apropos of Donegall's urban Belfast estate: '. . . It is the wish of the family to create as many freeholds as they can, and therefore I shall make all the future building leases for three lives or 99 years concurrent. . . .'[3] In other words, the leases would be for three lives or 99 years, *whichever was the longer*. This would mean that the chattel element in the lease could not impinge on the freehold; and if the term of years out-lasted the term of lives, the lease would cease to be freehold for the remainder of the term of years, unless new lives were inserted.[4]

The Fosters commonly let land on leases with the alternative of years and lives, but they themselves leased no land on these terms. Most of their estate—between 5,000 and 5,500 acres out of a total in the early nineteenth century of nearly 7,000—

[1] Thomas Knox to Abercorn, 28 Jan. 1792, Abercorn MSS., P.R.O.N.I. T.2541/IB1/3/8.

[2] Giles Jacob, *A New Law Dictionary, Corrected by Owen Ruffhead and J. Morgan*, 10th edn. (Dublin, 1773), entry under 'freehold'.

[3] William Lyon to Chichester Skeffington, 11 Mar. 1802, F.P. D.562/2852.

[4] One election petition stated an objection to leases which 'gave the tenants the chance of 31 years, if the lives should fall within that term'—*Case of William Brownlow, to be heard on 6 December 1753*, F.P. T.2519/4/227. Presumably, these peculiar leases gave the tenant an *additional* 31 years, if the three lives should all drop within the original 31-year period.

was in fact owned in fee simple. With minor exceptions, it was all freehold. This applied even to their estate of over 1,000 acres in co. Meath, where they were never politically active. The principal weak point in their Louth estate was that more than 1,000 acres of it—the townland of Carrickbaggot—was leased for three lives only, without a covenant for perpetual renewal. But this was a weak point mainly in economic terms: in political terms, while the lives ran, the land was just as much freehold as the fee simple land which comprised virtually all the rest of their Louth estate.[1] The heavy preponderance of the freehold element in the whole estate was almost certainly the result of deliberate policy. For example, their 800 acres in Corrstown and Newtown Monasterboyce, near Dunleer, had originally been leased by them for 999 years, but they had subsequently, and no doubt for political reasons, got the lease converted into lives renewable.[2] Much of their non-freehold land which remained non-freehold, together with other politically useless assets like impropriate tithes, they had off-loaded on to cadet branches of the family, who had to be provided for somehow. In terms of income, these cadet branches were generously provided for. The net rental of their property in co. Louth was £8,500 at the very least in the early nineteenth century;[3] which was probably more than the contemporary net rental of John Foster's estate. Where however the cadet estates could not compare with Foster's was in their freehold element: in 1821 they could muster only 40 freeholders as compared to his 420. This cannot have been an accident.

[1] These conclusions about the Foster estate have been reached by collating the following:
  (*a*) Rental of the Foster estate, 1778–82, *C.L.A.J.* x. 222 ff.
  (*b*) Ditto, *c.* 1820, F.P. D.562/1468.
  (*c*) Statement of Lord Ferrard's title to his unsettled estates, 1836, Kirk MSS., P.R.O.N.I. D.2121/7/33.
  (*d*) Brief in Lord Massereene *v.* Lord Ferrard, [1838], F.P. D.1739/3/15.

[2] Lease of Corrstown from Stephen Ludlow to John Foster, 11 Dec. 1703, F.P. D.562/5119; rough abstract of Lord Massereene's title to lands in Louth and Meath, [*c.* 1880], F.P., Chilham deed room.

[3] This minimum figure is arrived at by adding up the rentals mentioned in the following letters:
  (*a*) J. L. Foster to Foster, 15 Oct. 1810, F.P. D.562/2235.
  (*b*) Henry Foster to John Page, 19 Dec. 1810, F.P. T.2519/4/1680.
  (*c*) J. L. Foster to Peel, 8 July 1826, Peel MSS., B.L. Add. MS. 40388, fols. 7–10.

It was also possibly no accident that his Louth acreage so heavily out-numbered his Meath. Concentration in one county was a valuable political asset, since proprietorship thinly spread over several would have meant that he was a major interest in none. Other politically minded landowners could boast at least an equal degree of concentration. William Brownlow of Lurgan, M.P. for co. Armagh, for example, left at his death in 1794 land worth £6,000 a year in co. Armagh, where his political ambitions had lain, and £1,300 a year in co. Monaghan, where he had had none. An even more striking example is the Duke of Leinster, virtually all of whose estate (popularly reckoned at 80,000 acres in the 1790s, though much of it must have been let in perpetuity) was concentrated in co. Kildare, where he claimed to return both members.[1] From Foster's point of view, the important thing was that the Foster estate was more heavily concentrated in Louth than those of the next-biggest interests there. The Earl of Clermont was the largest landowner in the county; but the co. Monaghan estate which he enjoyed in right of his wife (and which later passed to Lord Rossmore) was at least as valuable, if not as extensive, as his patrimonial Louth property. His younger brother, James Fortescue, was in a similar situation. Though more generously provided for than most younger sons, his property was of limited political advantage to him since it was almost equally divided between Louth and Meath. This was the result of the partition made in 1741 by his father, Thomas Fortescue, and John Foster the Elder, of their 4,500-acre estate straddling the Louth/Meath border; Fortescue had taken the Meath half, and the cannier—or perhaps just luckier—Foster had taken Collon. Had the arrangement been the other way round, the subsequent political roles of the two families in Louth would probably have been inverted. Another victim of thinly spread proprietorship was Balfour. In addition to property in Meath and Drogheda, he owned roughly 3,800 acres in Louth and another 3,800 acres in Fermanagh.[2] If all the land he owned had been concentrated in Louth,

[1] J. Turner to Lord Gosford, 5 Nov. 1795, Gosford MSS., P.R.O.N.I. D.1606/1/165; Bolton, *Union*, p. 183; *Public Characters of 1799–1800* (London, 1799), pp. 332 f.
[2] Rent book for Balfour's Louth estate, [*c.* 1770], Balfour MSS., N.L.I. MS. 9543; rental and valuation of Balfour's Fermanagh estate, 1815, Erne MSS., P.R.O.N.I. D.1939/2/17.

he would have been the second-largest landowner in the county. As it was, he was only the fourth-largest and did not cut much of a political figure there, and even less of a political figure in Fermanagh. Lord Clanbrassill is an even better example of the same phenomenon. He owned land in cos. Louth, Meath, Down, Galway, Tipperary, Kilkenny, and Wexford; but his Louth estate was his largest single unit, and Louth was the only county in which he was a major political interest. Inexplicably, the Louth estate was never placed under settlement, and so became encumbered with all his numerous debts. When he died in 1798, a private Act of Parliament was required to preserve it intact by empowering his executors to sell the scattered settled property. Indeed, it was not until 1816 that the Louth estate and the political interest which went with it were protected by settlement.[1] Clanbrassill, like Clermont and Balfour, owned more land than Foster. But Foster had the advantage over them all in terms of concentration.

The situation of his estate was advantageous, not only from the point of view of its concentration in the one county, but from its proximity to two other constituencies, Dunleer and Drogheda. Many county interests did not possess this advantage, particularly those in counties like Fermanagh, Sligo, Leitrim, Cavan, and Monaghan, which contained only one or two boroughs. The situation of part of the Foster estate within the boundaries of Dunleer borough had been an important factor in the successful Foster take-over bid for one of its seats. This was moreover an unqualified advantage, because the Foster tenants with a freehold qualification derived from land within the boundaries of Dunleer, were able to vote, by virtue of that qualification, in elections for Louth. This runs counter to modern ideas of constituency boundaries, but it is really less illogical than many facets of the unreformed electoral system. The freehold was not essentially a rural qualification; it could as easily relate to urban property. Moreover, in most of the Irish boroughs (and Dunleer was no exception), the borough franchise was not related to possession of property, or even to residence, within the borough; and in most, the freeholders of

[1] *Dublin Evening Post*, 24 Dec. 1789 and 10 June 1790; *Lady Roden's Diary*, p. 166; MS. opinion of Thomas Lefroy, [*c.* 1838], Roden MSS., P.R.O.N.I. Mic. 147, vol. 4.

the borough, if they voted in borough elections at all, voted by virtue of qualifications other than their freeholds. The exceptions were county boroughs like Drogheda, and manor boroughs like Mallow, where the freeholders voted in the borough, as freeholders, and therefore could not vote in the county by virtue of the same qualification.[1] Since Dunleer was neither a county nor a manor borough, its freeholders were not precluded from voting in co. Louth. The overlap between Dunleer and co. Louth would have led to considerable economies in the distribution of patronage, if the same tenants had been electorally necessary in both constituencies. This, however, was not the case: the Fosters controlled Dunleer, not through the votes of their tenants there, but through the votes of friends and relations not resident in the borough.[2] It was in fact the overlap between Louth and Drogheda which led to the economies in patronage.[3] This overlap had its one dangerous aspect—the greater political awareness and effectiveness of the Catholic voters of Drogheda.[4] But on the whole it redounded to the Fosters' advantage, the

[1] It has long been known that borough freeholders voted in county elections in England, because of the controversy over this matter during the Reform Bill debates in 1832 (Gash, *Politics in the Age of Peel*, pp. 91 ff.). The question has not yet been investigated in the case of Ireland, although on the face of it, it is unlikely that the unreformed electoral system in the two kingdoms should have differed on a fundamental point like this; also, one section of the Irish Reform Act (2 & 3 Will. IV, c. 88, s. 4) implies that in Ireland borough freeholders had hitherto voted in the county. A number of manuscript references show that this was the case, the most explicit being a letter from James Johnston to Lord Bective, 28 Oct. 1812, which refers to 'every freeholder in a county whose freehold lay in a city or town' (Headfort MSS., Headfort House, Kells, co. Meath, F/9/37). Under the English Reform Act, borough freeholders continued to vote in the county, as a counterpoise to the £50 tenants-at-will enfranchised by the famous Chandos clause: the Irish Reform Act had no Chandos clause, and in Ireland borough freeholders and other voters qualified to vote in both the borough and the county, ceased to vote in the county.

[2] List of the freemen of Dunleer, 1783, F.P. D.562/4629.

[3] See pp. 189 f.

[4] This kind of interaction between constituencies could occur where they did not overlap at all and indeed were hundreds of miles apart, for example in the Beresford strongholds of cos. Londonderry and Waterford. These two constituencies were as far apart politically as they were geographically. At the time of the Catholic Emancipation crisis, the different tactics which the Beresfords employed in the two exposed them to the charge of being 'Protestants in the North and Catholics in the South'; and at the 1830 general election they had cause to complain that the election address of their opponent in Londonderry had done him no good there, but them much harm in Waterford. See Primate Beresford to Duke of Wellington, 27 July 1830, Pack-Beresford MSS., P.R.O.N.I. D.664/A/212.

more so as they had the sense to bale out of Drogheda before, in all probability, it had seriously over-taxed their strength.

In building up and supervising their influence in Drogheda they were helped, not only by the fact that their estate and seat were situated only seven miles from the town, but also by the fact that both Collon and Drogheda were within thirty Irish miles of Dublin, where in the years before the Union Foster spent most of the time he was away from home. Drogheda, in fact, lay on his route from Dublin to Collon. In the years after the Union, London to a considerable extent replaced Dublin as his second home; but attendance at Westminster for an Irish member, even for an office-holder like Foster, only covered the months between the end of December and June or July.[1] In the years 1801, 1803, and 1807 he did not go over at all, and after his retirement from office in 1811, his attendances became infrequent.[2] His official and parliamentary duties, therefore, did not significantly interfere with personal supervision of his local interest, both in Louth and Drogheda; which was as well, as neither his son, Thomas Foster, nor his nephew, John Leslie Foster, was readily available for such supervision, and the agent permanently on the spot at Collon was not of suitable social standing for the task. For Foster, as a medium-sized landowner with heavy political commitments at both national and local level, it was a great advantage that his estate and local interest should have been situated only thirty miles from the capital.

Even more important than the situation of the Foster estate was the extent to which it had been improved. The main testimony on this point comes from Arthur Young, even though there is good reason for thinking that he exaggerated the increase in the rental which the improvements effected. Contributory testimony comes from Lord Sligo, whose own family had received almost as honourable a mention from Young as the Fosters. In 1807 Sligo reported to Foster how '. . . for twenty miles from your house we saw and felt the influence of your power and example; and I assure you, if I were to impose a duty on every man of fortune in Ireland,

---

[1] Occasionally the government tried to get him over before the Christmas recess; see, for example, Richmond to Foster, 10 Dec. 1810, F.P. D.562/11495.

[2] William Houghton to Foster, 29 Aug. 1818, F.P. T.2519/4/1581.

it would be to pass through Collon and see what improvement and beauty it was within the life of man to accomplish .. . .'[1] The more improved the estate, the more numerous the freeholders it could accommodate. However, in the absence of detailed information about the improvements, if any, carried out by the Fosters' rivals in Louth, it is hard to assess this element in the Foster interest. Young had words of praise for Ravensdale, the seat of James Fortescue, which he declared to be 'beautiful in itself, but trebly so on information that before he fixed there it was all a wide waste'. How far this panegyric would have been applicable to the estate of his largely absentee brother, the Earl of Clermont, is, however, a different matter. Even at Ravensdale, Young noted that rents were no more than 10s. an acre, and 2s. to 5s. on mountain land: figures which should be compared with Chief Baron Anthony Foster's statement, also recorded by Young, that 21s. was currently the average rent for land under corn in co. Louth, and that 10s. had been the average twenty-five years before, in 1750. As late as 1819, James Fortescue's son, the 2nd Lord Clermont, who had inherited the property of both his father and his uncle, was still drawing only 10s. an acre from it, and in 1828 the position seems to have been no better. Indeed, his income from his co. Louth estate in the 1820s was not much more than the Fosters', although he owned possibly double their acreage. This would suggest that, in spite of Young's testimony, the estate was either unimproved or unimprovable, although it must be remembered that part of it, the manor of Ballymascanlan, was let in perpetuity and was therefore beyond the Fortescues' economic (and political) control.[2] On the whole, it seems fair to conclude that they were less deserving of Young's praise than Lord Clanbrassill, who received none. In 1772, another traveller noted that the most improved 500 acres of Clanbrassill's estate would let for £4 4s. an acre, and in 1793 the whole was yielding a higher rental on a smaller acreage than the Fosters';[3] this however was due, not so much to Clanbrassill's improvements, as to the fact that his estate

---

[1] Sligo to Foster, 2 June 1807, F.P. D.207/70/20.
[2] Young, *Tour*, i. 151, 154 f.; Lord Dufferin to Thomas Skeffington, 10 June 1819, F.P. D.562/3426.
[3] Quoted in Maxwell, *Country and Town*, p. 196; *Lady Roden's Diary*, p. 166.

was predominantly urban. Of the improvements, if any, carried out by Balfour, nothing is known.

A comparison between the number of acres and the number of freeholders which the four leading interests in co. Louth could boast, gives some idea of the importance of the Fosters' improvements to the Foster interest. The 2nd Lord Clermont, with an estate of well over 11,000 acres, had at least 150 freeholders—probably many more—in the 1820s; Balfour, with 3,800 acres, had some 235 in 1821; Lord Roden, with just over 4,000, had some 320 in 1821; and Foster, with roughly 5,500, had some 420 (excluding the 40 freeholders supplied by the cadet Fosters) in the same year.[1] Comparison between Foster and Lord Clermont cannot fairly be made because of imperfect information about the number of the latter's freeholders. Comparison between Foster and Balfour shows that the former's lead in freeholders was much longer than his lead in acres. Comparison between Foster and Lord Roden shows that the lead in freeholders was only a little longer; but again this was because the Clanbrassill estate in Dundalk was predominantly urban, and therefore more densely populated than Foster's predominantly rural property. It is tempting to adduce, as a measure of the importance of the Fosters' improvements, the fact that the freeholders on their estate outnumbered the freeholders in a county town like Dundalk. But this would be misleading. No doubt there were more than 320 freeholders in Dundalk; the 320 represented only those who were within Roden's economic and political control. The rest were the sort of people who had opposed Lord Clanbrassill from 1782 onwards, and who opposed the landlord, anti-Emancipationist candidates at the Louth election of 1826. They presumably leased their Dundalk property either in perpetuity or on long leases—the kind of terms which alone would encourage tenants to sink capital into building and which the Clanbrassills had been anxious to grant since the 1730s.[2] A straight comparison cannot therefore be made between Foster and Roden, because of the great difference in the leasing policy

---

[1] J. L. Foster to Lord Oriel, 19 Nov. 1822, F.P. D.207/74/123; *Louth Freeholders 1821*, P.R.O.N.I. T.2519/14/1.

[2] (Unsuccessful) private bill to enable Lord Limerick to lease land in Dundalk for more than 31 years, 2–8 Mar. 1736, House of Lords R.O. Main Papers.

on their respective estates: on the Foster estate perpetuities were unknown, except on their urban property in Drogheda, and the longest lease was for three lives. However, it is fair to assume that only improvements as sweeping as the Fosters' would have enabled them easily to out-number the 320 free-holders whom Roden could call his own.

To put the Fosters, and indeed the other leading interests in co. Louth, into their proper perspective, it is necessary to turn to other counties; Louth, after all, was the smallest in Ireland. In co. Armagh, for example, the leading interest numerically in 1789 was the Cope family of Loughgall, with 450 freeholders[1]—a number which must have greatly exceeded the contemporary Foster total. Yet, though the Fosters were able to hog the representation of Louth, the Copes during the second half of the eighteenth century had to share the repre-sentation of Armagh with four other county families, and got noticeably the leanest share at that. Again, a certain Sir Samuel Hayes could field 300 freeholders in co. Donegal in the 1790s[2]— a number which presumably exceeded the contemporary Clanbrassill total in co. Louth. Yet Hayes, so far from being the second-biggest interest in his county, was the merest also-ran. These figures show that what was politically decisive was not the number of freeholders on a man's estate, but the relation-ship which this bore to the numbers on other estates in the same county constituency. Cope, Hayes, and at least the first three interests in Louth—Foster, Clanbrassill and Clermont— were all in the same league in terms of freeholders. Yet Cope, because Armagh was so much larger in size and contained, not surprisingly, more numerous family interests than Louth, had to be content to take his place in a rota of representation; and Hayes, because Donegal was so very much larger in size and contained not only more numerous but more powerful family interests than Louth, had to be content to play a minor, supporting role. The Fosters' 420 freeholders would have been lost in the Donegal electorate of well over 6,000 in 1815.[3] Indeed, the Fosters' 420 freeholders were in danger of being

---

[1] Statement of the voting strengths of the leading interests in co. Armagh, 7 June 1789, Gosford MSS., P.R.O.N.I. D.1606/1/139.

[2] Thomas Knox to Abercorn, 23 Mar. 1790, Abercorn MSS., P.R.O.N.I. T.2541/IB1/1/4.

[3] *Commons' Journals* (Ireland), lxx, App., 1058 ff.

lost in the 1821 Louth electorate of 2,830. However, although he had only one-sixth of the electorate, Foster was protected in 1821 by his alliance with Lord Roden. On a double voting system, two interests who could muster roughly 750 double votes were in a strong tactical position, even in an overall electorate of 2,830, since it was unlikely that a much more broadly based opposition would be able to muster and discipline its forces as effectively. This was particularly true in the political circumstances of co. Louth in 1821. Some members of the old independent interest were still strongly anti-Emancipationist; Balfour, although an Emancipationist, hesitated to appeal to the Catholic vote; Lord Clermont, if his registries had been in better shape, might have been prepared to appeal to the Catholic vote (as he had done briefly two years before), but as an absentee who had tried to set up an unknown English nephew, he cannot have been in much favour with the independent interest. The upshot was that, although the registered electorate had grown most alarmingly since the last period of danger for Foster, 1779–85, it was still unlikely that a coalition could be formed against him.

The compactness of the alliance with Roden, who was not related to Foster and had little common ground with him beyond a community of sentiment on Emancipation, requires some comment. In the days when a Foster and Fortescue had sat together for Louth, the county representation had looked deceptively like a family affair. However, it was not kinship, but freeholders, which caused the Fosters and the Fortescues to ally, just as it was freeholders which decided the shift within the alliance in the decade 1761–71. In Louth, as presumably in most counties, ties of kinship criss-crossed each other in a complex pattern; the Fortescues were no more closely related to the Fosters than they were to Lord Clanbrassill and to several members of the independent interest (see Appendix, Table Four). In Louth, and presumably in most counties, it was the arithmetic of the double-voting system which more than anything else dictated the political alliances. This arithmetic was simply that, wherever possible, two leading interests of approximately equal strength should form a junction, and each guarantee his second votes to the other. Indeed, if a single candidate was confronted by a junction, it was to his advantage to find a 'running horse' or 'faggot', no matter how weak in freeholders, on whom his own double votes and all the double votes he could procure, might be spent safely and without advantage to his opponents. In the celebrated co. Down election of 1790, the territorially and numerically powerful Downshires set up just such a faggot, to prevent their second votes from going to one or other member of the junction formed against them. In the co. Armagh election of 1797, a candidate who was confronted by a junction was advised to 'set up a person to take off his second voices'.[1] If there was some hope of this arithmetic working in the case of a faggot, it was obviously almost certain to work in a case where the three leading interests in a county were united in a coalition. What was unusual about Louth was not that the big three—Foster, Clermont, and Clanbrassill—came together and were successful in carrying the county, but that they stuck together for a very long time—1745–1809. In most counties, the landed structure was such that a coalition among the big three would have been all-powerful; but in most, the fact that there were only two seats to satisfy three families, would have produced jealousies and probably a rift, from which other leading interests or the independent interest would have been the gainers.[2] In Louth there was no other leading interest, except Balfour. Also, the Clermonts and Clanbrassills between 1745 and 1798, and the Clermonts and Rodens from 1798 to 1800, could muster only one suitable candidate in the main branch of their families at any one time; and so far was the Union from intensifying the pressure on the representation of

[1] Jupp, *Co. Down Elections*, p. 183; James Harden to Gosford, 13 July 1797, Gosford MSS., P.R.O.N.I. D.1606/1/194. There are various references to the existence of a convention, particularly in Ulster, that a landlord should ask his tenants for only one vote, and leave them to cast their second as they pleased— see, for example, Mrs. McTier to Dr. William Drennan, 19 Jan. [1776], Drennan MSS., P.R.O.N.I. D.591/1A. However, the prevalence of junctions suggests that this convention was not widespread. The most difficult thing of all, from the landlord's point of view, was to get tenants to cast 'plumpers' and 'sink', or waive, their second votes, although this was the tactic which the Fosters seem to have been forced into trying at the 1826 election.

[2] For example, there was a *renversement des alliances* among the leading interests in co. Armagh between the 1753 by-election and the general election of 1761; and in the late 18th and early 19th century, there were frequent 'revolutions' in the politics of co. Kerry—William Brownlow to Sir Archibald Acheson, 4 Nov. 1760, Gosford MSS., P.R.O.N.I. D.1606/1/29; Robert Day to Glandore, 2 Aug. 1796, Talbot-Crosbie MSS., N.L.I.

Louth that, on two occasions after its passing, 1806 and 1825, Clermont and Roden could not muster even one suitable candidate. The consequence was that they had no strong personal or family reason for challenging the Fosters' claim to monopolize one of the two county seats, firmly based as it was on the Fosters' superiority in freeholders.

This superiority in freeholders derived from the Fosters' improvements. In assessing the importance of this factor, it is helpful to compare the Fosters, not just with the other leading interests in Louth (who like the Fosters benefited from its smallness), but with leading interests in other counties. This comparison is complicated by the fact that reliable acreage and freeholder figures are distinctly hard to come by, particularly the two in combination, and particularly a freeholder figure which, like the Fosters' 420-odd, represents the interest concerned at full stretch. The difficulty of getting reliable figures explains why the six interests chosen for the comparison have really little in common with the Fosters, except an equal degree of documentation in this respect. The one which has most in common with them is Lord Rossmore, whose family had 500 freeholders and well over 8,000 acres in co. Monaghan in 1807 (much of it urban property, so the same reservation has to be made as in the case of Lord Roden in Dundalk).[1] Two points are noteworthy about Rossmore: first, he had a bigger acreage than the Fosters; second, he had fewer freeholders, relative to his acreage, than they. The same applies to the other interests in the comparison, all of whom were much larger landowners than either Rossmore or the Fosters: the 2nd Marquess of Hertford, with something less than 50,000 acres and 1,350 freeholders in co. Antrim in 1802; the 2nd Viscount O'Neill, with some 30,000 acres and 1,040 freeholders in the same county in the same year; Lord Abercorn, with 26,000 acres and between 763 and 850 freeholders in co. Tyrone in the period 1795–1806; the 3rd Marquess of Downshire, with over 60,000 acres and some 3,400 freeholders in co. Down in 1812; and the 1st Earl of Londonderry, with roughly half the acres and half the freeholders in the same county in the same year.[2]

---

[1] See p. 282, *n.* 2.

[2] Calculations by Lord Macartney of the number of freeholders on each estate in co. Antrim, 1802, Macartney MSS., P.R.O.N.I. D.572/21/101, fols. 80–1;

Comparison between landowners of this size and the Fosters is far-fetched. However, they at least resemble the Fosters in being reasonably improving and owning reasonably fertile estates: no meaningful comparison could be made between the Fosters and the proprietors of the meaninglessly vast wastes of Connaught. What emerges from the comparison is, again, the significance of the Fosters' improvements in terms of the number of freeholders they could field relative to their acreage (in comparing the Fosters with the two co. Down magnates, it must be remembered that freehold creation in co. Down, as will be seen, had probably been carried well beyond the limit of economic prudence). The result of the comparison with Lord Hertford is particularly striking, because Hertford's estate included the substantial town of Lisburn. However, what also emerges from the comparison is that the Fosters were not by Anglo-Irish standards particularly large landlords. Indeed, very few county interests of anything like their longevity owned such a small estate. The smallness of Louth is therefore a point which should not be pressed too far: Louth was small, but its leading proprietary interests were not large, and not much of its land was Church land and thus neutralized for political purposes.

If the relative strength of the Fosters in terms of freeholders is remarkable, it is also at first sight remarkable that all these estates, the Foster included, were not much stronger in this respect. Freehold tenures were very common in Ireland— indeed, in his speech on the Catholic Relief Bill in 1793, Sir Laurence Parsons had declared, with some exaggeration, 'almost all the lands of the country are let for lives'.[1] The only monetary qualification for the franchise was that the freehold should yield to the tenant 40/– a year above the rent he paid and all other charges, and this figure had been fixed as long ago as Henry VI's reign. Much had happened to the value of money in the intervening centuries, as one parliamentary re-former reminded the Earl-Bishop of Derry in 1783:

. . . When the law for that purpose first passed, 40/– a year was

half year's rental of the manor of Killultagh [the future Hertford estate], 1719–23, P.R.O.N.I. D.427/1; rental of the O'Neill estate, 1831, P.R.O.N.I. T.2024/2; James Hamilton to Abercorn, 24 Jan. 1795 and 5 Feb. 1806, Abercorn MSS., P.R.O.N.I. T.2541/IA1/21/1, IA2/15/3; Jupp, *Co. Down Elections*, pp. 179, 189, 191.

[1] Quoted in Lecky, *History of Ireland*, iii. 155.

a good income. The possessor was an independent man. But what alteration has since occurred? Time has changed the value of money and the value of life's necessaries; it has changed everything but the law. What was then independence is now beggary. A 40/- freeholder without a trade could not support a family without alms. 'Tis his trade makes him independent, not his freehold. . . . His 40/- would not provide him and his family potatoes and salt for three months. . . .[1]

Since the monetary qualification for the franchise was so low, it is obvious that the Fosters could have had many more than 420 freeholders if they had leased out their estate in neat 40/- parcels or—and this is how in practice it could have been effected—if they had encouraged the process of sub-dividing holdings which was endemic among Irish tenants, and at the expiry of each head lease had made direct tenants of those who had been sub-tenants previously, thus realizing the maximum political potential of their estate and ensuring to themselves complete and direct control over each individual tenant. In other words, they could have practised what the agriculturalist, Edward Wakefield, called 'political agronomy'.[2]

   The one obstacle to the practice of 'political agronomy' was economics. All landlords had to think twice before they did anything which either impaired the fee simple value of their estate or lowered the income which they drew from it annually: a freeholder was not just a voter, he was a tenant farmer to whom the landlord entrusted a part of his land, and on whom he depended for a part of his income. This consideration must have operated particularly strongly in the case of the Fosters, who had a tradition of improvement to live up to and a heavy burden of debt to struggle under. Significantly, John Leslie Foster was a stern critic of 'political agronomy'. Writing to Peel in 1828, he pointed out that the financial rewards to be derived from possession of parliamentary interest at constituency level had been so attractive forty years earlier that many landlords had pursued them to the detriment of the efficient management of their estates. The re-enfranchisement of the

---

   [1] 'Catholicus' to the Earl-Bishop, [November 1783, or later], Bruce MSS., P.R.O.N.I. D.2798/5/17.
   [2] Quoted in W. A. Maguire, *The Downshire Estates in Ireland, 1801–1845* (Oxford, 1972), p. 125.

Catholics in 1793 provided further stimulus towards the multiplication of holdings and of freeholders, and the wartime boom
in agricultural prices served to cushion landowners who responded to the stimulus against the worst economic effects of such
a leasing policy. Then, closely following the peace and the
post-war depression, came economical reform; so that the
rewards of 'political agronomy' were whittled away at the very
time when landowners were beginning to feel its full economic
ill-effects. By this time, however, it had become very difficult
for them to retrace their steps and reverse their policy; having
encouraged sub-division for so long, they could not now dis-
courage it without apparent harshness.[1] In this John Leslie
Foster was undoubtedly correct. The most notorious practi-
tioner of 'political agronomy' was Lady Downshire, who in the
period 1801–9 created a 'warren of freeholders' on the vast co.
Down estates of her son and ward, the 3rd Marquess; and recent
work on the Downshire estates has shown what a slow and difficult business it was for the 3rd Marquess, when he came into
his inheritance, to undo what his mother had done. Another
co. Down example of the same thing is the Annesley estate in
and around Castlewellan. In the early nineteenth century this
estate was 'sub-divided . . . for the purpose of creating 40/–
freeholders', and in 1843, nearly fifteen years after the abolition
of the 40/– freehold franchise, this sub-division was cited as a
major cause of the estate's unproductiveness.[2]

Prior to the 1793 Act, the practice of 'political agronomy'
was probably extremely rare, even in Ulster, where the majority
of the population was not disqualified from the franchise on
religious grounds. One early example, that of co. Antrim at
the time of a by-election in 1725, is particularly striking;
at that date Lord Hertford's forebear had only 40 or 50 freeholders on exactly the same estate as Lord Hertford's, and other
very large landlords had only a couple each. This of course
reflects the important economic problem of the late seventeenth

---

[1] J. L. Foster to Peel, 16 Dec. 1828, Peel MSS., B.L. Add. MS. 40397, fols. 384–
94. As an ex-Chief Secretary, Peel probably did not have to be told all this. In
1813 he had exclaimed in exasperation that the Irish members received ten times
the favours of the English.

[2] Maguire, *Downshire Estates*, pp. 125 ff.; report of the master in chancery on
the estate of the Earl Annesley, a minor and ward of chancery, 1843, Annesley
MSS., P.R.O.N.I. D.1503/2/32.

and early eighteenth century, that landlords found it difficult to get good tenants except on highly disadvantageous terms (significantly, Lord Massereene's 150 freeholders—the largest number on any co. Antrim estate in 1725—were described as 'lives renewable').[1] Later in the century, in 1780, Hercules Langford Rowley, another co. Antrim magnate, whose family owned large property in, and from time to time represented, both cos. Antrim and Meath, was clearly not practising 'political agronomy', as he declared it to be a principle with him never to interfere with the terms on which his head tenants sub-let their land.[2] In the year of the 1793 Act, Lord Charlemont, whose family from time to time represented co. Armagh, had 1,100 tenants on his Armagh estate; but in 1789 he had been able to muster only 250 freeholders (and there is no reason to think that the tenurial structure of his estate had changed markedly in the short intervening period).[3] What is known about the size and composition of Ulster electorates prior to 1793, suggests that estates were very far from being leased out in neat 40/– parcels. At the celebrated co. Armagh by-election of 1753, for example, only 1,159 people voted, of whom 676 were 40/– freeholders and 483 £10 freeholders;[4] at the equally hotly contested co. Antrim general election of 1776 (for which the poll-book from the deputy-sheriff's court, where nearly half the electorate polled, survives), 660 of the voters in the deputy-sheriff's court were 40/– freeholders and 415 were £10 freeholders.[5] Outside Ulster, 40/– freeholders were understandably less numerous, because of the religious disqualification of the majority of the population. At the co. Galway by-election of 1753, for example, an almost equally celebrated contest as contemporary Armagh, roughly 700 people voted, of whom roughly half were 40/– freeholders and half £10 freeholders (the roughness derives from the fact that

---

[1] Arthur Dobbs to Michael Ward, 5 July 1725, Castle Ward MSS., P.R.O.N.I. D.2092/1/2/121.

[2] Rowley to the Earl-Bishop of Derry, 5 Aug. 1780, Bruce MSS., P.R.O.N.I. D.2798/3/29.

[3] Revd. Edward Hudson to Charlemont, 10 Aug. 1793, Charlemont MSS., R.I.A., 2nd ser. 2, vi. 56; see also p. 293, n. 1.

[4] Copy of the Armagh poll-book, 1753, Brownlow MSS., P.R.O.N.I. T.2736/1.

[5] Deputy court poll-book for the co. Antrim election, 1776, Young MSS., P.R.O.N.I. D.1634/L/1.

the figures were in dispute);¹ and in co. Clare in 1768, there were only 57 40/- freeholders to 448 £10 freeholders, and although there were further contests in 1776 and 1783, and a consequent rise in the electorate, the 40/- element did not rise very much in proportion to the £10.² In overwhelmingly Catholic counties like Galway and Clare, it is not surprising that an exclusively Protestant franchise should have produced a small and fairly affluent electorate. Indeed, the preamble of an Election Act of 1785 stated that the great cause of confusion at elections and of prolongation of polls was the large number, not of 40/-, but of £10, freeholders.³

The figures do not, however, tell the whole story. Because of the presence of the domestic linen industry in Ulster (and elsewhere, including Louth), many 40/- freeholders must have enjoyed an extra-agricultural source of income. These were the 40/- freeholders whose trade made them independent, according to the Earl-Bishop's correspondent, and they were the 40/- freeholders about whose fate Foster waxed pathetic when a uniform £10 franchise for voters of both religions was proposed in 1793; Foster argued that the Ulster linen weavers, the Protestant backbone of the country, would not be able to farm a £10-freehold successfully, and would neglect their trade in the unsuccessful attempt.⁴ For another reason, too, electorates were probably more affluent than the surviving figures suggest, and not just in Ulster or because of linen. The 40/- freeholder was a man who fell into a particular category of electoral registration, not a man whose freehold produced to him precisely 40/- a year. Under the Irish registration system (which will be discussed in more detail later on), a distinction was drawn between different categories of freeholders, and different rules were prescribed for the different categories. From 1728 to 1745, the distinction lay between freeholders of under and over

---

¹ *Case of Robert French and Charles Daly* . . ., in connection with the subsequent co. Galway election petition, [pre 11 Dec. 1753], F.P. T.2519/4/215.

² Co. Clare poll-books, 1768, 1776, and 1783, Inchiquin MSS., N.L.I. MSS. 14793–5. In the predominantly, though not overwhelmingly, Catholic county of Louth, the breakdown of the poll at the 1767 by-election was 314 £10 freeholders, 275 40/- freeholders, and 50 rent-chargers; the last category were likely to have been considerably more affluent than many of the £10 freeholders—brief on behalf of Stephen Sibthorpe, 5 Feb. 1768, F.P. D.562/1214.

³ 25 Geo. III, c. 52, s. 1.

⁴ *Parl. Reg.* (Irish), xiii. 342.

£10; from 1745 to 1785, it lay between 40/– and £10 freeholders; from 1785 to 1786, there was no distinction at all;
from 1786 to 1795, it lay between 40/– and £100 freeholders;
and from 1795 to 1829, a three-tiered distinction obtained:
40/–, £20, and £50.[1] What must be remembered is that a 40/–
freeholder was a man whose land was worth between 40/–
and the next monetary category; from 1786 to 1795, in particular, a 40/– freeholder was a man with land worth anything up to £100. Moreover, economic considerations must
have played an important part in deciding the category in
which a freeholder registered himself, or allowed his landlord
to register him. To register as a £10 freeholder, meant admitting
to his landlord that he was making £10 a year out of the landlord, and might mean that the level of his rent would be the
subject of unwelcome revision next time his lease fell in.
Landlords, on their side, would try to get tenants to register
in whatever category was realistic, because the rules of registration were less exacting for the more affluent category, and in
their case there was less chance of votes being lost on technicalities; but, since tenants were wont to make registration day the
occasion for a plea for an abatement of rent, and to protest
that hard times precluded them from swearing to a £10 or
£20 qualification without perjuring themselves and endanger-
ing their immortal souls, landlords probably did not push this
matter very far. At the Galway election of 1753, for example,
several voters who were objected to because of defects in their
registry as 40/– freeholders, turned round and voted as £10
freeholders (who were not required to be registered until 1785).
In spite of the closeness of the scrutiny at this election, they
were not objected to the second time.

On the whole, therefore, because tenants had a sound economic
reason for down-grading themselves, because the 40/– qualification was a minimum, not an absolute, and because many
40/– freeholders had other sources of income besides their
land, the electorate prior to 1793 must have been more affluent
and independent than the few surviving poll-books would
suggest. Indeed, in spite of the much greater prevalence of
freehold tenures in Ireland than in England, the Irish electorate,

---

[1] 1 Geo. II, c. 9, s. 7; 19 Geo . II, c. 11, s. 2; 25 Geo. III, c. 52, s. 1; 26 Geo.
III, c. 23, s. 1; 35 Geo. III, c. 29, ss. 30, 37.

again prior to 1793, cannot have been as socially and economically inferior to the contemporary English electorate as is commonly supposed (nor Irish electoral practices, particularly in the matter of the conduct and duration of polls, as markedly more impure[1]). One practical objection to the 'Catholic rabble' potentially enfranchised by the 1793 Act (which Foster did not make, because he was arguing primarily on constitutional grounds), was not that it was Catholic, but that it was rabble; and in the case of some counties, notably in Connaught, the effect of the Act was eventually to transform a largely nominal 40/- franchise into a nearly actual one. There was, of course, considerable variation from county to county (Louth being an extreme case of the Act's making no difference to the size and composition of the electorate for years after its passing): a variation which cannot be explained on grounds of population, but which is to be explained rather on the grounds of the varying degrees of competition between Protestant proprietary interests which existed from one county to another (the exceptional case of Louth helps to prove this rule). However, it is likely that even in counties where competition was most fierce, economic considerations were not completely ignored. In 1822, the 2nd Earl of Rosse, who as Sir Laurence Parsons had pointed out the dangers of the 1793 Act at the time, and had advocated a £20 franchise for Catholics combined with full Emancipation, thus described its effects, probably with particular reference to King's County, where he resided: '... Forty years ago, the lands of Ireland were let in farms of 500 or a [*sic*] 1,000 or 1,500 acres: now landlords, finding that they

---

[1] In England a 15-day limitation to the duration of polls obtained, and the absence of any such limitation in Ireland occasioned much righteous English indignation after the Union, and led eventually to Ireland's being placed on the same footing as England by the Election Act of 1820. In fact, there had existed under Irish legislation a less narrow, practical limitation to the duration of polls, in that the poll could not go on beyond the day on which the writ was returnable. Also, Irish legislation made provision for what was lacking under English legislation until 1832: more than one polling place, where the need arose. An Act of 1775 provided for a second (or deputy-sheriff's) court in any county where more than 400 freeholders had polled at the previous election, and the comprehensive 1795 Act provided for as many polling places as there were baronies and half-baronies in a county. It was not the inadequacy of Irish legislation, but the delayed-action effects of the 1793 Act, which turned Irish polls into something of a scandal. A measure which in the end brought about an approximate quadrupling of the electorate, was bound to burst the confines of the old electoral code.

can get higher rents and get more voters, let them to Catholics in portions of 20, 30 and 40 acres, and these, as they multiply fast, again sub-divide them among their sons and daughters ...'[1] What is significant is that the, no doubt short-sighted, economic consideration of 'higher rents' was at least a contributory inducement to the landlords; also, an agricultural unit of 20 acres, though small, was far larger than was necessary to confer the minimal 40/- qualification. It is probable that, even after 1793, there were few counties where 'political agronomy' was carried so far that landlords leased out land in 40/- parcels.

'Political agronomy' on anything remotely like that scale, was obviously a disastrous policy from the economic point of view. However, the running of an estate and the running of a political interest were not necessarily conflicting activities. For example, the Fosters' policy of not granting perpetuities was sound in both economic and political terms.[2] This makes it hard to assess the extent to which a politically minded landlord—Foster or anyone else—was influenced in his leasing policy by political considerations, or subordinated economic considerations to them. There was nothing inherently undesirable, from the economic point of view, in a freehold lease. For example, the agent on a co. Monaghan estate which had never been exploited politically, welcomed the 1793 Act on the purely economic ground that it would encourage Catholic tenants to take longer leases; and in 1729, an agent on a Queen's County estate had expressed the view that a three-life lease was better than one for 31 years '. . . for the keeping up of improvements; for when it is for a term of years, the tenants are apt to let things go to rack'.[3] In certain circumstances, it would be to the landlord's advantage that a holding should be due to revert to him at a specified and predictable time; in other circumstances, this would not be to his advantage, particularly if it led the tenant to over-work the land during the last years of his tenure. Long leases encouraged sub-division, short

---

[1] Rosse to Redesdale, 30 Mar. 1822, Redesdale MSS., P.R.O.N.I. T.3030/13/1.

[2] The same, generally speaking, is true of joint or communal occupation of land, which the Fosters intervened on several occasions to correct.

[3] Very Revd. Lorcan O'Mearain, 'The Bath Estate, 1777–1800', *Clogher Record*, vi (1968), 572; Henry Hatch to Col. Flower, 3 Feb. 1729, Ashbrook MSS., N.L.I. MS. 11476/2.

leases discouraged improvement; so the very unpredictability of the term of a freehold lease could have its advantages. In any case, complicated tables of calculation existed on the basis of which a landlord could predict, with reasonable precision, how long a life of such-and-such an age was likely to last.[1]

It is therefore impossible to generalize about these matters; all depended on the particular needs and customs of each individual estate. For example, the tenants on the Abercorn estate in co. Tyrone in the middle of the eighteenth century claimed that 21-year leases inhibited them from carrying out improvements, and asked their by no means politically minded landlord, the 8th Earl of Abercorn, to 'indulge' them in freehold leases. (The idea of 'indulging' a tenant with a freehold lease would have fallen strangely on the ears of Lady Downshire.) By the late eighteenth century, the situation on the Abercorn estate had been transformed. The landlord was then the very politically minded 1st Marquess of Abercorn. Those tenants who were not freeholders knew that he was anxious to build up his political interest, and on condition of their 'indulging' him by accepting freeholder leases, they huckstered for additional years to be added to their unexpired term, and for abatements of rent.[2] The same tactics were employed against the 3rd Viscount Palmerston (the future Prime Minister). Leases do not seem to have been common on the Palmerston estate in co. Sligo, and even those tenants who had invested heavily in building preferred the word of a Palmerston to a lease. This touching trustfulness was a source of great inconvenience to Palmerston, who decided in the period after 1817 to realize for the first time the political potential of his estate. He

---

[1] Bishop of Ferns to Egremont, 6 Feb. [1798], Petworth House MSS., P.H.A. 57/7. The Bishop of Ferns's testimony on this point may be suspect, as Fitzgibbon claimed that '. . . in managing the estate of his See, [he] avows that he acts solely upon a table of calculation which he bought for half a crown' (quoted in McDowell, *Fitzgibbon Letters from the Sneyd Muniments*, p. 311). Fitzgibbon seems to have garbled the Bishop's remark, as see lands could not of course be leased for lives. The Bishop was probably talking about Lord Egremont's huge estates in cos. Clare and Limerick, for which he acted as head agent—see A. P. W. Malcomson, 'Absenteeism in Eighteenth-Century Ireland', *Irish Economic and Social History Society Journal*, vol. i (1974), 31.

[2] Nathaniel Nisbitt to Abercorn, 24 Feb. 1748, and James Hamilton to Abercorn, 8 Sept. and 1 Nov. 1795, Abercorn MSS., P.R.O.N.I. T.2541/IA1/ID/44, /IA1/ 21/23, 26.

endeavoured to conceal the purpose of his change of policy
by avoiding the minimum freehold qualification of one-life
leases, and by choosing instead '. . . three old lives . . . in order
to secure the votes, and at the same time to give to the leases
the character of an act done in the ordinary course of things,
and not for electioneering purposes'. The tenants do not seem
to have been taken in, and Palmerston was no doubt forced
to make economic sacrifices to obtain his political ends.
The same sacrifices had been exacted from another co. Sligo
landlord in 1808, who complained, '. . . two villages refused
[to register] unless they got such lives as they would themselves nominate, although holding under an old lease and at
6s. the acre. . . .'[1] Even if no such sacrifices were exacted, the
actual process of making out the freeholder leases was '. . . a
tedious and expensive business, for there must not only be a
formal surrender on a half-crown stamp of the present lease,
and [*sic*] the printing and stamping of each pair of new leases
will cost 6/–, exclusive of preparing the surrenders and filling
the leases'.[2] In these unspectacular but significant respects,
landlords who would not have dreamt of going the lengths of
Lady Downshire or the Annesleys in building up their political
interest, would still find themselves subordinating economic
to political considerations.

The extent to which Foster subordinated one to the other
is uncertain. One thing, however, which is certain is that his
estate was not leased out in anything like neat 40/– parcels:
in 1821 it included four £50-freehold and fourteen £20-
freehold leases. Moreover, a fair proportion of the 420 freeholders with whom it was credited in that year are likely to have
been sub-tenants, not directly amenable to his control. Unfortunately, the printed freeholders' lists of the period 1821–7[3]
credit every freeholder on the Foster estate to Foster, regardless
of whether there was an intermediate landlord or not. Also, the
earliest full rentroll of the Foster estate does not come until
1838[4]—nine years after the raising of the freehold qualification

---

[1] G. Swan and James Walker to Palmerston, 29 Nov. 1817 and 5 Apr. 1819,
Palmerston MSS., Hampshire R.O.; John Nolan to Charles O'Hara, 22 Feb.
1808, O'Hara MSS., N.L.I.

[2] James Hamilton to Abercorn, 24 Jan. 1795, Abercorn MSS., P.R.O.N.I.
T. 2541/IA1/21/1. [3] See p. 137, n. 1.

[4] Brief in Lord Massereene v. Lord Ferrard, 1838, F.P. D.1739/3/15.

from 40/– to £10, and six years after the franchise had ceased, under the terms of the 1832 Reform Act, to be exclusively freehold-based. It would be more than risky to use evidence dating from 1838 as the basis on which to form conclusions about the tenurial structure of the estate in the first half of the 1820s.

The case of the Annesleys of course demonstrates that the tenurial structure of an estate did not change overnight, and was especially unresponsive to changes in electoral law. But this may be less true of the Foster estate, which had already undergone one dramatic change—not perhaps overnight—but within the very short period of two years, from the beginning of 1822 to the beginning of 1824. At the former date there had been roughly 420 registered freeholders on the estate (about the same as in 1821): at the latter, the number had dropped to 335. The reasons for the drop are hard to guess. They cannot have been political, since Foster had every possible motive for keeping up his voting strength; and he was clearly not at this stage preparing for a raising of the franchise from 40/– to £10 or £20, since the number of substantial middlemen on his estate fell, instead of rising, in the period between 1821 and 1824. Nor is the answer to be found in defective registration.[1] Instead, the only answer which seems to square with the known facts is that economic considerations made it impossible for him to keep up the total of 420 freeholders, which he had probably achieved for the first time only in 1821. Since 1814 the estate had been under trusteeship; and it was the trustee, not Foster, who was economically in control and had the responsibility of meeting the annual charges and satisfying the anxious creditors. After the 1826 election, as has been seen, the trustee refused to be deflected from his primary responsibility by political considerations, and it is reasonable to assume that in the period 1822–4 he insisted on a consolidation of holdings as the best means of extracting the maximum income from the estate. This can only have been effected by agreement with the tenants: the Fosters' freeholder leases were granted for the lives of so many different people that, short of famine or

---

[1] The registration of a 40/– or £20 freeholder was valid for eight years, and in 1822 there were no freeholders on the Foster estate whose registries dated from before 1817. For a discussion of the registration system see pp. 313 ff.

massacre, they could not possibly have dropped from 420 to
335 in the space of only two years. The drop was a continuous
process, since the number stood at only 270 by the time of the
election of 1826. Then, at some time after 1826, the process
was reversed. In December 1828 John Leslie Foster was able
to report to Peel that the Foster estate could field 360 freeholders out of a co. Louth total which he reckoned at 3,500;
he also added that, if the franchise were raised to £20, it could
field a still higher proportion of the county electorate, 60 out of
700.[1] As there had been only twelve freeholders with a qualification of £20 or more on the Foster estate in 1824, this latter
figure suggests that considerable consolidation of holdings had
been going on between then and 1828 (since 1825 at least, a
raising of the franchise had been a strong possibility, so that
political and economic considerations alike would have pointed
towards consolidation[2]). The rise in the number of 40/– freeholders by December 1828 is, conceivably, attributable to the
fact that the trusteeship had expired with Lord Oriel's death in
September.

   It may be unfair to suggest that, without the restraint of
trusteeship, the Fosters would have sacrificed economic to
political considerations. After all, Young, who visited Collon
just after the decade of bitter electioneering from 1761 to
1771, did not find (or at least did not record) any traces of the
ravages of 'political agronomy'. The fact that the Fosters'
improvements gave them a much higher yield of freeholders
to their acreage than that of any comparable estate, meant
that to some extent they escaped such a temptation. The main
concern of both Chief Baron Anthony and of John Foster
seems to have been to attract and hold on to good and improving
tenants; moreover, John Foster's preference for Protestant
tenants was so strong that he was prepared to advertise for
them, and hold out liberal inducements to them to settle at
Collon.[3] In a predominantly Catholic county like Louth, this

---

[1] J. L. Foster to Peel, 16 Dec. 1828, Peel MSS., B.L. Add. MS. 40397, fols.
384–94. For further comment on the fluctuations in the number of the Foster
freeholders during the 1820s see pp. 138 f., and for a full discussion of the trusteeship,
pp. 326 ff.

[2] See, for example, J. L. Foster to Oriel, 12 Apr. 1825, F.P. D.207/74/144.

[3] Young, *Tour*, i. 147 f.; Revd. [Bramtfield ?] to Foster, 3 Nov. 1807, F.P.
D.562/12518.

was obviously not the quickest or easiest way of building up the numbers of his freeholders (although it may have meant that those freeholders he had were politically more reliable). Another of his favoured devices for obtaining a good class of tenants was a fourteen-year probationary lease. If the tenant built a decent house and made other improvements, two lives with the alternative of twenty-one years were added to his lease; if not, the land was politically neutralized until the expiration of the fourteen-year term.[1] This was not a species of leasing policy which would have commended itself to a landowner obsessed with building up his political interest; nor indeed was the policy of granting a term of years as an alternative to a lease for a life or lives, although this was what Foster seems usually to have done. From the political point of view, the danger inherent in such a lease, as has been seen, was that the term of years might out-last the life, and the lease thus cease to be a freehold lease. This could often be rectified by granting a fresh lease. But sometimes the remaining term of years in the old lease was devised to a widow, a daughter, or a minor; which meant once again that the land was politically neutralized. In 1820, for example, there were sixteen leases on the Foster estate which were vested in the 'representatives' of somebody and which were noted as being temporarily unavailable as freeholder leases.[2] No doubt these were leases in which the term of years had out-lasted the term of life, and no doubt the 'representatives' were widows, daughters, or minors. This was a danger which Lady Downshire was careful to avoid: her leases were for the minimum freehold qualification of one life, and did not have the alternative of a term of years.

There are therefore quite a few indications that Foster's leasing policy was not uninfluenced by political considerations, but that it was not influenced by them to an extent which was economically damaging—except perhaps in the 1820s. Like the 1st Marquess of Abercorn, he was asked to reduce people's rents 'as low as I could register [as a 40/- freeholder]', and presumably complied except where the request was obviously

[1] Lord Kilmorey to Foster, 15 Oct. 1820, F.P. D.562/13518.

[2] State of the freeholder leases on John Foster's estate, [Aug. 1820], F.P. D.562/14680. In a similar list made by Oriel in October 1824, there is the laconic reference, 'Alex. Adams—his widow—freehold expired—17 years to come' (D.562/14687).

a try-on, or where the sum of money involved was significant.[1] Presumably he was also prepared to take limited steps towards coercing the politically recalcitrant among his tenantry—again like Lord Abercorn. In 1809, for example, the Abercorn agent asked for authority to tell those tenants who refused to register their freeholds that they '. . . must expect to receive such marks of displeasure as are usual and be charged for the privilege of cutting turf, and that as they have so long delayed to register, they must now be at the expense of it themselves, which otherwise would have been paid for them, as heretofore. . . .'[2] The Foster/Massereene MSS. do not furnish a precisely parallel case, but the measures taken by John Leslie Foster to compel his tenants to disclose who had burgled his house at Rathescar, near Dunleer, in 1821, give a good idea of what the usual 'marks of displeasure' consisted of. Foster's steward was directed

. . . to take up about two hundred cards distributed by Letitia [Mrs. J. L. Foster], which entitled the families to whom they are given to certain assistance from us. I also call in all debts due to me, and withdraw the privilege of people passing through the demesne. I also declare to the people that I will never again employ a man about Rathescar (save the bound tenants) until the robbers are prosecuted to conviction, informing them at the same time that, if I find the present bound tenants insufficient, I will bring in strangers and make bound tenants of them, so that the necessary number of labourers may be completed. . . .[3]

Privileges, perquisites, and 'assistance' of this sort were not part of the contractual relationship between landlord and tenant and were particularly numerous on the estates of enlightened and improving landlords like the Abercorns and the Fosters. John Leslie Foster was firmly of the opinion that they should be withdrawn as a punishment for political disobedience, particularly for voting against a landlord's wishes

---

[1] James McCabe to Foster, 4 Sept. 1820, F.P. D.562/13502. Dr. J. H. Whyte, in his article 'Landlord Influence at Elections in Ireland, 1760–1885', *E.H.R.* lxxv (1960), 741, quotes a number of examples of landlords being held to economic ransom by their tenants at election time.

[2] James Hamilton to Abercorn, 14 Dec. 1809, Abercorn MSS., P.R.O.N.I. T.2541/IA 2/18/23.

[3] J. L. Foster to Foster, 30 May 1821, F.P. D.207/74/86. 'Bound' tenants were presumably tenants who were 'bound', as part of the conditions under which they held their land, to perform labour services to their landlord.

at an election, and that the tenant should be plainly told that, unless he undertook to toe his landlord's political line in the future, he could expect no renewal of his lease at the expiration of its present term.[1] How effective such tactics would be is problematical. John Leslie Foster's reprisals of 1821 were all very well when the matter at issue was robbery, since robbery was something which would arouse much less popular sympathy among the rest of the tenants than political disobedience. Indeed, Foster was hopeful in 1821 of being able to get the parish priest of Dunleer to excommunicate the robbers: there would have been no hope of getting him to excommunicate freeholders who had voted against Foster in 1826, especially since this particular priest had been active in inciting them to do so.[2]

In theory, there were various ways in which a landlord could punish a politically recalcitrant tenant, if the immediate withdrawal of privileges and the threat of no future renewal of his lease did not bring him to heel. If the tenant had been slack in complying with the covenants in his lease—like suit of court or to the landlord's mill—the landlord could enforce them with rigour; and if the tenant was in arrears with his rent the landlord could proceed—or threaten to proceed—against him by distraint, by process to recover the arrear, or by ejectment. Indeed, as a last resort, the landlord could precipitate an arrear by making him an 'English tenant': that is to say, suspending the 'hanging gale' and obliging him to pay his half-yearly rent on the nail, instead of six months later. This was the step which Lord Oriel wanted to take against those tenants (few though they in actual fact were) who had defied him at the 1826 election. But his trustee clearly did not like the thought of a man as heavily indebted as Oriel embarking on a species of agrarian warfare; and, as far as is known, nobody on the Foster estate was made an English tenant.[3] The plain fact of the matter was that, unless he was prepared to disregard economic considerations, a landlord's power to punish tenants for political disobedience was limited. It was

[1] J. L. Foster to Peel, 16 Dec. 1828, Peel MSS., B.L. Add. MS. 40397, fols. 384–94.
[2] J. L. Foster to Oriel, 30 May 1821, and Revd. W. H. Foster to Oriel, 15 June 1826, F. P. D.207/74/86, /73/51.
[3] Oriel to W. P. Greene, 3 Dec. 1826, F.P. T.2519/4/1609.

generally accepted that covenants in leases were in practice unenforceable and depended on the voluntary co-operation of the tenant; and the various methods of proceeding against a tenant in arrears were, thanks to combinations among tenants and complications in the law, slow, expensive, cumbersome, and uncertain (though much less so after the law was modified in 1816 and again in 1820).[1] A landlord who launched into reprisals against politically disobedient tenants had to be fairly sure in advance that he would be successful in evicting those of them whom he failed to bring to heel; for no one wanted to see his land in the hands of tenants who knew they could expect no renewal, and were therefore bent on extracting the maximum advantage out of it during the unexpired term of their leases.

In all these respects, the landlord's attempts at coercion were likely to misfire, and the more likely to do so, the more numerous were the tenants concerned. Indeed, the aspect of the 1826 election which was characteristic of the normal political relationship between landlord and tenant was, not Oriel's abortive reprisals, but the probably spontaneous and sincere expressions of regret which the agent received from many of the offenders.[2] A study of the politics of co. Down in the period 1783–1831 has led to the conclusion that there was more of deference than dependence in a tenant's political obedience to his landlord,[3] and widely though Louth differed politically from the neighbouring county of Down, there is a great deal in the Foster/Massereene MSS. to endorse that conclusion. Unless the circumstances were exceptional—which those of the 1826 election were—and unless the landlord was heavy-handed or oppressive—which Oriel was not—tenants followed his political lead without constraint and almost as a mark of respect. The triumphal arches erected at Collon after the

[1] On the question of covenants, see Maguire, *Downshire Estates*, pp. 115 f., and on the question of proceedings against tenants in arrears, pp. 52 ff. In 1794, Foster had written, apropos of an unsatisfactory agent: '. . . I much fear he is very ignorant of tenants and tenants' customary rights. He seems to rely on law for everything, and I never knew a wise landlord go to law with a poor tenant . . .; experience may teach him that confidence and fair words will answer better than distrust and resort to law. . . .' (Foster to Sheffield, 11 Aug. 1794, *Anglo-Irish Dialogue*, p. 16.)

[2] W. P. Greene to Oriel, 13 July 1826, F.P. D.562/5080.

[3] Jupp, *Co. Down Elections*, p. 197.

1826 election, bearing the legend, 'Glory, Collon tenantry, in your fidelity to your landlord', and the newspaper account of the occasion which described Oriel as the 'happy landlord of a happy tenantry', were perhaps ill-timed, but were not without substance.[1]

It was not the recalcitrance of tenants, but the rigours of the registration system, which constituted the biggest single menace to Oriel's interest in Louth, or indeed to any county interest anywhere. Without meticulous attention to the electoral register, particularly in the period after 1795, he would have been deprived of the political advantages inherent in the structure and situation of his estate, and accruing from the leasing policy which he pursued. The compulsory registration of freeholders was something peculiar to the Irish electoral system. In England a man had to be a payer of Land Tax to qualify as a 40/– freeholder: in Ireland there was no Land Tax, and therefore no check on the authenticity of his claim to vote. This defect was remedied by an Election Act of 1728, which provided that the 40/– freeholder had to have registered his freehold at least six months before the election at which he tendered his vote. This Act laid the foundation for a system of registration which was progressively tightened as the century wore on. Another Act, of 1795, laid it down that freeholders already on the register had to re-register every eight years, unless their freeholds were worth £50 a year or more; and a further Act, of 1805, increased from six months to one year the period which had to elapse between registration or re-registration and the actual exercise of the franchise.[2] The effect of the re-registration clause of the 1795 Act on the electorate of co. Kerry, where a by-election was imminent in 1796, is graphically described in the following letter from one of the candidates:

. . . I yesterday became acquainted with the additional strength gained to us by the Catholic interest, or at least Lord Kenmare's. It will be in future stronger than I had an idea of, but if O'Hara's[3] Bill is in force, it is now almost nothing. Of this fact, most luckily, everyone here is ignorant, and it is supposed, and the Catholics

---

[1] *Saunders News Letter*, 7 July 1826.
[2] Peel to J. L. Foster, 12 Dec. 1826, J. L. Foster MSS., P.R.O.N.I. T.2519/7/1; 1 Geo. II, c. 9, s. 6; 35 Geo. III, c. 29, s. 31; 45 Geo. III, c. 59, s. 4.
[3] Its promoter, Charles O'Hara, M.P. for co. Sligo; see pp. 156 (*n.* 1), 340.

themselves think, they can poll for me this time 310 voters. . . . At the general election . . . nothing can possibly oppose us. Lord Kenmare will by that time have 800 undoubted voters, and I shall have more than 250. At present, in truth, all Lord Kenmare's tenants have no votes, a few gentlemen of fortune and a dozen or two of 40/– registered freeholders excepted. Literally, hardly a single Catholic has conformed to the Registry Act. My interest is reduced to nothing, and in fact the whole tenantry of the county are this time precluded from the voting. . . .[1]

To some extent the dramatic effect of the 1795 Act on the electorate in Kerry was due to the fact that it was a new measure, unheard-of or imperfectly understood by those affected by it. However, even after it had been in operation for some time, it was still catching major county interests in its toils. At the co. Donegal general election of 1806, for example, two of the leading interests, Lords Erne and Mountjoy, were reduced to virtually nothing by defective registry.[2] The surprisingly low poll of Drogheda freeholders in 1807, as has been seen, can also probably be attributed to the same cause.

One of the most spectacular victims of the registration system was the Abercorn interest in cos. Tyrone and Donegal. Lord Abercorn succeeded to the family titles in 1789 and to estates which, from the point of view of their political potential, had been much neglected by his politically apathetic predecessor. The potential was vast, but the next general election could not be far away, and all new freeholders created by Abercorn must, even as the law stood before the Acts of 1795 and 1805, be registered at least six months before the election at which they tendered their votes. As Abercorn lamented to the Chief Secretary, to whom he seriously suggested that the Government might delay the general election until the freeholders were valid:

. . . With more time before me, I should have very little doubt of securing the election of a friend of my own in each of the Counties of Tyrone and Donegal. In the County of Tyrone I have, I think (though my rentroll is not at present before me), near £17,000 a year: in Donegal I have at least one of the best estates. I am now

[1] H. A. Herbert to Glandore, [late? 1796?], Talbot-Crosbie MSS., N.L.I.
[2] John James Burgoyne to Abercorn, 15 Nov. 1806, Abercorn MSS., P.R.O.N.I. T.2541/IA4/1/8.

executing deeds which will enable me to make some (I am told many) hundred freeholders. . . . But the misfortune is that any freeholders I could make will not be capable of voting so soon as the elections must take place. . . .[1]

This was by no means the end of Abercorn's misfortunes with the registration system. These and subsequent freeholder leases were granted for one life only, with the alternative of a term of years, and Abercorn for economic reasons deliberately chose 'a decayed life', that of his elderly agent. Thereafter, the state of the agent's health was closely watched, and minor details, such as the fact that he had fallen downstairs, faithfully reported to Abercorn. ('. . . He was . . . much bruised, but thank God he is almost quite recovered, and in such spirits at our registering that he swears he will live out two elections yet. Although I think he is going fast, especially his intellect, yet I think him a good life for a year or two . . .')[2] In spite of this vigilance, the agent out-smarted them all by dying unexpectedly not long before the general election of 1806, with the result that a very large number of Abercorn's freeholders in both Tyrone and Donegal were 'suddenly extinguished'.[3] Worse was to follow: although the provisions of the 1805 Election Act did not come into operation until 1809, the general election of 1806 was followed by another only five months later. Under the 1795 Act, this did not give Abercorn time to resurrect his dead freeholders. Much the same happened to the Ponsonby family, who lost a sizeable proportion of their voting strength in co. Londonderry because of the death of Fox, on whose life many of their leases depended, just before the general election of 1806.[4]

It was the unpredictability of elections which put the sting into the registration system: a sting which was largely absent prior to the 1795 and 1805 Acts. Until the Octennial Act of 1768, the only compulsion to dissolve the Irish Parliament was provided by the demise of the Crown; but as an Act of 1728 provided that Parliament need not be dissolved for six months

---

[1] Abercorn to Hobart, [late 1789–early 1790], ibid. /IK/11/9.
[2] James Hamilton to Abercorn, 13 Jan. 1806, ibid. /IA1/15/1.
[3] Abercorn to Admiral Pakenham, 9 Nov. 1806, ibid. /IK/19/21.
[4] 45 Geo. III, c. 59, s. 12; collection of election squibs relating to the co. Londonderry election of 1806, Lenox-Conyngham MSS., P.R.O.N.I. D.1449/8.

after that event,[1] and six months was the registration period established by the rudimentary Registration Act of the same year, the demise of the Crown held no great terrors for electoral interests, until the establishment of a one-year registration period by the 1805 Act. Between 1728 and the passing of the Octennial Act in 1768, the only general election which took place, that of 1761, was in fact occasioned by the demise of the Crown (and was held over six months after that event); the government never repeated the disastrous experiment of 1713, by dissolving Parliament when there was no compulsion to do so. After 1768, general elections became more frequent (though, if the long reign and long Parliament of George II are set aside, there were as many general elections, including that for James II's Parliament, in the forty years prior to his accession as there were in the forty years after his death). However, after 1768 general elections became, not only more frequent, but more predictable, taking place at regular intervals of seven rather than eight years. Prior to the Place Act of 1793, by-elections took place only if a member went mad, was expelled the House, took holy orders in the Church of Ireland, was made a peer or a judge, or quite simply died. Moreover, prior to 1771, the Speaker could not issue a writ for a by-election during the parliamentary recess, which meant that there was a flurry of by-elections at the start of every session, averaging twenty-three (or a simultaneous turnover of nearly one-twelfth of the House) during George II's reign. This amounted to a mini general election, and could be an important sounding-board for popular opinion during times of political crisis, notably in 1753. But, since the parliamentary recess lasted for roughly a year and a half out of every two years, by-elections were seldom unpredictable events, and most local interests had as much leisure to prepare for them as the Fosters in 1766–7.[2] They became much more unpredictable after 1771, and rather more frequent after the Place Act in 1793. General elections, too, became much more unpredictable after the Union. Instead of following the convenient septennial pattern of 1768–1800, they took place erratically in 1802, 1806, 1807, 1812, 1818, 1820, 1826, 1830, 1831, and 1832. The tightening of

---

[1] 1 Geo. II, c. 7.
[2] McCracken, 'Central and Local Administration', pp. 84, 91.

the registration system thus coincided with a period of unpredictable elections, which meant that Foster or any other
electoral interest knew not the time nor the hour when a
maximum exertion would be required of him.

The problem lay not so much in the registration of tenants
who had been hitherto unregistered, or whose registrations had
lapsed through the expiry of their leases (for in such instances
the tenant had no vote as things stood, so Foster had nothing to
lose and everything to gain by registering him); the problem
lay rather in choosing the right time to re-register existing
freeholders. This had to be done within the statutory period
of eight years, otherwise their registries expired; but if an
election took place within a year (or up to 1809, within six
months) of their re-registration, they were debarred from
voting at it. Timing was, therefore, of the essence. If Foster
were caught denuded of freeholders at the time of an election,
there was no chance of his being able to conceal the fact;
for publicity was another unwelcome facet of the registration
system. Registrations could be made four times a year, after
quarter sessions, and anyone who had some to make applied
for an adjourned sessions of the peace to be held at a market
town convenient to his estate. The clerk of the peace dealt
with registrations, and was obliged by law to keep an electoral
register which anyone could examine at a small fee, and which,
after 1820, had to be printed annually under the terms of the
Election Act of that year.[1] To some extent this element of
publicity was an asset to the leading interests in any county,
because it made possible a counting of heads without the expense
of a poll. In this way contests were averted in Louth, probably
in 1761 and certainly in 1820. But its general effect was to keep
county interests consistently under their full potential strength,
because each took its cue from the other, and none wanted to
stake its all on the one sessions of the peace. A rare exception was
Lord Roden who, as has been seen, registered 224 of his 320 freeholders 'in one batch' at an adjourned sessions in May 1825. All of
these were eligible to vote at the 1826 election by only a month.[2]

---

[1] Extracts from the various election acts insofar as they related to the duties of
the clerk of the peace, 17 Feb. 1811, F.P. D.562/14655; 1 Geo. IV, c. 11, s. 30.
[2] Revd. W. H. Foster to Oriel, 14 June 1826, F.P. D.207/73/136; *List of Co.
Louth Freeholders Registered between Lent 1825 and Lent 1826*, P.R.O.N.I. T.2519/14/5.

Up to 1821 Foster was less seriously affected by the exigencies of the registration system than most county interests, or at least than his leading rivals in co. Louth. This was because of his own longevity as M.P. for the county, and also because of his inability, in spite of incessant solicitation, to get himself created a peer in the years between 1811 and 1821. During the fifty-three years that he represented Louth, his Fortescue or Jocelyn colleague changed five times. Within the same period the Fortescues and Jocelyns had to weather five by-elections, and Foster only one. All this was changed in 1821 when Foster, at the age of almost eighty-one, was at last gratified with his long-sought peerage. (One side-effect of his ennoblement which, though not of major importance, is worth mentioning, is that he was now debarred from writing canvassing letters, and only the most discreet use could be made of his name by others; this was the more awkward in view of the fact that he was the only member of the family semi-permanently on the spot at Collon in the years after 1821.)[1] His wife, Lady Ferrard, now aged eighty-five, was already a peeress in her own right; so the death of either of them would remove their only son, Thomas Skeffington, from the House of Commons. In spite of this, Skeffington rather than his cousin, John Leslie Foster, was chosen as the Foster candidate in 1821, probably because at the time of the by-election Lady Ferrard was 'again better and

[1] There was a standing order of the Irish House of Commons against certain 'persons' (this must mean peers) concerning themselves in elections for the lower House, which was often appealed to in election petitions—see, for example, *Commons' Journals* (Ireland), vii. 34. But some peers were extremely incautious. Lord Clermont, as has been seen, allowed his name to be used publicly in 1819; and as late as 1859 the absentee 1st Lord Leconfield allowed his agent to circularize the tenants with a printed letter informing them that Leconfield would 'thank' them to vote for a particular candidate in a co. Limerick election (circular letter from Wainwright Crowe to the Leconfield tenantry, 20 Apr. 1859, Petworth House MSS., P.H.A. 1668/1). But, on the whole, most peers were more circumspect. After the 1768 election in co. Tyrone, for example, Lord Abercorn suggested that a 'treat' be given to the tenants in his name, but then queried whether this was 'proper' (Abercorn to James Hamilton, 24 May 1768, Abercorn MSS., P.R.O.N.I. T.2541/IK8/2/34). The most striking example of circumspection is that of Foster's nephew, John Maxwell Barry, at the co. Cavan election of 1826. By that time Barry had succeeded to the family title as 5th Lord Farnham, and he warned his candidate for the election to '. . . Take particular care always to speak in your own name and never to use mine respecting the election' (Farnham to Henry Maxwell, 29 May 1826, Farnham MSS., N.L.I.). As an ex-Speaker of the House of Commons, Lord Oriel was probably no less circumspect than his nephew.

Lord Oriel . . . as stout as possible'.¹ Skeffington was elected
without opposition, but it was obvious that a further by-election
would 'in the course of nature very soon come'.² It came with
the death of Lady Ferrard at the beginning of 1824. John Leslie
Foster's unopposed return at the ensuing by-election provided
only a momentary respite. Lord Oriel still had the rising dissatisfaction of the old independent interest and the failing
health of John Leslie Foster's colleague, John Jocelyn, to worry
about. Then, two years later, the futility and irrelevance of such
worries were revealed at the dramatic general election of 1826.

It is interesting to trace how Oriel worked his registries so as
to meet the difficult circumstances of the period from, say,
1818 to 1827. For a start he almost never—either then or at any
other period—inserted the life of a Foster in his freehold leases:
a fatal policy if the death of the Foster concerned, as well as
extinguishing the lease, would precipitate a by-election.
(The only member of the family whom he ever used as a life
in a lease of any significance was his daughter, Lady Dufferin,
a politically harmless choice.) In the timing of his registrations,
as well as in the choice of lives for leases, he also showed considerable shrewdness. It was usual to hold a big registration
immediately after a general election, when the next one was, or
seemed to be, a remote prospect. Yet, because of the King's
advanced age, Oriel did virtually no registering after the 1818
general election, nor in 1819 either.³ This meant, presumably,
that he was at the same electoral strength as in 1818, when the
King died and a general election was sprung on him in March
1820. At the first sessions after this he registered some 125
freeholders, who were out of action for the by-election in
August caused by the death of Lord Roden. The 125 were
however back in play well before the by-election of September
1821, when the Fosters' own seat was at stake; so, too, were
some 168 freeholders whom Oriel had registered between
July and September 1820, although the September registries
were eligible to vote only by a matter of days.⁴ In the period

¹ F. T. Foster to Augustus Foster, [Aug. 1821], Vere Foster MSS.
² Chichester Fortescue to Balfour, 15 July 1821, Balfour MSS., N.L.I. MS.
10368.
³ State of the freeholder leases on John Foster's estate, [Aug. 1820], F.P.
D.562/14680.
⁴ *Louth Freeholders, 1821*, P.R.O.N.I. T.2915/14/1.

1821–2 he realized what was probably the maximum electoral potential of his estate, 420 freeholders. Thereafter, as has been seen, the number fell sharply, but this was nothing to do with the registration system, which he continued to handle with considerable skill. Between the 1821 by-election and the beginning of 1824, he registered no freeholders in Louth, presumably because of the uncertain health of Lady Ferrard, and only in Meath, where her health was immaterial, did he register a substantial number (89 in 1823[1]). It was not until after her death and the successful outcome of the by-election of February 1824 that he once again attended to his Louth registries, registering 66 freeholders in October 1824 and a further 27 in February 1825 (this 27 tallies roughly with the 28 freeholders on the 1824 list who had been registered eight years previously, in 1817, and whose registries were about to expire in any case).[2] In April 1825, John Leslie Foster wrote from London to warn him that a Franchise Bill was under consideration which would raise the qualification for the freehold franchise, but preserve all existing 40/– freeholders for the duration of their registries (this abortive bill was one of the celebrated 'Wings' of the contemporary Emancipation Bill). He therefore urged his uncle 'to re-register all expiring voters without a moment's delay'.[3] It was no doubt this report which induced Lord Roden to re-register his 224 in May 1825. It had no such effect on Oriel, who presumably did not want to run the risk that his depleted force of 270 freeholders (as compared with the 420 of 1822) would be incapacitated at the next general election by immature registry—as Roden's 224 very nearly were. Ignoring Foster's advice and Roden's example, Oriel registered no freeholders until after the election was over, and then renewed the registries of the whole 270 in two large instalments, one in September 1826 and the other in December.[4]

Although on this occasion, and indeed throughout the period 1817–27, Oriel always guessed right, handling the registration system was nonetheless a guessing-game in which the stakes were uncomfortably high, and it is not surprising

[1] List of Oriel's freeholders in co. Meath to be registered, 1823, F.P. D.562/ 14698.
[2] Statement of how Oriel's tenantry voted, [*c.* July 1826], ibid. /14698.
[3] J. L. Foster to Oriel, 12 Apr. 1825, F.P. D.207/74/144.
[4] *Louth Freeholders, 1827*, P.R.O.N.I. T.2915/14/6.

to find him complaining of its impolicy during the debate in Parliament on his Irish budget of 1804.[1] Yet, because of its complexities, because of the value of inside information about the timing of general elections or the likelihood of changes in the franchise, and because of the provision which existed for adjournments of sessions to any market town (for example, Collon or Dunleer), it is obvious that the system must have redounded to the advantage of the leading interests in any county, and to the disadvantage of the minor interests and the substantial yeomanry. The psychological effect of the registration processions from the great estates to the nearest market town, must have been considerable in itself; which perhaps suggests one contributory reason for the failure of most of the great landlords to re-establish their old pre-eminence when the qualification for the franchise was raised to £10 in 1829. If the registration system had a purifying effect on elections, it did not have a democratizing one. Individual voters who were not organized by their landlords or who, like many of the Dundalk freeholders, were independent of landlord control, probably had little idea of how it worked. A case in point is a Dundalk freeholder called John McCollum, who was an excise officer frequently consulted by Foster and employed by him as a clerk in the Irish Exchequer Office in London in 1805. A letter McCollum wrote Foster at the time of the 1806 Louth election shows that even a man of his education, intelligence, and standing completely misunderstood the system.[2] If he was in the dark, how much more so must ordinary, barely literate 40/– freeholders have been—until of course the Catholic Association enlightened them in the years between 1826 and 1829. The registration fee, which stood at 4/– in 1805, was in itself a deterrent. It was the custom on the large estates for the landlord to pay this fee, just as he paid the costs of executing freeholder leases;[3] and here again the system favoured the more

[1] *Parl. Debs.*, ii. 881 f.

[2] Foster to Pitt, 29 June 1805, Chatham MSS., P.R.O. 30/8/328, fol. 65; McCollum to Foster, 3 Nov. 1806, F.P. D.562/4339.

[3] Anonymous letter to Vesey FitzGerald, 20 May 1813, Vesey FitzGerald MSS., N.L.I. MS. 7818, pp. 301–2. This letter states that the registration fees for 40/– freeholders were always paid by their landlords, and implies that those of £20 and £50 freeholders were not. On the Abercorn estate some attempt was made to get 'the most respectable tenantry' to pay their own fees—with what success is unclear. The great majority of the Abercorn tenants certainly had their fees paid

affluent leading interests at the expense of the minor ones. Another deterrent was religious scruples about swearing on the Book, which was a necessary part of the registration process for all freeholders except Quakers, who by a special concession were allowed to make an affirmation. Large landlords could, and did, overcome these scruples by threatening their tenants with the usual 'marks of displeasure';[1] but small men independent of landlord control presumably stuck to their guns, and stayed away.

The need for inspired guesswork and the 'distressing casualties' of the 1826 election, when Oriel lost 105 votes out of his reduced total of 270 through the most trivial technicalities of wording, should be treated as isolated instances of the registration system working to his disadvantage. The 'distressing casualties' were the result of pure carelessness; and in a county where there had not been a contest since 1768, it is not surprising that mistakes had crept into the registries. Up to then he had probably benefited greatly from the carelessness and the mistakes of others. At the time of the 1806 general election, for example, when, it is true, he had allowed his own registries to dwindle to only 60, the minor county interests who collectively constituted the independent interest could muster only a couple of freeholders each; this applied even to Balfour, who was a major interest and a short-lived candidate at the election.[2] In the years between 1820 and Oriel's compromise with the independent interest in 1825, defective registry on the part of the latter (and of Lord Clermont, who had only 13 freeholders in 1821 and 40 in 1824) seems to have been a major factor in saving Oriel from a contest which he might not have won. In general, the adverse effects of the registration system on a leading county interest—be it Lords Erne, Mountjoy, Abercorn,

for them—see James Hamilton to Abercorn, 21 Aug. 1805, 13 Jan. and 14 Dec. 1809, Abercorn MSS., P.R.O.N.I. T.2541/IA2/14/6, 15/1, 18/23. Lord Palmerston tried initially to get his tenants to pay the costs of executing the freeholder leases, but had to abandon the attempt; it is not clear whether in the end he paid the registration fees also.

[1] James Hamilton to Abercorn, 19 Dec. 1809, 2 and 27 Jan., and 24 Feb. 1810, ibid. 18/23-5, 35. On Matthew Fortescue of Stephenstown's estate, 18 out of 32 £10 freeholders refused to register in 1830, possibly on religious grounds (Fortescue to William Lewery, 4 Sept. 1830, Pyke-Fortescue MSS., P.R.O.I.).

[2] Rochfort to Foster, 30 May 1806, F.P. D.207/33/95; 1806 election correspondence, F.P. D.562/4332-73.

or Oriel—are easy to document, while the beneficial effects
are not. The main beneficial effect lay in the number of small
interests or individual voters whom the system either discouraged
or effectively prevented from voting in elections. In Louth,
which up to at least 1815 had an abnormally low registered
electorate, even in proportion to its small size, this factor
was probably very important.

From the point of view of a leading county interest, therefore,
the advantages of the registration system on the whole outweighed the disadvantages. In any case, the system was something which all leading interests had equally to contend with—
like the economic dangers of 'political agronomy'—and was
not unique to Foster. Where Foster was, if not unique, at
least a little unusual, was in the extent of his indebtedness.
As things turned out, his indebtedness never quite reached
crisis point; he did not, for example, suffer the misfortune of
that princely bankrupt, the 2nd Earl Verney, who lost the
Buckinghamshire election of 1784 because his opponents displayed his recently distrained furniture on the hustings.[1]
However, Foster's indebtedness was at least a confusing and
compromising factor in his local interest, and on balance probably counteracted the exceptional advantages he enjoyed
through the structure and situation of the Foster estate.

Since at least 1740 the Foster family had never been free
of debt; their indebtedness, as has been seen, was almost inherent in their newness as a family. However, it was not until
John Foster's time, and in particular until 1792, when he borrowed in one go sums totalling £23,000 from the banking
family of La Touche,[2] that the situation became alarming.
The subscription at the time of the Union gave unwelcome
publicity to his financial difficulties, but in the end brought
no relief. In 1805, ironically at the very time when he was
introducing the Irish budget at Westminster, his stock at
Collon came near to being distrained by the sheriff of Louth
in satisfaction of several judgement debts. At this stage his

---

[1] Lady Verney (ed.) *Verney Letters of the Eighteenth Century from the MSS. at Claydon House* (2 vols., London, 1930), ii. 281. Verney was eligible to be a candidate in an English election because he was an Irish peer.

[2] Brief in Lord Massereene v. Lord Ferrard, 1838, F.P. D.1739/3/15. Unless otherwise attributed, the succeeding information about the Fosters' finances is drawn from this source.

total debts amounted to at least £50,000,[1] of which £16,000 represented the unpaid marriage settlements of his aunt and his daughter. By 1810 the figure had increased to £72,000. Advantage was, therefore, taken of Thomas Foster's marriage at the end of the year, to draw up a comprehensive family settlement which was intended to disentangle once and for all the mesh of indebtedness by making both John and Thomas Foster tenants-for-life of the vast majority of the Foster estate. No statement is available of the relative value of the property settled and left unsettled in 1810; but in 1838 the former was bringing in £6,349 a year net and the latter £1,469. Since these figures exclude land which was unsettled because it had been bought in the period between 1810 and 1838, they give a good idea of the ratio of settled to unsettled property established in 1810. The settled property was charged with mortgage debts incurred under the previous family settlement of 1777, and amounting to £28,000; the unsettled with the remainder of the Fosters' debts—£44,000 in all.

The intention and the effect of the settlement was drastically to reduce John and Thomas Foster's borrowing power (and, as has been seen, their freedom to manœuvre in Drogheda politics). It gave them no authority to increase the debt of £28,000 on the settled property, except for the specific purpose of raising a sum of £5,000 as a provision for Thomas Foster's younger children. At the same time, it considerably decreased the size of their unsettled property, by settling for the first time land which John or Thomas Foster had held in fee prior to 1810, and upon which they had been able, because they held it in fee, to run up mortgage or judgement debts. A mortgage debt was a debt secured upon a particular piece of land: a judgement debt was a debt which was a lien on the debtor's freehold pro-

---

[1] J. L. Foster to Foster, 3 and 13 May 1805, F.P. D.562/1634, 1619. At the end of the previous year, Lord Redesdale had written, no doubt with much exaggeration: Foster's '. . . necessities are so great, whilst his dishonesty is so notorious, that no man would pay for his patents [of office], which therefore passed the Seal so as to make his seat in Parliament questionable; and he lives in a ready-furnished house, though he has a much better house in Dublin unfurnished, the sheriff having stripped it by executions, no tradesmen being willing to trust him for new furniture, and the owner of the house knowing that if a chair or a table belonging to him [the owner] were put into it, a new execution would sweep away the article the next day. . . .' (Redesdale to Perceval, 17 Dec. 1804, Redesdale MSS., P.R.O.N.I. T.3030/7/30.)

perty in general. The Fosters' £44,000 worth of debt was a mixture of both, although judgement debts predominated. With the consent of their creditors this now became a charge solely on the land left unsettled by the 1810 settlement, which was designated as 'indemnity' land, and was if necessary to be sold in order to satisfy the demands upon it. No doubt the creditors only agreed to accept this lesser security in the expectation that sales of land would soon follow. If so, they were to be disappointed, because none of the indemnity land had in fact been sold even by 1838. Prestige and politics combined to prepossess the Fosters against selling, if by shuffling and procrastination they could stave it off. Yet without selling, they could only with the greatest difficulty keep up interest payments on their various borrowings. In 1825, for example, when Lord Oriel was hoping to be able to raise a loan of £20,000, John Leslie Foster wrote discouragingly to him: '. . . there is not a doubt that you could satisfy the most fastidious lender as to the principal, by the assignment of the certain securities affecting your estate. But as to the interest, I do not see how you can meet their terms. . . .' The problem was that any lender would require security 'which the family settlements would not admit of', and that there was 'no unsettled estate to resort to'.[1]

The difficulty of keeping up interest payments was accentuated by the post-war slump in agricultural prices, which tended to render obsolete a settlement conceived at a time of war-time optimism; in or around 1820 the net rental of the Foster estate was just under £9,000,[2] but by 1838 it had dropped to roughly £8,000. The difficulty was further accentuated by John Foster's retirement from office in 1811, followed by Thomas Foster's dismissal from it two years later. This meant not only a loss of income but a loss of borrowing power. Office, though it failed to resolve the Fosters' financial difficulties, had at least provided the short-term advantage of extended credit. Dublin bankers did not under normal circumstances lend on mortgage

---

[1] J. L. Foster to Oriel, 5 Nov. 1825, F.P. D.207/74/173.

[2] Rental of the Foster estate, [c. 1820], F.P. D.562/14568. Unfortunately no rental has survived for the period when the settlement was drawn up. This 1820 rental at first sight looks as if it relates to an earlier period, because it is undated and written on paper marked 1805. However, it includes a small estate called Funshog which the Fosters did not acquire until roughly 1820 (J. L. Foster to Oriel, 19 Nov. 1822, F.P. D.207/74/123).

to private individuals;[1] yet the La Touches had lent large sums to Foster, partly no doubt because of private friendship and community of political sentiment,[2] but partly perhaps because Foster, with influence over the placing of government loans and lotteries, was a man who could profitably be singled out for special treatment. Foster's command of other forms of patronage had also no doubt recommended him to many people with money to lend, as a person whom it might be worthwhile to place under an obligation. Certainly, as has been seen, a suspiciously high proportion of the more valuable patronage at his disposal went to people to whom he owed money.[3] It would be unsubtle to conclude from this that he repaid in patronage what he could not repay in cash. Many of these people were personal friends to whom it was only natural that Foster, as a fairly bad risk, should have had to turn for financial help; and it was equally natural that he should have wanted to use his patronage for the benefit of his friends. Because his private credit had been strengthened by his public situation, his departures from office, or at least from the government fold, tended to precipitate crises in his financial affairs. Shortly after he went into opposition in 1799, his anti-Unionist allies found it necessary to pass the hat round for him; shortly after he was extruded from office in 1806, he found himself compelled to sell his life-pension in compensation for the abolition of the speakership; and shortly after John and Thomas Foster's final departure from office in the period 1811–13, John Leslie Foster could see that, true to form, another 'crash' was 'impending'.[4] To avert the crash, the whole Foster estate, whether settled or indemnity property, was conveyed in trust to the Fosters' kinsman, Lord Chief Justice Downes, afterwards 1st Lord Downes. The trust was to last for the life of John Foster, and during its existence Downes was to satisfy the demands for interest payments,

[1] Large, *Irish Landowners*, pp. 22 f.
[2] Foster to Peter La Touche, 31 July 1809, F.P. T.2519/4/1636. The La Touches were strongly anti-Emancipationist; all but one of them were anti-Unionists; and Foster and they were also united in wanting an absentee tax in 1797–8.
[3] Some of them were political allies as well, for example, Edward Hardman. See Wellesley to Foster, 28 Oct. 1807, F.P. D.207/35/24, and Hardman to Foster, 18 Feb. 1811, F.P. D.562/12684.
[4] J. L. Foster to Foster, 20 Jan. 1814, F.P. D.207/74/3.

pay Thomas Foster's maintenance of £1,680, and allow John Foster the residue. Yet, drastic though this measure was, it produced little or no improvement in the Fosters' financial situation. In 1838, ten years after the expiration of the trust, the debts still stood at £72,000.

Financial difficulties inevitably had an adverse effect on a political interest, and if the difficulties were acute the effect could be disastrous. For example, Lord Clanbrassill's Louth estate was placed under a receivership by the Court of Chancery in 1780, because he had allowed an arrear of £6,000 to accrue on a mortgage debt of £40,000.[1] Receiverships could be politically disastrous, because they severed the link between landlord and tenant, and compromised the authority of the former. The Fosters avoided one, firstly, because they did their best to ensure that every mortgage on their estate was 'vested in a friend';[2] and secondly, because they submitted voluntarily, before worse befell, to a trusteeship exercised by a friend of their own choosing. Nevertheless, all their ingenuity could not prevent debts on the scale of theirs from trenching upon their political interest. Even a friendly and patient mortgagee was a nuisance politically, because his name had to feature on every lease affecting the part of the estate where his mortgage lay. Almost all of the Foster estate was affected by mortgages, and several parts of it by more than one. This made the execution of leases a slow business, although the requirements of the registration system made it desirable that they should be executed with the minimum of delay. With the setting up of the trust in 1814, the process was further slowed up by the need to make Lord Downes a party to every lease.[3]

In other respects, too, the trusteeship proved politically inconvenient. No doubt it was all to the good that Downes's heir and successor as trustee, the 2nd Lord Downes, restrained Lord Oriel from making English tenants of his recalcitrant freeholders in 1826, since the economic effects of such an action, to say nothing of the adverse publicity which the Catholic Association would have given it, were bound to be damaging.

[1] *Statement of Lord Roden's Title*, pp. 235–45.
[2] George Pentland to Oriel, 4 Dec. 1822, F.P. D.562/14047. One mortgagee was certainly an enemy—Ogle, whose family held a mortgage on the Foster estate from at least 1778 to 1810.
[3] J. L. Foster to Oriel, 1 May 1822, F.P. D.207/74/107.

However, Oriel had been indiscreet enough to declare to the tenants concerned that he intended to wreak this form of vengeance; which meant, as he himself lamented to Lord Downes's agent, that '. . . my character is involved, if your delay shall receive the construction which it naturally must, that I hesitate to act or enforce the intentions I have declared . . .'[1] Nor was this the only respect in which the trusteeship interfered with his political authority over his tenantry. Just before the election, Lord Downes's solicitor had made a most unfortunate blunder by posting a notice to the tenantry in which he referred to the Foster estate as 'the estates late of the Rt. Hon. Lord Oriel'. How he ever made such a silly slip is hard to imagine; but the slip, for all its silliness, was a contributory factor to the Fosters' discomfiture, although it was great hyperbole in Oriel to say that 'it nearly proved fatal to John Leslie's election'.[2] At a time when the tenants were torn between the distress-warrant and the Cross, it was unfortunate that anything should have happened to weaken the deterrent power of the former.

Financial difficulties had a further and more obvious effect on the Foster interest, in that they prevented the Fosters from increasing their territorial stake in Louth. The vast majority of their estate in both Louth and Meath had been acquired in the period up to 1750, before they ever sat or attempted to sit for Louth. Thereafter, they made only small additions to the estate. Some of their rivals in Louth were not under similar restrictions. Lord Clermont, for example, was showing interest in expanding his Louth property in the early nineteenth century. So too, either at this time or later, were the Bellews, who bought the Dunleer estate which had formerly belonged to the Fosters' old landlords there, the Tenisons, and which had been warmly recommended to the Fosters as well-situated to round off their own Dunleer estate.[3] It was not, however, either the Bellews or Lord Clermont who caused the main flurry

---

[1] Oriel to W. P. Greene, 3 Dec. 1826, F.P. T.2519/4/1609.

[2] *Notice from W. H. Griffith to the Tenants on Lord Oriel's Estate*, 6 June 1826; Oriel to Griffith, 4 July 1826, F.P. D.562/5074, 5077.

[3] Memorandum about Killaly, co. Louth, [c. 1 July 1813], Pyke-Fortescue MSS., P.R.O.I.; Pentland to Oriel, 30 Nov. 1825, F.P. D.562/14437; Pentland to Foster, 18 Aug. 1819, F.P. D.562/13329; rough abstracts of the Massereene title to lands in Louth and Meath, [c. 1880], F.P. Chilham deed room.

in the land market in Louth; it was a number of newcomers to the county, prominent among whom were Edward Callaghan or O'Callaghan, who was probably a conformed Catholic,[1] and a rich West Indian merchant called Thomas Fitzgerald, who established himself at Fane Valley, co. Louth. Both were active during the early 1820s in buying land and building up freeholders, and both were Emancipationists. In 1822 Callaghan had no freeholders to his name, but by 1824 he had 100; and Fitzgerald boasted that he had £60,000 to lay out on land in co. Louth, and seems to have made his purchases primarily for the political interest they carried with them.[2] He must have spent his money to good effect, because at the general election of 1833 he realized his ambition to represent the county.

Just as changes in the landownership of Louth had heralded the political emergence of the Fosters in the 1740s, so similar changes, only this time in an unwelcome direction, heralded their eclipse. The newcomers were doing their purchasing in the years 1815–21, the very period when the registered Louth electorate was making its dramatic ascent from 850 to 2,830; and it is hardly fanciful to associate the newcomers with this movement. By 1822 the Fosters recognized that '. . . without some material exertions on our part, our interest will soon be in a more critical situation than we have hitherto contemplated. . . .'[3] One exertion, however, of which they were virtually incapable, was increasing their own territorial strength. They did, it is true, acquire in 1820 or 1821 a small estate capable of being stocked with thirty or forty freeholders. But with this single exception, the only territorial boost which their interest received in this period came from the considerable purchases of land made by Lord Oriel's nephew by marriage, William Drummond Delap, another rich West Indian. In 1820, for example, Delap spent £31,000 on an estate which had previously been in the hands of an antagonist of the Fosters, and he may

---

[1] J. L. Foster to Oriel, 19 Nov. 1822, F.P. D.207/74/123. J. L. Foster called him 'O'Callaghan', but the printed freeholders' lists of the 1820s do not use the 'O'. There were O'Callaghans in co. Louth, but they had a long tradition of attachment to the Foster interest.

[2] D'Alton, *Dundalk*, pp. 226, 234 ff.; Pentland to Foster, 27 Apr. and 18 Aug. 1819, F.P. D.562/13290, 13329.

[3] J. L. Foster to Oriel, 19 Dec. 1822, F.P. D.207/74/123.

have made other purchases as well.¹ Nevertheless, his activities were not of themselves sufficient to redress the balance. The compromise of 1825 with the independent interest was almost certainly inspired by the recognition that, by then, a higher proportion of the land in co. Louth than ever before was in the hands of politically active and potentially hostile landowners. Since financial difficulties precluded Oriel from counteracting this process by buying more land, he had no alternative but to ally himself with the least objectionable of his rivals.

Financial difficulties had the final effect of depriving him of flexibility and resilience in the matter of election expenditure. Election expenditure is a term capable of almost indefinite extension. For example, it can be made to comprise all the methods resorted to by an M.P. to nurse a constituency in between elections—donations to local charities, reductions of rent to give tenants a 40/– qualification, disposal to others of jobs worthy of a gentleman's acceptance which might well have been given to a member of his own family, and so on. Extended this far, the term ceases to mean anything. Indeed, it only has meaning if confined to money spent on actual elections or on petitions arising out of them. The most striking point about the Foster interest in co. Louth is that it required only minimal election expenditure in this sense of the term. During the seventy years of their ascendancy, the Fosters had to shoulder the burden of one short-lived election petition and of only three contests—leaving out of the reckoning the contests of 1755 and 1835, which fall outside the period of their ascendancy. Few county interests of anything like their longevity got off so lightly.

Like figures for freeholders, figures for election expenditure are not easy to come by, and the subject lends itself much more than that of freeholders to inflated estimates. Lord Sligo was very probably exaggerating when he informed the Castle in 1802 that it had cost his family '£50,000 and fifty years of constant residence, to obtain the representation of Mayo'.²

---

¹ J. L. Foster to Foster, 25 Jan. 1819, and Thomas Skeffington to Foster, 14 June 1820, F.P. D.207/74/53, T.2519/4/1722. The antagonist was Wallop Brabazon of Dunany, a relation and political ally of Balfour.

² Sligo to Marsden, 21 July 1802, S.P.O. 620/18A/7. By 'representation' Sligo seems to have meant both seats for Mayo, which he claimed that he had controlled up to the 1802 general election.

The figures for the expenditure on the notorious co. Down election of 1790 have been removed from the realms of pure legend, and it appears that that election and its 1805 sequel cost the Downshire family something in the region of £60,000[1] (the 1797 and 1802 general elections were uncontested in Down). It certainly cost the Beresford family £15,000 to fight the 1826 election in their traditional stronghold of co. Waterford against even more formidable opposition than the Fosters met in Louth, and unlike the Fosters they lost the election.[2] Also unlike the Fosters, they came back fighting at the general election of 1830, and this time they won, though at what cost is unrecorded. At that same election the enormously wealthy 3rd Marquess of Hertford offered his candidate in co. Antrim a float of £20,000 'for a commencement of a canvass', and 'support in money without limit'.[3] As in the matter of acreage, it may seem absurd to compare the Fosters, for whom an expenditure of a few hundred pounds in the mid-1820s was 'a serious consideration',[4] with these four Marquesses and great territorial magnates. At the same time, the four Marquesses (Sligo, Downshire, Waterford, and Hertford) are the Fosters' peers, in that they are among the few interests who possessed the same sort and length of hegemony in their respective counties of Mayo, Down, Waterford, and Antrim as the Fosters did in Louth.

To some extent, of course, the four Marquesses were just magnificent spenders—particularly Hertford—and perhaps spent beyond what the difference in scale between electioneering in their counties and in Louth necessarily required. For this reason, it is necessary to attempt a comparison between the Fosters and interests in other counties who did not have, proportionally, their territorial and numerical strength, but who were closer to the Fosters in the size of their estates and the extent of their means. Even when compared with these lesser

[1] Shannon to Boyle, 2 July 1790, Shannon MSS., P.R.O.N.I. D.2707/A/3/3/4; Jupp, *Co. Down Elections*, p. 183.

[2] George Meara to Primate Beresford, 3 July 1830, Pack-Beresford MSS., P.R.O.N.I. D.664/A/151.

[3] Hertford to Revd. William Cupples, 3 July 1830, Johnston-Smyth [Cupples] MSS., P.R.O.N.I. D.2099/5.

[4] Oriel to Ferrard, 2 Oct. 1825, F.P. D.562/3383. The remark was made, not about election expenditure, but about the fees on the patent of an earldom, after which at this time Oriel was pathetically hankering.

interests, the Fosters still got off lightly in the matter of election expenditure. Unfortunately, there is no information about what they spent on the by-elections of 1755 and 1767, but the £1,500 which was their half of the expenses of the 1768 general election, compares extremely favourably with the minimum of £1,700 which Claudius Hamilton, a defeated candidate in co. Tyrone in the same year, had spent before the poll even began. Tyrone of course had perhaps five times Louth's electorate in 1768: between 2,500 and 3,000 voters.[1] But Clare had a smaller electorate, and in Clare Sir Lucius O'Brien spent £2,000 in 1768, and won, while in Meath John Dutton spent £2,000 in the same year, and lost.[2] Neither of these candidates, it is true, had the advantage of the economies which a junction of interests must have made possible. All the same, the successful junction in co. Tyrone in 1768, James Stewart of Killymoon and Armar Lowry Corry, spent £3,000 each[3]—double what the Fosters spent at that election. None of these comparisons is straight, just as no two counties are identical. The comparisons are drawn at random, on the basis of what reliable figures for expenditure on the 1768 election are available, though they do in fact cover a fair spectrum of county constituencies. They suggest that the Fosters' expenditure in Louth, even allowing for the expense of the ensuing lawsuits, was nothing out of the ordinary. The other candidates in the comparison spent more on the actual election, and secured nothing like the Fosters' long-lived ascendancy in their respective counties, if indeed they or their families succeeded in the future in being elected at all. (The case of Armar Lowry Corry's family, it should be noted, is complicated by the fact that the head of the family was a peer from 1781 onwards, and the eldest son a minor between 1781 and 1795, and again between 1802 and 1822.) The only candidate in the comparison who at all

[1] Claudius Hamilton to Abercorn, 29 June 1768, Abercorn MSS., P.R.O.N.I. T.2541/IA1/8/71.

[2] O'Brien to Charlemont, 2 June 1775, *H.M.C. Charlemont MSS.*, i. 330; co. Clare poll book, 1768, Inchiquin MSS., N.L.I. MS. 14793; Large, *Irish Land-owners*, p. 43. The number of votes cast at the 1768 Clare election was 496, of whom 48 were disallowed on a scrutiny. I have found no figure for the Meath poll in that year, but in 1781 the registered electorate of the county stood at 2,243— P.R.O.I. M.1364.

[3] Account of Stewart's and Corry's expenses on the co. Tyrone election, 1768, Stewart MSS., P.R.O.N.I. D.3167/2/10.

resembles Foster in his future role in his county is Lowry Corry's partner at the 1768 election, James Stewart of Killymoon: he sat for Tyrone, uninterruptedly and without contest, from 1768 to 1812, and bowed out in the latter year when a contest which he would have lost was imminent.[1] He also resembled Foster in the less healthy respect that he would have been financially very vulnerable if he had had to fight another contest during his tenure of the seat.

Because there was no contest in Louth between 1768 and 1826, it is not absolutely clear what the effect of one would have been. However, events in Drogheda provide some indication. The £2,500 which Thomas Foster spent in 1807, he could just about afford at that point in time, because by the terms of the family settlement of 1777 he was due to inherit the Foster estate in fee on the death of his father.[2] This remainder in fee enabled him to run up debts—no doubt he had to in order to win the 1807 election—and at least placed him on a firmer financial footing than the other possible contenders for the Drogheda seat. The settlement of 1810, however, changed all this by giving him nothing more than a tenancy-for-life to look forward to, which left him in what his brother-in-law, Lord Dufferin, later called a state of 'perfect thraldom'.[3] His position was nonetheless more enviable than his father's. He could always hope that his eldest son, to whom the estate would descend in fee after his death, would be prepared when he came of age to execute a re-settlement letting Thomas Foster's personal debts in upon the settled property. Such re-settlements were not uncommon, and money could be, and in Thomas Foster's case was, raised in anticipation of them— this was what caused the sordid lawsuit of 1838 between Thomas Foster, then Lord Ferrard, and his eldest son, Lord Massereene. To John Foster, however, no such recourse lay open, because he was almost certain to be dead before Thomas Foster's eldest son came of age. This explains why John Foster, though the head of the family and far and away its leading political light, was unable to prevail on Thomas Foster to contest Drogheda in 1812 and again in 1818 (if, indeed, he

[1] *Address from Stewart to the Electors of co. Tyrone*, 20 Oct. 1812, ibid. /2/227.
[2] Statement of John Foster's title, 12 May 1808, F.P. D.207/8/6.
[3] Dufferin to Ferrard, 25 Aug. 1831, F.P. T.2519/4/2127.

really wanted him to). Neither father nor son held the family purse strings after 1810, but the son came nearer to doing so than the father. The result was that Thomas Foster's unadventurous policy towards Drogheda was the course pursued. It was almost certainly the right policy in any case. What is striking about the Fosters' expenditure on Drogheda in 1807 is that, like their expenditure on Louth in 1768, it was fairly modest. In 1807 it would have cost Thomas Foster £5,000 to have been returned for a close borough whose patron had offered the nomination to the Government, and even then he would have been subject to a 'positive restriction of supporting their measures'.[1] It may be that it cost him a further £2,500 to nurse Drogheda during the life of the 1807 Parliament; but even so, it was a matter of no small importance to a family circumstanced as the Fosters were, whether they were called upon for £5,000 at one go, or in easy stages. At a co. Donegal by-election in 1808, when the maximum electorate was 2,600, it was reckoned that the contest would cost the winner between £6,000 and £8,000;[2] and this is not an unreasonable sum, granted the superior prestige of representing a county as opposed to a close borough.

In other words, and to put it at its bluntest, the Fosters were in Parliament on the cheap. This was true even of Drogheda, and especially true of Louth, where their uncontested return must have cost them each time only a few hundred pounds on fees to the sheriff and on a token 'treat'. The effect of the Union in increasing the value of the remaining Irish seats and the pressure upon them, has already been discussed; the sums which candidates were prepared to spend, particularly on county elections, had presumably increased accordingly (not that there was ever much logic in such matters).[3] This meant that

---

[1] John Maxwell Barry to Foster, 1 May 1807, and Sligo to Foster, 2 May 1807, F.P. D.207/52/17, 70/19.

[2] James Hamilton to Abercorn, 5 Jan. and 1 Feb. 1808, Abercorn MSS., P.R.O.N.I. T.2541/2/17/1, 10.

[3] It would be logical to assume that the actual cost of contesting elections rose in proportion to the rise in county electorates after 1793. But the figures already quoted for the 1768 election suggest that there was no strong correlation between cost and size of electorate: in particular, Sir Lucius O'Brien's £2,000 spent on an electorate of only 440 (allowed voters) sounds like very bad value. Again, the celebrated co. Armagh by-election of 1753 cost William Brownlow £5,000 (excluding the presumably enormous cost of the subsequent petition) on an

the Fosters, with their notorious financial difficulties and limited ability to face a contest, had become something of a freak among Irish parliamentary families, especially among county members who enjoyed anything like their longevity. The notoriety of their financial difficulties is an important point. It was not uncommon for families so circumstanced to be deliberately frightened out of their county seat, or at least forced into sharing it, by a weaker interest with a longer purse.[1] In Louth there must have been several purses longer than the Fosters'. The Rodens and the Balfours, it is true, were themselves in financial difficulties. But the Bellews do not seem to have been so; the Emancipationist newcomers with political ambitions cannot have been so; and Lord Clermont, who was hostile to the Fosters from 1809 to 1824, certainly was not. To this extent, the Foster interest survived for the good, negative reason that nobody between 1768 and 1826 opposed it. There is no information about the Fosters' expenditure in 1826, but the fact that the popular candidate spent at least £2,000 gives some idea of its likely level. After the 1826 contest the Fosters lay low (although they had other than financial reasons for doing so), and when they took the field again at the 1835 general election the ensuing expenditure contributed to the most serious financial crisis they had yet undergone, which culminated in the 1838 lawsuit. This epilogue to the Foster interest in Louth, though

electorate of less than 600; this compares very favourably with the presumptive cost of the co. Donegal by-election of 1808, which seems to have been a no less bitter contest and was fought on a much higher electorate (account of Brownlow's expenses in 1753, P.R.O.N.I. T.2718/1). It is probable that the unenfranchised tenants of at least the leading interests were included in the freeholders' 'treats'; which would mean that election expenditure would not necessarily rise if and when the unenfranchised became enfranchised. (For example, in 1768 the Fosters and Fortescues paid for six times more dinners than there were voters at that election.) Also, the level of expenditure was surely dictated, not so much by the number, as by the status, of the voters? As has been seen, all but 57 of the 448 Clare voters were £10 freeholders. Such voters would expect to be 'treated' in the style to which they were accustomed; beer in the 18th century seems to have cost practically nothing, wine cost sums which bear some relation to present-day prices. In the matter of travel, too—which usually came next to the pubs in any election bill—voters of some substance would cost large sums in carriage-hire and turnpike tolls.

[1] See, for example, Dean Thomas Graves to Glandore, 29 June 1794, Talbot-Crosbie MSS., N.L.I. This letter describes, among other things, how H. A. Herbert of Muckruss, co. Kerry, was frightened into withdrawing from a by-election by the threat of expense.

ignominious, was appropriate. The Fosters had always lacked financial resilience. At any time since at least the 1790s, two contests which fell, like those of 1826 and 1835, within a comparatively short space of time, would almost certainly have chased them out of the representation of the county, since the annual charges on their estate were so high and their borrowing power so confined, that they were incapable of sudden, heavy expenditure. As it happened, the Foster interest was already eclipsed by the time financial prostration set in, but financial prostration might easily have been the cause of its eclipse.

This chapter has so far counted acres, examined registry books, and inquired into finances. In the first two respects the Fosters were either better endowed, or else no worse endowed, than any other leading county interest; in the last respect they were certainly worse endowed, but since their weakness was never exploited, this mattered little. Yet it has become plain that acres, freeholders, and money, even in combination with 'jobs of all sorts', do not fully account for the longevity of the Foster interest in Louth. In an important sense, the Fosters were elected by default: a large proportion of the potential electorate of the county remained unregistered until at least 1815 and, both before and after that date, circumstances did not favour the formation of an opposition powerful enough to defeat them. What was decisive in Louth politics up to 1821 and indeed beyond, was not real estate factors, but John Foster's personal calibre and personal venerability. If a member of the Fortescue or Jocelyn family, rather than Foster, had possessed these personal attributes, he rather than Foster would no doubt have been the dominant interest in the county, in spite of Foster's superiority in freeholders. The personal attributes of the candidates had always been an important factor in Louth elections. In 1767, when Foster was nothing but the eldest son of the biggest single interest in the county, his claims to the seat were admitted by the independent interest, and he would not have been opposed in 1768 if he had been available to stand in 1767, or if the Fosters had not persisted—quite rightly, as things turned out—in setting up the ridiculous Sibthorpe. (Equally ridiculous was the candidature of Lord Jocelyn in 1806, and this would have produced a contest but for the strength of Lord Roden's registry at that time.) When to Foster's local claims as the representative of the biggest political interest in the county were added his subsequent claims on national grounds, he became an extremely strong candidate. With the passage of time, the length of his service as M.P. for Louth almost became a claim in itself. Just as, in the period 1785–1800, it would have been an extreme step to oppose the Speaker, so in the period after 1811, when the Foster interest was much more vulnerable, it would have been an extreme step to oppose a member of Foster's standing, who had expressed no notion of retiring, and who ultimately became the Father of the House. It would also have been an extreme step to have opposed a man who was venerable, not just on account of the length of his service, but on account of the part he had played on the highly emotive question of the Union. In any case, in spite of the advanced age Foster had reached (eighty-one) by the time he retired, he was still credited with a certain amount of influence over economic measures affecting Ireland right up to the end,[1] and compared with the great majority of the faceless Irish members, was still an active and useful representative. His personal interest in Louth, in other words, remained dominant after his real or territorial interest had ceased to be so.

It was this kind of personal interest, or personal popularity, which in many counties determined that the leading interests were not to rotate in the county representation, but that one was to dominate it to something like the same extent as Foster. In co. Armagh, with its five fairly equally balanced interests (all of them as strong or stronger in real estate than Foster), it was the personal popularity of William Brownlow which determined that he should sit without contest or interruption from 1753 to his death in 1794. Significantly, Brownlow was the archetype of the independent country gentleman, and had missed being elected Speaker by only four votes in 1771. If

---

[1] See, for example, Peter La Touche to Foster, 12 July 1820, F.P. D.562/15981. Dr. A. J. B. Hilton informs me that Foster was probably the first person to suggest breaking with the traditional system of import duties on foreign corn, and to propose instead a system of 'contingent prohibition': total prohibition when home prices were below a certain level (84/– or 80/–), and total freedom to import when they were above it. Ministers objected to this device, but the English land-lords preferred it to the old system and it was enacted, at 80/–, in 1815. I am grateful to Dr. Hilton for his help on this and other points.

this is not proof in itself of the importance of his personal popularity, corroborative proof may be found in the facts that his son had to fight a contest in 1795 in order to win the seat at the by-election caused by his death, and had to decline a contest at the general election of 1797. Brownlow Senior is in one sense an unfair comparison with Foster, because he was usually on the opposition side over the popular issues of the day and, apart from his views on his constituents' right to instruct him, was usually a politically popular member: he is a fair comparison in the more important sense that he was a landlord of roughly the same size (though, granted that Armagh was much bigger than Louth, not of the same proportionate size), and that if attention were not drawn to his high personal calibre he would pass for just another landlord.[1] The same is true of John O'Neill, later 1st Viscount O'Neill, M.P. for co. Antrim, 1783–93. O'Neill was a landlord of much greater actual, and much smaller proportionate, acreage than Foster. But beyond giving him a head start over other popular candidates, his acreage had little to do with his election in 1783. He himself declared in an address of thanks that it had been 'inspired *by the bottom*', and at his next election, in 1790, both his colleague and he deliberately refrained from drawing 'materially' on the votes from their own estates. The principal ingredients in O'Neill's success were his (very moderate) Volunteering, his courting of the Presbyterian vote, his prestige as the representative of the kings of Ulster, his princely hospitality, and the perhaps unique independent-mindedness of the Antrim electorate.[2] The O'Neill family soon became established as the semi-hereditary representatives of Antrim, or divisions of Antrim; but this should not obscure their popular beginnings.

Moreover, the importance of personal popularity can be seen even more clearly in the case of some exceptional county members, who were much smaller landlords, in actual as well

[1] Malcomson, *Foster and the Speakership*, p. 278; Dr. Alexander Halliday to Charlemont, 31 Jan. 1795 and 13 July 1797, Charlemont MSS., R.I.A., 2nd ser., vii. 62, and viii. 45; Charlemont to James Stewart, 10 Aug. 1797, Stewart MSS., P.R.O.N.I. D.3167/1/68; O'Connell, *Politics and Social Conflict*, pp. 175 f.

[2] Mrs. McTier to Dr. William Drennan, [Sept. ? 1783], Drennan MSS., P.R.O.N.I. D.591/94; Halliday to Charlemont, 9 June 1790, Charlemont MSS., R.I.A., 2nd ser., v. 36.

as proportionate terms, than Foster, and yet enjoyed a considerable run in the representation of their counties. The example of James Stewart of Killymoon, M.P. for co. Tyrone from 1768 to 1812, has already been quoted; Stewart's long and uncontested run can be explained partly on the ground of the divisions which subsisted between the great county magnates, Lords Abercorn, Belmore, Caledon, and Northland, but mainly on the ground of his popularity among the gentry and the Presbyterian yeomanry and tenantry.[1] Co. Wexford, a county where there was no dominant proprietary interest, produced two colourful and, in proprietary terms, improbable, M.P.s in the last third of the eighteenth century: Sir Vesey Colclough, M.P. from 1766 to 1790, and George Ogle, M.P. from 1769 to 1797. Colclough was something of an old rogue, who cast off his legitimate issue, and lived with a mistress and their children in the family seat, which bore the Wordsworthian name Tintern Abbey, but was falling about their ears; shortly after his death, his estate was producing a mere £1,600 a year (and a mere 164 freeholders), though it had probably boasted a higher rental at the time he succeeded his father in the county representation.[2] Ogle, too, was in serious financial straits, having 'run out a very good estate'. He was a 'Patriot' M.P., but his interest in the county long survived his acceptance of a pension from the Government in 1784. His uncompromising opposition to Emancipation may have contributed to its eclipse, but almost immediately secured his election for the open but very Protestant constituency of Dublin City.[3] Clearly, both Colclough and Ogle possessed an appeal for their constituents which real estate factors cannot explain. The same is not so true of two other long-serving M.P.s with slender

[1] Address of the Presbyterian ministers and elders of the province of Ulster to Stewart, 28 June 1782; John Stewart to Stewart, 12 May 1796; Stewart's calculations of his income and expenditure, Jan. 1804; and newspaper cutting about Stewart's being driven out of the representation of Tyrone by 'mighty Lords', [post 20 Oct. 1812]—Stewart MSS., P.R.O.N.I. D.3167/2/37, 122, 180, 229.

[2] John to Caesar Colclough, 30 Jan. and 5 Feb. 1795, and 17 Nov. 1796; Caesar Colclough to Messrs. Reeves, 9 Dec. 1796—Colclough (McPeake) MSS., P.R.O.N.I. T.3048/C/18.

[3] Lady Courtown to Sydney, 4 Aug. [1782], Sydney MSS., N.L.I. MS. 52/K/1B; Blaquiere to Jenkinson, 14 July 1780, Liverpool MSS., B.L. Add. MS. 38214, fols. 95–6; Johnston, *Irish Parliament, 1784–7*, p. 195; John to Caesar Colclough, 4 Apr. 1796, Colclough MSS., P.R.O.N.I. T.3048/C/18; Bolton, *Union*, p. 73.

proprietary pretensions: Charles O'Hara, M.P. for co. Sligo from 1783 to 1822, and the Knight of Kerry, M.P. for Kerry, 1795–1831. O'Hara was not a large landlord, and his estate was so heavily encumbered that he actually lacked the £600-freehold qualification necessary for a county member; the curious feature of Sligo politics was that O'Hara was the candidate of the independent interest, but was also backed by the Earl of Kingston, who was probably the largest proprietor in the county.[1] Much the same applied to the Knight of Kerry. He owned a few thousand much-encumbered acres, but attracted independent support through his ability and charm, and, more practically, the support of the largest county magnate, the Earl of Kenmare. The important point in both cases is that there were plenty of other candidates competing for the support of Lords Kingston and Kenmare, and personal factors almost certainly caused the preference to be given to O'Hara and the Knight of Kerry (the Knight of Kerry even succeeded in retaining the regard of O'Connell until he joined the Duke of Wellington's Government in 1830).[2] Like the Knight of Kerry's, Vesey FitzGerald's Emancipationist politics were a vital asset in an overwhelmingly Catholic constituency; but in Clare as in Kerry, every serious candidate had to be an Emancipationist, and the wonder is not that Vesey FitzGerald was outrun by O'Connell in 1828, but that as a smallish and heavily encumbered landlord, he succeeded in holding his seat against large proprietary interests between 1818 and that date.[3] Likewise, real estate factors do not explain why General G. V. Hart, a very small co. Donegal landlord (or rather head tenant) held a county seat against the large proprietary interests there from 1812 to 1832.[4]

[1] Sir Henry King to O'Hara, 2 Jan. 1783; Dr. Walker King to O'Hara, 3 Dec. 1800; O'Hara to King, [?4] Jan. 1803; half-year's rental of O'Hara's estate, Nov. 1814; Daniel Webber to Charles K. O'Hara (O'Hara's son and successor), 12 Aug. 1824—O'Hara MSS., N.L.I.

[2] Memoir of Maurice FitzGerald, Knight of Kerry, by his son, Peter, Knight of Kerry, Feb. 1868; Kenmare to Knight of Kerry, 3 Jan. 1796 and 12 Aug. 1811; O'Connell to Knight of Kerry, 15 May 1815 and 7 Apr. 1830—FitzGerald MSS., 5/83, 10/64, 82, 13/14.

[3] Vesey FitzGerald to J. O. Vandeleur, 10 June 1817; William Stamer to Vesey FitzGerald, 11 May 1818; E. S. Hickman to Vesey FitzGerald, 19 Feb. 1820—Vesey FitzGerald MSS., N.L.I. MSS. 7853, pp. 240–2, 7854, pp. 126–8, and 7858, pp. 68–9.

[4] Hart to his brother, John, 9 Oct. 1812, Hart MSS., P.R.O.N.I. D.3077,

These exceptional county members do not compare with Foster as landlords: they have been discussed merely to illustrate that, in certain circumstances, personal popularity could prevail, even when not accompanied by significant landlordism, just as the cases of Brownlow and O'Neill illustrate that significant landlordism was not decisive unless accompanied by personal popularity. In counties where none of the interests possessed personal popularity of this level, a rotation of interests in the county representation was the norm, with the lion's share going to the interest which was prepared to spend most time, trouble, and money on electioneering. There were only a few counties where one landlord owned such a high proportion of the land that he could hold one seat in an unshakeable grip through the votes of his own tenantry alone. Examples, and probably an exhaustive list, are co. Kildare, the Duke of Leinster's stronghold; co. Wicklow, that of the absentee Lord Fitzwilliam; and co. Down, that of the 'proud Leviathan',[1] Lord Downshire. Yet even in these three extreme cases, there were limits to the electoral authority of the landlords concerned. Leinster and Fitzwilliam were wont to boast that they could return both members for their respective counties, but both, during the eighteenth century, used their great influence almost invariably on behalf of other local families— the very people who would have opposed them if they had tried to make their boast good. There were six other landlords in co. Wicklow who would individually have been powerful in most other counties, and collectively could easily have kept the Fitzwilliams out of the second seat for Wicklow, if the Fitzwilliams had tried to pursue a monopolizing policy; and the Leinsters, in spite of the moderation of their policy, met with increasing opposition in co. Kildare as the century wore on, and were not altogether successful in controlling the people they claimed to return.[2] Even the Downshires, prior to

temporary bundle E/2. This letter, which seems to be written with complete candour, reveals among other things that Hart was surprised to find himself warmly supported by the leading proprietary interest, Lord Conyngham, and did not know why Conyngham had decided in his favour. They were both generals, and had been on the staff in Ireland at the same time, which probably had much to do with the decision, as did the minority of Conyngham's eldest son.

[1] Cornwallis to Ross, 24 Oct. 1799, *Cornwallis Correspondence*, iii. 141.
[2] The names of those returned for cos. Wicklow and Kildare during the 18th

1776, had been content to take their place in the usual kind
of rotation in the representation of their county; and their
dominance thereafter was due to the enormous trouble and
expense to which they were prepared to go, and in particular
to Lady Downshire's 'political agronomy'. Even after her
'political agronomy', the Downshire estate accounted for no
more than one-quarter of the co. Down electorate, and in
1790 it had accounted for only 18% (roughly the same as the
Foster estate in Louth in 1821).[1] In spite of this sometime
similarity to the Downshires, Foster's place is really with the
next rank of county magnates, the people who, if they exerted
themselves, could hold one seat, not in an unshakeable grip,
but in one which would be hard to shake: Lord Sligo in
Mayo, Lord Clanricarde in Galway, Lord Waterford in
Waterford, Lord Hertford (and Lords Antrim and O'Neill
successively) in Antrim, Conolly in Londonderry, and so on.
Once again, the striking thing is the disparity, in terms of
acreage, between Foster and the company he keeps; and once
again this is a reminder that Louth was possibly no smaller
in proportion to other counties than Foster was in proportion
to other county interests. The strength of his grip on Louth
was due, not primarily to Louth's smallness, but to his own
personal popularity.

There were, of course, political ingredients in this personal
popularity, particularly from 1792 onwards. But it is reasonable
to place the emphasis on the personal, not the political. Between
1779 and 1785 Foster had not been politically popular, and
indeed his interest may have survived only because the Fortescues did not waver in the direction of Volunteering, and Lord
Clanbrassill ceased to do so after the attack on his control of
Dundalk borough. Foster's stand on the dead issue of the
Union redounded entirely to his political popularity, but his

century speak for themselves. Other particularly pertinent references are: Bolton,
Union, p. 38; Lord Rockingham [Fitzwilliam's predecessor in the estate] to Charle-
mont, 25 Nov. 1760, *H.M.C. Charlemont MSS.*, i. 266; W. Wainwright to Fitz-
william, 21 Mar. 1790, Aspinall transcript from the Fitzwilliam MSS., Sheffield
City Library, for which I am indebted to Dr. P. J. Jupp; Lady Louisa Conolly to
Duchess of Leinster, 22 Oct. 1775, printed in Brian Fitzgerald (ed.), *The Corre-
spondence of Emily, Duchess of Leinster* (3 vols, Dublin, 1949–57), iii. 158; Maurice
Keating to [?], 23 June [1799], S.P.O. 513/73/4; and Duke of Leinster to Thomas
Tickell, 7 Jan. 1802, Tickell MSS.

[1] Jupp, *Co. Down Elections*, p. 191.

stand on the live issue of Emancipation became a threat and a danger after 1813. The fact that Emancipation did not become a live issue in Louth elections until 1826, and the regard for Foster evinced on that occasion by even the demagogue, Sheil, and the loyalty to him evinced by his tenants, are convincing proofs of his personal popularity. In the same year, Lord George Beresford, the defeated candidate in co. Waterford, put in a similar plea for the 2nd Marquess of Waterford:

. . . If ever Protestant landlord was calculated, by the influence of rank, property or character, to counteract the spiritual interference of the Romish priesthood, it was my deceased brother. . . . Intimately acquainted by a long residence with the local interests of his county, unceasingly devoted to the promotion of its welfare, and mixed up with all its important business, he had improved into a feeling of personal attachment, the respect which was due to his station and public virtues. . . . I assert with confidence and with pride that the late Marquess of Waterford was deservedly popular. . . .[1]

The threnody of an unseated paternalist is obviously a suspect piece of evidence; but whatever the truth of Lord George Beresford's remarks, it is important to know that it was as paternalists that this great Ascendancy proprietary interest saw themselves. Foster had earlier, in his first speech on the Union, stated his views on the paternalist role of the Ascendancy:

. . . I have ever understood that the example of the upper ranks was the most effectual means of promoting good morals and habits among the lower orders; that their attention to the education, the health, and the comforts, as well as the protection they afforded the lower ranks, all which can only arise from residence, were the surest mode of conciliating their affections as well as improving their manners; that if every estate and every village afforded a benevolent protector, an easy and impartial dispenser of justice, and allayer of the little feuds which headstrong passions, untamed by education, are too apt to carry to the last excesses, the lower orders would learn, not only obedience and veneration to the laws, but would feel attachment to the country which afforded them such blessings. . . .[2]

[1] Draft of a speech by Beresford, allegedly made at Armagh, but probably at Coleraine or elsewhere in co. Londonderry, 5 Oct. 1826, Primate Beresford MSS., Armagh Diocesan Register; photocopies in P.R.O.N.I., ref. T.2772/7/6C.
[2] *Foster's Speech of 11 Apr. 1799*, p. 64.

This paternalist outlook is not congenial to the twentieth century; but it clearly struck a responsive chord in at least one Collon tenant, who did not hesitate to appeal to Foster when her husband began to '. . . lead me a very uneasy life-time by turning me out of doors at unreasonable hours and [by] upbraidings of a delicate case . . .'[1]

There is every reason to suppose that, once the bitter contests of the decade 1761–71 were over, Foster, even when most unpopular politically, was never personally unpopular. If the absorptions of high office did not make him neglect the essential drudgery of maintaining his registries, so neither the absorptions nor the glamour of high office made him neglect the equally important personal side to maintaining a local interest. His refusal to stand for re-election *in absentia* in 1804 illustrates well his attention to this personal side. His return to power in 1804 was one of the most important moments in his career, and at the time it must have seemed the supreme moment. Yet he was not so carried away by it that he was prepared to do violence to the feelings of his constituents. Instead, he waived his much-needed official salary for two months, and laid himself open to the opposition pleasantry that a chancellorship of the Irish exchequer, apparently shared by Corry and him, was as great a monstrosity as a cow with two heads, particularly as the two '. . . seemed to be actuated by the most adverse spirit, and to be nothing less than butting against each other. In this state, how was the House to distinguish? . . . Which was that whose lowings they were to listen to, as conveying the true oracle? . . .'[2] The difficulty in 1804 was, of course, that he was away from Louth at the time of his appointment to office, and could not leave London because of the imminence of the Irish budget (this did not happen again in 1807): in more usual circumstances, the proximity of Louth to Dublin and, after the Union, the part-time nature of his attendance at Westminster, helped him in keeping up the personal side of his relationship with his constituents, as they helped him in keeping up his registries.

Basically, however, he was successful with the personal side because he had a genuine zest for this sort of thing. He was at ease and in sympathy with his constituents, a country gentleman

[1] Mrs. Anne Goodlow to Oriel, 1 Aug. 1821, F.P. D.562/1444.
[2] *Parl. Debs.*, ii. 1001 ff.

living among country gentlemen, and living, moreover, in a style which even by local, co. Louth standards was far from grand. In 1799, by which time political popularity had been added to personal, a Unionist canvasser of the area reported to the Castle that the higher circles in Louth were 'pretty generally under the influence of the Speaker', although some progress might be made with 'the middling class'.[1] Another Unionist visitor to Louth in 1799 expressed no such reservations about the extent of Foster's influence and, by implication, attributed it to paternalism rather than politics:

> . . . Armagh, I fancy, will return Cope, a notorious Unionist. Monaghan is indifferent and cold, and will not catch the fire of that prince of country gentlemen, Dick Dawson [a significant phrase as an *introit* to a discussion of Foster]. And as to Louth County, one can only wonder at the moderation of its resistance, considering the very just and well-deserved ascendancy of the Speaker, the best Grand Juror, Magistrate, improver and country gentleman in the Kingdom. I spent a very pleasant day and night at Collon, and was in danger of being perverted by the hospitality of the owner of that charming place. . . .[2]

Obviously, anything as elusive as Foster's paternalist style, and in particular his manner towards his constituents, is extremely hard to capture or document. Something of its tone may be divined from a letter he wrote to Edward Hardman's son in 1821; Hardman had written to congratulate him on his elevation to the peerage, and Foster replied with heavy humour (humour was not his strongpoint): '. . . Remember, you must not belord me more than once in a letter, and never belordship me, no more than you would hitherto have besirshipped me. . . .'[3] In 1824, one of his Burgh relations, to whom years earlier he had given much-needed assistance through his command of patronage, recalled:

> . . . At the time of the overthrow of our fortunes, he not only exerted himself to serve us, but entered into our feelings with a tenderness far more endearing to gratitude than any service . . .; while he was

[1] James Dawson to Robert Marshall (Castlereagh's private secretary), 16 July 1799, Castlereagh MSS., P.R.O.N.I. D.3030/1370.
[2] Judge Robert Day to Knight of Kerry, 22 Aug. 1799, FitzGerald MSS. 7/17. Day was the circuit judge for that year.
[3] Oriel to Hardman, 24 July 1821, F.P. D.562/13689.

in London, and the state of public affairs rendered the business of a statesman peculiarly oppressive, he wrote all the authentic news almost weekly to Sir John [the writer's husband]; and so dear is kindness to the kindly heart, that this consideration for his desolated feelings and secluded situation excited in his breast even stronger exertions of gratitude than the other important service. . . .[1]

It is of course a commonplace that murderers are often excellent family men; and the testimony of a relation who was under strong obligations to Foster must be treated with caution, particularly as an indication of the nature of his relationship with his constituents. At the same time, it is useful to know that this pleasing and unfamiliar side of his character existed, particularly since its existence is belied by a great volume of hostile contemporary testimony. His letter to Hardman is particularly suggestive: by 1821, the Hardman family had ceased to be either politically or financially necessary to Foster, and he had provided for them well. There is thus no reason for suspecting that his down-to-earth tone towards them was anything but genuine. Interestingly, the Belfast radical, Dr. William Drennan, who bitterly disliked him politically, recorded this sort of tone as characteristic of him: describing a chance meeting in about 1786, Drennan wrote that Foster 'chatted with me very familiarly, just as he does with everybody'.[2] Drennan's opinion would have been echoed by the horde of linen drapers, revenue officers, road-surveyors, and no doubt Louth constituents, who were regularly treated to a bed at Collon; also by the official subordinate who wrote to Foster on the occasion of his retirement in 1811 (when he presumably had no further reason to ingratiate himself with Foster), expressing '. . . the feeling that all of our Department will probably never again experience the same gentlemanlike ease in official communication; nor shall I meet with that warm friendship and kindness which, since I had the honour of acting under you, I have at all times received. . . .'[3] Foster's

---

[1] Lady Macartney to Lady Dufferin, 1 May 1824, F.P. D.207/73/232. Her husband, Sir John Macartney, M.P. for Naas, co. Kildare, in the 1797 Parliament, had been a prominent anti-Unionist. Barrington commends his indifference to personal or financial considerations, and his opposition to the Union did in fact contribute greatly to the 'overthrow' of his fortune.

[2] Drennan to Mrs. McTier, [1786 ?], Drennan MSS., P.R.O.N.I. D.591/224.

[3] William Gore to Foster, 25 Feb. 1811, F.P. D.562/15099.

perhaps most attractive characteristic was his ability to evoke loyalty and affection in inferiors, subordinates, and dependants:[1] a characteristic which contrasts sharply with his knack of raising the hackles of many of his ministerial colleagues, particularly those of them who were Englishmen.

Like many radicals, Dr. Drennan was susceptible to the condescensions of the great; and condescension was of the essence when it came to maintaining a local interest. The greater the height from which a local magnate condescended, the greater the impact of his condescension. This point was made trenchantly to the 3rd Marquess of Londonderry by his agent in 1825, who described maintaining an interest in the admittedly very different conditions of co. Down as a

Herculean task. . . . There are so many independent squires and squireens, all of whom, as well as their wives and daughters, require the nicest management. For the Marquess to keep up the interests of his family, it would be necessary that he should . . ., not only entertain the heads of houses, but enter into the most familiar intercourse with them, surprise the breakfast table of one in the morning, the dinner of another in an evening, chat with the ladies, view all the imaginary improvements of the house, farmyard, farm, etc., and enter into all the domestic concerns of the whole family. . . .[2]

Foster did not have the high rank or the broad acres of the Londonderrys. But in the period 1777–1811 he did have the asset of high office. It was his 'mongrel capacity' of Minister and country gentleman which gave his condescension its impact, the more so as condescension in his case was probably not strained or artificial. One of the many Louth squires to whom he addressed canvassing letters in 1806, replied in terms which illustrate the importance of this asset well: '. . . you are not only the most fit person to fill the Representation of Louth, but also the most able and judicious Chancellor of the Exchequer this Nation ever had, and your being deprived of that Office a public loss. . . .'[3] Burke, who had nothing good to say about him, seems to have thought that there was constitutional impropriety in a Speaker executing 'the office of an active

[1] See, for example, Foster to John Croker, 13 Nov. 1809, F.P. D.207/71/16; Corry Junior to Foster, [c. 20 Jan. 1812], F.P. D.562/6606.
[2] Jupp, *Co. Down Elections*, p. 192.
[3] Neal McNeale to Foster, 4 Nov. 1806, F.P. D.562/4343.

magistrate in a county not thirty miles from the Capital'.[1]
Whether or not this was true, the impact locally of the keen
interest taken by a man of his national prominence in all
matters of local concern, and in particular the impact of his
readiness to expose his person by careering round the county
at the head of his yeomanry corps in the dark days of 1797 and
1798, can easily be imagined.[2] Louth was proud of having the
first commoner of Ireland as its representative, the more so as
Foster was always down-to-earth, affable and approachable;
and locally he continued to be called 'the Speaker' by many
people, long after the office and the Parliament to which it
related had been abolished.[3]

His personal popularity in the constituency derived, therefore, in large measure from the fact that he was at once local
worthy and national figure. What he did in national politics
was much less important than what he was. His copious correspondence on local matters with local people produced a much
greater effect for being written by a 'great' man, perhaps
'. . . while he was in London, and the state of public affairs
rendered the business of a statesman peculiarly oppressive . . .'
Obviously, the local recipients of his letters were not such
small men that they were completely bowled over at receiving
a letter from the Speaker of the Irish House of Commons or the
Chancellor of the Irish Exchequer: probably these people, or
most of them, belonged to the higher circles in Louth, not
even to 'the middling class'—squires rather than squireens. Yet,
granted the smallness of Louth, the higher circles must have
included some fairly small landowners. A case in point is
Daniel McNeale of Rosemount. McNeale was a faithful Foster
adherent, but his adherence was costly, not only in patronage,
but in the time and trouble which Foster had to spend writing
letters to him, or writing letters to the government on his
behalf.[4] In view of the time and trouble spent on him, it is
surprising to learn that he could command an absolute maximum of only twenty-five votes in Louth, and probably the

[1] Edmund to Richard Burke, 10 Nov. 1792, *Burke Correspondence*, vii. 286 f.
[2] 'Recollections of a beloved father' by Lady Dufferin, [*c.* 1828], F.P. T.2519/
4/1819. See also a letter from Spencer Huey to John Forbes, 1 July 1788, printed
in T. J. Kiernan (ed.), 'Forbes Letters', *Analecta Hibernica*, No. 8 (1938), 344 ff.
[3] Malcomson, *Foster and the Speakership*, p. 272.
[4] See particularly Lord Manners to Oriel, 28 Feb. 1823, F.P. D.562/3947.

actual number was less.[1] In general, Foster's papers give a striking impression of how time-consuming and troublesome it was to have a local interest to nurse. Many of his papers—perhaps as much as two-thirds of the total—have been destroyed, but the destruction was, as far as is known, accidental; and though he sorted and filed them during the years of his retirement, he made no attempt to weed out the less important, and destroy them. This means that a bundle of tradesmen's accounts for the 1770s has had as good a chance of survival as papers relating to major matters of politics or economics; it means also that what has survived gives a rough-and-ready idea of the amount of time which he spared from the more pressing and important duties of office to devote to matters of purely local, though not necessarily of electoral, concern. The amount of time which he did spare, and the comparative triviality of many of the local matters on which he spent it, are alike remarkable: police, presentments, mail-coach routes, turnpike roads, gaols, hospitals, yeomanry, and so on. In 1740, one local magnate had been reminded, apropos of the borough of Charleville, co. Cork, that 'without much application, good words and kind promises, few people have success in elections.'[2] If this was true of a corporation borough, it was even truer of a county. In Louth, Foster was not sparing of 'application, good words and kind promises', and they made the greater impression on his constituents because of his high position in the life of the nation. This was the secret of his personal popularity.

It is easy to overlook simple things like Foster's country-gentleman ethos, and the fillip which his career in national politics gave to local pride. Yet these things were important, even in the days of the unreformed Parliament. The assumption is often made that, in a period when political issues were not usually decisive of elections (though in Louth they were clearly an important element), there was nothing to fill the vacuum thus created but real estate factors—jobs, freeholders, registries, and hard cash; and Ireland, much more than England, has been the victim of this assumption. It is not borne out in the case of Louth, nor in many—probably most—other Irish counties.

[1] McNeale to Foster, 9 July 1821, F.P. D.562/13676.
[2] Quoted in Malcomson, *Newtown Act*, p. 334.

CHAPTER EIGHT

John Foster: Rearguard of the Ascendancy

In 1822, Lord Rosse observed, '. . . At any time when it is really necessary, I will go over and do my best' in the House of Lords by openly stating his views on Emancipation and the Catholic Question generally. '. . . But until then I wish to keep quiet, as I should involve myself in contests in this County [King's], which it is prudent to avoid except upon a real emergency. . . .'[1] Prudential motives of this kind did not prevent Foster, or John Leslie Foster, from going over and doing their best in Parliament. Foster kept the Emancipation issue out of Louth elections and, after 1813, out of Louth politics; but in the years after his retirement from office it was not fears for the electoral repercussions in Louth, but his wife's failing health, followed by his own, which prevented him from going over and doing his best more often (the last time was in 1821[2]).

Whether the arena was that of local politics or national politics, whether his strategy was discreet paternalism or declared partisanship, whether the issue was Catholic Relief, Catholic Emancipation, or the Union, Foster was consistent in identifying and pursuing the interests of the Anglo-Irish Ascendancy, as he conceived both them and it. Basically, his conception of the Ascendancy was the *status quo* of 1782; and 1782 marked his *ne plus ultra*, not because of the Constitution established in that year, but because of the Catholic Relief Acts passed. The Constitution of 1782 was a child which he merely adopted, and certainly had not fathered. In 1799–1800 he defended it as loyally as its father, Grattan,[3] but in reality what he was defending was not the Constitution of 1782, nor even the Irish Parliament, but the Ascendancy. His behaviour immediately

---

[1] Rosse to Redesdale, 7 May 1822, Redesdale MSS., P.R.O.N.I. T.3030/13/4.
[2] Lady Dufferin to Lady Ferrard, 4 Apr. [1821], F.P. T.2519/4/1740.
[3] *Foster's Speech of 11 Apr. 1799, passim.*

after the Union, shows that it was the Ascendancy which he was defending at the time, and also shows his ability to identify the new interests of the Ascendancy after a dramatic shift in the political kaleidoscope. In February 1801, when Pitt's moral commitment to round off the Union with Catholic Emancipation transpired, Foster wrote:

... The Union has accomplished for them [the Irish Catholics] the Reform without which they could never hope to be of consequence in Parliament. The Emancipation now projected takes away their disability. They will soon feel how little they will be in Britain, how great they would be here [Ireland]. They will look to restoring the Parliament and to filling the vacancies [left] by the purchased Boroughs with popular elections, in which they will hope for a majority; and if this comes to pass, a Catholic Government and consequent separation will be the effect. ...

In another letter he added the trenchant sentence: '. . . I shall not be surprised if the loyal men who opposed . . . [the Union] by their advice shall be its supporters by their arms . . .'[1] For himself, Foster saw it as his duty, in the altered circumstances of the years after 1801, to support the Union by taking office in the United Parliament. In 1802 he attacked the methods by which it had been carried, but he did not attack the Union itself; and though he apparently exclaimed in the House in 1811, 'Take back your Union', this was in the heat of debate and also of intoxication. Lecky argued in 1886 that Grattan, had he been alive then, would not have desired the restoration of the Irish Parliament:[2] Foster ceased to desire it in 1801. Highly as he valued the Irish Parliament, in the last resort it was for him only a means to an end; the end was the maintenance of the Ascendancy and (for Foster) its inseparable concomitant, the British connection. After 1801 the Union was the only remaining means to that end.

Foster was unusual among Irish politicians of the period 1782–1801, in that he was opposed to all incursions on the *status quo* of 1782—Place, Pension, and Responsibility measures (almost certainly), Catholic Relief, parliamentary reform, the

---

[1] Foster to Sheffield, 5 and 13 Feb. 1801, *Anglo-Irish Dialogue*, pp. 36 f.

[2] Quoted in Patrick Buckland, *The Anglo-Irish and the New Ireland* (Dublin, 1972), p. 8. The 'Take back your Union' anecdote is told by Henry Grattan Junior (*Life*, v. 422) in the context of the Repeal agitation of *1810*, but see Pole to Richmond, 25 May *1811*, Richmond MSS., N.L.I. MS. 65, fol. 773.

Union. Most people, at one time or another, and for different reasons and upon different terms, supported at least one or two of these. Yet these people, too, would have considered themselves as in some sense upholders of the Ascendancy; they differed from him primarily because they were prepared to contemplate measures to renovate the Ascendancy, so as to make it less offensive to Irishmen who were not Anglo-Irish (especially the Catholics), and/or to make it more defensible against the British government. Foster stands out, not because he upheld the Ascendancy—since that was more or less common form—but because his definition of the Ascendancy was so narrow and rigid that, on all the political issues affecting the Ascendancy, he could behave only as a rearguard. The term 'Anglo-Irish Ascendancy' is a historian's term, which can be defined as the historian chooses; and for purposes of this study it has been defined as the *status quo* of 1782 and what was left of it after 1792–3 and 1800, since that was Foster's definition. But another term, 'Protestant Ascendancy', was used by contemporaries, and merits examination. In November 1792, Richard Burke mentioned that Protestant Ascendancy was a new term,[1] and the way in which it was bandied about in the debates on the Catholic Relief Bill earlier in the year, suggests that he was right. Because it was a new term, it was liable to considerable variety of individual interpretation. For example, in December 1792 one of Lord Abercorn's members used it in contra-distinction to 'Protestant supremacy'.[2] In the debates on the Relief Bill of 1792, many members declared their commitment to Protestant Ascendancy, including several Opposition members, notably Grattan and the Ponsonbys. The following is Grattan's definition:

. . . The Protestant Ascendancy, I conceive to be twofold: first, your superiority in relation to the Catholic; second, your strength in relation to other objects. To be the superior sect, is a necessary part, but only a part of your situation. To be a Protestant State, powerful and able to guard yourself and your island against those dangers to which all States are obnoxious, is another part of your situation. . . . It would be my wish to unite the two situations—a strong State

[1] Lecky, *History of Ireland*, iii. 125.
[2] George Knox to Abercorn, 13 Dec. [1792], Abercorn MSS., P.R.O.N.I. T.2541/IB1/3/35.

with the Protestant at the head of it. But in order that the head of the State should be secure, its foundation should be broad. Let us see how far the Protestant Ascendancy in its present condition is competent to defend itself. Can it defend itself against a corrupt Minister? . . . I need not tell you, for you already know, as the Protestant Parliament is now composed, that which you call the Protestant Ascendancy is a name. . . . There is another danger to which, or to the fear of which, your divisions may expose the Protestant Ascendancy: I mean an Union. . . . From all this, what do I conclude? That the Protestant Ascendancy requires a new strength, and that you must find that strength in adopting a people, in a progressive adoption of the Catholic body . . .[1]

It might be argued that Grattan was merely paying lip-service to the Protestant Ascendancy in order to assuage the prejudices of Protestant squires against the Catholics. But Grattan was slow and hesitant in his advance towards the Catholics in 1791–3—he did not unequivocally declare his support for full Catholic Emancipation until the course of debate on the 1793 Bill, and was not the first member to do so.[2] Indeed, his advance looks as if it was dictated by his fear that the Irish Parliament, and Grattan personally, would be 'outrun' in the 'race for the Catholic' by the British Government. Foster saw, and said, that the race was on; but he considered that the British Government would be obliged to call it off if the Irish Parliament refused to join in. More important, Foster was rooted to the already outworn notion that the interests of the Anglo-Irish Ascendancy and those of the British government were one and the same. He therefore could not view the Ascendancy in Grattan's two-fold sense—'your superiority in relation to the Catholic; . . . your strength in relation to other objects'; he could not view the British government as an object in relation to which the Ascendancy needed to be strong. More specifically, he saw the policy of Catholic Relief as an aberration on the part of the British Government of 1793, not as an intimation of a Union.

In passing the Catholic Relief Act of 1793, the Irish Parliament followed Grattan's, not Foster's, line. It would be rash

[1] *A Report on the Debates in Both Houses of the Parliament of Ireland on the Roman Catholic Bill Passed in the Session of 1792* (Dublin, 1792), pp. 113 ff.
[2] George Knox to Abercorn, 6 Feb. [1793], Abercorn MSS., P.R.O.N.I. T.2541/IB1/4/10.

to generalize about the motives which actuated the majority of a Parliament of 300. But one important, and perhaps dominant, motive was that the concessions proposed by the British Government would be less damaging to the Ascendancy than a situation in which the Catholics continued to regard the Irish Parliament as their enemy and the British Government as their only friend. It must be remembered that Edmund Burke, perhaps the most ardent advocate of political concessions to the Irish Catholics, considered that re-enfranchisement, combined with Catholic Emancipation, would make no appreciable difference to the Irish representation 'for a long series of years', if at all.[1] Burke's first-hand knowledge of Ireland had ceased with the 1760s, and he was probably less perceptive than those few people, on both sides of the question, who saw as early as 1793 that Protestant candidates had '. . . been labouring, by strong declarations in favour of the Catholics, to form an interest in Catholic counties which should secure a return for themselves'.[2] However, it was easy for the generality of members of the Irish Parliament to convince themselves, once the British Government had shown its hand in December 1792, that the concession of the vote on a 40/– qualification was daft rather than dangerous, and therefore something for which the Irish Parliament should at the last minute steal as much gratitude as possible from the British Government. To some, notably the Ponsonbys, who had opposed the concession of the vote in 1792, the logic of the political situation in 1793 was that they should 'outrun' the British Government by supporting full Catholic Emancipation; and the Ponsonbys adduced the divisive policy of the British Government as one of their motives for so doing.[3] The first motion in favour of Emancipation in 1793 was made by Lord Abercorn's political following; so it is particularly instructive to look at Lord Abercorn's course on the Catholic Question prior to that time. It might be expected that he would have used such influence as he had with Pitt in favour of unlimited Catholic Relief: he had, in fact, done no such thing. In December 1791 and January 1792, he had

---

[1] Burke to Fitzwilliam, [*c.* 26 Sept. 1794], *Burke Correspondence*, viii. 22.
[2] George Knox to Abercorn, 9 Feb. 1793, Abercorn MSS., P.R.O.N.I. T.2541/IB1/4/11.
[3] *Parl. Reg.* (Irish), xiii. 327.

dissuaded the British Government from thinking of conceding the vote; in late October 1792 he wanted the British Government to state their determination to support the Irish Parliament (precisely the line of Lord Westmorland and the Irish Cabinet), and the Irish Parliament to pass a Convention Act; it was only after the British Government had agreed to receive the petition from the Catholic Convention, that Abercorn changed his tack. He granted audience to the Catholic delegates himself, and instructed his members not only to support, but to propose, Emancipation—presumably greatly to the annoyance of Pitt. Since Abercorn was virtually an Englishman (though he described himself as an Irishman), enjoyed a personal relationship with Pitt, and scouted 'the silly . . . phrases of Protestant interest and Protestant Ascendancy', it is remarkable that he reacted and acted in this way.[1] It is much less remarkable that other political interests and individual members with a more narrowly Irish outlook, should have done likewise. The conservative and 'Ascendancy' principles on which the supporters of Catholic Relief and even Emancipation acted, cannot be sufficiently emphasized.

Foster was hostile, not only to Catholic Relief, but to another, more constructive proposal for strengthening the Ascendancy which was made in 1793: parliamentary reform. Just as many members of the Irish Parliament supported even full Emancipation in 1793 on conservative and 'Ascendancy' principles, so many supported parliamentary reform—including some great borough proprietors like Lord Shannon and the Beresfords. Indeed, there was considerable danger in 1793 that a backlash of Protestant resentment at the British Government's alleged betrayal of the Irish Parliament would have carried a reform on aristocratic lines.[2] An aristocratic parliamentary reform was not a contradiction in terms. One obvious shortcoming of the unreformed electoral system in Ireland, as in Great Britain, was that it did not do what it purported to do—represent property. In Ireland, for example, two of the greatest borough proprietors, Lords Shannon and Ely, were weak in landed

[1] Abercorn to Thomas Knox, 5 Jan. 1792; Abercorn to Hobart, 26 Oct. [1792]; Abercorn to Hobart, 15 Dec. [1792]; Abercorn to George Knox, 17 Dec. [1792]—Abercorn MSS., P.R.O.N.I. T.2541/IK/12/2, 64, 72, 73.
[2] George Knox to Abercorn, 17 Jan. 1793, ibid. IB1/4/2.

property; some of the greatest landed proprietors had no borough interest—Lords Altamont (later Sligo), Antrim, Clanricarde, Fitzwilliam, and Lansdowne, to name only the greatest; many very considerable landed proprietors were represented only by the kind of rotation which was characteristic of the politics of most counties; and many of the borough proprietors, for example the Ruxtons of Ardee, were poor men who had no alternative to selling their seats or bargaining for their votes. The proposers of parliamentary reform in 1793 were the Ponsonbys (who were running a race of their own against Grattan), and the Ponsonbys were the aristocratic party *par excellence*. In 1792, George Ponsonby had complained, 'it is a favourite theme to accuse this side of the House as an aristocracy'.[1] In 1789 it had been reported that the Prince of Wales had promised William Ponsonby the speakership 'and the *conduct of the House of Commons*';[2] and if political circumstances had permitted, William Ponsonby would have reverted to Undertaker type, instead of taking up the various reforming measures which were almost forced upon him in the early 1790s. In January 1793 George Knox reported to Lord Abercorn that the partisans of the Ponsonbys were talking '. . . openly of the connection with England being dissolved, and exult in it as a just punishment on the English Ministry for attempting to govern this country without the assistance of the aristocracy. . . .'[3] Henry Grattan Junior recurred to this theme as late as 1810; he lamented the 'want of a good, wholesome aristocracy in Ireland', and in proof of this stated the view that the Ponsonbys had no power left by 1795, because 'a race of upstarts set up by the Castle were the rulers of the day'.[4] Of course, much of this was myth; in social background Foster was an upstart by comparison with the Ponsonbys, but as has been seen, in terms of the electoral interest which they could command in their own right, he was as much an aristocrat as they.[5] However, the point of substance which emerges through the myth, is that the Ponsonbys, and Henry Grattan

---

[1] *Roman Catholic Debates of 1792*, p. 219.
[2] Buckingham to Grenville, 28 Mar. 1789, *H.M.C. Dropmore MSS.*, i. 440.
[3] See p. 355, *n.* 2.
[4] Henry Grattan Junior to James Grattan, Nov. 1810, Grattan MSS., N.L.I. MS. 2111.
[5] See pp. 195 ff., 205 f.

Senior, saw parliamentary reform as a means of making the Irish Parliament more aristocratic, not more democratic, and as a means of strengthening it against the Castle and the British Government. This was very much a conservative and 'Ascendancy' point of view. Interestingly, it was shared by Lord Abercorn, English-orientated though he was. Abercorn favoured a parliamentary reform which would make Parliament more truly representative of property by adding one member to the representation of each county: he opposed the Ponsonby plan of 1793 because he considered it insufficiently aristocratic, or rather 'a wretched trick of borough aristocracy to pilfer popularity with one hand and electioneering influence with the other'.[1] It was not a point of view shared by Foster, who could not see how the Ascendancy could be strengthened by a weakening of the British connection. If Foster had been presented with the alternatives of an aristocratic parliamentary reform and a Union, it is hard to know which he would have chosen.

What has been so far suggested is that those Irish politicians who were on the opposite side to Foster over the political issues affecting the Ascendancy, were seeking to renovate rather than to wreck it. They differed from him primarily because theirs was the more flexible, constructive, and also opportunist, approach. There were differences, too, between Foster and those whose approach more closely resembled his, notably Fitzgibbon and Beresford—differences of emphasis most of the time, and a diametrically opposite political course at the time of the Union. Part of the explanation is that neither Fitzgibbon nor Beresford possessed Foster's aggressive Anglo-Irish patriotism. Fitzgibbon was Anglo-Irish by adoption, but Old English by descent; and Beresford, though Anglo-Irish, was English-orientated as a result of his family and political connections, and of his own thought-processes. By at least 1793 Fitzgibbon had despaired of the separate Anglo-Irish State and Parliament;[2] and Beresford, though only a lukewarm Unionist in late 1798, had always thought of himself as the prop of 'English government' in Ireland, and in 1799–1800 acted consistently with that role. At the time

---

[1] Abercorn to Thomas Knox, 26 Jan. [1793]; Abercorn to George Knox, 1 Apr. [1793]—Abercorn MSS., P.R.O.N.I. T.2541/IK/13/17, 36.

[2] Clare to Auckland, [5 June 1798], printed in Falkiner, *Lord Clare*, p. 151.

of the Union, Fitzgibbon's invectives against the Irish character, and particularly the Irish Catholic character, were among the speeches which Foster described as 'painful to me, as an Irishman, to hear'.[1] He would have been equally pained if he had known that in 1779–81 Beresford's consistent advice to his contacts in British ministerial circles had been that it was not for the advantage of 'English government' to appoint Irishmen to key offices in Ireland; or if he had read Fitzgibbon's diatribe in a letter to William Eden about 'the madness and folly of my countrymen' in rejecting the revised commercial propositions in 1785: '. . . God Almighty bless them! If my lot had not been cast amongst the fools, I could see them running to the Devil with perfect indifference. But I have acquired vicious habits of regard for the pitiful spot of the Globe which I hate myself for not being able to shake off . . .'[2] Characteristic of Foster, and foreign to Fitzgibbon and Beresford, was Foster's declaration during the Union debates: '. . . But you are to be improved into British manners and British customs? Idle talk! Much as I admire Britain, I am not ready to give up the Irish character or to make a sacrifice for the change . . .'[3] By 'Irish' and 'Irishman' he meant, of course, Anglo-Irish and Anglo-Irishman.

However, there was more to the differences between Foster, Fitzgibbon, and Beresford than family background and personal orientation. These three, though they may perhaps be collectively described as the brains behind reactionary politics in the Ireland of the 1790s, responded with different emphasis and a different degree of conviction to the various changes which impended. All were upholders of the Ascendancy, but only Foster upheld it above all else. The British connection, not in the last resort the Ascendancy, was Fitzgibbon's God— Westmorland's jibe that he had no other God but English government, intended to imply time-serving, in fact went to the root of Fitzgibbon's political faith. Because he was not Anglo-Irish, and because he was possessed of a ruthlessly logical cast of mind,

---

[1] *Foster's Speech of 17 Feb. 1800*, p. 1.

[2] Beresford to Robinson, 13 Dec. 1779 and 27 June 1781, *Beresford Correspondence*, i. 116, 164; Fitzgibbon to Eden, 22 Aug. 1785, quoted in R. B. McDowell, 'Some Fitzgibbon Letters from the Sneyd Muniments in the John Rylands Library', *Bulletin of the John Rylands Library*, 32 (1952), 310.

[3] *Foster's Speech of 11 Apr. 1799*, p. 67.

Fitzgibbon could actually envisage a situation in which a parliament of 'giddy', irresponsible, small-minded planters would constitute a menace to the British connection;[1] he hoped that his influence would avert that situation; but if his influence did not, what was left of it would be thrown into the scale of the British connection. Similarly, even if British governments were being giddy and irresponsible, in the last resort they must be supported and served. This was the situation which confronted Fitzgibbon in 1793. Characteristically, his response was to send a verbal, and apparently private, message to Pitt in January. He was ready '. . . to grant everything short of seats in Parliament, Corporations and Sheriffs, and to give a qualified right of carrying arms, if the British Cabinet would agree to put a final bar to future demand. . . .' Back came the inflexible answer 'that the only pledge Great Britain could give was to resist every attack on the Act of Settlement and the Church Establishment'.[2] (This was a pledge not worthy of the name; Fitzgibbon prophesied attacks on both the Act of Settlement and the Church establishment—the former incorrectly—but not even Fitzgibbon expected them in Pitt's, or his own, lifetime.) The important point is, not that Fitzgibbon's move was largely unsuccessful, but that it was in character for him to make it. Equally, it was in character for Foster publicly to criticize the British Government of 1793, but to continue to admit no distinctness of interests between the British government generally and the Anglo-Irish Ascendancy; in Foster's political faith, the two stood or fell together. Beresford, in contrast to both Foster and Fitzgibbon, was a politician to whom the term political faith is inappropriate. He felt, with Fitzgibbon, a paramount allegiance to the British connection, but felt it with much less conviction; perhaps because of his lack of strong conviction, he was also more receptive than either Foster or Fitzgibbon to the constructive ideas for shoring up the Ascendancy—for example, to the aristocratic parliamentary reform of 1793. At bottom, he simply enjoyed solving problems,

---

[1] 'Giddy' was one of Fitzgibbon's favourite adjectives; see, for example, Fitzgibbon to Eden, 29 Aug. 1784, *Fitzgibbon Letters from the Sneyd Muniments*, p. 301.

[2] [Edward Cooke's] 'Memorandum of the conversation which passed with Mr. Dundas at Wimbledon in the presence of Mr. Pitt', 21 and 22 Jan. 1793, Melville MSS., N.L.I. MS. 54A/74.

working hard, and reaping the rewards of his labours. Matters personal to himself were the only things he felt strongly about—his reputation no less than his material wellbeing (hence the duel he fought with Fitzwilliam). His absorption in small things is ludicrously apparent in a letter he wrote in August 1795, drawing Pitt's attention to the fact that, if Beresford became First Lord of the Treasury instead of Chief Commissioner of the Revenue, he would still be liable for expensive official entertaining, and would lose the 'house, coals, candles, etc.' which were perquisites of his existing office.[1] The example of Fitzgibbon, Beresford, and Foster is a reminder that the role of the reactionary is neither static nor simple; no less than the advocate of change, he has a variety of options and priorities among which to choose; and the consequence of his choice may be to separate him essentially from those with whom he would seem, superficially, to have much in common.

Politically, Foster was the most complete reactionary of the three. His great strength was that, when it came to the bit, he was capable of adapting himself to much-hated and bitterly resisted change, and of identifying where the best interests of the Ascendancy lay in the new political circumstances; typical of this cast of mind was his comment on the Union just after it came into effect: 'even so carried, it is the law; we are bound'.[2] His great weakness was that he opposed change, possibly in 1792–3 and certainly in 1799–1800, with a root-and-branch rigidity which deprived him of any practical influence over the shaping of the measures concerned, so that he afterwards had to accept *in toto* things which at the time he might have been able to modify in part. Yet this was a weakness to which anyone acting from intense conviction and not blessed with clairvoyance was bound to be liable. The twentieth-century historian, handicapped by hindsight, and also by an inability to comprehend the intensity of the convictions of men like Foster, is all too readily able to see where he went wrong: it was a mistake for him (and the rest of the Irish Cabinet) to charge the Catholic Committee in 1792 with being unrepresentative of Catholic opinion, since that charge forced

[1] Beresford to Rose, 25 Aug. 1795, Chatham MSS., P.R.O. 30/8/325, fol. 115.
[2] Foster to Sheffield, 13 Feb. 1801, *Anglo-Irish Dialogue*, p. 37.

on the election of the Catholic Convention later in the year;[1] it was a mistake for him to ignore or reject in 1793 the possibility of a special £10 or £20 franchise for Catholic voters; it was a remarkable mistake for him to use the argument in 1793 that, if Catholics were allowed to elect members of Parliament, there could be no logic in denying them the right to be elected; more generally, it was a mistake for him to ignore the fact that, through being left unresolved, the Emancipation issue was wrecking paternalist local politics more effectively, and sooner, than any other issue could have done; it was a mistake for him to employ his telling and prescient arguments against the provisions of the Union in 1799, and especially in 1800, in the form of speeches on the floor of the House, since this in itself meant that the Government could not accept them without loss of face; and, finally, it was a mistake for him to oppose the Union with such effect and with such an emphasis on the real and uninfluenced sense of the country, that the Government was almost forced, first into flirtation with, and then into moral commitment to, the Catholics. However, at the time, he was bent on defeating these measures, not on palliating their effects; like everyone else then and for years afterwards, he was more fearful of independent, middle-class Catholic voters than of dependent Catholic 40/– freeholders; and though he dreaded what vote-catching Protestant candidates and ignorant British governments might do, he could not help predicating even for them some participation in his convictions. The only way in which he could have deferred the demise of the Ascendancy was by conducting a strategic withdrawal; but it is unhistorical to criticize him for not seeing this, and for fighting a series of rearguard actions.

Outside the political sphere, however, in his own chosen sphere of economic affairs, a very different Foster is apparent: constructive, flexible, hardly conciliatory (since that was not in his nature), but certainly not reactionary. Foster's emphasis on economic affairs, and particularly on the economic role of the Irish Parliament, was partly a matter of personal aptitude and inclination. It was also partly the result of his appreciation that the most important aspect of public business in Ireland open to the Irish politician was '. . . the consideration of its

---

[1] Richard to Edmund Burke, [*c.* 8 Sept. 1792], *Burke Correspondence*, vii. 201.

internal economy and its aptitude to various improvements . . .', as Lord Camden pointed out to Castlereagh in 1796.[1] However, the real significance of his emphasis on economic affairs is that he saw in prosperity not just a palliative, but a cure for political discontent; the search for prosperity, in other words, was the obverse and positive side to his negative resistance to any and every political encroachment on the *status quo* of 1782. Prosperity was a cure rather than a palliative because, in Foster's eyes, the ill was socio-economic, not political. It was his conviction that the great mass of the Catholic people were 'incompetent' even to understand the Emancipation issue. In March 1795, for example, he wrote: '. . . Every address, petition, etc., with which the papers abound, is the fabrication of the Dublin [Catholic] Committee, to awe the Kingdom and frighten England. The mass of the Papists in the Country know nothing and care nothing about the Claims, and may even dislike them . . .'; and again, in May: '. . . The truth is that the lower Papists are no way interested in aggrandizing the superiors of their own religion by hazarding their lives to get them into Parliament, and those of the best property are too loyal to suffer them to rise on such a purpose. . . .'[2] There is nowhere a policy statement from Foster that the best way to kill Emancipation was with economic kindness. But his paternalist record in co. Louth, and the success with which he kept the Emancipation issue out of Louth elections, speak for themselves. Also, his letters teem with a juxtaposing of political news and reports on the state of the harvest, weather, and so on. At first, this juxtaposing seems accidental; but close reading of, for example, the long run of letters to Lord Sheffield, conveys the strong impression that it is deliberate and reflects an instinctive thought-process.[3] An isolated, but more explicit, instance occurs in a letter to Perceval, written in June 1811: '. . . as to this Country [Louth], I never saw more content nor less disposition to think of politics or Popery or Protestantism. Every man gets full employment, and there is plenty of work even for women and children. . . .'[4] However, the most explicit

---

[1] Camden to Castlereagh, 22 Mar. 1796, Castlereagh MSS., P.R.O.N.I. D.3030, vol. 4, p. 1009.

[2] Foster to Sheffield, 26 Mar. and 6 May 1795, *Anglo-Irish Dialogue*, pp. 18 ff.

[3] See, for example, Foster to Sheffield, 1 Aug. [1795], ibid. 15.

[4] Foster to Perceval, 22 June 1811, Perceval MSS. in the possession of Mr.

instance of all—a virtual policy statement—is Foster's response to a letter from Auckland of October 1798, in which Auckland, at Pitt's behest, had sounded out his views on the Union:

. . . If I understand you right, you propose this measure as an expedient for carrying on the Government of this Kingdom, which you apprehend to be in danger from the state of the Country and the disposition of the people. I own to you, I do not see the danger, if the Government supports the Constitution and its establishments firmly and decidedly . . . I think the great difficulty in governing Ireland arises from a want of the knowledge of the comforts of life in the lower orders, and of course a want of educaton, of veneration for the Laws which promote and protect wealth, and a want of industry or exertion to procure it. This difficulty has been gradually lessening for the last fifteen years, during which the Country was increasing into wealth and prosperity beyond even our most sanguine expectations. . . . I should fear any measure which goes to undo the work to which the sudden rise of our prosperity is generally attributed here—I mean the independence of our Legislature—would have the very opposite effect [to that of tranquillizing the country]. . . .

This view—that political problems are best met with economic solutions—is surprisingly modern, and certainly is not associated with 'Ascendancy' politicians of the late eighteenth century. In the same letter, Foster provides a very practical example of it: his plan (which had been ignored or rejected by Cornwallis) for tranquillizing the country by employing the defeated and pardoned rebels, at government expense, on public works, until such times as compensation to the loyalists and a general return of confidence to the employers of labour, rendered such emergency measures unnecessary. Pitt himself, who found the rest of Foster's letter unsatisfactory, commented on this part of it: 'His idea of finding employment for the disbanded rebels seems to me a very judicious one.'[1]

Foster was extreme and unique in the constructive political possibilities he saw in a successful economic policy. But the other members of the Irish cabinets in which he served, attached an importance to economics, and devoted an attention to them, which has surely been underestimated by historians?

David Holland, the Barn, Milton Street, Polegate, Sussex; Foster's copy of this letter (F.P. D.207/69/31) is damaged and suffers from slight loss of text.

[1] Foster to Aukland, 21 Oct. 1798, and Pitt to Auckland, 28 Oct. 1798, Sneyd MSS., P.R.O.N.I. T.3229/2/36, 38.

Fitzgibbon is a case in point. Fitzgibbon was no more interested in economics than he had to be as the drafter of economic legislation while Attorney-General, 1783–9. Yet, in his reaction to the failure of the commercial propositions, which historians have tended to view as a political fiasco rather than as an economic set-back, Fitzgibbon went straight to the economic heart of the matter: '. . . Whether we may hereafter recover our senses, and discover that the recollection of Mr. Grattan's splendid periods is but a slender compensation for poverty and the most absolute dependence on Great Britain, which is most certainly our present condition, I cannot take upon me to say. . . .'[1] Moreover, historians have perhaps thought of the economic policy pursued in the period 1782–1800 too much in terms of the measures which were taken to boost and protect Irish manufactures and agriculture. This was certainly an important element in the policy, and one which is rightly associated with Foster. However, it was an element which is not above criticism, and the trend of modern scholarship has been to cast doubt on the effectiveness of 'prosperity by Act of Parliament'.[2] For example, Foster can probably be accused of smothering the Irish linen industry with attention, at a stage when, as Lord Hardwicke sourly remarked in 1802, it was 'no longer in its infancy'.[3] Foster can also probably be accused of exaggerating the economic case for a separate Irish Parliament and, more generally, the efficacy of protectionism; the war-time recession in most sectors of Irish trade and industry was not something which the indifference of the United Parliament caused or the vigilance of a separate Irish Parliament could have averted, although it was undoubtedly accentuated by the taxation made necessary by the financial provisions of the Act of Union. Likewise, the post-war agricultural slump was not caused by the United Parliament, and would probably have been beyond the remedy of a separate Irish Parliament.

Perhaps the more important, and certainly the more indisputably successful, element in the economic policy of the

---

[1] Fitzgibbon to Eden, 29 Aug. 1785, printed in Falkiner, *Lord Clare*, p. 144.

[2] See, for example, L. M. Cullen, *An Economic History of Ireland since 1660* (London, 1972), pp. 95 ff.

[3] Hardwicke to Wickham, 20 Mar. 1802, Wickham MSS., P.R.O.N.I. T.2627/5/E/12.

period 1782–1800, was the measures passed regulating Ireland's external trade with Great Britain, other parts of the Empire, the United States, and France. The Constitution of 1782 provided no machinery for a harmonizing of British and Irish interests in this wide sphere. In a sense, the Constitution of 1782 increased Ireland's bargaining power: Foster's Corn Law of 1784 was made possible by the hard economic fact that Great Britain had just recently become an importer, instead of an exporter, of corn, but it is questionable whether a British Privy Council which retained the right to amend Irish legislation would have allowed him to enact the law on terms so favourable to Ireland.[1] In a more important sense, however, the Constitution of 1782 weakened Ireland's bargaining power. By failing to recognize Great Britain's right to legislate for Ireland in matters of external trade, it left Great Britain free to legislate without regard to Ireland. In fact, Ireland had no bargaining power, and was reliant on British goodwill. All depended on skilful negotiation between the Irish cabinet and the English 'men of business', like Charles Jenkinson, William Eden, and George Rose, and on tactful draftsmanship, which would keep Irish legislation in line with British, without arousing the hypersensitivities of the Irish Parliament in constitutional matters. The failure of the commercial propositions was a failure of negotiation and draftsmanship; and its effect, combined with the success of the Anglo-French commercial treaty of 1787, was to make France rather than Ireland for a short time Great Britain's most favoured nation. But this was an isolated, though spectacular, failure, which was offset by a substantial amount of unobtrusive success. The success was achieved, and was unobtrusive, because the constitutional hypersensitivities of the Irish Parliament were not aroused; but precisely because they were not aroused, historians, with their emphasis on the political, have not laid sufficient stress on the achievement.

One striking instance of the men of business on each side of the Irish Sea—in this case Jenkinson and Foster—seeking to break through prejudice and to identify and harmonize the substantial interests of the two kingdoms, occurred some

---

[1] I am indebted for this point to Professor J. C. Beckett. For Foster's views on the effect of his Corn Law, see Foster to Westmorland, 31 Dec. 1790, *Anglo-Irish Dialogue*, pp. 76 ff.

years before the Constitution of 1782. In June 1777 Jenkinson wrote to the Lord Lieutenant, Lord Buckinghamshire:

. . . I am clearly of opinion that the corn of Ireland should be allowed to be brought to the British market in preference to all foreign corn whatsoever. Great Britain by her laws has made it necessary for Ireland to become a corn country more than she otherwise would have been, so that justice as well as policy requires that we should give her in this respect all reasonable encouragement; and as Your Excellency [i.e. Foster] very well observed, the corn of Ireland lies particularly convenient for the supply of that part of England which is not a corn country, and which is most in want of corn for the cheap supply of its numerous manufacturers. . . . As to the time of obtaining this favour, I am sorry to say that the present is not the most proper, when the price of all sorts of grain is reasonable, and is likely to become much cheaper before the meeting of Parliament in Winter; so that the Country Gentlemen would be more likely to take the alarm on that account; and if the favour was obtained, much benefit could not be expected from it by the Irish in the present moment. . . .[1]

This remarkable letter anticipates, not just Foster's Corn Law of 1784, but the reciprocal preference which was established, on Jenkinson's rather than Foster's terms, in 1792.[2] The difficulty of finding a 'proper' time, and the need to assuage prejudices on both sides of the Irish Sea, account for the long time-lag. Later in the year of Jenkinson's letter, 1777, another letter which deserves extensive quotation was written to Lord Buckinghamshire, this time by Lord North, who was by instincts a man of business rather than a prime minister:

. . . The British Parliament, to do them justice, thinks [*sic*] liberally enough about Ireland, and are generally willing to adopt measures beneficial to that Kingdom. But the difference in the burthens in the two Kingdoms, and the distinct footing on which they stand, makes [*sic*] it often difficult to reconcile their interests . . . Till a Union can be effected (which the prejudices of both Nations will, I am afraid, for ever prevent), no King or Ministry will be able to persuade the British Parliament to encourage the woollen or any other staple manufacture of this Kingdom, in Ireland. But in other articles they will, perhaps, be more complaisant. The great objection to most of the propositions in Your Excellency's

[1] Jenkinson to Buckinghamshire, 7 June 1777, Heron MSS., N.L.I. MS. 13035/7.   [2] See pp. 59 f.

letter is that they would give a door to counterband [*sic*] trade which would effectually defeat all the provisions of our laws. . . .[1]

There were other British prejudices and myths, too—the cheapness of labour and provisions in Ireland, the preference given to Irish linen in the British market, which was viewed as '. . . an advantage to Ireland infinitely greater than any which England derives from Ireland, and [which] ought to stand as an equivalent for many disadvantages. . . .'[2] But, basically, apart from the reference to wool, Lord North's letter could have been written at any time between 1782 and 1800: the Constitution of 1782 accentuated the 'distinct footing' on which the two kingdoms stood, and Pitt's successful measures against smuggling accentuated British fears that Ireland would act as a 'counterband' back door into England. North's letter encapsulated the heavy burden of prejudice with which the English men of business had to contend throughout the period 1782–1800; and the Irish men of business had their burden, too, though it was mainly of a constitutional and political nature. The interpretative and almost educational role which each fulfilled was the role, not just of men of business, but of men of goodwill.

A striking example of this role is provided by the British and Irish Navigation Acts of 1786 and 1787. These were the work of Jenkinson, but as he had drafted the provisions relating to Ireland, they would have suffered the fate of the commercial propositions. Commenting on the British Bill in May 1786, Fitzgibbon wrote:

. . . as Mr. Jenkinson's Bill is framed, it will be impossible that we can, by any Clause to be added to it, postpone its operation as to this Country. As the Bill now stands, it certainly imports to bind this Country generally, and as it now stands, I do not see how it will be practicable to register any ship in Ireland. . . . I can't but suggest the impolicy of repealing any of the former Navigation Laws at present, which in the situation of the two Countries, the British Parliament cannot re-enact for Ireland; and it would seem that every object of Mr. Jenkinson's Bill might be attained by enacting new regulations, without in any sort shaking the Laws which are now received in Ireland.[3]

---

[1] North to Buckinghamshire, 13 Oct. 1777, ibid. MS. 13035/13.
[2] Richard Atkinson to Pitt, 21 Nov. 1784, Chatham MSS., P.R.O. 30/8/321, fols. 205–10.   [3] Fitzgibbon to Orde, 5 May 1786, Bolton MSS., N.L.I. MS. 15867/2.

The more courtier-like Hely-Hutchinson wrote: '. . . I have considered with the utmost diffidence a Bill prepared by one of the ablest men, and one of the warmest friends of Ireland, in the British Empire. Perhaps the most experienced British Members have not yet got into the habits of preparing Bills with a view to the present state of both Countries.'[1] It was, in fact, the Lord Lieutenant, the Duke of Rutland, who wrote (to Pitt) stating the objections from the Irish point of view in their full force and vigour; 'I am persuaded', he concluded, 'you will not urge the Irish Government to an unnecessary attempt, which must involve their ruin.' Jenkinson complied. However, the separate Irish Bill which he drafted for the Irish session of 1787 still contained clauses which, in the view of the Irish Cabinet, were 'likely to create cavil and mis-representation'. The Irish Cabinet re-drafted the offending clauses, in a manner which Jenkinson, now Lord Hawkesbury, conceded was '. . . judicious and well-calculated to remove objections on your side the water, and [which] cannot I am sure be in the least degree disapproved of here. When the measure is completed, I shall from that moment consider the two Kingdoms once more united, so far as relates to maritime policy and Naval power. . . .'[2] The Bill passed, after little opposition, except from Grattan, who 'incautiously committed himself upon the subject before he perfectly comprehended it';[3] and the episode closed with an exchange of thanks and con-gratulations between the English and Irish men of business. The story was repeated over the Anglo-French commercial treaty in the same year, 1787. In this instance, the negotiations for Ireland's inclusion in the treaty were greatly facilitated by the good personal relations subsisting between Beresford, Fitzgibbon, and Foster, on the one hand, and the British negotiator, Eden. (There was almost, however, a last-minute hitch over Irish linen, which Fitzgibbon blamed on 'the blundering stupidity of that old Balderdash Bitch, Lord Sydney', the British Home Secretary.[4]) The story was again repeated over the commercial adjustments of 1792–3. But the example

[1] Hely-Hutchinson to Orde, 2 May 1786, ibid. MS. 15867/1.

[2] Hawkesbury to Fitzgibbon, 19 Mar. 1787, Liverpool MSS., B.L. Add. MS. 38309, fol. 144.

[3] Fitzgibbon to Hawkesbury, 2 Apr. 1787, ibid. Add. MS. 38221, fol. 317.

[4] Fitzgibbon to Eden, 4 Apr. 1787, printed in Falkiner, *Lord Clare*, p. 147.

of the Navigation Acts of 1786–7 is the clearest and best-documented, and will suffice.

In all these negotiations, Foster, for all his fundamental goodwill towards Great Britain, stood out among the members of the Irish Cabinet as the one who was most aggressively 'patriotic' in driving a hard bargain for Ireland. As Isaac Corry, then an opposition admirer of Foster, observed during the Irish debate on the revised commercial propositions, '. . . I know the battles he has fought on the other side of the water in favour of the commerce of this Country, and will bear testimony to it; and I expected as much from him. . . .'[1] Foster always spoke in terms of the Empire and the common good of Great Britain and Ireland, appealed to 'the good sense and mutual interest of each Country', and expressed his detestation of 'the mistaken policy of treating the two Countries as rivals'.[2] Yet, in Foster's Empire, Ireland was almost the co-equal partner of Great Britain. Departing from the common forms of the period (which Sir Boyle Roche jumbled together in his famous 'bull'), Foster did not call Great Britain 'the Mother Country' or Ireland 'the Sister Kingdom'; he talked about the 'brotherly' affection between the two kingdoms, and called them 'the two great members of the Empire'.[3] More specifically, in his blueprints for the commercial propositions, composed in September 1784, he claimed as a matter of right that Great Britain should re-interpret the Navigation Act to permit the importation of British colonial goods into Great Britain via Ireland.[4] To this, without mentioning Foster's name, Pitt took direct and pointed exception: '. . . I think it is universally allowed that, however just the claim of Ireland is not to have her own trade *fettered and restricted*, she can have no claim to any share, beyond what we please to give her, in the trade of *our Colonies*. They belong (unless by favour or by compact we make it otherwise) *exclusively to this country*. . . .'[5] Granted this fundamental

---

[1] Quoted in Revd. N. D. Emerson, 'Mr. Speaker Foster', *C.L.A.J.* vi (1927), 120.
[2] *Foster's Speech of 11 Apr. 1799*, p. 51; Foster to Sheffield, 12 Apr. [1790], *Anglo-Irish Dialogue*, p. 9. [3] *Foster's Speech of 11 Apr. 1799*, pp. 48, 109.
[4] Foster to Orde, 15 Sept. 1784, Melville MSS., P.R.O.N.I. T.2627/2/2/6. This is Dundas's copy: Pitt's copy is in the Chatham MSS., P.R.O. 30/8/328, fols. 33–7. In January 1783, the Lord Lieutenant, Lord Temple, had privately put forward the same argument, perhaps under Foster's tuition—Temple to Grenville, 3 Jan. 1783, *H.M.C. Dropmore MSS.*, i. 179.
[5] Pitt to Rutland, 6 Jan. 1785, *Pitt–Rutland Correspondence*, p. 60.

divergence of view, it is surprising that the commercial propositions came so near to succeeding—or rather, the fact that
they did, is a tribute to Foster's 'Ministerial Patriotism'.
Neither Pitt nor anybody else on the British side of a negotiation
in which Foster was concerned ever doubted the strength of
his patriotism: during the negotiations over the Anglo-French
commercial treaty, the less patriotic Beresford was driven to
exclaim to Eden that Foster thought '. . . nothing is concerned
in this Treaty but [Irish] linen . . .'[1]

The jibe illustrates strikingly the difference between Beresford
and Foster. In a negotiation between Great Britain and Ireland,
the English-orientated Beresford could see both the British and
Irish points of view, and his letters as a result often read like
a discussion paper drawn up by a modern civil servant to indicate
the various options open to his political masters. On the question
of Ireland's proposed participation in the East India Company's
monopoly in 1793, for example—while Foster rode 'his hobby
as to the East Indies as hard as ever'—Beresford wrote to
George Rose:

> . . . The Company certainly are the most competent judges of what
> may be the value of permanent confirmation of their Charter by
> Ireland, and whether it is worth their putting themselves to an
> acknowledged inconvenience and expense by having a warehouse
> in Ireland for the supply of India goods. If this could be conceded,
> we think that [the Irish] Government could carry a permanent
> confirmation of the Charter: if it cannot, endeavour must be made
> to continue the annual prohibition of importing tea into Ireland
> except from England, for which purpose it will be necessary to
> supply us with arguments to show the inconveniencies which would
> result from establishing a warehouse, etc, in Ireland. . . .[2]

In a negotiation with the 'brother' kingdom it was not Foster's
way to indicate at the outset that he was prepared to retreat,
or to provide a plan of campaign for his British opposite
number. Though the two men were the acknowledged economic
experts in the Irish Parliament, Foster was anxious to carry the
economic role of that Parliament further than Beresford. This

---

[1] Beresford to Eden, 13 Sept. 1786, and Eden to Foster, 26 Apr. 1787—Auckland
MSS., B.L. Add. MSS. 34422, fol. 256, 34424, fols. 348–9.
[2] Beresford to Rose, 3 May 1793, Chatham MSS., P.R.O. 30/8/325, fol. 94.
For the quip about Foster's 'hobby' see p. 59, *n.* 4.

was probably because Beresford did not see the constructive political possibilities which Foster saw in a successful economic policy. In practical terms, it meant that Foster was prepared to press for economic measures which, while they would conduce to the advantage of the Empire as a whole, would not necessarily conduce to the advantage of Great Britain: Beresford was not.

The Catholic Relief Act of 1793 impelled Beresford in the direction of parliamentary reform, and convinced Fitzgibbon of the necessity of a Union. Politically, Foster stood still. With his stronger and deeper emphasis on economic factors, he was presumably able to regard the commercial concessions of that year, which were the fulfilment of much of his economic policy, as to some extent an offset to the 'unaccountable changes in our Constitution'.[1] He was not especially myopic in his optimism, and particularly in not foreseeing the possibility of a Union. In September 1794, for example, Edmund Burke declared: '. . . The concessions made to Ireland by Great Britain, both constitutional and commercial, have completely exhausted the fund of compensations which might be offered as a balance to the heavy weight of prejudice entertained in that Country against an Union. Nothing—literally nothing at all—remains on the part of England, as an object of Negotiation. . . .'[2] This was a high-flown exaggeration; in practical terms, the equalization of the duties between the two kingdoms still remained to be conceded, and nearly was conceded in 1793 and again in 1795. If Foster thought seriously about the possibility of a Union—and he must have done so—he may have made the calculation that a few more years of the Irish Parliament, and a few more concessions from Great Britain to Ireland, would weaken the case for a Union to the point of impossibility. However, 1793 was a crucial date, not just because of the Catholic Relief Act, but because of Great Britain's entry into the war. Again, Foster was not especially myopic in not foreseeing the effects of the war. In February 1793, for example, Lord Abercorn, who was much nearer to the fountainhead of British government than Foster, observed blithely: '. . . We are now at war with the French. Probably, for the first month, the advantage will be on their side: after

---

[1] Foster to Sheffield, 1 Aug. [1793], *Anglo-Irish Dialogue*, p. 13.
[2] Burke to Fitzwilliam, [c. 26 Sept. 1794], *Burke Correspondence*, viii. 21.

that, never fear, we will maul them.'[1] It was, in fact, the Irish economy rather than the French army, which was about to be mauled. The economic and fiscal effects of the war, combined later with the financial provisions of the Act of Union, put paid to Foster's economic policy and Ireland's prosperity. In 1790, Parnell had boasted that 'he did not think it possible for any Nation to have improved more in her circumstances since 1784. . . .' But the effect of the war was to increase the expenditure of the Irish Government five-fold between 1793 and 1800, from £1,363,388 a year to £6,854,804, the rise being almost entirely attributable to military expenses, particularly from 1795 onwards, when Ireland itself became seriously disturbed. In 1788 Parnell had boasted that 'the Public Funds in this Country have been higher here [*sic*] these several years past than in England . . .' But by 1798 the Irish Government was heavily dependent on the credit of the British Government to keep itself afloat.[2] This dependence became complete in the years after the Union, leaving no alternative to financial amalgamation, which Foster was almost certainly advocating by 1811. The combination of the war and the financial provisions of the Act of Union left the chancellor of the Irish exchequer with virtually no room for manœuvre; not only was there no longer any hope for an economic solution to political problems, but Foster's unavoidably stiff budgets became in themselves a major source of unrest and dissatisfaction. As he wrote to Perceval in August 1810: '. . . The whole fury of the Press is as yet to be levelled at me—most unaccountably, were I their ultimate or real aim. But the Government, the Union, and British Connection are the objects which the agitators are advancing to through the Taxes, as the surest of all subjects to raise discontents upon. . . .'[3]

It has been necessary to lay heavy emphasis on the importance which Foster attached to economic policy, on the considerable success which attended the Irish cabinet's and his economic policy up to 1793, and on his hopes that positive political benefits would derive from the continuing success of that policy:

[1] Abercorn to Alexander Young, [11 Feb. 1793], Abercorn MSS., P.R.O.N.I. T.2541/IK/13/23.

[2] These quotations and figures are taken from Dunraven, *Finances of Ireland*, pp. 29, 43.

[3] Foster to Perceval, 12 Aug. 1810, F.P. D.562/2101.

otherwise, his rearguard reaction to the political issues of the day would be blameable for an unconstructiveness which not even intense conviction could excuse. It would be a reaction inconceivable in a man of Foster's high intelligence. However, the wider focus will be lost if too much attention is concentrated on Foster personally. The common ground between Foster and virtually all the Irish politicians in seeking to uphold some kind of Ascendancy, was not translated into common action against the British government, because Irish politicians were all prisoners of a defective political system—a political system whose defects had, if anything, been accentuated by the Constitution of 1782.

Under the Constitution of 1782, the British government retained two methods of controlling the Irish Parliament: the first was the direct and politically emotive method of not 'returning' a bill which had passed both Irish Houses; the second was the indirect and less politically emotive method of 'managing' the Irish Parliament—and the House of Lords required good management as well as the House of Commons, as the Lord Lieutenant, Lord Buckingham, pointed out in 1788–9.[1] The first method was not resorted to as an engine of control. Buckingham urged in 1788 the desirability of keeping up 'the practice of rejecting in the English Privy Council', but on this and other occasions the British government fought shy of the practice unless it was justified and indeed necessitated by purely technical considerations of draftsmanship.[2] After 1782 the British government was forced to make up in patronage what it had lost, or did not venture to assert, in prerogative. After 1782 it was also forced to rely much more heavily than before on the services of Irish politicians. This was partly because Irish legislation could no longer be amended in England—Fitzgibbon's 'old Balderdash Bitch' Lord Sydney wrote, with remarkable insensitivity, to the Lord Lieutenant in 1784: '... Let me impress upon you to advise your friends to be more attentive to the contents of Bills, now they do not admit of alterations; for the inaccuracies in them are very numerous.'[3] The greater reliance on Irish politicians was also partly dictated by the increasing

[1] Buckingham to Grenville, 18 Nov. 1788 and 13 May 1789, *H.M.C. Dropmore MSS.*, i. 372, 467 ff.
[2] Buckingham to Grenville, 2 Apr. 1788, ibid. 315; Sydney to Buckingham. 12 Apr. 1788, P.R.O., H.O. MSS. H.O. 100/23, fols, 228–9.
[3] Sydney to Rutland, 6 May 1784, *H.M.C. Rutland MSS.*, iii. 93.

volume of parliamentary business, which the establishment of annual sessions both recognized and accentuated. But, above all, it was dictated by the failure of the Constitution of 1782 to provide any machinery whereby Great Britain could regulate Ireland's relations with foreign powers and other parts of the Empire. The failure of the commercial propositions, and the success of the Navigation legislation of 1786–7, are the best examples of the crucial importance of sound Irish advice in this sphere. Yet, in spite of this, after 1782 as before, the relationship between the Irish politicians and the Irish Administration remained totally *ad hoc*. The Irish cabinet was not a cabinet in even the contemporary British sense of the term; it was a panel of experts, often not even *ex officio* experts, assembled by the lord lieutenant at his discretion. The members of the Irish cabinet were not there because collectively they could command a majority in the Irish Parliament. The Irish administration—the lord lieutenant and the chief secretary— were not there for that reason either: they were there because they had been appointed by the British government, to which alone they were responsible, and so ultimately to the British, certainly not to the Irish, Parliament. If the Irish administration was defeated in the Irish House of Commons, the result was—not a change of Irish administration and Irish cabinet— but deadlock, until the Irish administration succeeded in re-establishing its majority. This was precisely what happened early in 1789. The effect on the Irish politicians of this defective political system was twofold. The Irish politicians who were normally to be found in office and government developed a mentality which made it difficult for them to distinguish between British government generally and the particular British government of the day, and made them very reluctant to go into opposition to the latter. Likewise, the Irish politicians who were normally to be found in opposition did not oppose with a view to replacing the existing Irish cabinet; this they could not hope to do, unless there was a change of government or policy in Great Britain, and it is significant that, up to 1799, the only two successful Irish oppositions, those of 1785 and 1789, were fuelled by the expectation of a change of government in Great Britain. In this way both government and opposition politicians were the prisoners of the system: they were accustomed to individual, not collective, bargaining; and when surprised by a measure like the Catholic Relief Bill of 1793, they were incapable of collective action.

The effects of the system were intensified by an accident: the long duration of Pitt's first ministry, which roughly coincided with the life of the Constitution of 1782. Ironically, at the start of his ministry, the great threat to Irish political stability seemed to be the short durations and frequent changes of British government. When the Fox–North Coalition had come to power earlier in 1783, their Lord Lieutenant, Lord Northington, had restored stability by refraining from the 'General Sweep'[1] of Irish supporters of the previous administration which the Duke of Portland had perpetrated in 1782. Thus, the Fox–North Coalition, 'unnatural' in terms of British politics, produced in Ireland the nearest thing to a broad-bottomed Irish cabinet, embracing politicians of as varied a political complexion as Grattan and John Scott, the one an 'upright and temperate *demagogue*', the other the 'uniform drudge of every Administration'.[2] It also brought Fitzgibbon to the fore, initially (and this is almost incredible, in the light of later events), as Yelverton's under-study in the House of Commons. Fitzgibbon half expected Pitt to make a general sweep.[3] However, the new British Government saw and stated explicitly that

. . . It was of the utmost importance to the Government of both Countries to show that the change of Administrations here was not to affect the affairs of Ireland, and that those who were recommended by a Lord Lieutenant at the eve of his departure from Dublin as persons who had supported the united interests of both Countries, were to be appointed immediately to their offices, for fear of riveting an opinion, which had its rise from recent transactions, that support in one Administration was to be looked upon as a demerit to their successors. . . .[4]

---

[1] This phrase occurs in a letter from Francis Hardy to John Forbes, 22 Jan. 1789, quoted in Kelly, *British and Irish Politics in 1785*, p. 557.

[2] Mornington to Grenville, 23 July 1782, *H.M.C. Dropmore MSS.*, i. 163; Grattan, *Life*, i. 401.

[3] Fitzgibbon to Eden, 12 Jan. 1784, *Fitzgibbon Letters from the Sneyd Muniments*, p. 301.

[4] Sydney to Sir Lucius O'Brien, 11 June 1784, Sydney MSS., N.L.I. MS. 52/J/7.

It is extremely important to remember that, when Pitt made it an 'indispensable' condition of Lord Fitzwilliam's appointment in 1794 that there should be a '. . . Full security that Lord Fitzgibbon and all the supporters of Government shall not be displaced on the change, nor while they continue to act fairly in support of such a System as shall be approved here . . .',[1] he was not acting from any particular partiality towards Fitzgibbon and the then Irish Cabinet, but in consistency with a principle which he had enunciated at the outset of his ministry. However, the very length of his ministry meant that the principle, valid in 1784, had perhaps ceased to be so by 1794. In 1797 Lord Fitzwilliam wrote: '. . . I think that the salvation of Ireland . . . *does not depend upon measures, but upon men,* [and] that concessions meanly made by persons hostile to the concessions, would do no good—it would be throwing away what would be the means of grace in other men's hands. . . .'[2] To some extent, this remark demonstrates Whig genius for rationalizing rapacity. However, the largely changeless continuity of the Irish Cabinet of 1784, or at any rate the abiding predominance of Fitzgibbon, Beresford, and Foster, undoubtedly took much of the grace out of the Catholic Relief Act and the other concessions of 1793. It also closed the important viceregal safety valve, that lords lieutenant expiated in their persons the sins of a defective system of government. Up to 1782 the pattern had generally been that lords lieutenant departed amid opprobrium and their successors arrived amid applause; thus, even Lord Buckinghamshire, soon to be the most discredited and disgraced lord lieutenant of the period 1777–1811, at the outset of his Administration had the pleasure of pitying and patronizing his departing predecessor, Lord Harcourt.[3] This safety valve no longer operated when lords lieutenant came and went, but the Irish Cabinet endured, seemingly, for ever.

As far as is known, only one suggestion for remedying the defective system was ever made; this was by Lord Mornington,

[1] Pitt to Westmorland, 19 Oct. 1794, Chatham MSS., P.R.O. 30/8/325, fol. 63.

[2] Fitzwilliam to William Ponsonby, 20 May 1797, Aspinall transcript from the Fitzwilliam MSS.

[3] Buckinghamshire to Germain, 2 Feb. and 20 Sept. 1777, Heron MSS., N.L.I. MS. 13035/2, 11.

in a memorandum to Grenville of September 1789.[1] Mornington's proposal was to the effect that the lord lieutenant should
be withdrawn from the political sphere, and should become
the king's representative alone, instead of a cross between
king's representative and 'Minister'; the Irish politicians who
could command a majority in the Irish Parliament, should
be made departmental Ministers, responsible to that Parliament,
and the patronage of those departments, most of which now
vested in the lord lieutenant direct, should be theirs to dispose
of; this loss of patronage would be no loss to the British government, since as things stood none of the patronage of Ireland,
except two of the vice-treasurerships and a few pensions, could
be diverted to British political purposes. This bold and interesting plan derived in some particulars from Mornington's
personal pique at the Rutland Administration and hopes of
attaining Irish office at the hands of Grenville. But in essentials
it was a blueprint for responsible cabinet government in Ireland.
Late eighteenth- and early nineteenth-century British governments did not act on abstractions of that kind in their handling
of Irish affairs. Grenville's brain-child, the second chamber of
the Canadian legislature established by the Canada Act of
1791, was eminently such an abstraction. But Canada was
geographically so remote that government by blueprint was
possible, and at times even unavoidable. Ireland was sufficiently
far away for most British Ministers (Grenville was an exception) to have no personal knowledge of it, but near enough
for government from-hand-to-mouth, or at least for government of the sort that sufficed for contemporary Great Britain—
a government which responded to events rather than anticipated them. Responsible, cabinet government was still in the
process of evolution in Great Britain itself, and indeed the
period from 1783 onwards was a crucial phase in the process.
So the British Government of the day cannot reasonably
be blamed for failing to impose such a system on Ireland.
If Ireland had attained responsible, cabinet government, and
the Constitution of 1782 thus been made a workable political
institution, this would have had to arise naturally out of some
political event or situation, not artificially out of a blueprint.
The political situation of 1792–3 almost brought it about.

[1] *H.M.C. Dropmore MSS.*, iii. 541 ff.; the date is my conjecture.

Since May 1792 Pitt had been in negotiation with the Duke
of Portland's wing of the British Opposition, whom he hoped
to rally to the approaching war-effort. One of the offices
which he had indicated would be made available to a Portlandite was the lord lieutenancy of Ireland;[1] and because the
Oppositions in the two countries were considerably intertwined,
as he knew to his cost, a coalition embracing Ireland as well
as Great Britain seemed a hopeful strategy. 'Internal' reform,
the reinterpretation of the Navigation Act, and participation
in the East India Company's monopoly, were the baits to the
Irish Opposition; the Catholic Relief Bill was also, to some
extent, a bait to the Grattanite part of the Irish Opposition—
those very few members who had shown themselves sympathetic
to political concessions to the Catholics during the debates of
1792. As Henry Grattan Junior noted innocently, it 'happened
fortunately' that Grattan and most of the rest of them were in
London in November/December 1792; and he also noted that
they had at least one interview with Dundas.[2] Another person
who happened fortunately to be in London was the hoary,
but far from venerable, Hely-Hutchinson, who also favoured
political concessions to the Catholics (partly because this line
accorded with his electoral interests in Cork City). In mid-
December 1792 the British Government finally made up their
minds that a Catholic Relief Bill should be introduced as a
government measure, instructed the Lord Lieutenant, Lord
Westmorland, accordingly, and invited the Irish Cabinet to
London to discuss the details. The Irish Cabinet refused to go[3]
—which, incidentally, suggests that they were not the time-
servers that they have been misrepresented as being. Their
refusal gave Pitt a freer hand to negotiate with the Irish Opposition. The Responsibility Bill which the Irish Opposition
introduced at the start of the 1793 session seemed also to
Pitt and Dundas to provide an opportunity for offering more
attractive terms than heretofore. When the Irish Administration warned Pitt and Dundas that the Bill, as it stood, would
'. . . take the patronage from the Lord Lieutenant as much as
possible, and . . . give the conduct of affairs to Irish Parliamentary leaders . . .', Pitt and Dundas replied that '. . . they

---

[1] Campbell, *Lives of the Chancellors*, vi. 213.   [2] Grattan, *Life*, iv. 77.
[3] See p. 359, *n*. 2.

did not see insuperable objections, as they were convinced that public opinion would sooner or later have a similar influence upon the Administration of Ireland to that which it has in England, and that consequently Administration must be ultimately conducted according to the sentiments of the House of Commons, which would by this means have a great influence in the choice of the Ministers of the Crown. . . .'[1] In other words, if the establishment of an Irish treasury board led to responsible, cabinet government for Ireland, and made the lord lieutenant a figurehead instead of the Minister of the country, Pitt and Dundas were content.

They were content because, at this point in time, it looked as if Pitt would 'not long have much to do with' Irish politics (as Lord Abercorn wrote to him on the very day that Dundas and he gave their comments on the Responsibility Bill);[2] in other words, Ireland was about to become the province of the Portlandites. A few days later, a most significant but studiously opaque correspondence was opened up with Grattan by the new Lord Chancellor of England, Lord Loughborough. Loughborough had taken office, nominally so that he could act as the bridge over which the Portlandites marched into government, but actually because he could not wait to get his hands on the Great Seal. Using Hely-Hutchinson as an errand boy, Loughborough wrote to Grattan at the end of January inviting him to come to London for '. . . a fair and candid discussion of the several points which seem necessary to settle the situation of Ireland in a just conformity to England . . .'; and when Grattan replied unenthusiastically, Loughborough became rather more explicit:

. . . We have marked with attention, and without jealousy, the progress of your improvement. We must be weak and short-sighted indeed, not to observe that the Administration must be adapted to the change of situation, and must be founded on the firm basis of public confidence and esteem; that, to be respected, it must be responsible, and cannot subsist by favour and protection from any external support. . . .[3]

---

[1] See p. 359, *n.* 2.
[2] Abercorn to Pitt, 22 Jan. 1793, Abercorn MSS., P.R.O.N.I. T.2541/IK/13/12.
[3] Loughborough to Grattan, 30 Jan. and 21 Feb. 1793, Grattan, *Life*, iv. 107 ff.

The strong implication of Loughborough's second letter was that those members of the existing Irish Cabinet who were not indisposed to internal reform, were to be 'the co-adjutors of the conference'; so it looks as if Pitt still shrank from a general sweep. This helps to explain why Grattan held aloof. He would not even attend a conference which took place in Dublin between members of the Irish Cabinet, Hobart, and the Ponsonbys; the unconstructive reason he gave for his refusal was that he would not meet Fitzgibbon.[1] Not even the Ponsonbys could be persuaded to take office, and instead Grattan and they, as has been seen, outran the terms of the Catholic Relief Bill by advocating Emancipation. These circumstances, combined with the continuing aloofness of the Portlandites in Great Britain, caused Pitt to turn again to the old Irish Cabinet, and particularly to Fitzgibbon. Fitzgibbon had earned golden opinions from Lord Westmorland for 'his spirit and the discountenance he gave to the cabals and hobby-horses' which threatened the Irish Administration during the 1793 Session, particularly the aristocratic parliamentary reform.[2] When he went to London in April, he was well received by Pitt, and their mutual commitment to the principle of a Union established a bond between them. However, the immediate purpose of Fitzgibbon's mission was to press for the conversion of the Hereditary Revenue into a Civil List granted for the King's life.[3] This was an old chestnut of the Irish Opposition, who had in the past advocated a slavish imitation of Burke's British Civil List Act of 1782 without, as Fitzgibbon had been able to demonstrate in 1789, regard to the different circumstances of Ireland.[4] Fitzgibbon's aim in now taking up a favourite opposition measure was drastically to reduce the discretion of the proposed treasury board. Fitzgibbon's proposal was, not only that the Hereditary Revenue should be converted into a Civil List, but also that the rest of the revenue be appropriated to specified purposes, with the effect that the treasury board would become 'measurers, not Ministers'.[5] Pitt must have yielded to his

[1] Westmorland to Pitt, [pre- 18? Feb.? 1793], Chatham MSS., P.R.O. 30/8/331, fols. 191–4.
[2] Westmorland to Pitt, 2 Apr. 1793, ibid. fols. 122–3.
[3] Ibid.   [4] *Parl. Reg.* (Irish), ix. 299.
[5] Anonymous memorandum [probably by Fitzgibbon] criticizing the proposed

arguments. Probably he required little convincing; after all, the political situation which had led him to toy with responsible, cabinet government for Ireland no longer obtained, and a Union had all along been his first preference in any case.

The fumbling move towards responsible, cabinet government in 1792–3 was a unique occurrence. There were other moves towards broadening the bottom of the Irish cabinet, or changing its composition entirely. The former was attempted, disastrously, under Lord Fitzwilliam, and the latter would probably have happened if the Prince of Wales had become the unrestricted Regent of Ireland in 1789, or if anything had ever come of the various schemes that he should acquire political experience and a sense of responsibility by being appointed to the lord lieutenancy. However, in all these experiments and schemes, nothing was ever said of entrusting all or some of the patronage of the Crown in Ireland to Irish parliamentary leaders; and without such a development the composition of the Irish cabinet might have been changed, but the defective political system would have remained. It was allowed to remain because, broadly speaking and with the exception of 1792–3, it suited the interests of the British government better than anything which could have been substituted for it.

At the outset of his ministry, Pitt was so far from wanting to turn the Irish cabinet into responsible Ministers that, even as things were, he did not trust the Duke of Rutland in their hands. Reporting a conversation he had had with Archbishop Robinson of Armagh in September 1784, Lord Sydney wrote to Pitt:

... He thinks that the measures for the Irish Government ought to be settled here, for this reason: that a Lord Lieutenant, left to himself, looks too much to gaining Irish popularity during *his own time*. ... I agree with him that the measures to be taken in Ireland ought, after full communication with the Lord Lieutenant, to be decided upon and directed here: as to arrangements of men and officers [*sic*], that ought to be left to the Lord Lieutenant. ...[1]

Responsibility and Place and Pension Bills, [Feb.–Apr. 1793], Melville MSS., N.L.I. MS. 54/5; Fitzgibbon to Hobart, 4 Apr. 1794, Chatham MSS., Cambridge U.L. Add. MS. 6958/1428; Westmorland to Pitt, 17 Apr. 1794, Chatham MSS., P.R.O. 30/8/331, fols. 226–8.

[1] Sydney to Pitt, 6 Sept. 1784, Sydney MSS., N.L.I. MS. 52/J/3.

Rutland's behaviour seemed to the British Government to fulfil these forebodings. Writing to Sydney in the same month, September 1784, he showed that he had so far imbibed the views of his Irish Cabinet that he actually cracked a joke about that sore subject, Foster's Libel Act, which he called a 'masterpiece of *despotism and tyranny* for which my Administration has been so justly condemned'.[1] When sounding him out about the feasibility of carrying a parliamentary reform in Ireland, Pitt at the beginning of the next month pointedly observed: '. . . it must have naturally happened that the persons with whom you have necessarily most habits of intercourse must be those who are most interested against any plan of Reform; that is to say, those who have the greatest share of present Parliamentary interest. . . .'[2] In reply, Rutland carefully omitted the other adverse opinions he had received from the Irish Cabinet, but enclosed that of Lord Earlsfort (formerly John Scott) who, he correctly pointed out, had no parliamentary interest.[3] Over the commercial propositions, too, Rutland's echoing of the opinion of the Irish Cabinet that Pitt's cherished 'imperial concerns' should be left out, clearly caused dismay in Whitehall, and drew from Sydney the following admonition in April 1785:

> . . . I am now writing to Your Grace a letter of a most private kind, and therefore venture to hint to you that, even among those who have received the most distinguished marks of favour from Government, there are some who appear to lean so entirely to the side of popularity in Ireland as to lay embarrassments in the way of accommodation, where the real interest of Ireland is not concerned. . . .[4]

This, by eighteenth-century standards sharp, rebuke reveals the gulf which separated British and Irish politics and politicians, a gulf which was not inappositely represented by the Irish Sea. In Ireland, there were virtually no politicians who represented the Pittite combination of efficiency and 'liberalism'. Fitzgibbon, Beresford, and Foster were all efficient administrative reformers, but that was the extent to which they

---

[1] Rutland to Sydney, 2 Sept. 1784, *H.M.C. Rutland MSS.*, iii. 135.
[2] Pitt to Rutland, 7 Oct. 1784, *Pitt–Rutland Correspondence*, p. 46.
[3] Rutland to Pitt, 14 Nov. 1784, *H.M.C. Rutland MSS.*, iii. 148.
[4] Sydney to Rutland, 15 Apr. 1785, ibid. 200.

were imbued with the Pittite reforming spirit. Their advice was coloured by High Protestant preconceptions—not that that became a defect in the British Government's eyes until 1791. They tended to favour draconian measures, like the Libel Act and Foster's fines for illicit distillation. Moreover, they were not even exempt from the vice of running after Irish popularity. It is ironical that the British Government of the day should have brought this last charge against men who have gone down in Irish nationalist history as quislings. However, at the time, the whole political focus was different on opposite sides of the Irish Sea. The British politicians sent to serve in Ireland saw things differently from the British politicians at home, not simply because they were second-rate people under the thumb of their Irish advisers, but also because they to some extent participated in the Irish focus. This process can be seen at work on Rutland's Chief Secretary, Orde, who was by no means second-rate or uncritical of his Irish advisers. Writing in March 1784 on the subject of Foster's Corn Law, he is evidently struggling to come to a true appraisal of Foster in the Irish, as opposed to the British, context:

. . . There are certainly strong reasons against granting the whole export bounty for Dublin, because of the bounty on inland carriage to it; but such a proportion as may put it on a footing with the rest of the Kingdom, it is certainly entitled to. Yet, I will not venture to determine that it will be allowed in the House, such prevalence has self-interest upon this point. I am convinced, however, that Mr. Foster upon the whole thinks right about this subject, and has in view the *most feasible* means of getting rid of the inland bounty . . . I sincerely hope that he has still greater and more liberal notions, and is only restrained by the impossibility of success to any hasty proposition. I am not afraid of the consequences to Great Britain. . . .[1]

Rutland himself was far from being second-rate. His drinking habits were a cause for concern, but otherwise he was arguably the most capable and successful of Pitt's lords lieutenant. The lovelessness of the relationship between Pitt's ministry and its Irish cabinet was most apparent in 1791-3, when the British Government was sharply divided from the Irish Cabinet on the most important issue of the day, Catholic

[1] Orde to Shelburne, 8 Mar. 1784, Aspinall transcript from the Lansdowne MSS. at Bowood, kindly placed at my disposal by Dr. P. J. Jupp.

Relief, and when the British Government had very good reason to think that it was not being properly represented by its Irish representatives, the Lord Lieutenant and Chief Secretary. But it is important to note that the lovelessness was there long before Catholic Relief was even heard of, and under the comparatively capable Rutland Administration. Indeed, it was endemic in the political situation, a facet of the loveless marriage of convenience between the British government and the Anglo-Irish Ascendancy. The unsuccessful and successful commercial measures of the period 1784–7 taught Pitt the value and, on the whole, the soundness of his Irish Cabinet's advice. But if, prior to 1792–3, he gave thought to the defective political system in Ireland—and it is probably unhistorical to expect him to have done so—he may have concluded that it was no bad thing, from the point of view of the British government, that Irish advice should continue to come from a panel of experts, not from a set of responsible Ministers with collective bargaining power against him.

The lovelessness of the relationship between the British Government and the Irish Cabinet is most clearly to be seen in Pitt's personal relations (which they must be called, for want of an alternative term) with Foster, Beresford, and Fitzgibbon. Pitt and Foster first met in November 1784. Significantly, they met under the unfavourable auspices of a very back-handed introduction from Orde, who (as has been noted) was far from being the pawn of his Irish advisers. Orde warned Pitt: '. . . it may be well to listen to him for the sake of information, but at the same time to be cautious of acceding too readily to his suggestions. I venture to recommend above all things a seeming confidence in his candour and liberality . . .' A few days later, he added that Foster would be anxious to make a merit of obtaining better terms for Ireland than his colleague, Beresford; '. . . some, therefore, of his suggestions, attributed to the Irish Nation, are merely the workings of his own busy mind, and are to be received accordingly. . . .'[3] During the ensuing negotiations over the commercial propositions, Pitt dealt as much as possible with Beresford in preference to Foster, in spite of the fact that it was

---

[1] Orde to Pitt, 1 and 6 Nov. 1784, Chatham MSS., P.R.O. 30/8/329, fols. 178, 180–1.

Foster who was Chancellor of the Exchequer and, next to Orde, would be responsible for piloting the propositions through the Irish House of Commons; in this, Pitt seems to have been following his own inclination, as well as acting on Orde's hint. In 1789, Foster complained to Orde: '. . . since you were here [1787] I have not had any intercourse with either . . . [Pitt or Lord Hawkesbury] or with any Ministerial man. When I was in London last year, they all forgot they had ever seen me, and your friend Rose mistook me for a Custom House Officer. . . .'[1] The mistake is easily comprehensible, as Rose was proverbially short-sighted, and Foster, out of speaker's robes, was simian and unimpressive in appearance; but significantly, Rose made no mistake about Beresford, whom he thought 'the pleasantest man in business that I have ever met with'.[2]

Foster, on his side, was almost pathetic in his admiration for Pitt—'a wonderful man', 'a prodigy of talents and integrity'.[3] These remarks, it should be noted, were made to Lord Sheffield at a time when Sheffield was in opposition and still a Pitt-hater, so they were certainly not made with a view to their being repeated to Pitt, nor is there any reason to doubt that they represented Foster's sincerely held opinion. Even when Pitt attacked Foster personally in 1799, Foster's angry public reaction included one expression of continued respect ('I look on him as the greatest Minister for Finance that ever existed in any country'), and his private reaction was sorrowful; in August 1799 he could find it in his heart to write to Lord Camden—and his subsequent conduct does not suggest that he was attempting a change of political tack—'. . . You kindly wish to soften any asperity in my mind towards Mr. Pitt, and I thank you; but I assure you, I feel none. I regret exceedingly his change of sentiment towards me, and I lament it the more because I ever looked to him with respect and esteem . . .' The 'misunderstanding' between Foster and Pitt over the Union revealed a more profound misunderstanding on Foster's part of Pitt's attitude towards him. Foster expected

---

[1] Foster to Orde, 25 Dec. 1789, F.P. D.562/8114.

[2] Rose to Orde, 7 Aug. 1785, Ashbourne, *Pitt*, p. 71. I am indebted to Dr. P. J. Jupp for the point about Rose's short sight.

[3] Foster to Sheffield, 24 Dec. [1785] and 23 Aug. [1786], *Anglo-Irish Dialogue*, p. 7.

that some consideration would be given to, or gratitude shown for, his '. . . thirty-eight years' continued support of Government in Parliament, the greater part of which time I was happy in enjoying much of the confidence of Administration, and was always a zealous and active friend . . .'[1] But the fact was that up to the Union crisis he was little more than a name in British ministerial circles, kindled no warmth in British ministerial breasts, and was therefore treated by Pitt as a mercenary who had been well-paid but had mutinied. (It was ironical, and no doubt profoundly irritating to Pitt, that the precedent for the subscription got up by the Ponsonbys and the Dublin bankers for the payment of Foster's debts in 1799, was the subscription got up by the London bankers and others for the payment of Pitt's debts in 1789; in refusing the money, Foster too was acting on the previous Pittite precedent.[2])

It is not surprising that Foster and Pitt should have misunderstood each other, and the attitude of each to the other. They did not meet in private company until 1804, and prior to 1802 Pitt had never even seen Foster in action in Parliament. Significantly, the British parliamentary reporter, 'Memory' Woodfall, who had seen him in action in the Irish Parliament in 1785, immediately pronounced him 'one of the readiest and most clear-headed men of business I ever met with'; this is significant, not just because Woodfall was a good judge, but also because he was an Englishman.[3] Presumably Foster made the same impression on Pitt—perhaps not in 1802, when he was fighting on difficult ground—but in the early part of 1804. Now that he had first-hand knowledge of Foster, both as a man and as a man of business, and now that the issues of the Union and Emancipation no longer sundered them, Pitt may even have come to see what had hitherto been visible only to Irishmen—that Foster was in many respects an Irish

---

[1] *Foster's Speech of 11 Apr. 1799*, p. 58; Foster to Camden, 3 Aug. 1799, Pratt MSS., K.A.O. U.840/O.81/4.

[2] Ehrman, *Pitt*, p. 657. It is indicative of the extent of Pittite irritation that Canning drafted a very machiavellian motion on the subject of Foster's subscription, for use in the Irish House of Commons—Helen Landreth, *The Pursuit of Robert Emmet* (London, 1949), p. 409. Because Foster was Speaker there was constitutional impropriety in the subscription.

[3] Woodfall to Eden, 16 Aug. 1785, *Auckland Correspondence*, i. 80.

Pitt. The policies which Foster pursued as Chancellor of the Irish Exchequer under Pitt, made the resemblance closer still: Foster's enquiry board of 1804 was based on a purely Pittite model, and his whole emphasis on reducing the cost of collecting the revenue rather than increasing its gross yield, had been Pitt's formula for British peace-time finance between 1783 and 1793.[1] When Foster tendered his resignation in June 1805, Pitt went so far as to say that he was 'most anxious, both on public and personal grounds, that it may be still possible to induce you to re-consider your determination.'[2] Too much, however, should not be read into this: Grattan observed at the time that Foster 'had nobody for him but Pitt, and Pitt gave him up for his convenience, as he did and must have done with regard to Lord Clare';[3] and Pitt's letter to Foster began formally with 'Dear Sir', as the few letters with which Pitt favoured Foster, Beresford, and Fitzgibbon always did.

With Beresford, Pitt had something more closely resembling a personal relationship. He seems to have sincerely felt the outrage of Beresford's dismissal in 1794, and came to his rescue as soon as the current crisis over Holland permitted; also, Beresford was probably the only Irish politician to whom Pitt wrote direct when canvassing for support in the early spring of 1804.[4] Their relationship is hard to define, because it was also personal in the sense that it was based on personal rather than epistolary contact. From time to time both Foster and Fitzgibbon inflicted on Pitt long and unsolicited expositions of their views on Irish policy: Beresford, a suppler diplomat than either of them, recognized that letter-writing was not Pitt's *forte*, and that he received very many more letters than he answered. Beresford, therefore, almost always communicated with him indirectly via Rose or Eden, relying on their sense of timing for the impression which his views made on Pitt. Perhaps the best indication of Beresford's standing with Pitt is that in 1784, when Beresford's brother-in-law, Lord Townshend, was pressing for a marquessate, he employed

---

[1] Ehrman, *Pitt*, pp. 256, 289 ff., 296; Abbot to Redesdale, 19 July 1804, Redesdale MSS., P.R.O.N.I. T.3030/2/8.

[2] Pitt to Foster, 29 June 1805, Chatham MSS., P.R.O. 30/8/102, fol. 200.

[3] Grattan to McCan, 15 July 1805, Grattan, *Life*, v. 271.

[4] Auckland to Beresford, 21 Jan. 1795, and Pitt to Beresford, 11 Apr. 1804, *Beresford Correspondence*, ii. 61 f., 285 ff.

as his intermediary with Pitt, not a fellow-Englishman, but Beresford.[1]

Unlike Beresford, and like Foster, Fitzgibbon was an object of suspicion rather than affection to Pitt and the British Government; where Foster was suspect because of his economic patriotism, Fitzgibbon was suspect because of his intemperance. Lord Charlemont nicknamed him 'Sir Petulant',[2] and his tendency to over-react to demonstrations of popular feeling helped to keep in business the often politically bankrupt Irish Opposition; this applied particularly to his proceeding by the doubtful legal process of attachment against sheriffs who had convened meetings to elect delegates to a national congress in 1784, and later to his high-handed behaviour over a disputed election to the Dublin lord mayoralty in 1790. Even the pliant Camden remarked in 1801, with marvellous euphemism, that Fitzgibbon was '. . . a person who, with various endowments and great virtues, could not return discretion of language amongst his qualifications for great situations . . .'[3] Fitzgibbon's tooth-and-nail support of Lord Buckingham during the Regency crisis in 1788–9 ought to have provided mitigation of these faults, and did in fact elicit that rarity, a letter of thanks from Pitt, and one which still more remarkably stated '. . . how happy I feel personally at such a moment in being embarked in the same boat with you . . .'[4] Unfortunately for Pitt's reputation, the letter was not spontaneous, but was inspired by a plea from Buckingham 'that Pitt would write him [Fitzgibbon] three lines of flattery'.[5] Soon afterwards, Pitt resisted Buckingham's recommendation that Fitzgibbon be appointed Lord Chancellor, and only agreed to the appointment after Buckingham had indignantly rejected a series of mediocre Englishmen and one Scot recommended by the British Government.[6]

---

[1] Townshend to Beresford, 27 Dec. 1784, *Beresford Correspondence*, i. 261 f.

[2] Charlemont to James Stewart, 3 Aug. 1790, Stewart of Killymoon MSS., P.R.O.N.I. D.3167/1/34.

[3] Memo. by Camden on Pitt's resignation in February 1801, Pratt MSS., K.A.O. U.840/O.127.

[4] Pitt to Fitzgibbon, 23 Feb. 1789, printed in J. R. O'Flanagan, *Lives of the Lord Chancellors of Ireland* (2 vols., Dublin, 1870), ii. 190.

[5] Buckingham to Grenville, 18 Feb. 1789, *H.M.C. Dropmore MSS.*, i. 413.

[6] Buckingham to Grenville, 30 Dec. 1788 and 13 May 1789, ibid. 393 ff. 467 f.

After 1793, there was a political, but hardly a personal, bond between Pitt and Fitzgibbon. Moreover, even over the Union, of which Fitzgibbon has been called the architect and the mainspring, what is remarkable is how little influence he actually wielded: he did not think a Union should be attempted in 1799, or before peace was made with France; Pitt had decided that it should be carried on narrowly Protestant lines, *before* Fitzgibbon arrived in London to impress this view upon him, although Fitzgibbon no doubt had some corroborative influence on the decision; Fitzgibbon thought that the best procedural approach was to pass acts appointing commissioners to negotiate the terms on behalf of the two kingdoms—Pitt's first thought, too, but one from which he departed in the event; and Fitzgibbon seems to have endeavoured, in vain, to overcome Pitt's *'very ill-placed'* 'scruples' about admitting from the outset the principle of compensation for disfranchised boroughs—a principle admitted by Pitt in 1785, and admitted even by the United Irish parliamentary reformers in 1793.[1] Up to 1791, and the sudden appearance of the policy of Catholic Relief, Fitzgibbon in some sense thought of himself as Pitt's man in Ireland; when acknowledging Pitt's letter of thanks of 1789, Fitzgibbon repeated, and mixed, Pitt's nautical metaphor: '. . . I shall always feel unshaken confidence when I am embarked on the same ground as you. . . .'[2] But after 1791–3 there could only be coincidence, not harmony, of sentiment between them. Fitzgibbon could no longer behave towards Pitt with that deference to which Pitt was accustomed, even from British politicians. In February 1801, for example, the anti-Emancipationist Eden, now Lord Auckland, after much soul-searching, wrote Pitt a long and

---

[1] Clare to Auckland, 3 July 1798, Falkiner, *Lord Clare*, p. 152; Pakenham, *Year of Liberty* pp. 339 f.; Clare to Auckland, 23 Dec. 1798, *Auckland Correspondence*, iv. 74; Pitt to Camden, 28 May 1798, Pratt MSS., K.A.O. U.840/O.190/A/6; William Elliot to Lord Minto, 11 Jan. 1799, Aspinall transcript from the Minto MSS. The remark about Pitt's very ill-placed scruples was made by Elliot, a Scottish Whig, who was then one of the Under-Secretaries at the Castle, but by no means a member of the 'Castle clique': Elliot favoured the inclusion of Emancipation in the terms of the Union. His opinion on the subject of borough compensation is, therefore, particularly significant, as is the fact that Pitt ignored it. By delaying the recognition of the principle until after the Government's defeat in January 1799, Pitt converted a norm of contemporary political thinking into a bribe.

[2] Fitzgibbon to Pitt, 2 Mar. 1789, Chatham MSS., P.R.O. 30/70/153.

restrained letter in which he ventured to dissent from Pitt's opinion; Fitzgibbon's reaction, by contrast, was to descend on Downing Street in person, and obtain two separate interviews, in both of which he inveighed against Pitt's 'Popish projects'.[1]

In February 1799 one of Lord Downshire's members quipped: '. . . The S[peaker] and Pitt answering each other is like Phillidor and the Spaniard playing chess at Madrid and London. . . .'[2] In a way, the comment encapsulated a communications problem which had existed between Pitt and his Irish cabinet since 1784. The paradox of the whole period is that, while there were Irish Foxites, and even Irish Portlandites, there were no Irish Pittites, with the possible exception of Beresford. There were not many English Pittites either— possibly only Grenville, Dundas, and ardent young followers of Pitt like Canning. In 1801 Lord Auckland found that he was not one of the number, though he had been close to Pitt for a considerable time, and Pitt had almost married his daughter. If Pitt commanded the respect of members of his Irish cabinet, without responding to the warmth into which they sought to translate that respect, then that was not untypical of his relationship with nearly all British politicians. However, it mattered more in his relationships with the Irish politicians, because these were already hampered by the Irish Sea, and could less well afford the additional obstruction of Pitt's personality. Of the three ablest and most influential members of the British Government—Grenville, Dundas, and Pitt himself—who were also the three who took most interest in Irish policy, only Grenville had ever been across the Irish Sea. What was unfortunate, though perfectly understandable, is that at a time when great political ability was in short supply (and, arguably, it always is), there was no meeting of minds between these three and the three ablest Irish politicians on the government side—Foster, Beresford, and Fitzgibbon. In such a meeting, Foster, Beresford, and Fitzgibbon would surely have held their own, as they more than did against Pitt's lords lieutenant and chief secretaries. These lords lieuten-

[1] Auckland to Pitt, 31 Jan. [1801], and Pitt to Auckland, 31 Jan. 1801, *Auckland Correspondence*, iv. 122 ff.; Clare to Shannon, 13 Feb. 1801, Shannon MSS., P.R.O.N.I. D.2707/A/2/2/156.

[2] Robert Johnson to Downshire, 19 Feb. 1799, Downshire MSS., P.R.O.N.I. D.607/G/75.

ant and chief secretaries were of the stuff of which the rank
and file of Pitt's British cabinets were made, and Westmorland,
Hobart, Camden, and Pelham did in fact sit in Pitt's or Addington's cabinets subsequently to their service in Ireland. In towering over them, Foster, Beresford, and Fitzgibbon were towering
over the generality of British politicians as clearly as did Pitt,
Grenville, and Dundas. However, not only was there not a
meeting of minds between the big three in each kingdom; there
was, if anything, a battle between them for the minds of the
lords lieutenant and chief secretaries. That such a battle was on,
was apparent to all in 1791–3; but basically it was being fought
non-stop between 1784, and the appointment of Lord Cornwallis and the decision in favour of a Union in 1798.

Since this was the case, it is necessary to consider why the
British Government did not change the composition of its
unloved Irish cabinet. The change need not have involved the
bold, constitutional experiment of responsible, cabinet government which was in contemplation in 1792–3; it could have
been a superficial, window-dressing kind of change, by which
one or two of the old stagers were replaced by members of the
Opposition—in·other words, the sort of cabinet which had
existed briefly under Lord Northington and which came into
even briefer existence under Lord Fitzwilliam.

Certainly, the members of the Irish Cabinet of the 1790s
(excluding the Fitzwilliam interlude), who have earlier been
defined as Foster, Beresford, Fitzgibbon, Parnell, and Agar,
would not only have put up no collective resistance to such a
change; they would positively have welcomed it. The Irish
Cabinet of the 1790s was riven with personal rivalries. The
experts of which it was composed resembled *prime donne*
in the display of their expertise. Fitzgibbon and Beresford
generally acted together (apart from anything else, they were
brothers-in-law); so did Foster and Parnell (Parnell was
content to be Foster's under-study); Agar, on the other hand,
was a solo performer (probably because he alone had an
association with the British Opposition which, although he
was the High Protestant churchman *par excellence*, almost resulted in his promotion to the Archbishopric of Armagh under
Fitzwilliam).[1] These three sections of the Irish Cabinet

[1] Beresford to Auckland, 15 Nov. 1794, *Beresford Correspondence*, ii. 44.

competed with each other for the attention of successive administrations, their mutual suspicions and antagonisms sometimes expressing themselves in the mild form of the 'little jealousies'[1] apparent between Foster and Beresford in late 1784, and fomented wittingly or unwittingly by Orde and Pitt; and sometimes in the ludicrous form recorded by Camden in 1797: '[Beresford] . . . has taken great pains to show that the annihilation of the duty on beer has not tended to increase the manufacture of that article, whilst on the other hand the Speaker is moving every day for papers to endeavour to show that the measure is an advantageous one. Being fresh from Beresford, I am apt to think he is in the right. . . .'[2] Sometimes, however, the suspicions and antagonisms could take a much more serious form—for example, the parliamentary run on Beresford in October 1794, which was partly inspired by Foster, and which concerned Beresford's alleged corruption as a member of the Dublin wide streets board. Under Fitzwilliam, parliamentary committees were set up to investigate, not only the wide streets board, but also Beresford's administration of the Revenue, and it would seem that Foster was as prominent in the latter investigation as in the former. By August 1795 matters had reached such a pitch that Beresford was contemplating a move to the first lordship of the treasury (in the end he was acquitted by both parliamentary committees, and remained at the head of the Revenue); from the fact that Camden at this stage considered it 'awkward' for Beresford and Thomas Foster to sit at the same board, it would seem that John Foster was still associated in the witch-hunt.[3] Beresford's own correspondence reveals only one instance of friendly cooperation between himself and Foster, and includes many unflattering references to Foster. Foster's personal relations with Fitzgibbon were notoriously bad. In February 1791,

---

[1] Orde to Rutland, 30 Nov. 1784, *H.M.C. Rutland MSS.*, iii. 152.

[2] Camden to Pelham, 7 Feb. 1797, Pelham MSS., B.L. Add. MS. 33102, fols. 156–7.

[3] Douglas to Pitt, 16 Oct. [1794], Chatham MSS., P.R.O. 30/8/327, fol. 248; Fitzgibbon to Beresford, 18 Apr. 1795, Beresford to Carlisle, 27 Apr. 1795, and Beresford to Auckland, 5 Mar. 1796, *Beresford Correspondence*, ii. 104, 107, 102 f.; Ashbourne, *Pitt*, pp. 216 f; Camden to Pelham, 25 Aug. 1795, Pelham MSS., B.L. Add. MS. 33101, fols. 229–30. Sylvester Douglas's opinion, expressed in the letter cited above, was that in the wide streets board business Beresford had been irregular, though not dishonest.

after Foster had joined in an opposition attempt to get rid of Beresford's 'complicated and oppressive' restrictions on brewing, Lord Shannon reported:

... This business ... brought on a serious quarrel in the Irish Cabinet ...; and the Lord Chancellor, after expressing himself to me in very strong terms on the Speaker's conduct, said Government ought to drive him from the Chair and put Billy P[onsonby] into it, and that in a fortnight. These two always hated each other, but the Speaker is, I understand, jealous at not being more a Minister. ...[1]

Since Lord Shannon was Ponsonby's brother-in-law, and at this time allied with him in opposition, Fitzgibbon's diatribe was tantamount to a political overture; and in fact, Fitzgibbon was always inclined towards the Ponsonbys, who felt a 'personal attachment' to him as late as the end of 1794.[2] Parnell, Fitzgibbon considered 'the most brutal, blundering, inefficient financier in the habitable World', and sided with the Lord Lieutenant in resisting Parnell's exploitation of the treasury board in 1794.[3] On his side, the good-natured Parnell seems to have been comparatively free from this spirit of internecine rancour: in January 1795, Beresford heard that, at a drunken dinner which Parnell gave for the Ponsonbys and others, '... Sir John got into an argument, and swore that they never did so silly a thing as turn me out, and was pleased to speak of me as an efficient and honest servant of the Crown. ...'[4] Parnell's good opinion of Beresford is interesting; so too is a comment made in February 1797 that there had been 'not a little difference' between Parnell and Foster.[5] This, however, was probably only a temporary difference. Not only were Parnell and Foster normally in alliance; they both were

[1] Shannon to Lord Boyle, 15 Feb. 1791, Shannon MSS., P.R.O.N.I. D.2707/A/3/3/9. Foster's views on the Irish brewing industry prevailed in the end—Donoughmore to Foster, 6 Apr. 1807, F.P. T.2519/4/336. I am indebted for this latter reference to Mr. T. R. McCavery.

[2] Thomas Knox to Abercorn, 30 Jan. [1792], Abercorn MSS., P.R.O.N.I. T.2541/IB1/3/9; T. L. O'Beirne to Portland, 23 Aug. 1794, Aspinall transcript from the Fitzwilliam MSS.

[3] Fitzgibbon to Auckland, [Jan.] 1799, *Fitzgibbon Letters from the Sneyd Muniments*, p. 305; Fitzgibbon to Hobart, 4 Apr. 1794, Chatham MSS., Cambridge U.L. Add. MS. 6958/1428.

[4] Beresford to Auckland, 19 Jan. 1795, *Beresford Correspondence*, ii. 60.

[5] John Stewart to Abercorn, 27 Feb. [1797], Abercorn MSS., P.R.O.N.I. T.2541/IB2/2/5.

well-disposed to Grattan, in the same way that Fitzgibbon was well-disposed to the Ponsonbys.

Thus, at cabinet level, there was a good deal of fluidity in the Irish political situation—a fluidity based on the Irish administration's freedom to bargain with individuals, not on the possibility of the individuals bargaining collectively with the Irish administration—but a good deal of fluidity nonetheless. The fact that broadly speaking the same people were in cabinet for most of the 1790s, and indeed for most of the period 1784–98, obscures but must not conceal this essential fluidity. These people remained the 'ins' for a variety of reasons, of which a sense of collective identity was not one.

For a start, when Pitt came to power at the end of 1783, all British politicians were still reeling from the shock of the agitations which had extorted the Constitution of 1782, and which had frightened the Patriots and Whigs in the Duke of Portland's Cabinet out of completing the settlement with some provision for commercial and 'imperial concerns'. Compared with nineteenth-century Irish agitations, those of the early 1780s seem a genteel and élitist business. But they were not so regarded at the time, either by the British government or by conservative Irish politicians like Foster (nor in reality were they[1]). The loss of the American colonies had put the British government into a frame of mind in which it could regard the loss of Ireland as a serious possibility. So many things which were conceivable under the Constitution of 1782 never came to pass, that it is hard now to remember that it left Ireland at perfect liberty, for example, to accredit ambassadors to foreign courts, or to build its own navy: the British government was very much alive to these dangers, and in stipulating for a contribution from Ireland towards the naval expenses of the Empire, Pitt's Government was in part motivated by a desire to obviate the second.[2] The British government was also very much alive to the danger of employing Patriots and Whigs in cabinet. The lesson of the Portland Administration was that such Irish politicians were hopelessly addicted to 'the corrupt

---

[1] For the social and political implications of the Volunteers, see D. H. Smyth, 'The Volunteer Movement in Ulster: Background and Development, 1745–85', Q.U.B. Ph.D. thesis, pp. 66 ff.

[2] Sydney to Rutland, 1 Feb. 1785, *H.M.C. Rutland MSS.*, iii. 169, 172.

love of a flimsy and precarious popularity' (in Fitzgibbon's telling phrase),[1] and the opposition to the commercial propositions mounted by Grattan and the Ponsonbys, all of whom had been prominent under Portland, only reinforced the lesson. In March 1783 Lord Temple (the future Buckingham), who was himself liable to the charge of running after Irish popularity, solemnly declared: '. . . my firm opinion is that we shall always find it necessary to look to the old Court here, and not to those whom every gale will turn . . .'[2] In less spectacular instances than that of 1782, the Patriots and Whigs had proved themselves unreliable, if not actually treacherous. Years later Buckingham recalled to Pitt:

. . . You well remember the spirit and letter of the compact when we opened the W. India trade to her [Ireland], and you know the infamous deviation from it proposed in 1783 by Grattan and the Crown Lawyers, Yelverton and Kelly, in L. Northington's Government, and carried against Parnell and Beresford and Foster, who stated the fraudulent valuation of their duties on sugars, compared with those of G. Britain. . . .[3]

It is highly significant that Parnell, Beresford, and Foster should have acted in this instance as the champions of British interests and the upholders of the compact with Great Britain. The outcome of the commercial propositions must surely have demonstrated to the British Government that even Foster's economic patriotism was not, by Irish standards, immoderate and dangerous?

Moreover, while there was well-founded doubt about the inclination of Patriots and Whigs to conduct themselves in cabinet with reasonable regard to British interests, there was also doubt about their ability to get the necessary business of government done. Were there, really, any men of business in their ranks? It may be significant that the two successive Patriot Attorneys-General, Hussey Burgh and Yelverton, both escaped to the well-remunerated safety of chief judgeships as fast as they could—something which the next Attorney-General, Fitzgibbon, declined to do in 1786.[4] Hussey Burgh

---

[1] *Clare's Speech of 1800*, p. 41.

[2] Temple to Grenville, 1 Mar. 1783. *H.M.C. Dropmore MSS.*, i. 198.

[3] Buckingham to Pitt, 13 Feb. [1790?], Chatham MSS., P.R.O. 30/8/325, fol. 176.

[4] Fitzgibbon to Eden, 10 Jan. 1786, Falkiner, *Lord Clare*, p. 145; Orde to Rutland, 31 May 1786, *H.M.C. Rutland MSS.*, iii. 303.

and Yelverton both needed the money badly, and Fitzgibbon did not. However, it is also likely that Hussey Burgh and Yelverton found the transition from opposition orator to government spokesman uncongenial. Whatever their motives, they and one or two others of lesser note, like Thomas Kelly, had their chance of front-bench political office, and threw it up. Fitzgibbon has been charged with time-serving; but it must always be remembered that he chose and stuck to 'the hurricane sphere'—as did Foster. William and George Ponsonby are possible examples of men of business in the Patriot and Whig ranks; George acquired important experience of business in Anthony Foster's former office of First Counsel to the Revenue Commissioners, 1782–9, and William had by no means insignificant administrative responsibilities as Joint Postmaster General, 1784–9; indeed, even when in opposition, the Ponsonbys displayed a certain glibness and professionalism which grated on the country gentlemen.[1] However, the Ponsonbys cannot really be called Whigs until they wrong-footed themselves on the Regency in 1788–9. Up to then, and arguably for long after, they were simply the most numerous and (next to Lord Ely) least scrupulous of the aristocratic parliamentary interests in the House of Commons. A more serious candidate as a Patriot or Whig man of business is John Forbes. Forbes has been credited with a sound and detailed grasp of the *minutiae* of public accountability.[2] However, it should be noted that an anonymous memorandum, almost certainly the work of Fitzgibbon, successfully drove a horse and cart through the draftsmanship of Forbes's Responsibility Bill of 1793;[3] so Forbes's claims are at least not beyond dispute. Grattan, clearly, has no claims. Two examples have been quoted of his failure to understand the substance of measures.[4] When Grattan turned to the tithe question in 1786, Fitzgibbon, who was still on fairly friendly terms with him, observed cruelly: 'if I know him, the deeper he goes there, the faster he will stick'.[5] Grattan was not even a ready speaker. Commenting on his speech on the commercial propositions

---

[1] *Roman Catholic Debates of 1792*, p. 99.
[2] Kiernan, *Financial Administration*, pp. 279 ff.   [3] See p. 380, *n.* 5.
[4] See pp. 57, 368.
[5] Fitzgibbon to Orde, 15 Sept. 1787, Bolton MSS., N.L.I. MS. 15883/9.

in August 1785, Lord Camden (a good English judge of the subject) wrote: it 'smells a little too much of the lamp. It reads better as a pamphlet than I fancy it could be heard as a speech. . . .'[1] (Yet, resort to the lamp had not given Grattan mastery of the subject.) Grattan's oratory is characterized by complex and often overstrained antithesis—a style which no one speaking *ex tempore* could have affected, and which people must have found very difficult to follow at first hearing. At one crucial moment in the Regency debates, when he was taken by surprise, he actually seems to have been lost for words.[2] There were various reasons for Grattan's reluctance to serve in cabinets. But fear of exposing his deficiency in business must surely have been among them? Stress has already been laid on the increased importance of Irish men of business in the day-to-day workings of government since the Constitution of 1782. It is probable that the Ponsonbys, Grattan, and Lord Fitzwilliam recognized this too, and sought to humour Foster, not just because they wanted him out of the speakership, but also because they thought that they could not quarrel with both Foster and Beresford and still carry through the equalization of duties, which was part of the agreed programme of the Fitzwilliam Administration.[3] There were stronger practical than political obstacles to a general sweep.

Grattan was not the only important Patriot politician who was disinclined to contribute to a broadening of the Irish cabinet by at least lending his name to it: Lord Charlemont and Forbes shared his flamboyant coyness in this respect. This section of the Opposition was haunted by the spectre of Henry Flood's vice-treasurership, which was reinvoked by Grattan's unparliamentary (and carefully rehearsed[4]) denunciation of Flood in 1783. They never took office, even when administrations which they supported were in power, considering themselves (in the sententious words of Henry Grattan Junior)

---

[1] Camden to Robert Stewart, 4 Oct. 1785, Pratt MSS., K.A.O. U.840/C.173/95.

[2] Buckingham to Grenville, 20 Feb. 1789, *H.M.C. Dropmore MSS.*, i. 414.

[3] See p. 60.

[4] Duke of Chandos to Flood, 9 Nov. 1783, printed in *Original Letters . . . to the Rt. Hon. Henry Flood*, ed. 'T.R.' (London, 1820), pp. 123 f. In this letter, Chandos describes Grattan's conduct as that of an 'assassin', which implies that Chandos considered Grattan's speech to have been prepared in advance. A comparison of the two speeches shows that Flood's was the much rougher, and therefore probably *ex tempore*, performance; Grattan's has all the precision of premeditation.

'too high to be sold to any Government'.[1] This was an unfortunate attitude. A 'mixed' government of Pittites and
Portlandites worked well in Great Britain after 1794, in spite of
the Fitzwilliam débâcle, and some kind of 'mixed' government
would seem to have been still more appropriate to the circumstances of Ireland. However, even when Rockinghamite Whig
elements were in power in Great Britain in 1782–3, and
the composition of the Irish Cabinet reflected this fact to a
greater or lesser extent, Charlemont and Grattan could not be
prevailed upon to take office; and although Forbes would have
taken the solicitorship-general under Portland if it had been
available for him, he appears to have refused it under the
much less Whiggish Administration of Northington.[2] Under
Fitzwilliam in 1794–5 the situation was different, because of the
rapacity of the Ponsonbys: Charlemont would not have taken
office, Forbes certainly would, but only Grattan was given the
opportunity to refuse.[3] Once it was clear that they were not
going to be baulked of the Constitution of 1782, Charlemont,
Grattan, and Forbes had given free-lance support to the
Portland and Temple Administrations, frequently (though
much less frequently under Temple) participating in cabinets,
and Grattan had given free-lance support to Lord Northington
and even in 1784, to the Duke of Rutland. All three, but particularly Grattan and Forbes, were prominent members of
the Fitzwilliam Cabinet; and without holding office Grattan
and Forbes played a semi-ministerial role in the House of
Commons. However, apart from Grattan in 1784, none of them
gave even free-lance support to Pittite administrations, far
less participated in their cabinets. The idea of such participation may seem far-fetched. But it has already been noted that
the Foster/Parnell section of the existing Irish Cabinet was
well-disposed to Grattan, and to some extent these sentiments
were reciprocated. Henry Grattan Junior's *Life* of his father,
which usually echoes his father's views on people, consistently
speaks of Foster with sorrow rather than with anger, portraying
him as both economic wizard and fallen angel; and in 1801

---

[1] Grattan, *Life*, ii. 224. For Charlemont's objections to taking office, see
Malcomson, *Speaker Pery*, p. 59, *n* 77.

[2] Forbes to Adair, 15 June 1782 and 30 July 1794, Adair MSS., B.L. Add. MS.
53802—unfoliated.

[3] Charlemont to Stewart, 2 Dec. 1794, Stewart MSS., P.R.O.N.I. D.3167/1/59.

it was noted that '. . . Grattan . . . ever kept up great intercourse with the supporters of Government and, odd to say, that
class whose alleged corruption was the great ground of his
clamour. . . .'[1] Even Charlemont, who was apt to turn political
into personal quarrels (as he did with Grattan himself), had
nothing harsher to say of Foster's candidature for the speakership in 1785 than: '. . . whatever good private qualities he
may have, as a public man" [he] is certainly inadmissible on
my principles . . .'[2] In practical terms, neither Charlemont
nor Grattan is likely to have been much loss, since Charlemont
shared the infirmity of 'my ever-beloved Marquess' (Rockingham) and could barely bring himself to utter a word in Parliament, and like Grattan he had only a slender grasp of detail or
business; but the moral effect of their presence in office, or at
least in cabinet would have been considerable. Forbes was a
greater practical loss. Strangely, although he was an Irish
Portlandite, he never seems to have recognized the existence
of the Pitt–Portland Coalition in Great Britain. In 1795,
when Camden offered him a seat on the treasury board,
which now existed by virtue of Forbes's Responsibility Act
passed earlier in that year, he refused the offer because it had
not come direct from Portland and, apparently, because
Camden was a Pittite. Next year he accepted a West Indian
governorship (which was the best Portland could do), bade
farewell to Ireland and the possibility of achieving anything
further there, and was killed by the West Indian climate in
1797.[3]

In 1780, Forbes had expressed the view that it was virtually
impossible for the Irish Opposition to co-operate with the
British.[4] In his subsequent conduct he ran counter to this view,
as did most Irish opposition politicians. Indeed, in Fitzgibbon's
eyes, the biggest single defect in the Irish political system,
after the Constitution of 1782 as before, was the tendency of the
British and Irish oppositions to co-operate,[5] which naturally
led Irish politicians who were free from Grattan's, Charlemont's, and Forbes's temperamental or conscientious aversion

---

[1] Grattan, *Life*, ii. 13 ff.; Henry Alexander to Abbot, 13 Nov. 1801, Colchester
MSS., P.R.O. 30/9/1, part 3/1.
[2] Charlemont to Stewart, 20 Aug. 1785, Stewart MSS., P.R.O.N.I. D.3167/1/16.
[3] Forbes to Adair, 12 Jan. 1796, Adair MSS., B.L. Add. MS. 53802.
[4] Forbes to Adair, 6 Feb. 1780, ibid.   [5] *Clare's Speech of 1800*, pp. 49 f.

to office, to trammel themselves with engagements to the British opposition: true to his apprenticeship under Lord Northington, Fitzgibbon favoured a broadening of the bottom of the Irish cabinet, and feared any narrowing of the lord lieutenant's area of selection. In June 1784, Fox declared his intention of making his harvest in Ireland, and did so with considerable success over the commercial propositions. However, there was no clear alignment of the oppositions until the Regency crisis. On that occasion the Irish Opposition was joined by many traditional supporters of the Castle. But the almost immediate recovery of the King, and Buckingham's success in bullying or buying virtually all the traditional supporters except Lord Shannon back to their old allegiance, had the effect of polarizing Irish politics along British party lines. The appointment of Lord Fitzwilliam in 1794 promised to end this polarization, but in fact accentuated it. The recall of Fitzwilliam drove all the important Irish Whigs (except, for a while, the Duke of Leinster) into embittered and increasingly fruitless opposition, culminating in secession on the Foxite model in 1797. In May of that year, when Pitt tried to open a negotiation with Grattan and the Ponsonbys, via Fitzwilliam and of course without the knowledge of his Irish Cabinet, he met with a stony response; the Irish Whigs insisted on the proscription of Fitzgibbon and the existing Irish Cabinet, and in any case were reluctant to take office except as a result of a change of government in Great Britain, and at the hands of Fox, not of Pitt.[1]

The important point about this process of polarization is that all the running was made by the British and Irish oppositions: Pitt and his lords lieutenant were on the whole patient and indulgent in their attitudes to Irish politicians whose connections lay with the British opposition; for example, Rutland and Buckingham (up to the Regency crisis) put up with much political waywardness from the Ponsonbys and the Duke of Leinster. It so happened that the principal family connections which criss-crossed the Irish Sea were between Irish politicians and opponents of Pitt, not between Irish politicians and his supporters.[2] Even the youthful Castlereagh is not an exception:

[1] William Ponsonby to Fitzwilliam, 29 May 1797, Aspinall transcript from the Fitzwilliam MSS.   [2] See p. 27.

in the early 1790s his step-grandfather, Lord Camden, sat in Pitt's Cabinet, but his grandfather, Lord Hertford, was in opposition until 1793. Even Agar, as has been mentioned, had connections with the British Opposition, which jerked him into opposition over the Regency: his uncle, Welbore Ellis, originally a Northite, suffered under the unpleasant nickname of 'Fox's jackal', and was in opposition until the Pitt–Portland Coalition in 1794. The twist which such family connections gave to Irish politics was an important matter of accident. However, it was probably in the nature of the political connection between Great Britain and Ireland for British and Irish oppositions to have more in common than British governments and their leading Irish supporters; British oppositions often acted irresponsibly where Irish issues were concerned, but British governments could not, because on them lay the heavy responsibility for maintaining the British connection. When the Rockingham Whigs came to power in 1782, they realized for the first time the seriousness of the game they had been playing with the Irish Opposition, but were not able to convince the Irish Opposition that it had all been a game. Likewise, if the Prince of Wales had had time in 1789 to accept the Regency of Ireland and to appoint a lord lieutenant, that lord lieutenant would probably have endeavoured to resist some of the reforming measures proposed to him by the Irish Whigs, and perhaps the principle which they intended to impose on him that they were the arbiters of who should constitute his cabinet. When a British opposition became a British government, it saw Irish politics in a different light: it was partly *because* Pitt was in power from 1783 to 1801 that there were no Irish Pittites during that period.

The Ponsonbys, though subject to the tendency common to all potential opposition groups, require special consideration. Unquestionably Foxite by 1797, they had deserted Pitt for Fox in 1785 and again in 1788–9; but like the other Irish opposition groups they had not scrupled to desert Fox for Pitt, or at any rate Portland, in 1794–5. Of the Ponsonbys it can probably be said that, up to 1795, they were actuated by love of office, not by love of Fox. Indeed, they would joyously have assumed the role of the Irish Pittites, if Pitt had given them any encouragement. In November 1787, George Ponsonby had the bad taste to use the death of the Duke of Rutland as the pretext for making a tender of their services to Pitt:

> . . . In the last conversation which I had with him [Rutland] upon political affairs, he told me that you had been so good as to interest yourself in my behalf, and warmly to recommend to him an attention to my advancement. I now beg leave to return you my most sincere thanks for this kindness, and to assure you that I feel it the more sensibly . . . as flowing spontaneously from your own unsolicited friendship . . . I can assure you that this Country does not contain any man or set of men who were more truly and firmly attached to the Duke of Rutland in his lifetime than myself and my family and friends, or who are more desirous to support your Government, administered as it was by him. I do not know what system you mean to pursue with respect to this Country, but so far as I can collect from my Lord Sydney's letter to the late Lord Northington, it is the plan of your Administration not to suffer any change in the persons who administer the King's Government here, to produce any change in the mode of governing, but to continue the same just and equitable conduct towards this Country and the supporters of its Government, from one Representative to another. Upon this point, I take the liberty of an old friendship to request a particular communication from you, as such a declaration from you will enable my family to give a decided and I hope powerful support, let whosoever come over here as Lord Lieutenant. . . .[1]

In considering this letter, it has to be remembered that the Ponsonbys had done more than most to wreck Pitt's cherished commercial propositions, the most important measure of the Rutland Administration; that, though their opposition had been forgiven them, they continued to be unreliable and a thorn in Rutland's side; and that they were on a number of occasions a thorn in his successor's side, before they finally went into opposition over the Regency and were dismissed from their offices.[2] If Pitt did not answer this letter—and there is no evidence that he did—his failure need not, for once, be imputed to neglect. During the abortive and perhaps half-hearted negotiations of the spring of 1797 it was reported that Pitt would make 'no difficulty about Removals—the bitter

---

[1] George Ponsonby to Pitt, 11 Nov. 1787, Chatham MSS., P.R.O. 30/8/329, fols. 372–3. The letter began, 'My Dear Sir', a familiarity which Fitzgibbon rarely permitted himself in a letter to Pitt, and Foster and Beresford never. Even Dundas was only on 'My Dear Sir' terms with Pitt until the day of Pitt's death.

[2] Buckingham to Grenville, 22 Mar. 1789, *H.M.C. Dropmore MSS.*, i. 436.

pill is the Admissions'.[1] It was perhaps in Pitt's nature to feel gratitude less strongly than resentment; but he certainly had reason to feel resentment at the conduct of the Ponsonbys.

In the apparent absence of Ponsonby Papers, it is hard to be fair to that conduct. However, it should be noted that William Ponsonby, who was animated by a semi-hereditary ambition for his father's old office, the speakership, was eleven years older than his brother, George, and only five years younger than his hitherto successful rival, Foster. William Ponsonby would not have become Speaker in the course of nature, and this made him impatient of 'fasting and mortification'.[2] Moreover, he was an impatient man at the best of times. In 1797, Edmund Burke complained that Ponsonby '. . . seems to be guided by nothing but his passions. He is by his natural temper perhaps the most vehemently irritable and habitually irritated of any person whom I have ever heard of—I mean of a man conversant with publick affairs; and he is even yet more hot in deliberation and council than he is in debate. . . .'[3] Ponsonby was not a man to be satisfied with emoluments (of which his connections and he enjoyed at least their fair share in 1782–9), and probably not with the fluctuating and uncertain extent of influence which was accorded to the individuals who composed the Irish Cabinet, as it stood. He seems to have been a man who sought to engross power, not to share it. Hence his readiness to risk what power he had on the chance of a change of British government in 1785 and 1788–9; hence also his rashness and rapacity in 1794–5. Because of his avidity for the speakership, and because of the traditional feud between the Beresfords and the Ponsonbys, it was natural that he should attack Beresford, not Foster. But the Fitzwilliam Administration was guilty of great precipitancy and inconsistency, as well as breach of engagement, in dismissing Beresford (who was well-disposed to retire), in offering him a pension equivalent to his full salary (the terms Beresford obtained when he retired honourably in 1802, but in 1794–5 a contravention of the Pension Act), and subsequently in charging him with malversation (a crime which, if it could have been proved against

---

[1] See p. 400, *n.* 1.
[2] Robert Day to Lord Glandore, 6 July 1790, FitzGerald MSS., 5/19.
[3] Burke to French Laurence, 1 June 1797, *Burke Correspondence*, ix. 364.

him, would have deprived him of the right to any pension at all).[1] Besides, in 1794–5 as in 1806,[2] the Beresfords were not at all anxious for battle with the Ponsonbys. The day before Beresford's dismissal, his brother, Lord Waterford, had called at the Castle to offer their support to the new Administration.[3] This was not necessarily an interested support; Lord Waterford was not strongly, if at all, anti-Emancipationist, and even after Beresford's dismissal would not join in the opposition to Grattan's Emancipation Bill, although he allowed the rest of his family connection to do so.[4] From the Emancipationist point of view, therefore, Ponsonby never did so silly a thing as turn Beresford out. In August 1790, Lord Donoughmore had written to his father, Hely-Hutchinson: '. . . certainly, the English Minister cannot like the furious race his friends in Ireland have been running, if he looked at Irish characters with English eyes . . .'; and elsewhere in the same letter he censured Fitzgibbon and Beresford for 'hard driving'.[5] While Pitt had many reservations about 'his friends', the Regency crisis and the Fitzwilliam débâcle must have convinced him that the real hard drivers were the Ponsonbys. It was not the exclusiveness, and certainly not the sense of collective identity, of the existing Irish Cabinet which kept the Ponsonbys out of office; rather it was the Ponsonbys' own shameless and compulsive office-seeking.

There was one other possibility for a partial displacement or a general sweep of the existing Irish Cabinet; this was Lord Abercorn and his political following. Abercorn had inherited his uncle's Irish estates and electoral interest in 1789, and lost no time in extending the latter and assembling about himself a small group of young men of ability and ambition, headed by the Knox brothers and E. H. Pery. Although this was a unique, and perhaps self-defeating, way of going about it, his aim seems to have been to establish himself as Pitt's Irish

---

[1] See, for example, Fitzgibbon to Beresford, 26 Mar. 1795, *Beresford Correspondence*, ii. 88 ff.

[2] See pp. 235 f.

[3] Memo. by Lord Westmorland on the Fitzwilliam débâcle, Feb. 1795, Chatham MSS., P.R.O. 30/8/331, fol. 320.

[4] Fitzgibbon to Beresford, 14 Feb. 1795, *Beresford Correspondence*, ii. 75; John Pollock to Westmorland, 15 Apr. 1795, Westmorland MSS., S.P.O. fol. 111.

[5] Donoughmore to Hely-Hutchinson, 6 Aug. 1790, *H.M.C. Donoughmore MSS.*, p. 324.

oracle, and more specifically to get himself appointed Lord Lieutenant. His outrunning of the British Government in 1792–3, which has already been discussed, almost certainly wrecked what chances he ever had. But, prior to that, Abercorn himself rightly or wrongly thought that an Abercorn viceroyalty was a serious possibility. He alluded plainly enough to it in June 1791 in a letter to Thomas Knox: '. . . The point which I know you have most at heart relative to me will, I think, not take place, unless you can give us [presumably Pitt and him] reasons to over-balance ours, but we may consider what are else the best and fittest objects to keep in view. . . .'[1] It was an unspoken rule of British government in Ireland not to appoint Irishmen to the lord lieutenancy. But largely absentee Irish proprietors—Lord Hertford in 1765–6 and indeed Fitzwilliam—were not deemed to be disqualified on the ground of Irishness, and Lord Buckinghamshire's family connections in Ireland, which greatly contributed to his troubles, had not been deemed a bar to his appointment. Rutland, Westmorland, and Camden were all appointed to the lord lieutenancy partly on the strength of their Cambridge friendship with Pitt, and Abercorn, too, was a Cambridge friend.[2] The obvious attraction of an Abercorn viceroyalty from Pitt's point of view was that Abercorn appeared not to be a man whom every Irish gale would turn, while at the same time his mind was not closed to reforming measures. Indeed, Abercorn's party had been formed on the Pittite principles

. . . that upon the topics of Pensions, Police, and other questions of expense and job, our line should be strenuously, explicitly, and manfully to oppose Whig Club plausibilities, brought forward insidiously and obnoxiously for purposes of faction, disunion, and embarrassment . . .; at the same time professing that we hate jobs and improper expenditure of the Public Money as much as the most *soi-disant* Patriot of them all, and that . . . we feel and we avow ourselves ready and willing to co-operate, whenever Government shall upon mature consideration bring forward plans tending to limit, as England has done (but not servilely copying her), an improperly extended Pension List . . .; or should Government delay

[1] Abercorn to Thomas Knox, 30 June [1791], Abercorn MSS., P.R.O.N.I. T.2541/IK/11/150.
[2] Ehrman, *Pitt*, p. 17.

so long to bring forward such plans as to give just cause of doubt whether it ever meant it at all, we shall think ourselves authorized to come forward with such plans ourselves, etc, etc. . . .[1]

This approximated to Dundas's pious, and hypocritical, hope of governing Ireland on a less corrupt system.[2]

An Abercorn viceroyalty would certainly have been an interesting phenomenon, although it is hard to speculate on what its outcome would have been. Abercorn's ambitious young men had the contempt of youth for virtually all the established political figures in Ireland—the existing Irish Cabinet (particularly Beresford and Fitzgibbon), Grattan, the Ponsonbys, and so on. They would thus have been disposed to form themselves into a self-sufficient and exclusive cabinet, although it is doubtful for how long they could have sustained such a system, as none of them had any experience of office or practical administration. If Abercorn had abetted them, he would have been behaving more as the leader of an Irish party, which he strengthened by means of the patronage of the Crown, than as the king's representative in Ireland. This would have made it intellectually possible for traditional supporters of British government to go into opposition to him— the one thing which had not been intellectually possible for Beresford and Scott in 1777–80, when they had intrigued against Lord Buckinghamshire, but had not openly opposed him in Parliament. Perhaps an Abercorn viceroyalty would have fomented in the early 1790s the dramatic *renversement des alliances* which took place, too late, in 1798–9, when Foster and Parnell combined in opposition with Grattan and the Ponsonbys. The next opportunity for such a salutary *renversement* came with Lord Fitzwilliam, but was lost by 'hard driving'. It is possible that it would have been lost under Abercorn because Abercorn would have failed to drive hard enough: for all his early 'liberalism', by 1798 he had fallen largely under the influence of Fitzgibbon;[3] perhaps experience of government would only have accelerated his enthusiasm for 'the old Court'. It is all speculation, but speculation justified

[1] Abercorn to Pery, 3 Mar. [1791], Abercorn MSS., P.R.O.N.I. T.2541/IK/11/111.

[2] See p. 242.

[3] Lord Bathurst to Camden, 13 Mar. 1798, Pratt MSS., K.A.O. U.840/O.198/2.

by the need to break free from the notion that there was anything inevitable about the monotonous political alignments of
the period 1784–98. The abortive plan of 1792–3 for responsible, cabinet government, and its more academic precursor,
Lord Mornington's blueprint of September 1789, held out the
only hopes of a permanent and on-going disruption of the
monotony. However, the best hope for temporary relief was
probably Lord Abercorn, not Grattan, Burgh, Yelverton,
Lord Charlemont, Forbes, the Ponsonbys, and the other more
celebrated alternatives to the Irish Cabinet as it stood.

Because of the frustration of these hopes, and the unattractive-
ness to the British Government of all the alternatives, except
perhaps Lord Abercorn, the existing Irish Cabinet was allowed
to remain. It was almost always unloved by the British Government, but by and large it was appreciated as the least of the
available evils, and it was not actively disliked except in
1791–3. Those years apart, the Irish Cabinet was not necessarily less 'liberal' and less reforming than the British Government wanted it to be; the differences between them were
more subtle, and had much to do with the timing of events and
the implications for Great Britain of particular Irish measures.
Thus, in 1784, Foster's Libel Act was deemed too draconic by
the British Government mainly because it ran counter to
English legal practice. In other respects the British Government was at least as disposed to tough measures as the Irish
Cabinet: indeed, Fitzgibbon was assured of the King's 'entire
approbation of every part of your conduct' in regard to the
National Congress,[1] though his conduct was dubious on both
legal and political grounds. At this stage, Pitt favoured parliamentary reform for Ireland, but partly for the illiberal reason
that it would '. . . unite the Protestant interest in *excluding the
Catholics from any share in the representation or Government of the
country . . .*',[2] and mainly because Irish parliamentary reform
was consistent with his then British policy. When his British
parliamentary reform measure was defeated in 1785, he lost
interest in Irish parliamentary reform, and had set his face
against it by 1793. (Likewise, his espousal of Catholic Relief

---

[1] Rutland to Fitzgibbon, 1 Oct. 1784, O'Flanagan, *Lives of the Chancellors*, ii. 176.
[2] Pitt to Rutland, 7 Oct. 1784, ibid. pp. 44, 47. These are two different letters
of the same date.

in 1791, though a reversal of his previous Irish policy, was consistent with his then British policy, as enshrined in the British Catholic Relief and Canada Acts of that year.) Thus, between 1785 and 1791, there was no material difference between the British Government and the Irish Cabinet over reform of the Irish representative system, and there was substantial agreement between them over law and order measures as well. The terms of Fitzgibbon's draconic Whiteboy Act of 1787 had been discussed between Pitt and him late in 1786, and Fitzgibbon introduced it in the Irish House of Commons as an Irish adaptation of the time-honoured English Riot Act, which till then had had no Irish counterpart.[1] Even the measures of 1793, with the sole and very important exception of the Catholic Relief Act, had the support of all or some of the Irish Cabinet. They included draconic Convention and Gunpowder Acts, the handiwork of Fitzgibbon; economic measures which, as has been seen, were originally the brain-children of Foster; and the Militia Act, which was also strongly favoured by him.[2] Foster was either indifferent or hostile to the Place and Pension Act and the Civil List Act, and Parnell introduced them in the House of Commons with '. . . such an appearance of humbug . . . and in some particulars such ignorance of the subject . . .' that it would seem that he was hostile.[3] Fitzgibbon's attitude, however, was quite different. The Civil List, as has been seen, was his idea; and in 1789 he had advised the passing of the Opposition's Pension Act, which was very similar in its terms to the Act of 1793, and also resembled the Place and Pension Act of that year in that it gave the government the power to vacate seats.[4]

Moreover, the passing of the conciliatory measures of 1793, combined with the Opposition's reaction to them and Pitt's discovery that Fitzgibbon, at any rate, was committed to a Union, had the effect of strengthening the position of the Irish Cabinet. The alternative Irish politicians to them were now

---

[1] Orde to Rutland, 24 Oct. and 6 Nov. 1786, *H.M.C. Rutland MSS.*, iii. 351, 354; *Parl. Reg.* (Irish), vii. 161.

[2] For Foster's attitude to and part in these measures, see pp. 85 f., 255.

[3] George Knox to Abercorn, 13 June 1793, Abercorn MSS., P.R.O.N.I. T.2541/IB1/4/21.

[4] Buckingham to Grenville, 12 and 14 Mar. 1789, *H.M.C. Dropmore MSS.*, i. 429 f., 433.

shackled to Catholic Emancipation and to some sort of parliamentary reform, neither of which was acceptable to the British Government. Catholic Emancipation was acceptable in principle, but the British Government were afraid of its 'tending to diminish the prospect of attaining the desirable object of a Union';[1] and parliamentary reform was no longer acceptable, because of its implications for Great Britain, and to a lesser extent because it would jeopardize the British government's influence over the Irish Parliament. These views were not rigid or consistently held. For example, Pitt seems to have been prepared to concede Catholic Emancipation and at least to consider parliamentary reform, as the means of bringing Grattan and the Ponsonbys into government in 1797.[2] However, by and large, the British Government remained opposed to both. They were also, by and large, not indisposed to whatever coercive measures the worsening security and military situation in Ireland seemed to require. In a sense, they regarded the concessions of 1793 as closing the conciliation account with Ireland. They had legislated boldly, generously, and with perhaps unique disregard for the English consequences of Irish acts; the Irish Catholics had been placed on a greatly more favourable footing than their English counterparts (who did not, for example, get the vote until 1829); if the Irish Catholics were not conciliated, everything possible had been done to conciliate them, and they must abide the consequences. Dundas participated in the optimism of the Burkes that the Irish Catholics would feel themselves bound by ties of gratitude and affection to the British Crown: Pitt and Grenville were probably colder, harder, and more realistic in their attitude.[3] When Fitzgibbon, by then Lord Clare, made his celebrated speech in February 1798 in reply to the Whiggish general, Lord Moira, and in the course of it justified the infliction of (admittedly mild) torture as a means of extorting information about concealed arms, the speech was greeted by the British Government, not with embarrassment and

---

[1] Dundas to Loughborough, 12 Jan. 1801, printed in Campbell, *Lives of the Chancellors*, vi. 351; Camden to Pitt, 1 June 1797, Pratt MSS., K.A.O. U.840 O.156A/19.

[2] See p. 400, *n.* 1.

[3] For the attitude of Pitt's brother, see Chatham to Camden, 8 June 1797, Pratt MSS., K.A.O. U.840/C.102/3.

distaste, but as one 'of infinite advantage . . . both here and in
Ireland.'[1] When Clare's speech was followed soon afterwards by
Abercromby's general order, Pitt's reaction was to blame the
general order for '. . . holding out a change of system, and
giving colour and credit to those attacks from Lord Moira
which were beginning to be thought of as I believe they deserve
. . .'[2] The subsequent quarrel between the British Government
and the Irish Cabinet was not a quarrel about military policy,
but a quarrel about the Irish Cabinet's attempt to decide who
should be commander-in-chief in Ireland.[3] On Dundas's
part, it is true, it was a quarrel about military policy as well.
But, then, on this as on most Irish issues, Dundas was uniquely
'liberal'. At the height of the Abercromby crisis, the Duchess of
Devonshire wrote to him: '. . . You alone can do good, for you
are the only person I have met with for a long time who has
power, and yet seems to feel the necessity of not staking everything on coercion. . . .'[4] The Duchess was here voicing the
Whig, opposition view of her husband; but she was also drawing
on information derived from her brother, who was a member of
Pitt's British Cabinet. There was, thus, not much substance
in the view plausibly and trenchantly propounded by the
visiting Whig, Lord Wycombe, in June 1798 that the government of Ireland was 'made up of English imbecility and Irish
ferocity very oddly mixed up together'.[5] If, as is commonly
asserted, the draconian measures taken by the government of
Ireland between 1795 and 1798 really precipitated an avoidable rebellion, and really undermined the military competence of the loyalist forces to deal with it,[6] the burden of
responsibility rests as much with the British Government as
with the 'overbearing, sanguinary faction which farmed the
country', as Wycombe miscalled the Irish Cabinet.

Furthermore, what is really significant is that, in the period

[1] Grenville to Clare, 16 Mar. 1798, *H.M.S. Dropmore MSS.*, iv. 130. See also
Lord Bathurst's letter (cited in p. 406, *n.* 3), which seems to be recording Pitt's
reaction.

[2] Pitt to Camden, 13 Mar. 1798, Chatham MSS., P.R.O. 30/8/325, fols. 5–6.

[3] See pp. 72 ff.

[4] Duchess of Devonshire to Dundas, [post-24 Mar. 1798], Melville MSS.,
N.L.I. MS. 54A/83A.

[5] Wycombe to Lady Holland, 21 June 1798, Holland MSS., B.L. Add. MS.
51682—folio numbers provisional.

[6] See particularly Pakenham, *Year of Liberty, passim.*

1791–3, when the Irish Cabinet was most actively disliked by
the British Government, the British Government did not derive
or seek inspiration for their policy of Catholic Relief from
Irish politicians of a different political stamp. It has already
been suggested that the Irish Opposition, and other elements
in the Irish Parliament, were as good as impelled through
Catholic Relief into Catholic Emancipation by the conduct of
the British Government. Certainly, the policy of even Catholic
Relief was first espoused by the British Government, not the
Irish Opposition. When a deputation of Irish Catholics approached Grattan for support in July 1791, he referred them
to Hobart; and in December 1791 Lord Abercorn had no fear
that the concession of 'political equality' (by which he seems to
have meant the concession of the vote) could be carried, as it
'. . . would not only be a very unpopular measure with Parliament, but particularly resisted by the principal of their [the
Irish Catholics'] Opposition friends . . .'[1] Even when some of
the Irish Opposition had been compelled the length of conceding the vote, and were in London at the end of 1792 conducting some sort of negotiation with the British Government,
their views on the terms of the proposed Relief Bill went entirely unheeded. Years later, in 1829, the 2nd Earl of Donoughmore, Hely-Hutchinson's son, recalled how Grattan, Forbes,
and he had tried unavailingly to get the intended property
qualification for the vote considerably raised:

. . . They [the Catholic Committee] sent over their petition to the
King by five Delegates. Mr. Pitt and Lord Melville [Dundas]
determined that they should be restored to the franchise, unqualified,
and enjoyed just as the Protestants did. Grattan, Forbes, and myself
sent a message to Lord Melville deprecating this act, and telling
him that it would be impossible to answer for the consequences of
what numbers of the pauper population of Ireland might acquire
the right of voting [sense?]; that we were even sure that the respectable part of the C. Community and the people of property did
not wish for such an extension of franchise. But all our opposition
was of no avail, as the Scotch Gentleman [Dundas] thought he
knew Ireland a great deal better than we did; and he entrenched
himself by talking of general principles, and all that nonsense which
pretended statesmen make use of, when they are entirely ignorant

[1] Grattan, *Life*, iv. 41; Abercorn to Thomas Knox, 26 Dec. [1791], Abercorn
MSS., P.R.O.N.I. T.2541/IK/11/199.

of the nature of a question, and give you words and not arguments in support of their opinions. . . .[1]

Foster was by no means the only Irish politician who regarded the Act as an example of 'counsels devised in England without sufficient knowledge of our situation'[2]—in this case, without sufficient knowledge of the prevalence, or rather predominance, of 40/– freehold leases in Ireland. In matters of high policy— and the Union is the next instance—the British Government ignored, not just the advice of the Irish Cabinet, but all Irish advice. In 1791–3, when the Irish Cabinet were most obviously set aside and ignored, they were still in no worse a situation than the Irish alternatives to them.

Basically, although the unloved and largely unavoidable Irish Cabinet enjoyed a long tenure of power, it was a form of power which was merely subsidiary. They managed the day-to-day business of government extremely well; and if they were at variance with the British Government on issues of high policy, that did not alarm the British Government over-much, since on issues of high policy they did not require Irish advice—only Irish assistance. The complex relationship between the British Government and the Irish Cabinet is reduced to simplicity in two episodes: the summonses to London which the Irish Cabinet received in December 1792 and in October/November 1798, on both occasions to embellish and be made party to a decision which had already been taken.

The effect on the Irish Cabinet was that they acquired over the years an attitude to politics which was semi-bureaucratic. Even during the convulsion of the Union crisis, Foster expressed regret and almost surprise that the Irish Administration did not consult him on economic affairs; and after the convulsion was over he wrote sadly, 'my habits in life have been to support Government, and if I am prevented from continuing them, I am too old to adopt others'.[3] Beresford found it easier than the others to adapt himself to a semi-bureaucratic role. He had much in common with the pure man of business of the English type, and men like John Robinson, George Rose, and even William Eden were men of no political allegi-

[1] Donoughmore to Knight of Kerry, 11 Feb. [1829], FitzGerald MSS., 18/102.
[2] Foster to Sheffield, 7 July 1798, *Anglo-Irish Dialogue*, p. 26.
[3] Foster to Sheffield, 12 Dec. 1799 and 5 Feb. 1801, ibid. pp. 33, 36.

ance, or at least of a political allegiance which was eminently transferable. Foster, too, had something in common with this type—less than Beresford, but more than Fitzgibbon. He was not primarily a House of Commons man—no one could be so described who was prepared to leave what he called the 'bustle of business and debate'[1] for the infrequently broken taciturnity of the speakership. Though extremely effective in debate, he was effective in a way which was at least as appropriate to the lord lieutenant's cabinet as it was to the floor of the House; as a Whiggish commentator on the Irish Parliament observed in 1790, he was 'rather a sensible reasoner than a sublime orator', and 'the best-informed man in the House'.[2] These were the very qualities which gave him persuasiveness behind the scenes. His expertise in economics and finance was such that, although his wider influence might vary from administration to administration, he was at least guaranteed some influence in this sphere, and he accepted with a good grace whatever influence he was accorded. Almost as much as the largely non-political under-secretaries, he was a permanent Castle fixture. One lord lieutenant made him his 'Minister', others leant on him 'more in Finance than in politics', but whatever happened, he was still there. With the exception of the period 1779–80, he was not singled out by any administration for special marks of favour and confidence; which meant that he was never subjected, by the rotation natural in such circumstances, to special marks of disapprobation and disgrace by another—even in 1794–5.

To some extent Foster was a man of easy political virtue. Certainly, like most politicians of practical ambition, he loved power and office, and clung to them tenaciously. However, he believed, or made himself believe, that his primary motive in clinging to them was the well-being, particularly the economic well-being, of Ireland; and if he usually thought of the country and himself as one and the same thing (a fault imputed to Speaker Ponsonby, a man infinitely less well-equipped than Foster to advance the country's well-being[3]),

[1] Foster to Eden, 17 Sept. 1785, Auckland MSS., B.L. Add. MS. 34410, fol. 113.
[2] 'Falkland' [Revd. John Scott], *Review of Principal Characters in the House of Commons of Ireland* (Dublin, 1789), pp. 129 ff.
[3] Malcomson, *Foster and the Speakership*, 295n. See also p. xxii.

this too is a thought-process common to most politicians of practical ambition, and particularly to politicians who belonged to the Anglo-Irish Ascendancy. This 'Ascendancy' thought-process was perhaps best expressed by Edmund Burke's friend, Charles O'Hara Senior, in the late 1760s: '. . . The politics in Ireland come within very narrow compass. Being well with England, and obtaining by slow and imperceptible degrees some few commercial advantages, is our external object . . .'; and again: '. . . This Kingdom is so circumstanced that it never can be effectually served but by the aid of Government. Opposition, therefore, can be but preventive, never availing for the promotion of its [Ireland's] interests, and therefore not eligible but in cases of necessity. . . .'[1] Foster was old enough to have imbibed this 'Ascendancy' thought-process of the 1760s. His attitude to office and government was simple and pragmatic; he saw them as the place he must be if he was to have the power to palliate bad measures and, every now and then, to introduce good ones (he himself was, of course, the arbiter of what was bad and what was good). Enough good measures were passed, even in 1793, to sustain this attitude, and actually to give it continued validity. Even at the close of Foster's generally frustrating years of office after the Union, in 1810, he had the substantial satisfaction of being able to get an act passed reimposing the transit duties on foreign linen, and undoing 'the injustice and impolicy and surprise of 49 George III, c. 98'.[2] Earlier, his most famous office, the speakership, had given him occasional opportunities to strike direct, if unimportant, blows on behalf of the Ascendancy. The following arch reply to a letter he received from Camden in December 1795 about the wording of the King's Speech for the forthcoming session, shows that he knew how to employ the rapier as well as the bludgeon:

. . . the words, *other institutions of public education*, plainly seem to allude to the Popish College [Maynooth], and Your Excellency must not smile if I object to the coupling it with the Protestant Charter Schools. It was originally [?right] to mention it as a new

---

[1] O'Hara to Charles O'Hara Junior, 26 May [1768 ?] and [Oct. 1766–Aug. 1767], O'Hara MSS., P.R.O.N.I. T.2812/15/25, 14.

[2] Foster to Vesey FitzGerald, 13 May 1813, and Vesey FitzGerald to Peel, 6 Oct. 1813, Vesey FitzGerald MSS., N.L.I. MS. 7818, pp. 289–90, and MS. 7820, pp. 206–8.

subject, but there is no reason to give it a fixed place in the Speech, though you do intend, very properly, to continue a yearly allowance to it. The Nonconforming Ministers have not been so honoured. . . .[1]

Whether his weapon was rapier or bludgeon, and usually it was the latter, he never despaired of palliating bad measures, until the arrival of Lord Cornwallis in 1798. Then, for the first time, he withheld his advice and sulked—not that he would have been listened to anyway. One thing can be said for Foster: his love of power and office may have been unhealthy, but it derived from his ambition to do good; his conception of good may have been narrow, but at least good, as he conceived it, was the object.

If Foster's semi-bureaucratic attitude to politics and government was valid in the sense that he retained some power to do good, as he conceived it, right up to his last retirement in 1811, it was old-fashioned and unrealistic in the sense that politics in Ireland in the 1780s, and particularly in the 1790s, no longer came within the narrow compass of the 1760s. In the 1760s, England had been as anxious to be 'well with' the Anglo-Irish Ascendancy as the Ascendancy was to be well with England: by 1791 England, or at any rate Dundas, had come to regard the Ascendancy as only 'one description of Irishmen', who could no longer be supported by England in their desire for 'monopoly or pre-eminence'.[2] In the 1790s, measures vitally trenching on the Ascendancy, which would have been inconceivable in the 1760s, were not only conceivable, but were passed. In their response to those measures the Irish Cabinet were hampered, perhaps to some extent by easy political virtue, but more profoundly by the semi-bureaucratic habits they had formed, and by the intellectual difficulty they experienced in distinguishing between British government generally and the particular British Government of the day.

[1] Foster to Camden, 31 Dec. 1795, Pratt MSS., K.A.O. U.840/O.97/1. The offending words were changed to 'other institutions of public charity and improvement'. Foster, however, did not succeed in his other point that 'in Church and State' should be tacked on to the phrase 'most excellent Constitution'. See *Commons' Journals* (Ireland), xvi. 166 f. The Opposition moved an unsuccessful amendment to the address, in favour of the equalization of duties between Great Britain and Ireland.

[2] Dundas to Westmorland, 26 Dec. 1791. quoted in Lecky, *History of Ireland*, iii. 40.

Their response to the Catholic Relief Bill of 1792 was to yield their vote, but not to sacrifice their opinion—this un-heroic expression was used by Agar in the House of Lords.[1] Much the same happened in 1793. Fitzgibbon's private attempt in January to come to a compromise with the British Government over the terms of the Relief Bill, has already been discussed. It seems to have been a well-kept secret; but even to those not in the know, his general behaviour suggested that he was not going to go all lengths in opposition to the Bill. In the same month, January, George Knox reported to Lord Abercorn: '. . . The Chancellor talks as if he was on the point of resigning, which I think he is not, having never con-sidered him to be a man of real pride and firmness. . . .'[2] The prediction was correct, although reverence for the British connection almost certainly influenced Fitzgibbon's course more significantly than the alleged want of real pride and firmness. In his speech on the Bill in the House of Lords, Fitzgibbon declared that he was in principle opposed to it, but that in the present state of agitation in the country he could not advise its rejection. Like Fitzgibbon, Parnell in the end spoke in constrained support of the Bill, and Beresford probably voted for it, though he did not speak. Even Foster and Agar, though they spoke and voted against it, did not, it seems, endeavour to concert an opposition to it; and one passage in Foster's speech certainly does not suggest opposition *à l'outrance*:

. . . He never blamed the Irish Government, nor did he blame them now; the measure began in Britain. But he should never cease to think it was extreme folly or indiscretion in the British Ministry to rouse the question here. He would add that, much as he feared its fatal consequences, and much as he opposed it, yet should it pass into a law, it would then be his duty from that moment to give up his own opinions, to embrace it as the Law of the Land, and to do everything that an individual could do to render it beneficial and effectual. . . .[3]

George Knox imputed a more sinister and underhand course of conduct to Foster and Fitzgibbon. In early February,

---

[1] *Roman Catholic Debates of 1792*, p. 244.
[2] George Knox to Abercorn, 24 Jan. 1793, Abercorn MSS., P.R.O.N.I. T.2541/IB1/4/5.   [3] *Parl. Reg.* (Irish), xiii. 345.

Knox '. . . thought I could observe the Chancellor and the Speaker working, the one secretly, the other openly through the medium of Maxwell [John Maxwell Barry] to overturn the present Administration, and to make this Bill the instrument of that purpose. . . .'[1] However, in view of the different courses pursued by Fitzgibbon and Foster during the subsequent stages of the Bill, in view of Westmorland's expressed admiration of Fitzgibbon's conduct and Hobart's expressed admiration of Foster's speech,[2] and in view of the continued good personal relations between Fitzgibbon and Foster on the one hand, and Westmorland and Hobart on the other, Knox's suspicion is unlikely to have been well-founded. Besides, as a supporter of the Bill, and indeed of full Catholic Emancipation in 1793, he had a natural bias towards exaggerating the darkness of Fitzgibbon's and Foster's designs. The chief of these designs, in the case of both Fitzgibbon and Foster, was to make a set-piece speech placing on record their sentiments in the most powerful and convincing manner possible, in the hope that they were thereby setting up an intellectual barrier to 'the further progress of innovation'. The hope was not wholly vain: Fitzgibbon's speech, the less effective of the two, was reprinted as late as 1813 by some English anti-Emancipationists who were '. . . convinced that it contains the most constitutional and irresistible arguments against the subversion of the Constitution now meditated . . .'[3]

The Catholic Relief Bill of 1793 was the only issue affecting the Ascendancy on which there was a straight confrontation between the Irish Cabinet and the British Government. In 1795 the situation was much more confused. In January, and up to the middle of February, the attitude of the British Government to Fitzwilliam's Emancipation Bill was uncertain, as was the degree of authorization and support which Fitzwilliam had from London. Through Lords Auckland and Westmorland, the Irish Cabinet may well have been aware of the hostility of the King, and the likelihood of Fitzwilliam's being disavowed. 'In the beginning of the business'—which

[1] George Knox to Abercorn, 6 Feb. [1793], Abercorn MSS., P.R.O.N.I. T.2541/IB1/4/10.   [2] See pp. 380, 67.
[3] *The Speech of the Rt. Hon. John, Earl of Clare . . . on the Second Reading of the Bill for the Relief of His Majesty's Roman Catholic Subjects in Ireland, March 13, 1793*, new edn. (London, 1813), pp. 8, 5.

presumably means January—Fitzgibbon and Foster had prevailed on him to declare that the Emancipation Bill was 'open for both Houses, and that it was not a measure of Government'.[1] Also, both Beresford and Agar were peculiarly circumstanced in early 1795, in that neither of them had any self-interested motive for supporting Fitzwilliam's measures; Beresford had just lost his office, and Agar had just been disappointed of the Archbishopric of Armagh. On the issue of the Union, too, there was not a straight confrontation between the Irish Cabinet and the British Government; on that issue the Irish Cabinet were themselves divided. The only one of them who displayed easy political virtue was Agar. Beresford is a doubtful case. Ever the bureaucrat in the service of 'English government', he supported the Union, partly because that was his cast of mind, and partly because his brother, Lord Waterford, had been a convinced Unionist since long before the failure of the commercial propositions in 1785: there is probably no good reason to impute unworthier motives to Beresford; one of his sons opposed the Union, and resigned his office in consequence.[2] Fitzgibbon supported the Union from conviction, because he thought it would be carried on exclusively Protestant lines. Foster and Parnell likewise opposed it from conviction, although less worthy motives, which need not be taken seriously, were imputed to both. Foster's and Parnell's opposition to it is, therefore, the sole instance of individual members of the Irish Cabinet bolting from their semi-bureaucratic harness and freeing themselves from their reverence for British government.

Because Parnell took his cue from Foster, it is Foster's conduct over the Union, and the nature and extent of his opposition to it, which especially demand examination. He himself wrote to Sheffield in March 1799: '. . . your old friend . . . , in maintaining an opinion which he could not yield, upon one single point, . . . is no more a leader or in cabal or joined with any man to oppose Government at large, than he was on the Catholic Question in 1793 . . .'; and in August 1799 he wrote to Camden:

[1] See p. 70, *n.* 1.
[2] Waterford (then Lord Tyrone) to Beresford, 15 June 1785, and Beresford to Auckland, 6 Feb. 1799, *Beresford Correspondence*, i. 268, and ii. 211.

. . . I might think it unjust and hard that Government should withdraw all intercourse and connection with me, . . . and I might also complain that their papers are employed in misrepresenting me as a leader of Party and in general Opposition. . . . Let them speak, act, or write as they please, I have been too long in the habit of supporting Government, and [am] too much convinced of the necessity of doing so, ever to be driven by them into Party or Opposition. . . . I am happy that it was not I who quit them. I should no more have thought of doing so, than I did on the Popery Question . . .[1]

The implied abhorrence of 'Party' and 'General Opposition' is not surprising, granted that Foster had been born in 1740, and was almost old enough to be Pitt's or Fox's father; even by contemporary British standards his outlook was not particularly 'old-fashioned'.[2] Basically, his argument was an independent country gentleman's argument: government was to be supported in its proper sphere of raising the supplies and in general conducting the king's business, but was not necessarily to be supported if it went outside this sphere and touched on matters of principle or conviction.[3]

---

[1] Foster to Sheffield, 20 Mar. 1799, *Anglo-Irish Dialogue*, p. 30; Foster to Camden, 3 Aug. 1799, Pratt MSS., K.A.O. U.840/O.81/4. Camden had earlier written to Foster appealing to his semi-bureaucratic bent: '. . . if the principle is carried, I trust we shall not be deprived of your assistance and support in the details; and I confess I see no inconsistency, but indeed the mark of a high mind, in rendering that which has been decided, even contrary to one's own opinion, to be right, as advantageous (under the circumstances) as it can be. . .'; Camden to Foster, 25 July 1799, Pratt MSS., K.A.O. U.840/O.184/5. The inelegance of language was Camden's: the sentiments were Foster's except on questions affecting the Ascendancy.

[2] For the significance and prevalence of party in late eighteenth century Great Britain, see Paul Kelly, 'British Parliamentary Politics, 1784–6', *Historical Journal*, xvii. No. 4 (1974), 733–55, *passim.*

[3] The independent country-gentleman outlook is explicit in William Stewart of Killymoon's canvassing letter to the 8th Earl of Abercorn on the occasion of the co. Tyrone election of 1768: '. . . In general, I have supported Government and seldom agreed to any of the popular motions, made only to distress the Administration. If I have done as a Country Gentleman ought to do, I think I may rely on Your Lordship's very powerful protection'; Stewart to Abercorn, 16 Feb. 1768, Abercorn MSS., P.R.O.N.I. T.2541/IA1/7/18. John Forbes strongly disliked what he himself called 'the independent country gentlemen', who he considered had a horror of 'the people' and were in fact amphibious animals, part-Whig and part-Tory (Forbes to Adair, 6 Feb. 1780. Adair MSS., B.L. Add. MS. 53802). In this letter he goes on to express the fear that the independent country gentlemen will co-operate with Lord North's minions (as Foster did) to resist the modification of Poynings's Law. In contrast to this, a roughly contemporary letter from

What is significant, however, is that Foster's opposition, for all his disclaimers, was not an independent country gentleman's kind of opposition. His alliance with Grattan and the Ponsonbys reeked of 'Party' (though it is true that he had previously co-operated uneasily with them in government): for example, it made it necesssary for Foster to declare in the House that the Catholics, like the Protestants, were 'interested' in the constitution and Parliament of their country, and that the Irish Parliament was more competent than 'a distant Parliament sitting in a distant land' to 'discuss every question of Irish concern', including 'the religious question'.[1] This was a far cry from his language of 1793. No doubt he would have argued that it was the 1793 Act which had given the Catholics their interest in the constitution and Parliament. He could also have argued that he was going no further than asserting the competence of the Irish Parliament to 'discuss' the Catholic Question; but the implication of his words was that the outcome of the discussion would be favourable to the Catholics. Moreover, although his opposition was not 'General', and was concentrated 'upon one single point', it was not confined to rejecting proposals put by the Irish Administration before the House, but anticipated these proposals, sought to take legislative initiatives, and even sought to pledge the Administration against its own measure. The attempted legislative initiatives, especially the Regency Bill, were in part inspired by the tactical desirability of getting the House into committee on some pretext or other, so that Foster could speak; but they had the effect of disquieting the anti-Unionist country gentlemen (including Foster's colleague, William Charles Fortescue), who were prepared to divide against a proposal of the Administration, but reluctant to divide in favour of a proposal of the Opposition. In mid-February 1799 Beresford reported, significantly: '. . . As to the

Castlereagh's father describing the carrying of the Short Money Bill in November 1779 (which the writer supported), talks indiscriminately about 'us patriots' and 'us country gentlemen', and describes how 'we' took possession of the treasury bench for a joke, and from there mimicked 'the style of a country gentleman in opposition'; Robert Stewart to Camden, 27 Nov. 1779, Pratt MSS., K.A.O. U.840/C.492/5. Clearly, 'country gentleman' and 'independent country gentleman' are terms capable of widely varying interpretation.

[1] *Foster's Speech of 11 Apr. 1799*, p. 112, and his *Speech of 17 Feb. 1800*, pp. 37 f.

Speaker, he must see he is not able to carry his point. He cannot but perceive that the country gentlemen are afraid of him and Ponsonby, and he sees the error of having brought forward the question of Union, and not being content with the victory he had . . .'[1] Foster usually had a surer feel of the pulse of the country gentlemen than Beresford, but his convictions on the question of the Union carried him further, and nearer to 'General Opposition', than a late-eighteenth-century opposition dared go.

If Foster's opposition to the Union was comparatively 'modern' in this respect (and remarkably so for a politician like Foster), it was 'old-fashioned' in another: this was his insistence that the Union was not the sort of measure which the Administration should push unless it had 'the real sense of the country' behind it. In other words, Foster thought it should be 'open for both Houses', as Fitzwilliam had made Emancipation in 1795. This idea that certain measures could not with propriety be made 'measures of Government' was certainly not unique to Foster. In January and February 1793, when fumbling for guide-lines for a parliamentary following which he was not at hand to guide in person, Lord Abercorn came up with two parallel distinctions: one between 'economic subjects' and 'Constitutional Reforms'; the other between 'Government measures' and 'great measures'.[2] Things like Catholic Relief, Catholic Emancipation, and parliamentary reform belonged, in Abercorn's eyes, to the latter category in both distinctions, and he was ready to go into opposition if Lord Camden's Administration violated the distinction by dismissing George Knox from office for supporting Emancipation in 1795.[3] Lord Abercorn was not a profound political thinker, nor was the leader of another parliamentary following, the slow-witted and fundamentally honest 2nd Marquess of Downshire, who was fumbling less lucidly for a similar distinction in February 1795: '. . . In support of Government in matters of the Empire, I am decided; but as to internal regulation which must affect the Empire, I am against. Popery

[1] Beresford to Auckland, 18 Feb. 1799, *Beresford Correspondence*, ii. 117; Bolton, *Union*, pp. 120 ff.
[2] Abercorn to George Knox, 22 Jan. and 2 Feb. 1793, Abercorn MSS., P.R.O.N.I. T.2541/IK/13/10, 19.
[3] Knox to Abercorn, 5 June 1795, ibid. /IB1/6/34.

Reform, no consideration can induce me to approve, much more to support. Loss of popularity, loss of Public Opinion, loss of property, loss of life, are trifles in comparison of self-approbation. . . .'[1]

This discussion of what measures were properly 'measures of Government', went on in Great Britain too. Pitt had already drawn his famous distinction between 'the man and the Minister'; his Cabinet had agreed to differ over parliamentary reform in 1784–5 (a question which of course generated much less heat in Great Britain than it did in Ireland, or than the Catholic Question or the Union did there); and the term 'open question' was to reappear as the formula by which the British Cabinet held together, in spite of their differences over Catholic Emancipation, between 1812 and 1827. However, there was only a verbal resemblance between the 'open question' in the British context of 1812–27 and in the Irish context of 1795.[2] In the British context, it was a solution to a problem of government: in the Irish context it was a solution to a problem of opposition—how to oppose particular measures without going into 'General Opposition', how to oppose the British Government of the day without opposing British government. Pitt distinguished between the man and the minister for the sound, practical reason that the King would not allow him to propose, with the coercive power of the Crown, certain measures which Pitt wanted to propose; Catholic Emancipation was made an 'open question' between 1812 and 1827 because the Crown opposed it, and yet could not form a government which did not include some of its supporters. In the hands of Pitt and Lord Liverpool, the 'open question' was thus a practical response to a particular set of political circumstances: in the hands of Foster, Abercorn, and Downshire, it was an intellectual attempt to exclude certain questions from the sphere of government, whatever the political circumstances—an attempt to keep the politics, or rather the government, of Ireland within the 'very narrow compass'

---

[1] Downshire to John Reilly [his political manager], endorsed 11 Feb. 1795, Downshire MSS., P.R.O.N.I. D.607/C/72.

[2] It must, therefore, be put down to coincidence that Castlereagh would seem to have been the originator of the idea of the 'open question' in the British context; see Castlereagh to Lord Hertford, 27 June 1811, Hertford MSS., B.L. Egerton MS. 3260, fols. 213–25: photocopies in P.R.O.N.I., ref. T.3076/2/55.

of Charles O'Hara's day. Downshire had decided that Catholic Emancipation was a matter of 'internal regulation', and he expected to be allowed to act on his private judgement, even if Pitt decided that it was a 'matter of the Empire'. For a number of very important reasons, there was no British counterpart to the idea of the 'open question' in this distinctively Irish sense. The first was the difference between Great Britain and Ireland in the intensity with which political convictions were held; this derived largely from the fact that the ruling class in Great Britain was much less precariously based and much less vulnerable than the Anglo-Irish Ascendancy. The second reason was that in Great Britain Pitt was denied the coercive power of the Crown in proposing measures which their opponents would have considered ought to have been left 'open for both Houses': in Ireland, he was granted that coercive power. In practice, he did not need it till the Union; Westmorland dismissed no office-holders for opposing the Catholic Relief Act of 1793, and Camden dismissed neither George Knox nor anybody else for supporting Catholic Emancipation in 1795. Foster mistook practice for principle; which is why so intelligent a man made such silly remarks about the harshness of the dismissals of 1799.[1] The third reason for there being no British equivalent of the Irish 'open question', was that it was an idea which appealed peculiarly to government-orientated upholders of the Anglo-Irish Ascendancy; it provided them with a formula for opposing the British Government of the day while still supporting British government. However, it was an idea which was foredoomed to failure in practice. It was the British Government of the day, not the Irish politicians, who had the power to decide whether a question should be 'open' or not. Even if this had not been so, the Irish politicians would have differed sharply from each other in their decisions about different questions. Foster almost certainly considered that Camden should not have left Emancipation 'open' in 1795, and should have dismissed George Knox; quite certainly, Abercorn did not consider the Union a question which should have been left 'open', because Knox, who was the only anti-Unionist among Abercorn's members, resigned his office rather than compromise

[1] See p. 81.

the Administration in its policy of dismissal.[1] Obviously, Fitzgibbon did not consider the Union an 'open question' either.

The idea of the 'open question', as interpreted by Foster and Fitzgibbon in 1795, was thus foredoomed to failure, and was almost antithetical to the same term, as interpreted by the British Cabinet after 1812. However, another of the Irish Cabinet's ideas was to influence British politics on the Emancipation issue right up to 1829; this was the idea that giving the royal assent to Emancipation was contrary to the king's coronation oath. Fitzgibbon and the English Chancellor, Lord Loughborough, are known to have come up with this early in 1795,[2] but their respective contributions to it, and to implanting it in the King's mind, have been misconceived. From the abundant evidence, it is tolerably clear that Loughborough acted as little more than Fitzgibbon's agent in this dubious transaction. On 14 February and 2 March 1795, Fitzgibbon wrote two letters to Beresford (who was then in London protesting in person against his dismissal) embodying, in slightly inconsistent forms, the coronation oath argument, and suggesting that he draw various points in the argument to the attention of Dundas, Loughborough, and Auckland.[3] Beresford and Auckland were on intimate terms, as were Auckland and Loughborough. Beresford must have passed at least the second letter to Auckland, and Auckland have passed it to Loughborough, because on 27 May Loughborough wrote to Auckland returning to him 'Lord Fitzgibbon's letters, which I think entitled to very great consideration' (one of these may have been a letter of 24 March, which Fitzgibbon had written to Auckland direct).[4] On 5 March, Loughborough

---

[1] George Knox to Wickham, 2 Jan. 1804, Wickham MSS., P.R.O.N.I. T.2627/5/Q/238.

[2] *Auckland Correspondence*, iii. 303 f.; Ashbourne, *Pitt*, pp. 199 f.; Bolton, *Union*, p. 19. The first two sources suggest that the ex-Lord Lieutenant, Westmorland, was Fitzgibbon's intermediary with the King, and thus that the Fitzgibbon and Loughborough intrigues were independent, concurrent operations. What is more probable is that Westmorland played a supporting role in a combined operation. Elsewhere (iv. 116 f.) the editor of the *Auckland Correspondence* reaches conclusions which agree in substance with what follows.

[3] *Beresford Correspondence*, ii. 72 f., 75 f.

[4] Loughborough to Auckland, 27 May 1795, *Auckland Correspondence*, ii. 304 f. Fitzgibbon to Auckland, 24 Mar. 1795, *Fitzgibbon Letters from the Sneyd Muniments*, pp. 302 f.

wrote a memorandum to the King on the subject.[1] This memorandum embodied all but one of Fitzgibbon's points in his letter to Beresford of 2 March, which would just have had time to arrive, and it contained many striking verbal echoes. One of Fitzgibbon's points which reappears in Loughborough's memorandum would have occurred only to an Irish lawyer: '. . . whether a repeal of any of the English Statutes adopted by that Act [the modification of Poynings's Law in 1782] in this Country [Ireland] is not a direct violation of the compact then made by the Parliament of Ireland with Great Britain. . . .' Another of Fitzgibbon's points, which he had made with characteristic overstatement, reappears in a mealy-mouthed form in Loughborough's memorandum; where Fitzgibbon had threatened the lord chancellor of England with the loss of his head, Loughborough wrote: '. . . The Chancellor of England would perhaps incur some risk in fixing the seal of England to a bill for giving the Pope a concurrent ecclesiastical jurisdiction with the King . . .' The only point of substance in Loughborough's memorandum which does not occur in Fitzgibbon's letter is, whether '. . . a repeal of the Act of Supremacy and the establishing the Popish religion in any of the Hereditary Dominions [could] be invidiously construed as amounting to a reconciliation with the Church of Rome? . . .' This point is made, almost in so many words, in Fitzgibbon's subsequent letter to Auckland of 24 March, and may also have been made in a 'conference' which Fitzgibbon states he had had, apparently with Auckland or with Auckland and others, in early February.[2] Indeed, it appears that the ever-impatient Fitzgibbon regarded his letters to Beresford and Auckland merely as reminders of what he had said during this 'conference'.

The formulation of the coronation oath argument did not defeat Emancipation in 1795; the King's mind was already made up, and his hostile opinion had been expressed in a paper composed a month earlier, on 5 February. It is extremely likely, however, that Fitzgibbon's (and Beresford's) presence in London, and his 'conference' in early February, had much

---

[1] Campbell, *Lives of the Chancellors*, vii. 285 f.

[2] Fitzgibbon to Beresford, 2 Mar. 1795, *Beresford Correspondence*, ii. 75 f. Fitzgibbon had preceded Beresford to London to campaign against Fitzwilliam.

bearing on this paper. The King believed in the myth of Irish jobbery, and had no special regard for the Irish Cabinet. Yet, his paper to a considerable extent argues the anti-Emancipationist case from their point of view, and from the point of view of the Anglo-Irish Ascendancy in general. The following extracts are particularly striking:

... It is but fair to confess that the whole of this plan [of Emancipation] is the strongest justification of the old servants of the Crown in Ireland for having objected to the former indulgences that have been granted, as it is now pretended those have availed nothing, unless this total change of political principles be admitted. . . . One might suppose the authors of this scheme . . . are actuated alone by the feverish inclination of humiliating the old friends of English government in Ireland, or from the desire of paying implicit obedience to the heated imagination of Mr. Burke. . . .[1]

'Old servants of the Crown in Ireland' and 'old friends of English government in Ireland', are the warmest and most affectionate epithets ever bestowed on the Irish Cabinet by highly placed British figures of the 1790s. It is probable that from 1795 to the Abercromby crisis in 1798, the Irish Cabinet had a firm friend in the King. Certainly, he eagerly swallowed the coronation oath argument. Having failed to extract a decisive confirmation of its validity from Loughborough, the King copied the Loughborough memorandum almost verbatim in his own hand, the argument from the Act of 1782 included, and submitted it in this disguised form to Lord Kenyon, the Chief Justice of the King's Bench, and to the Attorney-General, Sir John Scott.[2] They replied to this and a subsequent communication of 14 March by picking holes in some of the legal arguments, but concluded by resting the whole question on '. . . the judgement of the person who takes the Coronation Oath, [which] must determine whether any particular statute proposed does destroy the government of the Established Church. It seems that the Oath, couched in the general terms

---

[1] Printed, without date, in Campbell, *Lives of the Chancellors*, vii. 287. Campbell assumes, erroneously, that the King's paper post-dated Loughborough's memorandum of 5 March.

[2] The King's correspondence with Kenyon is printed in H. Philpotts (ed.), *Letters from His Late Majesty to the Late Lord Kenyon on the Coronation Oath, with His Lordship's Answers . . .* (London, 1827), pp. 5 ff. The King's first letter and enclosure is printed in *H.M.C. Kenyon MSS.*, pp. 542 f.

in which it is found, does not preclude the party sworn from exercising a judgement . . .' This opinion, combined with a less non-committal re-statement of Loughborough's views,[1] determined the King on his line of attack if the issue of Emancipation should again be raised. His paper of 5 February had argued the anti-Emancipationist case largely as a matter of policy: in 1801 it was all a question of conscience. There was almost certainly no tampering with the King's conscience in 1801: none was needed, as Fitzgibbon had already struck a temporarily decisive blow for the Anglo-Irish Ascendancy in 1795.[2]

To what extent other members of the Irish Cabinet, besides Beresford, seconded Fitzgibbon's successful intrigue, is not absolutely clear. Agar certainly did. On 14 March, the King submitted to Kenyon a supplementary 'state of the question, as drawn by a Right Reverend Prelate' of the Church of Ireland, who turns out, as might well be supposed, to have been Agar.[3] Through Lord Sheffield, Foster had a confidential channel of communication with Loughborough; but no letter from Foster to Sheffield on the subject of the coronation oath survives, and Sheffield was out of town at the time, and in the throes of his second marriage.[4] It would therefore seem that Foster (and Parnell) played no part in this high-level intrigue;

---

[1] This memorandum, dated 10 Mar. 1795, is printed in A. Aspinall (ed.), *The Later Correspondence of George III* (5 vols., Cambridge), ii. 317 ff. It is a re-statement designed to give the impression that the queries concerning the coronation oath originated with the King.

[2] One practical objection to the coronation oath argument was that, in 1689, when the Coronation Oath Act was passed, Irish Catholics were not excluded from Parliament; they were by the time of the Union with Scotland, and the article of that Union 'securing the Church of England as by Law established' was Fitzgibbon's second line of defence. In this respect, the Union in 1800 strengthened the coronation oath argument, as Catholics had been excluded from the English Parliament in 1689. However, there was more of emotion than logic in the argument, and there was certainly no logic in its timing. Fitzgibbon could have argued just as well that the 1793 Act re-enfranchising the Irish Catholics was a violation of the coronation oath; and if he was right in stating that the repeal of all or part of the Act of Uniformity constituted such a violation, then George III had violated it already by assenting to section 3 of the British Catholic Relief Act of 1791 (31 Geo. III, c. 32).

[3] Archbishop of Canterbury to the King, 19 Mar. 1795, Aspinall, *Later Correspondence*, ii. 322.

[4] Foster to Sheffield, 7 Jan. 1795, *Anglo-Irish Dialogue*, p. 16. There are no more letters until mid-March, and they contain no reference or allusion to Loughborough or the coronation oath.

which is not surprising. Foster's lack of English connections, apart from Sheffield and his viceregal contacts of the 1790s, has already been emphasized. Because of his aristocratic background, Beresford had been familiar with the art of lobbying great men in London since the mid-1760s. Agar's connections in British politics have been discussed. Fitzgibbon had no connections of his own, except perhaps with Auckland, who was primarily Beresford's friend; but Fitzgibbon had the whole Beresford network of connections at his disposal. However, Fitzgibbon mounted the backstairs of St. James's Palace in 1795, not simply because he had English connections to facilitate his ascent, but because he had come to see, with a clarity and conviction unique in the Irish Cabinet, that it was from Whitehall, not Dublin Castle, that all the really important policy decisions came. This was the lesson of 1792–3. The Catholic Relief Act of 1793 would probably not have been carried, at any rate in 1793, if Lord Westmorland had not lost his nerve in December 1792. Westmorland was pathetically anxious about his political future in Great Britain, which depended wholly on Pitt, his only patron and protector. In March 1794, he wrote abjectly to Pitt: '. . . Whenever you make your arrangements that I may come away, I rely that you will arrange for me a proper situation. I must say, I look to a seat in your Cabinet. You told me I should not descend when I came here. . . .'[1] Westmorland was probably aware that the lord lieutenancy of Ireland had been on offer to the Portland Whigs since May 1792. He was hurt that his request for the Garter was not immediately granted, and attributed to this delay the Catholic Convention's decision to by-pass him and present their petition to the King direct.[2] When the British Government decided that the petition should be received, Westmorland treated the decision as an intimation of his own approaching political ruin, swiftly back-pedalled, and 'represented that a change of sentiment was taking place among the Protestants'—as Pitt and Dundas mercilessly reminded him in January 1793.[3] The lesson of this dramatic volte-face

[1] Westmorland to Pitt, 30 Mar. 1794, Chatham MSS., P.R.O. 30/8/331, fols. 216–17.

[2] Westmorland to Pitt, 7 Dec. 1792, quoted in Lecky, *History of Ireland*, iii. 114.

[3] See p. 359, *n.* 2.

was not lost on Fitzgibbon. When Fitzgibbon set off for London in April 1793, Westmorland's letter recommending him to Pitt shows that Fitzgibbon had quite simply not troubled to explain to Westmorland that the purpose of Fitzgibbon's Civil List scheme was to stifle the Irish treasury board at birth.[1] Obviously, Fitzgibbon had realized that the decision would be Pitt's, and that it was a waste of time even to discuss the matter with Westmorland. Just as he by-passed Westmorland and went straight to Pitt in 1793, so in 1795 he by-passed Pitt and went straight to the King.

Not even Beresford and Agar saw and acted on the necessity of going straight to the British fountainhead in the way that Fitzgibbon did: Foster and Parnell saw it only dimly, and acted on it not at all. Yet, in a sense, Foster's and Parnell's resort to the idea of the 'open question' in 1799 resembled in essentials Fitzgibbon's exploitation of the coronation oath argument in 1795. Foster's and Parnell's opposition to the Union was straightforward and almost heroic: Fitzgibbon's opposition to Emancipation in 1795 was underhand and ignoble. However, both were attempts—the former unsuccessful, the latter successful for some time to come—to prevent the measures concerned from being made 'measures of Government', to keep the compass of government narrow, to solve, or rather to avoid, the old problem of how to oppose the British Government of the day without opposing British government.

This is an essential resemblance apparent only to the historian; it is there, but so too are crucial dissimilarities between Fitzgibbon, Beresford, and Agar, on the one hand, and Foster and Parnell on the other. Foster and Parnell had it in common that they were the least cosmopolitan, least English-orientated, members of the Irish Cabinet; both were down-to-earth, plain-spoken country gentlemen, Parnell to the point of inelegance; both conducted business, be it private or public, in the gregarious and hospitable fashion which Barrington has immortalized as characteristic of their class; and both lived greatly beyond their means, another characteristic of their class. Henry Grattan Junior, relying presumably on his father's recollections of Foster at Westminster, praised Foster's manner of conducting parliamentary business as that of a country

[1] See p. 380, *n.* 2.

gentleman, while Isaac Corry's was that of an upstart, who fawned before the English members, 'begging pardon of the House for taking up their time with Irish affairs'.[1] Foster's style of life during the recess, and the size of his estate, were likewise those of a country gentleman; and he owed his election to the speakership in large measure to his popularity with 'the country gentlemen' and even with 'the independent gentlemen in opposition' in the Irish House of Commons.[2] Just as Foster lacked the facility of Beresford, the born aristocrat, in his dealings in the unfamiliar sphere of British politics, so Foster succeeded in being elected Speaker, and Beresford twice had to withdraw his pretensions. Foster was a typical product of the Anglo-Irish landed class, in spite of Redesdale's sweeping statements about the unacceptability of the Irish Cabinet even to the class which produced it. Foster belonged to that Cabinet, not only because of his practical ability as a man of business, but also because of his considerable, though unascertained, influence in the House of Commons; and his influence in the House derived, in large measure, from his ability to rationalize what in other members of his class was prejudice, and give articulation to what in them was instinct. At the time of his first speech against the Union, in April 1799, the point was specifically made by one well-informed English observer: '. . . Out of doors his arguments will have great weight with those who violently opposed the Union from passion and prejudice, and were wholly at a loss for argument . . .'[3] Years earlier, Lord Buckinghamshire, when arguing Foster's superiority over the other would-be economic experts in the Irish Parliament (Beresford included), pointed out that Foster had the 'talent' of rendering economic affairs 'perspicuous to moderate understandings'.[4] Presumably he had in mind the 'moderate understandings' of the Irish country gentlemen. Parnell's political existence as Chancellor of the Exchequer can no doubt be explained on the same ground.

Unfortunately, since Foster was a member of the Anglo-Irish landed class (not just a spokesman, as Carson was to be

[1] Grattan, *Life*, v. 106.
[2] Malcomson, *Foster and the Speakership*, pp. 275 ff.
[3] Bishop of Ferns to Lord Egremont, 17 Apr. 1799, Petworth House MSS., P.H.A. 57/21.
[4] Buckinghamshire to Heron, 12 Apr. 1779, Heron MSS., N.L.I. MS. 13037/8.

in the late 1890s), he participated in that class's limitations of view, and failed to project himself and his ideas into the context of British, as opposed to Irish, politics. Although he thought, politically and economically, in terms of the Empire, he perhaps never grasped in the years after the outbreak of the war the extent of the danger which Ireland's internal divisions constituted for the Empire as a whole, or at least never grasped the importance which British politicians attached to that danger. The lesson of the Catholic Relief Act of 1793 was that the Irish Parliament might swallow even something as indigestible as a Union, if it was prescribed from Whitehall. Foster failed to learn the lesson, perhaps misled by the temporary triumph of his views on Emancipation in 1795. Significantly, when his views (and Fitzgibbon's) were quoted at the meeting of the British Cabinet held to conduct a *post mortem* on the Fitzwilliam débâcle, Pitt took them up '. . . with some sort of avidity. . . , but soon abandoned . . . [them] on its being observed that some allowance must be made in the weight of these opinions for the known prejudices of the persons by whom they were given. . . .'[1] It was Foster's failure that his views were always received with allowances, and then abandoned, in the one quarter which counted. On the intellectual level, he recognized that this was the one quarter which counted. At about the time of the British Cabinet's *post mortem*, he wrote to Sheffield: '. . . It is very natural they [the Irish Catholics] should ask everything, if they are told, it is only ask and have. But if they be firmly told that this is no time to ask, they will be as meek as lambs, and if the Protestants know they won't be betrayed by English instructions, they will tell them so without bigotry or passion. . . .'[2] He warned the Irish supporters of Catholic Relief in 1793 that the Catholics would feel no gratitude to them, as it was notorious that the measure had been 'suggested to this Kingdom from abroad' (an interesting phrase for a fervent upholder of the British connection to use); and in his speech on the Union in February 1800, referring to 'religious jealousies', he exclaimed, 'British, not Irish, counsels roused them! and British, not Irish, counsels now propose this Union. . . .'[3] On the level of

---

[1] Portland to Pelham, 28 Mar. 1795, Pelham MSS., B.L. Add. MS. 33101, fol. 165. [2] Foster to Sheffield, 14 Mar. 1795, *Anglo-Irish Dialogue*, p. 17.
[3] *Parl. Reg.* (Irish), xiii. 332; *Foster's Speech of 17 Feb. 1800*, p. 38.

personality, however, he seems to have had difficulty in breaking free of the 'petty, provincial politics . . . of Ireland' (as Camden loftily described them to Castlereagh).[1] Perhaps Foster's was a nature which preferred to remain a big fish in a small pond. Whatever the reason, his political activity was largely confined to the Castle and the Irish cabinet, in a political situation controlled from Whitehall. In practice, this almost certainly made no difference whatsoever to the course of late-eighteenth-century Irish history. After all, the more English-orientated and more realistic Fitzgibbon achieved nothing except the catching of a conscience most willing to be caught, Fitzgibbon's advice was as much discounted by the British Government as Foster's, and as has been noted, Fitzgibbon's influence on even the Union was negligible.

Fitzgibbon died so soon after the Union that it is impossible to say what his post-Union role and influence would have been: Foster alone of the old Irish Cabinet established himself at Westminster, staging there a quite remarkable come-back, and returning to office at an age when most men would be retiring. However, his aggressive (and audible) provincialism remained—Wilberforce, who had met him before the Union, called him 'Mr. *Spaker*', and Chief Secretary Wickham commented in 1802 that the British Opposition had been 'more astonished at the strength of Mr. Foster's brogue than convinced by his arguments'.[2] Foster was not of the generation, nor did he have the inclination or the English connections, to transfer himself into British politics in the way that Castlereagh, George Ponsonby, and the Wellesleys succeeded in doing. Instead, he saw himself as an ambassador for Ireland, who went to Westminster because the Union had made it necessary for him to 'quit Ireland for the chance of serving it'.[3] Writing to an English member as late as 1811, he explained that he had 'laid it down as a general rule, being an Irishman, not to interfere in private bills here'; and in the previous year he had described himself, in a private letter to an English connec-

---

[1] Camden to Robert Stewart, 16 Oct. 1790, Castlereagh MSS., P.R.O.N.I. D.3030/F5.

[2] Wilberforce to Mornington, 20 Apr. 1799, Wellesley MSS., B.L. Add. MS. 37308, fol. 230; Wickham to Hardwicke, 22 Mar. 1802, Hardwicke MSS., B.L. Add. MS. 35713, fol. 38.

[3] Foster to Sheffield, 17 May 1801, *Anglo-Irish Dialogue*, p. 40.

tion, as 'an Irishman . . . conversant only in Irish affairs'.[1] This intense and almost blinkered concentration on Irish affairs was probably one of the things which recommended him to Pitt in 1804. Certainly, it was not as a result of any change in Foster, or in his political course, that the man who had been discredited in the eyes of the British Government in March 1798, was allowed to become 'the Viceroy over the King's Vicegerent' in 1804–5. Grattan, for one, recognized that it was still the same Foster; referring to Foster's resignation in July 1805, he wrote: '. . . Foster has ridden too hard: the same violent spirit that made him torture the rebels, has overturned himself . . .'[2]

Not only was it the same Foster; to some extent the reason for his tenure of office at Westminster was the same as the reason for his continuing membership of the Irish cabinet between 1777 and 1798: his assistance was wanted in doing the day-to-day business of government, and now, in particular, the Irish parliamentary business. In theory, the Union had reduced the burden of the Irish parliamentary business. There was no longer a separate Irish Parliament to be managed, and the Irish representation had been reduced from 300 to 100. In practice, however, this reduced burden was allowed to become unbearable, because very little was done to prevent it from falling almost exclusively on one man—the chief secretary. During the parliamentary session, the chief secretary was needed in two places at once, Westminster and Dublin, and he usually compromised by spending only part of the session at Westminster. In Dublin, there were a number of people to fill his place when he was absent. The lord lieutenant was permanently resident there; so were the under-secretaries (who ceased to sit in Parliament after the Union), and the lord lieutenant's private secretary or secretaries. The lord chancellor and the law officers were not so permanently resident in Dublin, and sometimes attended Parliament. But Lord Clare's plan for the lord chancellor to attend Parliament from January to the close of the session, and be represented judicially in Dublin by the master of the rolls,[3] was not acted on by his successors; and the

[1] Foster to Montague Burgoyne, 18 Mar. 1811, and to Sir George Dallas, 19 Sept. 1810, F.P. D.562/11766 and T.2519/4/1098.
[2] See p. 110, n. 2.
[3] Clare to Castlereagh, 14 Nov. 1800, printed in O'Flanagan, *Lives of the Chancellors*, ii. 270 ff.

law officers needed to be in Dublin if they were to carry out the onerous duties of their offices, keep up their private practices at the bar, and entitle themselves to their official fees, which constituted almost the whole of their official incomes (the attorney-general's salary was a mere £88).[1] Under these circumstances, it was at Westminster that the chief secretary stood most in need of help, and the help had to come from other quarters than those so far mentioned—most obviously from the chancellor of the Irish exchequer, who was allowed to assume and retain a crucial supporting role in the conduct of the Irish parliamentary business. The only sustained attempt to spread the burden more widely was the use made of the services of C. M. Ormsby, First Counsel to the Irish Revenue Commissioners, between 1802 and 1806; Addington had Ormsby returned to Parliament in 1802 so that he could provide the legal assistance in Parliament which the law officers usually were not available to provide. But the experiment was not altogether successful. Ormsby's office carried with it duties which could not be entirely neglected; like the law officers, most of his official income came from fees, and the Second Counsel to the Commissioners understandably took the view that, if he was doing Ormsby's work, he should receive Ormsby's fees; moreover, Ormsby tended to range himself first with Corry and then with Foster,[2] so that in practice his presence at Westminster strengthened, rather than weakened, the chancellor of the Irish exchequer's position *vis-à-vis* the chief secretary. Because the chancellorship of the Irish exchequer had been allowed in this way to assume an importance by no means intrinsic to it, it was natural for Pitt to appoint to it the most widely acknowledged expert in Irish economics and finance: at the time of Pitt's return to power in 1804, there could be no question that that was Foster.

This same acknowledged expertise in Irish economics and finance had given Foster his continuing place in the old Irish Cabinet. However, his position in Whitehall was weaker than his position in Dublin Castle. Superficially strong, it was

[1] John Stewart to Abercorn, 21 Jan. and 1 Feb. 1803, Abercorn MSS., P.R.O.N.I. T.2541/IB3/4/1, 4. See also p. 212.

[2] Wickham to Corry, 24 Jan. 1803, Wickham MSS., P.R.O.N.I. T.2627/5/H/49; Henry Alexander to Lord Caledon, 17 and 18 Oct. 1805, Caledon MSS. P.R.O.N.I. D.2433/C/6/5, 6.

strong mainly by default—default of another arrangement being made for providing the chief secretary with the parliamentary support he needed. The wonder is that this was not done; for strife between the chancellor of the Irish exchequer and the other members of the Irish administration was almost endemic. Dublin Castle was very frequently critical of chancellors of the Irish exchequer, when they were out of easy reach at Westminster, for departing from instructions and taking unauthorized initiatives; and the chancellors of the Irish exchequer very frequently rebutted these criticisms with counter-charges of their own. It was the post-Union equivalent of Whitehall's pre-Union dread that lords lieutenant and chief secretaries would succumb totally to the influence of the Irish cabinet. The most stormy and rancorous chancellorship of the Irish exchequer was Foster's between 1804 and 1805, when he was First Lord of the Irish Treasury as well. But there was a basic lack of delimitation between the powers and duties of the chancellor of the Irish exchequer and those of the chief secretary, which would almost certainly have made itself felt had no Irish treasury been established, and certainly did make itself felt when the chancellor of the Irish exchequer was not first lord. It was a major problem in the case of three out of the four chancellors of the Irish exchequer in the period between the Union and the abolition of the office in 1817, and it might well have become a major problem in the case of the one exception,[1] Newport, had his term of office not been so short. Significantly, it was a major problem in the case of Foster's sometime protégé, Vesey FitzGerald, in whom the British government at last found a 'practicable' Irish politician, and who was on very good personal terms with the Chief Secretary and Lord Lieutenant of the day.[2] Yet, at any time between 1801 and 1817, the British government was free to alter

[1] For an example of the harmony prevailing between Newport and the Government over even the vexed issue of the powers of the treasury board, see Lord Grenville to Duke of Bedford, 1 Aug. 1806, *H.M.C. Dropmore MSS.*, viii. 253.

[2] Vesey FitzGerald to Peel, [July? 1813?] and 14 July 1813; Lord Liverpool to Vesey FitzGerald, 4 Oct. 1813; and Lord Whitworth and Peel to Vesey Fitz-Gerald, (both) 23 Jan. 1817—Vesey FitzGerald MSS., N.L.I. MSS. 7813, pp. 247–9, 7820, pp. 17–20, 7813, pp. 228–30, 7853, pp. 17, 86–7. The wish for a 'practicable' Irish politician (i.e. not Foster) was expressed by Perceval in 1811—W. W. Pole to Duke of Richmond, 16 Mar. 1811, Richmond MSS., N.L.I. MS. 65, fol. 751.

the specification for its Irish administration, and eliminate its dangerous, or at any rate inconvenient, dependence on the one Irish politician and office-holder.[1] It could have put the lord-ships of the Irish treasury to more constructive use than it did.[2] It could have appointed a chief secretary whose strong-point was economics and finance (Charles Long is a case in point), and recruited complementary support among Irish politicians whose strengths lay in other directions. Early in 1803, the Government had actually almost made up their minds to abolish the chancellorship of the Irish exchequer, or at any rate its political functions, which were after all as recent in date as 1784. Of this decision Foster stated his approval.[3] To fill the vacuum thus created, the Government planned to retire the Attorney-General, John Stewart, compensate him with a sinecure office and a lordship of the Irish treasury, and employ him to assist the chief secretary with the conduct of the Irish parliamentary business.[4] Stewart was in fact retired, but the rest of the plan was never put into operation, and the chancellor of the Irish exchequer remained the chief secretary's number two. Another possibility open to the government was to appoint an Englishman to the chancellorship of the Irish exchequer—the Talents, in fact, considered George Tierney in 1806.[5] Since there was no longer an Irish Parliament whose colonial sensitivities had to be respected, an Irish chancellor of the Irish exchequer was no longer a *sine qua non*, and the office itself was actually dispensed with in 1811–12. All these—and more—possibilities were open; the government had no compelling need of an Irish, or any, chancellor of the Irish exchequer, and certainly no compelling need of Foster.

There was, thus, an element of window-dressing in the con-tinuation of the office, and in the continued appointment of Foster and other Irishmen to it. It is tempting to equate window-dressing with cynicism; and there was, indeed, cynicism in the decision to retain Foster in 1810, so that he—a native—should

---

[1] See, for example, Hardwicke to Yorke, 28 Feb. 1806, Hardwicke MSS., B.L. Add. MS. 35706, fol. 327.

[2] See pp. 213 f.   [3] See p. 88.

[4] See p. 434, *n*. 1.; also, John Stewart to Abercorn, 2 May 1803, Abercorn MSS., P.R.O.N.I. T.2541/IB3/4/10; Marsden to Wickham, 25 Jan. and 10 Feb. 1803, Wickham MSS., P.R.O.N.I. T.2627/5/K/6, 20.

[5] Grattan, *Life*, v. 288. Tierney's father had been born in Limerick.

bear the odium of the unpopular budget of that year, which otherwise would have fallen on the British Government and, more generally, on the Union.[1] However, the window-dressing, cynical at times, was also statesmanlike and well-intentioned. In September 1803, after Emmet's insurrection, Castlereagh wrote to Wickham:

> ... I do most earnestly advise you to manage Foster, and every man of station in the Country, as well as you can. There is no danger at present in their power: there is much in their separation from Government, inasmuch as it gives to the Government an appearance of distinctness from the natural interests of the Country, which will always be turned against them with effect when anything awkward happens. . . .[2]

As an Irishman, Castlereagh was perhaps peculiarly sensitive to Irish colonial sensitivities. But there is reason for thinking that all the British governments of the immediate post-Union period participated to some extent in this view. Why else should Henry Alexander have been made Chairman of Committees in 1801? If Foster had shown a more conciliatory disposition, he might well have been made Speaker in 1802.[3] The chairmanship of committees and speakership were, of course, comparatively harmless offices, and withdrawn from the specifically Irish sphere: British governments, generally speaking, saw more danger than Castlereagh in giving to Irish politicians influence over Irish affairs, although they recognized, with him, the need to sweeten the Union by giving the Irish politicians prominence—prominence, but preferably not influence. The experiments with the low-ranking C. M. Ormsby and the low-calibre John Stewart can perhaps be seen as attempts to give prominence to Irish politicians who would be unlikely to constitute a danger; the experiment with Foster in 1804 can certainly be seen as a bold departure from previous timidity. Foster was made Chancellor of the Irish Exchequer in 1804, not only because of his practical utility, but because of the hoped-for moral effect of his appointment on Ireland and the Irish members. It was another example of

[1] See p. 372.
[2] Castlereagh to Wickham, 6 Sept. 1803, Wickham MSS., P.R.O.N.I. T.2627/5/G/52.
[3] Malcomson, *Foster and the Speakership*, p. 281.

the stress which late-eighteenth-century and early-nineteenth-century governments laid on the quality, as well as the quantity, of the support they attracted to themselves.[1] At any time since the Union, Foster's appointment to office would have been a symbol of the extinction of the Union as a political issue. In May 1804, its moral effect was heightened because at that point in time Foster's reputation at Westminster was probably at its peak, thanks to his conduct during the earlier part of the session, particularly on the currency committee. In early April, the Dowager Lady Downshire had written:

. . . I trust Mr. Foster will persevere in his patriotic exertions. Without the active interference of well-informed, independent Irish Members, I fear little can be done for Ireland, on account of the general want of particular information and knowledge of its interests, which the English Members cannot be supposed to possess. But no disposition in the Government or Parliament is wanting to meet and relieve all its wants, and therefore much good is to be hoped for and expected. . . .[2]

Lady Downshire was predisposed to Foster, who had been an ally of her martyred husband at the time of the Union; as an Englishwoman by birth, she perhaps credited the British Government with better intentions towards Ireland than most Irish commentators would have done; also, the British Government to which she referred was Addington's, which she supported to the last, not Pitt's. With these reservations, however, her remarks may be treated as a reflection of the spirit of optimism and goodwill towards Ireland which were symbolized by Foster's appointment to office by Pitt.

Foster's appointment may also have symbolized a reaction on Pitt's part against the earlier Addingtonian optimism that Ireland could be purified, conciliated, and saved only by means of English appointees. Hardwicke, Abbot, and Wickham all took this view, but its most extreme manifestation was Lord Clare's English successor as Lord Chancellor of Ireland, Lord Redesdale. As John Mitford, Redesdale had been the author of the British Catholic Relief Act of 1791. He was professionally as well as politically well qualified for the lord chancellorship,

[1] See pp. 204 f., 223 ff.
[2] Lady Downshire to John Reilly, 9 Apr. 1804, Downshire MSS., P.R.O.N.I. D.607/I/22.

because he was probably the best equity lawyer in England, and a close friend of the Lord Chancellor of England, Lord Eldon, with whom he could be expected to collaborate closely on the assimilation of the law in the two kingdoms. Moreover, his appointment put the Addington Administration to great inconvenience, because he was Speaker of the House of Commons at the time, and not only did the appointment vacate the speakership, but the Government's choice of Abbot as his successor vacated the chief secretaryship too.[1] Hitherto, the Englishmen appointed lord chancellors of Ireland had been second- or third-rate, and no loss to English law or British politics: in appointing Redesdale, the Addington Administration sacrificed English to Irish considerations, in a sincere and well intentioned attempt to get the best possible man for the job. For all this, the appointment was most unfortunate in its consequences. Redesdale soon proved to be still more intemperate and imprudent in his language than Lord Clare. Worse still, his experience of Ireland transformed his earlier 'liberalism' on the Catholic Question into a paranoic dread of the political designs of the Irish Catholic Church. This exploded into publicity just after Emmet's insurrection, when the leading member of the conservative Catholic aristocracy, Lord Fingall, applied to Redesdale for the commission of the peace for co. Meath. Redesdale signed the commission, but also embroiled himself in a protracted correspondence with Fingall, in which he questioned the loyalty of any Catholic to a Protestant State; he also had the extreme insensitivity to observe that Fingall's 'distinguished loyalty' had *probably* excluded him from receiving in advance information about the intended insurrection.[2] This correspondence got into print early in 1804, and was castigated in the House of Commons by, among others, Pitt's acolyte, Canning. There is a most significant contrast between Redesdale's behaviour and that of Clare, who had also had correspondence with Fingall about co. Meath J.P.s. In 1801, Fingall had recommended to Clare a man who, from his name, was probably a Protestant; but Clare, in his reply, had as good as invited Fingall to nominate Catholics: '. . . I shall always be happy to attend to any recommendation from

[1] E. B. Mitford, *Life of Lord Redesdale* (London, 1939), *passim*.
[2] Ibid. pp. 124 ff.

you, . . . and in future you have only to send any recommendation you may wish to forward to me to Mr. Dwyer [the
Chancellor's secretary], and the appointment shall take place
of course [i.e. as a matter of course]. . . .'[1] Pitt would have
known nothing about this previous correspondence. But it was
a commonplace that Englishmen appointed to Irish office
often went more Irish than the Irish themselves; the English
lord chancellors of the previous century had tended to fall in
love with the Penal Code or run after Irish popularity, or
both; and Archbishop Robinson of Armagh, another Englishman, had been a prey in the 1780s to much wilder apprehen-
sions about the Irish Catholics than any member of the then
Irish Cabinet.[2]

At the very time that Redesdale's correspondence with
Fingall was published in Dublin, Pitt was getting to know
Foster in London; and although this is pure speculation, it
would be surprising if it did not occur to Pitt that a native
politician like Foster, whatever his 'prejudices', would never
have involved himself and the Government in a scrape of this
kind. It may also have occurred to Pitt that a native politician
like Foster, who naturally did not subscribe to the conciliatory
policy of Redesdale and the Hardwicke Administration on law
and order issues, would not have involved the Government in
the far more serious scrape of Emmet's insurrection. Not only
did the Pittite Canning attack the Irish Administration for their
alleged laxity and negligence at the time of the insurrection;
the Pittite Castlereagh, who held office under Addington until
Pitt's second ministry was formed in May 1804, and did his best
to repel Canning's attack in the House, was also privately of
the opinion that the charge was well-founded.[3] As a result
of Emmet's insurrection and the indiscretions of Redesdale,
the changeable tide of British political thinking was turning
towards Foster in the spring of 1804, just as it had turned away
from him in March 1798.

It must again be stressed that this is pure speculation. But
speculation is the only guide to what was in Pitt's mind in the

---

[1] Clare to Fingall, 1 Oct. 1801, Fingall MSS., N.L.I. MS. 8023/6. For Clare's
possible clash with Foster over the appointment of Catholic J.P.s, see pp. 249 f.

[2] Robinson to Orde, 19 Jan. 1785, Bolton MSS., N.L.I. MS. 16350, fols. 71–2.

[3] G. Hume and A. P. W. Malcomson (ed.), *Robert Emmet: the Insurrection of July
1803* (H.M.S.O., Belfast, 1976), No. 198.

spring of 1804, when he appointed Foster, not only to the chancellorship of the Irish exchequer, but to an unprecedented and potent combination of that office with the first lordship of the Irish treasury; Phillidor and the Spaniard, now that they had come together, conducted their negotiation by word of mouth, and neither has left an account of the terms of the arrangement or the motives for his actions. At the time, the ineffective Chief Secretary, Nepean, reported to Lord Hardwicke that Pitt's eyes had been opened from the outset to the danger inherent in Foster's appointment:

. . . There cannot be the smallest doubt that Mr. Foster will endeavour to possess himself of as much power and authority as possible, and I see difficulties in keeping it down. His disposition is, however, very well known, and it is not a failing of the present Government to allow persons to possess powers to which by their Employments they are not fully entitled. I have taken care to have Your Excellency's opinion on this subject fully and completely understood, so that ignorance cannot possibly be pleaded hereafter. . . .[1]

However, one possible source of misunderstanding was that the word-of-mouth negotiations between Pitt and Foster were conducted largely via Lord Camden. In 1796, when Lord Lieutenant, Camden had urged on Pitt the division of the revenue boards and other measures to make more effective the treasury's control over the Revenue.[2] Charles Long was later to take the view that the root cause of the clash of authorities which ensued in 1804–5, was that the Responsibility Act of 1795 was inappropriate to post-Union conditions;[3] by this he probably meant that, before the Union, the defects of the Act had not mattered much in practice, because all the key office-holders concerned—the lord lieutenant, chief secretary, first lord of the treasury, and chancellor of the exchequer—were in the one place at the one time, Dublin Castle, and so were forced by proximity into co-operation. It may be that Camden briefed Pitt badly, because Camden was thinking in terms of pre-Union conditions. On the other hand, there may have been

---

[1] Nepean to Hardwicke, 2 June 1804, Hardwicke MSS., B.L. Add. MS. 35715, fol. 68.
[2] Camden to Pitt, 10 Feb. 1796, Chatham MSS., P.R.O. 30/8/326, fol. 62.
[3] Long to Foster, 26 Oct. 1805, P.R.O., H.O. MSS. H.O. 100/131, fol. 259.

more policy than muddle in Camden's role: before Pitt's resignation in 1801, Camden had proposed that the lord lieutenancy should be abolished, and replaced by a secretaryship-of-state for Ireland whose holder (who by implication was to be Camden himself) should be part-resident in Dublin and part-resident in London.[1] Pitt's reaction to this plan is unknown. But the period 1801–4 had witnessed very serious clashes of authority between the Lord Lieutenant and the Home Secretary, and between the Lord Lieutenant and the Commander of the Forces in Ireland. It may well be that, in the spring of 1804, Pitt regarded the lord lieutenancy, institutionally, as under review, and Hardwicke, personally, as on probation.

Considerations of practical politics must also have influenced Pitt. The leading characteristic of the 100 Irish members at Westminster, certainly up to 1820, was their readiness to transfer their allegiance from one ministry to another: this might have been guessed, but was not yet proven, in the spring of 1804. Hence the activity of the Pittites in canvassing for Irish support against Addington; and, in fact, if a considerable majority of the Irish members had not transferred their allegiance to Pitt, his weak second ministry would never have got off the ground.[2] Under these circumstances, Pitt may have attached undue importance to securing the services of Ireland's leading, perhaps only, elder statesman; and since Foster would not take the chancellorship of the Irish exchequer on its own, it had to be accompanied by the first lordship of the Irish treasury. The importance was certainly undue, if Pitt expected Foster's appointment to swing Irish votes; it is a significant fact that Pitt, who appointed as his Chancellor of the Irish Exchequer the hero of the anti-Unionist struggle, was weaker in Irish support than the Talents, who appointed the fairly obscure Newport, who had not even sat in the Irish Parliament.[3] However, Foster was at least important as a symbol, and his appointment as a gesture—as Lady Downshire's remarks make plain. Pitt may also—and this is pushing speculation to its uttermost bounds—have sighed for a 'strong man' who would prevent his ministry from being buffeted and riven by

---

[1] Camden to Pitt, 1 Aug. 1800, Pratt MSS., K.A.O. U.840/C.30/6.
[2] Jupp, *Irish M.P.s at Westminster*, p. 71.   [3] Ibid.

the problems of Ireland, as the Addington ministry had been, at a time when it desperately needed to concentrate its attention on the war in Europe. Pitt had long since found his 'strong man' for Scotland in the person of Dundas, whom he was soon to lose; and Irish commentators were wont to draw comparisons, not only between Foster and Pitt, but also between Foster and Dundas.[1] Ironically, the resemblance between Foster and Dundas became uncomfortably close in the autumn of 1805; in June a motion for Dundas's impeachment had been carried, because of defalcations committed by the Paymaster of the Navy, Alexander Trotter, for which Dundas, as Treasurer of the Navy, was held accountable: in September the discovery of a defalcation of some £13,000 in the Irish linen board funds, for which Foster's protégés, the Corrys, were responsible, invited comparison between James Corry Junior and Trotter, and between Foster and Dundas.[2] In the spring of 1804, however, if the comparison between Foster and Dundas struck Pitt, it would have held out the hope that, in Foster, Pitt had found a man who might make Ireland as little troublesome to the British government as Dundas had made Scotland. Foster was the only surviving Irish politician of real and proven calibre who was interested in Ireland purely for its own sake, and did not seek to make British political capital out of his expertise in Irish affairs; if Foster, because he was an Irishman, made a more successful 'Minister' for Ireland than Hardwicke had hitherto proved to be, then let him become 'the Viceroy over the King's Vicegerent'. Something of this may have been in

---

[1] Redesdale to Perceval, 23 May 1805, Redesdale MSS., P.R.O.N.I. T.3030/7/31.

[2] Report of the Commissioners of Accounts on the linen board accounts, 2 Sept. 1805, S.P.O. 537/275/1—I am indebted for this reference to Dr. H. Gribben; Henry Alexander to Caledon, 17 Oct. 1805, Caledon MSS., P.R.O.N.I. D.2433/C/6/4; James Corry Junior (the Secretary to the linen board) to Foster, 9 Aug. 1796, deposition of Corry, 11 Jan. 1806, and Corry to J. C. Beresford, 15 Jan. 1806—F.P. D.562/9055, 6339, 6344. It was Corry's father and predecessor who had committed the fraud, and all Corry was doing was concealing it until he could raise the money to make restitution in full (which he eventually did). However, for all his protestations to the contrary, Foster had in fact known about the fraud since 1800 or 1801, if not 1796; and it appears that this embarrassing fact would have come out as a result of Corry's examination before a committee of the linen board, if the chairman of the committee, J. C. Beresford, had not hushed it up. J. C. Beresford was Beresford's son, so it is ironical that he should have spared Foster after Foster's persecution of his father in 1794-5.

Pitt's mind in the spring of 1804; there is no evidence for what was in his mind, and perhaps it is a mistake to seek to rationalize what was there. Much of Pitt's behaviour during his second ministry was irrational and erratic, and the terms of Foster's appointment may simply be an early symptom of loss of grasp.

From the start, there was no possibility of Foster's becoming the Irish Dundas: Dundas had been given charge of the patronage of Scotland, and Hardwicke retained charge of the patronage of Ireland. Foster never denied that the lord lieutenant was the 'Minister' in the sphere of patronage:[1] all he claimed was that the dismissal of offending revenue officers was not a matter of patronage, but a necessary part of the treasury's 'control and superintendence'. In 1806, an in-coming office-holder whose office commanded a large volume of departmental patronage, was clearly informed '. . . that although the applications from individuals were to be made directly to him, . . . yet that in cases where Parliamentary interests were in question, he was to attend to the wishes of Government. . . .'[2] The same invariable rule must have applied to even as high-ranking an office-holder as Foster was when Chancellor of the Irish Exchequer and First Lord of the Irish Treasury. In practice, the use he made, and the extension he gave, to the patronage of the treasury was not aimed at increasing his influence with the Irish members, but at strengthening the treasury's 'control and superintendence' by placing reliable people (some of them his wife's poor relations) in key positions in the Irish bureaucracy.[3] Irish members who happened to be friends of Foster might use him as an intermediary with the Irish Administration or the British Government; but if their application were successful, it would be spelt out to them that their obligation was to the Government, not to Foster. As has been noted, Owen Wynne did not even use Foster as an intermediary in the spring of 1804, and nor had Edward Hardman in 1801–3 (although, in Hardman's case, a subsidiary motive must have been Foster's and his desire to play down the closeness of their political connection).[4] Foster would almost certainly have concurred with Wickham's already-quoted view that '. . . the formation

---

[1] See p. 92.
[2] Grenville to Elliott, 1 Apr. 1806, *H.M.C. Dropmore MSS.*, viii. 75.
[3] See pp. 278 f.   [4] See pp. 218, 171 ff.

of a *Party* on Irish politics only is a thing impracticable . . . as long
as Government has any favours to grant or any titles to bestow
. . .'[1] Nor is there any evidence that he ever attempted to form
such a party. His violent clash with the 1st Earl of Donoughmore in 1804[2] was a clash between the treasury and the revenue,
of which Donoughmore was Chief Commissioner; through
that professional go-between, Lord Sligo, Donoughmore made
overtures for a compromise arrangement over the division of
the boards, sought a political alliance between the Hely-
Hutchinsons and the Fosters, and in particular offered John
Leslie Foster the Hely-Hutchinson interest in the College.
Foster's indifference to these proposals caused Lord Sligo
to remonstrate with him: '. . . If you think of measures only,
without considering men, depend upon it, you will find your
mistake, and the error will be more to be lamented, because
you will not only lose the men, but the measures also . . .'[3]
However, Foster was right in concentrating on measures,
not men. The only man, effectively, who mattered for Foster
was Pitt; and a political alliance with the Hely-Hutchinsons
or any other Irish parliamentary interest was worth little and
would not have lasted long, in a situation where the Irish
patronage machine remained tightly under the control of the
lord lieutenant.

It was, therefore, as inevitable as anything in history ever
is, that Foster would not become the Irish Dundas, and that
his appointment, on the terms on which he was appointed,
would involve Pitt's ministry in even more acute problems
of Irish government than had beset Addington. It is, however,
at first sight surprising that Foster should have stood higher
in the estimation of the English members than he did in that of
the Irish,[4] and that he should have failed—as he seems to have
done—to assemble around him at least an *atelier* of politically
talented Irish M.P.s. The explanation does not lie wholly in
the prostitution of the Irish members practised by the British
government: it lies partly in considerations of generation.
Foster was not only an elder, but an elderly, statesman—in
1806, George Knox (who was a generation younger) remarked,
almost with surprise, '. . . old Foster . . . has still great weight in

---

[1] See p. 88 *n.* 2.   [2] See p. 20.
[3] Sligo to Foster, [March ? 1805], F.P. D.207/70/4.   [4] See p. 93.

Ireland . . .'[1] Moreover, the Irish members were unusually young: in 1804, the average age of the non-Irish members was roughly forty-six, and that of the Irish members forty-one.[2] At sixty-four, Foster was the third-oldest of them, and he became the second-oldest when Beresford died in 1805. The Irish members had a sharp eye to 'the reversionary interest', were politically unreliable on questions concerning the Prince of Wales, and were therefore likely to have diagnosed Foster as a bad reversionary bet. For much the same reasons as they were youthful, the Irish members were lacking in political talent—'inevitable' House of Commons men, for the most part, listlessly performing the political functions of their social station. All but fifteen of the Irish members who sat at Westminster between 1801 and 1820, came from families who had sat in the Irish Parliament; and these were the very families which, because of their parliamentary interest, had been widely ennobled. In 1805, Lord Dunlo, who had been considered for the chancellorship of the Irish exchequer in 1803,[3] succumbed to his father's earldom of Clancarty; and in 1807, at the very time he was being considered as a possible alternative to Foster,[4] Sir Laurence Parsons succumbed to his uncle's earldom of Rosse. Examples of talented Irish politicians who were in the wrong House could be multiplied. Again, the excesses of patronage which had carried the Union, lumbered many Irish politicians with offices which, after the Union, were either legally or geographically incompatible with a seat in Parliament; Beresford was exceptional in that he gave up his office and retained his seat, and that was because he had reached retiring age anyway. For Irish politicians, the Union resolved the identity-problem of who was a politician and who was a bureaucrat: politics lay at Westminster and the bureaucracy in Dublin. Not only the under-secretaries, but the law officers and many experienced Irish parliamentarians, opted for bureaucracy. As a further deterrent to politics, there was the

---

[1] George Knox to Abercorn, 21 Sept. 1806, Abercorn MSS., P.R.O.N.I. T.2541/IB3/12/24.

[2] I am indebted for these figures to Mr. Roland Thorne of the History of Parliament Trust.

[3] Wickham to Hardwicke, 6 Feb. 1803, Wickham MSS., P.R.O.N.I. T.2627/5/E/111.

[4] See p. 101.

increased difficulty, which successive governments did nothing to remedy, of finding a seat.[1] It can almost be said that, because of peerages, offices, and the shortage of seats, a generation of potential Irish talent was lost—the generation below Foster's. The Irish politicians who distinguished themselves at Westminster were either considerably less than a generation younger than him—Grattan, George Ponsonby, Corry, and Newport— or considerably more than a generation younger than him— the Knight of Kerry, Sir Henry Parnell, Vesey FitzGerald, John Leslie Foster, and, youngest of all, Thomas Spring-Rice. Possible exceptions are Henry Alexander, who gave up politics for a post in the government of the Cape; George Knox, who held office only briefly, and then lost his seat; and John Maxwell Barry, who was never more than a Lord of the Irish Treasury. The only important exceptions are Castlereagh, who cannot be counted as an Irish politician, as George Ponsonby initially can; and Plunket, who made only the briefest appearance at Westminster during the years of Foster's official career there. The parliamentary record of the Irish members, and perhaps even the course of Foster's career at Westminster, might have been very different if so much potential Irish talent had not been buried in the Irish peerage, the Irish bureaucracy, and the seatless wilderness.

Foster's second term of office at Westminster merely repeated, in lower key, the themes of his first. The first has more symbolic than practical significance; but it symbolizes much. It marks the last opportunity which Foster had to shore up the position of the Ascendancy by economic means. By then, the policy was probably unrealistic, nor was this a real opportunity to implement it: the war and the financial provisions of the Act of Union, the controversy over the powers of the Irish treasury, and the probable incompatibility of revenue reform with the on-going political exploitation of revenue patronage[2]—each of these was an insuperable obstacle to Foster's policy of killing Emancipation with economic kindness. His first term of office at Westminster also symbolizes the sameness of Irish politics, or rather of the disadvantages under which Irish politicians laboured, before and after the Union. After the Union, Foster had no bargaining power with the British government because

---

[1] See pp. 212 ff.   [2] See pp. 244 f.

he had no power-base among the Irish members, just as the Irish Cabinet before the Union had had no collective bargaining power because the considerable measure of support which they enjoyed in the Irish Parliament was never ascertained. Again, after the Union the Irish politicians, devoid though they were of the power to head an Irish 'party' or to influence high policy, were still objects of suspicion to the British governments who employed them, just as they had been before the Union, when they had been capable of being rather more troublesome, though still hardly dangerous. The best Irish minds and the best English minds were now free to meet, without the distorting interposition of the lord lieutenant as the essential channel of communication; but mistrust and misunderstanding were as prevalent as they had been before the Union. This suggests that the mistrust and misunderstanding between Irish and English politicians was psychological, indeed pathological. Finally, Foster's first term of office at Westminster symbolizes, not only the lovelessness of the marriage between the British government and the Anglo-Irish Ascendancy, but the unequal inter-dependence of the two; Pitt found Foster merely useful, but Foster depended upon Pitt. However, although Foster was politically mistaken in the short term in thinking that the inter-dependence was more nearly equal than the British government of his day would have admitted, in the long term he was to be proved not so far wrong. The British government of his day considerably accelerated the political demise of the Ascendancy; but British governments of the future were never to find another 'description of Irishmen' who suited and served their purposes nearly so well. The Irish Unionists of the late nineteenth and early twentieth centuries were more broadly based, socially and denominationally, than the old Ascendancy had been. But their relationship with even British Conservative governments was to be no less loveless, and no more fruitful, than the marriage of convenience between the Ascendancy of Foster's day and the British government of Pitt's.

APPENDIX

GENEALOGY OF THE BURGHS OF BERT AND OLDTOWN

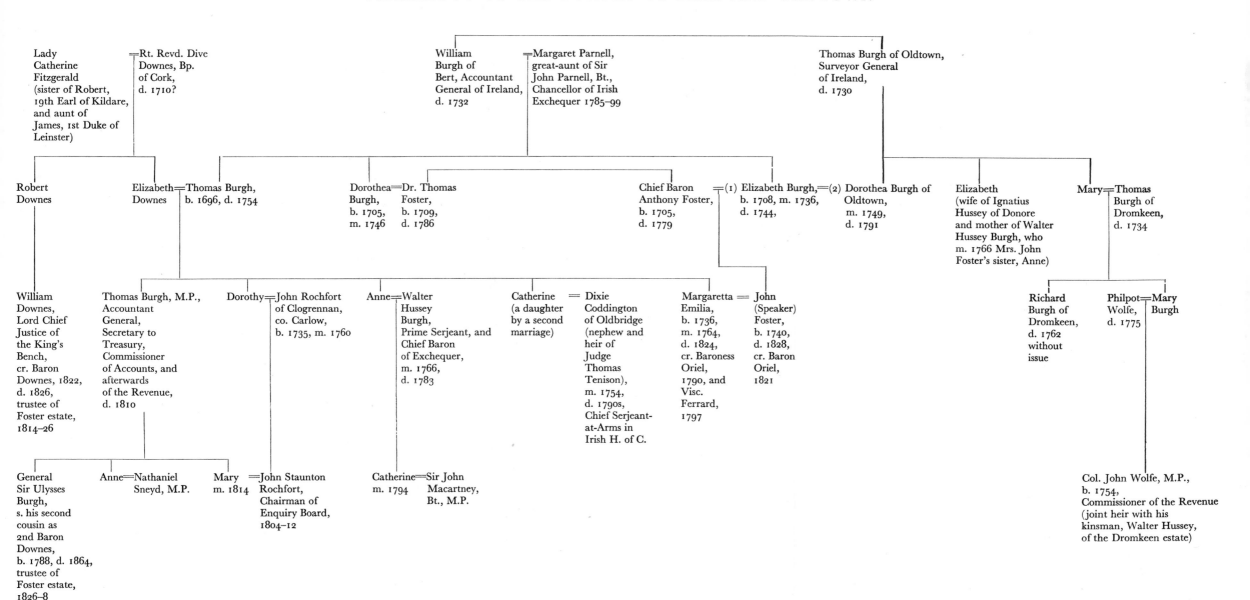

TABLE FIVE

THE FOSTERS' INCOME FROM OFFICIAL SOURCES

Name	Office	Income	Year
Anthony Foster	First Counsel to the Commissioners of the Revenue	£1,100[1]	1760–6
,, ,,	Chief Baron of the Exchequer	£1,000 plus fees and allowances[2]	1766–77
,, ,,	Commissioner of Accounts	£500[3]	,,
,, ,,	Pension on retirement	£1,000[4]	1777–9
John Foster	Chairman of Committees	£500[5]	,,
,, ,,	,, ,,	£500	1779–84
,, ,,	Customer of Dublin Port	£1,000	,,
,, ,,	Chancellor of the Exchequer	£2,500[6]	1784–5
,, ,,	Commissioner of Accounts?	£500[7]	,,
,, ,,	Speaker	Salary, £4,000 fees, £1,000[8]	1785–93
,, ,,	,,	£5,000	1793–8
Thomas Foster	Colonel of the Louth Militia	£1,000[9]	,,
,, ,,	,, ,,	£1,000	1798–9
,, ,,	Commissioner of the Revenue	£1,000[10]	,,
John Foster	Speaker	£5,000	,,
,, ,,	,,	£5,000	1799–1801
Thomas Foster	Colonel of the Louth Militia	£1,000	,,
,, ,,	,, ,,	£1,000	1801–4
John Foster	Compensation for the abolition of the speakership	£5,000[11]	,,
,, ,,	,, ,,	£5,000	1804–6
,, ,,	Chancellor of the Exchequer	Salary, £1,200 fees, £1,000[12]	,,
	First Lord of the Irish Treasury (but apparently with the salary either of the Second Lord or of a supernumerary Lord)[14]	Either £800 or £1,200 (probably the latter)[13]	,,
Thomas Foster	Colonel of the Louth Militia	£1,000	,,
,, ,,	,, ,,	£1,000	1806–7
John Foster	Compensation for the abolition of the speakership (sold for £30,000 some time in 1806)[15]	£5,000	,,

TABLE FIVE (*cont.*)

Name	Office	Income	Year
John Foster	Chancellor of the Exchequer	£2,200	1807–11
,, ,,	Second Lord of the Irish Treasury	£800[16]	,,
,, ,,	Supernumerary, after 1809 Second, Lord of the British Treasury	£1,600[17]	,,
Thomas Foster	Supernumerary Lord of the Irish Treasury	£1,200[18]	,,
,, ,,	Colonel of the Louth Militia	£1,000	,,
,, ,,	,, ,,	£1,000	1811–13
,, ,,	Supernumerary Lord of the Irish Treasury	£1,200	,,
,, ,,	Colonel of the Louth Militia	£1,000	1813–16
Anthony Foster John Foster Thomas Foster	Total official income	£212,900[19]	1760–1816

N.B. The italicized figures are conjectural.

Notes on Table Five

1. Godfrey Lill to Viscount Townshend, 7 June 1768, Townshend MSS., N.L.I. MS. 394/40. This, Lill makes clear, was if anything an underestimate. In 1828, just after its abolition, John Leslie Foster, who had held it up to then, estimated its income as £4,000 a year, and said that it was the most valuable of the law offices of the Crown, except for the attorneyship-general (J. L. Foster to Peel, 3 May 1828, Peel MSS., B.L. Add. MS. 40396, fols. 203–5).
2. Establishment of Ireland, 1787, F.P. D.562/1823. The fees and allowances constituted the bulk of the income.
3. Rowley Lascelles, *Liber Munerum Publicorum Hiberniae* (2 vols., London, 1852), i, Part 3, pp. 51, 78). The £500 came from fees and was therefore variable.
4. See note 2.
5. Johnston, *Irish House of Commons in 1791*, p. 31.
6. Orde to Pitt, 13 Aug. 1786, Chatham MSS., P.R.O. 30/8/329, fol. 277; Pelham to Northington, 9 Jan. 1784, Pelham MSS., B.L. Add. MS. 33101, fols. 17–18.
7. Lascelles, *Liber Munerum*, i, Part 3, pp. 51, 78. These fees may be included in the fees of the chancellorship of the exchequer, since Foster was an *ex officio* Commissioner of Accounts.
8. Estimate of parliamentary grants, 1784, F.P. D.562/9401C; estimate of the fees for passing bills in the British and the Irish Houses of Commons during the session of 1794, F.P. D.562/7581; Porritt, *Unreformed House*, ii. 403. Lord Annaly, writing to the Earl-Bishop of Derry on 12 March 1771. said that Ponsonby had lost to himself and his family £6,000 a year through resigning the speakership (Babington & Croasdaile MSS., P.R.O.N.I. D.1514/1/5/9).

9. The pay of a militia colonel under the Act of 1793 establishing the Irish militia was eight and sixpence per day spent on duty with his regiment—*Commons' Journals* (Ireland), vol. 16, Appendix, p. xii. It is therefore impossible to calculate precisely what Thomas Foster's pay amounted to. In addition to his pay he had the clothing account for his regiment, out of which it was estimated in the 1790s that a colonel could make for himself roughly £1,000 a year—McAnally, *Irish Militia*, p. 249. In 1807, or later, the colonelcy of the Sligo was stated to be worth £1,000 a year—Charles O'Hara to Charles K. O'Hara, 13 July [c. 1807], O'Hara MSS., N.L.I. In view of these uncertainties, Thomas Foster's pay and perks as Colonel of the Louth have been reckoned at the round figure of £1,000 a year from 1793 to 1816, when the regiment was disembodied. He remained its Colonel until his death in 1843.
10. Hardwicke to Pelham, 26 Sept. 1801, Pelham MSS., B.L. Add. MS. 33114, fol. 53.
11. Draft deed of sale (never actually executed) between Foster and David La Touche, 12 Jan. 1803, F.P. D.562/9238.
12. Return of all salaries, fees, and emoluments of officers of the Irish treasury, 2 Oct. 1804, F.P. D.562/14843.
13. Marsden to Wickham, 10 Feb. 1803, Wickham MSS., P.R.O.N.I. T.2627/5/K/20.
14. The conflicting evidence on this point is: Nepean to Hardwicke, 24 May and 2 June 1804, Hardwicke MSS., B.L. Add. MS. 35715, fols. 53, 78; Richmond to Hawkesbury, 6 June 1807, Whitworth MSS., K.A.O. U.269/1, p.33.
15. J. L. Foster to Foster, 8 July 1806, F.P. T.2519/4/264.
16. See note 13.
17. John Watson Stewart, *The English Directory for 1810* (Dublin, 1810), p. 118. There was no difference in salary between a supernumerary lordship and the second lordship of the British treasury. However, it may well be that Foster, because of the other offices he already held, did not receive the full £1,600 salary for either.
18. See note 13.
19. This is not an exact figure calculated to the precise date of appointment to, and resignation from, each office: in several instances the precise date is not known. Included in the total is the £30,000 raised by the sale of John Foster's compensation in 1806.

BIBLIOGRAPHY

A. PRIMARY SOURCES

1. *MS. Material*

ARMAGH DIOCESAN REGISTER, ARMAGH

Beresford MSS.: MSS. of Lord John George Beresford, Archbishop of Armagh, 1822–62; mainly of diocesan interest, but including some papers relating to the political interests of the Beresford family and therefore additional to the Pack–Beresford MSS. in P.R.O.N.I. (q.v.); photocopies in P.R.O.N.I. (T.2772).

BRITISH LIBRARY, LONDON

Adair MSS.: letters to Serjeant James Adair from John Forbes, M.P. for Drogheda, and others, 1780–96 (Add. MS. 53802).

Auckland MSS.: MSS. of William Eden, 1st Lord Auckland. These are of some interest for the period of Eden's chief secretaryship, 1780–2; but their main relevance lies in the fact that his regular correspondents, especially at the time of the Union, were such well-informed men as Lord Clare, Lord Sheffield, John Beresford, Edward Cooke, and John Lees (Add. MSS. 34419–20, 34422, 34424, 34454–5).

Buckingham MSS.: letter-books of the 1st Marquess of Buckingham, as Lord Lieutenant, 1782–3 and 1787–9 (Add. MSS. 40177–80, 40733).

Croker MSS.: MSS. of John Wilson Croker; nothing of relevance except a MS. diary of Croker's (Add. MS. 52471).

Hardwicke MSS.: MSS. of the 3rd Earl of Hardwicke as Lord Lieutenant, 1801–6 (Add. MSS. 35643, 35706, 35708, 35710–16, 35718, 35723–7, 35751, 35771–2, 35781).

Herries MSS.: MSS. of J. C. Herries, who as well as being Spencer Perceval's private secretary, briefly held private secretaryships in the Irish administration, 1805 and 1811; little relevant to Foster (Add. MSS. 57366–57469).

Hertford MSS.: MSS. of the 1st and 2nd Marquesses of Hertford (Egerton MSS. 3260–1); photocopies of the material of Irish interest in P.R.O.N.I. (T.3076/2).

Holland MSS.: letters from Lord Wycombe to Lady Holland, late 1790s (Add. MS. 51862).

Lismore Election Committee Minutes, 1791 (Egerton MS. 264).

Liverpool MSS.: MSS. of Charles Jenkinson, 1st Earl of Liverpool; not much of relevance (Add. MSS. 38214, 38219–21, 38309–10).

Newcastle MSS.: including letters to the 2nd Duke of Newcastle about Irish affairs, particularly from the Lord Lieutenant, the 3rd Duke of Devonshire, in the late 1730s (Add. MS. 32690).

456 *Bibliography*

Northington MSS.: letter-book of the 2nd Earl of Northington, as Lord Lieutenant, 1783–4 (Add. MS. 38716).

Peel MSS.: MSS. of Sir Robert Peel, 2nd Bt.; very useful for the period of Peel's chief secretaryship, 1812–18, and even more so for the letters he received while Home Secretary from J. L. Foster, 1826–9 (Add. MSS. 40181, 40185, 40207, 40224, 40225, 40278, 40280–1, 40388–9, 40396–9).

Pelham MSS.: MSS. of Thomas Pelham, 2nd Earl of Chichester, as Chief Secretary, 1783–4 and 1795–8, as Home Secretary, 1801–3, and in between times—especially during the Union crisis (Add. MSS. 33100–3, 33106, 33109, 33114); transcripts of the Irish material in the Pelham MSS. up to 1796 are available in P.R.O.N.I. (T.755).

Perceval MSS.: MSS. of Spencer Perceval as, among other things, Prime Minister, 1809–12; nothing directly relevant to Foster (Add. MSS. 49188, 49193).

Percy MSS.: letters from Thomas Percy, Bishop of Dromore, to his wife, 1798–1800 (Add. MS. 32335).

Robinson MSS.: correspondence between John Robinson, Secretary to the British Treasury, and the King about Irish affairs, 1776–80 (Add. MSS. 37833–5); see also *H.M.C. Abergavenny MSS.*

Southwell MSS.: MSS. of Edward Southwell as Secretary of State for Ireland, especially letters to Southwell from Dr. Marmaduke Coghill, 1722–35, which contain useful information about Anthony Foster's early political patrons (Add. MSS. 2112–3).

Vansittart MSS.: MSS. of Nicholas Vansittart as Chief Secretary, 1805 (Add. MSS. 31229–30).

Wellesley MSS.: MSS. of the 1st Marquess Wellesley; some useful correspondence about the management of Trim borough, 1797–8, and about the Union, 1798–1800 (Add. MSS. 37308, 37317).

Windham MSS.: MSS. of William Windham as Chief Secretary, 1783 (Add. MS. 37873).

BUCKINGHAMSHIRE COUNTY RECORD OFFICE, AYLESBURY

Buckinghamshire MSS.: MSS. of Robert Hobart, 4th Earl of Buckinghamshire, as Chief Secretary, 1789–93, and thereafter, including a list of the Irish Parliament in 1788 (D.M./H.); photocopies in P.R.O.N.I. (T.2627/1).

CAMBRIDGE UNIVERSITY LIBRARY

Chatham (Pretyman) MSS.: MSS. of William Pitt the Younger, partly additional to the Chatham MSS. in the P.R.O., but chiefly composed of non-contemporary copies of them (Add. MS. 6958).

EAST SUSSEX RECORD OFFICE, LEWES

Sheffield (Gage) MSS.: letters from Foster to the 1st Earl of Sheffield, which are the biggest and best source of information on his broad political thinking (AMS 5440); photocopies in P.R.O.N.I. (T.2965);

calendared in A. P. W. Malcomson (ed.), *An Anglo-Irish Dialogue: a Calendar of the Correspondence between John Foster and Lord Sheffield, 1774–1821* (Belfast, 1975).

GENEALOGICAL OFFICE, DUBLIN

Pedigree of the Burghs of Bert and Oldtown (MS. 176, pp. 467–79); photocopy in P.R.O.N.I. (T.2519/1).

Pedigree of Henry Foster of Cormie (MS. 165, pp. 428–9, 225–7); photocopy in P.R.O.N.I. (T.2519/1).

GLOUCESTER COUNTY RECORD OFFICE, GLOUCESTER

Redesdale MSS.: MSS. of the 1st Lord Redesdale, as Lord Chancellor of Ireland, 1802–6 (2002/C/7–9, /X12–14, 25); photocopies in P.R.O.N.I. (T.3030).

HAMPSHIRE COUNTY RECORD OFFICE, WINCHESTER

Normanton MSS.: MSS. of Archbishop Agar of Cashel, 1st Earl of Normanton; nothing on Irish politics (21 M. 57).

Palmerston MSS.: co. Sligo estate and electioneering correspondence of the 3rd Viscount Palmerston, particularly for 1817 and thereafter (38 M. 60).

Wickham MSS.: MSS. of William Wickham as Chief Secretary, 1802–4 (38 M. 49/1, 3); photocopies in P.R.O.N.I. (T.2627/5).

HOUSE OF LORDS RECORD OFFICE

Draft of an unsuccessful Dundalk estate bill, 1736 (Main Papers Series).

HUNTINGTON LIBRARY, SAN MARINO, CALIFORNIA

Emly (Pery) MSS.: MSS. of E. S. Pery, Foster's predecessor as Speaker; photocopies or non-contemporary MS. copies in P.R.O.N.I. (T.3087, T.3052).

KENT ARCHIVES OFFICE, MAIDSTONE

Pratt MSS.: MSS. of the 1st Marquess Camden as Lord Lieutenant, 1795–8, and thereafter (U.840); photocopies of only part of this collection are available in P.R.O.N.I. (T.2627/4), so citation is made from the originals in K.A.O.

Whitworth MSS.: MSS. of the 1st Earl Whitworth as Lord Lieutenant, 1813–18, incorporating some papers of his predecessor, the 4th Duke of Richmond, Lord Lieutenant, 1807–13 (the rest of which are in the National Library of Ireland, q.v.); U.269/O.214.

LIBRARY OF CONGRESS, WASHINGTON

Reports, attributed to Sir Henry Cavendish, of debates in the Irish House of Commons, 1776–89; there are 82 vols. in all, of which only the first four have been drawn upon; microfilm in P.R.O.N.I. (Mic. 12).

LONGFORD–WESTMEATH LIBRARY, MULLINGAR

Howard Bury MSS.: political and estate papers of the 2nd and 3rd Earls of Charleville; photocopies in P.R.O.N.I. (T.3069).

LOUTH COUNTY LIBRARY, DUNDALK

Register of Louth Freeholders, 1821–2, 1824–7; photocopies in P.R.O.N.I. (T.2519/14). These are printed, but are apparently the only surviving set; so they have been counted among the manuscript sources.

NATIONAL LIBRARY OF IRELAND, DUBLIN

Ashbrook MSS.: estate correspondence of the Flowers of Castle Durrow, Queen's County (MS. 11476).

Aylmer (Brodigan) MSS.: MSS. of Thomas Brodigan, secretary to the Catholic Committee of Drogheda (unsorted collection).

Balfour MSS.: MSS. of the Balfour family of Townley Hall, co. Louth (MSS. 9543–4, 10360, 10367–8, 10370).

Beaufort MSS.: MSS. of the Revd. D. A. Beaufort, Vicar of Collon (MSS. 8778–80, 13176).

Blaquiere MSS.: MSS. of Sir John Blaquiere, 1st Lord De Blaquiere, as Chief Secretary, 1772–6, and thereafter (MS. 877).

Bolton MSS.: MSS. of Thomas Orde, 1st Lord Bolton, Chief Secretary, 1784–7 (particularly MS. 16350).

Buckingham MSS.: MSS. of the 1st Marquess of Buckingham, as Lord Lieutenant, 1782–3 and 1787–9, and thereafter (MS. 5022, Joly MSS. 39–40).

Domvile MSS.: including, for some reason, papers of the Gardiner family, Viscounts Mountjoy, mostly about co. Dublin politics (MSS. 9399, 11848).

Farnham MSS.: MSS. of the 2nd Earl and the 5th Lord Farnham (Foster's nephew, formerly John Maxwell Barry), about co. Cavan politics (MSS. 11497–8 and unsorted).

Fingall MSS.: particularly the MSS. of the 8th Earl of Fingall, the Catholic leader (MS. 8021).

Forbes MSS.: MSS. of John Forbes; not much about Drogheda (MSS. 978, 10713).

Foster MSS.: 25 copies of letters from Foster, 1819 (MS. 4128); photocopies in P.R.O.N.I. (T.2519/3—q.v.).

Heron MSS.: MSS. of Sir Richard Heron, 1st Bt., as Chief Secretary, 1777–80, incorporating many of the papers of the 2nd Earl of Buckinghamshire, Lord Lieutenant at the same time (MSS. 5168, 13035, 13037–9, 13048, 13050–1, 13053, 13054).

Inchiquin MSS.: co. Clare poll-books, 1768, 1776, and 1783 (MSS. 14793—5).

List of the Irish Parliament, 1783 (MS. 2098); photocopy in P.R.O.N.I. (T.3035).

Lord Lieutenant's Union Correspondence: a miscellaneous collection, fully described in Bolton, *Union*, p. 224 (MS. 886).

Melville MSS.: part of the papers of Henry Dundas, 1st Viscount Melville, among other things as Home Secretary, 1790–4, and of his son, Robert,

2nd Viscount, as Chief Secretary, 1809; another part of this collection is in N.L.S. (q.v.); MSS. 54–55A.

Newport MSS.: MSS. of Sir John Newport, 1st Bt., mostly as Chancellor of the Irish Exchequer, 1806–7; there are other Newport MSS. in the Q.U.B. Library (q.v.); MS. 976.

O'Hara MSS.: MSS. of Charles O'Hara, M.P. for co. Sligo, 1783–1822, about local politics and family finances (unsorted collection). A further section of this collection remains in family possession and has been photocopied by P.R.O.N.I. (T.2812).

Pakenham Mahon MSS.: MSS. of the Mahon family of Strokestown, co. Roscommon, Lords Hartland; a good deal of material about local politics (MSS. 10081–95).

Richmond MSS.: MSS. of the 4th Duke of Richmond as Lord Lieutenant, 1807–13 (MSS. 58–75A).

Stratford MSS.: MSS. of the 2nd Earl of Aldborough, including material on Baltinglass borough and co. Wicklow politics (unsorted collection).

Sydney MSS.: MSS. of Thomas Townshend, 1st Lord Sydney, Home Secretary, 1782–3 and 1783–9 (MSS. 51–2).

Talbot-Crosbie MSS.: family and political MSS. of the co. Kerry magnate, the 2nd Earl of Glandore (unsorted collection).

Townshend MSS.: some MSS. of the 4th Viscount Townshend as Lord Lieutenant, 1767–72 (MSS. 394, 8009).

Vesey FitzGerald MSS.: MSS. of William Vesey FitzGerald as Chancellor of the Irish Exchequer, 1812–16, and about co. Clare and general politics (MSS. 7813–59).

Wicklow MSS.: family and political MSS. of the Howard family, earls of Wicklow (unsorted section); photocopies of part of this unsorted section in P.R.O.N.I. (Mic. 146).

NATIONAL LIBRARY OF SCOTLAND, EDINBURGH

Elliot of Wells (Minto) MSS.: MSS. of William Elliot as Chief Secretary, 1806–7 (MSS. E.W. 21–42).

Melville MSS.: a further section of the MSS. of the 1st Viscount Melville (MSS. 64, 68, 1051); photocopies of the few items of Irish interest in P.R.O.N.I. (T.2627/2). P.R.O.N.I.'s calendar of these items has been published in *Eighteenth-Century Irish Official Papers in Great Britain: Private Collections, Vol. 1* (Belfast, 1973), pp. 249 ff.

PUBLIC RECORD OFFICE, LONDON

Chatham MSS.: MSS. of William Pitt the Younger (30/8/325–31).

Colchester MSS.: MSS. of Charles Abbot, 1st Lord Colchester, as Chief Secretary, 1801–2, and thereafter (30/9/1/1, /1/2, /2/1).

Home Office MSS. (especially H.O. 100/1, /9, /75, /85, /122–3, /125, /129–31); available on microfilm in P.R.O.N.I. (Mic.224).

Treasury MSS.: minutes of board meetings, 1807–11 (T.29/89–110).

PUBLIC RECORD OFFICE OF IRELAND, DUBLIN

Meath freeholders list, 1781 (M. 1364).

Pyke-Fortescue MSS.: estate papers of the Fortescues of Stephenstown, Dundalk, co. Louth (Accession No. 1004).

PUBLIC RECORD OFFICE OF NORTHERN IRELAND

Abercorn MSS.: MSS. of the 8th Earl and the 1st Marquess of Abercorn, both relating to local politics in cos. Donegal and Tyrone, and the latter providing a whole new slant on national politics as well (T.2541).

Anglesey MSS.: correspondence of Sir Nicholas Bayly, 2nd Bt., and his grandson, the 1st Marquess of Anglesey, with the agents on their Louth estate, including incidental political comment; also, MSS. of the 1st Marquess as Lord Lieutenant, 1828–9 and 1830–3 (D.619).

Annesley MSS.: MSS. of the 2nd Earl Annesley, Chief Commissioner of Excise, 1805–10 (D.1854/4), and co. Down estate papers of the Annesley family (D.1503).

Babington & Croasdaile MSS.: incorporating part of the MSS. of Frederick Hervey, Earl-Bishop of Derry, 1768–1803 (D.1514/9); see also Bruce MSS.

Bedford MSS.: MSS. of the 4th Duke of Bedford as Lord Lieutenant, 1756–61 (T.2915).

Belmore MSS.: estate, family, and political papers of the Earls Belmore, including late-eighteenth-century building accounts for Castle Coole, Enniskillen, co. Fermanagh, and co. Tyrone election material for the 1870s (D.3007).

Blair MSS.: including correspondence about Newry politics in the 1770s (D.717).

Brownlow MSS.: account-book of William Brownlow of Lurgan showing his expenses at the co. Armagh by-election of 1753, and a copy of the poll at that election (T.2718/1, T.2736/1).

Bruce MSS.: incorporating most of the remaining MSS. of the Earl-Bishop of Derry (D.2798).

Caledon MSS.: political papers of the 2nd Earl of Caledon, including some papers of his father-in-law, the 3rd Earl of Hardwicke, as Lord Lieutenant, 1801–6 (D.2433).

Cassidy MSS.: MSS. of the Revd. Mark Cassidy, agent of the Marquesses of Londonderry, including some material on co. Down politics (D.1088).

Castlereagh MSS.: MSS. of Viscount Castlereagh, later 2nd Marquess of Londonderry, as Chief Secretary, 1798–1801, and before and after (D.3030).

Castle Ward MSS.: MSS. of the Wards of Castle Ward, Strangford, co. Down, Viscounts Bangor, including material on local politics in co. Down and elsewhere (D.2092).

Cleland MSS.: MSS. of the Revd. John Cleland, Cassidy's predecessor as the Londonderry family's agent, including useful comment on the Fitzwilliam Administration (D.714).

Coddington MSS.: MSS. of the Coddington family of Oldbridge, co. Meath, including the Dunleer corporation book, 1709–1811, and a volume of maps of the Louth estate of Viscount Massereene and Ferrard, 1863 (T.2519/12).

Colclough (McPeake) MSS.: MSS. of the Colclough family of Tintern Abbey, Enniscorthy, co. Wexford; useful for co. Wexford politics (T.3048/C).

Downshire MSS.: MSS. of the 1st and 2nd Marquesses of Downshire; invaluable for politics in the various constituencies where the family had influence, and for the events of the Union crisis (D.607, D.671).

Drennan MSS.: correspondence between Dr. William Drennan and his sister, Mrs. Martha McTier, and brother-in-law, Samuel McTier; the years between 1783 and 1793 are especially relevant (D.591).

Drennan–Bruce letters: letters from Drennan to the Revd. William Bruce (D.553).

Dufferin MSS.: including MSS. of Foster's daughter, Anna, and son-in-law, the 2nd Lord Dufferin (D.1071/A/112, /B/C/29).

Dunraven MSS.: MSS. of the Hon. Windham Wyndham Quin, M.P. for co. Limerick, 1807–20 (D.3196); the other Dunraven MSS. cited are described under Private Collections.

Erne MSS.: MSS. of the Earls Erne, containing information about the co. Fermanagh estate of the Balfour family of Townley Hall, co. Louth (D.1939).

Foster/Massereene MSS.: as the name implies, this is really two collections in one; but of the total of well over 25,000 documents, roughly 22,000 relate to the Foster family, so the collection has been cited throughout as F[oster] P[apers], followed by the reference number. The vast majority of it is in P.R.O.N.I., and is divided into the following sections:

1. *c.* 4,500 papers (F.P. D.207).
2. *c.* 18,000 papers (F.P. D.562).
3. *c.* 200 papers (F.P. D.1739).
4. *c.* 2,500 papers (F.P. T.2519/4—photocopies in P.R.O.N.I., originals in Lord Massereene's possession).
5. *c.* 150 papers (F.P. D.2681).

There is no logical reason for these five sub-divisions, nor any very clear-cut distinction in subject-matter between them. They merely reflect the fact that the Foster/Massereene MSS. have been deposited in piecemeal batches in P.R.O.N.I. over the period 1927–71.

There are two further batches of the collection elsewhere than P.R.O.N.I.:

6. *c.* 25 copies of letters from Foster, 1819, in N.L.I. (q.v.); photocopies in P.R.O.N.I. (T.2915/3).
7. *c.* 500 deeds and legal papers in Lord Massereene's possession at Chilham Castle, Kent (cited as F.P., Chilham deed room). These have not been copied by P.R.O.N.I.

Garstin MSS.: notes by J. Ribston Garstin on the Dunleer corporation, *c.* 1900 (T.2519/10).

Gosford MSS.: MSS. of the 1st Earl of Gosford; useful for co. Armagh politics and for the Union (D.1606).

Hart MSS.: MSS. of Gen. G. V. Hart, M.P. for co. Donegal, 1812–32, and of his elder brother, John Hart of Ballynagard, co. Londonderry; collection in the process of being sorted (D.3077).

Johnston of Kilmore MSS.: diary of Francis Johnston, the architect; informative about building in co. Louth in the 1790s (D.1728/27).

Johnston-Smyth (Cupples) MSS.: including MSS. of the Revd. William Cupples about co. Antrim elections, *c.* 1830 (D.2099/5).

Kirk MSS.: MSS. of the Kirk family of Carrickfergus; useful on the finances of the Fosters, who borrowed money from them in the 1840s (D.2121).

Leinster MSS.: including some political papers of the 2nd Duke of Leinster and a considerable quantity of political papers of the 3rd Duke (D.3078/3, 11).

Lenox-Conyngham MSS.: MSS. of the Lenox-Conyngham family of Springhill, Moneymore, co. Londonderry; useful on Dundalk and co. Londonderry politics (D.1449/8, 12).

Macartney MSS.: MSS. of Sir George Macartney, Earl Macartney, Chief Secretary, 1768–72; useful also for the period 1778–80 and for co. Antrim politics, particularly at the general election of 1802 (D.572).

O'Hara MSS.: MSS. of Charles O'Hara (q.v. under N.L.I.) and also of his father, Charles O'Hara Senior (T.2812).

Pack-Beresford MSS.: MSS. of Lord John George Beresford, Archbishop of Armagh, relating to the Beresford family's electoral interest in cos. Londonderry and Waterford (D. 664/A).

Roden MSS.: MSS. of the 2nd Earl of Clanbrassill and the 1st and 2nd Earls of Roden (Mic.147).

Ross MSS.: three documents relating to the 1826 Louth election (T.2519/11).

Rowan-Hamilton MSS.: MSS. of the Rowan-Hamilton family of Killyleagh, co. Down, including legal and estate papers of the Tichborne, Aston, and Tipping families of co. Louth (D.50–151).

Shannon MSS.: MSS. of Henry Boyle, 1st Earl of Shannon, and of his son, the 2nd Earl; some references to the Foster family, and important insights into the niceties of borough proprietorship (D.2707).

Stewart of Killymoon MSS.: MSS. of James Stewart, M.P. for co. Tyrone, 1768–1812 (D.3167).

Young of Fenaghy, co. Antrim, MSS.: including a deputy court poll book for the co. Antrim general election of 1776 (D.1634/L/1).

Bibliography

QUEEN'S UNIVERSITY, BELFAST, LIBRARY
Newport MSS.: further MSS. of Sir John Newport, mostly post-1820 (MS. 7).

ROYAL IRISH ACADEMY, DUBLIN
Burrowes MSS.: MSS. of the Whig anti-Unionist, Peter Burrowes, including some 'strays' of doubtful provenance (MS. 23 K. 53).

Charlemont MSS.: MSS. of the 1st Earl of Charlemont, including a great deal of local detail about the politics of cos. Antrim, Armagh, and elsewhere, omitted from the *H.M.C. Report* (q.v.); MS. 12 R. 1–30.

J. L. Foster MSS.: letters, mainly from Peel, to J. L. Foster, with a few letters from the Earl-Bishop of Derry, to his son-in-law, John Thomas Foster (MS. 23 G.39); photocopies in P.R.O.N.I. (T.2519/7).

STATE PAPER OFFICE, DUBLIN
Official Papers, 1790–1831 (507, 509, 510, 513, 519, 521, 524, 526–30, 534, 537, 544, 550, 577).

Private Official Correspondence book, 1789–93.

Rebellion Papers, 1796–1807 (620/7, 13, 18, 24–6, 29, 56–61, 66).

Westmorland Correspondence, 1789–1808.: MSS. of the 10th Earl of Westmorland, as Lord Lieutenant, 1790–4.

WEST SUFFOLK RECORD OFFICE
Grafton MSS.: MSS. of the 3rd Duke of Grafton, particularly letters to him from the Irish Lord Chancellor, Lord Lifford (/423).

PRIVATE COLLECTIONS
Apsley House MSS.: MSS. of the 1st Duke of Wellington as Chief Secretary, 1807–9; also papers on Trim borough, co. Meath, 1790. Part of Wellington's chief secretaryship papers have been published, and photocopies of the more important of the unpublished papers are available in P.R.O.N.I. (T.2627/3); by permission of the Duke of Wellington.

Aspinall transcripts: transcripts made by the late Professor A. Aspinall in connection with the work of the History of Parliament Trust from the Chatsworth, Fitzwilliam, Grey of Howick, Holland, Minto, Sidmouth, and other collections; most of the transcripts relating to Irish politics are currently (1977) in the possession of Dr. P. J. Jupp, who is responsible for the Irish section of the 1790–1820 volumes of the History of Parliament, and who kindly placed them at my disposal.

Congleton MSS.: including MSS. of Sir John and Sir Henry Parnell, 2nd and 3rd Bts.; by permission of Lord Congleton, Ebbesbourne Wake, near Salisbury, Wiltshire.

Conyngham MSS.: including some family and political papers of the 1st Marquess Conyngham (nothing relating to the Fosters or to Drogheda); in the possession of the Marquess Conyngham, Slane Castle, Slane, co. Meath.

Courtown MSS.: estate, family, and political papers of the Earls of Courtown, including material on co. Wexford politics in the 1820s and 1830s; by permission of the Earl of Courtown; now (1978) deposited in the T.C.D. Department of MSS.

Dropmore (additional) MSS.: part of the papers of W. W. Grenville, later Lord Grenville, mainly as Chief Secretary, 1782–3; additional to the Dropmore MSS. in the B.L. and to the *H.M.C. Dropmore MSS.* (q.v.); by permission of the late Mrs. O. J. Fortescue, Ethy House, Lostwithiel, Cornwall.

Dunraven MSS.: title-deeds and other legal papers; by permission of the Earl of Dunraven, Adare Manor, Adare, co. Limerick.

FitzGerald MSS.: P.R.O.N.I.'s calendar of this collection is to be published under the title, *The FitzGerald Papers: a Calendar of the Papers of Robert and Maurice FitzGerald, Knights of Kerry, 1750–1850*, and the reference numbers relate to this calendar; by permission of Mr. Adrian FitzGerald, 16 Clareville St., London S.W.7.

Foster/Massereene MSS.: legal and estate papers, mostly of the Foster family (cited as Chilham deed-room MSS.); by permission of Viscount Massereene and Ferrard, Chilham Castle, Chilham, Kent.

Headfort MSS.: including papers relating to co. Meath politics in the early nineteenth century, but nothing specifically relating to Louth or the Fosters; by permission of the Marquess of Headfort, Headfort House, Kells, co. Meath. The reference numbers relate to P.R.O.N.I.'s calendar of this collection.

Holloden MSS.: MSS. of the Vigors, Wilson, and associated families; by permission of Miss Faith O'Grady, Holloden, Bagenalstown, co. Carlow.

Perceval (Holland) MSS.: further MSS. of Spencer Perceval, including some Foster–Perceval correspondence (duplicated in the Foster/Massereene MSS.); by permission of Mr. David Holland formerly of the House of Commons Library.

Petworth House MSS.: MSS. of the Wyndham family, earls of Egremont, later Lords Leconfield, the absentee proprietors of large estates in cos. Clare and Limerick; by permission of Lord Egremont and the West Sussex R.O., Chichester, who administer the collection.

Rossmore MSS.: including letters to the 2nd Lord Rossmore, mainly from his son, the Hon. H. R. Westenra, M.P. for co. Monaghan; by permission of Lord Rossmore, Keeper's House, Rossmore Park, Monaghan. The reference numbers relate to P.R.O.N.I.'s calendar of this collection.

Shee (Neall) MSS.: MSS. of Sir George Shee, 1st Bt., among other things as Under-Secretary at the Home Office, 1801–3; by permission of Capt. Richard Neall, 57 Orchard Avenue, Chichester, Sussex.

Spencer Bernard MSS.: MSS. of Scrope Bernard, as private secretary to the Lord Lieutenant, 1782–3 and 1787–9, and as Under-Secretary at the Home Office thereafter (T.2627/6); by permission of the late Mr. J. G. C. Spencer Bernard, Winchedon House, near Aylesbury, Bucks.

P.R.O.N.I.'s calendar of this collection has been published in *Irish Official Papers: Private Collections*, Vol. 1, pp. 195 ff.

Tickell MSS.: MSS. of Thomas Tickell about co. Kildare politics; by permission of the late Major-General Sir Eustace Tickell; now in the possession of Major-General M. E. Tickell, The Old Vicarage, Branscombe, Seaton, Devon.

Vere-Foster MSS.: MSS. of John Thomas Foster and his descendants, some of which were made available to me by permission of Mrs. A. C. May of Glyde Court, Ardee, co. Louth.

Waterford MSS.: mainly estate papers of the earls of Tyrone and marquesses of Waterford, including some early nineteenth-century political material relating to co. Londonderry; apparently no surviving correspondence of the 1st and 2nd Marquesses.

2. *Printed Material*

ABBOT: *Diary and Correspondence of Charles Abbot, Lord Colchester*, ed. Lord Colchester (3 vols., London, 1861).

AUCKLAND: *The Journal and Correspondence of William, Lord Auckland*, ed. Bishop of Bath and Wells (4 vols., London, 1861–2).

BERESFORD: *Correspondence of the Rt. Hon. John Beresford*, ed. William Beresford (2 vols., London, 1854).

BOULTER: *Letters Written by His Excellency Hugh Boulter, D.D., Lord Primate of All Ireland, etc.* . . . (2 vols., Dublin, 1770).

BUCKINGHAM: *Memoirs of the Courts and Cabinets of George III*, ed. Duke of Buckingham (4 vols., London, 1853–5).

BURKE: *Correspondence of Edmund Burke*, ed. T. W. Copeland and others (9 vols., Chicago/Cambridge, 1958–70).

CASTLEREAGH: *Memoirs and Correspondence of Viscount Castlereagh*, ed. Marquess of Londonderry (vols. i–iv, London, 1848–9).

CORNWALLIS: *Correspondence of Charles, 1st Marquess Cornwallis*, ed. Sir C. Ross (vols. ii–iii, London, 1859).

DRENNAN: *The Drennan Letters*, ed. D. A. Chart (Belfast, 1931).

ELDON: *The Public and Private Life of Lord Chancellor Eldon*, ed. Horace Twiss (3 vols., London, 1844).

FLOOD: *Original Letters . . . to the Rt. Hon. Henry Flood*, ed. 'T.R.' (London, 1820).

FORBES: 'Forbes Letters', ed. T. J. Kiernan, in *Analecta Hibernica*, No. 8 (1938).

FOSTER: *The Two Duchesses: Georgiana Duchess of Devonshire, Elizabeth Duchess of Devonshire*, ed. Vere Foster (London, 1898).

GEORGE III: *Letters from His Late Majesty to the Late Lord Kenyon on the Coronation Oath, with His Lordship's Answers* . . ., ed. Henry Philpotts (London, 1827).

GEORGE III: *The Later Correspondence of George III*, ed. A . Aspinall (vol. ii, Cambridge, 1963).

GEORGE IV: *The Correspondence of George, Prince of Wales, 1770–1812*, ed. A. Aspinall (vol. ii, London, 1964).

GRATTAN: *Memoirs of the Life and Times of the Rt. Hon. Henry Grattan*, ed. Henry Grattan Junior (5 vols., London, 1839–46).

GRENVILLE: *The Correspondence of Charlotte Grenville, Lady Williams Wynn*, ed. R. Leighton (London, 1920).

HARDWICKE: *The Viceroy's Post-Bag*, ed. M. McDonagh (Dublin, 1904).

LENNOX: *Life and Letters of Lady Sarah Lennox*, ed. Countess of Ilchester and Lord Stavordale (2 vols., London, 1902).

MALMESBURY: *Diaries and Correspondence of James Harris, 1st Earl of Malmesbury*, ed. Earl of Malmesbury (4 vols., London, 1844).

MOORE: *Memoirs, Journal, and Correspondence of Thomas Moore*, ed. Lord J. Russell (8 vols., London, 1853–6).

MOUNT CASHELL: *An Irish Peer on the Continent, 1801–3*, ed. T. U. Sadleir (London, 1920).

PITT–RUTLAND: *Correspondence between the Rt. Hon. William Pitt and Charles, Duke of Rutland*, ed. Duke of Rutland (London, 1890).

ROCKINGHAM: *Memoirs of the Marquess of Rockingham and his Contemporaries*, ed. Earl of Albemarle (2 vols., London, 1852).

RODEN: *The Diary of Anne, Countess Dowager of Roden*, ed. Earl of Roden (Dublin, 1870).

ROSE: *Diary and Correspondence of George Rose*, ed. L. Vernon-Harcourt (2 vols., London, 1860).

SIDMOUTH: *Life and Correspondence of the Rt. Hon. Henry Addington, 1st Viscount Sidmouth*, ed. G. Pellew (3 vols., London, 1847).

VERNEY: *Verney Letters of the Eighteenth Century from the MSS. at Claydon House*, ed. Lady Verney (2 vols., London, 1930).

WELLINGTON: *The Supplementary Despatches, Letters and Memoranda of Arthur Wellesley, 1st Duke of Wellington*, ed. Duke of Wellington (vol. v, London, 1860).

PUBLICATIONS OF THE HISTORICAL MANUSCRIPTS COMMISSION

Abergavenny MSS. (MSS. of John Robinson), *10 Report, Appendix vi.*

Carlisle MSS. (MSS. of the 5th Earl of Carlisle as Lord Lieutenant, 1780–2), *15 Report, Appendix vi.*

Charlemont MSS. (MSS. of the 1st Earl of Charlemont), *12 Report, Appendix x,* and *13 Report, Appendix vii* (2 vols.).

Donoughmore MSS. (MSS. of John Hely-Hutchinson, Secretary of State, 1777–94), *12 Report, Appendix ix.*

Dropmore MSS. (MSS. of W. W. Grenville, Lord Grenville), vols. i (*13 Report, Appendix iii*) and vii–ix (these last are not Appendices to any Report).

Emly MSS. (MSS. of E. S. Pery, Speaker of the House of Commons, 1771–85), *8 Report, Appendix i*, and *14 Report, Appendix ix* (2 sections).

Kenyon MSS. (MSS. of Lord Chief Justice Kenyon), *14 Report, Appendix iv.*

Lonsdale MSS. (MSS. of the 1st Earl of Lonsdale), *13 Report, Appendix vii.*

Lothian MSS. (MSS. of the 2nd Earl of Buckinghamshire as Lord Lieutenant, 1776–80).

Rutland MSS. (MSS. of the 4th Duke of Rutland as Lord Lieutenant, 1784–7), *14 Report, Appendix i*, vol. iii.

Stopford-Sackville MSS. (MSS. of Lord George Germain, 1st Viscount Sackville), vol. i.

Vernon Smith MSS. (MSS. of Joseph Smith, Pitt's private secretary from 1787), *12 Report, Appendix ix.*

NEWSPAPERS

Belfast Evening News, 1786.

Belfast News Letter, 1761, 1768, 1776, 1783, 1790, and 1797 (nothing specifically on Louth or Drogheda elections).

Drogheda Morning Post, 26 July 1826.

Dublin Evening Post, 1779, 1783, 1789, 1790, 1793, 1799, 1826, and 1831.

Faulkner's Dublin Journal, 1761, 1768, 1779, and 1782.

Freeman's Journal, 1826.

Saunders's Dublin News Letter, 1826 and 1830–1.

PARLIAMENTARY PROCEEDINGS, REPORTS, SPEECHES, STATUTES, ETC.

Debates:

The Parliamentary History of England from the Norman Conquest to 1803 (36 vols., London, 1806–20); continued as *The Parliamentary Debates from the Year 1803 to the Present Time*, 1803–20 (41 vols., London, 1804–20); cited as *Parl. Hist.* and *Parl. Debs.*

The Parliamentary Register, or History of the Proceedings of the House of Lords and Commons [of Great Britain], 1774–1806 (89 vols., London, 1802–6); cited as *Parl. Reg.*

The Parliamentary Register, or History of the Proceedings and Debates of the House of Commons of Ireland, 1781–97 (17 vols., Dublin, 1782–1801); cited as *Parl. Reg.* (Irish)

A Report of the Debates in Both Houses of the Parliament of Ireland on the Roman Catholic Bill Passed in the Session of 1792 (Dublin, 1792).

A Report of the Important Debate in the House of Commons of Ireland on Thursday April 11 1799 on the Regency Bill, including the Admirable Speech of the Rt. Hon. John Foster (Dublin, 1799).

A Detailed Report of the Speeches in Both Houses of Parliament on the Irish Roman Catholic Petition, from the 25th of March 1805 ... to the 14th of May following ... (London, 1805).

Journals:

Journals of the House of Commons of the Kingdom of Ireland, 1613–1800 (19 vols., Dublin, 1796–1800).

Members:

Return of the Names of the Members Returned to Serve in Parliament, Part ii, Parliaments of the United Kingdom, 1801–74, and Parliaments of Ireland, 1559–1809, 1878–9 [H.L. 180], xi.

Reports:

Municipal Corporations (Ireland), Appendix to the First Report of the Commissioners (Part ii: Conclusion of the North-Eastern Circuit and Part of the North-Western Circuit), 1835 [28], xxviii, pp. 357 ff.

Speeches:

The Speech of the Late Rt. Hon. John, Earl of Clare . . . on the Second Reading of the Bill for the Relief of His Majesty's Roman Catholic Subjects in Ireland on March 13, 1793, new edn. (London, 1813).

Speech of the Rt. Hon. William Pitt in the House of Commons, Thursday January 31 1799, 4th edn. (London, 1799).

Speech of the Rt. Hon. John Foster . . . Delivered in Committee on Thursday the 11th Day of April 1799 (Dublin, 1799).

The Speech of the Rt. Hon. John, Earl of Clare . . . on a Motion made by Him on Monday, February 10, 1800 (Dublin, 1800).

Speech of the Rt. Hon. John Foster . . . Delivered in Committee on Monday the 17th Day of February 1800 (Dublin, 1800).

Substance of the Speech of the Rt. Hon. John Foster in Committee on the Irish Budget on May 7 1806 (London, 1806).

Statutes:

Owen Ruffhead (ed.), *The Statutes at Large . . . of the Parliament of England, afterwards of Great Britain, from Magna Charta to the Union of Great Britain and Ireland* (18 vols., London, 1763–1800).

A Collection of the Public General Statutes Passed in the Parliament of Great Britain and Ireland, 1801–69 (74 vols., London, 1801–69); the volumes up to 1832 are the relevant ones.

The Statutes at Large Passed in the Parliaments Held in Ireland, 1310–1800 (20 vols., Dublin, 1789–1800).

B. SECONDARY SOURCES

[ANON.], The Book of Dundalk (1946).

ASHBOURNE, LORD: *Pitt: Some Chapters of His Life and Times* (London, 1898).

BALL, F. E.: *Judges in Ireland, 1221–1921* (2 vols., London, 1926).

BARRINGTON, SIR JONAH: *Personal Sketches of My Own Times* (3 vols., London, 1827–32).

BARRINGTON, SIR JONAH: *The Rise and Fall of the Irish Nation* (Dublin, 1833).

BARTLETT, T.: 'The Townshend Administration in Ireland, 1767–72' (Q.U.B. Ph.D. thesis, 1976).

BAYLEY, JOHN: *Summary of the Law of Bills of Exchange, Cash Bills and Promissory Notes*, 3rd edn. (London, 1813).

BECKETT, J. C.: *The Making of Modern Ireland, 1603–1923* (London, 1966).

BECKETT, J. C.: *The Anglo-Irish Tradition*, (London, 1976).

BODKIN, M. (ed.): 'Notes on the Irish Parliament in 1773', *Proc. R.I.A.*, vol. 48, Sec. C, No. 4 (1942–3).

BOLTON, G. C.: *The Passing of the Irish Act of Union* (Oxford, 1966).

BUCKLAND, PATRICK: *The Anglo-Irish and the New Ireland* (Dublin, 1972).

CAMPBELL, LORD: *Lives of the Lord Chancellors* (7 vols., London, 1848).

CHILDE-PEMBERTON, W.: *The Earl-Bishop: the Life of Frederick Hervey, Bishop of Derry and 4th Earl of Bristol* (2 vols., London, 1922).

CHRISTIE, I. R.: *The End of North's Ministry, 1780–82* (London, 1958).

CLERMONT, LORD: *A History of the Family of Fortescue in All Its Branches* (London, 1869).

CLONCURRY, LORD: *Personal Recollections of His Life and Times* (London, 1859).

CROOKSHANK, ANN, and THE KNIGHT OF GLIN: *Irish Portraits, 1660–1860* (London, 1969).

CULLEN, L. M.: *An Economic History of Ireland since 1660* (London, 1972).

D'ALTON, JOHN: *A History of Drogheda* (Dublin, 1844).

D'ALTON, JOHN: *A History of Dundalk* (Dundalk, 1864).

DELANY, V. T. H.: *Christopher Palles* (Dublin, 1960).

DUNRAVEN, EARL OF: *The Finances of Ireland before and after the Union* (London, 1912).

EDGEWORTH, R. L.: *Memoirs of His Own Life*, ed. Maria Edgeworth (2 vols., London, 1820).

EMERSON, REVD. N. D.: 'Mr. Speaker Foster', *C.L.A.J.* vi (1927–8), pp. 117 ff., 199 ff.

ENGLEFIELD, D. J. T.: 'The Irish House of Parliament in the Eighteenth Century', *Parliamentary Affairs*, ix (1956).

FALKINER, H. L.: 'Lord Clare', in *Studies in Irish History and Biography* (London, 1902).

'FALKLAND' [REVD. JOHN SCOTT]: *The Parliamentary Representation of Ireland* (Dublin, 1790).

'FALKLAND' [REVD. JOHN SCOTT]: *A Review of the Principal Public Characters in the House of Commons of Ireland* (Dublin, 1789).

FETTER, F. W. (ed.): *The Irish Pound 1797–1826: a Reprint of the Report of the Committee of the British House of Commons on the Condition of the Irish Currency* (London, 1955).

FITZGERALD, B.: *Lady Louisa Conolly, 1743–1821: an Anglo-Irish Biography* (London, 1950).

FITZGERALD, J.: 'The Organization of the Drogheda Economy, 1780–1820' (U.C.D. M.A. thesis, 1974).

FITZGIBBON, E.: *Earl of Clare: Mainspring of the Union* (London, 1960).

FOSTER, R. F.: *Charles Stewart Parnell: the Man and His Family* (Brighton, 1976).

FROUDE, J. A.: *The English in Ireland in the Eighteenth Century* (3 vols., London, 1881).

GASH, N.: *Politics in the Age of Peel: a Study in the Technique of Parliamentary Representation* (London, 1953).

GASH, N.: *Mr. Secretary Peel: the Life of Sir Robert Peel to 1830* (London, 1964).

GRAY, D.: *Spencer Perceval: the Evangelical Prime Minister, 1762–1812* (Manchester, 1963).

HARDY, F.: *Memoirs of the Political and Private Life of James Caulfeild, Earl of Charlemont* (London, 1810).

HARLOW, V. T.: *The Founding of the Second British Empire*, vol. i (London, 1952).

HILTON, A. J. B.: *Corn, Cash, Commerce: the Economic Policies of the Tory Governments, 1815–30* (Oxford, 1977).

HUME, G., and MALCOMSON, A. P. W. (eds.): *Robert Emmet: the Insurrection of July 1803* (H.M.S.O., Belfast, 1976).

HUNT, W. (ed.): *The Irish Parliament in 1775* (Dublin, 1907).

HYDE, H. M.: *The Rise of Castlereagh* (London, 1933).

JOHNSTON, E. M.: *Great Britain and Ireland, 1760–1800* (Edinburgh, 1963).

JOHNSTON, E. M. (ed.): 'The State of the Irish House of Commons in 1791' *Proc. R.I.A.*, vol. 59, Sec. C., No. 1 (1957).

JOHNSTON, E. M. (ed.): 'The State of the Irish Parliament, 1784–7', ibid., vol. 71, Sec. C., No. 5 (1971).

JOHNSTON, E. M.: *Ireland in the Eighteenth Century* (Dublin, 1974).

JUPP, P. J.: 'Irish Parliamentary Representation, 1800–20' (Reading Ph.D. thesis, 1966).

JUPP, P. J.: 'Irish Parliamentary Elections and the Influence of the Catholic Vote, 1800–20', *Historical Journal*, x (1967).

JUPP, P. J.: 'Irish M.P.s at Westminster in the Early Nineteenth Century', *Historical Studies*, vii (London, 1969).

JUPP, P. J.: 'Politics and Parties in Great Britain and Ireland, 1782–1820' (unpublished paper read to the U.C.D. Historical Society, 1969).

JUPP, P. J.: 'Co. Down Elections, 1783–1831', *I.H.S.* xviii (1972).

JUPP, P. J. (ed.) *British and Irish Elections, 1784–1831* (Newton Abbot, 1973).

KELLY, P.: 'British Parliamentary Politics, 1784–6', *Historical Journal*, xvii, No. 4 (1974).

KELLY, P.: 'British and Irish Politics in 1785', *E.H.R.* xc, No. 356 (July 1975).

KIERNAN, T. J.: *History of the Financial Administration of Ireland to 1817* (London, 1930).

LANDRETH, H.: *The Pursuit of Robert Emmet* (London, 1949).

LARGE, D. (ed.): 'The Irish House of Commons in 1769', *I.H.S.* xi (1958).

LARGE, D.: 'The Wealth of the Greater Irish Landowners, 1750–1815', *I.H.S.* xv (1966).

LECKY, W. E. H.: *History of Ireland in the Eighteenth Century* (5 vols., London, 1903).

LINEN BOARD: *Proceedings of the Trustees of the Linen and Hempen Manufactures of Ireland, 5 Jan.–5 July 1809* (Dublin ?, 1810).

LONGFORD, E.: *Wellington: the Years of the Sword* (London, 1969).

McANALLY, H. M.: *The Irish Militia, 1793–1816: a Social and Military Study* (London, 1949).

McCRACKEN, J. L.: 'Central and Local Administration in Ireland under George II' (Q.U.B. Ph.D. thesis, 1941).

McCRACKEN, J. L.: 'Irish Parliamentary Elections, 1727–68', *I.H.S.* v (1942).

McCRACKEN, J. L.: 'The Struggle between the Irish Administration and Parliament, 1753–6', *I.H.S.* iii (1942–3).

McDOWELL, R. B.: *The Irish Administration, 1800–1964* (London, 1964).

McDOWELL, R. B.: *Irish Public Opinion, 1750–1800* (London, 1944).

McDOWELL, R. B.: *Public Opinion and Government Policy in Ireland, 1801–46* (London, 1952).

McDOWELL, R. B.: 'Some Fitzgibbon Letters from the Sneyd Muniments in the John Rylands [now in the Keele University] Library', *Bulletin of the John Rylands Library*, vol. 34, No. 2 (1951–2).

MAGUIRE, W. A.: *The Downshire Estates in Ireland, 1801–45* (Oxford, 1972).

MALCOMSON, A. P. W.: 'Election Politics in the Borough of Antrim, 1750–1800', *I.H.S.* xvii (1970).

MALCOMSON, A. P. W.: 'The Struggle for Control of Dundalk Borough, 1782–92', *C.L.A.J.* xvii (1970).

MALCOMSON, A. P. W.: 'The Foster Family and the Parliamentary Borough of Dunleer, 1683–1800', *C.L.A.J.* xvii (1971).

MALCOMSON, A. P. W.: 'John Foster and the Speakership of the Irish House of Commons', *Proc. R.I.A.*, vol. 72, Sec. C, No. 11 (1972).

MALCOMSON, A. P. W.: 'The Earl of Clermont: a Forgotten Co. Monaghan Magnate of the Late Eighteenth Century', *Clogher Record*, xiii (1973).

MALCOMSON, A. P. W.: 'The Newtown Act: Revision and Reconstruction', *I.H.S.* xviii (1973).

MALCOMSON, A. P. W.: *Isaac Corry, 1755–1813: 'an Adventurer in the Field of Politics'* (Belfast, 1974).

MALCOMSON, A. P. W.: 'Absenteeism in Eighteenth-Century Ireland', *Irish Economic and Social History Journal*, i (1974).

MALCOMSON, A. P. W.: 'Speaker Pery and the Pery Papers', *The North Munster Antiquarian Journal*, xvi (1973–4).

MANNING, J. A.: *The Lives of the Speakers of the House of Commons* (London, 1851).

MAXWELL, CONSTANTIA: *Country and Town in Ireland under the Georges* (Dundalk, 1949).

MITFORD, E. B.: *Life of Lord Redesdale* (London, 1939).

NAMIER, L. B.: *The Structure of Politics at the Accession of George III* (2 vols., London, 1929).

NAMIER, L. B.: *England in the Age of the American Revolution* (London, 1961).

O'CONNELL, M.: *Irish Politics and Social Conflict in the Age of the American Revolution* (Philadelphia, 1965).

O'FLANAGAN, J. R.: *Lives of the Lord Chancellors of Ireland* (2 vols., Dublin, 1870).

O'MEARAIN, VERY REVD. L.: 'The Bath Estate, 1777–1800', *Clogher Record*, vi (1968).

O'NEILL, THERESA V.: 'The Sixth Parliament of George III, 1798–1800' (U.C.D. M.A. thesis, 1943).

O'REGAN, W.: *Memoirs of the Legal, Literary, and Political Life of . . . John Philpot Curran* (London, 1817).

O'SULLIVAN, H. (ed.): 'Two Eighteenth-Century Maps of the Clanbrassill Estate, Dundalk', *C.L.A.J.* xv (1961).

PAKENHAM, T.: *The Year of Liberty: the Story of the Great Irish Rebellion of 1798* (London, 1969).

[PALMERSTON, LORD]: *The New Whig Guide* (London, 1819).

PARES, R.: *King George III and the Politicians* (Oxford, 1964).

PHILLIPS, W. A.: *A History of the Church of Ireland* (3 vols., Oxford, 1933).

PLOWDEN, F.: *The History of Ireland from Henry II to the Union* (2 vols., Dublin, 1812).

PLOWDEN, F.: *The History of Ireland from the Union to 1810* (3 vols., Dublin, 1811).

PORRITT, E. and A.: *The Unreformed House of Commons* (2 vols., London, 1903).

Public Characters of 1798–9, 3rd edn. (London, 1801).

Public Characters of 1799–1800 (London, 1799).

REYNOLDS, J. A.: *The Catholic Emancipation Crisis in Ireland, 1823–29* (Yale, 1954).

RIDGEWAY, W.: *Reports of Cases upon Appeals and Writs of Error since the Restoration of the Appellate Jurisdiction, 1784–6* (3 vols., Dublin, 1795–8).

SAYLES, C. O. (ed.): 'Contemporary Sketches of Members of the Irish Parliament in 1782', *Proc. R.I.A.*, vol. 56, Sec. C, No. 3 (1954).

SIMMS, J. G.: 'County Louth and the Jacobite War', *C.L.A.J.* xiv (1959).

SIMMS, J. G.: 'Irish Catholics and the Parliamentary Franchise, 1692–1728', *I.H.S.* xii (1960–1).

SMYTH, D. H.: 'The Volunteer Movement in Ulster: Background and Development, 1745–85' (Q.U.B. Ph.D. thesis, 1974).

STANHOPE, EARL: *Life of the Rt. Hon. William Pitt* (4 vols., London, 1861–2).

TEMPEST, H. G. (ed.): 'Rental and Account of Collon Estate, 1779–81', *C.L.A.J.* x (1943).

TRAINOR, B. and CRAWFORD, W. H.: *Aspects of Irish Social History, 1750–1800* (H.M.S.O., Belfast, 1969).

WALKER, B. M.: 'Irish Parliamentary Election Results, 1801–1922' (volume at present in draft, to be published as an ancillary to the *New History of Ireland*).

WALL, MAUREEN: 'The United Irish Movement', *Historical Studies*, v (London, 1965).

WALPOLE, S.: *The Life of the Rt. Hon. Spencer Perceval* (2 vols., London, 1874).

WATSON, J. S.: *The Reign of George III, 1760–1815* (Oxford, 1963).

WHITLAW, J. A. G., 'Anglo-Irish Commercial Relations, 1779–85, with Special Reference to the Negotiations of 1785' (Q.U.B. M.A. thesis, 1958).

WHYTE, J. H.: 'Landlord Influence at Elections in Ireland', *E.H.R.* lxxv (1960).

WRAXALL, SIR N. W.: *Posthumous Memoirs of His Own Times* (3 vols., London, 1836).

YOUNG, A.: *A Tour in Ireland* (2 vols., Dublin, 1780).

C. REFERENCE WORKS

BURKE's *Dormant, Abeyant, Extinct and Forfeited Peerages of the British Empire* (1883).

BURKE's *Landed Gentry of the United Kingdom* (1862).

BURKE's *Peerage and Baronetage* (1933).

BURTCHAEL, G. D., and SADLEIR, T. U. (eds.) *Alumni Dublinenses* (Dublin, 1935).

C[OCKAYNE], G. E.: *The Complete Peerage*, ed. V. Gibbs and others (13 vols., London, 1910–40).

COLLINS's *Peerage of England*, ed. Sir E. Brydges (9 vols., London, 1812).

COTTON, H.: *Fasti Ecclesiae Hibernicae* (2 vols., Dublin, 1851).

Dictionary of National Biography (Oxford, 1917–49).

HUGHES, J. L. T.: 'The Chief Secretaries in Ireland, 1561–1921', *I.H.S.* viii (1952–3).

HUGHES, J. L. T.: *Patentee Officers in Ireland, 1173–1826* (Dublin, 1960).

JACOB, G.: *A New Law Dictionary, Corrected by Owen Ruffhead and J. Morgan*, 10th edn. (Dublin, 1773).

LASCELLES, R.: *Liber Munerum Hiberniae, 1152–1827* (2 vols., Dublin, 1852).

LESLIE, J. B.: *Clogher Clergy and Parishes* (Enniskillen, 1929).

LEWIS, S.: *A Topographical Dictionary of Ireland* (2 vols., London, 1837).

PLAYFAIR, W.: *British Family Antiquity* (9 vols., London, 1809–11).

POWICKE, F. M.: *Handbook of British Chronology* (London, 1939).

SMYTH, C. J.: *Chronicle of the Law Officers of Ireland* (London, 1839).

Townland Index: *Census of Ireland, 1901, Consisting of a General Topographical Index with an Alphabetical Index to the Townlands and Towns of Ireland* (2 vols., Dublin, 1904).

WATSON'S *Gentleman's and Citizen's Almanack* (Dublin, 1747–1840).

INDEX

(Where a person, place or subject is not specifically mentioned by name, the page reference is given in brackets)